Lecture Notes in Computer Science 12185

More information about this series at http://www.springer.com/series/7409

Sakae Yamamoto · Hirohiko Mori (Eds.)

Human Interface
and the Management
of Information

Interacting with Information

Thematic Area, HIMI 2020
Held as Part of the 22nd International Conference, HCII 2020
Copenhagen, Denmark, July 19–24, 2020
Proceedings, Part II

 Springer

Editors
Sakae Yamamoto
Tokyo University of Science
Tokyo, Japan

Hirohiko Mori
Tokyo City University
Tokyo, Japan

ISSN 0302-9743   ISSN 1611-3349   (electronic)
Lecture Notes in Computer Science
ISBN 978-3-030-50016-0   ISBN 978-3-030-50017-7   (eBook)
https://doi.org/10.1007/978-3-030-50017-7

LNCS Sublibrary: SL3 – Information Systems and Applications, incl. Internet/Web, and HCI

This Springer imprint is published by the registered company Springer Nature Switzerland AG
The registered company address is: Gewerbestrasse 11, 6330 Cham, Switzerland

Foreword

The 22nd International Conference on Human-Computer Interaction, HCI International 2020 (HCII 2020), was planned to be held at the AC Bella Sky Hotel and Bella Center, Copenhagen, Denmark, during July 19–24, 2020. Due to the COVID-19 coronavirus pandemic and the resolution of the Danish government not to allow events larger than 500 people to be hosted until September 1, 2020, HCII 2020 had to be held virtually. It incorporated the 21 thematic areas and affiliated conferences listed on the following page.

A total of 6,326 individuals from academia, research institutes, industry, and governmental agencies from 97 countries submitted contributions, and 1,439 papers and 238 posters were included in the conference proceedings. These contributions address the latest research and development efforts and highlight the human aspects of design and use of computing systems. The contributions thoroughly cover the entire field of human-computer interaction, addressing major advances in knowledge and effective use of computers in a variety of application areas. The volumes constituting the full set of the conference proceedings are listed in the following pages.

The HCI International (HCII) conference also offers the option of "late-breaking work" which applies both for papers and posters and the corresponding volume(s) of the proceedings will be published just after the conference. Full papers will be included in the "HCII 2020 - Late Breaking Papers" volume of the proceedings to be published in the Springer LNCS series, while poster extended abstracts will be included as short papers in the "HCII 2020 - Late Breaking Posters" volume to be published in the Springer CCIS series.

I would like to thank the program board chairs and the members of the program boards of all thematic areas and affiliated conferences for their contribution to the highest scientific quality and the overall success of the HCI International 2020 conference.

This conference would not have been possible without the continuous and unwavering support and advice of the founder, Conference General Chair Emeritus and Conference Scientific Advisor Prof. Gavriel Salvendy. For his outstanding efforts, I would like to express my appreciation to the communications chair and editor of HCI International News, Dr. Abbas Moallem.

July 2020   Constantine Stephanidis

HCI International 2020 Thematic Areas and Affiliated Conferences

Thematic areas:

- HCI 2020: Human-Computer Interaction
- HIMI 2020: Human Interface and the Management of Information

Affiliated conferences:

- EPCE: 17th International Conference on Engineering Psychology and Cognitive Ergonomics
- UAHCI: 14th International Conference on Universal Access in Human-Computer Interaction
- VAMR: 12th International Conference on Virtual, Augmented and Mixed Reality
- CCD: 12th International Conference on Cross-Cultural Design
- SCSM: 12th International Conference on Social Computing and Social Media
- AC: 14th International Conference on Augmented Cognition
- DHM: 11th International Conference on Digital Human Modeling and Applications in Health, Safety, Ergonomics and Risk Management
- DUXU: 9th International Conference on Design, User Experience and Usability
- DAPI: 8th International Conference on Distributed, Ambient and Pervasive Interactions
- HCIBGO: 7th International Conference on HCI in Business, Government and Organizations
- LCT: 7th International Conference on Learning and Collaboration Technologies
- ITAP: 6th International Conference on Human Aspects of IT for the Aged Population
- HCI-CPT: Second International Conference on HCI for Cybersecurity, Privacy and Trust
- HCI-Games: Second International Conference on HCI in Games
- MobiTAS: Second International Conference on HCI in Mobility, Transport and Automotive Systems
- AIS: Second International Conference on Adaptive Instructional Systems
- C&C: 8th International Conference on Culture and Computing
- MOBILE: First International Conference on Design, Operation and Evaluation of Mobile Communications
- AI-HCI: First International Conference on Artificial Intelligence in HCI

Conference Proceedings Volumes Full List

http://2020.hci.international/proceedings

Human Interface and the Management of Information Thematic Area (HIMI 2020)

Program Board Chairs: **Sakae Yamamoto, Tokyo University of Science, Japan, and Hirohiko Mori, Tokyo City University, Japan**

- Yumi Asahi, Japan
- Shin'ichi Fukuzumi, Japan
- Michitaka Hirose, Japan
- Yen-Yu Kang, Taiwan
- Keiko Kasamatsu, Japan
- Daiji Kobayashi, Japan
- Kentaro Kotani, Japan
- Hiroyuki Miki, Japan

- Ryosuke Saga, Japan
- Katsunori Shimohara, Japan
- Takahito Tomoto, Japan
- Kim-Phuong Vu, USA
- Marcelo M. Wanderley, Canada
- Tomio Watanabe, Japan
- Takehiko Yamaguchi, Japan

The full list with the Program Board Chairs and the members of the Program Boards of all thematic areas and affiliated conferences is available online at:

http://www.hci.international/board-members-2020.php

HCI International 2021

The 23rd International Conference on Human-Computer Interaction, HCI International 2021 (HCII 2021), will be held jointly with the affiliated conferences in Washington DC, USA, at the Washington Hilton Hotel, July 24–29, 2021. It will cover a broad spectrum of themes related to Human-Computer Interaction (HCI), including theoretical issues, methods, tools, processes, and case studies in HCI design, as well as novel interaction techniques, interfaces, and applications. The proceedings will be published by Springer. More information will be available on the conference website: http://2021.hci.international/.

General Chair
Prof. Constantine Stephanidis
University of Crete and ICS-FORTH
Heraklion, Crete, Greece
Email: general_chair@hcii2021.org

http://2021.hci.international/

Contents – Part II

Supporting Work, Collaboration and Creativity

Information in Intelligent Systems and Environments

Contents – Part I

Service Design and Management

Recommender and Decision Support Systems

Enhancing Peoples' Training Experience: A Gym Workout Planner Based on Soft Ontologies

Rita de Cássia Catini[1,2], Paulo Cesar de Macedo[2], Julio Cesar dos Reis[3] (iD),
and Rodrigo Bonacin[1,4(✉)] (iD)

[1] UNIFACCAMP, Campo Limpo Paulista, SP, Brazil
ritacatini@gmail.com
[2] São Paulo State Technological College - FATEC, Mogi Mirim, SP, Brazil
paulo.macedo@fatec.sp.gov.br
[3] Institute of Computing, UNICAMP, Campinas, SP, Brazil
jreis@ic.unicamp.br
[4] Information Technology Center Renato Archer - CTI, Campinas, SP, Brazil
rodrigo.bonacin@cti.gov.br

Abstract. The development of novel interactive systems for supporting our daily activities (*e.g.*, gym training activities) demands flexible and dynamic ontologies for knowledge representation and application support. In this paper, we propose a soft ontology-based architecture for dealing with decision support and recommendation under dynamic and uncertainty situations, including those related to gym training activities. Our architecture considers users' characteristics and group's feedback (*e.g.*, comments, evaluation, sensor data and results) to develop and evolve flexible ontological structures using a Fuzzy RDF approach for implementing soft ontologies. The architecture was implemented by the OntoGymWP application, which provides suggestions of gym workout plans based on users' features and social feedback represented in Fuzzy RDF ontologies. These ontologies are used to semantically encode: users' profile; shared concepts from the domain for each group of users; and training plans for each individual. The implemented proof of concept reveals the viability of the architecture, as well as its potentiality in providing suitable gym workout plans based on extensible and flexible ontologies.

Keywords: Soft ontology · Decision support · Recommendation systems · Fuzzy RDF · Personalization

1 Introduction

As Web technologies have been increasingly integrated into people's routine, there is a need for software applications to dynamically support their daily activities. However, various human activities are flexible as well as belong to open domains, which includes dealing with subjective interpretations and ill-defined concepts. Computer-based support for those activities requires adaptable and

© Springer Nature Switzerland AG 2020
S. Yamamoto and H. Mori (Eds.): HCII 2020, LNCS 12185, pp. 3–21, 2020.
https://doi.org/10.1007/978-3-030-50017-7_1

dynamic solutions, making it crucial that computers deal with information on the Web in a proper way.

Several software applications support people interested in improving their physical performance. Typically, they use data from their databases or/and inputs from a physical education professional to infer suggestions of training. Usually, this analysis (anamnesis) includes the history and the desired goal; professionals indicate the training to be performed according to their own knowledge and skills. Nevertheless, existing computational support solutions are limited in terms of analyzing social feedback and users' social tagging associated with the various training activities.

Semantic Web technologies have been applied for supporting various users' activities on the Web. Ontologies are the core elements of this technology [1] because they are used to represent domain knowledge in a human and machine interpretable format. Most frequently ontologies are designed to deal with well-defined concepts. As a consequence, these ontologies may not be able to represent uncertain and open domains. Literature presents studies of flexible and iteratively developed ontological structures, such as soft ontologies [18], which focus on dealing with dynamically evolving and hard to define domains in a more suitable and precise way.

In this work, we argue that soft ontologies can be valuable to enhance peoples' training experience, by providing a flexible and expansive representation of the social feedback on training activities. According to Kaipainen et al. [18], hard ontologies (i.e., ontologies with fixed categories and rigid hierarchical structures) are not able to deal with applications, which include subjective and unstructured content, such as those related to folksonomies. Collao et al. [6] argued that soft ontologies can be applied to specialized tasks in an open interpretation approach. They allow users to interact with data from their own perspective, i.e., without presenting taxonomy or categorization to the curator's viewpoint.

This article presents a conceptual architecture, the design and a software prototype of a Ontology-based Gym Workout Planner (OntoGymWP) as an implementation of this architecture. This prototype takes advantage of soft ontologies to represent and analyze users' feedback and explores it to suggest training activities. We propose a fuzzy RDF [32] approach for implementing soft ontologies. In particular, they are used to represent users' profile, shared concepts from the domain for each group of users (e.g., belief values related to each physical activity) and training plans for each individual. On this basis, graph algorithms are used to determine groups, as well as to suggest personalized training plans based on group and individual feedbacks.

We experimented this proposal in practical illustrative scenarios. Obtained results indicate how the proposal can contribute to enhance users' experience according to users' profile and social feedback of the composed plan. The conducted implementation and evaluation contributed to indicate the limitations the approach and open research problems.

The remaining of this paper is structured as follows: Sect. 2 describes the background and literature review on soft ontologies. Section 3 details the conceptual architecture and the ideation of the OntoGymWP. Section 4 presents the design and implementation of the proposed system in addition to illustrative practical scenarios. Section 5 concludes the paper and indicates future investigations.

2 Background and Related Work

This section presents the background of the proposed approach focusing on RDF and Web Ontologies (Subsect. 2.1), and soft ontologies (Subsect. 2.2). Subsection 2.3 presents the related work on developing and using soft ontologies.

2.1 RDF and Web Ontologies

The semantic Web can be understood as an extension of the traditional Web by including semantic representations and interpretation mechanisms. This implies in the development of a new paradigm for information retrieval and sharing [14]. Berners-Lee *et al.* [1] proposed the semantic Web architecture, where the Resource Description Framework (RDF) [12] is a key element because it is used to define web resources, properties and their relationship on the Web [29].

An RDF statement consists of triples $(t = (s, p, o))$, as follows:

- *Subject (s):* Anything with a Uniform Resource Identifier (URI), that is, the Web resource to be described;
- *Predicate (p):* it is the property related to this resource;
- *Object (o):* it is the value of the property or another resource;

Ontology is another important concept of the Web semantic. Web ontologies are means for the formal representation of domain semantics. In ontologies, relevant entities and relationships that emerge from domain analyses and observation are modeled for machine-interpretation semantic representation [30]. Web ontologies extend the Web syntactic interoperability to the semantic interoperability [13]. This allows formalizing a shared representation of a domain, which can be used by humans and computational systems. The Web Ontology Language (OWL) is the W3C standard for ontology description in the Semantic web [31]. OWL ontologies are typically based on hierarchical structures, properties, logical axioms and class instances.

2.2 Soft Ontologies

According to Kaipainen *et al.* [18], conventional formal ontologies are not suited to deal with the dynamically nature of various new interactive technologies. These ontologies, named hard ontologies, are defined according to prefixed hierarchies usually based on domain modelers' experience. However, several applications are based on ill defined concepts and unstructured data. In some context (*e.g.*, folksonomies), it is difficulty to establish an apriori fixed and rigid structure of concepts.

The concept of soft ontologies was created to support the development and use of ontologies when it is difficult to determine relationships and organize knowledge [22]. Kaipainen *et al.* [18] use the term soft ontology as dynamically flexible and inherently spatial metadata sets to deal with ill defined domains. A soft ontology supports an open interpretation of content, without a fixed curators' view [6].

The properties of a soft ontology are spatially defined (*ontodimensions*) in multidimensional *ontospaces* [18]. In this sense, the (*ontodimensions*) define in which an information domain "is" or exists. *ontospaces* are used to relate entities of a domain and their similarity (proximity in a *ontosapce*) [25].

2.3   Related Work: Developing and Using Soft Ontologies

The review presented in this subsection is based on systematic review procedures suggested by Kitchenham [20]. Five scientific databases were used in this review (ACM DL, IEEE Xplore, SpringerLink, Science Direct and Google Scholar), The following string was used to query the databases: "soft ontology" OR "soft ontologies". The review was conducted in May 2019 and included full papers from the last 10 years written in English.

The review resulted on 19 papers related to our key research question (after the application of inclusion and exclusion criteria): *What techniques have been used to develop and use soft ontologies?*. This main question was broken down into four specific issues. In the following, we present these specific questions and highlight existing literature approaching them.

Q1: How soft ontologies have being developed and used for expanding the potential of applying ontologies in the analysis and representation of ill-defined and non-deterministic domains?

The majority of the studies do not focus on developing techniques for soft ontologies. In fact, only three of the selected investigations have addressed this issue. Bonacin, Calado and Dos Reis [3] focused on the construction of a meta-model for ontology networks, including soft ontologies. A RDF Fuzzy approach was used to develop the soft ontologies.

Although Rajaonarivo, Maisel and De Loor [28] do not directly mention the term soft ontology, they proposed an ontology that adapts from user' interaction for the construction of an enactive system. The user proximity, interactive proximity and semantic proximity measures are used in their proposal.

Kaipainen and Hautamäki [17] explored a new perspective where conceptualization is left under the responsibility of users' knowledge. They presented an ontospace model based on similarity models with multiple descriptive dimensions. In their approach, entities of an information domain are described in terms of their respective coordinates.

Additionally, we highlight the work of Lombello, Dos Reis and Bonacin [21] published after this review. A RDF fuzzy based approach was used to represent concepts of the domain under uncertain and evolving situations. Their work is the technological basis for the development of the ontology used in the system presented at this work.

Q2. *How the soft ontology concept is defined or formalized?*

In addition to the work in [18] (described in the last subsection), we highlight two other studies that provide a better definition and understanding of the soft ontology concept.

Vera *et al.* [22] presented the theoretical and practical comparative of soft and hard ontologies, including key aspects such as how knowledge is obtained and represented in each case. Caglioni and Fusco [4] argued that more flexible models to represent uncertain are needed. The work presented three ontology families that differ from description logic based ontologies: Fuzzy Ontologies, Possibilistic Ontologies, and Probabilistic Ontologies.

Q3. *Which and how the "subconcepts" of soft ontologies were defined and used?*

Some of the "subconcepts" used by Kaipainen *et al.* [18] is further detailed in other studies. Kaipainen *et al.* [19] detailed the use of *ontospace, ontodimensions* and *ontocoordinates* in enactive systems. The authors argue that use of ontologies that can be dynamically updated and restructured is a better representation of knowledge in this context. Pugliese and Lehtonen [26] used the concept of *ontospaces* to propose a framework that allows body interaction between a human and a virtual character in an enactive loop. System behaviors are created by mapping the human's *ontospace* into the virtual character's *ontospace*.

Dietze and Domingue [9] explored conceptual spaces and *ontodimensions* to link the representations of symbolic knowledge and data collected from a sensor network for weather forecast. Dietze *et al.* [8] applied these concepts to represent connections between data sensors and medical ontologies.

Ye, Stevenson and Dobson [33] explored conceptual spaces to promote semantic interoperability by capturing semantics shared by different types of knowledge domains. Their goal was to support communication, reuse and sharing of ontologies between systems. Dietze and Tanasescu [10] used conceptual spaces to address ontology mapping issues to facilitate the integration of heterogeneous knowledge models.

Kaipainen [16] discussed the constitutions of using the concepts of *ontospaces* and *ontodimensions* in the construction of a multi-perspective media. Pugliese, Tikka and Kaipainen [27] explored *ontospaces* in a solution for freely interactive narratives that can be told (narrated) in multiple ways.

Q4. *Which studies address the use of soft ontologies as part of tools for applied problems?*

Dietze *et al.* [7] proposed the use of soft ontologies as a way to calculate similarity between symbolic representation of semantic web services. Their objective was to provide automatic web service orchestration based on dynamic semantic descriptors.

Justo *et al.* [15] proposed the use of an ontology network, which includes soft ontologies to improve the empathy of interactive bots. Martinez *et al.* [23] and Vera *et al.* [22] argue that soft ontologies can be used in the development of ontology for educational areas. Soft ontologies provide further flexibility to represent educational situations/issues. Blasch *et al.* [2] presented situations in which hard and soft ontologies act together for content alignment in Geographic Information Systems.

Our work proposes, as presented by Bonacin, Calado and Dos Reis [3] as well as Lombello, Dos Reis and Bonacin [21], the use of a fuzzy RDF approach to develop soft ontologies (as the answer to *Question 1*). Our ontologies are formalized in terms of weighted graphs (*Question 2*), and we explore the concepts of *ontospace* and *ontodimensions* (*Question 3*) in the development of a decision support application/Workout (*Question 4*). We contribute with a comprehensive solution that explores the use of soft ontologies in a novel decision support architecture applied to an workout planner.

3   Exploring Soft Ontologies in the Design of a Workout Planner

This section presents our proposal by including a conceptual architecture (Subsect. 3.1), which is application independent (*i.e.*, it can be applied to various decision support systems). We then present the conception and design of a Gym Workout Planner (focus of this paper) based on the proposed architecture (*cf.* Subsection 3.2).

3.1   A Decision Support Architecture Based on Soft Ontologies

The conceptual architecture allows to understand how a soft ontology can be used in a decision support application as well as its requirements. Through this model, the solution phases are established. Table 1 presents the key components of our architecture, which are used throughout this section. Our graph representation is based on [32], where standard RDF graphs are expanded to include intermediate nodes representing disjunctive and conjunctive fuzzy attributes, whose values are represented by the weights of the edges. RDF standards link in a structured form a directed, labeled graph, where edges represent the named link between two resources, represented by the graph nodes[1].

Figure 1 illustrates the conceptual architecture based on soft ontologies. This figure presents the execution flow from the users profiles (item #1 of Fig. 1) to the generation of a individual decision graph for a specific user (items #6 and #7 of Fig. 1). In the following, we present a brief explanation of the Fig. 1 model:

– Based on the profile data of a set of registered users, described using Fuzzy RDF (item #1 of Fig. 1 and Table 1), a group definition algorithm (item #2 of Fig. 1 and Table 1) creates groups of users with similar characteristics (item #3 of Fig. 1 and Table 1).
– The information collected of each group member (*e.g.*, feedback, actions, sensors data) generates and updates a subset of a soft ontology, using fuzzy RDF graphs (item #4 of Fig. 1 and Table 1). This graph represents unique ontological space (ontospace), as compared with graph of other groups.

---

[1] https://www.w3.org/RDF/.

Table 1. Architectural components of a soft ontology based architecture

#	Component	Description
1	User profile in (fuzzy) RDF	Set of user' profile descriptions using Fuzzy RDF
2	Group definition algorithm	Algorithm for the definition of users' groups, for instance, by calculating the similarity of user's profiles using graph-based similarities
3	Groups with similar users	Groups of users created by the component #2
4	Fuzzy RDF – graphs with concepts for each group	Subset of the soft ontology with adjusted weights for a specific group of users
5	Decision algorithm	The algorithm used for decision making based on graphs representing the groups (Component #4)
6	Individual decision graph	RDF graph describing the decision
7	Specific user's profile	Fuzzy RDF model describing an user profile

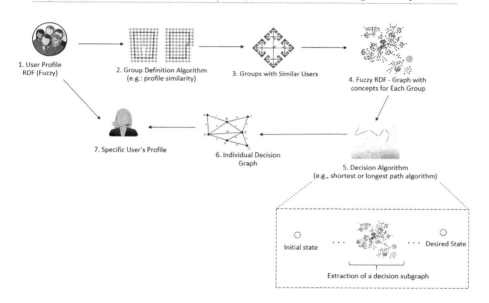

Fig. 1. Architecture overview.

– In the sequence, decision algorithms (item #5 of Fig. 1 and Table 1) are used to analyze a graph representing a group (last item). This determines the best decision for a specific user inside the group, for instance, a set of actions to be performed by a system (or robot), changes in an interactive interface, recommended actions for a domain experts, or a gym workout plan. A shortest path algorithm, for instance, can be used to determine the best path between an initial state and a desired state in a group graph with sequences of actions/states.

– An individual user' graph (item #6 of Fig. 1 and Table 1) is used to describe the decision to be taken. For instance, in case of a shortest path algorithm, this graph may contain a sequence of actions to be taken. The decision is then presented to an user (item #7 of Fig. 1 and Table 1).

Figure 2 illustrates the inclusion of a new user according to the proposed architecture. When a new user (item #1 of Fig. 2) registers in a system, the group definition algorithm (item #2 of Fig. 2) processes to which group this user belongs to. New groups can be created at this time according to the parameters used by the algorithm (and required by the application). In this case, a new set of user groups (item #3 of Fig. 2) and a new graph representing the group are created (item #4 of Fig. 2). Otherwise, the user is inserted in an exiting group and consider the existing group graph. The decision algorithm (item #5 of Fig. 2) is executed and the individual decision graph is created (item #6 of Fig. 2).

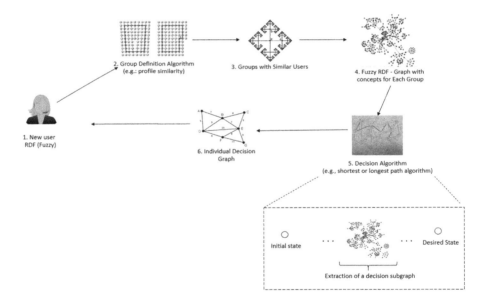

Fig. 2. Process for including a new user.

Figure 3 describes how the soft ontology (through group graphs) is updated. The architecture defines two types of updates.

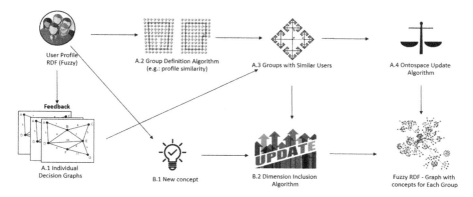

Fig. 3. Update and extension of soft ontologies.

A) Feedback-based update: This case refers to the update of Fuzzy RDF values of an existing concept in an *ontospace*. This process is described as follows:

– When an user receives his/her individual decision graph, (s)he provides a feedback related to this decision. This feedback may include explicit acts (*e.g.*, accept or reject a decision) or indirect ones (*e.g.*, sensor data, action consequences, body expressions). The feedback results are source of changes to the individual decision graph (item #A.1 of Fig. 3). For instance, when someone decides to take a different action (from the suggested one), this action is updated at the individual decision graph by changing their weights (*e.g.*, decreases the weight of the suggested action and increases the weight of the action taken).

– After a predetermined time, the individual decision graphs (item #A.1 of Fig. 3) are used to update (through group graphs) the soft ontology. To this end, it is necessary to re-evaluate the homogeneity of the groups (item #A.3 of Fig. 3), using the group definition algorithm (item #A.2 of Fig. 3). The groups with similar users and the individual graphs are used by the *ontospace* update algorithm (item #A.4 of Fig. 3). Different *ontospace* update algorithms and strategies can be used as needed. For example, a straightforward alternative is to adjust the weights of the group graph according to the average of the weights of the individual graphs.

B) New concept update: This case occurs due to the need of inclusion of a new *ontodimension* on the soft ontology, as follows:

– Starting from the need of including a new concept (item #B.1 of Fig. 3), a dimension inclusion algorithm (item #B.2 of Fig. 3) is responsible for including a concept in the group Fuzzy RDF graphs, *i.e.*, in our soft ontology. This is accomplished by the inclusion of new RDF triples, including the concept and its relationships. The addition of a new concept can be general and applicable to all groups, or the inclusion can be assigned to specific groups.

- Dimension inclusion algorithm (item #B.2 of Fig. 3) assigns a weight (fuzzy values) to the new RDF triples. Default values can be used in the absence of information about the new concept; or they can be determined from a complex analysis of previous groups' data (out of scope of this paper).

It is important to note that the proposed architecture is application independent. It can be applied to a wide range of application including decision support related to fuzzy concepts and rich feedback (*e.g.*, in social networks, learning environments, interaction with assistant robots, etc.).

3.2 The Conception of a Gym Workout Planner

At this stage, we emphasize the conception of the OntoGymWP by using the architecture presented. Based on soft ontology and associated technologies, a software prototype was designed to automatically generate training plans for gym users. The OntoGymWP aims at providing a more personalized and dynamic way to suggest training plans according to users' characteristics and needs.

Initially, a hard ontology was modeled by the involved researchers (authors of this paper) to be used as an initial model. The objective of this ontology was to mitigate the cold start problem [24], since initially we had no weights or knowledge about the specific context of users. The fuzzy weights and flexible structures are created during the system usage.

We defined a process for suggesting a gym-training plan for a specific user as follows:

- The system determines groups with similar characteristics by using dissimilarity algorithms for weighted graphs over the users' profile (fuzzy RDF representations);
- Each group is represented by a soft ontology (also implemented using fuzzy RDF) including activities and belief values related to these activities, in which lower values are attributed to activities more accepted by the group. Physical activities of the same type are described by disjunctive nodes. These soft ontologies are dynamically updated and expanded according to the users' (groups) feedback and input from physical education professionals;
- The system composes a training plan by using weighted graphs path algorithms over the soft ontology structure and values;
- The suggested plan is presented to the user. Physical education professionals may change the suggested plan. Such changes can be used as feedback to the system recalculate the ontology fuzzy values;
- The user executes the activities and provides feedbacks, which update his/her plan, the group ontology and his/her profile.

In our constructed prototype, four algorithms are used to execute the described process:

1. A dissimilarity calculation algorithm for weighted graphs (to define similar groups). We implemented an adapted version of the algorithm presented in [5].

2. A decision algorithm. Since our group graphs contains training activities and belief values related to these activities, we adopted an adapted version of the Dijkstra algorithm [11] to calculate the shortest path. A path goes through a set of activities including one of each type (they are described by disjunctive nodes) with the lower sum of assigned weight. This path describes a training plan for an specific user.

3. An *ontospace* update algorithm, which updates the values of the fuzzy RDF graph according to user's feedback. If there is a positive feedback from a group member about a suggested activity, it is multiplied by a factor that decreases its value, and other related activities are multiplied by a factor that increases their values (*i.e.*, lower values are attributed to activities more accepted by the group). If the feedback is negative, the suggested activity has a value multiplied by a positive factor.

4. Dimension inclusion algorithm. In our system, this new dimension concerns new training activities. If other activities of the same type already exist, then it is placed in a disjunctive node of the RDF Fuzzy model (*i.e.*, in our system only one activity per type is suggested in a plan). The initial assigned value for an new activity is the average of the other activities values in a given of user. The activity is then made available in the system via the soft ontology. The group's feedback adjusts the weight over time. In another case, if it is an activity of a different type (*i.e.*, it introduces a new type of activity in the system), then it is the only option with a default weight of 1.

4 Studies with the Ontology-Based Gym Workout Planner

The OntoGymWP was constructed with the objective of evaluating the architecture proposed in this work. Subsection 4.1 describes the main characteristics of this prototype. Subsection 4.2 discusses our findings, limitations and open challenges.

4.1 The Ontology-Based Gym Workout Planner

The first version of OntoGymWP does not aim to be a complete workout planner. The focus of the current version of our prototype is on the suggestion of training plans based on soft ontology context. The OntoGymWP was implemented using PHP[2], Java[3] and Javascript[4] technologies. These technologies are highly popular in the development of Web systems, and they have adequate support for RDF standards required to our study.

The Protégé platform[5] was used to model the initial hard ontology, which contains an initial domain/application representation to avoid the cold start

---

[2] https://www.php.net/.

[3] https://www.java.com/.

[4] https://www.w3.org/standards/webdesign/script.

[5] https://protege.stanford.edu/products.php.

problem [24]. For instance, training suggestion plans for those users whose profiles have less than 70% of similarity to any other user registered in the system is previously defined on this hard ontology (according to their features). Figure 4 presents the core classes created to describe a fitness center. Other concepts of the infrastructure, such as equipment, activities and professionals, are also represented in this ontology.

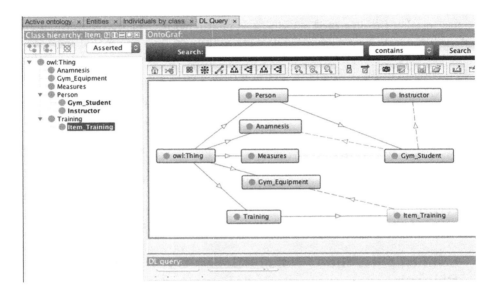

Fig. 4. Core classes of our OWL ontology describing a fitness center.

For evaluation purposes, we generated a fictitious database with 300 registered gym users to validate and test the system in use. The *Generatedata*[6] was used for this purpose. The generation parameters were defined with the support of a physical education professional.

Figure 5 presents the OntoGymWP homepage, where users can access the main functionalities of the OntoGymWP prototype, including: add a new athlete; use a search interface to select athletes; access the similarity calculation results (for a selected athlete); visualize the similarity graph/Fuzzy RDF;, visualize groups' graphs/Fuzzy RDF (with 30 most similar users); and generate the individual training for a selected athlete.

The user registration interface includes a form with the following fields: (1) personal data (*e.g.*, name, gender, age); (2) features from the anamnesis performed by an expert (*e.g.*, weight, height, regular physical activities); and, (3) objectives defined together with an expert (*e.g.*, fitness, weight loss, preparation for professional sports, muscle mass gain).

---

[6] https://www.generatedata.com/.

Fig. 5. OntoGymWP homepage.

The search interface is used to search an athlete and select him/her; or to search a group of athletes with similar characteristics to the selected one. In this case, the system lists groups of athletes in a similarity rank from the most similar to least similar (*i.e.*, from the lowest dissimilarity value to the highest one).

Figure 6 presents the groups' graphs visualization interface. This visualization includes the 30 most similar athletes. The user can select athletes, visualize and compare the individual's characteristics of each athlete (ellipses at the left side of Fig. 6) as well as the activities performed (ellipses at the right side of Fig. 6). This interface allows the user to visualize the fuzzy RDF source file and download it for external use.

Figure 7 presents a fuzzy RDF subgraph of the activities executed by the group with similar characteristics of the selected users. Weights are readjusted according to the preferences/feedback of the group members. These values present in the edges are used by the decision algorithm to select the activities to be suggested to an individual athlete. Disjunctive and conjunctive nodes, as well as edges names were removed for visualization purposes.

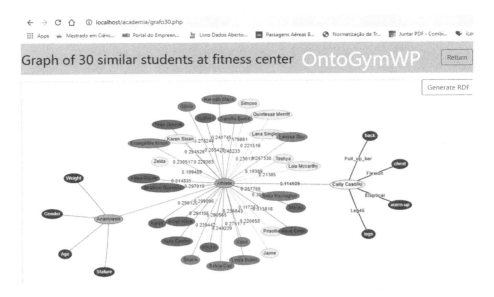

Fig. 6. Example of graph with the most similar athletes.

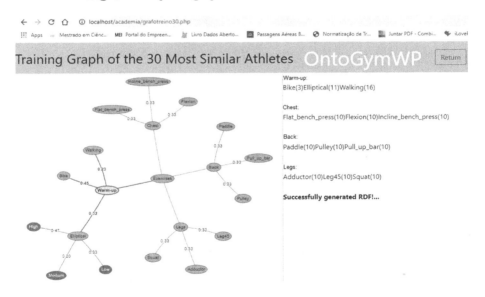

Fig. 7. Example of Group Fuzzy RDF activity subgraph.

The values at the edges represent the degree of belief of the adequacy of an activity to a certain group of athletes described as RDF triples: $(t = (s, p, o)[n])$; n is a value of belief of adequacy to the group, where n is [0...1]. For example, in Fig. 7 some of the represented triples are:

1. *(Bike, typeof, Warm-up) [0.45]:* 0.45 represents the belief that *Bike* can be selected as preferred *typeof Warm-up* for this group;
2. *(Flexion, typeof, Chest) [0.33]:* 0.33 represents the belief that *Flexion* can be selected as preferred *typeof Chest* exercise for this group;
3. *(High, intensityof, Elliptical) [0.47]:* 0.47 represents the belief that *High* can be selected as preferred *intensityof Elliptical* exercise for this group.

The adopted decision algorithm chooses the best path in this graph to propose a training plan. An adapted version of the Dijkstra algorithm [11] selects the best path[7] in the graph containing all the type of exercises and intensity. The plan is then suggested to the selected athlete. As Fig. 8 shows, this plan can be changed by an expert (or by the athlete). These changes are considered as part of the feedback, which is used to change the individual and group Fuzzy RDF graphs.

Fig. 8. User interface of an individual training plan suggestion and change.

4.2 Discussion

New interactive applications demand flexible and expandable models capable of representing knowledge under uncertainty. Soft ontologies [18] are suited to deal with the dynamic nature of these applications because its structure is not conditioned to fixed hierarchies or rigid pre-defined knowledge representation models. These ontologies rely on concepts such as ontological dimensions and space to provide flexible representations.

This paper contributed with a conceptual architecture and application that explores soft ontologies in the context of a gym workout planner. Our ontologies were implemented as Fuzzy RDF graphs. This is a novel solution, and our

---

[7] We use the complement values to calculate the shortest path.

investigation contributed by presenting a viable proof-of-concept of a conceptual architecture that implements soft ontologies in planning recommendation systems.

The conceptual architecture proposed is generic and can be reused for future work in other applications. It includes a set of steps, structures for representing knowledge and algorithms that can be adapted and applied to problems involving personalized decision making based on users' feedback (explicit or not).

The OntoGymWP allowed to evaluate the use of soft ontologies in a challenging scenario. We found that it was possible to automate, in a personalized way, the suggestion of training to athletes, based on their profiles and feedback from group of similar users. The ontology provided the flexibility to introduce new concepts and adapt the training plan in a dynamic and flexible way over time.

Some simplifications were adopted in the construction of the first version of the OntoGymWP prototype. This aimed to be a proof of concept for our architecture. One of the simplifications was to adopt an activity of each type in the training plan. Other simplifications refer to the scope of the profile and decision support functionalities. In addition, it is important to mention that the OntoGymWP, at this stage, does not aim to be an enactive system [19].

New versions of the OntoGymWP can incorporate body sensors, evaluate body expressions (e.g., using computer vision techniques) and on the fly social reactions for further enhancing user's experience. These elements can be used as feedback (as supported by our architecture) and trigger the reconfiguration of the ontology based on them. Also, advanced machine learning technologies can be incorporated to provide the analysis of the feedback and guide the evolution of the ontologies (in the weights for instance). More sophisticated algorithms and action plans can be explored using the same architecture. These extensions require further studies, as well as dealing with conceptual and technological challenges in related areas.

5   Conclusion

Soft ontologies are useful to represent knowledge about dynamic and uncertain domains. Such a characteristic is required by several contemporary interactive systems. In this paper, we presented a soft ontology based architecture for implementing decision support and recommendation systems. The solution leverages features in interactive systems towards personalized user's experience. Our architecture uses a Fuzzy RDF approach to implement soft ontologies, and it considers the users' similarities and their feedback to adapt flexible ontologies. This architecture was implemented by the OntoGymWP application, which provides gym training plan suggestions according to users' profile and dynamic feedback. As a prof of concept, the software application showed the viability of the proposed architecture, as well as reveled possible improvements and challenges. Next steps of this research includes to improve the OntoGymWP to incorporate features of enactive systems and to carry out empirical studies on fitness center, including experts' feedback and practical result analysis.

Acknowledgements. This work was partially financed by Coordenação de Aperfeiçoamento de Pessoal de Nível Superior – Brazil (CAPES/PROSUP) and the São Paulo Research Foundation (FAPESP) (Grants #2015/16528-0 and #2017/02325-5) (The opinions expressed in here are not necessarily shared by the financial support agency.)

References

1. Berners-Lee, T., Hendler, J., Lassila, O.: The semantic web. Sci. Am. **284**(5), 28–37 (2001)
2. Blasch, E.P., Dorion, E., Valin, P., Bosse, E., Roy, J.: Ontology alignment in geographical hard-soft information fusion systems. In: 2010 13th International Conference on Information Fusion, pp. 1–8 (2010). https://doi.org/10.1109/ICIF.2010. 5712081
3. Bonacin, R., Calado, I., dos Reis, J.C.: A metamodel for supporting interoperability in heterogeneous ontology networks. In: Liu, K., Nakata, K., Li, W., Baranauskas, C. (eds.) ICISO 2018. IAICT, vol. 527, pp. 187–196. Springer, Cham (2018). https://doi.org/10.1007/978-3-319-94541-5_19
4. Caglioni, M., Fusco, G.: Formal ontologies and uncertainty in geographical knowledge. J. Land Use Mobil. Environ. (TeMA) (2014). https://hal.archives-ouvertes. fr/hal-01906704
5. de Castro, L.N., Ferrari, D.G.: Introdução à mineração de dados: conceitos básicos, algoritmos e aplicações, 1 edn. Ed. Saraiva (2016)
6. Collao, A.J., Diaz-Kommonen, L., Kaipainen, M., Pietarila, J.: Soft ontologies and similarity cluster tools to facilitate exploration and discovery of cultural heritage resources. In: Proceedings of 14th International Workshop on Database and Expert Systems Applications, pp. 75–79, September 2003. https://doi.org/10. 1109/DEXA.2003.1232001
7. Dietze, S., Benn, N., Domingue, J., Conconi, A., Cattaneo, F.: Two-fold service matchmaking – applying ontology mapping for semantic web service discovery. In: Gómez-Pérez, A., Yu, Y., Ding, Y. (eds.) ASWC 2009. LNCS, vol. 5926, pp. 246–260. Springer, Heidelberg (2009). https://doi.org/10.1007/978-3-642-10871-6_17
8. Dietze, S., Benn, N., Domingue, J., Orthuber, W.: Blending the physical and the digital through conceptual spaces. In: OneSpace 2009 Workshop at Future Internet Symposium (FIS) (2009). http://oro.open.ac.uk/23019/
9. Dietze, S., Domingue, J.: Bridging between sensor measurements and symbolic ontologies through conceptual spaces. In: 1st International Workshop on the Semantic Sensor Web (SemSensWeb 2009) at The 6th Annual European Semantic Web Conference (ESWC 2009), June 2009
10. Dietze, S., Tanasescu, V.: Spatial groundings for meaningful symbols. In: Workshop on Matching and Meaning 2009 at The AISB 2009 Conference (2009). http://oro. open.ac.uk/23070/
11. Dijkstra, E.W.: A note on two problems in connexion with graphs. Numer. Math. **1**(1), 269–271 (1959). https://doi.org/10.1007/BF01386390
12. Gandon, F., Schreiber, G.: RDF 1.1 XML syntax, February 2014. http://www.w3. org/TR/2014/REC-rdf-syntax-grammar-20140225/
13. Hazman, M., El-Beltagy, S.R., Rafea, A.: A survey of ontology learning approaches. Int. J. Comput. Appl. **22**(8), 36–43 (2011)
14. Jain, V., Singh, M.: Ontology based information retrieval in semantic web: a survey. Int. J. Inf. Technol. Comput. Sci. (IJITCS) **5**(10), 62–69 (2013)

15. Justo, A., dos Reis, J.C., Calado, I., Bonacin, R., Jensen, F.: Exploring ontologies to improve the empathy of interactive bots. In: 2018 IEEE 27th International Conference on Enabling Technologies: Infrastructure for Collaborative Enterprises (WETICE), pp. 261–266. IEEE Computer Society, Los Alamitos, June 2018. https://doi.org/10.1109/WETICE.2018.00057. https://doi.ieeecomputersociety.org/10.1109/WETICE.2018.00057

16. Kaipainen, M.: Perspective-relative narrative media and power. In: Proceedings IADIS International Conference e-Society 2010, Porto, Portugal, 18–21 March 2010, pp. 553–556. IADIS Press (2010)

17. Kaipainen, M., Hautamäki, A.: Epistemic pluralism and multi-perspective knowledge organization: explorative conceptualization of topical content domains. Knowl. Organ. **38**(6), 503–514 (2011)

18. Kaipainen, M., Normak, P., Niglas, K., Kippar, J., Laanpere, M.: Soft ontologies, spatial representations and multi-perspective explorability. Expert Syst. **25**(5), 474–483 (2008)

19. Kaipainen, M., Ravaja, N., Tikka, P., Vuori, R., Pugliese, R., Rapino, M., Takala, T.: Enactive systems and enactive media: embodied human-machine coupling beyond interfaces. Leonardo **44**, 433–438 (2011)

20. Kitchenham, B.: Procedures for performing systematic reviews. Technical report TR/SE-0401, Department of Computer Science, Keele University, UK (2004)

21. Lombello, L.O., dos Reis, J.C., Bonacin, R.: Soft ontologies as fuzzy RDF statements. In: IEEE 28th International Conference on Enabling Technologies: Infrastructure for Collaborative Enterprises (WETICE), pp. 289–294 (2019). https://doi.org/10.1109/WETICE.2019.00067

22. del Mar Sánchez Vera, M., Fernández, J.T., Sánchez, J.L.S., Espinosa, M.P.P.: Practical experiences for the development of educational systems in the semantic web. J. New Approach. Educ. Res. **2**(1), 23–31 (2013). https://doi.org/10.7821/naer.2.1.23-31. https://naerjournal.ua.es/article/view/v2n1-4

23. Martinez-Garcia, A., Morris, S., Tscholl, M., Tracy, F., Carmichael, P.: Case-based learning, pedagogical innovation, and semantic web technologies. IEEE Trans. Learn. Technol. **5**(2), 104–116 (2012). https://doi.org/10.1109/TLT.2011.34

24. Middleton, S.E., Alani, H., Shadbolt, N.R., De Roure, D.C.: Exploiting synergy between ontologies and recommender systems. In: Proceedings of the 3rd International Conference on Semantic Web - Volume 55, SemWeb 2002, pp. 41–50. CEUR-WS.org, Aachen, DEU (2002)

25. Pata, K.: Participatory design experiment: storytelling swarm in hybrid narrative ecosystem, pp. 482–508. IGI Global, Hershey (2011). http://services.igi-global.com/resolvedoi/resolve.aspx?doi=10.4018/978-1-60960-040-2.ch029

26. Pugliese, R., Lehtonen, K.: A framework for motion based bodily enaction with virtual characters. In: Vilhjálmsson, H.H., Kopp, S., Marsella, S., Thórisson, K.R. (eds.) IVA 2011. LNCS (LNAI), vol. 6895, pp. 162–168. Springer, Heidelberg (2011). https://doi.org/10.1007/978-3-642-23974-8_18

27. Pugliese, R., Tikka, P., Kaipainen, M.: Navigating story ontospace: perspective-relative drive and combinatory montage of cinematic content. In: Expanding Practices in Audiovisual Narrative, pp. 105–128 (2014)

28. Rajaonarivo, L., Maisel, E., De Loor, P.: An evolving museum metaphor applied to cultural heritage for personalized content delivery. User Model. User Adap. Inter. **29**(1), 161–200 (2019). https://doi.org/10.1007/s11257-019-09222-x

29. Sahraoui, K., youcef, D., Omar, N.: Improvement of collaborative filtering systems through resource description framework. In: Proceedings of the International Conference on Intelligent Information Processing, Security and Advanced Communication, IPAC 2015. Association for Computing Machinery, New York (2015). https://doi.org/10.1145/2816839.2816863
30. Staab, S., Studer, R.: Handbook on Ontologies, 2nd edn. Springer, Heidelberg (2009). https://doi.org/10.1007/978-3-540-92673-3
31. W3C OWL Working Group: OWL 2 Web Ontology Language Document Overview (2012). https://www.w3.org/TR/owl2-overview/
32. Yanhui Lv, Ma, Z.M., Yan, L.: Fuzzy RDF: a data model to represent fuzzy metadata. In: 2008 IEEE International Conference on Fuzzy Systems (IEEE World Congress on Computational Intelligence), pp. 1439–1445 (2008). https://doi.org/10.1109/FUZZY.2008.4630561
33. Ye, J., Stevenson, G., Dobson, S.: A top-level ontology for smart environments. Pervasive Mob. Comput. **7**(3), 359–378 (2011). https://doi.org/10.1016/j.pmcj.2011.02.002

Music Interpretation Support System - Integration Support Interface of Impressions from Listening to Music and Reading Its Score

Tomoko Kojiri$^{(\boxtimes)}$ and Akio Sugikami

Kansai University, 3-3-35, Yamate-cho, Suita, Osaka 564-8680, Japan
`kojiri@kansai-u.ac.jp`

Abstract. To play music with individuality, it is important for performers to interpret the music from their own viewpoints with impressions for each bar. However, especially in introductory music education in Japan, teachers mainly teach their students how to play notes correctly without training performers on how to interpret the music. In music interpretation, performers need to form impressions for each bar. The aim of our research is to provide an environment that helps performers form an impression for each bar in the score. Impressions can be obtained from two viewpoints: from the notes or the musical symbols that make up the bars and from their roles in the song as a whole, which is usually grasped from listening to the entire piece. Our research develops a music interpretation support system where performers can consider impressions for each bar from both of these aspects: by reading the notes and musical symbols and refining these impressions by listening to the entire piece. We also developed a mechanism to promote awareness of inconsistency in the derived impressions.

Keywords: Music interpretation support · Impression attachment · Awareness of inconsistency · Representation of impression changes

1 Introduction

Beginner musicians (performers) often start with reading the score. Many pay attention only to the notes and musical symbols on the score, and then try to play the sound accurately according to the score. However, strictly playing the sound according to the score results in a performance that lacks expressiveness and emotional impact [1]. Such a performance is the result of playing without considering the atmosphere that the music tries to convey. To grasp the music's intended atmosphere, the performer must interpret the music by forming an impression of each part of the score while reading it and express these impressions in their performance.

In some parts of the score, musical symbols called expression terms are attached to express the atmosphere of the music. However, these expression terms are not inscribed on every bar in the score. Where they are missing, it is necessary for the performer to consider the impression by interpreting the scores. However, performers, especially in Japan, are not trained to interpret scores to consider impression. The purpose of this

© Springer Nature Switzerland AG 2020
S. Yamamoto and H. Mori (Eds.): HCII 2020, LNCS 12185, pp. 22–38, 2020.
https://doi.org/10.1007/978-3-030-50017-7_2

study is to develop an environment that supports performers in forming impressions of each part of the score.

Some studies for creating an automatic performance instrument tried to develop a mechanism to provide interpretation of scores to achieve an expressive performance [2]. These studies were able to give one interpretation of the scores; however, this interpretation was not unique. Differences in interpretation lead to individuality in performances. Therefore, our aim is to support performers in achieving their own interpretation and to promote playing music according to their own tastes.

To interpret music, it is necessary to read the score. There are studies that support reading scores. In Watanabe et al., the relations of scores among multiple instruments in an orchestra score, such as melodies or accompaniments, were demonstrated by analyzing their measures [3]. Kornstädt's system supported performers' analyses of scores by providing search functions based on pitch, rhythm, and harmony [4]. These studies supported easily reading notes and musical symbols that are clearly written on the scores, but this information is not enough to promote the performers' own interpretations.

Several researches attempted to create a mechanism that can handle music based on impressions. Kaji et al. applied the user's interpretation of music in searches. This allowed the web system to gather impressions of parts of a score from many people. It also developed a search mechanism for music based on the attached impressions [5]. In this system, users added impressions only on the parts of scores where they formed impressions, so impressions were not given to all bars. On the other hand, Yang's system allowed users to attach images that represent the atmosphere of the music [6]. Since only one image can be attached to one score, it was not able to represent detailed impressions of the scores. To play music, impressions should be attached to all bars. In addition, these studies did not support interpreting the scores.

The aim of our research is to provide an environment that helps performers form an impression of each bar in a score. These impressions can be obtained from two viewpoints. One is from the notes or musical symbols that make up the bars. The other is from their roles in the entire song, which is usually grasped from listening to the whole piece. If the impression obtained from the notes or musical symbols is regarded as bottom-up, the impression obtained by listening to the music can be regarded as top-down. Performers need to consider both the bottom-up and the top-down impressions and decide how to perform each bar.

In the writing field, Shibata et al. proposed a framework for writing sentences from both top-down writing that refines sentences from the overall concept and bottom-up writing that summarizes fragmented sentences [7]. We introduce this idea into our research. We developed a music interpretation support system where performers can consider impressions of each bar from two aspects: reading the notes and musical symbols and refining their impressions by listening to the music. In addition, we developed a mechanism for highlighting inconsistent impressions derived by both approaches. By capturing music from both the top-down and bottom-up aspects using this system, performers are able to think about the impression not only from a narrow range of only notes and musical symbols, but also from the construction of the entire piece.

2   Approach for Interpreting Music

2.1   Information on Musical Score

When playing a musical instrument, the performer reads and plays the score. Information on the score includes musical notes and musical symbols. Notes represent pitch and sequences of notes form a melody. Musical symbols include dynamic symbols, velocity symbols, expression terms, and so on. Dynamic symbols describe the strength for playing a sound, e.g., *p* for playing softly and *f* for playing strongly. Velocity symbols indicate the speed at which the notes should be played. Expression terms represent the atmosphere or mood of the music. They are impression clues for each bar, but are not included on every bar.

2.2   Trials for Adding Impressions

We investigated how performers attach impressions to music. We asked two university students with piano experience to read the "Burgmüller 25 Practice Song Op.100 No.1 La Candeur" piano score and consider how they would perform it. We requested that they write down comments about how they would perform on the bars where they intended to add emotions. The score annotated by one the collaborators is shown in Fig. 1. In the score, musical symbols were attached to 15 bars with no musical symbols attached to the remaining eight bars.

There were 10 bars where comments were added by the collaborators, and nine of these had musical symbols. The only bar that did not have a musical symbol had the same comment as the former bar that had a musical symbol. This indicates that the performers form impressions when reading a score. In addition, the bars that do not have musical symbols tend to be performed with impressions similar to the preceding bars.

Fig. 1. Example of adding impressions

2.3   Overall Framework for Music Interpretation Support System

Our investigation showed that performers use musical symbols to indicate their impressions. In addition, they use the same impression for the bars that form a series of a melody. This suggests that the bottom-up impression attachment (*bottom-up approach*) consists of two steps: reading the musical symbols and attaching an impression to the bar, and integrating bars that form a melody and attaching an impression to them.

On the other hand, performers form impressions of an entire musical piece by listening to it. If the song consists of several parts with changing tunes, there may be an impression attributed to each part. Therefore, the top-down impression attachment (*top-down approach*) also consists of two steps: forming an impression for a group of bars, and dividing the group into smaller groups and attributing a detailed impression to them.

With the top-down approach, it is difficult to consider impressions for each bar. On the other hand, with the bottom-up approach, it is difficult to consider the impression of an entire musical piece because musical symbols are only given to some bars. If performers are able to form impressions that satisfy both the top-down and bottom-up approaches, such impressions may match the impressions of hearing music while satisfying the musical symbols in the scores. Therefore, this research develops a music interpretation support system with which a performer can consider impressions that satisfy both the top-down and bottom-up approaches.

An overview of the system is shown in Fig. 2. The system holds music data, such as scores and sound files. Musical scores are written in MusicXML format [8]. When the title of a musical piece is selected, MuseScore 2 [9] is executed and the score of the music is displayed on its interface. The impression attachment interface provides an environment where performers can attach impressions by the top-down and bottom-up approaches, respectively. In addition, it also represents the musical symbols attached on the music data, which are extracted by the musical symbol extraction mechanism, for supporting the bottom-up approach. The impression-inconsistency judgment mechanism alerts performers when there is an inconsistency in the impressions given by the top-down and bottom-up approaches.

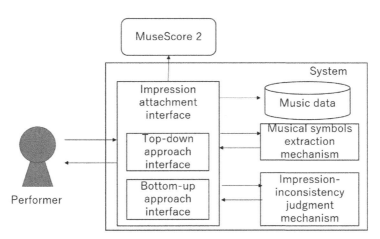

Fig. 2. System overview

3   Impression Attachment Interface

3.1   Impression Graph

The proposed support system provides an interface where performers can consider impressions for each bar both from the top-down and bottom-up approaches. To produce a consistent impression, we need a representation method for describing impression.

Music is regarded as a story that is expressed by the composer using sound. In Japanese language education, the interpretation of the emotions of the characters in a story is represented by a line graph called the emotion curve [10]. The emotion curve expresses the ups and downs of the characters' emotions along the transition of the story's scenes. By visualizing the emotions with a graph representation, the story can be interpreted easily. Since the impression of music is similar to the emotions in a story, we introduce a line graph to illustrate the changes in impression, which we call an "impression graph."

The impression graph represents changes in impression in the music with the vertical axis representing the impression of the music and the horizontal axis representing the bar numbers. The impression of the music can be represented in several ways. Hevner expressed the impression of the music using eight adjective groups [11]. Huang et al. used two axes of joy and activity [12]. We express impression according to degrees of positive/negative, since it is difficult to play music based on multiple emotions. We prepared five degrees, slightly weaker, weaker, medium, slightly stronger, and stronger, prepared for positive/negative, respectively. In addition to these five degrees, we also set neutral, which is just between positive and negative.

Figure 3 shows an example of an impression graph. In the vertical axis, 0 means neutral. The positive direction represents the positive degree; the higher the number is, the higher the positive degree. Conversely, the negative direction indicates the negative degree.

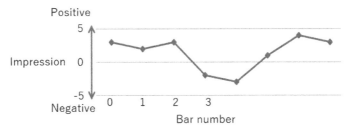

Fig. 3. Impression graph

3.2   Impression Attachment Interface

When considering the impression from a top-down approach, the performer listens to the music and divides the bars into groups based on changes in impression, and attributes an impression to the groups. By listening to the music repeatedly, the performer notices that the impression changes even more in a group and divides the group into smaller groups of bars. To attach impressions along with such steps, the top-down approach interface provides an environment where the performer can divide the group of bars into small groups that he/she thinks have the same impression and can attach impressions for these groups. In addition, according to the impression attached to each group, the impression graph is updated so that bars in the same group have the same impression degree. An example of creating an impression graph based on the top-down approach is shown in Fig. 4. In Fig. 4, bars were first divided into three groups and impressions were attached to each group (Fig. 4a). When bars 2–4 were divided into two groups, such as groups of 2–3 and 4, and different impressions were attached to each group, the impression graph was updated according to the newly attached impression degrees (Fig. 4b).

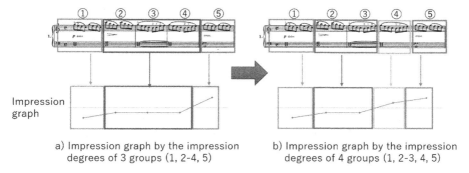

a) Impression graph by the impression degrees of 3 groups (1, 2-4, 5)

b) Impression graph by the impression degrees of 4 groups (1, 2-3, 4, 5)

Fig. 4. Example of updating impression graph based on top-down approach

On the other hand, the bottom-up approach relies on musical symbols in the bars to express impressions. First, impressions are attached to bars that contain musical symbols. Since there are phrases in the score, a group of bars can be created according to the phrases and the same impressions are given to the bars within a group that do not have musical symbols. After reading the scores repeatedly, the performer notices larger phrases that contain several small phrases, integrates the small groups into one

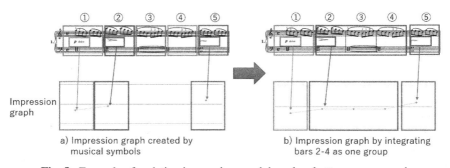

a) Impression graph created by musical symbols

b) Impression graph by integrating bars 2-4 as one group

Fig. 5. Example of updating impression graph based on bottom-up approach

bigger group, and attaches one impression to the bigger group. The bottom-up approach interface provides an environment where the performer can combine individual bars to form a group of several bars and attach an impression for each group. The interface also updates the impression graph based on the attached impression. An example of updating the impression graph based on the bottom-up approach is shown in Fig. 5. Since there are musical symbols at bar numbers 1, 2, and 5, the impressions are determined for these bars first (Fig. 5a). If a performer creates a group of 2 to 4 bars, the impression attached to bar 2 is also attached to bars 3 and 4 (Fig. 5b).

4   Impression-Inconsistency Judgment Mechanism

Global changes in impression can be drawn with the top-down approach and fine-level impressions can be considered with the bottom-up approach. To play the music, unique impressions should be attached to each bar that can satisfy both approaches. However, when creating impression graphs from both approaches, their values are not always the same.

The impression-inconsistency judgment mechanism grasps the groups of bars and their impression degrees and alerts the user if there are any large differences. It calculates the average degrees of the bars within a group that are attached from the top-down and bottom-up approaches, and provides a notification message if their average degrees are larger than the threshold. The impression graphs in Fig. 6a are inconsistent. Let us assume that the performer created a group of 1–4 bars with the top-down approach. The average impression degree of the group from this approach is 4, while that from the bottom-up approach is −2.75. If the threshold for detecting the difference is set at 2, this group is detected as an inconsistent group.

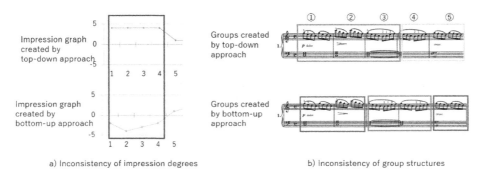

a) Inconsistency of impression degrees   b) Inconsistency of group structures

Fig. 6. Example of inconsistency

The reason for the differences in the impression degrees sometimes comes from the differences in the groups created by the top-down and bottom-up approaches. The differences in the ranges of the groups mean that the impressions drawn by listening do not match the impressions acquired by reading the scores. In such case, a unique impression cannot be attached. If the ranges of the groups from the top-down and bottom-up approaches are not the same, or not included by the other, the mechanism notifies of the difference. Figure 6b is an example of an inconsistency in created groups. Let us assume that the performer created two groups of 1–3 and 4–5 from the top-down approach and three groups of 1–2, 3–4, and 5 from the bottom-up approach. In this case, bars 3 and 4 are appreciated differently; they are regarded as belonging to different phrases from the top-down approach, but are regarded as forming one phrase by the bottom-up approach. In this case, bars 1 to 5 are considered inconsistent.

5   Prototype System

We implemented a support system for attaching impressions in the programming language C#. Figure 7 shows the interface. The interface includes a music selection unit, an impression graph display unit, a top-down approach unit, a bottom-up approach unit, a musical symbols display unit, and an impression check button.

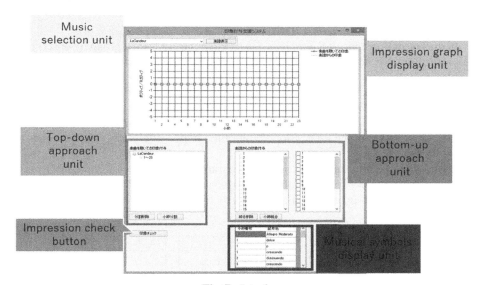

Fig. 7. Interface

When a song is selected from the song selection section drop-down list, the musical symbols are extracted from the score and displayed in the musical symbols display unit. At the same time, MuseScore 2 shows the score and the music can be listened to through MuseScore 2's play function.

In the top-down approach unit, bars can be divided into groups by listening to the music and impressions can be attached to each group. The relations between the created groups are illustrated as a tree structure. Initially, a node representing a group that contains all bars is displayed as the root node. When a node representing a group is selected and the group division button is pressed, a group division form is displayed (Fig. 8a). When the start bar number and end bar number are inputted and the add button is pushed, a new node is created as a child node of the selected node in the top-down approach unit. Further division can be performed by selecting the generated node. The impression degree input form appears by double-clicking on the node in the top-down approach unit (Fig. 8b). In this form, the track bar is used to input impressions from negative to positive in 11 levels from −5 to 5. After the impression is inputted, the value is reflected in the impression graph of the impression graph display unit as a blue line.

a) Group division form   b) Impression degree input form

Fig. 8. Forms used for attaching the top-down impression

In the bottom-up approach unit, bars can be combined to form a group by observing the scores. Initially, nodes corresponding to each bar are displayed as leaf nodes of the tree structure. By double-clicking on a node, an impression degree input form, which is the same as in Fig. 8a, appears. When selecting the bars and pushing the bar integration button, a group is created and displayed as the parent node of the selected nodes. The impression degree is also inputted to the created node. After the impression is inputted, the value is reflected in the impression graph of the impression graph display unit as a yellow line.

Figure 9 shows an example of impression graphs in the impression graph display unit. Impression degrees from the top-down approach are indicated by the blue line and those from the bottom-up approach by the yellow line.

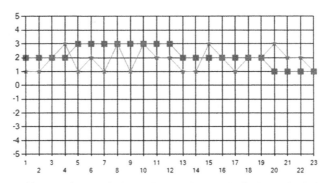

Fig. 9. Example of impression graphs in the impression graph display unit (Color figure online)

When the impression check button is pushed, the consistency of the group structures and the impression degrees are analyzed, and the notification message is generated by creating a new message window, if necessary. If the group structure is inconsistent, the notification message "The divisions of bars by listening to the music and by reading scores are different" appears. If the impression degrees are inconsistent, the "Are your impressions degrees consistent?" message appears.

6 Evaluation

6.1 Experimental Setting

We conducted an evaluation experiment of the proposed system with 13 university students $(A - M)$ who were able to read music. The subjects first completed the questionnaire in Table 1 (questionnaire 1). Question 1 asked the subjects whether they have experience playing musical instruments. Question 2 asked them to list the points to be aware of when starting to practice new music.

Table 1. Questionnaire 1 questions

ID	Question	Answer
1	Do you have experience playing musical instruments?	1. Yes/2. No
2	What do you consider when you start practicing a new song?	Free description

Next, after distributing the system manual to the subjects and explaining the purpose and usage of the system, the students used the system to provide their impression of the music. The target music was "Burgmüller 25 practice song Op.100 No.3 La Pastorale." As supplementary material, definitions of the musical symbols used in the score were provided. The threshold for detecting the differences in impression degrees was 2. We asked the subjects to answer another questionnaire while using the system to clarify the effective elements for having an impression (questionnaire 2), shown in Table 2. Question 1 asked why the music impression attachment method was switched to the top-down/bottom-up approach if the subject switched during the exercise. Question 2 asked about the factors in determining the impression degrees. The use of the system was terminated when the subjects were satisfied with their attached impressions.

After using the system, the subjects were asked to answer a third questionnaire (questionnaire 3), shown in Table 3. Question 1 asked how easy it was to express the impression of the music as positive or negative, and question 2 asked how easy it was to determine the impression degrees. Question 3 was designed to evaluate the effectiveness of the impression graph. Question 4 asked if the subject received a notification message during the use of the system and, if "Yes," the additional questions shown in Table 4 were provided.

Table 2. Questionnaire 2 questions

ID	Question	Answer
1	When you changed the manner of giving an impression, please provide all reasons for the change	1. To listen to the song/2. To read the score/3. Felt stuck/4. Other
2	When you decide the impression degrees, please select all elements that determined the value	1. Impression felt by song/2. Musical symbols in score/3. Sequence of music notes/4. Impression graph/5. Others

Table 3. Questionnaire 3 questions

ID	Question	Answer
1	Was it easy to express the impression of the music as positive/negative?	1. Yes/2. Somewhat yes/3. Somewhat no/4. No
2	Was it easy to decide the impression degrees?	1. Yes/2. Somewhat yes/3. Somewhat no/4. No
3	Did displaying the impression in an impression graph help you consider the impression of the song?	1. Yes/2. Somewhat yes/3. Somewhat no/4. No
4	Did the system point out inconsistencies during the experiment?	1. Yes/2. No

Table 4. Additional questions for question 4 of questionnaire 3

ID	Question	Answer
4-1	Were you convinced of inconsistencies that were pointed out by the system?	1. Yes/2. No
4-2	Did you change the impression value due to the inconsistency?	1. Yes/2. No

6.2 Results

The results of question 1 of questionnaire 1 show that all subjects had experience playing a musical instrument. Table 5 shows the answers to question 2 of questionnaire 1, describing the focus points for beginning practice. As shown in Table 5, the subjects who seemed to consider the impression of the music were subjects A, E, F, G, and M.

We begin by discussing the effectiveness of the top-down and bottom-up approaches. Tables 6 and 7 show the results of question 1 and question 2 of questionnaire 2. Table 8 shows the number of switches between the top-down/bottom-up approaches. Six out of the 13 people switched more than once, but seven switched only once. Subjects G, I, and J did not select 2 in Table 7, so they provided an impression only by listening to the music. On the other hand, subject F did not select 1 in Table 7, which means he

Table 5. Answers to question 2 of questionnaire 1

Subject	Points the subjects focus on in practicing a new song (*The target instrument*)
A	Sense (*piano*)
B	Whether the fingers can move properly (*piano*)
C	To play exactly to the music score, to play with the correct form (*piano*)
D	To enjoy music (*Electone*)
E	Listen to song before practicing to understand the role of the instrument (*timpani*)
F	To understand the whole flow of the song (*piano*)
G	To understand the whole flow of the song (*piano*)
H	To have the goal to practice (*piano*)
I	To be conscious of the movement of the fingers (*Electone*)
J	To read the score (*piano*)
K	To read the score repeatedly (*piano*)
L	To practice favorite parts first and then practice the other rest (*piano*)
M	To imagine the song and the role of the instrument by listening to the music (*piano*)

only used the impression acquired by reading the score. For these subjects, switching between the top-down and bottom-up approaches may not have been effective. However, other subjects considered the impression from both approaches. Therefore, making an

Table 6. Answers to question 1 of questionnaire 2

Answer	A	B	C	D	E	F	G	H	I	J	K	L	M
1		Y	Y						Y	Y	Y		Y
2	Y				Y		Y				Y		
3				Y	Y	Y							Y
4													

Table 7. Answers to question 2 of questionnaire 2

Answer	A	B	C	D	E	F	G	H	I	J	K	L	M
1	Y	Y	Y	Y	Y		Y	Y	Y	Y	Y	Y	Y
2	Y	Y	Y	Y	Y	Y		Y			Y	Y	Y
3	Y	Y			Y	Y					Y	Y	Y
4			Y			Y					Y	Y	
5													

impression from both the top-down and bottom-up approaches is effective for subjects whose impression cannot be determined solely by either.

Table 8. Number of switches between top-down/bottom-up approaches

A	B	C	D	E	F	G	H	I	J	K	L	M
3	8	1	4	3	1	3	1	1	1	10	1	1

We next focus on the effectiveness of displaying the impression as an impression graph. Table 9 shows the answers to questionnaire 3 and Table 10 shows the results of the additional questionnaire for question 4. Subject F did not answer the questions for 4-1 and 4-2 because the system did not send him any notification messages. From the results of question 1 in Table 9, with the exception of two participants (F and H), the subjects found it easy to express the impression of the music as positive or negative. However, as indicated by question 2, six of the subjects found it difficult to determine concrete values of impression. One reason for the difficulty may come from the complexity of expressing what is felt as a value. Subject F, who replied that it was not easy, commented, "It was difficult because I have not considered a concrete impression before." On the other hand, from question 3, all subjects except for F answered that it was useful to display the impression of the music in an impression graph. These results demonstrate that displaying the impression as an impression graph is effective from the viewpoint of positive and negative changes, but does not help determine the specific impression degrees.

Table 9. Answers to questionnaire 3

Question	A	B	C	D	E	F	G	H	I	J	K	L	M
1	2	2	2	2	2	4	2	3	2	2	2	1	2
2	3	2	3	3	2	4	1	2	2	2	3	2	3
3	2	2	2	1	1	4	1	1	2	2	1	1	1
4	1	1	1	1	1	2	1	1	1	1	1	1	1

Table 10. Answers to the additional questionnaire for question 4

Question	A	B	C	D	E	F	G	H	I	J	K	L	M
4-1	1	1	1	1	1	–	1	1	1	1	1	2	1
4-2	2	2	2	2	1	–	1	2	2	2	1	2	2

For our analysis of the effectiveness of the impression-inconsistency judgment mechanism, question 4 in Table 9 suggests that 12 out of the 13 subjects received notification messages while using the system. Nine subjects received alerts of inconsistency in group structure (*A, C, D, E, H, I, J, K,* and *M*) and three were alerted to inconsistencies in impression degrees (*B, G,* and *L*). For question 4-1, 11 out of 12 people were convinced of the presented inconsistency. However, only subjects *E, G,* and *K* modified their impression degrees after receiving the alert. Figure 10 shows the impression graphs for subject *G* before and after the notification messages were given. He received messages twice. One indicates the differences in impression degrees for bars 19–22 and 23–26 (Fig. 10a). After receiving the message, the impression degrees of the top-down approach in bars 19–22 and 23–26 were increased by two, respectively, to bring it closer to the bottom-up approach, and the inconsistency in bars 19–22 was resolved (Fig. 10b). After the second message was given for bars 23–26, the impression degrees of the bottom-up approach were reduced by two to bring it closer to the top-down approach and all the inconsistencies were resolved. For such subjects, the impression-inconsistency judgment mechanism effectively encouraged them to have unique impressions.

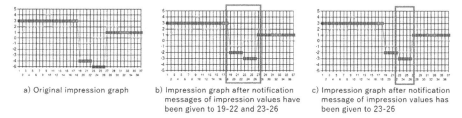

a) Original impression graph

b) Impression graph after notification messages of impression values have been given to 19-22 and 23-26

c) Impression graph after notification message of impression values has been given to 23-26

Fig. 10. Changes in impression degrees of subject *G*

The subjects who did not modify the impression degrees commented that "the impression I got from listening to the music was different from the impression from the score (so I cannot set a unified degree)" or "I thought both impressions were correct." The cause of these comments may be due to a lack of understanding of the meaning of the impression by the subjects. To play music, it is necessary to set a single impression for each bar. Since the subjects might not have understood the purpose of forming an impression, we conducted an additional questionnaire excluding subject *A*. We asked two questions: "Which impression will you use for performance, the impression obtained from the score or the impression obtained by listening to the music?" and "Do you think it is necessary to think about impressions from both top-down approach and bottom-up approach?" The subjects were allowed to answer this second question with free description reason. Table 11 shows the questionnaire results. Subjects *F, G, H, I,* and *K* were unable to answer the reason of the second question. All subjects responded that they would play using the impression acquired by listening to the music. In addition, eight of the subjects thought it important to consider the impression from the musical score as

Table 11. Answers to additional questions

Subject	Impression used for performance	Need for considering both impressions	Reason
B	Listening to song	Necessary	I can't understand the strength of each note and hand movement without looking at the musical score
C	Listening to song	Necessary	I need to grasp what the composer wants to convey from the music notes
D	Listening to song	Necessary	After capturing the image of the whole song, it is necessary to grasp small changes in the score
E	Listening to song	Necessary	There are some things I can understand from the score
F	Listening to song	Unnecessary	–
G	Listening to song	Unnecessary	–
H	Listening to song	Unnecessary	–
I	Listening to song	Unnecessary	–
J	Listening to song	Necessary	Because the score contains the thoughts of the person who created the song
K	Listening to song	Necessary	–
L	Listening to song	Necessary	I use both impressions for playing
M	Listening to song	Necessary	I obtain nuances in the music from the musical score

well, reasoning that this was "to get information from the score that cannot be obtained by listening to music." This answer indicates that, to form an impression from the score, it is still necessary to interpret the music.

7 Conclusion

In this research, to form impressions of the music to enhance the performance, we proposed a representation of impression changes as a graph structure, which we called an impression graph. In addition, we proposed a system where the performer can create impression graphs by listening to music and reading the musical score.

As a result of our evaluation experiment, we found that expressing the impression of the music with an impression graph with positive and negative axes is useful in interpreting the music, but it is difficult to determine concrete values. The current system allows impressions to be entered as concrete values, although there is a tendency to consider an impression by comparing the impressions of the preceding and succeeding bars. Therefore, it is necessary to consider an easy impression forming method, such as making it possible to attribute a relative impression, not an absolute value.

Many subjects stated that both the top-down and bottom-up approaches were useful. However, it was not possible to eliminate the inconsistency of impression degrees from the top-down and bottom-up approaches. According to our follow-up questionnaire, it has become clear that music will be performed by the top-down impression, so we need to modify the notification message to follow the top-down impression.

References

1. Juslin, P.N.: Communicating emotion in music performance: a review and a theoretical framework. In: Juslin, P.N., Sloboda, J.A. (eds.) Series in Affective Science. Music and Emotion: Theory and Research, pp. 309–337. Oxford University Press, New York (2001)
2. Liu, J., Hiraga, R., Igarashi, S., Sekiguchi, Y.: Computer-assisted music analysis system DAPHNE: -automatic analysis through realistic score sheets. SIG Technical reports of Information Processing Society of Japan, vol. 1999, No. 68, pp. 1–6 (1999). (in Japanese)
3. Watanabe, F., Hiraga, R., Fujishiro, I.: BRASS: visualizing scores for assisting music learning. In: Proceedings of the International Computer Music Conference, pp. 107–114 (2003)
4. Kornstädt, A.: The JRing system for computer-assisted musicological analysis. In: International Symposium on Music Information Retrieval, pp. 93–98 (2001)
5. Kaji, K., Nagao, K.: Mixa: a musical annotation system. In: Proceedings of the 3rd International Semantic Web Conference (2004)
6. Yang, X., Kobayashi, T., Ogura, K., Nishimoto, K.: How collectively gathered images relating to a musical piece affect creation of musical expressions. In: SIG Technical reports of Information Processing Society of Japan, vol. 2012-HCI-147, No. 27, pp. 1–8 (2012). (in Japanese)
7. Shibata, H., Hori, K.: A Framework to support writing as design using multiple representations. In: Proceedings of the 5th Asia Pacific Conference on Computer Human Interaction (2002)
8. MAKEMUSIC. Inc.: MusicXML for Exchanging Digital Sheet Music (2020). https://www.musicxml.com/
9. MuseScore (2020). "MuseScore." https://musescore.org/en

10. Reagan, A.J., Mitchell, L., Kiley, D., Danforth, C.M., Dodds, P.S.: The emotional arcs of stories are dominated by six basic shapes. EPJ Data Sci. **5**(1), 1–12 (2016)
11. Hevner, K.: Experimental studies of the elements of expression in music. Am. J. Psychol. **48**(2), 246–268 (1936)
12. Huang, S., Zhou, L., Liu, Z., Ni, S., He, J.: Empirical research on a fuzzy model of music emotion classification based on pleasure-arousal model. In: 37th Chinese Control Conference, pp. 3239–3244 (2018)

A Model of Decision Makings with Predictions

Tetsuya Maeshiro[1(✉)], Yuri Ozawa[2], and Midori Maeshiro[3]

[1] Faculty of Library, Information and Media Studies, University of Tsukuba,
Tsukuba 305-8550, Japan
maeshiro@slis.tsukuba.ac.jp
[2] Ozawa Clinic, Tokyo, Japan
[3] School of Music,
Federal University of Rio de Janeiro, Rio de Janeiro, Brazil

Abstract. This paper proposes a model of decision makings under strong constraints that explains the differences among novices and skilled persons. The model introduces the decision modules that are generated through experiences at the conscious level and gradually move to unconscious level. Predictions are executed in decision modules to evaluate the plausibility of decisions. While the multiple decision generation and evaluation is executed sequentially in novices, skilled persons are able to generate and evaluate decision candidates simultaneously, executed in parallel at the unconscious level.

Keywords: Decision making · Automatic process · Hypernetwork model · Multiple viewpoints · Skilled

1 Introduction

This paper presents a theoretical model of decision makings, particularly the decisions that require specialized knowledge and under constraints of time, available data quantity and quality, often limited very strongly in actual situations. Among these constraints, the time is possibly the most visible. Among many aspects to investigate decision makings, we focus on evaluation and the prediction of the target phenomena, the core mechanism of decision making processes.

This paper discusses the properties of prediction mechanisms involved in decision makings with strong time constraints and coordinations among multiple persons are required. Furthermore, we treat the decision makings where the behavior of other persons influence decisions, and predictions of uncertain future events have great weight of influence on decisions.

With the increasing complexity and amount of data related to daily events, the difficulty of decision makings is increasing for humans, even for skilled persons of the speciality of the events. One of difficulties is the filtering large amount of data. The difficulty increases when prediction capability is requested to accomplish decision makings, especially prediction about the future. Another difficulty

S. Yamamoto and H. Mori (Eds.): HCII 2020, LNCS 12185, pp. 39–54, 2020.
https://doi.org/10.1007/978-3-030-50017-7_3

is related to the intensifying complexity of the today's systems [1], which also leads to the first pointed problem of information amount, is the difficulty to correctly interprete the current status of systems. Furthermore, if anomalies occur, it is difficult to estimate the actual cause of the irregularities. Even more difficult task is to generate and execute decision makings in order to remedy the malfunctions of systems, as the prediction of influences of changes in a system's elements is involved.

In this paper, a system denotes any phenomena or entities that are represented with elements that constitute the target phenomenon or entity and relationships among elements. An element might be a physically existing or a virtual concept. Similarly, a relationship may have direct association with real or physical entities that connects the involved elements, or a conceptual interconnection for easier understandings of the elements' behavior without corresponding physical entities. We assume that states of some or all elements of the system are measureble. For other cases, the relationships are also measurable. These latter cases invoke a different kind of problem, which is the describability and the description model. Measurement of a relationship implies one of the following two cases. (1) the measured relationship, which connects two elements of the system, is treated as an element of the system. (2) Values or attributes are assigned to the relationship. However, since the theoretical basis of conventional system description is the graph theory [2], a system with measured relationship cannot be represented.

In some situations, there is a strong time constraints on decision makings, for instance medical treatments in emergency rooms, fighter pilot maneuvers in air combats, play decisions in continuously changing sports such as rugby and basketball. In these cases, decisions should be made instantly, and evaluations of decisions appear immediately, and the margin of error is usually very low, if not zero, as wrong decisions sometimes result in death of involved persons. Decisions to buy or sell stocks in financial market are another example, which involve gain and loss of money, in some cases of loss with severity equivalent to life loss. When making clinical decisions, prediction of the patients' future conditions is necessary. Medical treatment is a succession of decisions, some under strong time constraints and others not. Strong time constraints denotes timespan of seconds to minutes, where delayed decisions or wrong decisions imply patient's death.

In all above presented cases, prediction of future events and consequently their evaluations are necessary for the selection of acceptable decisions, though the weight of future predictions depends on the target problem. This paper treats decision makings with following conditions: big negative aspects of wrong decisions, necessity of predictions of future events, and strong time constraints.

The expression "strongly constrained" decision makings refer mainly the strong time constraints, where only a short time duration is allowed to make decisions and decisions are irreversible. The time duration in this paper denotes the time between the instant that a request for decision emerges and the instant that a decision should be made. For instance, a player holding a ball in a rugby match faces opponents rapidly advancing toward him. The player should decide whether to run forward with the ball or pass the ball to the ally to avoid the ball to be possessed by the opponent. In this case, the time duration of the decision starts when the player received the ball, and the deadline of the decision is the instant that opponents reach the player to tackle or to grab the ball. The not to decide decision is not an option because it is a 100% failing decision, as the player would be at least tackled and the ball will certainly be taken away. It is plausible to assume that 100% failure decision is not a decision. A more critical example is emergency medical treatments, where the patient may die if no decision is made. The time duration ranges from seconds to longer time, for instance days, but there always is a deadline.

Another aspect to consider is whether a person is specialized to the field that the decision is involved. We propose different models for novices and skilled persons. The basic mechanism is common for both, but the implementation is different. Our model is capable of explaining the transition from novices to skilled persons through training and learning experiences. The model is also capable of describing the intermediate levels between novices and skilled persons, or the level during the transition from the novice level to the skilled level. Conventional models of decision makings [3] are either general models and thus too conceptual or based on specific and limited cases. The RPD model [4] seems to be the best currently available model of decision makings of skilled persons under constraints, but partially due to its accordance with the observable human behavior, there is a gap from the brain function level. There is no clear connection between the functions of RPD and brain functions or granularity of functions described on the brain region level. Therefore, RPD is based on describable behavior. On the other hand, there are reports on decision makings from neuroscience [5–10], but the tasks tested in these experiments are simple, presenting another type of gap from the behavioral decision making models. The complexity of decisions investigated in behavioral studies are not simple aggregation of simple tasks studied in neuroscience.

2   Decision Makings Based on Predictions

The evaluation process of predictions is required for decision makings involving predictions. A single decision is selected among multiple candidate decisions based on some evaluation, and executed.

The simplest representation of a single decision is to represent the preconditions, the details of the decision, and the post-conditions which are the consequences of the decision making (Fig. 1). This is a description of single decision. The representation of actual decision making process is a combination of descriptions of one or more decision and another decision (decision-S) that denotes the selection of one decision to be executed (Fig. 2).

This is one possible description. Another description is to treat the decision selection decision-S as a kind of "meta" decision of decisions to be selected (decision-1··· decision-N), interpreting as a hierarchical structure with the decision selection decision-S on higher hierarchical level (Fig. 3).

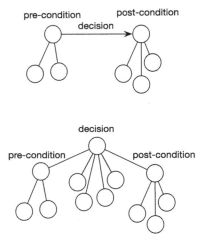

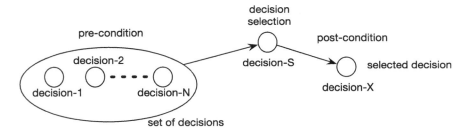

Fig. 1. Two simple represenations of a decision. Top is the representation of a decision as a relationship between pre-condition and post-conditions. Nodes attached to the pre-condition and post-condition nodes denote the attributes of the connected nodes. Bottom is the representation of the decision as a concept, where the pre-condition and post-condition nodes are the attributes.

Fig. 2. Representation of the selection of decision from a set of decisions

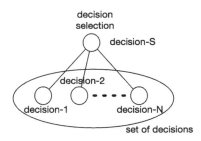

Fig. 3. Hierarchical representation of decision selection.

A more exact description would be to add details of each decision in Figs. 2 and 3. Details of decision-1 $\cdots$ decision-N can be added without problems, as attributes connected to nodes representing decision-1$\cdots$decision-N can be added (Fig. 4).

The details of the decision selection decision-S in Fig. 3, however, are different, because some interpretation ambiguities emerge. Theoretically, decision-S in Fig. 2 is a causal relationship between the set of decisions composed of decision-1$\cdots$decision-N and the selected decision decision-X. More precisely, the decision-X is one of decision-1$\cdots$decision-N, so the relationship is a singleton to the set of decisions (Fig. 5), where the edge representing the relationship points to the selected decision decision-X.

The necessity of predictions in medical diagnostics in clinical treatment is evident, as the treatment strategy differs according to the changes in patients' conditions. A complete set of examiniations is necessary, but it is not possible due to time and cost. Some specific examples are described in following sections.

2.1 Music Composition

We have been analyzing decision makings in music composition process. The prediction involved in the music composition process is the prediction of the sonority of the musical piece, and the emotion invoked in listeners, together with the evaluation by the listeners. The sonority denotes the sonority of the composed music when the musical piece is played with designated musical instruments, including the vocals.

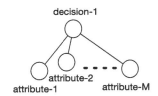

Fig. 4. Representation of attributes of a decision

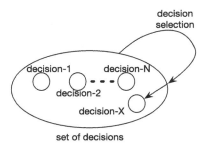

Fig. 5. Another representation of decision selection

Music composition processes were treated as sequences of decisions executed in composition, and each decision was represented using the [hypernetwork model]. Then decisions were related based on the similarities of concepts linked to decisions and structural similarities or discrepancies among decisions. The granularity of concepts associated with decisions are modified with homogenization process to equalize the detail level of concepts used in descriptions, executed simultaneously with the process to associate related decisions. After this process, an integrated representation of the whole composition process of one musical piece is obtained.

Since the decisions during the music composition are described during and after the composition of referred musical part, described mainly as a text written by the composer himself, the described content is focused on the thinking process related to the generation of musical notes to write on musical score. But there is always the prediction of the sonority aspects of the music to be composed, how the music sounds when played. The acoustic aspect is essential as the musical piece is evaluated by listening to it. Usually unconsciously, the sonority is predicted or imagined and evaluated by the composer himself, sometimes actually played using some musical instruments.

Then we have built a human machine integrated composition support system. The current use is mainly the study of self composition process and of other composers' creative process. The system is also used to assist the prediction of sonority and evaluation of musical passages during composition. Primary users are composers using mainly the music notation software as composition tool. A typical composition process consists of (1) generate a musical passage or notes, (2) judge if the introduced passage is "good", and if not, modify other passages or re-generate the passage.

The machine side consists of a database containing the passages assigned with the evaluation by multiple listeners, and a prediction module generated using the passages and evaluations.

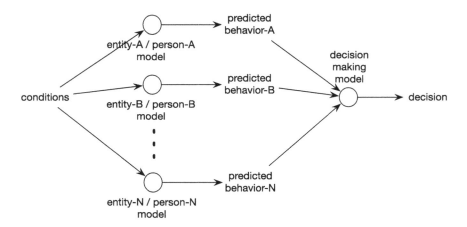

Fig. 6. Function diagram of decision making with predictions. "entity-A/person-A" denotes either a representation of an entity or of a person.

2.2   Product Development

Particularly for the creation of new products, for instance cosmetics, and the search of new problems, the crucial point is the introduction of new aspects. The aim is to provide products that embody novel aspects or concepts that the general public had no knowledge about. Otherwise the product would be a mere secondhand copy of the previously existing products.

A novel feature that represents a new aspect to describe is necessary in creative generation of concepts and products. Another problem is that people get accustomed and bored over time even for novel products that excited them. This is a characteristic of "Kansei". The emotional aspect is variable, changing over times.

The prediction in this case is the reaction to the newly introduced feature (aspect) and how this reaction changes over time, both predictions are difficult for machines, and possible only by humans with today's techniques. The nature of prediction is different from music composition case, where both human and machine are able to predict. In new product creation, only human is able to predict using human imagination. Thus the represented models are different.

2.3   Novices vs Skilled Persons

Another specific case of the differences of detection ability between novices and skilled persons is accounting. Without thorough, detailed and time-consuming analyses, experienced accounting skilled persons are able to detect a flaw in accounting documents almost instantly, just by glancing the numbers, although the exact error cannot be pointed out. The experienced person can detect the existence of the flaw instantly, although cannot explain the nature or details of the flaw at that instant. The flaws are number related, and are not simple mistakes like typos. On the other hand, non-experienced persons, including not only the novices but also persons with some experience, can confirm the flaw only after thorough analyses of documents.

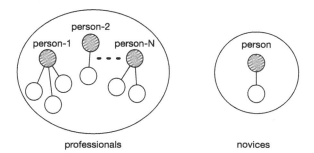

Fig. 7. Illustrative representations of other persons' models of skilled persons (left) and novices (right). Skilled Persons have multiple models, but novices have just a few general model. Squiggled nodes denote persons, and white nodes connected to squiggled nodes denote details or attributes of that person.

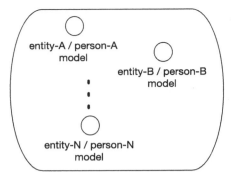

Fig. 8. A set of prediction models.

2.4 Integration of Predictions

In all examples discussed above, the integration of different predictions is necessary for the decision making, based on evaluations of predictions.

As discussed before, the prediction of other persons' behavior is important to make time constrained decisions in teams or groups consisting of multiple persons. Figure 6 is an illustrative function diagram of decision making. The decision is generated by the decision making model, which uses the predicted behaviors of all relevant entities or persons in the situation requiring the decision. The predicted behavior is generated by a model of the entity.

The prediction model is an integration of individual models entity/person-A, entity/person-B, ... (Fig. 8) and can be interpreted as a hierarchy of models (Fig. 9).

This is the simplest representation. Each prediction model has detailed descriptions using the hypernetwork model attached to specify the prediction model (Fig. 10).

Although individual models are represented separately as in Fig. 8, the use of hypermodel implies that the concepts used in descriptions are originated from "ocean" (Fig. 11), and many concepts are shared among descriptions of different

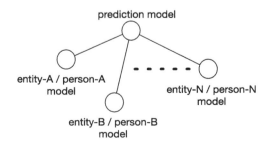

Fig. 9. Hierarchical structure of prediction models.

prediction model

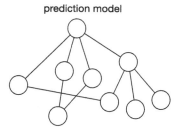

Fig. 10. Description of details of a prediction model

prediction models. The use of hypernetwork model enables the quantification of similarity and differences among prediction models. This quantitative similarity can be used to evaluate prediction models and to generate the prediction model of a new person or entity.

3   Model

This section presents the proposed model focusing on two aspects. One is the conceptual model describing the process flow and module architecture. The other one is the description of structural aspect, describing the functional units.

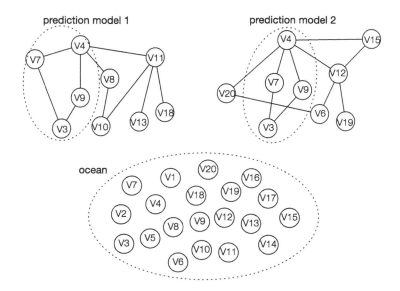

Fig. 11. Prediction models based on hypernetwork model. Dotted circles of "prediction model 1" and "prediction model 2" denote identical structure if the roles of hypernodes are ignored.

The main type of situation is those under strong time constraint and irreversible, i.e., a person should make correct decisions in short time, typically between seconds and minutes.

One fundamental difference between the model of skilled persons and novices is the accuracy of other persons' models and predictions of other persons' behaviors and actions. The other persons' models that skilled persons have is personalized, having different models for each individual (Fig. 7 (left)). On the other hand, novices have a generalized model for all individuals (Fig. 7 (right)). Furthermore, the detail level that novices have is low, resulting in a low prediction accuracy of behaviors due to low detail level and no individual factors incorporated into the model, because the necessary predictions are individual person's behaviors, and general (average) prediction is useless in actual decision makings.

To a team, such as ER (emergency room) medical team, rugby team in matches and jazz band, to function properly, accurate prediction of other team members' actions is crucial. All these example require time constrained and irreversible decision makings. Another fact to consider is that due to strong time constraints, there is no time for team members to discuss about the decision to make. The decision of a team member is to be understood by other members for the other members to make decisions based on that decision. Therefore, if one of members has inaccurate model of other members, that member's actions will be harmful for the team functionality, as that member's actions are at least unexpected by the other members. For instance, suppose a member holds the ball in a rugby match. Then the playing options are to hold the ball and move forward, to pass the ball to another member, and to kick the ball also to pass to another member. The purpose of the rugby team is to mark goals and win the game. If the member throws the ball to another member and that member was not expecting the pass, the probability to catch the ball without dropping it is low, because he expected that the member will kick the ball so he was already running forward to support the plays related to the kicked ball in the forward space.

It is plausible to assume that pre-planned decisions and plays (moves) are useless, and synchronization of plays is also impossible because no communication using detailed information is possible. The problem is that no actual play in the match can be expected and pre-planned before the match begins, as the number of possible plays and conditions are too numerous and practically infinite. Therefore, the players should be able to act at each instant by recognizing the conditions and deciding the moves that result in the win of own team.

The recognition-primed decision (RPD) model [4,11] states that skilled persons don't investigate or analyze the usefulness of multiple solution candidates before selecting the decision to execute, but the first choice is usually the best. This is a process opposite to novices, who study all the choices that comes to mind before selecting what to execute, and the size of the enumerated choices is usually fewer than the extensive enumeration of choices by the skilled persons.

Our experiments with rugby players suggest that RPD model is valid if considering the conscious level only, which the person recognizes and can describe. However, when integrating the unconscious level, skilled persons also consider multiple options, but they are discarded automatically at the unconscious level. Our experiments indicate that skilled persons consider multiple options, proved by the measurement of their attention movements, but often not described by themselves. The details of our experiment results will be presented elsewhere.

The prediction module is incorporated into our model (Fig. 12). The difference between the skilled person and the novice is the consciousness level of the prediction module. The novices has low prediction ability, implying fewer number of predicted facts and lower accuracy of predictions compared to skilled persons, besides the precarious selection process.

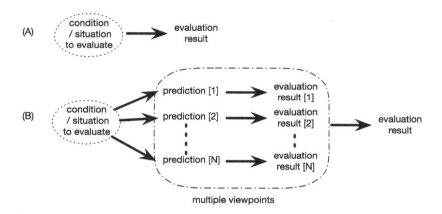

Fig. 12. Evaluation based on (A) single viewpoint or (B) multiple viewpoints.

The number of predictions in Fig. 12 reflects the ability of the person, or the degree of specialized skills that the person possesses. "prediction[i]" is the prediction result of aspect or viewpoint "i", and generally skilled persons handle more viewpoints than novices, i.e., the number of vewpoints is correlated with the specialization degree.

In our model, the main difference between novices and skilled persons is the degree of automation of prediction - evaluation process.

We predict that the cerebellum is also activated in decision makings, and its activity is higher for skilled persons. For novices, cerebellum activity should be very scarce, if no activity at all, as the ration of automated process through learning by experiences is small. The mechanism is similar to motor control, where the prediction of state is required for successful control and learning. The role of cerebellum is supervised learning, whereas other two types of learning, the reinforced learning and unsupervised are provided by basal ganglia and cerebral cortex respectively [12].

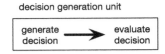

decision generation unit

Fig. 13. A single decision generation module.

Another fundamental difference between the skilled persons and novices is the sequence of decision generation (and prediction) and evaluation process. Novices generate a decision and evaluate it by thinking in conscious level, implying that the decision is evaluated after it is generated. Sometimes the decision would be edited or modified depending on the evaluation, but the process is sequential, executing ONE task at a time. On the other hand, we propose that decision generation – evaluation is executed as a single module/unit, and multiple generation - evaluation modules are executed in parallel. This is possible because the generation - evaluation is executed automatically on unconscious level.

We also propose the functional modularity of decision generation – evaluation process (Fig. 13).

Furthermore, we also propose that skilled persons treat decision evaluations as images and not as concepts. Such treatments enable processing of multiple and simultaneous evaluations.

The skilled persons present two differences in the architecture: (1) decision (prediction) generation – evaluation modules that function automatically without requiring conscious control; (2) activation of multiple predictor (decision generator) – evaluator modules that operates in parallel. The operation to discard unuseable decision due to low evaluation of prediction is also automatic.

Our model also incorporates not totally automatic/unconscious prediction-evaluation execution. The process for each predicted result goes through learning process that gradually moves the module to unconscious level (Fig. 14). Moreover, the internal structure of the module is not fixed and changes over time, improved by the learning and feedback process over time from new experiences. The advantage of our model is that it explains the functionalities of partially experienced persons, corresponding to the middle stage where the box representing a module is overlapped by the threshold between the conscious and unconscious levels, indicating that this decision generation - evaluation module is executed in both conscious and unconscious levels, or sometimes on either level. With increasing experiences by the person, the module gradually leaves the conscious level and enters into the unconscious level.

Table 1 summarizes the differences of the functions and features related to our model between novices and skilled persons (Fig. 15).

Conventionally, system modelling focused mainly on the entities, and relationships had secondary treatments. It might be related with our cognitive system, as we sense less difficulty when focusing on the elements that constitute a phenomena and how they are related, rather than emphasizing on the how the elements are related. Possibly due to this, we usually focus on the elements, and less attention is paid to the relationships or extracting only the relationships for the analysis is rare. Interactions have been represented indirectly using the descriptions of elements that act as interacting elements. However, indirect modeling is insufficient when analyzing the interactions and relationships themselves. Relationships can be fully analyzed if they are directly represented, and direct representation should generate insights directly related with interactions themselves.

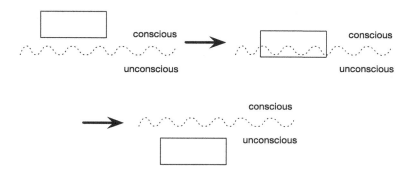

Fig. 14. Conceptual image illustrating a module belonging to the conscious level gradually entering the unconscious level through learning process. The initial stage represents the novices, and the third stage represents the skilled persons.

Table 1. Comparison of decision generation mechanisms of skilled persons and novices.

	Novices	Skilled persons
Number of prediction models	Single or Few	Multiple (Many)
Detail of model (granularity)	General	Detailed
Process level	Conscious (Manual)	Unconscious (Automatic)
Process speed	Slow	Fast
Execution	Sequential	Parallel

The system description consists basically of elements and relationships among elements. Conventional representation models used for system description are mathematically equivalent to graphs [2]. However, conventional models present following defects: (1) unable to represent N-ary relationships or relationships among more than two nodes; (2) unable to represent relationships among relationships; (3) unable to specify relationships or assign attributes; (4) unable to represent multiple facets of quantitative relationships. The hypernetwork model solves these issues.

The hypernetwork model allows integration and simultaneous description of multiple viewpoints to comprehend the target phenomena. Representation is viewpoint dependent, and representations are generated from the same set of elements. Its advantage is the comparison among different viewpoints to analyze the system. Details of individual relationships are described using the hypernetwork model [13,14]. Similar descriptions are impossible with other conventional models.

The proposed model can be discussed from the standpoint of Kahneman's system-1 and system-2 [15], where the thinking processes were classified into two types, fast or slow, while the former refers to intuitive decisions, and latter one denotes analytical and time consuming thinking process. The model of automatic decision generation and evaluation module of skilled persons is equivalent to the system-1 (fast) process, whereas the novices' sequential decision evaluation is equivalent to the system-2 (slow) process.

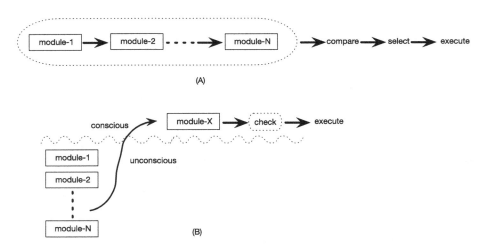

Fig. 15. Execution sequence of decision makings of (A) novices and (B) skilled persons.

4   Conclusions

This paper discussed the properties of decision makings under strong time constraints, often requiring decisions within minutes or even seconds, and decisions are irreversible, very difficult or even impossible to correct wrong decisions, further required when multiple persons are involved and predictions of their behavior influences the decisions.

This paper proposed a model of decision makings under strong constraints that explains the differences among novices and skilled persons. The model introduces the decision modules that are generated through experiences at the conscious level and gradually move to unconscious level. Predictions are executed in decision modules to evaluate the plausibility of decisions. While the multiple decision generation and evaluation is executed sequentially in novices, skilled persons are able to generate and evaluate decision candidates simultaneously, executed in parallel at the unconscious level.

The decision making model consists of multiple prediction models, each model corresponding to involved persons or entities that affect and are affected by the decisions. Multiple perspectives are used to represent prediction models and decisions because multiple aspects of the predicted behaviors and decision details are evaluated, implying that single viewpoint description is insufficient and inaccurate. The use of machines running machine learning to model predictions of involved intities and persons enable integrated human-machine system, where the human can concentrate on evaluation and selection of decisions.

Acknowledgments. This research was supported by the JSPS KAKENHI Grant Numbers 24500307 (T.M.) and 15K00458 (T.M.).

References

1. Clearfield, C., Tilcsik, A.: Meltdown: Why Our Systems Fail and What We Can Do About It. Atlantic Books, London (2018)
2. Berge, C.: The Theory of Graphs. Dover, Mineola (2001)
3. Klein, G.A., Orasanu, J., Calderwood, R., Zsambok, C.E.: Decision Making in Action. Ablex, Norwood (1993)
4. Klein, G.: A recognition primed decision (RPD) model of rapid decision making. In: Klein, G.A., Orasanu, J., Calderwood, R., Zsambok, C.E. (eds.) Decision Making in Action, pp. 138–147. Ablex, Norwood (1993)
5. Gold, J., Shadlen, M.: The neural basis of decision making. Rev. Neurosci. **30**, 535–574 (2007)
6. Uchida, N., Kepecs, A., Mainen, Z.: Seeing at a glance, smelling in a whiff: rapid forms of perceptual decision making. Nat. Rev. Neurosci. **7**, 485–491 (2006)
7. Harvey, C., Coen, P., Tank, D.: Choice-specific sequences in parietal cortex during a virtual-navigation decision task. Nature **484**, 62–68 (2012)
8. Lo, C., Wang, X.: Cortico-basal ganglia circuit mechanism for a decision threshold in reaction time tasks. Nat. Neurosci. **9**, 956–963 (2006)
9. Machens, C., Romo, R., Brody, C.: Flexible control of mutual inhibition: a neural model of two-interval discrimination. Science **307**, 1121–1124 (2005)
10. Shadlen, M., Kiani, R.: Consciousness as a decision to engage. In: Dehaene, S., Christen, Y. (eds.) From Cognition to the Clinic Research and Perspectives in Neurosciences, pp. 27–46. Springer, Heidelberg (2011). https://doi.org/10.1007/978-3-642-18015-6_2
11. Klein, G.: Sources of Power: How People Make Decisions. MIT Press, Cambridge (2017)
12. Doya, K.: Complementary roles of basal ganglia and cerebellum in learning and motor control. Curr. Opin. Neurobiol. **10**, 732–739 (2000)

13. Maeshiro, T., Ozawa, Y., Maeshiro, M.: A system description model with fuzzy boundaries. In: Yamamoto, S. (ed.) HIMI 2017. LNCS, vol. 10274, pp. 390–402. Springer, Cham (2017). https://doi.org/10.1007/978-3-319-58524-6_31
14. Maeshiro, T.: Framework based on relationship to describe non-hierarchical, boundaryless and multi-perspective phenomena. SICE J. Control Measur. Syst. Integr. **11**, 381–389 (2019)
15. Kahneman, D.: Thinking, Fast and Slow. Farrar, Straus and Giroux, New York (2011)

Decision Support System with Institutional Research: A Student-Centered Enrollment Advising System

Takeshi Matsuda[1]([⊠]), Yuki Watanabe[2], Katsusuke Shigeta[3], Nobuhiko Kondo[1], and Hiroshi Kato[4]

[1] Tokyo Metropolitan University, 1-1 Minami-Osawa, Hachioji, Tokyo 1920397, Japan
mat@tmu.ac.jp
[2] Tokyo University of Science, 1-3 Kagurazaka, Shinjuku-Ku, Tokyo 1628601, Japan
[3] Hokkaido University, Kita 8, Nishi 5, Kita-Ku, Sapporo, Hokkaido 0600808, Japan
[4] The Open University of Japan, 2-11 Wakaba, Mihama-Ku, Chiba 2618586, Japan

Abstract. In this paper, we propose an online dashboard system, Decision Support System with Institutional Research data (DSIR), developed for students who are looking for information on courses they are considering enrolling in. The system deals with three major factors that contribute to students' learning outcomes: the evaluation methods of courses, students' self-directed learning readiness (SDLR), and students' learning goals. The purpose of this study is to formatively evaluate the functions of DSIR. Specifically, we asked students to use its beta version to confirm visibility, under-standing of displayed contents, and usefulness in class selection. We then tried to clarify points in need of modification and functions to be developed. Participants highly rated DSIR in general, and most participants set their own goals by referring to the SDLR scale factor score. In addition, many participants selected courses by referring to the recommended courses dis-played on DSIR. Besides these real effects, our evaluation revealed the need to add explanations of terms and recommended course calculation methods and to devise display methods.

Keywords: Self-directed learning readiness · Course enrollment · Dashboard · Individualized recommendation

1 Introduction

1.1 Background

In this paper, we propose an online dashboard system, Decision Support System with Institutional Research data (DSIR), developed for students who are seeking useful information on their registration for a course. The system deals with three major factors that contribute to students' learning outcomes: the evaluation methods of courses, students' self-directed learning readiness (SDLR), and students' learning goals. It analyzes the collected data and forms two recommendation models. Then, it visually represents the

© Springer Nature Switzerland AG 2020
S. Yamamoto and H. Mori (Eds.): HCII 2020, LNCS 12185, pp. 55–64, 2020.
https://doi.org/10.1007/978-3-030-50017-7_4

results and produces two lists of recommended courses. The focus of this system is data-driven support for academic success in students' course selection and we expect it will reduce poorly informed course enrollment decisions at Japanese and other countries' universities.

We can point out the background and rationales to show and justify the efficacy of DSIR. First, elective courses account for a large portion of Japanese universities' curricula. Second, students do not have access to trustworthy information about a course until they receive the syllabus upon enrollment. Third, most universities in Japan do not have a substantive course numbering system that guides undergraduate students toward the mastery of the course [1]. Fourth and last, universities and their institutional research offices (hereafter, IR office) hold data and records that can be used for advising students, however they are used mostly for detecting at-risk students [2, 3]. As a result, many students face a lack of useful guidance for selecting courses. They there-fore depend on 'unofficial' versions of course guides that tend to be full of inaccurate information and rumor. The focus of DSIR is data-driven support for academic success in students' selection of courses.

1.2 Related Work

There are three major approaches to helping students choose appropriate courses and prior studies have been conducted in each area. The first approach is research on professional development programs as an academic advisor, and many successes have been reported, especially at National Academic Advising Association. For example, Gordon and Steel focused on undecided students, categorized such students, and introduced useful advising methods based on the theoretical frameworks, such as career construction theory, cognitive information processing theory and so on [4].

The second approach is based on data analysis. It involves the construction of a student model and the search for its application method. More specifically, conduct research on student decision-making support using various data. Wang and Orr, like Gordon and Steel, were interested in undecided students and used a large-scale institutional data set to demonstrate how to couple student and institutional data with predictive analytics for their academic success [5]. Some studies have focused on the relationship between the use of academic advising and student profiles. With reference to self-directed learning theory, Roessger et al. explored the relationship between the age of community college students and their use of academic advising services [6]. Most university students in Japan must decide on a major at the time of enrollment and their retention rate has been much higher than US students, so it is unlikely that Japanese universities will offer a student the same level of support in choosing courses. However, the globalization of the labor market means that the above studies are relevant to career support services, so using a lot of data can be important.

The third approach is to develop expert systems using unique algorithms and analysis methods. Examples include an intelligent web-based application that provides general advisory cases in special degree programs with semantic web expert system technologies [7], evaluation of a course recommendation model based on collaborative filtering [8], and an investigation into the effects of the pioneering and well-known advising system, SIGNALS [9]. System design and the interfaces of these systems were helpful in this research, as well as in their data processing. In recent years, research papers that integrate the second and third approaches by aggregating educational data and metadata and utilizing artificial intelligence (AI) have been published. In Japan, there have been various attempts to assist in course selection using ICT and big data, such as system for selecting courses using a goal-oriented learning support database that connects curriculum information and occupational characteristics data-bases [10], a course recommendation system using an open-source recommendation engine [11], and a system that automatically generates timetables based on the characteristics of courses analyzed from syllabi and student learning strategies [12].

In reviewing these prior and on-going studies and conducting a needs assessment of Japanese university students, we decided to proceed with development based on the following theories and practices:

1. Students' course selection criteria
2. Self-directed learning readiness scale (SDLRS)
3. Ability that students want to improve or their learning goals

Matsuda et al. classified three criteria for class selection based on student surveys: "credibility of credits," "interest in class content," and "external conditions (such as opening hours)" [13]. Among the criteria, the contents of the class are described in the conventional syllabus, which is shown to all the students. However, the meaning of external conditions varies greatly depending on a student's learning goal and cannot be changed by the student. Therefore, it is checked whether displaying the remaining credit acquisition possibility will help with the course selection. In this study, it is assumed that credit acquisition is composed of three elements: 1) the difficulty of the learning content itself, 2) the SDL readiness required for learning activities, and 3) the perceived difficulty of teacher evaluation. The course recommendation functions described below were designed based on these assumptions [14].

2 Purpose

The purpose of this study is to formatively evaluate the functions of DSIR. Specifically, we asked students to use its beta version to confirm visibility, understanding of displayed contents, and usefulness in class selection. We expected that DSIR could assist students in choosing courses, both in terms of SDLR characteristics and their own needs. We then tried to clarify points in need of modification and functions to be developed.

3 Methods

3.1 Developed System

As mentioned earlier, DSIR deals with three major factors that contribute to students learning outcomes: the evaluation methods or grade calculation standards of a course, students' self-directed learning readiness, and students' learning goals. It mounts the following functions to advise effectively:

- Collecting data from the syllabi of available courses, the SDLR level, and students' preference for what kind of skills or knowledge they want to gain from the course (Table 1 and Fig. 1);

Table 1. SDLRS items used in the developed system (*reverse item)

Factor	Item
1 Love of learning	I love to learn
	The more I learn, the more exciting the world becomes
	Learning is fun
2 Ability to use basic study skills and problem-solving skills	*I don't work very well on my own
	I can learn things on my own better than most people
	I can learn effectively both in a classroom situation and on my own
3 Acceptance of responsibility in learning	No one but me is truly responsible for what I learn
	*Even if I don't learn, I don't have the responsibility for it
	It's not others but myself who is responsible for my learning
4 Inquisitive mind	*I don't like dealing with questions where there's not one right answer
	*I always prefer well-known ways to learn to novel learning methods
5 Initiative and independence in learning	If there is something I have decided to learn, I can find time for it, no matter how busy I am
	I can learn almost everything that I need to know
6 Self-efficacy	I have a great deal of curiosity about everything
	I am good at thinking of unusual ways to do things
7 Positive orientation to the future	I like to think about my own future

- Analyzing the collected data and forming a recommendation model based on the student's SDLR and his or her choice of learning outcomes;
- Creating output by visualizing the results and indicating two lists of recommended courses (Fig. 2).

Based on the SDLRS developed by Guglielmino [15] as a DSIR measurement method, we present information related to unit availability using the Japanese version of a SDLRS developed by Matsuura et al. [16]. The Japanese SDLRS is composed of 58 items, and seven factors are extracted. Each item is answered using a five-stage Likert scale questionnaire, from "Almost never true of me" to "Almost always true of me." In this study, one to three items with high factor loading were extracted from the original question items corresponding to each factor. A total of 16 extracted items were used (Table 1).

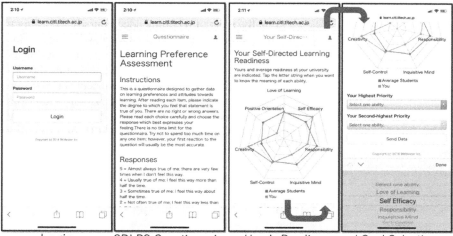

Login   SDLRS Questionnaire User's Readiness and Goal Selection

Fig. 1. Screenshots of DSIR

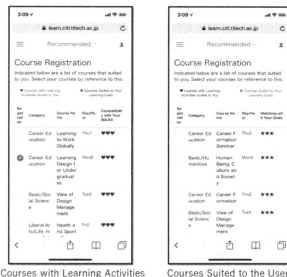

Courses with Learning Activities Courses Suited to the User's All Courses
Suited to the User   Learning Goals   the User Can Take

Fig. 2. Screenshots of DSIR (Course selection)

Regarding the visualization, the information displayed to students is as follows. First, a radar chart showing the degree of SDLR required by the class and the student's own SDLR is displayed. This radar chart also indicates the average values for students in the same department (right half of Fig. 1). Next, the syllabus of the class itself and data on past results are displayed, that is, the grade distribution and the credit acquisition probability of the course (Fig. 3).

Fig. 3. Explanation of a course

Finally, a list of recommended courses according to the student's goals and SDLR is displayed (Fig. 2). In a previous study [14], we developed a similar dashboard system that indicated determining factors in the level of difficulty of a course. Although the concept of this system was well-received at an academic workshop, a key point of critique was that it led students to "easy" courses and did not enhance their self-direction [13]. In response to this criticism, DSIR displays two lists of courses. One list shows the degree of conformance between a student's level of SDLR and the level that each course requires. The other list indicates the degree to which a student's learning objectives matches up with the stated learning outcomes of a course.

For students, "compatible courses with their SDLRS" and "suitable courses for their goals" are selected based on the compatible and target coincidence indices. The values of these indices are calculated using the following three types of seven-dimensional vectors based on the SDLRS [17]:

1. Student SDLRS Vector S: 7-dimensional vector with each score of seven items of the SDLRS
2. Student goal Vector T: seven-dimensional vector with the SDLRS item selected as the goal set to "1" and the unselected SDLRS item set to "0"
3. Course SDLRS Vector D: seven-dimensional vector with SDLRS items required by the course as "1" and other SDLRS items as "0"

In this system, the SDLRS item required by the course in the Vector D was subjectively judged based on the syllabus information and under certain guidelines. Since "compatibility" is the degree of matching between the student's readiness and the courses' required readiness, the cosine similarity between S and D was determined, and this value was used as an index. On the system, compatibility was divided into four levels with appropriate thresholds and displayed as icons as shown in Fig. 2. The thresholds were set at three points (average and average ± standard deviation) based on the distribution of responses in the preliminary survey. "Target match degree" is the degree of matching between the goal set by the student and the readiness required for a course. To find the target match degree, the inner product of T and D was calculated, and this value was used as an index. The overall degree of compatibility was represented by a number of heart-shaped icons.

Since a student can only select two goals, the dot product of T and D will take one of the values 0, 1, or 2. Based on this, the system uses three levels to display Since a student is only allowed to select two goals, the dot product of T and D will take one of the values 0, 1, or 2. Based on this, the system uses three levels to display icons using the number of stars as shown in the center screen of Fig. 2. On the screens showing "compatible courses" and "suitable courses", courses with higher indices, corresponding to the respective courses, are displayed preferentially.

In the case where multiple courses share the same rank, the one with the lower index is given priority, and courses with more diverse evaluation criteria are given priority.

3.2 Formative Evaluation

Formative evaluation experiments were conducted, and student volunteers tried the system at four universities, Tokyo Metropolitan University, Meiji University, Hokkaido University, and Tokyo University of Science. The results were analyzed, from which we expected to gain insight into what criteria students selected courses, as well as the relationship between SDLR and course selection.

A total of 51 undergraduate students tested the DSIR developed for smartphones, confirmed its usability and practicality, and described what functions they thought should be added and the necessary information to select courses. Students who participated in the evaluation were instructed to access DSIR using their own smartphone and work through the following list of procedures:

1. Answer the pre-use questionnaire.
2. Agree to the system terms, log in, and respond to the SDLRS survey (second screen from left in Fig. 1).
3. After confirming their own SDLR as indicated by a radar chart on the personal data screen (second screen from the right in Fig. 1), freely select courses from the list of all available courses.
4. Return to the personal data screen and select the two learning objectives.
5. Go to the recommended course list screen and add or delete the courses, referring to the list of "compatible courses" and "the courses that meet your goals."
6. Answer the post-use questionnaire.

These tasks took participants about 40 to 50 to complete. Once participants were free to choose courses, they were asked to set the goals they wanted to achieve in order to verify the effects and effects of DSIR.

4 Findings and Discussion

In addition to the participants' SDLRS and system operation logs, we also analyzed the results of the pre-/post- questionnaire. The main evaluation results are as follows.

4.1 Overall Evaluation and Understandings

In general, participants highly rated DSIR. Of the 51 participants, 44(86%) participants said they would use the system for actual course registration. Among the seven respondents who answered that they would not use the system, only one questioned the criteria for selecting the recommended course as the reason. Other participants who answered negatively mentioned that there were few elective courses in their departments or reported a fear that they would become dependent on the system.

A five-step Likert scale was used to assess degree of understanding of the graphics and data displayed on the personal data screen and recommended course list screen. Of the available responses, "I understood the meaning of self-efficacy " showed the lowest value at 3.45, and 8 out of 11 items exceeded four, which means they were generally well understood. The following items received particularly high ratings: "It was easy to compare the average of others with my learning tendency on the radar chart" (4.59), "I understood the meaning of the inquisitive mind" (4.47), and "I under-stood the meaning of the positive orientation" (4.47). As a whole, the display contents, which was written in simple, easy-to-understand language, were highly comprehended.

4.2 Effects of the System

At least two points were suggested as intended positive effects of DSIR. First, most participants might have set their own goals by referring to the SDLRS factor score displayed on the radar chart. In other words, the factors that were selected as the abilities to be acquired corresponded with those factors that often indicated low SDLRS scores. Specifically, 31 out of the 51 participants selected the two lowest-listed abilities as they would like to acquire as their goals. Only two participants did not choose either of the two lowest-listed abilities.

Second, many participants selected courses by referring to the recommended courses displayed on the system. On average, students selected 8.9 courses, of which an average of 2.6 had three heart icons and an average of 1.4 had three-star marks. Only seven participants did not include any recommended courses in their selection. Of these seven, two did not select any courses at the end, three chose only one course, and one chose only two courses, so in essence, only one participant ignored the recommended courses.

At the time of the first selection, that is, at the end of step 3 in the instructions, 18 participants selected at least one course with a three-heart icon, so more than half of the participants, 26 people, selected the recommended courses on the screen after that with the reference to the recommendation.

5 Future Work

The formative evaluations revealed that some parts of DSIR need improvement and new feature should be considered. The first is to add explanations of terms and recommended course calculation methods and to devise new display methods. This is because there was a difference in the degree of understanding of the displayed graphs and the data, and there were misunderstandings in the post-questionnaire that were made apparent in the free-written description of points for improvement and reasons for not using features. In fact, in the version of the application that participants evaluated, links to syllabus information of individual courses and glossary terms on graphs were available to users. However, since the participants were not aware that such operations could be performed, new information should be added to the interface along with features to access those data with intuitive operations.

The second area for improvement is in the additional development of a function to prevent registration errors. Specifically, the application should have a function that excludes courses offered during the time periods in which compulsory courses are set and a function for displaying how many courses will be required by the number of credits designated by the university. Many participants requested such convenience in the free-response items of the questionnaire. However, in order to develop these features, they must be able to cross-reference with the Student Information System database.

Third is the ingenuity of a method that will not leave DSIR unused. Using DSIR once at the beginning of each semester will neither elaborate the displayed content nor reflect the student's improvement in SDLRS. It is expected that with continued use, not only the contents of the application will be improved, but also the meta-cognition of the student users will be promoted as students input additional information and the SDLRS measurement function is developed further.

These improvements will be implemented in 2020.

Acknowledgment. This work was supported by JSPS KAKENHI Grant-Aid Grant Number 19H01717. We would like to thank Editage (www.editage.com) for English language editing.

References

1. The National Institution for Academic Degrees and Quality Enhancement of Higher Education, Guidelines for Internal Quality Assurance in Higher Education. (in Japanese). https://www.niad.ac.jp/n_shuppan/project/__icsFiles/afieldfile/2017/06/08/guideline.pdf. Accessed 31 Jan 2020
2. Funamori, M.: Does digital technology save higher education under massification process? Opportunities in MOOCs, big data in education, institutional research. J. Jpn. Soc. Inf. Knowl. **24**(4), 424–436 (2014). (in Japanese)
3. Kondo, N., Hatanaka, T.: Modeling of learning process based on Bayesian networks. Educ. Technol. Res. **42**, 57–67 (2018)
4. Schneider, H.A.: The Undecided College Student: An Academic and Career Advising Challenge, 4th edn. Johns Hopkins University Press, Baltimore (2015)
5. Wang, R., Orr, J.E.: Use of data analytics in supporting the advising of undecided students. J. Coll. Stud. Retention Res. Theory Pract. **22**, 76–84 (2019)
6. Roessger, K.M., Eisentrout, K., Hevel, M.S.: Age and academic advising in community colleges: examining the assumption of self-directed learning. Commun. Coll. J. Res. Pract. **43**, 441–454 (2019)
7. Henderson, L.K., Goodridge, W.: AdviseMe: an intelligent web-based application for academic advising. Int. J. Adv. Comput. Sci. Appl. **6**, 233–243 (2015)
8. Salehundin, N.B., Kahtan, H., Abdulgabber, M.A., Al-bashiri, H.: A proposed course recommender model based on collaborative filtering for course registration. Int. J. Adv. Comput. Sci. Appl. **10**(11), 162–168 (2019)

9. Main, J.B., Griffith, A.L.: From SIGNALS to success? The effects of an online advising system on course grades. Educ. Econ. **27**, 608–623 (2019)
10. Takahashi, Y., Shimizu, Y.: A methodology for constructing a career - oriented learning - support system with a multi - database system. Inf. Process. Soc. Jpn. SIG Tech. Rep. **2002**(41), 81–88 (2002). (in Japanese)
11. Minowa, H., Terasawa, T.: A recommender system to plan the college course selection. In: Proceedings of the 76th National Convention of IPSJ, pp. 615–616. Information Processing Society of Japan, Tokyo (2014). (in Japanese)
12. Hori, Y., Nakayama, T., Imai, Y.: A system for generating time schedules using spreading activation on a course network. J. Inf. Process. **52**(7), 2332–2342 (2011). (in Japanese)
13. Matsuda, T., Watanabe, Y., Shigeta, K., Kato, H.: Presentation of useful data for students' enrollment on courses - motivation, SDLRS and learning activities of students. In: Research Report of JSET Conferences JSET 15-1, pp. 169–176. Japan Society for Educational Technology, Fukuoka (2015). (in Japanese)
14. Matsuda, T., Watanabe, Y., Shigeta, K., Kato, H.: Development of student support system for data-driven course selection. In: Research Report of JSET Conferences JSET 15-5, pp. 225–230. Japan Society for Educational Technology, Fukuoka (2015). (in Japanese)
15. Guglielmino, L.M.: SDLRS-A. Ver. 1. Guglielmino & Associates, Florida (1998)
16. Matsuura, K., et al.: Development of Japanese-SDLRS for application. J. Jpn. Soc. Nurs. Res. **26**(1), 45–53 (2003). (in Japanese)
17. Kondo, N., Matsuda, T., Watanabe, Y., Shigeta, K., Kato, H.: Development of a course selection support system based on self-directed learning readiness and goal setting. In: Proceedings 7th Meeting on Japanese Institutional Research, pp. 100–105. Editorial Committee of MJIR, Tokyo (2018). (in Japanese)

Early Findings from a Large-Scale User Study of CHESTNUT: Validations and Implications

Xiangjun Peng[1], Zhentao Huang[1], Chen Yang[2], Zilin Song[1], and Xu Sun[1](✉)

[1] User-Centric Computing Group, University of Nottingham, Ningbo, China
xu.sun@nottingham.edu.cn

[2] Department of Computer Science, Syracuse University, Syracuse, USA

Abstract. Towards a serendipitous recommender system with user-centred understanding, we have built *CHESTNUT*, an Information Theory-based Movie Recommender System, which introduced a more comprehensive understanding of the concept. Although off-line evaluations have already demonstrated that *CHESTNUT* has greatly improved serendipity performance, feedback on *CHESTNUT* from real-world users through online services are still unclear now. In order to evaluate how serendipitous results could be delivered by *CHESTNUT*, we consequently designed, organized and conducted large-scale user study, which involved 104 participants from 10 campuses in 3 countries. Our preliminary feedback has shown that, compared with mainstream collaborative filtering techniques, though *CHESTNUT* limited users' feelings of **unexpectedness** to some extent, it showed significant improvement in their feelings about certain metrics being both **beneficial** and **interesting**, which substantially increased users' experience of serendipity. Based on them, we have summarized three key takeaways, which would be beneficial for further designs and engineering of serendipitous recommender systems, from our perspective. All details of our large-scale user study could be found at https://github.com/unnc-idl-ucc/Early-Lessons-From-CHESTNUT.

Keywords: Serendipity · Recommeder systems · User study

1 Introduction

Towards a more comprehensive understanding of serendipity, we have built *CHESTNUT*, the first serendipitous movie recommender system with an Information Theory-based algorithm, to embed a more comprehensive understanding of serendipity in a practical recommender system [16,24]. Although experimental studies on static data sets have shown that *CHESTNUT* could achieve significant improvements (i.e. around 2.5x), compared with other mainstream collaborative filtering approaches, in the incidence of serendipity, it remains necessary for a user study to be conducted to allow validations of *CHESTNUT* and impose further investigations into the concept of serendipity and the engineering of serendipitous recommender systems.

© Springer Nature Switzerland AG 2020
S. Yamamoto and H. Mori (Eds.): HCII 2020, LNCS 12185, pp. 65–77, 2020.
https://doi.org/10.1007/978-3-030-50017-7_5

Therefore, we carried out a large-scale user study around *CHESTNUT*, along with its experimental benchmark systems. To enable a detailed study, we first designed a plan to ensure all participants were capable of experiencing serendipity, by excluding the effects of any environmental factors as much as possible. We then launched the study, and invited 104 participants to contribute, from whom we collected extensive data and qualitative records from real-world users over a ten-month period.

Our initial results indicate that, although *CHESTNUT* limited users' feelings of "unexpectedness", when compared with item-based and user-based collaborative filtering approaches, it did show significant improvement in users' feelings about certain metrics being both "beneficial" and "interesting", which substantially increased their experience on serendipity. The low quantity of "unexpectedness", through our interviews, have been addressed due to relatively old movies from *CHESTNUT*.

Based on these preliminary statistics and context-based investigations, we summarized three key takeaways for future work, which lied on **the Design Principles of User Interfaces, Novel Integration of More Content-based Approaches** and **Introspection of Serendipity Metrics**. We believe they are extremely useful for further designs and engineering of serendipitous recommender systems.

More specifically, we have made three main contributions here:

(1) **A Large-scale User Study among *CHESTNUT* and two main-stream Collaborative Filtering Systems.** We have performed a large-scale user study among *CHESTNUT*, Item-based and User-based Collaborative Filtering approaches. Our study has lasted for around 10 months, which involved 104 participants across 3 countries. All details of our large-scale user study could be found at https://github.com/unnc-idl-ucc/Early-Lessons-From-CHESTNUT

(2) **Validations and Implications of the Improvements from *CHESTNUT* in Serendipity.** Through this study, we have validated the effectiveness of *CHESTNUT* in terms of serendipitous recommendations, compared with widely commercialized algorithms. Our initial results also indicates some limitations of our current end-to-end prototype, which has limited the performance of *CHESTNUT*.

(3) **Takeaways for Principles of Designs, Developments and Evaluations in Engineering of Serendipitous Recommender Systems.** Based on several implications from this study, we have summarized three key takeaways, as potential future work directions, to discuss about future principles of designs, developments and evaluations for serendipitous Recommender Systems.

This paper would be organized as follow. Section 2 would provide necessary background information and illustrate our motivation of this study. Section 3 would introduce details around this study, spanning from methodology to technical adjustments. Section 4 would report our initial results and relevant analysis from this study. Section 5 would present our discussion and introspection to motivate and stimulate potential principles and follow-up work in the future.

2   Background and Motivation

For a decade, serendipity has been understood narrowly within the Recommender System field, and it has been defined in previous research as "receiving an unexpected and fortuitous item recommendation" [13]. Such mindset have led to many efforts in the development and investigation of serendipitous recommender systems through modelling and algorithmic designs and optimizations, instead of rethinking the natural understanding of the concept. [1–3, 5, 6, 8–12, 14, 15, 17, 18, 20–22].

CHESTNUT was built to validate a novel insight around serendipitous recommender system, by merging **insight**, **unexpectedness** and **usefulness** to provide a more comprehensive understanding of serendipity, as the first user-centered serendipitous recommender system. In the context of movie recommendation, *CHESTNUT* enables connection-making between users through their directors' information (**cInsigt**), filter out non-popular and non-familiar movies (**cUnexpectedness**) and then generate recommendations through rating prediction (**cUsefulness**). The above three steps ensured relevance, unexpectedness and values respectively.

Although the theoretical support of *CHESTNUT* [24], its effectiveness [23] and practical system performance [16] has been examined earlier, **the missing validation from real-world users is still missing**. Also, a large-scale user study would also help to uncover several issues, which are not capable to be found through off-line evaluations, and enhance its practicality. Therefore, we have performed a large-scale user study since we believe such a study is essential, important and meaningful for both *CHESTNUT*-related work and the communities of Recommender Systems and Information Management.

3   Methodology

In this section, we introduce the research methods used in the *CHESTNUT* user study. Other than environmental factors, previous user studies of serendipity has pointed out that users' willingness to participate would undoubtedly affect their serendipitous experiences [23]. To allow us to collect satisfactory feedback, we scheduled face-to-face interviews as suggested by participants. However, we were unable to manage all interviews in this way, owing to geographical limitations. For those who couldn't attend in person, we applied a mobile diary method to record relevant details, which was a systematic method used in previous user studies on serendipity [19, 23].

3.1   Participants

In total, 104 undergraduate students were invited to take part in this user study, with each participant having made at least 30 movies' ratings. Although a previous study invited professional scholars to take part in serendipity interviews (i.e. because their speciality made experiencing serendipity easier), this study aimed to investigate serendipity within a more generalized group [23].

Table 1. Geographical distribution of participants

Affiliation	Number of participants	Country
Campus 1	79	China/United Kingdom
Campus 2	13	United States
Campus 3	4	China
Campus 4	2	China
Other campuses	6	China

Table 2. Personal information collection from participants

Affiliation	Average age	Male-to-Female ratio
Campus 1	19.468	33:46
Campus 2	20.769	5:8
Campus 3	18.750	3:1
Campus 4	20.000	1:1
Other campuses	19.000	5:1
All campuses	19.586	47:57

Table 3. Levels of involvements from participants

Affiliation	Average number of co-rated items
Campus 1	33.363
Campus 2	22.411
Campus 3	24.250
Campus 4	41.500
Other campuses	29.333
All campuses	32.362

Details about all participants' geographical distribution are reported in Table 1. Details about all participants' personal information are reported in Table 2. Details about the levels of involvements from participants are reported in Table 2. All participants' names reported in this study are aliases.

There are two things to be illustrated in Table 1: 1) The term **Countries** refers to those countries which the corresponding campus bases on; 2) The term **Other Campuses** refers to those campuses, which only has one participant (Table 3).

3.2   Procedure

Before the bulk of this study began, a pilot study was performed with two male participants on campus for a period of four days. The detailed experiment issues such as time arrangement, system functionality and interaction preparation, were all decided based on this pilot study.

The bulk of this study was then conducted. For each participant, there were two parts to the whole study - a pre-interviews and an empirical interviews. First, for the pre-interviews, each participant was invited individually to a short meeting (around 30 min), to introduce the purpose of study and to collect their own movie rating records. Since the majority of users do not use IMDb as their channel with which to manage their favorite movies, we had to perform this collection procedure within the interview, which also meant that participants could prepare in advance.

Second, for the empirical interviews, each participant made their own schedule in advance. During this stage, users were able to view their recommendation results from the website. Within the time period between the two interviews, we processed collected user profiles in ***CHESTNUT***, and placed their recommendation results online. During the interviews, participants were guided, both by the researchers and the system, to review their profiles, and to check and comment on their recommendation results step by step. We have sketched the interfaces in Figs. 1 and 2.

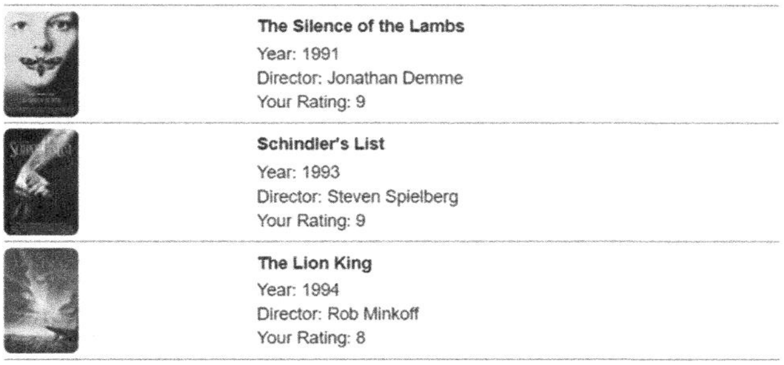

The Silence of the Lambs
Year: 1991
Director: Jonathan Demme
Your Rating: 9
Schindler's List
Year: 1993
Director: Steven Spielberg
Your Rating: 9
The Lion King
Year: 1994
Director: Rob Minkoff
Your Rating: 8

Fig. 1. User profile review page

Your Recommend List has been classified into three classess, you may click below button to sort them:
Recommend Type-A
Recommend Type-B
Recommend Type-C
Conclusion
13 Tzameti
Show Detail
Rating It
Next

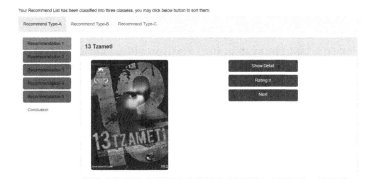

Fig. 2. User ratings and comment page

This user study has lasted for ten months because we followed the "user-centred" arrangements, and eac schedule was determined by the participants involved. In addition to **CHESTNUT**, we also set up two benchmark systems (i.e. an item-based and a user-based approach) and included their results together within this study. Each system produced five recommendation results, according to their submitted profiles. Since not every user could attend a face-to-face interview, we had to perform interviews via online applications (e.g. Wechat), where necessary.

3.3   Data Collection

Two types of data were collected: 1) the user experiences from all recommended movies, generated from all three systems. For each movie, the participants were able to rate feelings on whether the information they were presented with was "unexpected", "Interesting" and "Beneficial", according to the scale shown in Table 2. 2) under each page, the users also had the option to leave their comments on any of the movies, if they felt it was necessary (Table 4).

Table 4. Geographical distribution of participants

Rating	Context
5	Extremely
4	Quite A Bit
3	Moderately
2	A Little
1	Not At All

3.4   System Modifications

Previous studies on **CHESTNUT** applied the relatively small HeteRec 2011 data set from Movielens (i.e. 2113 users with 800,000 ratings) [4]. Since **CHESTNUT** is a memory-based collaborative filtering system, its baseline data set had to be expanded to adapt the system into a real-world scenario. We chose the most recent 30 years' movies and related ratings from ml-20m [7], which is one of the latest and largest data set from Movielens (i.e. 138471 users with 150,000,000 ratings).

4   Results

In this section, we will introduce the preliminary results and analysis, drawn from our user study. After collecting all feedback, we performed a series of preliminary analysises to examine the effectiveness of **CHESTNUT**. First, we will give a performance overview of **CHESTNUT** and its benchmark systems, which relied on data collected from online questionnaires (i.e. to sketch the level of users' feelings under the different metrics). Next, we will sketch out our perspectives as preliminary hypothesis, which will entail additional investigations and discussions around both serendipity and **CHESTNUT**.

4.1   Performance Overview

Our performance overview is divided into three parts, as arranged in the online questionnaires. We will examine the rating levels for whether the participants thought the information provided was "unexpected", "interesting" and "beneficial" separately. This was done for **CHESTNUT**, and for the item-based and user-based systems respectively.

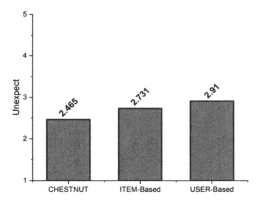

Fig. 3. Average rating of "unexpectedness"

First, we examined all participants' levels of "unexpected" feelings towards their results, as shown in Fig. 3. On the one hand, **CHESTNUT** performed the worst with regard to users' feelings of unexpectedness, with the level only reaching 2.465 on average. On the other hand, the user-based and item-based approaches achieved better ratings for this factor, with levels of 2.731 and 2.91 on average respectively.

We then explored the levels of feelings on relating to whether they found the information to be "interesting", and the results are shown in Fig. 4. In terms of providing interesting recommendation results, **CHESTNUT** achieved 3.523 on average. As for the user-based and item-based approaches, they only achieved average ratings of 3.163 and 2.881 respectively. The results support the fact that **CHESTNUT** is able to provide more interesting recommendation results.

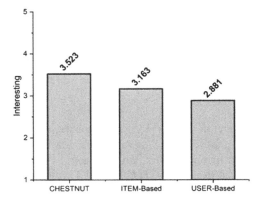

Fig. 4. Average rating of "interesting"

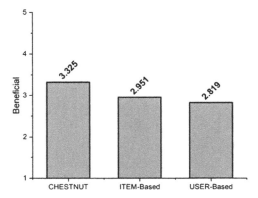

Fig. 5. Average rating of "beneficial"

Finally, we checked quantitatively the levels of feelings relating to whether they found the information to be "beneficial", as illustrated in Fig. 5. In this case, **CHESTNUT** achieved a rating of 3.325 on average, but the user-based and item-based approaches only reached 2.951 and 2.819 on average respectively. Similar to the results for how "interesting" the participants found the information, the results support the fact that **CHESTNUT** is able to provide much more beneficial recommendation results than the two conventional approaches.

4.2 Why Were the Results Not so "Unexpected"?

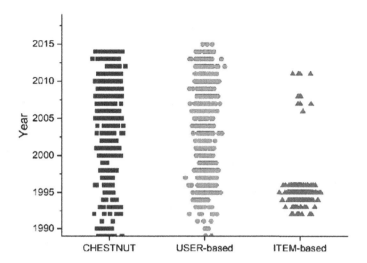

Fig. 6. Year distribution of recommendation results

The major concern of our user study is that results from **CHESTNUT** were not as highly rated in terms of their unexpectedness as we predicted. Normally, **CHESTNUT** has a particular functional unit (i.e. "cUnexpectedness") to ensure that all results are unexpected. However, during this study, **CHESTNUT** seemed to fail to make users feel that the results were unexpected.

Having looked further into this phenomenon, we found that, as participants claimed, they felt the results were unexpected when they encountered relatively old movies (i.e. those made approximately 20 years ago), because most only kept track of more recent productions. We further confirmed this by drawing the year distribution of recommendation results from different systems, as shown in Fig. 6. We believed this is the main reason why they outperformed than **CHESTNUT** in their "unexpected" ratings.

5 Discussions and Takeaways

Based on preliminary results and analysis from our study, we hereby discuss revealed issues and relevant takeaways, to stimulate novel insights and follow-up investigations. In general, there are three aspects, which we want to highlight:

- **Design Principles of User Interfaces.**
  The current User Interface design of **CHESTNUT** directly reflects high-level overview information of different items, which has indicated that general

design choices could potentially hurt users' capability to encounter serendipitous information. Particularly, in our case, the tag "year" has led to a lot of negative effects in the domain of "unexpectedness".

We believe future serendipity-oriented interfaces demands content-based interaction and personalized mechanisms. For instance, in the context of movies, we could use Movie Trailer as preview resources, and let users customize their interfaces by re-ordering the priority of displayed information as they prefer.

- **Novel Integration of More Content-based Approaches.**
  The current study of **CHESTNUT** has only been exploited with the setting of "Director", as the connection-making resources. Given the fact that Directors are dependent to active periods, levels of productivity and genres, it's reasonable to lead to "old movies appear frequently".
  We believe future studies among **CHESTNUT** and other serendipitous recommender systems would take the categories of information, as the guiding resources, into account. In **CHESTNUT**, we have already included support for other information categories in **cInsight**, such as Years and Genres. This would also impose novel integration of different content-based approaches together, which aims to provide personalized recommendation results.

- **Introspection of Serendipity Metrics.**
  The comparison between our real-world study and off-line evaluations have indicated that, there is a huge gap of current serendipity measures in the context of Recommender Systems.
  We believe this also imposes a lot of opportunities to develop novel schemes and frameworks for the validations of serendipitous designs and implementations. More specifically, the results from our experimental study and real-world feedback around **CHESTNUT** are extremely valuable, especially when combining both of them together.

Although we have addressed three aspects of our takeaways, we still believe there are a lot of challenges and opportunities beyond **CHESTNUT**. Hereby, we only provide reflections from our own experiences and we hope they would stimulate more interesting and novel ideas for serendipitous designs and engineering, in both Recommender Systems and other relevant communities.

6   Conclusion and Future Work

In this paper, we have presented our early findings from a large-scale user study of **CHESTNUT**, which involved 104 participants over a ten months period. According to our initial analysis, the results have shown that, compared with mainstream collaborative filtering techniques, though **CHESTNUT** limited users' feelings of **unexpectedness** to some extent, it showed significant improvement in their feelings about certain metrics being both **beneficial** and **interesting**, which substantially increased users' experience of serendipity. Based on them, we have summarized three key takeaways, which would be beneficial for further designs and engineering of serendipitous recommender systems.

Our future work will make variants of further in-depth studies, based on our summarized takeaways, to investigate both the concept of serendipity and the optimizations of **CHESTNUT** through these empirical data. Beyond **CHESTNUT**, we are particularly interested in bridging real-world feedback and off-line results for more sophisticated frameworks, to further validate many variants of other serendipitous recommender system designs and implementations.

Acknowledgement. We thank for valuable feedback and suggestions from our group members and anonymous reviewers, which have substantially improved the overall quality of this paper. In particular, we thank for our ex-member, Weikai Kong, for his great efforts in setting up and assisting to perform the bulk of this study. This research is generously supported by National Natural Science Foundation of China Grant No. 71301085 and Hefeng Creative Industrial Park in Ningbo, China.

References

1. Abbassi, Z., Amer-Yahia, S., Lakshmanan, L.V.S., Vassilvitskii, S., Yu, C.; Getting recommender systems to think outside the box. In: Proceedings of the 2009 ACM Conference on Recommender Systems, RecSys 2009, New York, NY, USA, 23–25 October 2009, pp. 285–288 (2009)
2. Adamopoulos, P., Tuzhilin, A.: On unexpectedness in recommender systems: or how to better expect the unexpected. ACM TIST **5**(4), 54:1–54:32 (2014)
3. Bhandari, U., Sugiyama, K., Datta, A., Jindal, R.: Serendipitous recommendation for mobile apps using item-item similarity graph. In: Banchs, R.E., Silvestri, F., Liu, T.-Y., Zhang, M., Gao, S., Lang, J. (eds.) AIRS 2013. LNCS, vol. 8281, pp. 440–451. Springer, Heidelberg (2013). https://doi.org/10.1007/978-3-642-45068-6_38
4. Cantador, I., Brusilovsky, P., Kuflik, T.: 2nd Workshop on Information Heterogeneity and Fusion in Recommender Systems (HETREC 2011). Proceedings of the 5th ACM Conference on Recommender Systems, RecSys 2011, New York, NY, USA, 2011. ACM (2011)
5. de Gemmis, M., Lops, P., Semeraro, G., Musto, C.: An investigation on the serendipity problem in recommender systems. Inf. Process. Manage. **51**(5), 695–717 (2015)
6. Ge, M., Delgado-Battenfeld, C., Jannach, D.: Beyond accuracy: evaluating recommender systems by coverage and serendipity. In: Proceedings of the 2010 ACM Conference on Recommender Systems, RecSys 2010, Barcelona, Spain, 26–30 September 2010, pp. 257–260 (2010)
7. Maxwell Harper, F., Konstan, J.A.: The movielens datasets: history and context. TiiS **5**(4), 191–1919 (2016)
8. Ito, H., Yoshikawa, T., Furuhashi, T.: A study on improvement of serendipity in item-based collaborative filtering using association rule. In: IEEE International Conference on Fuzzy Systems, FUZZ-IEEE 2014, Beijing, China, 6–11 July 2014, pp. 977–981 (2014)
9. Kamahara, J., Asakawa, T., Shimojo, S., Miyahara, H.: A community-based recommendation system to reveal unexpected interests. In: 11th International Conference on Multi Media Modeling (MMM 2005), 12–14 January 2005, Melbourne, Australia, pp. 433–438 (2005)

10. Kawamae, N.: Serendipitous recommendations via innovators. In: Proceeding of the 33rd International ACM SIGIR Conference on Research and Development in Information Retrieval, SIGIR 2010, Geneva, Switzerland, 19–23 July 2010, pp. 218–225 (2010)
11. Lee, K., Lee, K.: Using experts among users for novel movie recommendations. JCSE **7**(1), 21–29 (2013)
12. Lee, K., Lee, K.: Escaping your comfort zone: a graph-based recommender system for finding novel recommendations among relevant items. Expert Syst. Appl. **42**(10), 4851–4858 (2015)
13. McNee, S.M., Riedl, J., Konstan, J.A.: Being accurate is not enough: how accuracy metrics have hurt recommender systems. In: Extended Abstracts Proceedings of the 2006 Conference on Human Factors in Computing Systems, CHI 2006, Montréal, Québec, Canada, 22–27 April 2006, pp. 1097–1101 (2006)
14. Oku, K., Hattori, F.: Fusion-based recommender system for improving serendipity. In: Proceedings of the Workshop on Novelty and Diversity in Recommender Systems, DiveRS 2011, at the 5th ACM International Conference on Recommender Systems, RecSys 2011, Chicago, Illinois, USA, 23 October 2011, pp. 19–26 (2011)
15. Onuma, K., Tong, H., Faloutsos, C.: TANGENT: a novel, 'surprise me', recommendation algorithm. In: Proceedings of the 15th ACM SIGKDD International Conference on Knowledge Discovery and Data Mining, Paris, France, 28 June–1 July 2009, pp. 657–666 (2009)
16. Peng, X., Zhang, H., Zhou, X., Wang, S., Sun, X., Wang, Q.: CHESTNUT: improve serendipity performance in movie recommendation by an information theory-based collaborative filtering approach. In: Proceedings of the 22th Springer International Conference on Human-Computer Interaction (HCI 2020) (2020)
17. Schedl, M., Hauger, D., Schnitzer, D.: A model for serendipitous music retrieval. In: Proceedings of the 2nd Workshop on Context-Awareness in Retrieval and Recommendation, CaRR 12, 2012, Lisbon, Portugal, 14–17 February 2012, pp. 10–13 (2012)
18. Semeraro, G., Lops, P., de Gemmis, M., Musto, C., Narducci, F.: A folksonomy-based recommender system for personalized access to digital artworks. JOCCH **5**(3), 11:1–11:22 (2012)
19. Sun, X., Sharples, S., Makri, S.: A user-centred mobile diary study approach to understanding serendipity in information research. Inf. Res. **16**(3) (2011)
20. Taramigkou, M., Bothos, E., Christidis, K., Apostolou, D., Mentzas, G.: Escape the bubble: guided exploration of music preferences for serendipity and novelty. In: Seventh ACM Conference on Recommender Systems, RecSys 2013, Hong Kong, China, 12–16 October 2013, pp. 335–338 (2013)
21. Yamaba, H., Tanoue, M., Takatsuka, K., Okazaki, N., Tomita, S.: On a serendipity-oriented recommender system based on folksonomy and its evaluation. In: 17th International Conference in Knowledge Based and Intelligent Information and Engineering Systems, KES 2013, Kitakyushu, Japan, 9–11 September 2013, pp. 276–284 (2013)
22. Zhang, Y.C., Ó Séaghdha, D., Quercia, D., Jambor, T.: Auralist: introducing serendipity into music recommendation. In: Proceedings of the Fifth International Conference on Web Search and Web Data Mining, WSDM 2012, Seattle, WA, USA, 8–12 February 2012, pp. 13–22 (2012)

23. Xiaosong Zhou, X., Sun, Q.W., Sharple, S.: A context-based study of serendipity in information research among Chinese scholars. J. Doc. **74**(3), 526–551 (2018)
24. Zhou, X., Xu, Z., Sun, X., Wang, Q.: A new information theory-based serendipitous algorithm design. In: Yamamoto, S. (ed.) HIMI 2017. LNCS, vol. 10274, pp. 314–327. Springer, Cham (2017). https://doi.org/10.1007/978-3-319-58524-6_26

CHESTNUT: Improve Serendipity in Movie Recommendation by an Information Theory-Based Collaborative Filtering Approach

Xiangjun Peng, Hongzhi Zhang, Xiaosong Zhou, Shuolei Wang, Xu Sun[⊠], and Qingfeng Wang

User-Centric Computing Group, University of Nottingham Ningbo China, Ningbo, China
xu.sun@nottingham.edu.cn

Abstract. The term "serendipity" has been understood narrowly in the Recommender System. Applying a user-centered approach, user-friendly serendipitous recommender systems are expected to be developed based on a good understanding of serendipity. In this paper, we introduce **CHESTNUT**, a memory-based movie collaborative filtering system to improve serendipity performance. Relying on a proposed Information Theory-based algorithm and previous study, we demonstrate a method of successfully injecting insight, unexpectedness and usefulness, which are key metrics for a more comprehensive understanding of serendipity, into a practical serendipitous recommender system. With lightweight experiments, we have revealed a few runtime issues and further optimized the same. We have evaluated **CHESTNUT** in both practicability and effectiveness, and the results show that it is fast, scalable and improves serendipity performance significantly, compared with mainstream memory-based collaborative filtering. The source codes of **CHESTNUT** are online at https://github.com/unnc-ucc/CHESTNUT.

Keywords: Serendipity · Recommeder systems · Information Theory

1 Introduction

In an era of an increasing need for personalized recommendations, serendipity has become an important metric for achieving such a goal. Serendipitous recommender systems have been investigated and developed, to generate such results for their customers. Such systems can now be found in certain applications, such as in music recommendation [21].

However, as a user-centric concept, serendipity has been understood narrowly within the Recommender System field, and it has been defined in previous research as "receiving an unexpected and fortuitous item recommendation" [20]. The understanding of serendipity, as a user-centered concept, has been a gap for a while. Until recently, an awareness of this gap has led a conceptual bridge, which

© Springer Nature Switzerland AG 2020
S. Yamamoto and H. Mori (Eds.): HCII 2020, LNCS 12185, pp. 78–95, 2020.
https://doi.org/10.1007/978-3-030-50017-7_6

introduced serendipity from Information Research into Recommender Systems, by proposing an Information Theory-based algorithm [36]. To further investigate this algorithm, it needs to be implemented as an end-to-end recommender system, but it is difficult to do so.

The challenges of transferring this conceptual bridge into a real-world implementation are two-fold. Firstly, it is demanding to inject the understanding appropriately, since the implementation may forfeit the algorithm design, to develop such a run-time system. Secondly, even though the implementation can recommend serendipitous information, it is demanding to ensure an overall enhanced user experience. For example, the overall system performance may compromise a user's experience, if the system response time is slow, since serendipity is a very sensitive feeling.

Thus, it is important, that serendipitous systems are designed with an accurate understanding of the concept, while delivering a high level of performance. Hence, we present *CHESTNUT*, a state-of-the-art memory-based movie recommender system to improve serendipity performance. Whereas prior research has produced many serendipitous frameworks, it has focused on applying algorithmic techniques, rather than transferring a basic understanding of serendipity into the system development (Sect. 3).

We have addressed the issues of developing serendipitous systems by following a user-centered understanding of serendipity (Sect. 3) and focusing on runtime failures while making predictions (Sect. 5). Furthermore, we have optimized *CHESTNUT* by revisiting and updating **significance weighing** statistically to ensure a high level of system performance.

More specifically, we have made three main contributions here:

(1) *CHESTNUT* **Movie Recommender System.** *CHESTNUT* applies an Information Theory-based algorithm, which aims to combine three key metrics based on a user-centered understanding of serendipity: insight, unexpectedness and value [36]. With regard to these metrics, *CHESTNUT* has three key functional units, respectively: 1) **cInsight** performs the "making connections" to expand a target user's profile, to collect all target-user-related items (Sect. 3.1); 2) **cUnexpectedness** filtered out all expected items from all target-user-related items, with the help of a primitive prediction model (Sect. 3.2); and 3) **cUsefulness** evaluates the potential value of those candidate items through prediction, and generates a list of recommendations by sorting them from high to low (Sect. 3.3). In addition, while developing *CHESTNUT* we revealed key implementation details (Sect. 4). The source codes of *CHESTNUT* are online at https://github.com/unncucc/CHESTNUT.

(2) **Optimizations of** *CHESTNUT*. Through system development, we observed that implementations following conventional methods could cause runtime failure in *CHESTNUT*. We have formulated this problem (Sect. 5.1), and optimized *CHESTNUT* in two ways: First, we adjust the conventional designs while generating predictions for memory-based collaborative filtering techniques (Sect. 5.2); Second, we revisited the conventional

optimization method, **significance weighting**, to further improve the performance and effectiveness of *CHESTNUT*, with updates based on statistical analysis (Sect. 5.3).

(3) **Qualitative Evaluation of *CHESTNUT*.** We conducted an experimental study to assess the performance of *CHESTNUT*, both a bare metal version and in optimized versions (Sect. 6). We have also benchmarked *CHESTNUT* with two mainstream memory-based collaborative filtering techniques, namely: item-based collaborative filtering and K-Neareset-Neighour user-based collaborative filtering from Apache Mahout. The results shows that *CHESTNUT* is **fast, scalable and extremely serendipitous**.

2   Background

CHESTNUT is built on a series of works, which aimed to understand serendipity, to quantify serendipity in many use cases and to introduce serendipity understanding into the Recommender System (i.e. would be illustrated in detail further). We have also draw inspiration from the implementation and optimization of memory-based collaborative filtering techniques to enhance the system performance [7–9,27].

Within the Recommender System field, serendipity has been understood as "receiving an unexpected and fortuitous item recommendation" [20]. Many efforts have been made in the development and investigation of serendipitous recommender systems [1–3,5,6,10–12,14,15,23,24,28,29,31–33]. Until recently, the main focus of the development of serendipitous recommender systems has centered on the algorithmic techniques that are being deployed, however, there are no existing systems which aim to bring an optional serendipitous user experience by applying a user-centered approach to the development of serendipitous recommender systems.

Unlike accuracy or other metrics, serendipity, as a user-centric concept, is inappropriate for taking this narrow view within this field. Understanding the serendipity has already raised considerable interest and it has been investigated for long in multiple disciplines [18,19,25,30]. For instance, to better understand this concept, a number of theoretical models have been established to study serendipity [16,17,26]. More recently, previous research has highlighted how "making connections" is an important point for serendipitous engineering [13]. Based on previous research outcome from Information Research, an Information Theory-based algorithm has been proposed to better understand serendipity in the Recommender System [36]. Furthermore, a systematic context-based study among Chinese Scholars has been conducted and proves the effectiveness of the proposed algorithm [35].

This proposed conceptual bridge, which is based on a more comprehensive understanding of serendipity by merging **insight**, **unexpectedness** and **usefulness**, has been partly developed and studied in a movie scenario with early tryouts [34]. To bring together the above aspects, the system is expected to work sequentially in three steps, as follows: it first expands the user's profile by "making connections"; it then filters out unexpected items, according to the expanded profile and the original one; finally, it predicts ratings to calculate the value of all selected items to the target user, and then make appropriate recommendations.

However, it is still unclear how the proposed algorithm could be developed as an end-to-end recommender system in a real-world scenario, which is very practical, effective and suitable to deploy. Based on previous investigations, we have implemented **CHESTNUT** in a movie recommendation scenario. Below, we have presented a comprehensive overview of three major components to ensure and balance the three given metrics: **insight**, **unexpectedness** and **usefulness** (Sect. 3). In addition, we have presented the implementation details (Sect. 4) and optimization choices made during the development of **CHESTNUT**, which have been employed to attempt to improve its reliability and practicality in the real world (Sect. 5).

3   *CHESTNUT* Overview

Before explaining the details of the implementation, we introduce the three major functional units of **CHESTNUT**, which were developed consequentially with due consideration of the three metrics of serendipity mentioned above. There are three major functional units in **CHESTNUT**: *cInsight*, *cUnexpectedness* and *cUsefulness*. These units function sequentially and ensure corresponding metrics, one by one.

3.1   cInsight

The design of *cInsight* aims to stimulate the "making connections" process, which is a serendipitous design from Information Research, to expand the profile of target users.

Details of the functional process of *making connections* are as followed. With the users' profiles uploaded[1], according to a *referencing attribute*[2], *making connections* would direct target users from their own information towards the most similar users in this selected attribute[3]. This whole process is denoted as a *level*. The repetition of this process, by starting from the output in the previous level, would finally end with an *active user* or a set of *active users*, when the similarity between *active user* and *target user* reaches the threshold.

cInsight is not parameter-free: there are two parameters which need to be set in advance. First, the *referencing attribute* should be determined as the metric for *making connections*, and it should be related information, such as side information categories[4]. Second, is the threshold to determine if the repetition shall end. Since more *levels* are formed by *making connections*, there is a larger

---

[1] Those users denoted as *target users*.

[2] Attribute(s) to guide making connections.

[3] Those users denoted as *active users*.

[4] In movie recommendations, for instance, it could be directors, genres and so on.

distance between *active users* and *target users*. This threshold aims to make sure *active users* are not too "far" from the *target user*. Here, the thresholds could be the mathematical abstractions of similarity[5]. *cInsight* performed the *making connections* process by starting with the *target user* profile. The repetitions of multiple *levels* would terminate and form a direction from *target users* to *active users*. *cInsight* would finally re-organize all *active users'* profiles[6] for further processing. Here, assuming *referencing attribute* is **director** of movies, an example would be introduced as a brief explanation of *making connections* process:

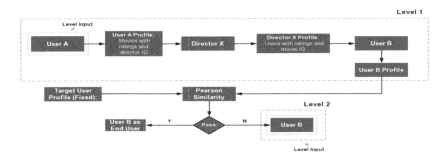

Fig. 1. An example of the connection-making process

For a *Target user* who will be recommended with serendipitous information, *cInsight* works by analyzing his or her profile, and selects corresponding information from the profile as the starting point, which will depend on which attribute has been selected to reference.

As Fig. 1 shows, the movie *Director D1*, who received the most movie ratings from *User A*, is selected as the attribute in this example. Then, according to *D1*, another *User B*, can be selected who is a super fan of *D1* and who contributes the largest number of movie ratings for *D1* throughout the whole movie database. If *User A* and *User B* satisfy the defined threshold on similarity, then *User B* is considered as the *active user* to recommend movies to *User A*. Otherwise, the algorithm continues to find another *User C*, by selecting another *Director D2*, on the basis of *User B*'s profile, until *User Z* is found to meet the threshold between *User Z* and the *Target user A*.

3.2   cUnexpectedness

After *cInsight*, all **relevant** items, generated by *making connections*, have been passed forward to *cUnexpectedness*. The design of *cUnexpectedness* aims to make sure all remaining items are indeed unexpected by the target user.

---

[5] For example, Pearson Correlation Similarity, and so on.
[6] More specifically, their items.

The functional process of *cUnexpectedness* proceeds in two steps, respectively. Firstly, it aims to identify what items a target user expects, based on a broader view of results from *cInsight*. Here, applying the primitive prediction model, *cUnexpectedness* expands the original target users' profiles into a **target-users-would-expect** profile. Secondly, based on the expected items generated by the first step, *cUnexpectedness* would remove all intersections between them and all items passed from *cInsight*[7]).

Here, we illustrate how the first step could be abstracted. The expected movie list (*EXP*) consists of two parts, namely those movies that could be expected by the users (*Eu*), and a primitive prediction model (*PM*) (e.g. those movies have been rated very high on average). And this are desribed in Eq. (1).

$$EXP = Eu \cup PM \tag{1}$$

Through *cUnexpectedness*, items from *cInsight* have been confirmed as being unexpected by the *target user*, which satisfies the need of **unexpectedness**.

3.3   cUsefulness

Following the guarantees of *cInsight* and *cUnexpectedness*, the final unit is to identify which items are valuable to target users, so *cUsefulenss* has been developed to achieve this goal. To evaluate potential movies' value towards target user(s), generating prediction scores is the methodology applied in **CHESTNUT**, conducted by *cUsefulness*. *cUsefulness* quantifies the value of each unexpected movie to target users by predicting how they would be rated by target users.

Since the development plan is collaborative-filtering based, the following equation, which is a conventional approach for prediction, is used to calculate the movie prediction score in *cUsefulenss*.

$$P_{a,i} = \bar{r_a} + \frac{\sum_{u \in U} (r_{u,i} - \bar{r_u}) \times W_{a,u}}{\sum_{u \in U} |W_{a,u}|} \tag{2}$$

In Eq. (2), $\bar{r_a}$ and $\bar{r_u}$ are the average ratings for the user a and user u on all other rated items, and $W_{a,u}$ is the weight calculated by the similarity values between the user a and user u. The summations are over all the users $u \in U$ who have rated the item i.

4   Implementation Details

After giving an overview of **CHESTNUT**'s architecture and exploring the functionalities of the major components, in this section we will introduce some implementation details while developing **CHESTNUT**, which enhanced the performance and practicality. **CHESTNUT** was developed in approximately 6,000 lines of codes in Java.

---

[7] Those items from *active users*, generated by the *target user*.

4.1   Similarity Metrics

As for the similarity metrics, during the development of **CHESTNUT**, *Pearson Correlation Coefficient* was selected as the similarity metric, which is described in Eq. (3).

$$W_{u,v} = \frac{\sum_{i \in I} (r_{u,i} - \bar{r_u})(r_{v,i} - \bar{r_v})}{\sqrt{\sum_{i \in I} (r_{u,i} - \bar{r_u})^2} \sqrt{\sum_{i \in I} (r_{v,i} - \bar{r_v})^2}} \tag{3}$$

In Eq. (3), the $i \in I$ summations are over the items that both users u and v have rated, $r_{u,i}$ is the rating of *u-th* user on the *i-th* item and $\bar{r_u}$ is the average rating of the co-rated items of the *u-th* user.

4.2   cInsight

cInsight expanded its profile through the *connection-making* process, after collecting the user's profile, which relies on the *referencing attribute* from this target user. According to the number of movies rated by the user with respect to this very attribute and users' effective ratings, the most related ones[8] has been selected. With this selection, another user's profile could be generated which covers all the users that have rated movies, with this *referencing attribute*. Through sorting by the number of effective scores on this director from different users, the largest was chosen as the next user. This process would be repeated until the similarity between *target user* and selected user reached a threshold, which had been set in advance.

In **CHESTNUT**, the *referencing attribute* has been set as *director* of movies, and the effective scores refer to those ratings above 4.0[9]. Moreover, this threshold has been set at 0.3[10]. These settings are based on "cInsight"-related studies previously [34].

4.3   cUnexpectedness

cUnexpectedness preserves the unexpected items by excluding those any expected items from all *active users'* items. Generating such expected items relies on the primitive prediction model.

In **CHESTNUT**, through the primitive prediction model, *cUnexpectedness* expanded the *target user's* profile in two respects: first, it added all series movies, if any of those had appeared within the *target user's* profile. Second, it also added the Top Popular Movies.

As Fig. 2 demonstrates, the work flow for generating the *target-user-expected* movies. While we implemented, we have specifically done in the following ways: for the first step, *cUnexpectedness* determines whether a movie belongs to a film series, by comparing their titles. To speed up this process, here we applied

---

[8] Information with regard to the *referencing attribute*.
[9] In this rating scale, the full mark is 5.0.
[10] Here, the similarity refers to *Pearson-Correlation Similarity*.

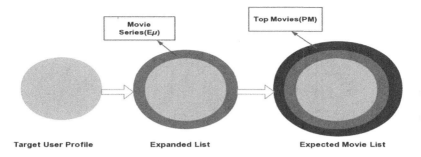

Fig. 2. Work flow of primitive prediction model

a *dynamic programming approach.* In the second step, we selected *Top Two Hundred* because we observed that there is an obvious fracture in this very number, through sorting counts from high to low, based on the number of ratings have been given in the whole data set.

4.4 cUsefulenss

cUsefulness is responsible for examining the potential value of all movies, which have been filtered by *cUnexpectedness.* In the very first prototype development, *cUsefulness* functioned as the same as other memory-based collaborative filtering techniques, by exploring target users' neighbors, finding one with the most similarities and generating predictions according to the method mentioned in Sect. 3.3. However, through lightweight tests, we observed how this have caused run-time failures. We will discuss about it in Sect. 5.

4.5 User Interface

For user interactions, a website has been developed as a user interface for **CHESTNUT**. After logging in, the user is able to view their rated movies, as shown in Fig. 3. For each movie, the interface would offer an image of the movie poster, the title, the published year, the director and the rating from this user.

The follow-up pages, which enable users to view results and give feedback, are organized very similarly. However, when viewing the results, users are able to gather more information via their IMDB links (e.g. for more details or trailers), to present their own ratings, to answer the designed questionnaire and to leave comments.

Fig. 3. The user interface

5   Optimization

In this section, we introduce some key insights for the related optimization of **CHESTNUT**. Through lightweight tests, we found out that **CHESTNUT** could only produce one to two results for almost every user. To improve the system's overall performance and deployability, we optimized **CHESTNUT** by applying a new significance weighting and reforming the prediction mechanism. We first explored the problem, and then introduced them respectively.

5.1   Problem Formulation

After breakdown evaluations of each component in **CHESTNUT**, we found that for every target user in the test set, only two to three items were predicted via *cUsefulness*, when the recommendation list was set to 1,000.

We believe this problem is two-fold. First, memory-based collaborative filtering relies on users' existing profiles to assist the prediction, and this method was directly conducted by searching co-rated items within the users' neighbors. However, with **CHESTNUT**, neighbor users are very unlikely to have co-rated items. From our observations, almost every user could not be supported by their top two hundred neighbors in **CHESTNUT**.

The second issue is more interesting. Owing to the characteristics of *Pearson-Correlation Coefficient*, the smaller the intersection between two users, the more the possibility that the value is higher. In other words, some similarities are not **trustworthy** and these led indirectly to **CHESTNUT's** runtime failures.

5.2   Mechanism Adjustment

Rather than searching a *target user's* neighbors from high similarity to low, *cUsefulness* applied a greedy approach to ensure the prediction process could proceed. Each time *cUsefulness* needs to make a prediction, it first selects all users who have co-rated *need-to-predict* items. Then, within this group, *cUsefulness* cross-checks to find if there are any neighbors. If so, *cUsefulness* regroups and ranks from high to low, according to the similarity. With these settings, *cUsefulness* would proceed and make predictions for as many items as possible.

This mechanism adjustment demonstrated its benefits. First, it optimized the overall system performance. Since prediction is the most time-consuming element of **CHESTNUT**, this adjustment ensured that the prediction would not reach a dead end, when finding predictable neighbors. Second, since it guaranteed the co-rated item in advance, it ensured that **CHESTNUT** would not have any runtime failures, caused by prediction interruptions.

However, this mechanism has intensified the formulated problem which mentioned previously. Since the computing sample size was smaller, owing to the features of serendipitous recommendation, the reliability of the similarity values would inevitably affect the overall recommendation quality.

5.3   Similarity Correction

We are not the first to recognize the necessity of similarity correction. Previous research has identified this kind of issue and has offered a solution known as **significance weighting** [8]. By setting a threshold, all similarity values, with fewer counts of co-rated items than this threshold, would divide a certain value to **correct** the value and maintain the exact similarity value.

In previous trials, **50** has been selected as the number for **significance weighting** to optimize the prediction process. However, in existing literature there is no explanation for how such a number has been obtained, and it appears to be a threshold obtained from previous experience. Since this threshold could be quite sensitive for the data set, we decided to explore and analyze its usage from a statistical perspective. As previously explained, the characteristics of Pearson-Correlation Coefficient could be too extreme when co-rated items are very limited (e.g. only one or two). Therefore, we have assumed the distribution shall be a normal distribution and we take advantage of the **Confidence Ratio** to illustrate this very problem.

All Pearson-Correlation values are computed and collected. All the values are then clustered and plotted on a new graph, with the average co-rated movie counters as y-axis and these values as x-axis. As shown in Fig. 4, it is evident that this nonlinear curve can be fitted into a *GaussAMP model*, which illustrates that the global Pearson-Correlation Coefficients approximate a normal distribution.

Inspired by the **Confidence Ratio** in a Normal Distribution, we defined the quantity of edge areas as the *unlikelihood*. This *unlikelihood* aimed to quantify the unreliability of similarity values from global views. Based on the results presented in Fig. 5, the Reliability, or the **Confidence Ratio**, could be abstracted as calculus mathematically. We then further selected four confidence ratios, in comparison with the initial value of **50**. According to the different ratios of the complete areas, determine the height reversely and apply into M and calculate the corresponding n, Table 1 could be obtained:

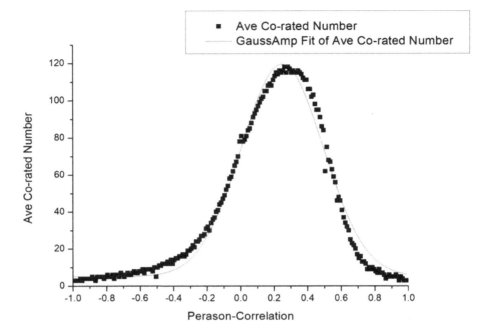

Fig. 4. Plotted pearson-correlation vs. ave co-rated number

Table 1. The average number of co-rated items under different ratios

Unlikehood	Confidence ratio	Average number of co-rated items
1%	99%	5.2
5%	95%	8.5
10%	90%	19.25
20%	80%	42.5
22.5%	77.5%	50

We substituted the obtained results with the **significance weighting** respectively, and applied this similarity correction to improve the reliability of these values, in all related components of *CHESTNUT*.

6   Experimental Study

In this section, we introduce details of *CHESTNUT's* experimental study. The *HeteRec 2011* data set was selected as the source data for this experimental evaluation. It contains *855,598* ratings on *10,197* movies from *2,113* users [4]. In addition, all users' k-nearest neighbors' data are also prepared in advance.

The experiment began by initializing the database and makes the supplement for information about directors of all the movies via a web crawler. Bearing in mind that some movies have more than one director, and there are no rules of distinction which are recognized by the public, only the first director was chosen during this process. After completion of the data preparation, **CHESTNUT** with different correction levels was run through each user in the database in turn.

Since **CHESTNUT** is a memory-based collaborative filtering system, to examine overall performances, we chose mainstream memory-based collaborative filtering techniques, namely: *item-based* and *user-based collaborative filtering* from **Mahout** as the benchmark [22].

All the implementations were conducted in Java and all the experiments were run on a Windows 10 Pro for Workstations based workstation Dell Precision 3620 with Inter Xeon E3-1225 processor (Quad Core 3.3 GHz, 3.7 GHz Turbo, 8 MB, w/HD Graphics P530) and 32 GB of RAM (4 × 8 GB, 2400 MHz, DDR4).

Our experimental study aimed to answer the following three questions:

(1) How much performance improvement can be achieved with **CHEST-NUT**, compared with mainstream memory-based collaborative filtering techniques?

(2) How many performance benefits have been gained with **CHESTNUT**, when different optimization levels are deployed?

(3) What tradeoffs are caused if **CHESTNUT** is optimized with **significance weighting**?

6.1   Recommendation Performance

We first demonstrated that **CHESTNUT** can significantly improve the **unexpectedness** of recommendation results and while maintaining its scalability. For this purpose, we varied the number of items in the recommendation lists from 5 to 1000, and each time increased the number by 5. As shown in Fig. 5, **CHEST-NUT** could perform unexpectedness between 0.9 and 1.0. However, *item-based* and *user-based collaborative filtering* could only perform unexpectedness within the ranges 0.75 to 0.8 and 0.43 to 0.6 respectively. This is because unexpectedness was one of the major goals set during the design and development of **CHESTNUT** (Fig. 7).

Figure 6 shows that **CHESTNUT** could continue its dominant performance in serendipity, which follows the same experiment settings. As benchmark systems, *item-based* and *user-based* systems perform serendipity within the ranges of 0.05 to 0.08 and 0.3 to 0.4, respectively. Nevertheless, **CHESTNUT** still outperformed these conventional systems in serendipity performance. There are two interesting observations within this series of experiments. One is that, although the *item-based* approach could produce more unexpected results than the *user-based*, the *user-based* approach provided more serendipitous recommendations.

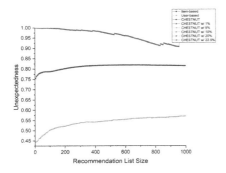

Fig. 5. Levels of unexpectedness in **CHESTNUT** and for benchmarks

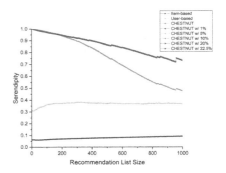

Fig. 6. Levels of serendipity in **CHEST-NUT** and for benchmarks (Color figure online)

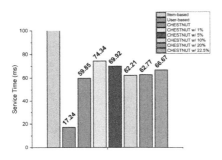

Fig. 7. Service time of **CHESTNUT** and for benchmarks

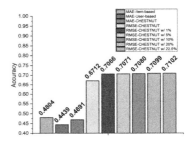

Fig. 8. Levels of accuracy in **CHEST-NUT** and for benchmarks

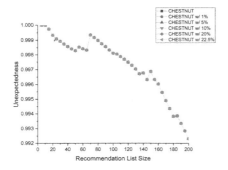

Fig. 9.   Unexpectedness   breakdown within **CHESTNUT**

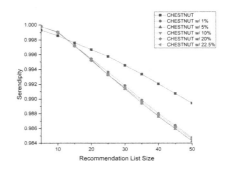

Fig. 10. Serendipity breakdown within **CHESTNUT**

The other interesting fact is that serendipity performance degraded gradually, when applying **CHESTNUT** without optimization. However, optimized versions of **CHESTNUT** performed better scalability. More details of this observation, will be discussed in Sect. 6.2.

As for time consumption, more details are provided in Fig. 9. It is necessary to highlight that, in the *item-based case*, approximately 10,000 ms were required, on average. However, the *user-based* approach did achieve very good performance, by consuming 17.24 ms on average. As for **CHESTNUT**, although it is slightly slower than the user-based approach, it is still much faster than *item-based* implementation. All versions of **CHESTNUT** could finish the service between 59.85 and 74.34 ms on average, which supports the assertion that **CHESTNUT's** performance is very competitive.

Finally, yet importantly, we have explored the accuracy of the recommendation results among the three systems. As their design goals, *item-based* and *user-based* approaches achieved 0.4804 and 0.4439 in **MAE**, which implies that they produce quite accurate results. However, for **CHESTNUT**, the results, irrespective of whether they are with or without the optimization, are less accurate than the benchmark systems.

6.2   Performance Breakdown

Based on Sect. 6.1, we observed the necessity to explore a performance breakdown analysis. We first examined the **unexpectedness** evaluations in detail. Different from previous settings, we took a closer view of **unexpectedness** performance, by narrowing the recommendation list size from 5 to 1,000 to 5 to 200. The most interesting observation is that, unexpected results were irrelevant to the optimization levels of **CHESTNUT**. As Fig. 9 shows, although there are variations in this metric, **unexpectedness** still remains over 0.992. However, we have found that **significance weighting** did not affect the **unexpectedness** performance at all, which indicates that the levels of optimization did not affect the performance of *cInsight*. This is because the threshold in *cInsight* served as the lower bound[11], and our optimization mainly aims to correct any extremely high similarities, which are caused by too small an intersection size between users.

However, optimizations do play a role in *cUsefulness*. To examine this in more detail, we maintained a very narrow view by setting the recommendation list size from 5 to 50. It has been observed that when a recommendation list size is smaller than 15, all optimized versions produce more serendipitous results than in the original version, although they were already very serendipitous. When the size is between 15 to 50, the situation was reversed. However, if we combined Fig. 10 with Fig. 6, the overall scalability of **CHESTNUT** is much weaker than the optimized versions.

This performance variation could be explained from two aspects. Since **CHESTNUT** could only make predictions within a small group compared to the other systems, and when there was no optimization, the predictions could be virtually high and this led to an obvious drift, as illustrated in Fig. 6 (the blue line). We believe that the most important benefit of optimization is that, it

---

[11] When the value is less than it, *making connections* terminates.

stabilizes serendipity performance and improves the scalability of the whole system, by improving the reliability of the similarity values.

6.3   The Tradeoff Caused by Optimization

Here, we have mainly focused on the tradeoff caused by Similarity Correction, since the other optimization aims to make *CHESTNUT* runnable. There are two main tradeoffs to discuss about.

First, there are some runtime overheads when values are corrected. As Fig. 9 shows, all optimized versions have a slight increase in the service time. As for the variations within these optimized versions, this is because if the correction rate were too high or too low, it would increase the computation difficultly and then cause overheads.

Second, we observed a very interesting situation. In the early investigations of **significance weighting**, researchers claimed that this approach was able to improve the accuracy of recommendations, and further investigation has supported that this very setting is effective [7–9]. However, optimized versions of *CHESTNUT* has conflicted with this. Figure 8 reveals a slight trend of accuracy loss, when the optimized levels were increased. We believe this is because of *CHESTNUT's* characteristics. What has been improved, via this optimization, is the trustworthiness of the similarity values. Unlike accuracy-oriented systems, it cannot be equal to the accuracy in serendipitous systems.

7   Discussion

Our experimental study revealed two main points for further discussions. First, *CHESTNUT* has been proven that it is applicable to deploy the Information Theory-based algorithm, as an end-to-end recommender system which can induce serendipitous recommendations. Especially, while the recommendation size is less than 50, *CHESTNUT* has dominated the serendipity performance, with close to the upper bound in evaluations. **Second, during the system implementation, it has been observed that *CHESTNUT* still needs optimizations via value corrections, to improve overall recommendation quality.** Through revisiting and updating **significance weighting** concepts, *CHESTNUT* has been optimized to improve the overall scalability and serendipitous recommendation performance, because of the reliability of similarity values has been improved greatly.

8   Conclusion and Future Work

In this paper, we have presented *CHESTNUT*, a state-of-the-art memory-based collaborative filtering system that aims to improve serendipitous recommendation performance in the context of movie recommendation. We implemented *CHESTNUT* as three main functional blocks, corresponding to the three main metrics of serendipity: insight, unexpectedness and usefulness. We optimized **CHESTNUT** by revisiting and updating a conventional method "significance weighting", which has significantly enhanced the overall performance of **CHESTNUT**. The experimental study demonstrated that, compared with mainstream memory-based collaborative filtering systems, **CHESTNUT** is a fast and scalable system which can provide extremely serendipitous recommendations. To the best of our knowledge, **CHESTNUT** is the first collaborative system, rooted with a serendipitous algorithm, which was built on the user-centred understanding from Information Researchers. Source codes of **CHESTNUT** is online at https://github.com/unnc-ucc/CHESTNUT.

The future work of **CHSETNUT** will focus on its extendibility. On the one hand, though **CHESTNUT** is not parameter-free, it wouldn't be difficult to extend into different usage context (e.g. shopping, mailing and etc.) since parameters of **CHESTNUT** could be obtained through our previous implementation experiences. On the other hand, as mentioned in Sect. 4, the *levels of connection-making* still rely on our previous experience and function as thresholds, which is the major limitation for system extension. We would further study **CHEST-NUT's** effectiveness and its extendibility through a series of large-scale user studies and experiments.

Acknowledgement. We thank for valuable feedback and suggestions from our group members and anonymous reviewers, which have substantially improved the overall quality of this paper. This research is generously supported by National Natural Science Foundation of China Grant No. 71301085 and Hefeng Creative Industrial Park in Ningbo, China.

References

1. Abbassi, Z., Amer-Yahia, S., Lakshmanan, L.V.S., Vassilvitskii, S., Cong, Y.: Getting recommender systems to think outside the box. In: Proceedings of the 2009 ACM Conference on Recommender Systems, RecSys 2009, New York, NY, USA, 23–25 October 2009, pp. 285–288 (2009)
2. Adamopoulos, P., Tuzhilin, A.: On unexpectedness in recommender systems or how to better expect the unexpected. ACM TIST **5**(4), 1–32 (2014)
3. Bhandari, U., Sugiyama, K., Datta, A., Jindal, R.: Serendipitous recommendation for mobile apps using item-item similarity graph. In: Banchs, R.E., Silvestri, F., Liu, T.-Y., Zhang, M., Gao, S., Lang, J. (eds.) AIRS 2013. LNCS, vol. 8281, pp. 440–451. Springer, Heidelberg (2013). https://doi.org/10.1007/978-3-642-45068-6_38
4. Cantador, I., Brusilovsky, P., Kuflik, T.: Second workshop on information heterogeneity and fusion in recommender systems (HetRec2011). In: Proceedings of the 2011 ACM Conference on Recommender Systems, RecSys 2011, Chicago, IL, USA, 23–27 October 2011, pp. 387–388 (2011)
5. de Gemmis, M., Lops, P., Semeraro, G., Musto, C.: An investigation on the serendipity problem in recommender systems. Inf. Process Manage **51**(5), 695–717 (2015)

6. Ge, M., Delgado-Battenfeld, C., Jannach, D.: Beyond accuracy: evaluating recommender systems by coverage and serendipity. In: Proceedings of the 2010 ACM Conference on Recommender Systems, RecSys 2010, Barcelona, Spain, 26–30 September 2010, pp. 257–260 (2010)
7. Ghazanfar, M.A., Prügel-Bennett, A.: Novel significance weighting schemes for collaborative filtering: generating improved recommendations in sparse environments. In: Proceedings of the 2010 International Conference on Data Mining, DMIN 2010, Las Vegas, Nevada, USA, 12–15 July 2010, pp. 334–342 (2010)
8. Herlocker, J.L., Konstan, J.A., Borchers, A., Riedl J.: An algorithmic framework for performing collaborative filtering. In: SIGIR 1999: Proceedings of the 22nd Annual International ACM SIGIR Conference on Research and Development in Information Retrieval, Berkeley, CA, USA, 15–19 August 1999, pp. 230–237 (1999)
9. Herlocker, J.L., Konstan, J.A., Borchers, A., Riedl, J.: An algorithmic framework for performing collaborative filtering. SIGIR Forum **51**(2), 227–234 (2017)
10. Ito, H., Yoshikawa, T., Furuhashi, T.: A study on improvement of serendipity in item-based collaborative filtering using association rule. In: IEEE International Conference on Fuzzy Systems, FUZZ-IEEE 2014, Beijing, China, 6–11 July 2014, pp. 977–981 (2014)
11. Kamahara, J., Asakawa, T., Shimojo, S., Miyahara, H.: A community-based recommendation system to reveal unexpected interests. In: 11th International Conference on Multi Media Modeling, (MMM 2005), Melbourne, Australia, 12–14 January 2005, pp. 433–438 (2005)
12. Kawamae, N.: Serendipitous recommendations via innovators. In: Proceeding of the 33rd International ACM SIGIR Conference on Research and Development in Information Retrieval, SIGIR 2010, Geneva, Switzerland, 19–23 July 2010, pp. 218–225 (2010)
13. Kefalidou, G., Sharples, S.: Encouraging serendipity in research: designing technologies to support connection-making. Int. J. Hum. Comput. Stud. **89**, 1–23 (2016)
14. Lee, K., Lee, K.: Using experts among users for novel movie recommendations. JCSE **7**(1), 21–29 (2013)
15. Lee, K., Lee, K.: Escaping your comfort zone: a graph-based recommender system for finding novel recommendations among relevant items. Expert Syst. Appl. **42**(10), 4851–4858 (2015)
16. Luo, J., Rongjun, Y.: Follow the heart or the head? The interactive influence model of emotion and cognition. Front. Psychol. **6**, 573 (2015)
17. Makri, S., Blandford, A.: Coming across information serendipitously - Part 1: a process model. J. Documentation **68**(5), 684–705 (2012)
18. Makri, S., Blandford, A., Woods, M., Sharples, S., Maxwell, D.: "Making my own luck": serendipity strategies and how to support them in digital information environments. JASIST **65**(11), 2179–2194 (2014)
19. McCay-Peet, L., Toms, E.G.: Investigating serendipity: how it unfolds and what may influence it. JASIST **66**(7), 1463–1476 (2015)
20. McNee, S.M., Riedl, J., Konstan, J.A.: Being accurate is not enough: how accuracy metrics have hurt recommender systems. In: Extended Abstracts Proceedings of the 2006 Conference on Human Factors in Computing Systems, CHI 2006, Montréal, Québec, Canada, 22–27 April 2006, pp. 1097–1101 (2006)
21. Murakami, T., Mori, K., Orihara, R.: Metrics for evaluating the serendipity of recommendation lists. In: Satoh, K., Inokuchi, A., Nagao, K., Kawamura, T. (eds.) JSAI 2007. LNCS (LNAI), vol. 4914, pp. 40–46. Springer, Heidelberg (2008). https://doi.org/10.1007/978-3-540-78197-4_5

22. Musselman, A.: Apache mahout. In Encyclopedia of Big Data Technologies (2019)
23. Oku, K., Hattori, F.: Fusion-based recommender system for improving serendipity. In: Proceedings of the Workshop on Novelty and Diversity in Recommender Systems, DiveRS 2011, at the 5th ACM International Conference on Recommender Systems, RecSys 2011, Chicago, Illinois, USA, 23 October 2011, pp. 19–26 (2011)
24. Onuma, K., Tong, H., Faloutsos, C.: TANGENT: a novel, 'surprise me', recommendation algorithm. In: Proceedings of the 15th ACM SIGKDD International Conference on Knowledge Discovery and Data Mining, Paris, France, 28 June–1 July 2009, pp. 657–666 (2009)
25. Pontis, S., et al.: Academics' responses to encountered information: context matters. JASIST **67**(8), 1883–1903 (2016)
26. Rubin, V.L., Burkell, J.A., Quan-Haase, A.: Facets of serendipity in everyday chance encounters: a grounded theory approach to blog analysis. Inf. Res. **16**(3) (2011)
27. Sarwar, B.M., Karypis, G., Konstan, J.A., Riedl, J.: Item-based collaborative filtering recommendation algorithms. In: Proceedings of the Tenth International World Wide Web Conference, WWW 10, Hong Kong, China, 1–5 May 2001, pp. 285–295 (2001)
28. Schedl, M., Hauger, D., Schnitzer, D.: A model for serendipitous music retrieval. In: Proceedings of the 2nd Workshop on Context-awareness in Retrieval and Recommendation, CaRR 2012, Lisbon, Portugal, 14–17 February 2012, pp. 10–13 (2012)
29. Semeraro, G., Lops, P., de Gemmis, M., Musto, C., Narducci, F.: A folksonomy-based recommender system for personalized access to digital artworks. JOCCH **5**(3), 1–22 (2012)
30. Sun, T., Zhang, M., Mei, Q.: Unexpected relevance: an empirical study of serendipity in retweets. In: Proceedings of the Seventh International Conference on Weblogs and Social Media, ICWSM 2013, Cambridge, Massachusetts, USA, 8–11 July 2013, (2013)
31. Taramigkou, M., Bothos, E., Christidis, K., Apostolou, D., Mentzas, G.: Escape the bubble: guided exploration of music preferences for serendipity and novelty. In: Seventh ACM Conference on Recommender Systems, RecSys 2013, Hong Kong, China, 12–16 October 2013, pp. 335–338 (2013)
32. Yamaba, H., Tanoue, M., Takatsuka, K., Okazaki, N., Tomita, S.: On a serendipity-oriented recommender system based on folksonomy and its evaluation. In: 17th International Conference in Knowledge Based and Intelligent Information and Engineering Systems, KES 2013, Kitakyushu, Japan, 9–11 September 2013, pp. 276–284 (2013)
33. Zhang, Y.C., Séaghdha, D.Ó., Quercia, D., Jambor, T.: Auralist: introducing serendipity into music recommendation. In: Proceedings of the Fifth International Conference on Web Search and Web Data Mining, WSDM 2012, Seattle, WA, USA, 8–12 February 2012, pp. 13–22 (2012)
34. Zhou, X.: Understanding serendipity and its application in the context of information science and technology. Ph.D. thesis, University of Nottingham, UK (2018)
35. Xiaosong Zhou, X., Sun, Q.W., Sharples, S.: A context-based study of serendipity in information research among Chinese scholars. J. Documentation **74**(3), 526–551 (2018)
36. Zhou, X., Xu, Z., Sun, X., Wang, Q.: A new information theory-based serendipitous algorithm design. In: Yamamoto, S. (ed.) HIMI 2017, Part II. LNCS, vol. 10274, pp. 314–327. Springer, Cham (2017). https://doi.org/10.1007/978-3-319-58524-6_26

Is This the Right Time to Post My Task? An Empirical Analysis on a Task Similarity Arrival in TopCoder

Razieh Saremi[✉], Mostaan Lotfalian Saremi, Prasad Desai, and Robert Anzalone

Stevens Institute of Technology, Hoboken, NJ 070390, USA
{rsaremi,mlotfali,pdesai9,ranzalon}@stevens.edu

Abstract. Existed studies have shown that crowd workers are more interested in taking similar tasks in terms of context, field and required technology, rather than tasks from the same project. Therefore, it is important for task owners to not only be able to plan "when the new task should arrive?" but also, to justify "what the strategic task arrival plan should be?" in order to receive a valid submission for the posted task. To address these questions this research reports an empirical analysis on the impact of similar task arrival in the platform, on both tasks' success level and workers' performance. Our study supports that 1) higher number of arrival tasks with similarity level greater than 70% will negatively impact on task competition level, 2) Bigger pool of similar open and arrival tasks would lead to lower worker attraction and elasticity, and 3) Workers who register for tasks with lower similarity level are more reliable to make a valid submission and 4) arriving task to the pool of 60% similar task will provide the highest chance of receiving valid submission.

Keywords: Task similarity · Task arrival · Crowdsourced software development · Worker performance · Competition level · Stability · Topcoder

1 Introduction

Crowdsourcing Software Development (CSD) requires decomposing a project to mini-tasks to put an open call for crowd workers [1, 2]. This fact raises two main questions for a project manager: 1- what is the best time to crowdsource a mini-task? and 2- how can I attract skillful workers to work on my mini task?

To answer project managers' questions, a good understanding of task characteristics, task arrival, and crowd workers' sensitivity to arrival tasks are required. Apart from CSD, crowdsourcing tasks are short, simple, repetitive, requires little time and effort [3]. While in CSD, tasks are more complex, interdependent heterogamous, and requires a significant amount of time, effort [4], and expertise to achieve the task requirements. Intuitively, higher demand for skilled workers effects on their availability and increase the task failure chances.

For example, in Topcoder [5], a well-known Crowdsourcing Software platform, on average 13 tasks arrive daily added to on average 200 existing tasks, simply more demand.

S. Yamamoto and H. Mori (Eds.): HCII 2020, LNCS 12185, pp. 96–110, 2020.
https://doi.org/10.1007/978-3-030-50017-7_7

Moreover, there is on average 137 active workers to take the tasks at that period which leads to on average 25 failed tasks. According to this example, there will be a long queue of tasks waiting to be taken. Considering the fixed submission date, such waiting line may result is starved tasks. Thus, task arrival policies will be one of the most important factors to avoid waiting time by assuring that there is enough available workers to take the task.

It is reported that crowd workers usually choose to register, work, and submit for tasks based on some personal utility algorithm, their skillsets and some unknown factors [6]. Crowd workers rather continue to work on similar context tasks based on their previous experience [7], task contexts include required technology, platform, and task type. Also, it is reported that one of the attractive attributes for a worker choosing a task is the monetary prize [8, 9]. By arriving a higher number of tasks, crowd workers will have a higher number of different choices for taking tasks. Therefore, a higher chance of task starvation or cancelation due to zero task registration or task submission form workers may occur. This fact creates a need for a similarity algorithm to cover all mentioned utility factors for a worker to take a task. We aimed to analyze task arrival in the platform and workers' sensitivity based on similar arrival tasks in the platform in order to minimize task waiting time and task failure.

Understanding the impact of similar available tasks on arrival tasks and available workers' performance and sensitivity becomes extremely important. There is a lack of study on the impact of open similar task on the new arrival tasks in the crowdsourcing market and workers' availability and performance in the field of software crowdsourcing. Considering the schedule reduction in crowdsourcing [10], software managers are more concerned about the risks of project success. In this study, we aim at approaching these gaps by investigating the following questions:

(i)   How does the number of available similar tasks impact on task failure?
(ii)   How do available similar tasks effect on task competition level?
(iii) How does the queue of available similar tasks impact on task stability?

We report the design and analysis results of an empirical study based on data gathered from Topcoder, the largest software development crowdsourcing platform with an online community of over 1 M crowd software workers [9].

The rest of the paper is organized as follows: Sect. 2 introduces the background and related work; Sect. 3 presents the design of the research conducted; Sect. 4 reports the empirical results to answer the three stated research questions. Section 5 discusses the results; and finally, Sect. 6 gives a summary and outlook to future work.

2   Background and Related Work

2.1   Task Similarity in CSD

Generally, workers tend to optimize their personal utility factor to register for a task [6]. It is reported that workers are more interested in working in similar tasks in terms of monetary prize [8], context and technology [7], and complexity level. Context switch generates reduction in workers' efficiency [7]. Besides the fact that workers usually register for a greater number of tasks than they can complete [11]. Combination of these two observations may lead to receiving task failure due to:

- Receiving zero registration for task based on low degree of similar tasks and lack of available skillful worker [8], and
- Receiving non-qualified submissions or zero submissions based on lack of time to work on all the registered tasks by the worker [14].

2.2 Workers Behavior in CSD

Software workers' arrival in the platform and their pattern of taking tasks to completion are the essential elements to shape the worker supply and demand in crowdsourcing platforms. For beginners, it takes time to improve and turn into an active worker after their first arrival [5, 12]. Therefore, most of them focus on registering and gaining experience for similar tasks. Existing studies show that by passing time, registrants gaining more experience, hence better performance is expected, and consequently, valid submissions is made [13, 14]. Yet there is a small portion of workers to manage not only to make a submission but also the submission passes the peer review and mark as a valid submission [15].

A typical issue related to workers is that some workers may decide to drop certain tasks after registering for competition or possibly become inactive due to various reasons, such as different time zones and geographical distributions, different native languages spoken by software workers and number of open tasks in the workers' list of tasks [16–18].

Generally, workers tend to optimize their personal utility factor to register for a task [6]. It is reported that workers are more interested in working in similar tasks in terms of monetary prize [8], context and technology [7], and complexity level.

2.3 Decision-Making in CSD

Software Online decision algorithms have a rich literature in operations research, economics, machine learning, and artificial intelligence, etc. Most of the existing work on crowdsourcing decision making is addressing problems in the general crowdsourcing markets. For example, many studies have applied machine learning techniques in learning worker quality and optimizing task assignment decisions [19], aggregating individual answers to improve quality [20, 21], and worker incentives [16]. Variety of modeling choices for repeated decision making in general crowdsourcing identified including quality of work, incentives and human factors, and performance objectives [22]. While a dynamic procurement model for crowdsourcing in which workers are required to explicitly submit their preferences has been presented [23]. The queuing theory was applied in real-time crowdsourcing to predict the expected waiting time and cost of the decomposed uploaded tasks [24]. In software crowdsourcing, only a few studies have focused on decision support for the software crowdsourcing market in terms of task pricing [6, 8, 25, 26], developer recommendations [11, 27], understanding worker behaviors [6, 14, 28, 29], and improve task scheduling [7, 31]. However, there is no consideration of the impact of similarity among the pool of available tasks on new arrival task status.

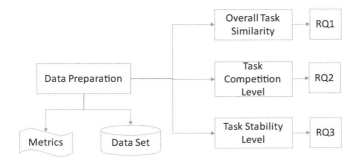

Fig. 1. Main flow of proposed framework and relationship to research questions

3   Research Design

3.1   Empirical Evaluation Framework

Driven by the resource-related challenges in software development, we design three evaluation studies to provide empirical evidence on the feasibility and benefits of CSD. The evaluation framework is illustrated in Fig. 1.

The three research questions in this study are:

RQ1 (Task Similarity Level): How does the number of available similar tasks impact on task failure?

This research question aims at providing a general overview of task similarity in terms of task arrival and available similar available tasks in the platform as well as its effect on task failure rate.

RQ2 (Task Competition Level): How does available similar tasks effect on attracting workers?

The consistency of worker availability will be measured by comparing two different similar tasks at the same time frame. The ratio of attracting workers in the platform in the same period of time with a specific similar task will be a good measure to indicate workers' availability and attraction.

RQ3 (Task Stability Level): How does the queue of open tasks impact workers' performance outcomes?

The ratio of receiving valid submission per task from workers in the same period of time with a specific similar task will be a good measure to indicate task success.

3.2   Dataset and Metrics

The gathered dataset contains 403 individual projects including 4907 component development tasks and 8108 workers from Jan 2014 to Feb 2015, extracted from the Topcoder website [9].

Tasks are uploaded as competitions in the platform, where Crowd software workers would register and complete the challenges. On average most of the tasks have a life cycle of one and a half months from the first day of registration to the submission's deadline. When the workers submit the final files, it will be reviewed by experts to check the results and grant the scores. In order to analyze the impact of task similarity of task success in the platform, we categorized the available data and defined the following metrics, as summarized in Table 1.

Table 1. Summary of metrics definition

Metric	Definition
Duration (D)	Total available time from registration date to submissions deadline. Range: $(0, \infty)$
Task registration start date (TR)	The time when a task is available online for workers to register
Task submission end date (TS)	The deadline that all workers who registered for the task have to submit their final results
Award (P)	Monetary prize (Dollars) in the task description. Range: $(0, \infty)$
# Registration (R)	The number of registrants that are willing to compete on the total number of tasks in a specific period of time. Range: $(0, \infty)$
# Submissions (S)	The number of submissions that a task receives by its submission deadline in a specific period of time. Range: $(0, \#registrants]$
Technology	Required programing language to perform the task
Platform	The associate platform that a task is performing in that
Task type	Type of challenge depends on the development phase
Task Status	Completed or failed tasks

3.3 Dataset Preparation

After data cleaning and removing tasks that were canceled per requestors wish, the number of tasks reduced to 4262 tasks. Because it is our interest to study task similarity effectiveness on task competition level and task stability level, we calculate, the number of similar arrival tasks per day as well as the number of open similar task in the platform per day. Then we clustered similar tasks to four groups of 60% task similarity, 70% task similarity, 80% task similarity, and 90% task similarity.

3.4 Empirical Studies and Design

Three analysis are designed based on the above metrics and proposed research questions, Fig. 1. Specifically, we are interested in investigating the following analysis in CSD:

RQ1 (Task Similarity Level):

Task Similarity Analysis: To analyze task similarity in the platform there is a need to understand the tasks' local distance from each other and task similarity factor based on it.

Def. 1: Task local distance ($D_i s_j$) is a tuple of all tasks' attributes in the data set. In respect to introduce variables in Table 1, task local distance is:

$$D_i s_j = (\text{Award, Registration date, Submission Date, Task type, Technology, Task requirement}) \tag{1}$$

Def. 2: Task Similarity Factor ($TS_{i,j}$) is a dot product and magnitude of the local distance of two tasks:

$$TS_{i,j,} = \frac{\sum_{i,j=0}^{n} Disi(Tj, Ti)}{\sum_{i,=0}^{n} \sqrt{Disi(Ti)} * \sum_{j=0}^{n} \sqrt{Djsj(Tj)}} \tag{2}$$

Similar Task Arrival: It is important to measure the number of similar arrival tasks as well as similar available tasks per day per newly arrived task. Then we will analyze the correlation between task status, and similar arrival task per task similarity cluster in the dataset. Therefore, there is a need to understand task failure and task success per similarity cluster.

Def. 3:: Task Failure (TF_j) per similarity cluster is the number of failed tasks (ft_i) in the platform, which arrived at the same calendar day in the same similarity cluster:

$$TF_j = \sum FT_i$$
$$\text{Where; } TS_{i,j} >= 0.9, 0.8, 0.7, 0.6 \tag{3}$$

Def. 4: Task Success (TSu_j) per similarity cluster is the number of completed tasks (ct_i) in the platform, which arrived at the same calendar day in the same similarity cluster:

$$TSu_j = \sum ct_i$$
$$\text{Where; } TS_{i,j} >= 0.9, 0.8, 0.7, 0.6 \tag{4}$$

In this part, we will be analyzing the impact of available similar tasks on task completing the level and the correlation of different degrees of task similarity on each other.

RQ2 (Task Competition Level): Workers' response on the same tasks in comparison with similar tasks will be analyzed in order to understand the task competition level to the same group of similar tasks.

Def. 5:   Task Competition Level, TCL (i,k), measures average registration for task i from registered similar arrival tasks

$$TCL_{i, k} = \sum_{k=1}^{n} (TRi)/n$$
$$\text{Where; } TSi, j \geq 0.6, 0.7, 0.8, 0.9 \tag{5}$$

RQ3 (Task Stability Level): Average valid submissions for task i in the same group of similar tasks illustrate task stability to be completed in the platform.

Def. 6:   Tsk Stability Level, TSL(i), measures average valid submissions of open tasks in workers queue in the same period of time that worker i take task j

$$TSL_{i} = \sum_{k=1}^{n} S(i)/n$$
$$\text{Where; } TSi, j \geq 0.6, 0.7, 0.8, 0.9 \tag{6}$$

4   Empirical Result

4.1   Task Similarity Level (RQ1)

Our analysis showed that on average 76 new tasks per week were posted on the platform. On average 2 tasks canceled by task owners' requests, 1 faced zero registration and 8 failed based on zero submission or non-qualified submissions. Such observation means 14% of task failure in the platform. We further looked at the task failure distribution in the platform based on the level of task similarity. Figure 2 presents the trend of task arrival per task similarity group. As it is clear all the task groups are following an increasing trend. While the group of tasks with the similarity of 60% and 70% is more centered around the mean, 80%, and 90% similarity are skewed towards lower than mean. The lower level of similarity provides higher diversity in terms of available tasks. This means that the pool of tasks with the similarity of 60% is providing a higher level of choice for workers to switch context and compete on new tasks. Also, it seems the lower similarity among tasks leads to a higher level of completion among available tasks in the platform.

Figure 3 illustrates the average failure ratio of tasks with respect to similar tasks arrival in the platform per week in four different similarity segments. As it presents, by increasing the task similarity level in the pool of available tasks, failure ratio increases. In the segment of 60% task similarity, failure ratio increases from 0% for less than 20 available tasks to 15% for more than 100 similar tasks. This ratio increased from 0% to almost 13% for the segment of 70% similarity. In the 90%, the similarity failure ratio increased from 4% for less than 20 tasks to 16% for more than 100 tasks. Interestingly,

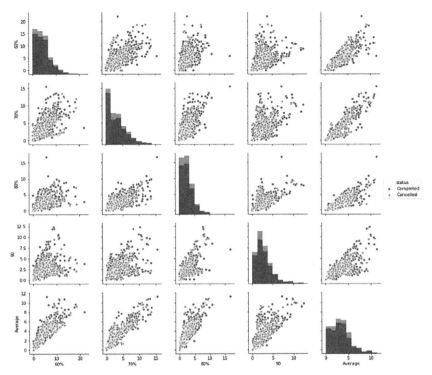

Fig. 2. Trend of task success per task similarity group

in the segment of 80% tasks, failure ratio was on average 20%. However, it dropped to around 17% for tasks in the range of 60 and 80, it again increased to 20% for more than 100 similar tasks available.

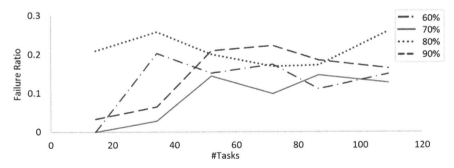

Fig. 3. Ratio of arrival similar task in the platform

Finding 1.1: Higher level of similarity among available tasks in the platform leads to a higher level of task failure ratio.

4.2 Task Competition Level (RQ2)

In order to a better understanding of the influence of task similarity on workers' attraction and consequently competition level, we studied the distribution of competition level of tasks in the different groups of task similarity. Figure 4 illustrates the probability density of competition level under each similarity group.

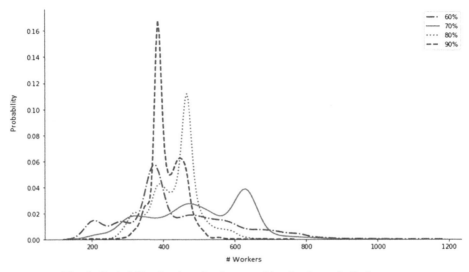

Fig. 4. Probability density of task competition level per similarity group

As it is clear in Fig. 4, tasks with the similarity of 90% attract a higher level of competition with bio-model probability. The highest probability of attracting workers to the competition level is 16% with an average of 190 workers and the second pick of attracting workers is 0.6% with an average of 280 workers. interestingly 90% task similarity cannot attract more than 580 workers per task. 80% task similarity is a tri-model with the highest probability of 11% and an average competition level of 300 workers, and the minimum probability of 0.2% with an average competition level of 100 workers. This category of tasks cannot attract more than 500 workers. 70% task similarity is a tri-model that would drop the probability of attracting workers in the competition to 0.4% with an average of 430 workers. Tasks with the similarity level of 70% can attract up to 700 workers. Interestingly, the 60% task similarity dropped competition level to 0.56% with an average of 180 workers and maximum of 980 workers.

Finding 2.1: Higher level of similarity among available tasks in the platform (i.e. 90% and 80% task similarity) leads to lower probability receiving registration per competition.

Finding 2.2: Lower level of similarity among available tasks in the platform (i.e. 60% task similarity) leads to a higher probability of receiving higher registration level per competition.

4.3 Task Stability Level (RQ3)

In order Task Stability level is another important factor in task outcome besides competition level. Therefore, we investigated a layer deeper and analyzed receiving valid submissions per task based on the open tasks in a different cluster of task similarity. Figure 5 illustrates the distribution probability of receiving valid submissions per task similarity group. As it is shown in Fig. 5, receiving valid submissions by tasks follows the polynomial distribution. Table 2 summarized the statistical analytics of the distribution of valid submissions ratio per task similarity group.

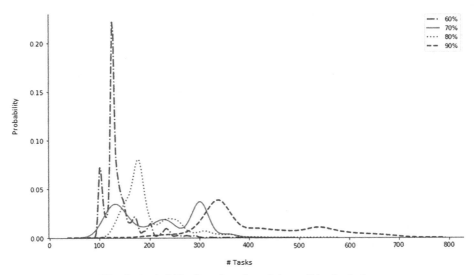

Fig. 5. Probability Density of receiving valid submission

Table 2. Summary of valid submission ratio

Metrics	90% Valid Sub	80% Valid Sub	70% Valid Sub	60% Valid Sub
Average	27.00	23.00	31.00	27.00
Min	24.00	10.00	22.00	15.00
Max	30.00	28.00	35.00	33.00
Median	28.00	26.00	33.00	30.00
Stdev	2.00	6.00	5.00	7.00

The probability of a task receives valid submission in the pool of tasks with the similarity of 90% is 5%. This means 350 tasks receive valid submissions. While the probability of receiving valid submissions for tasks with the similarity of 80% increased up to 7%, only 180 tasks in this group receive a valid submission. The cluster of tasks with the similarity of 70%, receiving valid task submission provides a tri-model in which two of them provides the probability of 4% with an average of 110 and 300 valid submissions respectively, and the third one provides the probability of 2% with an average of 230 valid submissions. Interestingly, tasks with a similarity of 60% lead to more than 20% probability of receiving valid submissions with an average of 110 valid submissions.

Finding 3.1: Lower level of similarity (i.e. 60%) among available tasks in the platform lead to a higher probability of receiving task stability.

5   Discussion and Evaluation

5.1   Similar Task Arrival

To successfully crowdsourced a software project in a crowdsourcing platform, besides understanding the task dependency in a project, it is important to identify the pattern of similar available tasks in the platform. The pool of available similar tasks would highly impact task competition level, task stability level and consequently project success. Also, facing a higher number of similar arrival tasks at the same time doesn't necessarily mean a bigger pool of available similar tasks and less chance of attracting qualified workers in the platform.

As it is shown in Fig. 1, arriving more than 100 available similar tasks in the platform will increase the chance of task failure up to 15%. Moreover, increasing task similarity ratio from 60% to 90% directly impacted on task failure. The increasing degree of task similarity in the platform would ease switching context for workers and lead to lots of failure tasks due to starvation or zero submissions [7, 30].

Our research showed that having multiple choices for workers will negatively impact on competition level and receiving qualified submissions, finding 1.1.

5.2   Task Competition Level

To assure of having a successful project in CSD, not only it is valuable to have a higher competition level to attract enough available qualified workers, but also it is important to have a good worker elasticity among different tasks. This fact makes the importance of knowledge workers' task registration patterns. Our study showed that generally a long line of active registered tasks per worker is negatively correlated with their submissions ratio. Besides having a high number of non-similar tasks in workers' basket indicates attracting a not qualified worker for the tasks, finding 2.1.

Moreover, finding 2.2 showed that, although a longer line of non-similar tasks in a worker's queue is not good, having a long line of similar tasks in workers' queue may lead to less worker elasticity [10]. This makes workers not be available to take a series of tasks of the same project or be very busy working on another similar and perhaps more attractive tasks and ignore other registered tasks.

However, 75% of workers retook the repeated task, and the project didn't face a high level of resource mismatching, team elasticity was low. Therefore, a bigger pool of open similar tasks in the platform is not always a good strategy for attracting qualified workers with high elasticity.

5.3   Task Stability Level

Our result presented that a higher number of available similar tasks means a higher number of different choices for a worker and a lower chance of receiving qualified submissions for a task. According to finding 3.1 workers with the lower queue of tasks are more reliable to retake task from the same project. This fact can be beneficial due to having some background and information about the project.

Since the different choice of task taking for workers will directly impact workers' availability to work on tasks, the higher queue of tasks generally and the queue of similar tasks especially represents a lower chance of receiving qualified submissions [30], and consequently means a higher chance of resource discrepancy. In order to overcome this issue not only a project manager should track open similar tasks in the platform upon task arrival, but it is also required to track workers' performance and activity in the platform in the same frame time.

5.4   Task Status Prediction

As finding 1.1 reports, the level of task similarity in the CSD platform directly impacts on task status. In order to prevent task failure as much as possible, a CSD project manager needs to predict the best time for posting the task. Therefore, in order to study the task failure level in the CSD platform, we build a prediction model using a time series analysis based on the dataset we used in this research. To build the model we used task arrival date, task similarity level with available tasks, task competition level and task submission level in the CSD platform and task status as the outcome of the prediction model. We have selected 4 configurations of task similarity i.e. 60%, 70%, 80%, and 90% respectively for the 30days of arriving tasks based on different similarity levels. For building and evaluating of the model we created two sets of the training set and sample set of data. The training set contains information required for a task where a worker actually registered and made a submission for the task earlier than the submissions date. Similarly, the testing set provides the same information but for all the tasks that were submitted on the deadline. The prophet library introduced by Facebook [32] was used for building and evaluating the predictive time series model.

Figure 6 illustrates the result of task valid submission prediction in the platform. As it is shown tasks with 60% similarity have a stationary prediction for making a submission, with an average of 135 submissions and the submission increased by passing time. Interestingly, while tasks with 70% and 90% level of similarity will not receiving a promising trend of receiving valid submissions, while tasks with 80% similarity are receiving valid submissions with an average of 180.

However, tasks with 60% similarity continue delivering valid submissions close to mean, tasks with 80% similarity experience a higher level of variation. It seems the best time for arriving a new task in the platform in order to have the highest chance of receiving valid submission is when there is the highest level of tasks with 60% similarity available in the pool of open tasks.

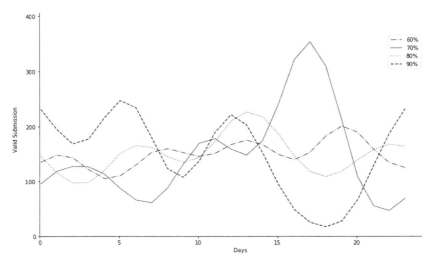

Fig. 6. Prediction of valid submission per task similarity group

5.5 Limitations

First, the study only focuses on competitive CSD tasks on the Topcoder platform. Many more platforms do exist, and even though the results achieved are based on a comprehensive set of about 5000 development tasks, the results cannot be claimed externally valid. There is no guarantee the same results would remain exactly the same in other CSD platforms.

Second, there are many different factors that may influence task similarity and workers' decisions in task selection and completion. Our similarity algorithm is based on known task attributes in Top coder. Different similarity algorithms may lead us to different but almost similar results.

Third, the result is based on task similarity only. Workers' network and communication were not considered in this research. In the future, we need to add this level of research to the existing one.

6   Conclusions

Task preparation is one of the most important issues in the crowdsourcing development world. Crowdsourced tasks perform by an unknown group of workers, who choose tasks based on personal and mostly unknown utility factors. This issue raises the concern about planning a task arrival on the platform. Task similarity impacts on task arrival indirectly. Our research shows that not only a higher level of similarity among available tasks in the platform negatively effects on task success but also the number of arrival similar tasks in the platform would impact competition level per task as well as workers' elasticity. Moreover, workers' queue of task impacts workers' discrepancy and their willingness to continue working on the same project's tasks.

This paper reports that 1) higher number of arrival tasks with similarity level greater than 70% will negatively impact on task competition level, 2) Bigger pool of similar open and arrival tasks would lead to lower worker attraction and elasticity, and 3) Workers who register for tasks with lower similarity level are more reliable to make a valid submission and 4) arriving task to the pool of 60% similar task will provide the highest chance of receiving valid submission.

In future, we would like to focus on the similar crowd worker behavior and performance based on task similarity level and try to analyze workers trust network as well as a task- worker performance network to report more decision elements according to task size and date of uploading, achievement level, task utilization, and workers performance.

References

1. Howe, J.: Crowdsourcing: Why the Power of the Crowd Is Driving the Future of Business. Crown Business (2008)
2. Surowiecki, J.: The Wisdom of Crowds. Random House, Inc. (2005)
3. Stol, K.-J., Fitzgerald, B.: Two's company, three's a crowd: a case study of crowdsourcing software development. In: 36th International Conference on Software Engineering (2014)
4. Chanal, V., Caron-Fasan, M.L.: The difficulties involved in developing business models open to innovation communities: the case of a crowdsourcing platform. Management **13**, 4 (2010)
5. Topcoder websit. http://www.Topcoder.com
6. Faradani, S., Hartmann, B., Ipeirotis, P.G.: What's the right price? pricing tasks for finishing on time. In: Proceedings Human Computation (2011)
7. Difallah, D.E, Demartini, G., Cudré-Mauroux, P.: Scheduling human intelligence tasks in multi-tenant crowdpowered systems. In: ACM (2016)
8. Yang, Y., Saremi, R.: Award vs. Worker behaviors in competitive crowdsourcing tasks. In: ESEM 2015, pp. 1–10 (2015)
9. LAtoza, T., Chen, M., Jiang, L., Zhao, M., Van der Hoek, A.: Borrowing from the crowd: a study of recombination in software design competitions. ICS-SE 2015, Florence, Italy, Crowdsourcing in Software Engineering (2015)
10. Saremi, R.L., Yang, Y., Ruhe, G., Messinger, D.: Leveraging Crowdsourcing For Team Elasticity: An Empirical Evaluation at TopCode, submitted
11. Yang, Y., Karim, M.R., Saremi, R., Ruhe, G.: Who should take this task? – dynamic decision support for crowd workers. In: Proceedings ESEM 2016, to appear
12. Kittur, A., et al.: The Future of Crowd Work, CSCW 2013, 23–27 February 2013, ACM, San Antonio, Copyright 2013
13. Saremi, R.L., Yang, Y.: Dynamic simulation of software workers and task completion, ICS-SE 2015, Florence, Italy, Crowdsourcing in Software Engineering
14. Archak, N.: Money, glory and cheap talk: analyzing strategic behavior of contestants in simultaneous crowdsourcing contests on Topcoder.com. In: Proceedings of the 19th International Conference on World Wide Web, WWW 2010, pp. 21–30. ACM, New York (2010)
15. Yang, J., Adamic, L.A., Ackerman, M.S.: Crowdsourcing and knowledge sharing: strategic user behaviour on taskcn. In: Proceedings of the 9th ACM conference on Electronic commerce, pp. 246–255. ACM, New York (2008)
16. Kaufmann, N., Schulze, T., Veit, D.: More than fun and money: worker motivation in crowdsourcing - a study on mechanical turk. In: Proceedings of 17th AMCIS (2011)
17. Marsella, S.C. Encode theory of mind in character design for pedagogical interactive narrative. Advances in Human-Computer Interaction, vol. 2014, Article ID 386928

18. Kulkarni, A., Can, M., Hartman, B.: Collaboratively crowdsourcing workflows with turko-matic. In: Proceedings of CSCW (2012)
19. Whitehill, J., Ruvolo, P., Wu, T., Bergsma, J., Movellan, J.: Whose vote should count more: optimal integration of labels from labelers of unknown expertise. Adv. Neural. Inf. Process. Syst. **22**(2035–2043), 7–13 (2009)
20. Mao, A., Procaccia, A.D., Chen, Y.: Better human computation through principled voting. In: Proceedings of the AAAI Conference on Artificial Intelligence, pp. 1142–1148 (2013)
21. Khanfor, A., Yang, Y., Vesonder, G., Ruhe, G.: Failure prediction in crowdsourced software development. In: 24th Asia-Pacific Software Engineering Conference (2017)
22. Slivkins, A., Vaughan, J.W.: Online decision making in crowdsourcing markets: theoretical challenges. ACM SIGecom Exchanges **12**, 4–23 (2013)
23. Karger, D., Oh, S., Shah, D.: Iterative learning for reliable crowdsourcing systems. In: 25th Advances in Neural Information Processing Systems (2011)
24. Singer, Y., Mittal, M.: Pricing mechanisms for crowdsourcing markets. In: Proceedings International WWWConference (2013)
25. Mao, K., Yang, Y., Li, M., Harman, M.: Pricing Crowdsourcing-Based Software Development Tasks, pp. 1205–1208. Piscataway, New Jersey (2013)
26. Alelyani, T., Mao, K., Yang, Y.: Context-centric pricing: early pricing models for software crowdsourcing tasks. In: PROMISE 2017, 63–72
27. Mao, K., Yang, Y., Wang, Q., Jia, Y., Harman, M.: Developer recommendation for crowdsourced software development tasks. In: SOSE, pp. 347–356 (2015)
28. Topcoder website: "10 Burning Questions on Crowdsourcing: Your starting guide to open innovation and crowdsourcing success." https://www.Topcoder.com/blog/10-burning-questions-on-crowdsourcing-and-open-innovation/. Accessed 14 Mar 2016
29. Zhang, H., Wu, Y., Wu, W.: Analyzing developer behavior and community structure in software crowdsourcing. Inf. Sci. Appl. **339**, 981–988
30. Saremi, R.: A hybrid simulation model for crowdsourced software development. In: CSI-SEAICSE, pp. 28–29 (2018)
31. Saremi, R., Yang, Y., Khanfor, A.: Ant colony optimization to reduce schedule acceleration in crowdsourcing software development. HCI, 5, 286–300 (2019)
32. Taylor, S.J., Letham, B.: Forecasting at scale. PeerJ Preprint 5:e3190v2 (2017). https://doi.org/10.2787/peerj.preprints.3190v2

User-Centred Design of a Process-Recommender System for Fibre-Reinforced Polymer Production

Thomas Schemmer[1]([✉]), Philipp Brauner[1], Anne Kathrin Schaar[1], Martina Ziefle[1], and Florian Brillowski[2]

[1] Human-Computer Interaction Center, RWTH Aachen University, Campus-Boulevard 57, 52074 Aachen, Germany
`{schemmer,brauner,schaar,ziefle}@comm.rwth-aachen.de`
[2] Institut Für Textiltechnik, RWTH Aachen University, Kackertstraße 9, 52074 Aachen, Germany
`florian.brillowski@ita.rwth-aachen.de`

Abstract. Today's production is massively influenced by fundamental digitalisation. IoP as the industrial realisation of the IoT idea is mainly based on the further processing and analysis of the accruing data volumes, e.g. sensor data, as well as the direct connection of integrated technical and human entities. For the technical implementation, this means that suitable infrastructures and concepts must be created that add value from the generated data.

Furthermore, the integration of human operators, from the shop floor to the management level, is a central challenge in the implementation of the IoP vision. Possible integration measures could be so-called recommender systems (RSS), which can offer a human operator data-based decision support in target situations. It is necessary to design and implement RSS according to the human operator's needs and capabilities to generate a real added value. In this paper, we present a design process for a support system in textile process planning. Corresponding evaluation results are shown and reflected regarding their added value.

Results show that the chosen user-centred design approach is suitable for the design of recommender systems for process planning of textile production chains, as it highlights usability conflicts early and helps identify additional feature requests. The expert evaluations run in this study revealed that the designed app concept could contribute to easier and better planning, especially in the area of fibre-reinforced polymer production.

Keywords: Fibre reinforced polymer · Recommender system · Industrial Internet · Cyber-Physical production systems · Human factors · Data lake

1 Introduction: Industry 4.0 and the Internet of Production

The digitalisation is reshaping society as a whole and modern production in particular. Today's vision of the Industrial Internet, Industry 4.0 [1, 2], or the Internet of Production (IoP) [3, 4] goes far beyond single cyber-physical production systems (where smart,

© Springer Nature Switzerland AG 2020
S. Yamamoto and H. Mori (Eds.): HCII 2020, LNCS 12185, pp. 111–127, 2020.
https://doi.org/10.1007/978-3-030-50017-7_8

computer-based controlling capabilities augment a production machine). It refers to tightly interconnected sensors, production machines, and management systems. The capturing of large volumes and varieties of data from planning, production, and use cycles of products poses tremendous challenges, but also exciting new possibilities. For example, data from past production cycles might be captured in data lakes and then analysed and used to optimise future production planning. Digital shadows as task and context-dependent, purpose-driven, aggregated, multi-perspective, and persistent datasets [3] and other constructions [5], are the foundation for novel forms of product, process, or shop floor planning and value creation in future production.

At present, a research gap regarding the role of the human operator in these new digitalised production environments can be observed. This research gap leads to the following questions: How must these systems and their interfaces be designed to support workers, and how can the valuable expertise of workers be captured, and integrated as a data source for future optimisations?

Human-machine interfaces will be central for integrating people into these novel socio-cyber-physical production systems [6]. In approaches implemented so far, interfaces exist in a range from a classical desktop application, over decision-support Systems (DSS) [7], to human-robot interaction [8, 9]. Furthermore, it can be assumed that irrespective of the type of interface, an increase in the complexity of the information for the human operator can be expected. To make this increasing complexity manageable for humans, a user-centred presentation of data and decisions, as well as targeted decision-support in complex decision-making or control-processes are needed [10].

Based on these assumptions and derived needs, this paper presents one concept for a user-centred design approach of a DSS application to be used in a prototypical textile manufacturing process. Section 1.1 illustrates theoretical considerations on DSS, as well as their opportunities and challenges in the context IoP. Subsequently, Sect. 1.2 focusses the users of such systems and their integration into the design process. Section 1.3 presents the use case, on which this work builds on. Both the need and the necessity of the user-centred design of DSS, as well as it's potential for the industry, are discussed.

Section 2 presents the unified research approach and the major research questions of the presented study. We present the results of the iterative development cycle in Sect. 3. This chapter includes the presentation of a requirement analysis with domain experts (see Sect. 3.1), an iterative prototyping design cycle (see Sect. 3.2), and the results of a user study with prototypical users and tasks (see Sect. 3.3). We discuss the results and implications of this work in Sect. 4.

1.1 Decision Support System in IoP Scenarios

User interfaces are the central link between humans and the technical and algorithmic components in an IoP. One specific type of interfaces are decision support systems that facilitate and enhance human decisions in work-relevant settings [11]. They give context-dependent support and suggestions to operators in specific decision-making situations [12]. Due to an increase in computing power, new DSS approaches can support human operators in sensitive and increasingly complex decision-making situations with targeted suggestions [12].

Yet, some central aspects must be considered for the design of useful DSS: First, advanced database management, with access to internal and external data, as well as knowledge and information on the framework conditions of use and management tasks are needed to provide specific support [13]. A second important aspect is the availability of powerful modelling functions that are accessed via a model management system [13]. The third aspect focusses on the user and the design of the user interfaces. A simple use of DSS interfaces, with interactive parts, suitable information visualisations, and the consideration of other usability relevant aspects should lead to a higher acceptance of such a tool in the work routine. One last meaningful aspect in the context of DSS is the consideration of worker inherent factors, such as trust in automation, information bias, and (professional) autonomy.

According to Madsen and Gregor (2000), *trust* is defined as a combination of willingness and confidence to follow the DSS [14]. In this context, willingness is related to affect- and cognition-based factors, whereas confidence is cognition-based [14]. *Information* bias is defined as the degree to which a human operator relies on the suggestions of the DSS [15]. *Autonomy,* as another relevant factor in the context of a successful implementation of DSS, addressees the need to ensure that users have the control over conditions, processes, procedures, or content of their works, as well as the capability for self-regulation [16].

Summarizing, DSS are an enabler for high performance of human operators, especially for complex decision tasks occurring in the context of an IoP. However, it is important to bear in mind that these advantages can only be utilised if the human operator actually uses the DSS, trust its suggestions, and can integrate it into the workflow. In order to address the criteria mentioned above, it has proven to be useful to make the development of software in general and DSS in particular user-centric (see Sect. 1.2).

1.2 User-Centred Design Approach

To ensure usable and accepted interactive systems, interface design should follow an iterative development process [17]. First, the functional and non-functional requirements from the users and other stakeholders should be gathered. Then prototypes are designed, implemented, and evaluated iteratively, e.g., starting with low-fidelity paper prototypes or small and easily modifiable apps [18]. Evaluating early prototypes with usability experts and—most importantly—with actual users is crucial, as this will generate feedback at early development stages, which can then be integrated into new interface prototypes. It is important to find a balance between functional complexity and fast production of prototypes: More functionality offers richer insights from evaluations but requires more work before generating feedback. If the usability of such a system is too low, it requires even more work to redesign or start over again. If the prototype functionality is too small, however, the usability might be easier to optimize, but many tests must be carried out. Figure 1 illustrates this typical workflow, including paper prototypes, low-fidelity apps, to the final product. Each of these prototypes requires a cycle of task and user analysis, design, implementation, and evaluation. The evaluation of each prototype generates information for the next prototype.

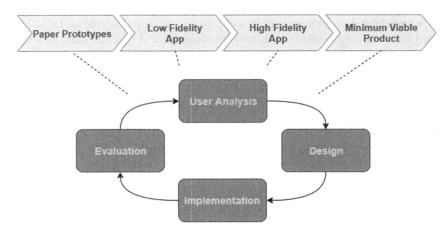

Fig. 1. Illustration of a user-centred design approach

One industrial sector in which this complexity is especially challenging is textile engineering. Due to a large share of manual tasks, a vast amount of possible operation steps, and complex materials, there is a great need in this industry for a successful implementation of IoT solutions.

1.3 Use Case: Manufacturing Processes in Textile Engineering

Based on the considerations made so far, this section illustrates a specific use case from textile composite production to indicate the potential of a decision support system and the challenges posed by complex processes, materials, and the user.

Regarding the background, the following should be mentioned: A typical task for textile engineers is the design of a multi-stage process chain for manufacturing components or products, with different production methods used at each process stage. Which methods are suitable at which position in the production chain depends on numerous factors, such as the shape of the product, the material selected, and the desired product properties. The process planning is complex because certain procedure steps fit together well, whereas others are technically incompatible, yield lower quality, or higher costs. Moreover, negative interactions between procedure steps can occur, which affect later stages of the manufacturing process. The planning of these processes therefore heavily relies on the planner's experience as well as intuitive decisions. Systematic planning guidelines do not exist or are difficult to apply due to the complex nature of composite processes. Currently, the planning of textile production chains is carried out manually and requires expertise about each potential process step. Due to the growing number of configuration options, it is becoming increasingly difficult for textile engineers to have the necessary expertise for all these steps and to apply this knowledge to the configuration tasks. Furthermore, the demographic change and thus a "retirement" of required, implicit knowledge particularly threatens the textile industry.

The described phenomena are particularly relevant in the specific case of textile fibre-reinforced plastics (FRP) production. Still, many lightweight parts are made of classic construction materials like wood, aluminium, or steel despite the high potential of composites. This rejection of FRP is due to a resource and scrap intensive nature of production processes, as well as the mainly manual production of components, which require highly specialised workers.

The described backgrounds call for an improvement in the future. A possible method to strengthen the potentials of FRP production could be automation or the support of the value core by technical tools. A user-oriented tool that supports workers in the form of a target decision support for process planning is a promising approach.

2   Research Approach and Questions for the Development of an Application for Process Planning in Textile Engineering

Due to the increasing complexity of processes, data, and decisions, DSS are essential to support operators in future production environments in general, and in particular in textile engineering. To optimally merge the capabilities of technical DSS's and human decision-makers, it is essential to design task, context, and user-adequate interfaces.

This chapter describes the applied user-centric development approach for the application. In particular, we focused on the following three research questions, which are numbered to enable discussion (see Sect. 4):

First, can the complex and specific area of process planning in the preform environment be supported by an interactive recommendation system (*Q1*)?

Second, can the general methodology of user-centred design be used for this very domain-specific area of software development (*Q2.1*), and what results will this approach achieve (*Q2.2*)?

Third, can these systems be used beyond decision support for experts (*Q3.1*), but also to systematically capture their expertise (*Q3.2*)? This additional information could potentially improve the quality of automated decisions and yield better recommendations.

Q1 and *Q2* will be answered in this paper, whereas *Q3* will only be discussed in the outlook. We will resolve the questions of additional features and knowledge extraction in a later iteration.

Combining both the research questions and the approach of user-centred design, we chose the following five development iterations. We discussed requirements with domain experts and designed two successive mock-ups. After other usability experts provided their feedback, we derived a paper-prototype that improved upon the usability flaws from the mock-ups. Lastly, we implemented a low-fidelity desktop app, that was then used in a usability evaluation. These steps are displayed in Fig. 2, a modified version of Fig. 3.

Fig. 2. The user-centred design cycle for the app

The results of the different iterations are presented within the next section.

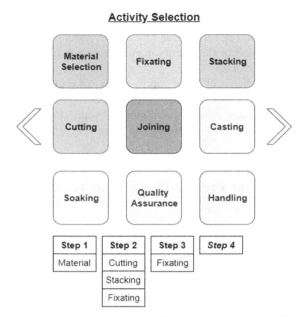

Fig. 3. First mockup as a Grid-based layout. Top: possible activities. Bottom: current step selections from the user. Arrows lead to the next/previous selection.

3   Results

This section presents the results of three design, developments, and evaluation iterations. We conducted a domain-expert interview with a focus on the analysis of functional and non-functional requirements (see Sect. 3.1). Next, we conducted a paper prototyping session (see Sect. 3.2) and evaluate the first functional prototype in a user study with domain experts (see Sect. 3.3).

3.1   Evaluation of Functional and Non-functional User Requirements

Methodological Approach. We started by conducting a use-case analysis with a focus on the identification of functional and non-functional requirements regarding fibre-reinforced polymer production. The chosen *methodological approach* was a semi-structured expert interview, divided into two main parts: In a *first step,* we asked the experts to describe the basic workflows within the field of fibre-reinforced polymer production. In a *second step,* the focus was on the identification of requirements, with special considerations on devices, complexity, and future users.

Sample. The sample of our interviews consists of N = 2 domain expert from textile engineering. Both participants had specific expertise in composite production with reinforced polymer production.

Results. Within the interviews, we could classify four categories of requirements (see Table 1). These different requirement categories (*RC*) influenced the development of all further prototypes. While *Technical Preconditions* are important, they are not within the scope of this paper, which is why they will not be discussed further. We will instead briefly touch upon the different process definitions that will be important for the *Navigation Capability* (*RC1*), as well as the categories of *Information Availability* (*RC2*) and *Configurability* (*RC3*).

Table 1. Four different requirement topics derived from the domain expert interview.

Requirement Category	Description
Navigation Capability	Users can navigate through the app comfortably
Information Availability	Users can get additional information and comparisons
Configurability	Users can create their processes, regardless of recommendations
Technical Preconditions	App requirements that derive from technical limitations

To plan the production process of a preform, users would select and get recommendations for steps and tools. A step is a selection of different activities (e.g. cutting and stacking), each with multiple associated tools (e.g. an electric scissor or a robot-assisted, ultrasonic knife), and multiple tool specifications. The whole production process is defined as a collection of steps. Each process follows a general sequence of material selection, stacking and alignment, cutting and draping, but differs widely depending on the material, form, and target criteria.

After selecting the available tools and intended steps, the users should get different process recommendations from these selections. Each of the process recommendations should have a different focus, e.g., maximising the expected workpiece quality or minimising production time. Upon selecting one recommendation, the corresponding process should be displayed to the users and saved for later analysis.

As future users are not necessarily well-experienced with FRP, additional information for each step and tool is suggested. Users should be able to easily comprehend the different activities, as well as clearly separate the benefits or drawbacks from them.

Maximising the choice of the users was defined as the overall goal of the app, as it should provide them with additional or often overlooked options. This range of alternatives includes the ability to create their own processes by rearranging every single step. While users should be shown the recommendations, they should not be bound by them. Feedback from the user about the completed process was only required if it didn't force the user to multiple actions. For example, pressing buttons each time a process step is completed to record the step's duration was deemed unnecessary, but evaluating the quality of a finished workpiece to rate the process chain would be worthwhile.

We categorise all feedback from the prototype iterations into the three *RC*.

3.2 Iterative Prototyping with Domain Experts

Based on the key results of the requirement analysis, we conducted a paper-prototyping iteration with expert reviews at the end of each iteration. The expert sample consists of experts from usability engineering and interfaces design (N = 2).

Methodological Approach. In total, we conducted three prototyping iterations. We based the *first iteration* upon a grid-layout, as all information is easily cluster-able (see Fig. 3). This initial design was evaluated as confusing by usability experts, especially since users could select multiple (conflicting) activities per step. The confusion led to the *second iteration,* where we chose a process-sequence design (see Fig. 4). While this improved the users' overview, it was evaluated as unclear for longer process chains. The usability experts recommended further clarification of the currently viewed steps within the process chain, which we added in *iteration three* (see Fig. 5 and following). Based on this, we build a low-fidelity prototype, which is discussed in the next section.

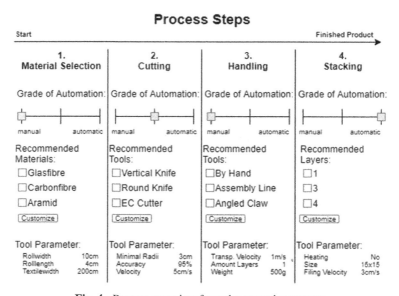

Fig. 4. Process overview from the second prototype

First Iteration. The first mockup's focus was to give users the maximum amount of choice. As all activities, tools or sub-tools were easily groupable, we chose the grid-based approach, highlighting the correlation (see Fig. 3). In the example, the user is selecting possible activities for the fourth step in the process chain. Each activity has its own button and a colour-coding: Green, yellow and red indicate the recommendation from our AI, from strong to weaker recommendations, whereas blue represents the current selection from the user. Gray coloured activities are neither recommended nor currently selected. If the user is content with the selection, he/she will click on the right-sided

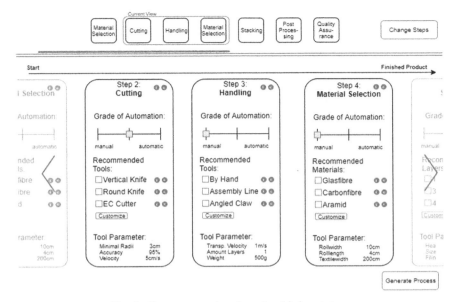

Fig. 5. Process overview from the third prototype

arrow to iterate through the next selected activity, choosing the activities' tools. If all tools were selected, users could then create a new step, restarting the selection process. In between each selection, the recommender system would get new input and give updated feedback. After the completion of the whole process with the available tools, at least one recommendation for the entire process would be generated.

Feedback from Usability -Experts: The grid-based approach might have worked for a mobile device, but initial tests raised multiple problems. The most important issue was that users would lose the overview of the current selection (*"For which activity is this tool that I'm currently selecting?"*). The navigation between multiple activities was rated as too complicated and going back to previous tool selections would possibly be confusing to the user *(RC1)*. Users were also confused about the multiple options: They expected to be able to choose only one *(RC3)*. This confusion was especially true for activities, as the recommendation for the next step was varying wildly. For example, choosing a material or ensuring quality in the same step would create too many alternatives in the user's mind, they were unable to follow their plan. This feedback led us to focus on the process chain itself and instead allow only a single activity per step.

Additionally, clustering information would leave unused space on a desktop screen to the left and right *(RC2)*. While more information—such as tool or activity descriptions—could be placed there, it would not fit into this design.

Second Iteration. The next prototype displayed the process chain as ordered columns next to each other, with each column displaying the recommended activity, tools, grade of automation and additional parameters. Figure 4 illustrates this design.

This prototype was again done as a mockup. Blue highlights tell the users that some form of interaction is desired or possible.

Users could change the order of steps with drag and drop or add new steps recommended by the system. Additionally, users are able to classify into automated or manual steps, further increasing the configuration capabilities.

Feedback from Usability-Experts: While this system could fill the entire screen and easily displayed additional information to the user, the main drawback was the maximum number of steps possibly shown *(RC2)*. For example, a common Full-HD screen with a resolution of 1920×1080 could display up to eight steps, without them being too narrow. Scrolling through all steps at a time would be tedious and confusing *(RC1)*, as steps could occur multiple times. The feedback led to the next iteration of the UI design, this time as a low-fidelity paper prototype.

Third Iteration. Figure 5 shows the main process configuration window of the third iteration. Compared to the previous prototype, the steps are clearly divided into their own section, increasing the attention focus of the user. Additionally, two more buttons *i* and *c* – for *info* and *compare*, respectively – were added to each step and tool. The info button opens a help panel to the left of the screen, whereas compare adds the step or tool to a comparing list. The user is then able to invoke the comparing, displaying a table with each of the parameters.

To provide a sense of overview over the process, we added greyed out steps to the left and right, indicating further steps. Moreover, we introduced a smaller and more compact step view at the top, including a highlighted current view displaying the visible steps. To navigate through the steps, users can click on an upper step button or the arrows pointing left or right.

Upon clicking the "Change Steps" button, users are forwarded to the window that Fig. 6 depicts. They are then able to switch steps with drag and drop, delete steps, or add new steps by dragging them from the lower half to the top half into the queue. On hovering over the new steps, arrows indicate the recommended position of the steps.

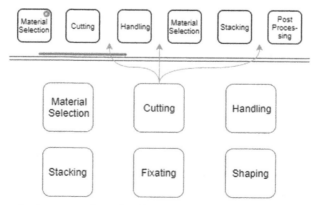

Fig. 6. Activity selection screen from the third prototype. Top: current process chain. Bottom: possible activities. Arrows indicate recommended insertion.

After selecting all steps and tools, users can finalise their recommendations. Afterwards, the app leads the users to a new window, where multiple process recommendations are derived from the users' selections (Fig. 7 shows such a recommendation). Each recommendation has a focus regarding either expected quality, costs or production time. Each step and the respective tool are displayed in order, highlighting possible problems by indicating the *fitness* of the steps in a colour-coded scheme. Currently, the program recommends one process as close to the user's selection as possible, while ensuring a high enough quality. Two other generated processes are less constrained and focus on achieving a high expected quality or a low cost of the end-product

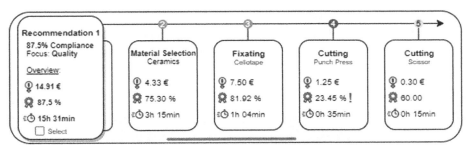

Fig. 7. One of the three process recommendations from the third prototype. Left: Summary of the recommendation. Right: Different steps rated regarding costs, quality and production time.

Feedback of Usability Experts: This prototype had no apparent flaws and was evaluated well by the experts. Next, we implemented it as a functional low-fidelity prototype to further evaluate the usability of the interactive system. We conducted a user study with domain experts, which we will discuss next.

3.3 Usability Evaluation

As a third step of the design process, we conducted a usability test of the functional low-fidelity prototype with archetypical users and domain experts from textile engineering (N = 4). All subjects had specific expertise in composite production. The study used simulated dummy data, as the recommendation system was not yet finished.

Methodological Approach. To evaluate the usability of the system, we have chosen a multimethod approach with a quantitative and a qualitative method: For the quantitative evaluation of the system's usability, we used Brook's System Usability Score (SUS) [19] that we complemented with a qualitative Think-Aloud study [20].

The SUS is a simple, standardised, and widely used questionnaire to evaluate interactive systems. SUS builds on ten-question items (such as "*I think the interface was easy to use.*") on a 5-point Likert scale. The normalised score reaches from 0 to 100 points (100, indicating high usability). Everything above 80 is defined as good usability; above 90 is nearly perfect. Having a score of 70 or lower indicates severe usability deficits. Although the SUS gives an overall score for systems that can act as a benchmark for the evaluation of future integrations, it does not highlight the particular problems and areas for improvements themselves [21].

Consequently, we conducted a Think-Aloud study with the domain experts before assessing the summative usability on the SUS survey. We assigned three tasks to the users. We designed the tasks to guide them through the app, while at the same time representing the most common use case. They had increasing complexity, starting at simply selecting a certain model file that should be built, to rating the different recommendations and choosing the best fitting one.

We discuss the qualitative results of the Think-Aloud study first, then the quantitative results from the SUS questionnaire. We conclude this chapter with a short synopsis of our key findings.

Think-Aloud Study. Analysing the user's feedback from the Think-Aloud experiments yielded additional feature or usability request. These were—additionally to the requirement categories—separated into three different sections, according to their occurrence (*occurrence category – OC*). Table 2 shows the different *OC*s.

Table 2. The different occurrence categories of feedback from the Think-Aloud study.

Occurrence Category	Description
Missing Features	Features that users wished for, but were not (yet) implemented
Misunderstood Features	Features that confused users, thereby reducing the overview and navigation capability
Overlooked Features	Features that were existing, but weren't used by the user

Domain-Experts Feedback. Some of these features in the three categories were minor, such as changing labels or highlighting the foci of recommendation screens *(OC1, RC2)*. One important missing element was a hover-preview when changing the grade of automation *(OC1, RC2)* – the AI changes the recommended tools or materials according to it. By including a preview window, users can see the changes before applying them, i.e. by releasing the mouse. Additionally, users requested more buttons for navigation throughout the app, such as *back* or *cancel* buttons for popups *(OC1, RC1)*. Another missing navigational feature was the ability to change the process step order by dragging the different steps *(OC1, RC1)*. Also missing were more highlights in the process recommendations, as users felt overwhelmed by the multiple recommendation screens without a clear flow of view *(OC1, RC1)*.

Misunderstood key elements were mostly inaccurate or misleading symbols, such as the quality or cost icons, as well as the compare button *(OC2, RC1)*. As the main app language is German, *c* for *compare* was a suboptimal choice, so we changed the compare button to two arrows targeting each other. Figure 8 shows all three icons before and after the change. Additionally, we introduced colour into the focus symbols, highlighting their importance.

Fig. 8. Icon progression, from before (top) to after evaluation (bottom). From left to right: *compare, quality, production cost*

The feature that caused the most perplexity was the AI's prototyped focus on quality, cost or production time *(OC2, RC2)*. While all users agreed that the options were suited and important, they didn't concur with the fixed focus scheme. Instead, they preferred a constrained range focus *(OC1, RC3)*, e.g., creating a process with a maximum cost of 15€. Multiple of these constraints should be possible, combining all three focus points.

The most surprising feature that was missed by the users was the colour grading according to the recommendation grade *(OC3, RC2)*. For example, in the process recommendation screen, each recommended step has a number displaying the order. This number is shaded in a traffic light system, coarsely dividing the different steps into recommended, suitable, and not recommended. None of the users recognised this, probably because the recommendation screen was lacking a clear view flow.

After the Think-Aloud experiment, users were encouraged to describe other details or desired features, that they didn't mention during the initial phase. The most common feature request was one for different mode of operation. Currently, the decision-support system is intended to create around five steps directly, giving the user an option to refine the process further. While this approach is a good middle ground, users wished for a *blank-slate* and a *fast-track* modus *(OC1, RC1/RC3)*. The *blank-slate* modus would only add the material selection step to a new process, giving the user much more freedom in the process creation. While theoretically possible with the *standard* mode, users would have to delete nearly all starting recommendations, which would be cumbersome. The *fast-track* modus, on the other hand, is planned to skip the step configuration from the user and instead directly present the final process recommendations, again constrained by the different focus points.

Another requested feature was the ability to compare the different recommendations directly *(OC1, RC2)*. Even though a user could read each step from all process recommendations, comparing every one of them would be unintuitive. The next iteration will therefore include diagrams and charts to compare the process chains among themselves, but also to compare all steps of a single process.

The gathered feedback, grouped into *OC/RC* pairs, is displayed in Fig. 9. This figure indicates that the next iterations should focus on adding information while increasing the clarity of the existing information display. Overall, the existing configurability and—in part—navigation are satisfactory to the user but still require additional features.

While the qualitative results indicated important features or flaws, they did not imply an overall satisfaction of the users about the app. Therefore, we included a quantitative SUS questionnaire into the study, which we discuss next.

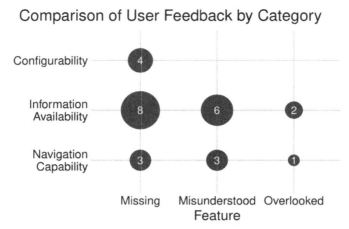

Fig. 9. Feedback from the Think-Aloud study, grouped by category pairs

SUS Result. The averaged SUS score was 77.6, which indicates a good, but improvable usability, as expected for a prototype. For comparison, [22] evaluated 21 existing productivity apps with a mean of 76.7. Overall, subject one differed most from all other participants, rating the app with only 48.2. It became clear in the Think-Aloud study that the subject didn't expect the AI recommendations to work. This negative expectation influenced the first question's rating (*"I think that I would like to use this system frequently."*) very negatively. On further investigation, the subject had similar hints about the usability as the other candidates.

In this chapter, we have seen the different iterations of the user-centred designed decision-support app, as well as the reactions and recommendations of users. The users quantitatively rated the app high but requested additional features or changes.

4   Discussion, Limitations and Outlook

The presented work is a first step towards a data-driven recommender system for planning preform production chains in textile engineering. This section discusses the current state of the project, its limitations, and provides a roadmap for future research. Research questions that were raised in Sect. 2 are referenced by their question indices (QX).

The current system recommends process configurations based on individual optimisation criteria and makes the decision rationale transparent to the operators. Overall, the iteratively developed prototype was well received by the participants in the user study; highlighting the importance of user-centred design and the integration of users as stakeholders into the development process. Further development iterations will focus on additional usability refinements, as well as the integration of additional functional features. Overall, user satisfaction and usability were high, especially for an early prototype ($Q2.2$). While this provides a promising result, further evaluations with integrated AI-recommendations and more subjects must be conducted.

Of course, this work is not without its limitations. First, the evaluations are based on rather small samples. Thus, we have to conduct additional user studies with more participants to get broader and deeper feedback on the developed prototypes. Yet, the preliminary findings suggest that there are no profound usability barriers, and future work can focus on continuously refining the user experience (*Q2*). Second, the current application builds on a small and limited test data set that does not yet represent the variety of process steps in the preform domain. Consequently, more process steps and alternatives will be included to facilitate advanced planning capabilities to the users. Nevertheless, the current interface design with the illustrated process flow and the suggested process steps will be able to represent the space of planning possibilities well and support the decision-makers in the planning process (*Q1*).

Future work will focus on the following aspects: First, an important milestone is the implementation of a working AI-based recommendation system. As discussed before, this AI will be based upon a knowledge graph [23] and data-driven recommendation that build on prior process data. Second, a pivotal question for the data-driven recommendation is the digitalisation of the implicit and explicit knowledge of experts, to create and continuously expand a large and high-quality database of process chains for future recommendations. For this, a suitable method of knowledge extraction has to be examined and implemented, and strategies for gratifying knowledge sharing must be developed and evaluated (*Q3.2*). Third, as outlined above, trust in interactive systems and process automation is crucial for acceptance and use. Future studies will evaluate if the system is trusted by users, which factors influence trust, and how trust can be increased by, e.g., explainable decision support.

5   Conclusion

The presented app is a key enabler to overcome conventional unsupported process planning and to establish a data-driven, more efficient, sustainable, and cost-aware production and planning process for composites.

Although the application is still in its infancy and not *yet* equipped with a powerful AI-based recommendation system, we have shown the approach is suitable to provide interactive recommendations for planning processes in the preform environment. Furthermore, we have shown that user-centred design can be used in this highly domain-specific problem space. It can increase the ergonomics, usability, and user experience of process planning applications in textile engineering in particular and production systems in general. Thus, the user-centred and participatory design will be a key enabler to develop accepted, usable, and useful interfaces for the IoP and the Industrial Internet.

The current findings suggest that the application can be used to provide smart decision support for preforming planning processes. A currently open question is if the experts' interaction with the system and their evaluation of the generated recommendations can be used for further optimizing the underlying knowledge base and to generate smart, data and expertise-driven recommendations.

In summary, this work is a first step towards a planning system that will harness the knowledge about the compatibility and association of different process steps, the experts' evaluation about possible process configurations, and prior experience from production monitoring to provide smart, persuasive, and user-centred decisions support for operators in an Internet of Production.

Acknowledgements. This research was funded by the German Research Foundation (DFG) within the Cluster of Excellence "Internet of Production" (EXC 2023, 390621612). The outstanding support of Imke Haverkämper is highly acknowledged.

References

1. Evans, P.C., Annunziata, M.: Industrial Internet: Pushing the Boundaries of Minds and Machine (2012)
2. Gilchrist, A., Gilchrist, A.: Introduction to the industrial internet. In: Industry 4.0., pp. 1–12. Apress (2016). https://doi.org/10.1007/978-1-4842-2047-4_1
3. Jarke, M., Schuh, G., Brecher, C., Brockmann, M., Prote, J.-P.: Digital shadows in the internet of production. In: ERCIM News, vol. 115, pp. 22–28 (2018)
4. Pennekamp, J., et al.: Towards an infrastructure enabling the internet of production. In: Proceedings - 2019 IEEE International Conference on Industrial Cyber-Physical Systems, ICPS 2019. pp. 31–37. Institute of Electrical and Electronics Engineers Inc. (2019). https://doi.org/10.1109/ICPHYS.2019.8780276
5. Tao, F., Cheng, J., Qi, Q., Zhang, M., Zhang, H., Sui, F.: Digital twin-driven product design, manufacturing and service with big data. Int. J. Adv. Manuf. Technol. **94**, 3563–3576 (2018). https://doi.org/10.1007/s00170-017-0233-1
6. Frazzon, E.M., Hartmann, J., Makuschewitz, T., Scholz-Reiter, B.: Towards socio-cyber-physical systems in production networks. Procedia CIRP **7**, 49–54 (2013). https://doi.org/10.1016/j.procir.2013.05.009
7. Philipsen, R., Brauner, P., Valdez, A.C., Ziefle, M.: Evaluating strategies to restore trust in decision support systems in cross-company cooperation. In: Karwowski, W., Trzcielinski, S., Mrugalska, B., Di Nicolantonio, M., Rossi, E. (eds.) AHFE 2018. AISC, vol. 793, pp. 115–126. Springer, Cham (2019). https://doi.org/10.1007/978-3-319-94196-7_11
8. Wang, X.V., Kemény, Z., Váncza, J., Wang, L.: Human-robot collaborative assembly in cyber-physical production: classification framework and implementation. CIRP Ann. - Manuf. Technol. **66**, 5–8 (2017). https://doi.org/10.1016/j.cirp.2017.04.101
9. Nikolakis, N., Maratos, V., Makris, S.: A cyber-physical system (CPS) approach for safe human-robot collaboration in a shared workplace. Robot. Comput. Integr. Manuf. **56**, 233–243 (2019). https://doi.org/10.1016/j.rcim.2018.10.003
10. Calero Valdez, A., Brauner, P., Schaar, A.K., Holzinger, A., Ziefle, M.: Reducing complexity with simplicity - usability methods for industry 4.0. In: 19th Triennial Congress of the International Ergonomics Association (IEA 2015), Melbourne, Australia (2015). https://doi.org/10.13140/RG.2.1.4253.6809
11. Power, D.J.: Decision Support Systems: Concepts and Resources for Managers. Greenwood Publishing Group, Westport (2002)
12. Harris, J.G., Davenport, T.H.: Research Report Automated Decision Making Comes of Age. (2005)
13. Shim, J.P., Warkentin, M., Courtney, J.F., Power, D.J., Sharda, R., Carlsson, C.: Past, present, and future of decision support technology. Decis. Support Syst. **33**, 111–126 (2002). https://doi.org/10.1016/S0167-9236(01)00139-7
14. Madsen, M., Gregor, S.: Measuring Human-Computer Trust
15. Parasuraman, R., Manzey, D.H.: Complacency and bias in human use of automation: an attentional integration. Hum. Factors **52**, 381–410 (2010). https://doi.org/10.1177/0018720810376055

16. Walter, Z., Lopez, M.S.: Physician acceptance of information technologies: role of perceived threat to professional autonomy. Decis. Support Syst. **46**, 206–215 (2008). https://doi.org/10.1016/j.dss.2008.06.004
17. International Organization for Standardization: ISO 9241-210:2010 - Ergonomics of Human-System Interaction - Part 210: Human-centred Design for Interactive Systems (2019)
18. Snyder, C.: Paper Prototyping: The Fast and Easy Way to Design and Refine User Interfaces. Morgan Kaufmann, San Francisco (2003). Elsevier Science
19. Brooke, J.: SUS - a quick and dirty usability scale. Usability Eval. Ind. **189**, 189–194 (1996)
20. Courage, C., Baxter, K.: Understanding Your Users - A Practical Guide to User Requirements Methods, Tools & Techniques. Morgan Kaufmann Publishers, San Francisco (2005)
21. A Practical Guide to the System Usability Scale : Jeff Sauro : 9781461062707
22. Lewis, J.R.: Measuring perceived usability: the CSUQ, SUS, and UMUX. Int. J. Hum. Comput. Interact. **34**, 1148–1156 (2018). https://doi.org/10.1080/10447318.2017.1418805
23. Gleim, L., et al.: FactDAG: formalizing data interoperability in an internet of production. IEEE Internet Things J. **7**(4) (2020)

Information, Communication, Relationality and Learning

A Long-Term Evaluation of Social Robot Impression

Saizo Aoyagi[1(✉)], Satoshi Fukumori[2,3], and Michiya Yamamoto[2]

[1] Faculty of Information Networking for Innovation and Design,
Toyo University, Tokyo, Japan
aoaygi@toyo.jp
[2] School of Science and Technology, Kwansei Gakuin University, Nishinomiya, Japan
[3] Faculty of Engineering and Design, Kagawa University, Takamatsu, Japan

Abstract. The impression of a social robot changes with long-term use due to novelty and familiarity effects. In this study, a psychological scale of the long-term change in impression of social robots was created through a long-term experiment focusing on characteristics and toolness of a social robot. Another long-term experiment using the created scale was performed to measure and compare changes in long-term impressions of Kiropi v2, RoBoHoN, and iPad. The results showed that scores corresponding to characteristics and toolness of the impression basically improved with each use. In addition, some impressions showed nonlinear changes due to novelty and familiarity effects. The results also showed differences between the robots, indicating that the impression of Kiropi v2 was the best.

Keywords: Human robot interaction · Social robot · Tablet-based robot · Long-term experiment · Impression evaluation

1 Introduction

A social robot is defined as a robot performing its functions by involving people [1]. In recent years, social robots have become widespread, such as Pepper of SoftBank Robotics [2] or RoBoHoN of SHARP [3]. These robots have various functions due to the development of artificial intelligence technology and are being commonly used. The authors' interest is in developing partner robots, which are an extension of social robots. Partner robots can not only communicate with people but also build close relationships with humans and support human activities on a daily basis in all aspects of life.

The authors focus on "characteristics" as one of the important factors for a robot to become a partner. In Japan, "character" generally means characters and their personalities in fictions such as anime and manga [4]. In addition, the characteristics of the robot refer to "some personality and presence" and "feeling of intelligence and intention" [5]. The robot does not need to actually have intelligence and intention. In addition, the image that ordinary people have

© Springer Nature Switzerland AG 2020
S. Yamamoto and H. Mori (Eds.): HCII 2020, LNCS 12185, pp. 131–144, 2020.
https://doi.org/10.1007/978-3-030-50017-7_9

of robots includes an element called characteristics. The authors developed a partner robot "Kiropi" and tried to add characteristics by attaching arm-formed hardware to tablet devices and confirmed that characteristics were felt through comparative experiments with iPads, etc. [6,7]. In the above experiment, each participant evaluated robots after using them only once.

Nevertheless, the impression of a social robot may change with long-term use. When a human repeatedly has contact with a social robot, there is a novelty effect in which the positive evaluation at the beginning decreases and a familiarity increases [8]. As a result, an experiment in which contact is made only once, as in the case of the above research, may result in overestimation at the beginning and ignore changes in impression due to long-term use. Thus, a robot meant for long-term use, such as a social robot, needs long-term evaluation.

In addition, the prior study [7] suggests that there are multiple aspects of impressions of robots that have not only characteristics but also "toolness." Toolness indicates that a robots is a convenient machine or a tool. The prior study did not assume that there were multiple aspects of impressions, so there were few evaluation items, and there is room for studying evaluation methods. To deeply understand the relationship between users and social robots, it is necessary to evaluate more diverse impressions.

The main purpose of this study is to clarify the change in impression over time by conducting a long-term experiment focusing on characteristics and toolness. At the same time, other robots on the market are evaluated to show the superiority of Kiropi. In addition, because there is no psychological scale for evaluating the long-term change in impression of social robots, the secondary purpose of this study is to create one.

2   Related Studies

2.1   Long-Term Experiment

Many long-term experiments using social robots or communication robots have been conducted. Communication robots are similar to social robots, robots whose main objective is communication with humans. For example, Leite et al. conducted a survey of this research area and reported many studies about four categories (health care, education, workplace and public space, domestic) of social robots [8]. Studies in this research area often involve qualitative analysis to clarify events about robots in real fields. Sung et al. investigated the process of domestic robot acceptance and proposed a framework of long-term interaction with social robots [9,10]. Tanaka et al. conducted a long-term observation experiment by placing a care-receiver robot acting as a student for children in a classroom of a nursery school [11]. Under such circumstances, there are few quantitative studies that use psychological scales. Exceptionally, De Graaf et al. described structural changes between impression factors before and after deciding to use a robot and during long-term use [12]. In addition, they analyzed the same experiment from the viewpoint of the reasons people stop using robots [13]. However, this series of studies includes only a single-condition experiment in a real home and involves no comparison. On the other hand, this study quantitatively compares the impressions of three differently designed robots, including Kiropi, using a psychological scale.

2.2   Novelty and Familiarity Effects

When people come into contact with objects repeatedly, there are contradictory phenomena where initially a high positive rating decreases or conversely increases [14]. As mentioned above, social robots are not exceptions to that [8]. The former is a novelty effect [15] where new things are highly evaluated, or a habituation where no reaction is seen after adaptation. The latter is a familiarity effect in which familiarity increases or a mere-exposure effect in which the evaluation improves simply through contact with the object [16].

The existence of these two-way effects is widely known, but their timing and how much they occur depend on the target object. Liao et al. [17] reported that the effects of novelty and familiarity depend on the type of object, such as faces, landscapes, and geometric figures, and also on the task, whether it involves passive viewing or active judgment. In particular, if people only look passively, familiar faces are preferred, and they have no preference for landscapes and geometric figures. If people make active judgments, familiar faces and novel landscapes are preferred. They have no preference for geometric figures. The above findings suggest that the design of the robot affects change in the impression during long-term use. Furthermore, to show that the impression of the robot and its change differ depending on the design, three designs (iPad, RoBoHoN [3], and Kiropi) are compared in a long-term experiment of the same task.

2.3   Characteristics and Toolness

Concepts close to characteristics and toolness are found in social robot studies. Sung et al. [10] found a "Learn/Adaptation Pattern" in which a robot is accepted as a partner and a "Use/Retention Pattern" in which a robot is regarded as a tool as patterns of long-term interaction with robots. These are considered to correspond to characteristics and toolness in the dimension of the relationship between a human and a robot. Kanda et al. [18] evaluated robot impressions and found four factors: fun, activity, intimacy, and performance evaluation (performance). The last two are considered to be characteristics and toolness.

In these studies, concepts close to characteristics and toolness were found, and measures to measure them were developed. However, there is no scale based on long-term experiments. In long-term experiments, the impression of the robot is thought to change, so even if the same items are used, the factors found and the factors linked to them compared using the scale made with the answers obtained in one evaluation may be different. Therefore, in this study, the authors use the adjective pairs used in the Japanese study [18] and perform factor analysis and scale construction using the results of long-term experiments.

Fig. 1. Appearance of Kiropi.

Table 1. Specifications of Kiropi.

Size	$310 \times 240 \times 113$ mm
Weight	1592 g
Motor	JR PROPO RBS582 $\times$ 8
Computer	Arduino Duemilanove
Tablet	Apple iPad2

3   Experiment 1: Creation of Psychological Scale for Evaluating Long-Term Change in Impression of Social Robots

3.1   Purpose and Method

An experiment to extract the factors of users' impression of a robot and to create a psychological scale for long-term change in impression was conducted.

Used Robots. Kiropi was developed in a prior study [7]. Figure 1 shows the appearance of Kiropi. Table 1 shows the specifications of Kiropi. Kiropi is basically an Apple iPad with robot arms. The eyes and mouth are displayed on the screen, as shown in Fig. 1. Kiropi has a voice memo function to record and play user speech. Kiropi's voice is created using a voice-generation software, CeVIO Creative Studio [19]. In addition, Kiropi moves its arms and changes its facial expression depending on human voice rhythm and loudness [20].

Task and Procedure. Five male university students (from 20 to 21 years old) participated. They are called participant 1 to participant 5 in this paper. The task of the experiment was to freely speak to Kiropi and record the voice. Figure 2 shows the experimental setup. In the experiment, participants completed the task two times in a week, at least one day apart.

Fig. 2. Experimental setup of experiment 1.

Table 2. Items of robot anxiety scale.

Anxiety toward communication capability of robots
Robots may talk about something irrelevant during conversation
Conversation with robots may be inflexible
Robots may be unable to understand complex stories
Anxiety toward discourse with robots
How I should talk with robots
How I should reply to robots when they talk to me
Whether robots understand the contents of my utterance to them
I may be unable to understand the contents of robots' utterances to me

The total experimental period was four weeks, and the task was done eight times in total. Before each instance of completing the task, except for the first time, participants played the voice recording and listened to it. After each instance of completing the task, participants responded to the questionnaire of adjective pairs of robot impression [18] and robot anxiety scale (RAS)[21]. RAS items for anxiety toward communication capability with robots (communication anxiety) and anxiety toward discourse with robots (discourse anxiety) were used in this experiment. Figure 2 shows the RAS items that were used. Participants responded to all questionnaire items using a visual analog scale (VAS). All VAS answers were converted to points from 101 to 0.

3.2   Results

Figure 3 and Fig. 4 show communication anxiety capability and discourse anxiety after eight tasks (#1 to #8), respectively. P1 to P5 refers to participant 1 to participant 5. All participants' answers tended to decrease. The overall trend was a tendency to decrease as the number of uses increased, although there was a difference among the participants. Anxieties of P2 and P3 decreased greatly at #2 and leveled off thereafter. On the other hand, both anxieties of P5 and discourse anxiety of P1 decreased significantly after #1. Communication anxieties of P1 and P4 and discourse anxiety of P4 leveled off and moved unstably up and down.

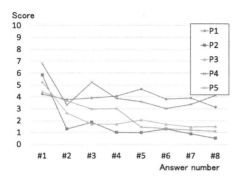

Fig. 3. Results of communication ability anxiety of RAS.

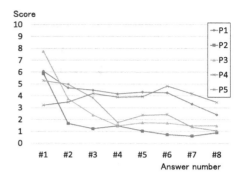

Fig. 4. Results of conversation anxiety of RAS.

Next, the scores of impression adjective pairs for all robots of the experiment were totaled for each item. A factor analysis was conducted using the scores. The factor axis was rotated using the promax method for the results of 28 items, and 27 items with a factor loading of 0.50 or more were selected for one or more factors. As a result, three factors were extracted. Table 3 shows the factor loadings of the three factors extracted.

Figure 5 and Fig. 6 show factor score changes of factor 1 and factor 2 respectively. P1 to P5 means Participant 1 to Participant 5. Each factor scores of participant 2, 3, and 5 shifted upward. Nevertheless, that of participant 1 showed a tendency to be flat, that of participant 4 showed a tendency to decrease.

3.3   Discussion

Figure 3 and Fig. 4 show that either the tendency to greatly decrease in #2 or the tendency to decrease as the number of uses increased after #3 was seen, except for the communication anxiety of P1 and P4 and discourse anxiety of P4, which tended to be flat. The former can be interpreted as the novelty effect and the latter as the familiarity effect. Therefore, it can be interpreted that only the novelty effect or the familiarity effect appeared depending on the person.

In addition, three factors of impression of social robots were extracted. The factor with the largest factor loading is named "Friendliness" because items are related to feelings of friendliness with communication partners (Fig. 5). Friendliness is considered to be equivalent to characteristics in the prior study [7]. Another factor is named "Performance" because items are related to machine performances (Fig. 6). Performance is considered to be equivalent to toolness in

Table 3. Factor loadings of adjective pairs.

Adjective pair		Factor 1	Factor 2	Factor 3
Warm	Cold	**0.96**	−0.06	−0.09
Likable	Dislikable	**0.90**	−0.06	0.09
Accessible	Inaccessible	**0.88**	−0.11	0.07
Kind	Cruel	**0.87**	0.04	0.12
Favorable	Unfavorable	**0.85**	0.13	0.08
Frank	Rigid	**0.85**	0.06	−0.10
Good	Bad	**0.81**	0.14	−0.24
Exciting	Dull	**0.79**	0.03	−0.01
Pretty	Ugly	**0.73**	−0.10	0.30
Safe	Dangerous	**0.73**	0.06	0.10
Friendly	Unfriendly	**0.71**	0.07	0.02
Distinct	Vague	**0.68**	0.27	−0.10
Pleasant	Unpleasant	**0.58**	0.16	0.26
Blunt	Sharp	0.10	**−0.88**	0.01
Rapid	Slow	0.00	**0.85**	0.07
Brave	Cowardly	−0.04	**0.82**	0.18
Quick	Slow	0.02	**0.79**	0.16
Cheerful	Lonely	0.06	**0.78**	0.15
Intelligent	Unintelligent	0.25	**0.75**	−0.51
Active	Passive	0.11	**0.69**	0.19
Full	Empty	0.34	**0.55**	−0.02
Interesting	Boring	0.48	**0.52**	−0.18
Humanlike	Mechanical	0.15	−0.09	**−0.75**
Agitated	Calm	−0.21	0.32	**0.68**
Complex	Simple	−0.11	−0.06	**−0.66**
Showy	Quiet	−0.28	0.27	**−0.66**
Light	Dark	0.18	0.34	**0.54**

the prior study [7]. These two factors appeared as a result of continuous use of the robot by humans.

Furthermore, changes in factor scores tended to decrease as the number of uses increased, indicating a possibility of converging to an impression of a robot over a long period of use.

Considering that each item of each impression adjective pair shown in Table 3 measures the factor with the highest load among the three factors, this is used as a psychological measure of long-term change in impression of social robots.

4   Experiment 2: Evaluation of Long-Term Change in Impression

4.1   Purpose and Method

An experiment was performed to measure changes in users' impressions of robots during long-term use of communication robots using measures constructed through experiment 1.

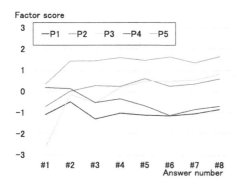

Fig. 5. Each participant's result of factor 1 (familiarity).

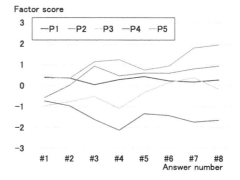

Fig. 6. Each participant's result of factor 2 (performance).

Used Robots. Three kinds of social robots (Kiropi v2, iPad, and RoBoHoN) were used as three conditions of the experiment to show differences in impressions depending on the design of robots.

Kiropi, used in experiment 1, had a metallic and angular design influenced by KHR-1 [22] by Kondo Kagaku. KHR-1 is a representative robot from the 2000s that triggered the popularization of robots not by experts or research institutions but by ordinary individuals in Japan. However, communication robots in recent years often have plastic and round exterior designs, such as RoBoHoN and Pepper. Therefore, aiming for a robot that is widely accepted, we decided to develop and use the next-generation robot, Kiropi v2, which reflects this trend. We made the exterior of the arm parts plastic and made the original iPad smaller.

Kiropi v2 has a modern appearance, inheriting the essential feature of Kiropi, a tablet with arms. Figure 7 shows the appearance of Kiropi v2. Table 4 shows the specifications of Kiropi v2. Kiropi v2 is basically an Apple iPad Air 2 with Sony electronic blocks [23] attached as arms. Kiropi v2 has voice recording and playing functions, the same as Kiropi used in experiment 1. The arm movement and the algorithm for generating the movement are the same as in experiment 1. Differences from experiment 1 are that the "news of today" button is displayed, and there is a news playback function.

The iPad in the experiment is an iPad with the Kiropi software, basically Kiropi v2 without the arm parts. The iPad has no moving parts and is close to a virtual agent, but in this study, it is called a robot for convenience.

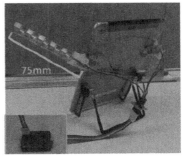

Fig. 7. Appearance of Kiropi v2.

Table 4. Specifications of Kiropi v2.

Size	$245 \times 255 \times 100\,\text{mm}$
Weight	1592 g
Motor	HiTEC HS-5035HD $\times 4$
Arm parts	SONY KOOV $\times 10$
Computer	Arduino Duemilanove
Tablet	Apple iPad Air 2

RoBoHoN is a robot with a telephone function designed by renowned robot creator Tomotaka Takahashi. Many similar robots by Takahashi, such as Sotaa [24], have been sold. This is also adopted as a comparison target with Kiropi v2 in the experiment because this is a standard design for commercial communication robots in Japan, and it is a design with a display like that of Kiropi. The same function of voice recording and playing was implemented in RoBoHoN so that it could perform the same tasks as Kiropi v2.

Task and Procedure. The experimental procedure and tasks were the same as in experiment 1, except for two differences. The first difference was using three conditions: Kiropi v2, iPad, and RoBoHoN. The second difference was adding a step of listening to "today's news" before the voice recording. This step mimics the general use of smart speakers today.

In the experiment, participants completed the task two times in a week, at least one day apart. The total experimental period was four weeks, and the task was completed eight times in total. Before each instance of completing the task, except for the first time, participants played the recorded voice and listened to it. After each instance of completing the task, participants responded to the questionnaire of adjective pairs of robot impression [18] and RAS [21].

The task of the experiment was to freely speak to Kiropi and record the voice. Before recording, participants listened to the news. After that, participants operated the recording button displayed on the screen and talked to the device about the news on the recording day, the progress of the research and study, and the private schedule and recorded the conversation. From the second time on, after listening to the news, before recording, participants touched the play button on the screen and played back the previously recorded content.

After each instance of completing the task, participants responded to the questionnaire of adjective pairs of robot impression [18] and RAS [21]. RAS items for communication anxiety and discourse anxiety were used in this experiment. Participants responded to all questionnaire items using a VAS. All VAS answers were converted to points from 101 to 0.

Eighteen university students (from 20 to 24 years old, 9 male and 9 female) participated. Participants were divided into three groups (conditions), each using a different kind of robot. It was an inter-group planning experiment.

4.2   Results

Averages and standard deviations of the scores of each item related to the anxiety and impression factors were calculated. Figure 8 and Fig. 9 show the average of communication anxiety and discourse anxiety of each condition after eight tasks. Error bars show standard deviations. The results of experiment 1 are also shown as "Kiropi" for reference. The overall trend was a tendency to decrease as the number of uses increased. There was a tendency to decrease greatly at #2.

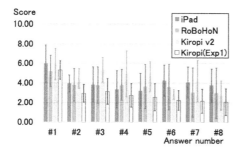
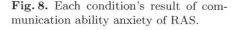
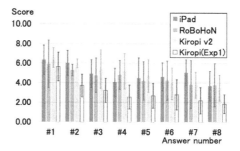

Fig. 8. Each condition's result of communication ability anxiety of RAS.

Fig. 9. Each condition's result of conversation anxiety of RAS.

Figures 10 and 11 show average scores of friendliness and performance of each condition after eight tasks. Error bars show standard deviations, and the results of experiment 1 are also shown as "Kiropi" for reference. Friendliness and performance show a tendency to increase. In particular, Kiropi v2 and RoBoHoN increased greatly at #2.

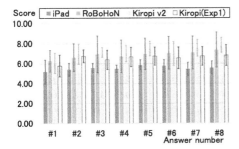

Fig. 10. Each condition's result of familiarity.

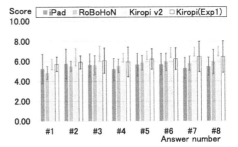

Fig. 11. Each condition's result of performance.

4.3 Discussion

Both types of anxiety about the robot decreased as the number of uses increased. Nevertheless, the tendency of the decrease was different between anxieties.

Discourse anxiety showed a relatively small decrease, and there was no difference between the types of robots. On the other hand, communication anxiety showed a relatively large decrease. Anxiety about the iPad did not decrease much, but anxiety about Kiropi v2 and RoBoHoN showed a particularly large decrease.

The reason for the difference between the robots could be that both Kiropi v2 and RoBoHoN have movable arms and moved them in accordance with the conversation. The importance of nonverbal communication such as gestures has been pointed out in human communication [20]. This is confirmed by the fact that gestures contributed to the reduction of anxiety in this experiment.

Only the communication anxiety of kuropi v2 showed a large decrease in #2, then increased and then decreased, as Fig. 8 shows. This high-low-high change can be interpreted as a novelty effect, its elimination, and the familiarity effect. The reason for this could be that participants were familiar with the designs of the iPad and RoBoHoN because they are commercially available, and they were already familiar, without novelty.

The 8th evaluation after the above process is referred to as "impression evaluation for long-term use." All robots evoke little anxiety, even if they are used for a long time, and Kiropi v2 has a particularly low anxiety design.

The friendliness and performance tended to increase significantly as the number of uses increased. In addition, there was a difference between the types of robots. Friendliness and performance were highest for Kiropi v2, followed by RoBoHoN and iPad. Also, Kiropi of experiment 1 was between the values of Kiropi v2 and RoBoHoN.

The friendliness and performance of all robots showed a decrease at #4 and then increased. This can be interpreted as the effect of novelty and its elimination, and the familiarity effect. Friendliness and performance showed a tendency to increase even if all robots were used for a long time, and Kiropi v2 has the design with the highest friendliness and performance.

The fact that the performance of Kiropi v2 was generally higher than that of RoBoHoN could be because Kiropi v2 has higher arm movement speed han RoBoHoN, and adjectives such as "quick" and 'fast" were included in the performance items.

The prior study suggested that the design of Kiropi had the effect of adding characteristics, but characteristics and toolness were in a trade-off relationship [7]. In this study, characteristics and toolness are considered to correspond to friendliness and performance. It cannot be said that the performance of Kiropi increased in the results of experiment 1. The scores for the friendliness and performance of Kiropi v2 were higher than those of Kiropi in experiment 2, indicating a clear increasing trend. It is suggested that the design of Kiropi v2 has been improved and the impression has become better than that of Kiropi.

5   Conclusion

In this study, a psychological scale of long-term change in impression of social robots' characteristics and toolness was created through experiment 1 using Kiropi developed in the prior study [6,7]. In addition, experiment 2, a long-term experiment of three types of robots, Kiropi v2 (with an improved design to match recent robot design trends), iPad, and RoBoHoN, was conducted to measure changes in impression using the created scale. As a result, scores of friendliness and performance of all robots showed a tendency to increase as the number of uses increased. In addition, some impressions could be interpreted as the effects of novelty and its elimination and familiarity. There was also a difference in impression among the robots, and the impression of Kiropi v2 was the best.

Regarding the robot's characteristics and toolness, the design of Kiropi v2, a tablet with arm parts, was evaluated as at least better than the iPad and as good as RoBoHoN in long-term use. This knowledge will contribute to the design of future social robots. In addition, the psychological scale created in this study is useful for social robot developers when they want to evaluate the impression of a robot in consideration of long-term use.

The limitation of this study was that the total number of participants in experiment 1 was 5 and that of experiment 2 was 6 in each group. In addition, because the factor of the robot type in experiment 2 was an inter-participant plan, it is not possible to exclude the difference of the participants assigned to each robot is affecting.

The authors hope that the knowledge obtained from this research will contribute to the development of a robot that can be a true and familiar partner.

Acknowledgement. We wish to thank the cooperation of Yusuke Okuda and Ryutaro Azuma who graduated from the School of Science and Technology, Kwansei Gakuin University. This work was supported by JSPS KAKENHI Grant Number 16H03225.

References

1. Yamauchi, S.: The Danish council of ethics: recommendations concering social robots (2016)
2. SoftBank Robotics Corp: Pepper for Biz. http://www.softbank.jp/robot/biz. Accessed 15 Jan 2020
3. Sharp Corporation: RoBoHoN. http://robohon.com. Accessed 15 Jan 2020
4. Odagiri, H.: Character Toha Nanika. Chikumashobo, Tokyo (2010). (in Japanese)
5. Sonoyama, T.: Introduction to Robot Design. Mynavi Corporation, Tokyo (2007). (in Japanese)
6. Yamamoto, M., Aoyagi, S., Fukumori, S., Watanabe, T.: KiroPi: a life-log robot by installing embodied hardware on a tablet. In: 2015 24th IEEE International Symposium on Robot and Human Interactive Communication (RO-MAN) (2015). https://doi.org/10.1109/ROMAN.2015.7333616
7. Okuda, Y., Aoyagi, S., Yamamoto, M., Fukumori, S., Watanabe, T.: KiroPi: a tablet-based robot with arm-shaped hardware for personality. Trans. Hum. Interface **2**(2), 209–220 (2018). (in Japanese)
8. Leite, I., Martinho, C., Paiva, A.: Social robots for long-term interaction: a survey. Int. J. Soc. Robot. **5**(2), 291–308 (2013). https://doi.org/10.1007/s12369-013-0178-y
9. Sung, J., Christensen, H. I., Grinter, R. E.: Robots in the wild: understanding long-term use. In: Proceedings of the 4th ACM/IEEE International Conference on Human Robot Interaction (HRI 2009), pp. 45–52 (2009)
10. Sung, J., Grinter, R.E., Christensen, H.I.: Domestic robot ecology. Int. J. Soc. Robot. **2**(4), 417–429 (2010). https://doi.org/10.1007/s12369-010-0065-8
11. Tanaka, F., Cicourel, A., Movellan, J.R.: Socialization between toddlers and robots at an early childhood education center. Proc. Nat. Acad. Sci **104**(46), 17945–17958 (2007)
12. De Graaf, M.M.A., Allouch, S.B., van Dijk, J.A.G.M.: Long-term evaluation of a social robot in real homes. Interact. Stud. **17**(3), 461–490 (2016)
13. De Graaf, M., Allouch, S.B., van Dijk, J.: Why do they refuse to use my robot?: reasons for non-use derived from a long-term home study. In: Proceedings of the 2017 12th ACM/IEEE International Conference on Human-Robot Interaction (HRI 2017), pp. 224–233 (2017)
14. Matsuda, K., Kusumi, T., Hosomi, N., Osa, A., Miike, H.: Effects of exposure frequency and background information on preferences for photographs of cars in different locations. Jpn. J. Psychol. **85**(3), 240–247 (2014). (in Japanese)
15. Fantz, R.L.: Visual experiences in infants: decreased attention to familiar patterns relative to novel ones. Science **146**, 668–670 (1964)
16. Zajonc, R.B.: Attitudinal efects of mere exposure. J. Pers. Soc. Psychol. Monogr. Suppl. **9**(2), 1–27 (1968)
17. Liao, H.I., Yeh, S.L., Shimojo, S.: Novelty vs. familiarity principles in preference decisions: task-context of past experience matters. Front. Psychol. **2**, 43 (2011)
18. Kanda, T., Ishiguro, H., Ishida, Y.: Psychological analysis on human-robot interaction. In: Proceedings IEEE International Conference on Robotics and Automation (ICRA 2001) (2001)
19. Frontier works Inc.: CeVIO creative studio. http://cevio.jp. Accessed 15 Jan 2020
20. Watanabe, T., Okubo, M., Nakashige, M., Danbara, R.: InterActor: speech driven embodied interactiveactor. Int. J. Hum. Comput. Interact. **17**(1), 43–60 (2004)

21. Nomura, T., Kanda, T., Suzuki, T., Kato, K.: Prediction of human behavior in human-robot interaction using psychological scales for anxiety and negative attitudes toward robots. IEEE Trans. Rob. **24**(2), 442–451 (2008)
22. Kondo Kagaku Co., Ltd.: KHR Series. https://kondo-robot.com/product-category/robot/khrseries. Accessed 15 Jan 2020
23. Sony Corporation, Sony Marketing Inc.: KOOV. https://www.sony.jp/koov/. Accessed 15 Jan 2020
24. Vstone Co., Ltd.: Sota. https://www.vstone.co.jp/products/sota/. Accessed 15 Jan 2020

Services Task Model Based Dialogue Scenarios Design Towards L2 WTC Support Oriented Dialogues Authoring Tool

Emmanuel Ayedoun$^{(\boxtimes)}$ (iD), Yuki Hayashi, and Kazuhisa Seta

Osaka Prefecture University, Osaka 5998531, Japan
eayedoun@ksm.kis.osakafu-u.ac.jp

Abstract. Prior studies have demonstrated that embodied conversational agents, which provide opportunities to simulate realistic daily conversation situations, could be effective in motivating second language learners to communicate in the target language. However, implementing such systems in various situations requires significant knowledge-engineering effort, which limits their widespread adoption and deployment. In this paper, we present a conceptual framework for dialogue scenario design based on an ontological model of service process. We provide an overview of a scenario authoring workflow and reduced number of activities that should be conducted by scenario designers to specify both the properties of the dialogue task structure and dialogue flow logic in the targeted conversation situation. We also discuss the benefits of embedding such a common service task structure in terms of reducing the authoring load of dialogue scenarios in various task-oriented service situations.

Keywords: Conversational systems · Authoring systems · Service-oriented dialogues · L2 communication

1 Introduction

To sustainably motivate second language learners to communicate in the target language, it is important to provide them with various opportunities to freely simulate and enjoy natural conversation in different realistic dialogue situations. This requires the design and implementation of a rich pool of different dialogue situations, particularly when there are limited opportunities for authentic face-to-face interactions; it also involves careful design of the different dialogue scenarios to the extent that a high degree of reality is achieved in interactions, similar to what learners are likely to experience in daily face-to-face situations.

Concerning this issue of degree of reality, task-oriented dialogue systems where a task should be accomplished in the target language are believed to have a clear potential for computer-assisted language-learning systems that place the student in a realistic situation [1]. For instance, in our previous works [2, 3], we developed an embodied conversational agent (CEWill) that provides second language learners with spoken dialogue

© Springer Nature Switzerland AG 2020
S. Yamamoto and H. Mori (Eds.): HCII 2020, LNCS 12185, pp. 145–163, 2020.
https://doi.org/10.1007/978-3-030-50017-7_10

opportunities in a restaurant context. CEWill was built following a knowledge-based approach in the task structure modeling and dialogue flow management, which enables it to achieve a deeper level of understanding and control of the conversation flow, increasing the degree of reality of interactions. However, adding a new conversation scenario to the system following this approach would require scenario designers to entirely hand-craft the dialogue task structure as well as the dialogue flow logic from scratch, and implement it in the system in the form of a dialogue script. Needless to say, this could easily become a time- and resource-consuming activity that requires significant knowledge-engineering effort and some degree of expertise about dialogue systems, in addition to proper domain knowledge. Hence, it is desirable to propose an alternative approach that could facilitate the rapid implementation of desirable dialogue scenarios in order to lower the dialogue scenario authoring barrier for non-programmers or educators, who are not necessarily knowledge or software engineers. Doing so would ultimately promote the availability of a richer pool of conversation scenarios for second language learners, which is desirable in terms of enhancing their engagement in communication.

In the following sections, we shed light on a conceptual dialogue scenario authoring framework to enable rapid specification of dialogue scenarios in various service domains. A detailed authoring workflow is presented to demonstrate the feasibility of the approach. The achievement of such a framework is expected to ultimately promote the availability of a richer pool of conversation simulation opportunities for L2 learners, and contribute to the diffusion of shared dialogue systems design principles, particularly for studies dealing with communicative aspects of language acquisition.

2   Related Works and Pertinence of Issue

Several recent reviews have noted the effectiveness of learning support systems and particularly intelligent tutoring systems (i.e., ITS), highlighting that well-designed systems can successfully complement or substitute other instructional models in many common academic subjects [4–6]. Hence, for the past years, extensive work has been conducted on developing authoring tools to speed up the development of learning support systems, reduce implementation workload, and lower the skill requirements.

However, as stressed by Woolf, despite all the positive evidence suggesting that learning support systems have already succeeded in finding use within education, research on authoring tools has been progressing slowly and ITS design has remained costly and complex [7]. Building an explicit model of anything is no easy task, and requires analysis, synthesis, and abstraction skills along with a healthy dose of creativity [8]. While authoring tools can significantly decrease the cognitive load involved in various design steps of a computer-based learning support system, reducing the entire design task to low-level decisions that yield a quality product remains difficult. In addition, Murray hinted at the challenging trade-off issue related to the extent to which the difficult task of authoring learning support systems could be scaffolded: ideally, a desirable authoring tool should be both specific enough to make authoring template-based, but general enough to be attractive to many educators [9]. This is an even more difficult issue when it comes to designing an authoring tool that could be used to design believable conversational agents across a wide range of different contexts, as would be desirable in the context of our study.

Authoring tools for conversation-based learning environments have focused on assisting non-technical users in the creation of pedagogical agent dialogues. AutoTutor [10] provides multi-agent conversational interactions to tutor students using the discourse patterns of a human tutor, and has been used across multiple domains including computer literacy and physics. To facilitate the application of AutoTutor to other domains, authoring tools have been developed to aid subject matter experts in creating dialogue-based tutors, such as the AutoTutor Script Authoring [11] and AutoLearn [12]. Another example of an authoring tool for agent dialogue is TuTalk [13], which was created to support the rapid development of agent-based dialogue systems by non-programmers. This tool facilitates the authoring of domain knowledge and resources required by the dialogue agent in the form of artificial intelligence (AI) planning techniques that address high-level goals of the dialogue system. Similarly, an authoring tool has been created for the Tactical Language and Culture Training System (TLCTS) that allows subject matter experts to create pedagogical dialogue for a foreign language learning training system at reduced cost and time [14].

However, despite the potential for increased student engagement and the reduced cost of creating lifelike virtual characters, pedagogical agents have not yet achieved widespread adoption in computer-based learning environments [15]. The available authoring tools environments, although certainly useful to implement pedagogical agents for specific domains, still seem to suffer from a lack or limited level of abstraction or versatility of their encapsulated initial domain knowledge, which in turn limits the reusability of their key components across different domains. Thus, a limiting factor in the widespread deployment of these conversational agents is a significant effort and the pedagogical agent expertise required to codify knowledge and behaviors into the ITS. For instance, a novice user may be overwhelmed and discouraged by an authoring tool that exposes too many necessary but general properties that could have rather been modelized under the hood in the authoring tool and reused automatically across different domains in a smart fashion. Achieving this level of versatility while still maintaining the authoring costs at an acceptable level for content creators is a challenging task, but certainly necessary to enable a more active and frequent use of authoring tools and learning support systems by educators who are not software engineers.

3 Goal, Challenges, and Requirements

As developed above, despite the availability of several learning support systems, such systems still struggle to find their way from the lab into actual learning environments due to the significant effort and pedagogical agent expertise required to codify knowledge and behaviors into them. Furthermore, available dialogue-based learning support systems are designed to carry on tutorial dialogues in specific subjects such as physics, computer literacy, or critical thinking. Tutorial dialogues achieved within such systems deal with replicating the dialogue moves of human tutors in teaching situations, which are dialogue situations quite different from the daily-life task-oriented dialogue scenarios targeted in the context of our present work.

3.1 Goal

In light of the aforementioned background, the goal of the work presented in this paper is to propose a conceptual framework to ease the design of dialogue scenarios over various conversation situations. This is expected to ultimately serve as a solid foundation toward the development of a dialogue system authoring tool that could facilitate the rapid implementation of our proposed embodied conversational agent (CEWill) over various dialogue situations. To this extent, our idea here is to target a suitable subset of dialogue domains that share a coherent structure at the task level and propose an approach to exploit this common task structure to provide domain-independent reusable dialogue task components. This is expected to facilitate the design process of the various dialogue scenarios falling under the hood of the target common task.

3.2 Challenges

To achieve this goal, and inspired by Murray's review of authoring tools [8], we summarize the challenges related to the design of dialogue scenarios in the context of the current study as follows:

A. **Decrease the effort** (time, cost, and/or other resources) for implementing various dialogue scenarios in CEWill;
B. **Decrease the skill threshold** for dialogue scenario modeling (i.e., allow actual educators and other people with non-programming skills to participate in the dialogue scenario design process);
C. Make possible **intuitive articulation and organization of the target domain knowledge**;
D. Contribute to the diffusion **of shared dialogue scenarios design principles** for studies dealing with communicative aspects of L2 acquisition.

3.3 Requirements

To address the above challenges, we have identified a number of core requirements for the desired dialogue scenario design framework.

1) **Embed a relevant level of domain-independent knowledge about task structure:** this refers to some generic knowledge about the common structure (i.e., model) of the different dialogue domains targeted by the system. Such knowledge, if pre-wired and embedded in the framework, could make authoring easier and more powerful by reusing the same structure across various instances of dialogue domains. In this way, dialogue scenario designers could simply focus on specifying domain-specific aspects of the dialogue flow, which will significantly lessen new scenarios' implementation effort and contribute to tackling Challenge A. Nonetheless, finding a relevant level of abstraction to the extent of providing a clear separation between domain-specific and domain-independent aspects of the task structure that could fit all possible dialogue scenarios is certainly a challenging (if not impossible) endeavor; hence, a reasonable compromise could consist in targeting an appropriate subset of related dialogue domains that share a number of generic properties.

2) **Make possible efficient work-flow and knowledge management:** this involves the system's ability to scaffold the dialogue scenario specification by allowing input using templates, data entry forms, pop-up menus, etc. Whenever the range of possible input values can be limited to a finite set, scenario designers should be allowed to select rather than type. There should also be a clear separation in the different types of information that scenario designers deal with: dialogue task structure, dialogue goals, dialogue flow, interface parameters, and so on. Scenario designers need to be supported throughout the overall design process and interactive prompts could be beneficial in terms of easing their work-flow. This is expected to contribute to addressing challenge B.

3) **Enable scenarios designers to visualize the structure of authored dialogue scenarios:** provide a user interface that allows designers to see both the static structure of the designed dialogue scenario and the dialogue control dynamics over possible dialogue paths. This could give designers a more precise idea of the possible actions in the designed scenario and allow them to make necessary refinements to achieve the desired dialogue scenario. This is expected to contribute to tackling challenge C.

4) **Facilitate content modularity, customization, and reusability:** this refers to the authoring tool's ability to allow modular authoring of the different components required to design a desired dialogue scenario and their storage as library structures so that they can be reused for multiple scenarios purposes, so as to take up challenge D. For instance, input processing, output processing, conversational strategies, etc. should be encapsulated in subcomponents with well-defined interfaces that are decoupled from domain-specific dialogue flow logic. Along this line, the tool should also make it easy to browse, search for, and reference content objects. Furthermore, since it is almost impossible to anticipate everything a designer may want, the tool should provide features for the extensibility of the existing components (i.e., customization).

4 Approach

To fulfill the requirement related to finding a relevant level of abstraction for knowledge about dialogue task structure (i.e., **requirement 1**), our idea is to focus on services (restaurant, hotel, travel-planning, etc.) that seem to share a certain degree of structure similarity at the task level, and build an authoring tool that embeds a generic service task structure model in order to facilitate the implementation of services-oriented dialogue scenarios across various services domains. Besides, focusing on services may offer L2 learners much in terms of desirable communicative practice and WTC support since learners are likely to face service-oriented dialogue situations in their daily lives.

4.1 Generic Structure of Service System Process

A service is present at a time t and location l if, at time t, an agent is explicitly committed to guaranteeing the execution of some type of action at location l, on the occurrence of a certain triggering event, in the interest of another agent and upon prior agreement, in

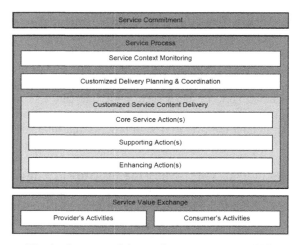

Fig. 1. Structure of the service system process [17]

a certain way [16]. According to Ferrario, despite the pervasiveness of the term service in the ordinary discourse, it is used in different ways across disciplines and, even within the same discipline, it is not rare to observe confusion and inconsistencies [17]. They further mentioned that given such a situation, service designers may not share a common semantic background, which could result in harming service interoperability. To overcome this issue, they adopted a high level of abstraction to propose a generic (ontological) model of services structure with the aim of facilitating a unified understanding of concrete services and their facets. For instance, with respect to the service delivery, they proposed that the central part of the service process is given by the customized service content delivery, which is the actual event in which one executes what has been promised in the service commitment; it is composed of the following:

- **Core service Actions:** are those actions that, in a sense, characterize a service for what it is and must necessarily be exposed to the customer, e.g., for a firefighting service, the action of extinguishing the fire;
- **Supporting Actions:** are actions necessary to the service but not explicitly mentioned as constituting the service, e.g., for a firefighting service, the action of driving to the place where the fire is to extinguish the fire is necessary, but it does not fight the fire itself as a core;
- **Enhancing Actions:** are actions meant to augment the value of the service. They can be considered as additional services actions that are connected to but not strictly included in the main service, e.g., for a firefighting service, the action of going to schools to provide advice on risk prevention.

We adopt this conceptualization of a service system process as proposed by Ferrario and his colleagues [17] as a baseline for our work, and further drill into the structure, properties, and relations of the three types of service actions (i.e., core service actions,

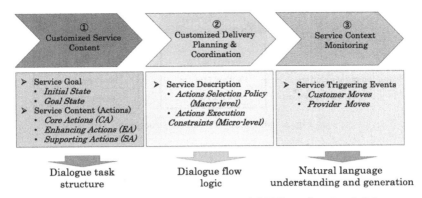

Fig. 2. From Ferrario's service process structure model [17] to a functional dialogue system

supporting actions, enhancing actions) to enable dynamic instantiation of such base structure for diverse service-oriented dialogue scenarios.

4.2 From Structure of Service Process to Service-Oriented Dialogue Scenarios Design

Based on the generic structure described in Fig. 1, we propose that the design of a service-oriented dialogue scenario in a given domain can be split into three main phases, each corresponding to the design of the three sub-processes of the service process, namely (Customized Service Content Delivery, Customized Delivery Planning & Coordination, and Service Context Monitoring) described in Fig. 1. This is a relatively straightforward and obvious approach since these three sub-processes form the core mechanism that orchestrates the execution of a given service [17]. On the other hand, keeping in mind that the finality of our work is to design actual dialogue scenarios that will be implemented for spoken language interactions with L2 learners, we are also required to satisfy the constraints of dynamic execution of service actions (i.e., dialogue management) and natural language processing (i.e., language understanding and generation in dialogue) that are proper to dialogue systems.

To meet these requirements, we propose the conceptual transition map shown in Fig. 2, which serves as a bridge connecting the static service process structure (theoretical perspective) presented above and aspects related to the dynamic nature of dialogue systems (practical perspective). Basically, we propose a design roadmap to fill the gap between Ferrario's service task structure model and service-oriented dialogue scenario dialogue system. We demonstrate how key mechanisms of a functional dialogue system may be achieved by authoring the three sub-processes of Ferrario's service system process structure. In the following sections, we provide details on our domain-independent design policy toward achieving rapid specifications of the dialogue scenario (i.e., Dialogue task and Dialogue flow logic) in the services domain. It is noteworthy that despite the importance of aspects related to Natural language recognition and generation in actual dialogue systems, these subjects are beyond the scope of this work. Nevertheless, such

Fig. 3. Model of service goal structure

mechanisms could be implemented by combining our proposed approach with external natural language understanding services such as Wit.ai and DialogFlow.

5   Modeling Dialogue Task Structure

The dialog task structure captures the goals and actions that will be performed to achieve the delivery of the target service. Thus, it is composed of the service goal structure on the one hand, and service actions structure on the other. To better illustrate our descriptions, we introduce an example that we will use continuously throughout this paper. We use a service that most people should be reasonably familiar with and that was implemented in our prototype system [2, 3]: the restaurant scenario.

5.1   Model of Goal Structure

We assume that a given customer is bound to a service (which is delivered within spatio-temporal requirements) by their desire to satisfy some Need(s) and in return their obligation to deliver some Reward (s) to the service provider. As such, the service goal consists of initial and final states of the service in terms of customer needs, provider reward, and spatio-temporal requirements within which the service delivery is conducted.

Figure 3 shows the resulting model of service goal structure. Here in this example, let us suppose that the service is intended to satisfy the customer Need (*Drink* and *Food*), in return for which a provider's Reward (*Pay*) must be fulfilled. Note that in this case, the learner's Position is specified as a spatial requirement for the service delivery as well. In sum, the figure shows the service goal model specified for service delivery in a restaurant context between the customer (i.e., learner) and provider (i.e., dialogue system) with their interaction starting at the entrance of the restaurant, and the goal being to satisfy the customer's Need (*Drink* and *Food*) while ensuring that the provider's Reward (*Pay*) is fulfilled and the interaction ending at the specified Position *(cashier)*. Note that (*X*) in front of a Need or Reward means that such Need or Reward has not yet been satisfied, while (*O*) is used to specify the opposite.

5.2   Model of Actions Structure

The service actions are intended to be carried out to move the interaction from its initial to final states as specified in the service goal.

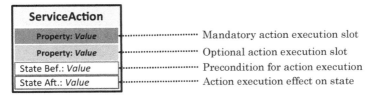

Fig. 4. Model of actions structure

Their execution triggers the actual dialogue between the service customer and provider. As shown in Fig. 4, we propose that the internal structure of each service action is composed of mandatory and optional slots that need to be filled through actual dialogue with the customer to enable the execution of a given service action. In addition, a service action can only be executed when some preconditions on the interaction state are satisfied; in the same vein, the execution of a given service action may update the interaction state through fulfillment of the customer's Need, the provider's Reward, or simply spatio-temporal requirement.

As mentioned in Ferrario's model, there are three types of services actions: Core Actions, Enhancing Actions, and Supporting Actions.

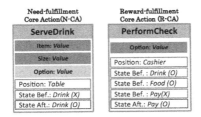

Fig. 5. Model of core actions types and structure

First, Core Actions (CA) are executed to handle a given customer's Need or to deliver a provider's Reward, so we distinguish Need-fulfillment Core Actions (N-CA) and Reward-fulfillment Core Actions (R-CA). With respect to the restaurant example, in Fig. 5 we present some examples of N-CA (*ServeFood*) and R-CA (*PerformCheck*) that could be specified in such a context for respectively handling the customer's Need (*Food*) and fulfilling the obligation to deliver the provider's Reward (*Pay*).

Next, Enhancing Actions (EA) are executed as "optional Core Actions" upon agreement with the customer. They are intended to augment the value of the service by satisfying additional Need(s) that the customer may have after delivery of the service's Need-fulfillment Core Actions. In the case of the restaurant scenario, a plausible Enhancing Action might be to propose a karaoke service *ServeKaraoke* after the customer has finished eating and drinking, as shown in Fig. 6. Upon agreement of the customer, the EA is executed similarly to a Core Action, according to the specifications of its internal structure.

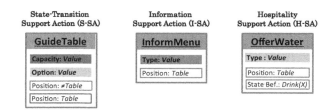

Fig. 6. Model of enhancing actions structure

Fig. 7. Model of supporting actions types and structure

Finally, Supporting Actions (SA) are responsible for aligning spatio-temporal requirements or performing actions that are necessary for the execution of CA and EA. Note that contrary to Core and Enhancing Actions, Supporting Actions are not intended to directly target customer's Need(s); in other words, their execution does not require fulfillment of Reward obligation toward the provider. We distinguish three types of Supporting Actions: State-transition Support Actions (S-SA) execution of which updates the values of spatio-temporal requirements, Information Support Actions (I-SA), which are performed to provide some information regarding the target core action, and finally Hospitality Support Actions (H-SA), which are other actions that are performed along with Core Actions to make the customer feel at ease. Figure 7 shows some examples of S-SA (GuideTable: this action has the effect of moving the customer to a position (i.e., Table) that is necessary for service delivery), I-SA (*InformMenu*: this action is performed to give some information regarding the nature of the proposed service), and H-SA (*OfferWater*: this action is executed to augment the quality of the proposed service) in a restaurant context.

On the basis of the aforementioned models, we assume that in order to perform a dialogue task structure specification for a given service domain, as well as the service goal (i.e., initial state and goal state), the work-flow should include specification of Core Actions (N-CA, R-CA), Enhancing Action (if necessary), and Supporting Actions (S-SA, I-SA, H-SA), as we will describe in Sect. 7.

Most goal-oriented dialogue tasks have an identifiable structure that lends itself to a hierarchical description of independent subcomponents [18]. This further leads to ease in design and maintenance, as well as good scalability properties for spoken dialogue systems. Our proposed model of dialogue task structure based on Ferrario's service process structure [17] can also be viewed as a hierarchical task representation that captures the nested structure of the dialogue task and thus implicitly represents context (via the parent relationship), as well as a default chronological ordering of the actions (i.e., left-to-right traversal). As shown in Fig. 8, this hierarchical plan-based representation does not prescribe a fixed order for the execution of the different actions (i.e., CA, EA, SA), which is rather determined based on user inputs, and encoded dialogue logic.

In the following section, we describe a model of dialogue flow logic enabling dynamic execution of the dialogue task structure (i.e., delivery of services actions toward the achievement of service goals).

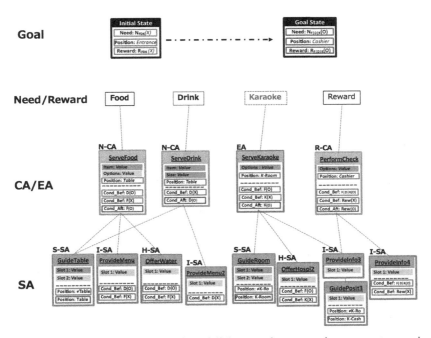

Fig. 8. Hierarchical task representation of dialogue task structure in restaurant scenario

6   Modeling Dialogue Flow Logic

To execute the dialogue task structure, we propose that the control of dialogue flow should be enforced at two levels: a macro-level and micro-level. The macro-level is concerned with the selection of the most appropriate service actions to execute based on the current dialogue state, while the micro-level deals with the proper execution of the target service action. More concretely, when a given service action has been selected at the macro level for execution, slot-filling tasks through actual dialogue moves for its execution are performed at the micro-level. In the following lines, we describe the key principles sustaining such dialogue flow logic and discuss how we can leverage the dialogue task structure and additional resources for its achievement.

6.1 Model of Macro-level Dialogue Flow Logic

As far as the macro-level (i.e., dynamic selection of CA, EA, and SA) is concerned, we propose that dialogue flow is determined by a combination of information on dialogue goals (as specified in the service goal), preconditions, and effects of defined service actions, and current dialogue state (i.e., Need (s)/Reward (s) have been satisfied and those that are still to be satisfied, status of spatio-temporal constraints).

The service goal structure (initial state, goal state) provides an overview of the Need (s) and Reward (s) to be satisfied for a successful interaction, as shown in Fig. 3. Based on this structure and the current dialogue state, the selection of a relevant Core Action (Fig. 5) can be achieved by referring to available Core Action(s)' effects constraints (i.e., which Need or Reward is to be satisfied via the execution of the target action). Furthermore, according to the current dialogue state, when a targeted Core Action's spatio-temporal preconditions constraints are not yet satisfied, relevant Supporting Action should be selected for execution to such extent. To illustrate this macro-level logic, let us refer to the dialogue task structure of the restaurant scenario shown in Fig. 8. Supposing, for example, that the Need *Drink* has not yet been satisfied, the relevant Core Action, which is *ServeDrink*, can be selected for execution. However, since Position: *Table* is a precondition constraint for the execution of *ServeDrink*, the Supporting Action *GuideTable* that has for effect to change Position to *Table* will be selected for execution. In this way, the selection of relevant service action can be orchestrated toward the achievement of the service goal.

The selection policy for Enhancing Actions is relatively similar to that described above for Core Actions; the difference here is that since the Need targeted by the execution of an Enhancing Action is optional, their selection must necessarily be preceded by an explicit Need confirmation or grounding during the interaction.

In sum, provided that dialogue task structure (service goal and actions structure) has been adequately specified, macro-level control of dialogue flow can be unfolded at runtime without any further authoring effort. At runtime, the dialogue state (i.e., Status of Needs and Rewards, status of spatio-temporal constraints) is regularly updated based on the selection and execution of service actions, as well as user inputs.

6.2 Model of Micro-level Dialogue Flow Logic

The micro-level control of dialogue flow involves actual execution of service actions that have been selected at the macro-level. This can be seen as slot-filling tasks where each service action is a form containing both mandatory and optional slots, as shown in Fig. 4. It follows that at the micro-level, the dialogue flow logic deals with specifying constraints for such slot-filling tasks. Slot-filling is about collecting certain bits of information or parameters from the customer before the target service action can be executed. To enable this, it is obvious that the nature or type of information expected for a given slot must be specified beforehand. This is to avoid, for example, situations where a slot expected to be filled out with information about *Size* is instead filled with information on *Menu*.

Moreover, while a predefined order for slot-filling is not always necessary, in some cases, such an order needs to be explicitly configured to preserve the naturalness of the interaction, and facilitate smooth action execution. For example, in the *ServeDrink* Core

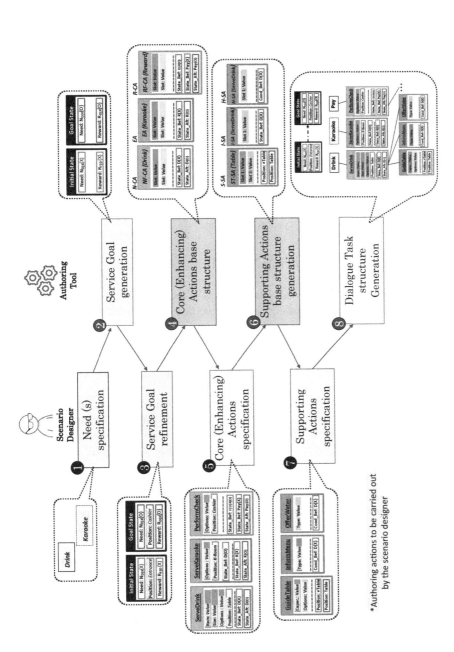

Fig. 9. Conceptual dialogue scenario authoring workflow (Color figure online)

Action case presented in Fig. 5, the slot *Size* cannot be filled before the slot *Item* because the size available for a given item may not be available for another one. In such a case, it would be desirable to specify that the slot *Item* is a prerequisite slot to the slot *Size*, for example.

Another factor that may come into play in the slot-filling process is the concept of mutual exclusivity between slots. In some cases, the filling of a given case indirectly allows the filling of another, so that in such a case it would be desirable to avoid redundancy in the slot-filling process by specifying mutual exclusivity constraints between slots. In addition, filling of all defined slots may not always be necessary to enable action execution. There may also exist some optional slots, as mentioned in Sect. 5.2.

In sum, to achieve control of dialogue flow at the micro-level, we propose that the dialogue flow logic specification should cover aspects related to slot-filling constraints such as slot type, filling order (prerequisite attribute), mutual exclusivity, optional or mandatory nature, as we will describe in the following section. At runtime, the micro-level dialogue state variables capture such constraints status and are regularly updated based on user inputs and subsequent system responses.

7   Simplified Scenario Authoring Workflow

The scenario authoring workflow provides an overview of the different activities that are conducted for specifying the properties of the dialogue task structure and flow logic in the targeted service domain.

In this section, we describe the authoring workflow from both the scenario designer and authoring tool perspectives. We also explain how the authoring tool actively supports the authoring process by guiding and facilitating the process behind the scenes, to fulfil the requirements evoked in Sect. 3.

In Fig. 9, we portrayed how the dialogue task structure and dialogue flow logic specifications of a dialogue scenario in a given service domain can be authored by conducting only four activities on the scenario designer side. These activities are presented on the left-hand side of Fig. 9 ((1), (3), (5), (7)), while right-hand side activities ((2), (4), (6), (8)) are to be executed behind the scenes by the authoring tool.

This hybrid approach is expected to consequently reduce the authoring effort by allowing system designers to focus solely on domain-dependent aspects of the target service domain dialogue scenario, while the authoring tool exploits the common underlying structure, to manage inter-domain commonalties, consistently to **requirement 1**.

Furthermore, by allowing input through the use of data entry forms for specifying service actions and making a separation among aspects related to dialogue task, flow logic, and natural language as we will explain below, we intend to make the authoring process more intuitive, to ease the work-flow for dialogue scenarios and satisfy **requirement 2**.

Moreover, the whole authoring process is designed to be executed via an interface in such a way that scenario designers can interactively participate in the authoring process, and visualize the authored dialogue structure, so as to satisfy **requirement 3**.

Finally, to satisfy **requirement 4** related to content customization and reusability, we designed the authoring workflow to provide a number of default settings for the basic structure of core, supporting, and enhancing actions. Scenario designers may reuse these available contents, customizing them according to the characteristics of their own contexts, as we will explain in the following paragraphs.

①. **Need Specification (Scenario Designer):** this is the first step in the dialogue scenario authoring process. Here, the scenario designer specifies the customer's primary and optional Need(s) that the service provider is committed to satisfying. For example, in a restaurant scenario, Drink and Food could be set as primary Needs, while Karaoke, which is not necessarily the main reason why a customer goes to a restaurant, could be set as optional. The reason for this distinction between primary and optional Needs is provided below.

②. **Goal Generation (System):** based on the Need(s) specified by the scenario designer, the authoring tool generates the basic template of the dialogue goal structure. This is achieved by generating a representation of initial and goal states based on the Needs specified by the scenario designer. By default, primary Need(s) are to be necessarily satisfied at goal state while optional ones are not necessarily to be fulfilled, as represented in the example in Fig. 9. In addition, Rewards slots are added as counterparts of defined Needs. By default, Pay is set as Reward for each of the defined Needs.

③. **Goal Refinement (Scenario Designer):** based on the automatically generated goal structure, the scenario designer may choose to refine both the initial and goal states of the interaction by adding some spatio-temporal requirements or modifying the desired starting and ending state criteria for the interaction. Note that in the example in Fig. 9, the scenario designer added a spatio-temporal requirement for the service delivery (i.e., position), which has different values at initial (i.e., Entrance) and goal (i.e., Cashier) state. This refinement of the goal structure enables scenario designers to clarify the big picture of the target service delivery process.

④. **Core and Enhancing Actions Generation (System):** at this point, the tool generates base structures of Core and Enhancing actions to be executed to satisfy Need(s) and Reward(s) specified in the Goal structure. The suitable types of actions are automatically set based on the nature of the target Need or Reward. For instance, N-CA are selected to satisfy primary Needs, while R-CA are employed for Rewards. EA are employed for optional Need(s). In this way, all defined Needs and Rewards are attributed to a specific Core Action or Enhancing Action. In the example presented in Fig. 9, Core Action N-CA (Drink) is generated to target the primary Need Drink, Enhancing Action EA (Karaoke) to target the optional Need Karaoke and finally R-CA (Pay) is generated to fulfill the Reward Pay. In addition to the type of Core Actions or Enhancing Actions, some constraints are also automatically generated and attached to each service action, as represented by green and red rectangles in the internal structure of each action in Fig. 9. The generation of these default constraints follows a simple principle, which can be stated in the following terms: A Core or Enhancing Action is executed to satisfy a Need or Reward. In practical terms, this supposes at least two things: first, the interaction state before the execution of a given Core or Enhancing Action should indicate that the target Need or Reward is not yet satisfied (i.e., content of green border rectangles); second, the execution of

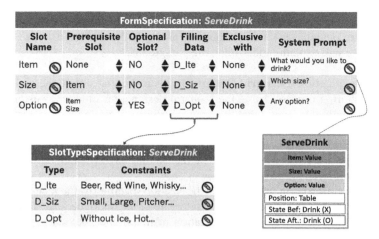

Fig. 10. Action slots specification interface

the Core or Enhancing Action triggers the satisfaction of the target Need or Reward (i.e., content of red border rectangles).

⑤. **Core and Enhancing Actions Specification (Scenario Designer):** Based on the automatically generated basic structure of Core and Enhancing Actions by the authoring tool, if necessary, the scenario designer can set additional spatio-temporal requirements or state constraints to the action. In addition, the scenario designer is requested to define slots that need to be filled in order to make possible delivery or execution of the target Core or Enhancing Actions during the interaction. To ease the handling of this essential activity, the scenario designer is prompted with a slot specification window, as illustrated in Fig. 10. In the FormSpecification window, the scenario designer can configure any number of form fields or slots by specifying several properties that will determine the flow of slot-filling tasks at runtime. Such properties include:

- Prerequisite slot: indicates which slots need to be filled before the current one; in the example provided in Fig. 10, the slot Item needs to be filled before the Size slot, while Item itself does not have any prerequisite prior to filling. The configuration of this property is conducted via selection among the list of defined (i.e., first column) slots.
- Optional slot?: indicates whether the slot's value is indispensable or not for the target service action execution; at least one slot is necessary for a given service action.
- Filling data: constrains the semantic type of the target slot. The configuration is conducted by selecting the appropriate type among the predefined ones. Scenario designers can still customize the existing slot types according to the restrictions of the target domain, or define new types from scratch via the SlotTypeSpecification window, as shown in Fig. 10.
- Exclusive with: shows mutual exclusivity relationships between two slots. This property can be useful in cases where the filling of a given case indirectly allows the filling of another so that in such a case it would be desirable to avoid redundancy in the

slot-filling process. Note that this property is symmetric so that when a given slot A is set to be exclusive with B, then B is also exclusive with A.

To further support the specification process and make authoring easier, the authoring tool may allow scenario designers to select predefined specification properties applicable to specific service actions or the whole domain. For instance, "Payment Mode" is a property that could be helpful to specify the order execution constraints existing between a Need-fulfilling Core Action (Enhancing Action) on the one hand, and Reward-fulfilling Core Action, on the other. Depending on the target service domain, the scenario designer may set Payment Mode with values such as Prepayment, PostPayment, or Pay-as-you-go. According to the selected value, execution constraints will be automatically added to the Reward-fulfilling and/or Need-fulfilling Core Action. For example, when the Pay-as-you-go mode is set, a Reward-fulfilling Core Action will be executed every time immediately after a given Need-fulfilling Core Action is executed. In this way, the scenario designer does not need to specify such execution preconditions constraints from scratch.

⑥. **Supporting Actions Generation:** basic structures of supporting actions are automatically generated and attached to each defined Core Action and Enhancing action. State-transition Supporting Actions (S-SA), which operate on state-temporal requirement, are only generated when the parent Core or Enhancing action have some spatio-temporal requirement. For example, in Fig. 9, S-SA (Table) is generated for the Core Action ServeDrink since the state-temporal requirement Position: Table was specified for ServeDrink. The basic structures of Information Supporting Action (I-SA) and Hospitality Supporting Action (H-SA) are also generated automatically for each Core and Enhancing Action. Note that by default, I-SA and H-SA inherit macro-level constraints (i.e., spatio-temporal requirements and precondition constraints) associated with their parent Core or Enhancing Action. This is because, for a given I-SA or H-SA to be executed, the dialogue state must be aligned in advance in a way that the parent Core Action is executable. Once again, this feature is expected to release scenario designers from the necessity of specifying execution constraints for I-SA and H-SA. However, it is still possible to modify these default settings according to the characteristics of the target domain. Note that while the specification of N-CA and EA requires the corresponding specification of some R-CA, this is not the case for SA, which once again should not be considered as explicit constituents of the service per se, but rather as "complimentary actions" (i.e., the customer is not bounded to any counterparty upon the delivery of such actions), which are orchestrated to facilitate the delivery of Core and Enhancing Actions.

⑦. **Supporting Actions Refinement:** this activity is similar to the refinement activity for Core and Enhancing Actions. The scenario designer can configure slot-filling policies for each supporting action via the slot specification interface shown in Fig. 10. Furthermore, since I-SA and H-SA are generated by default for all Core and Enhancing Actions, it is also possible to remove those that might be unnecessary.

⑧. **Dialogue Task Structure Generation:** the authored dialogue task structure for the target dialogue scenario is displayed as a hierarchical structure allowing the scenario designer to visualize and obtain a big picture of the authored domain knowledge. This can be seen as the semantic representation of the target scenario. Relations between customer Needs-provider Rewards and services Actions can be revisited by the scenario designer, to ensure that intended service delivery is achieved. For instance, the scenario designer may decide to go back through the aforementioned authoring activities and make appropriate revisions, add missing components, or even define new customer Needs, if necessary. Note that the generated dialogue domain allows for mixed-initiative interactions at the micro-level of flow control where a user can select any order and combination of fields to fill the slots defined for each service action, including a single turn or in multiple turns, as far as the slot-filling constraints are not violated. Otherwise, the system (dialogue manager) can still temporarily take the turn and control the conversation flow via some correction and grounding features implemented in DiMaCA (Section 4).

8   Conclusion

Given that second language learners' decision to initiate speech varies over time and across situations, a desirable conversational environment should offer learners the possibility of conversing efficiently in a variety of different social conversations situations.

However, implementing a realistic conversation scenario in a given domain (e.g., restaurant, hotel, flight booking) could easily turn out to be a time- and resource-consuming activity that requires significant knowledge-engineering effort and some degree of expertise about dialogue systems and the domain itself. Building on our previous works, which dealt with building a task-oriented natural conversation simulation environment for second language learners, the present study focused on the design of an authoring tool that could ease the implementation of new dialogue scenarios for the proposed system (i.e., CEWill) and similar dialogue systems. To reduce dialogue scenario authoring loads and allow actual educators and other stakeholders to actively participate in the system design process, we adopted a generic and reusable model of services process structure, which is expected to ease specification of dialogue scenarios in various service domains. A conceptual authoring workflow is presented to hint at the feasibility of the approach.

The achievement of such a framework is expected to ultimately promote the availability of a richer pool of conversation simulation opportunities for L2 learners, and contribute to the diffusion of shared dialogue systems design principles, particularly for studies dealing with communicative aspects of language acquisition.

References

1. Raux, A., Eskenazi, M.: Using task-oriented spoken dialogue systems for language learning: potential, practical applications and challenges. In: InSTIL/ICALL Symposium (2004)
2. Ayedoun, E., Hayashi, Y., Seta, K.: Web-services based conversational agent to encourage willingness to communicate in EFL context. J. Inf. Syst. Educ. **14**(1), 15–27 (2016)

3. Ayedoun, E., Hayashi, Y., Seta, K.: Adding communicative and affective strategies to an embodied conversational agent to enhance second language learners' willingness to communicate. Int. J. Artif. Intell. Educ. **29**(1), 29–57 (2018). https://doi.org/10.1007/s40593-018-0171-6. Springer

4. du Boulay, B.: Recent meta-reviews and meta–analyses of AIED systems. Int. J. Artif. Intell. Educ. **26**(1), 536–537 (2016)

5. Ma, W., Adesope, O.O., Nesbit, J.C., Liu, Q.: Intelligent tutoring systems and learning outcomes: a meta-analysis. J. Educ. Psychol. **106**(4), 901–918 (2014)

6. VanLehn, K.: The relative effectiveness of human tutoring, intelligent tutoring systems, and other tutoring systems. Educ. Psychol. **46**(4), 197–221 (2011)

7. Woolf, B.P.: Building intelligent interactive tutors: student-centered strategies for revolutionizing e-learning. Morgan Kaufmann, Burlington (2010)

8. Murray, T.: Authoring intelligent tutoring systems: an analysis of the state of the art. Int. J. Artif. Intell. Educ. **10**, 98–129 (1999)

9. Murray, T.: An overview of intelligent tutoring system authoring tools: updated analysis of the state of the art. In: Murray, T., Blessing, S.B., Ainsworth, S. (eds.) Authoring Tools for Advanced Technology Learning Environments, pp. 491–544. Springer, Dordrecht (2003). https://doi.org/10.1007/978-94-017-0819-7_17

10. Graesser, A.C., Chipman, P., Haynes, B.C., Olney, A.: AutoTutor: an intelligent tutoring system with mixed-initiative dialogue. IEEE Trans. Educ. **48**(4), 612–618 (2005)

11. Susarla, S., Adcock, A., Van Eck, R., Moreno, K., Graesser, A.C.: Tutoring research group: development and evaluation of a lesson authoring tool for AutoTutor. In: AIED2003 Supplemental Proceedings, pp. 378–387. University of Sydney School of Information Technologies Sydney, Australia (2003)

12. Preuss, S., Garc, D. Boullosa, J.: AutoLearn's authoring tool: a piece of cake for teachers. In: Proceedings of the NAACL HLT 2010 Fifth Workshop on Innovative Use of NLP for Building Educational Applications, pp. 19–27. Association for Computational Linguistics (2010)

13. Jordan, P.W., Hall, B., Ringenberg, M., Cue, Y., Rose, C.: Tools for authoring a dialogue agent that participates in learning studies. In: Luckin, R., Koedinger, K.R., Greer, J. (eds.) Artificial Intelligence in Education: Building Technology Rich Learning Contexts That Work, pp. 43–50. IOS Press (2007)

14. Meron, J., Valente, A., Johnson, W.L.: Improving the authoring of foreign language interactive lessons in the Tactical Language Training System. In: Workshop on Speech and Language Technology in Education, pp. 33–36 (2007)

15. Lester, L., Mott, B., Rowe, J., Taylor, R.: Design principles for pedagogical agent authoring tools. In: Sottilare, R., Graesser, A., Hu, X., Brawner, K. (eds.) Design Recommendations for Intelligent Tutoring Systems: Volume 3 - Authoring Tools and Expert Modeling Techniques. U.S. Army Research Laboratory, Orlando (2015)

16. Ferrario, R., Guarino, N.: Towards an ontological foundation for services science. In: Domingue, J., Fensel, D., Traverso, P. (eds.) FIS 2008. LNCS, vol. 5468, pp. 152–169. Springer, Heidelberg (2009). https://doi.org/10.1007/978-3-642-00985-3_13

17. Ferrario, R., Guarino, N., Janiesch, C., Kiemes, T., Oberle, D., Probst, F.: Toward an ontological foundation of services science: the general service model. In: 10th International Conference on Wirtschaftsinformatik, vol. 2, pp. 675–684 (2011)

18. Bohus, D., Rudnicky, A.I.: The ravenclaw dialog management framework: architecture and systems. Comput. Speech Lang. **23**(3), 332–361 (2009)

Educational Environment of Video System Using Superimposing Symbols to Support for Skill Training

Naka Gotoda$^{(\boxtimes)}$, Yusuke Kometani, Rihito Yaegashi, and Toshihiro Hayashi

Kagawa University, Hayashi-cho, Takamatsu-shi, Kagawa 2217-20, Japan
gotoda@eng.kagawa-u.ac.jp

Abstract. The body movement is composed of a series of postures, and it is possible for some learners to enhance the training effect by becoming conscious of the transitions from one posture to the next as movement. In the case of squats, the movement contains standing and flexing-posting posture factors, and the effect is enhanced by making them aware of the difference between ideal and current posture with some instructions. However, when watching general video teaching materials without coach by individuals, it is difficult for learners to be aware of movements and correct them. In this study, the system generates symbols to present instruction for the movements. The marker pointing movements are attached to a learner on the video by using AR marker to distinguish movement from a change of the posture. We developed and evaluated a video system to support so that a learner became conscious of the movement as improvement steps.

Keywords: Skill learning · AR · Wearable devices · Squat · Superimposed display

1 Introduction

In recent years, some people try to begin exercise to control the life style-related diseases. As simple exercise for health, there are strength training such as sit-ups, push-ups and squat. Among them, squats are whole body exercises that train not only the lower body but also upper body. In bending and stretching exercise like squat, it is necessary also to pay attention to the change when changing into the next posture, and exercise from some postures as well as a procedure and the posture [1]. By capturing the transition from one posture to the next as movement, and exercising while conscious of the transition of the posture, higher effects can be obtained.

Generally, learner has two chances to learn movement, one of the methods to receive the instructor's guidance at fitness gym, and to learn individually as we reference the video materials and texts. In the former case, the instructor coaches not only movement process but also to be aware of correction based on difference between the ideal movement and the current movement. In the latter case, one of the methods get video teaching materials from a video sharing site on the web [2]. In recent years, there are many videos

© Springer Nature Switzerland AG 2020
S. Yamamoto and H. Mori (Eds.): HCII 2020, LNCS 12185, pp. 164–174, 2020.
https://doi.org/10.1007/978-3-030-50017-7_11

produced by instructors, which are published free on the site. It is possible to imitate movements by using such videos, but it is difficult for them to be aware of movements and correct movements precisely by her/himself compared with the former case.

Under the system support by Okuno et al. [3], the learner watches and mimics a visual model which clarify directions for improvement as an emphasis deformation that requiring increase of the lacking element in the learner's action. The combination of instruction presentation and verbal expression helps the learner to understand how to modify the action. When showing linguistic expression, the influence on behavioral learning was seen by changing expression based on the index which Okuno et al. defined. Also, our approach tackles to emphatic visual model similarly, we developed the system that allows learners to learn and confirm gap between the ideal and the current by using the recorded video of their exercise, by giving guidance to places targets that are recognized as improvement movements, it provides the learning of movement environment where movement awareness and correction are possible.

On the other hands, small-sized microcomputers, sensors, and communication modules have been marketed inexpensively with the spread of IoT. Moreover, 3D printers and laser cutters allow individuals to prototype wearable devices easily. Additionally, by integrated with image recognition by AR/QR marker, the combination between video and sensor feedback information can be provided on specified position attached the markers. As more easy approach, a marker of a specific color (in this study, we call color marker) is easily available to realize by specified color sticker/ specialized suit [4]. Through the color recognition, the system can obtain a region or position of the body which is necessary to improve the condition (e.g. lower crotch in the squat). By incorporating a device in the color marker and enabling the correspondence between the position of the marker and the sensor. On the basis of such approach, it is possible to detect and treat with the additional information related to learner's movement, for each part of the body, that cannot be acquired from only the image recognition [5].

Regardless of simple and easy strength training such as squats, it is considered that people who exercise can repeat movements and acquire motion while try and error, so that they can be aware of the movement of each part of the body in movement. Figure 1 and 2 show the training process of searching for the target limit depending on the appearance or disappearance of failure/ establishment about posture hold as a result for better effect. Assuming that the center line is the target limit value of the load to be searched, in the case of no failure pattern and under the limit (see Fig. 1), it is considered that the squat always holds but it is difficult to approach to the limit value and get better effect. Under the condition that has a several failures under safe control without injury, it is possible to search for a place close to the limit value by repeating the practice that squats fail (see Fig. 2). The system makes this goal accessible by giving the learner guidance to induce failure. The learner learns with the goal of squat movement. The cause of failure to learn this movement is to break the balance. In this study, while learning squats, we develop and evaluate a video system to support the achievement of the goals of squats by letting learners break their balance.

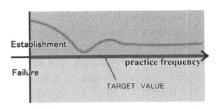

Fig. 1. A pattern of non-error training

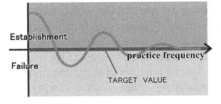

Fig. 2. A pattern of try and error training

2   The Learning Scenario by Motion Instruction

An object of learning is the "hindu squat": the full squat. The full squat is a basic squat and has the training effect of the upper body such as the abdominal and back muscles as well as the lower body. The basic posture of the full squat is defined by following four.

1. The arms are stretched in forward
2. Place and stand feet shoulder-width apart
3. The state and condition of toes are slightly turning outwards
4. Knee stretches to an extent not to bend too much
   (Stretch the knee not to stretch too much)

That movement has the following three.

1. Bend knees 90° to take four seconds while taking breath in
2. Hold the pose when bend knees 90°
3. Stretch knees to take four seconds while taking breath out

Matters to note in this movement has the following four.

1. Keep knees out of toes
2. Apply the empty weight whole the sole of the foot
3. Do not bend the back
4. Upper body shall be perpendicular to the ground

The learner can give high load to the thigh by being aware of these. The step definitions based on instruction of motion are follows.

1. Learn while imitating the basic posture
2. Learn the motion of flow of a goal while imitating
3. Acquire awareness of desired movements while achieving the movement conjunction with multiple part
4. Combine the awareness acquired in achieving the goal and learn the desired movement

If learner tries to achieve the goal focusing on each part of the body in Step 3, learner may need to climb over the basic learner have learned in Steps 1 and 2. In order to learn the target movement, there are stages to achieve multiple goals, and in order to achieve the goals, the learner may fail intentionally as a passing point and it may be necessary to try and error. In the case of personal learning, it is difficult to notice that it is necessary to break the situation once it has been learned, since basic pose and key point etc. are acquired as knowledge and learning is performed after that. In this study, we focus on the step 3 of the movement instruction and give the learner an instruction to induce the result of intentional failure as "error" owing to approach the success of knowing the optimal training bandwidth. We defined the condition to lose the balance as the failure.

1. Minimal the knees sticking out of standing position
2. The angle of inclination of the thigh is close to $0°$
3. Make the upper body vertical

In this learning scenario, the instructor attempt an demonstration, and the movement of the body is acquired by the color marker device, the photographed image, and the list of goals to be achieved are accumulated in the server as a teaching material. The learner selects the accumulated teaching material and performs a learning cycle, and tries and shot while wearing the color marker device. After an attempt, the learner confirms his or her attempt. The system promotes learner's motion correction and awareness based on marker-position and sensor data by presenting symbols. After the confirmation, the learner tries again and reflects the content of the instruction in the movement. By conducting this cycle, learners can achieve their selected goals.

3   Video System Using Superimposing Symbols

We developed a system for learning behavior. This system is composed of four sub-systems: color maker device, web API, web application and monitoring application. learners monitor the shooting data and logging data of the color marker device with a monitoring application. The learners use web application to look back (see Fig. 3).

3.1   The Color Marker Device

The color marker device is attached to a learner's body, and can be acquired by the acceleration, angular velocity, and magnetic sensor of the movement of the body part (see Fig. 4). The device was created using the NUCLEO series NUCLEO-F303K8, which is sold by ST micro as a microcontroller. As a sensor, we used MPU9250 of InvernSense, which has a 9-axis sensor equipped with acceleration, gyro and magnetic sensors of 3 axes. This device is used by the monitoring application and has commands to be executed during communication. This device connects to a PC using a USB cable. communication with the monitoring application is performed by serial communication. The baud rate is set at 11520 and sampling is performed at 220 Hz. The full scale is the acceleration sensor ± 2 [g], the angular velocity sensor ± 250 [°/ s], the magnetic sensor ± 4800 [μ T], the resolution is 16 bits for the acceleration and angular velocity sensors, and 14 bits for the magnetic sensor.

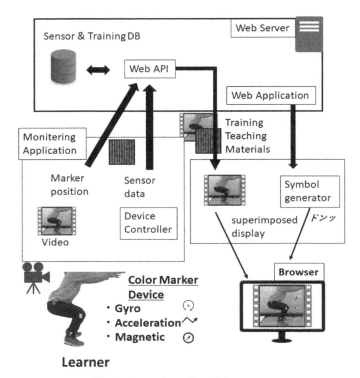

Fig. 3. A configuration of the system

Fig. 4. A color marker device integrated with several sensors

3.2 Web Application

The web application generates symbols that give instructions for correcting the movement of the learner from the results of the training set. The symbol will be presented with being superimposed on the learner's video. In order to make it possible to use even imitation in the early stages of learning, it is possible to browse the video training materials and simultaneously view and compare the current and past training sets. In the video display area of the screen, a symbol indicating guidance is displayed at an appropriate position according to the target, in accordance with the learner's action. The system instructs the ideal movement for improvement by changing the shape of the displayed symbol.

4 Experiment for System Evaluation

4.1 Experiment Condition

We conducted an experiment to confirm whether the proposed learning scenario could give learners guidance that would cause intentional failure. The learning of movement instruction was conducted over multiple sets. In addition, the experimental subjects were divided into two groups, with and without the symbol display, which superimposes the instruction by the symbol when the learner looked back on his or her own trial by watching the video between the sets.

The subjects are eight adult males (23 years old ± 1.5). The procedure of the experiment is the following nine steps.

1. Attach the color marker device to the subjects
2. Explain the procedure and cautions of squats
3. Explain the goal of squats in the experiment
4. Implementation and shooting of an attempt to squat two times in one set
5. Reflection learning
6. Repeat steps 6 and 7 five times
7. Post questionnaire

The color marker device is attached to the greater trochanter, knee and ankle (see Fig. 5). Each a color marker device is detected frame by frame through image recognition. In this training, while aiming at a motion to bend the knee as much as possible while keeping learner back straight, if a learner is about to lose balance, learner will rise without waiting for 4 s. If a learner rises, the movement is done at the same speed as descent. About the symbol presentation to the buttocks and the upper body symbol presentation, start presenting about 3 s before the knee is most bent in one squat of the learners, it is presented until about 2 s after the knee is most bent. The symbol of the knee is displayed, when the marker position on the image comes more than 60 px ahead of the standing position. An example of a series of flow of squats and changes in display timing and shape when displaying symbols is shown in Fig. 8. In this study, squat operation is repeated from T1 to T6. At T2, a symbol called " ドンッ (bump)" is displayed to call attention so that the knees do not go beyond the toes. In T3 and T4, in addition, the symbol " グッグ (jerk)" is displayed, and it is because the waist is dropped to the learner and the thighs are not parallel to the ground. T4 is when the buttocks are most down, where the " ドンッ (bump)" character is squeezed because the learner's knees are largely out in front. At T5, the " グッグ (jerk)" symbol disappeared, and at T6, the " ドンッ (bump)" symbol disappeared because the knee did not come out before the toes. In the example, the symbol for the upper body is not displayed. Figure 6 is an example of a symbol displayed on upper body. This symbol (" ぴーん (pin)") is displayed in place of " グッグ

(jerk)" when the thigh is parallel of the ground. In the symbol presentation on the knee, the text is contracted as the knee moves forward (rightward on the screen). Figure 7 is parameters of movement acquired from image. The stretching rate of the knee symbol is shown by formulas (1) and (2).

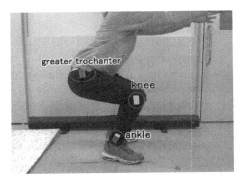

Fig. 5. Wearing positions of devices

Fig. 6. A symbol displayed on upper body

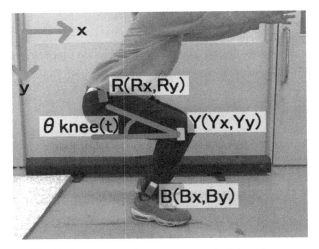

Fig. 7. Parameters of movement acquired from image

$$S_1x(n) = 0.3 + 0.5 \, (Yx_{max} - Yy(n)) \, / \, (Yx_{max} - Yx_{min}) \tag{1}$$

$$S_1y(n) = 1 + 2 \, (Yx(n) - Yx_{min}) \, / \, (Yx_{max} - Yx_{min}) \tag{2}$$

The symbol presented to the buttocks gives the impression of lowering the waist by stretching the shape of the symbol downward when the angle of inclination of the knee is large. The stretching rate of the buttocks symbol is shown by formulas (3) and (4).

$$S_2x(n) = 1 \tag{3}$$

$$S_2y(n) = 1.0 + 2\{1 - (\theta_{knee}(n) - 20)^2 / (max\theta_{knee} - 20)^2\} \qquad (4)$$

- "ドンッ (bump)" means the image that your knees hit the wall.
- "グッ (jerk)" means the image to lower the buttocks more.
- "ぴーん (pin)" means an image that raises the upper body more vertically.

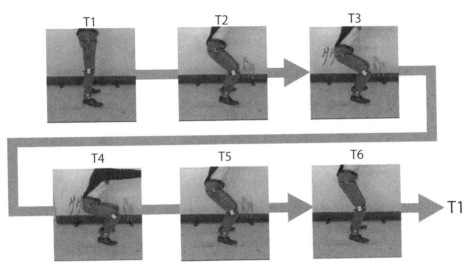

Fig. 8. Changes due to the passage of time in symbol display

4.2 Experimental Result

The movement of the subject with the symbol display and without the symbol display and the movement of the color marker are shown in the graph (see Fig. 9 and 10). The top left of the image is the origin, the y-axis is the vertical axis, and the x-axis is the horizontal axis in them. The x-coordinates about the yellow markers of two trainings including both the experimental and the control groups are shown. In the experimental group, it was found that the second training was to prevent the knee from coming forward of the toe compared with the first training. On the other hand, in the control group, no change was seen in the first and second times.

Besides we conducted a questionnaire about the learner's sense of balance each set (see Table 1). The questionnaire was conducted immediately after training set (see Table 2 and 3). Since the questionnaire was a form of answer on the ordinal scale, the Mann-Whitney rank sum test, which is a nonparametric test, was performed. As a result of the test with 5% on both sides, a significant difference was obtained depending on the presence or absence of symbol display. Therefore, it can be said that there was a difference in the sense of balance in the subjective squats of the learners of the group with instruction by symbol display and the group without symbol display. As a result of the questionnaire, the median of the group with instruction by the symbol display was 2 and the mode value was 2. The median of the group without symbols was 1.5 and the mode value was 1.

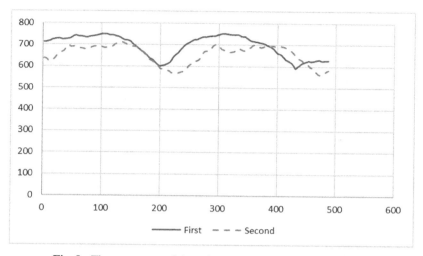

Fig. 9. The movement of the color marker with display of symbol

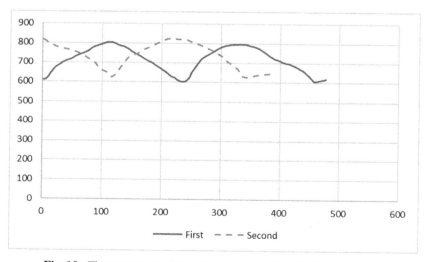

Fig. 10. The movement of the color marker without display of symbol

Table 1. The questionnaire about balance state in training

Q	How much balance was there when you raised your waist?
1	Afford enough
2	A little of margin state
3	No margin state
4	Felt that you had lost your balance
5	Lost your balance (moved your foot)

Table 2. The questionnaire for five sets (use symbols)

Subject	Set No.				
	1	2	3	4	5
A	1	5	2	5	3
B	1	2	2	5	3
C	1	1	5	2	2
D	1	2	5	2	2

Table 3. The questionnaire for five sets (no symbols)

Subject	Set No.				
	1	2	3	4	5
E	1	2	1	2	2
F	1	2	1	1	1
G	1	1	2	1	2
H	2	2	5	2	1

4.3 Consideration

The experimental results have shown that it was found that the learning by the symbol display using the proposal system causes a difference in the balance of squats felt by the learner. In the experimental group, they can be considered that training with high load and optimal bandwidth can be provided as focused training is repeated from the graph. As a result of the questionnaire, the group with the most frequent symbol display was larger. The system was able to show that the learners was able to be instructed to cause intentional failure to "break the balance" in squat training. The system could transmit the movement intention almost same about a waist and the knee compared with a proposal design. However, some symbols did not indicate the meaning of the individual symbols enough in order to be intuitively aware of the expected movement, and some subjects commented that they wanted to know the meaning of the symbols.

5 Conclusion

In this study, in the squat training, indicating the direction of correction related to the learner's movement is represented by a symbol. The support provided by superimposing the learner's body position on the image is proposed, and we conducted the experiment about the effectiveness of the proposal system. The system was able to show that the learners was able to be instructed to cause intentional failure to "break the balance" for new growth in squat training. Future tasks include how to transmit the meaning of symbols to learners, arrangement of words used for symbols flexibly for the purpose of improving intuitive comprehension.

Acknowledgement. This work was supported by JSPS KAKENHI Grant Numbers JP18H03344, JP19K12270 and 19K11463. In terms of system implementation and experiment, Mr. Takuya Ishioka and Mr. Takahiro Kumon contributed significantly on this work.

References

Hirasawa, Y., Ishioka, T., Gotoda, N., Hirata, K., Akagi, R.: Development of a promotion system for home-based squat training for elderly people. In: Yamamoto, S., Mori, H. (eds.) HCII 2019. LNCS, vol. 11570, pp. 492–501. Springer, Cham (2019). https://doi.org/10.1007/978-3-030-22649-7_39

Matsuura, K., Kanenishi, K., Miyoshi, Y., Terao, S., Gotoda, N., Yano, Y.: Development of the VLOG-BASED scenario with cybercommunities interest for experienced learning. In: Proceedings of IADIS International Conference on Web Based Communities, vol. 2007, pp. 272–275 (2007)

Okuno, K., Inamura, T.: Motion coaching with emphatic motions and adverbial expressions for human beings by robotic system - method for controlling motions and expressions with sole parameter. IEEE International Conference on Intelligent Robots and Systems (2011). https://doi.org/10.1109/IROS.2011.6094683

Sugawara, K., Yoshikawa, T., Matsuura, K., Karungaru, S., Gotoda, N.: A learning support system for integrated motor skill by organized training stages. In: Proceedings of 25th ICCE, pp. 451–456 (2017)

Ishioka, T., Gotoda, N., Christian, A., Kunieda, T., Yaegashi, R, Hayashi, T.: Suitable judgement assistance of visualization method for sensor log overlapping on daily video. In: Proceedings of the IADIS International Conference on Cognition & Exploratory Learning in Digital Age, pp. 168–176 (2018)

Appeal of Inconspicuous Body Movements During Spatial Invasion
Frequency Analysis of Movements

Yosuke Kinoe[(⊠)] and Yuna Akimori

Hosei University, 2-17-1, Fujimi, Chiyoda City, Tokyo 102-8160, Japan
kinoe@hosei.ac.jp

Abstract. This paper described a psychophysical study on inconspicuous but distinguishable characteristic body movements while a person encountered an uncomfortable spatial relation with the other. Based on empirical findings, this paper revealed the possibility of utilizing that the characteristic movement which met our three criteria as a new effective indicator in proxemics research.

We conducted four experiments, in which twenty-two participants in total participated. By combining the stop-distance procedure and motion capture technology, 3D movements of a participant's upper body were precisely obtained during a process of spatial invasion. All the obtained motion data were analyzed according to the detection criteria and the detection procedure based on time-frequency analysis. Firstly, the analysis revealed that at least some sort of the characteristic movements occurred at plural landmarks during a spatial invasion. Secondly, in most cases, those characteristic movements specifically happened *before* explicit physical reactions including the utterance of "stop". Thirdly, the results suggested that the characteristics of those movements were different from that of natural vibrations during "quiet standing" and from the movements during "just an utterance". Expanded studies toward a new theory development are underway.

Keywords: Personal space · Motion analysis · Frequency analysis

1 Introduction

1.1 Spatial Invasion to Personal Boundary

Personal space (PS) is a dynamic spatial component of interpersonal relations [4]. People possess and utilize it in everyday social situations. People like to be close enough to obtain warmth and comradeship but also like to be far enough away one another. Personal space can be defined as "an area individuals actively maintain around themselves into which others cannot intrude without arousing some sort of discomfort" [15].

Most of the time they are unaware of its sophisticated functioning, while they are comfortable with spatial relation with the other [10]. On the other hand, it seems that inadequate spacing in close proximity creates states of over arousal and tensions [4]. It sometimes results in a physical explicit behavior such as a fleeing [7].

© Springer Nature Switzerland AG 2020
S. Yamamoto and H. Mori (Eds.): HCII 2020, LNCS 12185, pp. 175–193, 2020.
https://doi.org/10.1007/978-3-030-50017-7_12

1.2 Related Literature

Proxemics on Approach Distance. Proxemics emphasizes research issues on the perception, use, and structuring of space. Over one thousand studies of personal space have been reported. A popular focus in proxemics has been approach distance [1, 5].

Stop-Distance Method. The "stop-distance method" was widely used to measure the approach distance and interpersonal distance between a dyad. In this method, in which a participant usually is studied in a laboratory, a participant is asked to say "stop" when he/she becomes discomfort with respect to a spatial relation with the other. An experimenter or a confederate stands apart from a participant, then slowly walks toward a participant until signaling to halt approaching. The remaining distance between a participant and an approacher is measured [6]. This method had been repeatedly tested and it is currently considered reliable and feasible in laboratory studies [4, 15].

On the other hand, when personal space is used on a daily basis, people utilize it on the base of *perceived*, not on the objective distances [4]. Although distance is an important variable in proxemics, it is an indirect and limited measurement of the factors that make up this invisible phenomena [5]. Yet of hundreds of empirical studies conducted on personal space, Gifford (2014) stressed there were few studies that investigated the *perceived* experience of personal space.

Vocal Behaviors. In order to learn the location of an invisible personal boundary, one of the simplest way is to keep approaching until a person verbalizes her/his discomfort [15]. Verbalizations and complemental vocal behaviors (e.g. angry vocal tone) are useful clues that indicate the point of time when discomfort occurs in a person. The stop-distance method combines both aspects of measurement, i.e. verbal behavior and approach distance.

Nonverbal Behaviors and Body Movements. It is known that the invasion of a personal boundary associates with discomfort and often leads to various form of compensatory explicit reactions which involve fleeing, turning-away and avoidance tendencies [15]. These explicit reactions can be observed as a sudden behavior. Because few study paid attention to reveal a process prior to the occurrence of these explicit reactions.

On the other hand, most studies on motion analysis have been concentrated typically on explicit physical movements, for example, musculoskeletal motions in sports and gait analysis. Few study paid attention to calm movements such as a quiet standing, except for a few exceptions such as CoM (center of mass)-based sway study on the fall risk of elderlies (e.g. [2, 14]).

The question here is what phenomena happen in individuals prior to the occurrence of physical explicit reactions or states. This paper investigates the perceived experience of personal space in this process. We shed light on inconspicuous but distinguishable vibrations of a participant's body during the process. Body movement cannot be translated as directly as verbal behavior, however, it may indicate something valuable about how a person is feeling about the current spatial relation. As Aiello [1] noted, the continued development of methodologies and measurement techniques is one of essential issues in proxemics research. We applied motion capture technology to meet it.

1.3 Research Hypothesis

Based on the existing literature in human proxemics as well as our previous study [10], we created our research hypothesis to be explored in this study.

Hypothesis. Persons perform inconspicuous but distinguishable characteristic vibrations at their specific body-parts when they begin feeling uncomfortable with interpersonal spatial relationship with the other person. This vibration happens in addition to their explicit physical responses to their discomfort.

Research Questions. This paper investigates whether any characteristic movement of a body occurs during a process of a spatial invasion. The following four research questions were established based on the hypothesis.

Q1. When persons are approached by the other person until they begin feeling uncomfortable, do they make any sort of physical movement?

Q2. How can we detect the occurrence of the above movement? How does the movement differ from natural sways?

Q3. When does the physical movement occur (e.g. at the same time of verbalization of discomfort, before it, after it)?

Q4. How does a body move (e.g. its speed, amplitude, duration, etc.)? Which parts of a body link during the above movement?

The primary objective of this paper is to investigate Q1 and Q2 as well as Q3, which mention the existence of the characteristic physical movement and require a methodology of distinguishing the target movements from the other ones. It was a hard problem.

1.4 Our Approach

Methodology for Capturing Target Phenomena

Stop-Distance Procedure + MoCap Technology. We combined two methods of different aspects from different domains. In order to determine the occurrence and the moment of feeling uncomfortable with her/his interpersonal distance to the other person, we employed *the stop-distance method*, which had been well-known method in Environmental Psychology. *Optical motion capture* technology was adopted in order to track 3D motion of a person's body very precisely within an one millimeter accuracy while she/he is approached by the other person. Figure 1 describes a set of anatomical landmarks of musculoskeletal system [13] chosen for motion analysis of an upper-body.

Study Design. In order to carefully reveal the phenomena of the characteristic movements of a body, we conducted four empirical studies from different viewpoints. Table 1 summarizes experimental settings and the number of participants of each study. Twenty-two participants in total (sixteen individuals) joined to the studies.

At first in the study 1, the detection procedure v1.0 and the criteria of the detection of the characteristic movements were defined. According to the procedure, we investigated

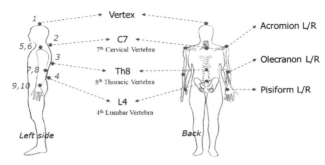

Fig. 1. The anatomical landmarks of an upper-body for MoCap. 1: Vertex, 2: C7 (Cervical Vertebra VII), 3: Th8 (Thoracic Vertebra VIII), 4: L4 (Lumbar Vertebra IV), 5/6: Acromion (L/R), 7/8: Olecranon (L/R), 9/10: Pisiform (medial wrist joint, L/R).

the occurrence of any characteristic movement of a body occurred during a process in which a person's personal boundary was invaded into by the other person.

On the other hand, the study 2 to 4 were designed for examining the *rebuttals* to our hypothesis. The study 2 examined the possibility that the characteristic movement of the study 1 might be the same as sways that naturally occurred while a participant quietly stood. No other person approached the participants there. The study 3 examined the possibility that a behavior of an utterance of "stop" might produce the characteristic movements of a participant. Finally, the study 4 investigated the occurrence of the characteristic movements *even* when a participant *didn't* verbalize her/his feeling of uncomfort during an approach by the other.

Table 1. Experimental settings of the study 1 to 4.

Study	Number of participants	Condition		Procedure
		Invasion by the other	Verbalization	
1	10	Yes	Yes	Stop-distance
2	6	No	No	Quiet-standing only
3	2	No	Yes	Verbalization only
4	4	Yes	No	Stop-distance

2   Study 1 – Detection of the Characteristic Movements

The objectives of the experiment were to examine the research questions: (Q1) when persons are approached by the other person until they begin feeling uncomfortable, do they make any sort of physical movement?; (Q2) how can we detect the occurrence of the movement?

In the study, the occurrence of the characteristic movement of a body were investigated, by creating the detection procedure v1.0 and a set of the criteria of the detection.

On the other hand, our previous studies indicated that our target phenomena of bodily movements during spatial invasion might be quite small ones that were hardly visible, which might disappear within a short duration such as a few seconds [9]. New analysis methods that satisfy both sensitivity and accuracy are needed. Frequency analysis can be expected as a useful starting point for investigating an overview of basic characteristics of those small body movements [10, 12].

2.1 Method

Participants. Ten university students (participant A1-10; age range: 20–23) participated.

Procedure. The stop-distance method was employed. Each participant was asked to stand quietly on a floor in an upright position, with her/his arms relaxed on either side of body, and the eyes opened. From the front direction, an assistant experimenter constantly approached the participant slowly (prox. a step per second) from a distance of 3.5 M. The participant was asked to verbalize "stop" quietly when she/he began feeling uncomfortable. The participant and an assistant experimenter were different gender, and were not an acquaintance. The participants were informed that the study dealt with spatial preferences. They gave their informed consent before the participation. The data collection was performed during daytime between December 2018 and December 2019, in Tokyo.

Measurements

Motion Data. 3D movements of 10 predefined musculoskeletal landmarks (Fig. 1) were captured from eight different directions by using the Simi motion system with synchronized high-speed video cameras (100 Hz). Standard deviation of motion tracking error with the calibration was 0.69 mm.

Video Recording and Time Stamp. Each participant's movement was recorded with time-stamp at a one-100th seconds accuracy. The recording contained additionally 2–4 s before and after an approach.

Interpersonal Distance (mm). Based on motion tracking data, an interpersonal distance was calculated by a 2D distance (i.e. x/y plane) between Vertexes of a participant and an assistant experimenter, according to the center-center model [8].

2.2 Results – Frequency Analysis of 3D Motion Data

All the participants of the study 1 made utterances of "stop" when they felt uncomfortable with spatial relations with an assistant experimenter. A process of an approach can tentatively be divided into six phases: (1) quiet-standing, (2) start of approaching, (3a) early phase of approach, (3b) later phase of approach (immediately before the verbalization), (4) the occurrence of verbalization, and (4b) immediately after the verbalization.

Frequency Analysis for Specific Points of Time (Time-Based Analysis)

Frequency analysis was conducted for each xyz direction of motion data captured from 10 predefined musculoskeletal landmarks of 10 participants. Figure 2 shows the results of frequency analysis for the movement in the front-back direction (Y) of the participant A2's Vertex at six key points of time. The charts show a pattern of each frequency component of the motion at the time of (a) quiet-standing, (b) start of approaching, (c) early phase of approaching, (d) later phase of approaching i.e. 3.45 s before the utterance, (e) the utterance of "stop", and (f) 1 s after the utterance. The vertical axis shows the intensity of frequency and the horizontal axis frequencies of movement.

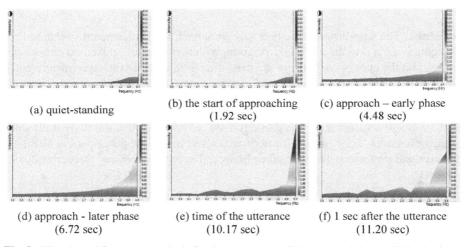

(a) quiet-standing	(b) the start of approaching (1.92 sec)	(c) approach – early phase (4.48 sec)
(d) approach - later phase (6.72 sec)	(e) time of the utterance (10.17 sec)	(f) 1 sec after the utterance (11.20 sec)

Fig. 2. Time-based frequency analysis for the movement of Vertex (participant A2) in the front-back direction at six specific points of time: (a) quiet-standing, (b) the start of approaching, (c) early phase of approach, (d) later phase of approach (i.e. 3.45 s before the utterance), (e) time of the utterance of "stop", and (f) 1 s after the utterance.

Figure 2 revealed that a pattern of frequency component of the movement of a specific landmark (i.e. Vertex) changed along phases of approaching. For example, a pattern of frequency component was apparently different between (a, b, c) vs. (d, e, f). Similar differences were observed also in other landmarks (e.g. Acromion), as well as in other participants. The phase model that consisted of six phases was adopted in our study. Our phase model explicitly distinguished an earlier and a later phase of approaching.

Time-Frequency Analysis of Motion in an Entire Process of Spatial Invasion to PS

Posture maintenance and control are fully dynamic and complicated process [11]. We performed a precise investigation about what kind of movement of each musculoskeletal landmark occurred while a person was approached by the other person.

The Vibration Characteristics Computation. We applied time-frequency analysis in order to identify an overall trend of a change pattern of each participant's motion during a process of approaching. The vibration characteristic computation calculates (a) the frequency of vibration occurrences at each specific frequency and (b) the time-frequency characteristics of vibration amplitude of motion.

Figure 3, 4 and 5 show examples of the results of time-frequency analysis of vibration characteristics of the movements of Acromion-left, Pisiform-left and C7, which were captured during the same entire process of approaching for the participant A2. In that session, an assistant experimenter started approaching at 1.92 s. and the participant A2 made an utterance of "stop" at 10.17 s.

The graduations of color shows the intensity of each frequency according to the indicator (band) at the right-side edge of a chart. If a chart shows the same color graduation, it indicates that the time-frequency characteristics of vibration amplitude of the movement of a target landscape is unchanged throughout an entire process of approaching. If a pattern of color graduation varies along elapsed time, it means a trend of the movement of a target landscape changed at that time.

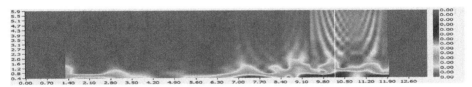

Fig. 3. Time-frequency chart for Acromion-left in the vertical direction (participant A2). The vertical axis shows frequency (Hz) and the horizontal one elapsed time (sec).

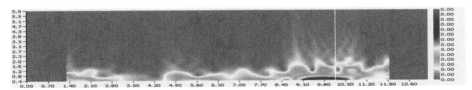

Fig. 4. Time-frequency chart for Pisiform-left in the vertical direction (participant A2). The vertical axis shows frequency (Hz) and the horizontal one elapsed time (sec).

Fig. 5. Time-frequency chart for C7 in the front-back direction (participant A2). The vertical axis shows frequency (Hz) and the horizontal one elapsed time (sec).

The analysis revealed the following.

- The time-frequency characteristics of vibration amplitude of the movement of a target landscape varied at several points of time in a process of approaching. The most significant changes of the time-frequency characteristics of landmark movements were typically identified at the phase of the utterance including the periods immediately before and immediately after the utterance.
- Especially, the time-frequency characteristics of vibration amplitude of the movement of a target landscape differed between the early phase of approaching and the phase of the utterance including the periods immediately before and after the utterance. This difference seemed to be characterized with the several components of different frequency ranges; for example, they contained a higher range around 3 Hz and a lower range around 0.8 Hz.
- The time-frequency characteristics of the movements temporarily became unstable at the moment when an assistant experimenter started approaching.

Detailed Time-Frequency Analysis for an Entire Process of Spatial Invasion to PS
In order to analyze time-frequency characteristics of movement of a target landscape more precisely, we created a set of detailed time-frequency charts below. Figure 6 shows an example of an analysis chart for the movement of Acromion-left in the vertical direction (participant A2). The vertical axis shows the intensity of each frequency and the horizontal one elapsed time. Figure 6 and Fig. 3 used the same motion data.

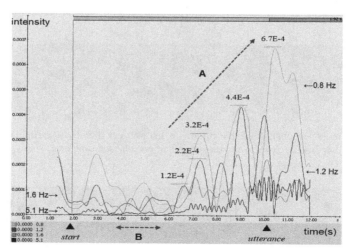

Fig. 6. Time-frequency chart for the movement of Acromion-left in the vertical direction (participant A2). A peak of the intensity of a specific frequency (e.g. 0.8 Hz) gradually increased along elapsed time, in a later phase of approaching (A). The intensity of higher frequency (e.g. 5.1 Hz) held very low prior to the above increase (B).

Based on the detailed time-frequency analyses of vibration characteristics of the movements of landmarks, the following two useful viewpoints were established.

Meaningful Increase of the Intensity of a Specific Range of Frequency. A series of peak of the intensity of each frequency gradually increased since a later phase of approaching until around the time of utterance of "stop". This gradual increase of the intensity significantly occurred at several specific frequencies such as 0.8 and 1.2 Hz. It was notable that a significant increase of the intensity of those frequencies of a specific landmark movement occurred before the participant verbalized "stop" (see part-A in Fig. 6).

Meaningful Suppression of the Intensity of a Specific Range of Frequency. On the other hand, the intensity of higher frequency such as 3.5 Hz and 5.1 Hz sometimes held very low for a while. The suppression was usually found prior to the above meaningful increase of the intensity of a specific range of frequency (see part-B in Fig. 6).

2.3   Criteria and the Detection Procedure of the Characteristic Movements

Based on detailed time-frequency analysis for landmark movements, the detection procedure v1.0 can be defined for identifying the occurrence of characteristic vibration pattern of landmark movement. This procedure was created typically for a situation where a person was approached by the other person.

The Criteria and the Detection Procedure v1.0. The following criteria were established based on the detailed time-frequency analysis of 3D motion data of the selected landmarks. The occurrence of the characteristic landmark movements was *detected* when all the criteria were satisfied. A set of parameters including frequency range and a timeframe used in the definition can be refined in further studies.

- *Criterion #1.* The intensity of a specific range of frequency increases more than 40% of the average of a series of peaks of late 3 s timeframe and continues increasing. The frequency range is assumed 0.4–1.6 Hz.
- *Criterion #2.* The intensity of a specific range of frequency is significantly suppressed and holds extremely low level for 1 s at least. This suppression is assumed to happen prior to the above increase. The frequency range is assumed 3.5 Hz and over.
- *Criterion #3.* The combinations of the above significant increment and suppression that satisfy the above criteria 1 and 2 happen at plural landmarks.

2.4   Results – Detection of Characteristic Movements During Spatial Invasion

Three hundreds charts of detailed time-frequency analysis for target landmarks (see Fig. 1) were created for each x/y/z dimension based on all the 3D motion data captured from 10 landmarks of 10 participants. According to the detection procedure v1.0, we performed the detection of the characteristic movement of the selected landmarks for all the participants A1-10. Table 2 summarizes the results.

Finally, the results revealed the following findings.

Table 2. The occurrence of the characteristic movement of the selected landmarks (study 1).

Phase	Landmarks	Participants										ratio
		A1	A2	A3	A4	A5	A6	A7	A8	A9	A10	
(A) Immediately before the utterance	Vertex	X	X	X	X	c1	c1	X	X	-	X	
	C7	c1	c1	X	c1	X	c1	X	X	X	X	
	Acromion L	X	X	X	X	X	c1	X	-	X	X	
	Pisiform L	X	X	X	X	X	-	X	X	-	X	
Summary of detection		yes	yes	yes	yes	yes	no	yes	yes	yes	yes	0.9
(B) At the moment of the utterance or immediately after it	Vertex	X	X	X	X	c1	X	X	X	X	X	
	C7	c1	X	X	c1	X	X	-	X	X	X	
	Acromion L	X	X	X	X	-	c1	-	-	-	X	
	Pisiform L	X	X	X	X	X	X	-	X	-	X	
Summary of detection		yes	yes	yes	yes	yes	yes	no	yes	yes	yes	0.9

(note) X: detected, c1: criterion 1 only, c2: criterion 2 only, -: no increment identified.

- The characteristic movements of landmarks were detected as for all the participants (10 of 10), in a duration between around 3 s before the utterance of "stop" or immediately after it.
- Especially, the characteristic movements were mostly detected at plural landmarks *before* the utterance of "stop" (9 of 10 participants). But, as for the participant A6, a meaningful suppression of the intensity of frequency range 3.5–5.1 Hz wasn't identified before the utterance.
- There were individual differences in landmarks that indicated the characteristic movement.

3 Study 2 – Testing Our Hypothesis (Quiet-Standing)

The study 1 revealed that the characteristic movements of participants' landmarks occurred specifically during a few seconds before the utterance of "stop" and at least, immediately after it. In order to build more rigid support for our hypothesis, the following rebuttals need to be examined.

- **Rebuttal-A.** The characteristic movement that satisfies the criteria-1, 2, and 3 is not unusual. It naturally occurs while a participant stands quietly.
- **Rebuttal-B.** The characteristic movement that satisfies the criteria-1, 2, and 3 is probably caused by a behavior of an utterance only; not by an influence of a spatial invasion by the other person.

The study 2 aims to examine the first rebuttal by conducting a controlled experiment. We investigated whether the characteristic movement occurred while a participant just stood quietly, without being approached by the other person. The absence of the characteristic movement during a quiet-standing will provide with a strong positive evidence to our hypothesis as well as a negative one to the rebuttal-A.

3.1   Method

Participants and Procedure. Six university students (participants A7-10 from the study 1 and new participants B1 and B2; age range: 20–23) participated in the study 2. Each participant was *just asked to stand quietly* on a floor in an upright position, with her/his arms relaxed on either side, and the eyes opened. *No one approached the participant*, nor stood in front of her/him.

Measurements. During quiet-standing, 3D motion data of 10 predefined musculoskeletal landmarks (Fig. 1) were captured with the same system as the study 1.

3.2   Results

Frequency analysis was conducted for each xyz direction of motion data captured for 10 predefined musculoskeletal landmarks (Fig. 1) of all the 6 participants. Time-frequency charts were created in order to identify an overall trend of a waveform of each participant's motion. For example, Fig. 7 and 8 show the results of time-frequency analysis of vibration characteristics of the movements of Acromion-left in the vertical direction while she (participant B2) stood quietly.

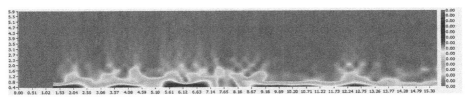

Fig. 7. Time frequency chart for Acromion-left, in the vertical direction (participant B2: quiet standing). The vertical axis shows frequency (Hz) and the horizontal one elapsed time (sec).

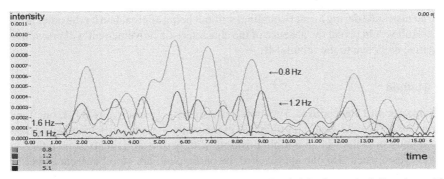

Fig. 8. Time frequency chart for the movement of Acromion-left in the vertical direction, which shows the intensity of specific frequency along elapsed time (participant B2: quiet standing).

According to the detection procedure v1.0, we performed a detection of the characteristic movement of the selected landmarks for each participant. Table 3 summarizes the results. The analysis revealed the following.

Table 3. The occurrence of the characteristic movement of landmarks (study 2: quiet standing).

Landmarks	Participants					
	A7	A8	A9	A10	B1	B2
Vertex	c1	-	-	-	c1	-
C7	-	-	c1	-	-	-
Acromion L	c2	-	-	c2	-	-
Pisiform L	-	c2	-	-	c1	-
detected?	no	no	no	no	no	no

(note) X: detected, c1: criteria 1 only, c2: criteria 2 only, -: no increment identified.

- Under the condition of "quiet standing", the characteristic movement of a landmark wasn't detected.
- 4 (of 24) cases showed a meaningful increase of the intensity of frequency range 0.8–1.6 Hz (i.e. criterion-1), as well as only 3 cases showed a meaningful suppression of the intensity of frequency above 3.5 Hz (i.e. criterion-2). However, they didn't happen together.

The results by a comparison of the study 1 and 2 indicated that the movement that satisfied all the above criteria didn't usually occur. The results indicated that the movements detected in the study 1 differed from natural sways during a quiet standing.

4   Study 3 – Testing Our Hypothesis (Utterance Only)

The study 3 aims to examine the rebuttal-B "the characteristic movement is caused by a behavior of an utterance only; not by an influence of a spatial invasion by the other". In order to test this, a controlled experiment was conducted.

We investigated whether the characteristic movement occurred when a participant made an utterance during a quiet-standing, without being approached by the other person. If the result would reveal the absence of the characteristic movement, it will provide with a negative evidence to the rebuttal-B.

4.1   Method

Participants and Procedure. Two university students (participants B1-2; one female and one male; age: 22 years) participated in the study 3. Each participant was asked to stand quietly on a floor in an upright position, with her/his arms relaxed on either side, and the eyes opened. No one approached the participant, nor stood in front of her/him. The participants were *just asked to verbalize "stop" quietly*, without spatial invasions. Data collection was conducted once for the participant B1 and repeated twice for B2.

Measurements. During quiet-standing including the utterance, 3D motion data of 10 predefined musculoskeletal landmarks (Fig. 1) were captured with the same system as the study 1.

4.2   Results

Time-Frequency Analysis of Landmark Movement During a Process of Utterance.
Time-frequency charts were created in order to identify an overall trend of a change
pattern of each participant's motion during a process of utterance. For example, Fig. 9
and 10 show the results of time-frequency analysis of vibration characteristics of the
movements of Acromion-left in the vertical direction (participant B2-2nd session). In
that session, the participant B2 made an utterance of "stop" at 5.02 s.

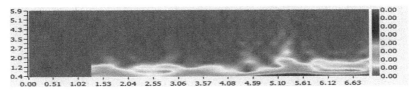

Fig. 9. Time frequency chart for Acromion-left in the vertical direction (participant B2-2: utterance only without spatial invasion). The vertical axis shows frequency (Hz) and the horizontal one
elapsed time (sec).

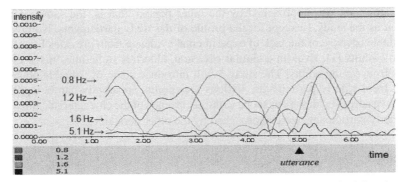

Fig. 10. Time-frequency chart for the movement of Acromion-left in the vertical direction, which
shows the intensity of specific frequency along elapsed time (participant B2-2: utterance only
without spatial invasion).

According to the detection procedure v1.0, we performed a detection of the characteristic movement of the selected landmarks for the participant B1 and B2 (2 sessions).
Table 4 summarizes the results. The analysis revealed that:

- In the study 3 under the condition of "only utterance without spatial invasion", the
  occurrence of the characteristic incremental vibration of landmark movement was not
  detected at any of the selected landmarks of any participant (B1, B2) between 3 s.
  before and 0.5 s. after the utterance.
- Contrary, in the study 1, the occurrences of the characteristic movements were detected
  at plural landmarks before the utterance as for 9 of 10 participants. By comparing the
  results of the study 1 and 3, they indicated negative to the rebuttal-B "the characteristic
  movement was caused only by a behavior of an utterance of stop".

Table 4. The occurrence of the characteristic movement of landmarks (study 3: utterance only).

	Phase					
	(A) Immediately before the utterance			(B) At the moment of the utterance or immediately after it		
	Participants			Participants		
Landmarks	B1	B2-1	B2-2	B1	B2-1	B2-2
Vertex	-	-	-	-	-	c1
C7	-	-	-	-	-	-
Acromion L	-	-	-	-	-	-
Pisiform L	-	-	-	-	-	-
detected?	no	no	no	no	no	no

(note) X: detected, c1: criteria 1 only, c2: criteria 2 only, -: no increment identified.

5 Study 4 – Testing Our Hypothesis (Elderly Adults)

In our recent research, we emphasize on spatial behaviors of elderly adults. The objectives of the study 4 is to investigate whether the characteristic movement occurred while an elderly participant was approached by the other person, that is, the same situational settlement as the study 1 except for the profile of the study participants. No prediction was available because of the lack of experimental evidence from previous literatures as for elderly adults [1]. Even in a similar occasion, elderlies sometimes make different behavior from young adults. The study 4 will introduce some of valuable phenomena obtained from elderly participants. Various viewpoints apparently can be applicable; however, we narrowed down our scope to the occurrence of the characteristic movements while elderly participants were approached by the other person.

5.1 Method

Participants. Four elderly adults (participants C1-4; three females and one male, age range: 70–83 years) participated in the study 4.

Procedure. The experimental settings including the stop-distance procedure were the same as the study 1, except that participants' profile of the study 4 was elderly adults. Each participant was asked to stand quietly on a floor in an upright position, with her/his arms relaxed on either side of body, and the eyes opened. From the front direction, an assistant experimenter constantly approached the participant slowly (prox. a step per second) from a distance of 3.5 M. The participant was asked to verbalize "stop" quietly when she/he began feeling uncomfortable. A pair of a participant and an assistant experimenter were different gender, and were not an acquaintance.

Measurements

Motion Data and Video Recording. According to the same procedure by employing the same system as the study 1, 3D motion data of 10 predefined musculoskeletal landmarks (Fig. 1) were captured during an entire process of approaching.

Interpersonal Distance (mm). An interpersonal distance was calculated by a 2D distance between Vertexes of a participant and an assistant experimenter.

5.2 Results

Three (i.e. C1, C2 and C3) of four participants didn't make any utterance of "stop" during an approach. In the analysis, we focused on motion data which were obtained from those three participants who didn't make any utterance of "stop". In those cases, an assistant experimenter had to halt when she/he couldn't walk any more due to an insufficient distance. The recording continued until the halt.

Time-Frequency Analysis of Motion During an Entire Process of Approaching

Frequency analysis was conducted for each xyz direction of motion data captured from 10 predefined musculoskeletal landmarks (Fig. 1). Time-frequency charts of the selected landmarks were created for the participant C1-3. Figure 11 and 12 show the results of time-frequency analysis of vibration characteristics of the movements of C7 in the front-back direction (participant C1). In this example, a process of approaching started at 12.3 s and halted at the end of the chart (24.5 s). The analysis revealed the following valuable findings.

- A peak of the intensity of each frequency gradually increased since a later phase of approaching until immediately before the end of approaching. This gradual increase of the intensity significantly occurred at relative lower frequencies such as 0.8 and 1.6 Hz.
- The intensity of higher frequency such as 5.1 Hz held very low for a while. The suppression was found prior to the above meaningful increase of the intensity of a lower range of frequency.
- The combination of the above significant phenomena happened at plural landmarks of the participant.

Fig. 11. Time-frequency chart for C7 in the front-back direction (participant C1). The vertical axis shows frequency (Hz) and the horizontal one elapsed time (sec).

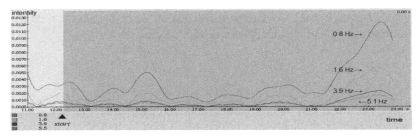

Fig. 12. Time-frequency chart for C7 in the front-back direction, which shows the intensity of specific frequency along elapsed time (participant C1).

5.3 Detection of the Occurrence of the Characteristic Movement of a Landmark

The same framework of the detection procedure v1.0 was basically applied to the study 4. In this study, some parameters of the detection criteria such as a frequency range were modified because of the difference in spatial behaviors between young participants and elderly participants.

Forty-five charts of detailed time-frequency analysis were created for each xyz dimension based on all the 3D motion data captured from the selected 5 landmarks of 3 participants. According to a modified version of the detection procedure v1.0, we attempted the detection of the characteristic vibration pattern of landmark movement as for the participant C1-3. Table 5 summarizes the results.

Table 5. The occurrence of the characteristic movement of landmarks (study 4: elderly adults).

Phase	Landmarks	Participants		
		C1	C2	C3
Approaching	Vertex	X	X	X
	C7	X	X	X
	Acromion L	X	-	-
	Olecranon L	X	X	X
	Pisiform L	X	X	-
Summary of detection		yes	yes	yes

As for all the participants C1-3, the characteristic movements were detected at plural landmarks of the participants in a later phase of approaching. The results suggested that a sort of the characteristic movements of participants' landmarks occurred *in spite of the absence of an utterance* of stop. This result provided our hypothesis with a positive evidence.

6   Discussion

The present paper presented fundamental but insightful data on phenomena during spatial invasion, although more participants and further studies will be needed. Our expanded studies for elderly persons as well as young students are under-way.

Revealing Small But Distinguishable Characteristic Movements

The unique focus of the present study was on inconspicuous but distinguishable movements during spatial invasion. In particular, the present study emphasized a very small movements whose amplitudes were estimated such as under 1 cm, whose frequencies hold relatively higher frequencies such as over 3 Hz. Those movements were hardly visible with eyes or a conventional motion analysis using global coordinates system (GCS). The challenge of the study was the development of the detection method.

Figure 13 shows a basic GCS chart that describes a translational motion of participant A2's Acromion-left in the vertical direction, which was created by using the same 3D motion data as Fig. 3 and 6 of the study 1. Standard deviation of motion tracking error with the calibration was 0.69 mm. According to Fig. 13, max amplitude in the vertical direction of translational motion of Acromion-left was approximately 3 mm in-between elapsed time at 7–10 s. Our detection procedure enabled making such small movements distinguishable.

Machine learning approach such as DNNs can be an alternative way of our future work; however, it was not currently adopted because of its drawback of the lack of transparency behind its behavior [3]. Our current aim was not on a mining but scientific discovery.

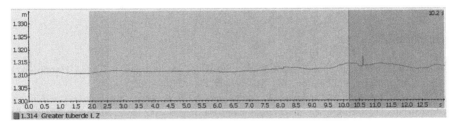

Fig. 13. Translational motion of Acromion-left in the vertical direction (participant A2) (GCS).

7   Conclusion

The present paper described an experimental study on perceived experiences of personal space while a person encountered an uncomfortable spatial relation with the other person. The primary contribution of the paper was to reveal empirical findings that indicated the possibility of utilizing a very small and inconspicuous body movement as an effective indicator in proxemics research. The second contribution was a methodological advancement.

In order to investigate a process of spatial invasion of a personal boundary, we integrated data collection methods of the stop distance and MoCap technology, and also created the initial version of the criteria of target characteristic movements and the detection procedure based on time-frequency analysis of 3D motion.

We conducted four experiments, in which twenty-two participants in total participated. The results revealed that, firstly, the characteristic movements were detected as for all the participants (10 of 10), in a duration between around 3 s before the utterance of "stop" or immediately after it. Secondly, especially in most participants (9 of 10 participants), the movements were detected at plural landmarks *even before* the utterance of "stop". Thirdly, the results indicated that the characteristic pattern of the movement while a participant encountered a spatial invasion was different from that of small vibrations during "quiet standing" and during "just an utterance" (the study 2, 3).

Further empirical studies and more participants are needed to enhance its specificity in reliability; however, these findings are expected to provide future researchers with helpful insights in proxemics study. Three extended research projects are underway. They involve an extended studies for elderlies in addition to young adults, methodological enhancement using advanced sensors, and finally, the development of expanded theory. Our methodology on the basis of nonverbal behavior is expected as a useful tool for investigating undiscovered phenomena which relate to a spatial invasion to personal boundaries, especially, it aims to support individuals who have a handicap of various kinds of linguistic abilities and emotional representations.

Acknowledgements. We thank all the study participants. We appreciate devoted support from AS, YK, MK and our lab members 2018–2019. We thank Dr. Mori and Dr. Yamamoto, who encouraged improving our early research framework.

References

1. Aiello, J.R.: Human spatial behavior. In: Stokols, D., Altman, I. (eds.) Handbook of Environmental Psychology, pp. 389–504. Wiley, New York (1987)
2. Bottaro, A., Casadio, M., Morasso, P., Sanguineti, V.: Body sway during quiet standing: is it the residual chattering of an intermittent stabilization process? Hum. Mov. Sci. **24**, 588–615 (2005)
3. Du, M., Liu, N., Song, Q., Hu, X.: Towards explanation of DNN-based prediction with guided feature inversion. In: Proceedings of ACM SIGKDD International Conference Knowledge Discovery and Data Mining, pp. 1358–1367 (2018)
4. Gifford, R.: Environmental Psychology, 5th edn. Optimal Books, Colville (2014)
5. Harrigan, J.A.: Proxemics, kinesics and gaze. In: Harrigan, J.A., Rosenthal, R., Scherer, K.R. (eds.) The New Handbook of Methods in Nonverbal Behavior Research, pp. 137–198. Oxford University Press, New York (2008)
6. Hayduk, L.A.: Personal space: where we now stand. Psychol. Bull. **94**(2), 293–335 (1983)
7. Hediger, H.: Studies of the Psychology and Behavior of Captive Animals in Zoos and Circuses. Butterworths Scientific, London (1955)
8. Kinoe, Y., Mizuno, N.: Dynamic characteristics of the transformation of interpersonal distance in cooperation. In: Zhou, J., Salvendy, G. (eds.) ITAP 2016. LNCS, vol. 9755, pp. 26–34. Springer, Cham (2016). https://doi.org/10.1007/978-3-319-39949-2_3
9. Kinoe, Y., Tatsuka, S.: Effect on postural sway of the invasion to preferable interpersonal distance. In: Yamamoto, S. (ed.) HIMI 2017. LNCS, vol. 10273, pp. 539–553. Springer, Cham (2017). https://doi.org/10.1007/978-3-319-58521-5_42
10. Kinoe, Y., Akimori, Y., Sakiyama, A.: Postural movement when persons feel uncomfortable interpersonal distance. In: Yamamoto, S., Mori, H. (eds.) HCII 2019. LNCS, vol. 11570, pp. 357–371. Springer, Cham (2019). https://doi.org/10.1007/978-3-030-22649-7_29

11. Loram, I.D., Maganaris, C.N., Lakie, M.: Paradoxical muscle movement in human standing. J. Physiol. **556**(3), 683–689 (2004)
12. Mori, H., Kinoe, Y.: Personal Communication at the HCII Conference 2019, Orlando, USA (2019)
13. Neumann, D.A.: Kinesiology of the Musculoskeletal System, 3rd edn. Elsevier, Amsterdam (2017)
14. Sieńko-Awierianów, E., Lubkowska, A., Kolano, P., Chudecka, M.: Postural stability and risk of falls per decade of adult life – a pilot study. Anthropol. Rev. **81**(1), 102–109 (2018)
15. Sommer, R.: Personal Space: The Behavioral Basis of Design, Updated edition edn. Bosko Books, Bristol (2008)

How to Emote for Consensus Building in Virtual Communication

Yoshimiki Maekawa$^{(\boxtimes)}$, Fumito Uwano, Eiki Kitajima, and Keiki Takadama

The University of Electro-Communications, Chofugaoka 1-5-1, Chofu, Tokyo, Japan
yoshimiki.maekawa@uec.ac.jp

Abstract. This paper reports a relationship between emotional expressions and consensus building in virtual communication. Concretely, we focus on emotions before consensus-building. To investigate the relationship, we employ Barnga which is one of card games for experiments. In Barnga, players cannot use language, and they have not the same rule. In addition, Barnga does not progress without consensus building, that is, the players are required to build a consensus sharing one's thought without language. Furthermore, we introduce an emotional panel which enables players to express emotional expressions in Barnga. The emotional panel have four variations which are happiness, anger, sadness and surprise. This paper conducts experiments with non-face-to-face condition which is similar to virtual communication. From the results, it is assumed that the anger expression is effective to build a consensus smoothly without forcing to change opinions of opponents in virtual communications.

Keywords: Consensus-building · Virtual communication · Emotion · Emotional expression · Human interface · Barnga

1 Introduction

In recent decades communication technologies have developed and we can communicate with our friends located far away with portable terminals easily. These technologies enrich our lives and become essential for us today. On the other hand, these communication services are based on virtual communication, that is, one of the non-face-to-face communications, then, information which we can convey is fewer than face-to-face communications. Such situations generate misunderstandings, flaming. What is worse, individuals are blamed and commits suicide. If all persons who communicate in virtual situations have the same way of thinking, the above problems might not occur, but the persons must have various insides. Therefore, solving the above problems is difficult and urgently necessary. Also, these problems can be said that the failure of consensus-building between persons who communicate each other. Consensus-building means that

Supported by Evolonguistics: Integrative Studies of Language Evolution for Co-creative Communication.

understanding or conjecturing intentions of opponents from their behaviors and heading to the same direction, so, building a consensus smoothly in the situations in which persons are not allowed to convey rich information is a clue of solving the problems.

Then, what information can we communicate in virtual situations? There are two types of information, that is, verbal information which is represented as text and utterance, and non-verbal information. Verbal information is used in now virtual communication, and it is effective to announce pre-organized information. However, it is difficult to describe one's inside which is very quantitative and to convey the inside to opponents rightly. In contrast, non-verbal information has been utilized since earlier than verbal information, so non-verbal information is expected to be able to convey one's inside intuitively. In fact, according to [1], non-verbal information builds impressions that affect behaviors toward opponents. From the above statements, it is assumed that it is important to convey ways of thinking or intentions to opponents with non-verbal information for promoting consensus-building in virtual communications.

The human has many channels that perceive non-verbal information. For example, distances between opponents, eyes and so on. In addition, especially, emotion is one of the primitive channels and is proved to relate with motivations of behavior and good relationships with opponents [2,3]. In other words, it can be possible to motivate behaviors toward opponents and build a consensus between the opponents by managing emotions. Occasionally, we cannot convey what we think to opponents by verbal information. In such a situation, emotions become useful ways to express ourselves and build good relationships with opponents.

This paper focuses on the role of emotions in virtual communications and investigates the usage of emotions for smooth consensus-building. Concretely, we employ Barnga [4] which is one of the cross-cultural games as virtual environments. In Barnga, players cannot convey verbal information and must build consensus to progress games. For experiments, we employ online Barnga in which the players can recognize only actions of the other players. Also, we introduce emotional panels to the online Barnga to enable to emote players' emotions, and the emotional panels have four variations: happiness, anger, sadness, and surprise. From the experimental results, we analyze the emotional panels which lead to smooth consensus-building.

This paper is organized as follows. Section 2 explains how to play Barnga, and Sect. 3 introduces the emotional panel which is an additional tool of Barnga. Section 4 develops on-line Barnga for a non-face-to-face experiment. Section 5 conducts experiments, and Sect. 6 discusses experimental results. Finally, Sect. 7 concludes this paper.

2 Barnga: Cross-Cultural Game

Barnga [4], developed by Thiagarajan, is a card game, and purposes to experience communications with people who have another cultural background artificially. Concretely, in Barnga, players play a card and decide the winner (this cycle is called Game in Barnga) based on different rules each other, *e.g.*, cards with Spade is stronger than other suits for one player, but another player's strongest suit is Heart and so on. In addition, players are not allowed to use language.

2.1   Game in Barnga

As we described, the cycle from playing cards to deciding the winner is called Game in Barnga. In addition, the number of winner selections is called Turn in this paper. We show the procedure of Game in Barnga as follows.

1. Game starts.
2. Each player play a card from their hand to a table.
3. Players select the winner whose played card is the strongest in the cards on the table, and the number of Turn is added by 1.
4. If the selections are matched, move to the procedure 5. If not, back to the procedure 3.
5. Game ends.

Figure 1 shows a flowchart of Game of Barnga. In the left figure, players play cards from their hands, *i.e.*, Player 1 plays 2 of DIAMOND, Player 2 plays 7 of DIAMOND, Player 3 plays 2 of SPADE, and Player 4 plays 4 of CRAB. In the right figure, on the other hand, players select the winner of Game, and colors of pictogram in balloons denote the kinds of players, that is, orange means Player 2, yellow means Player 3, blue means Player 1. In this case, the players select the winner again because winner selections do not match.

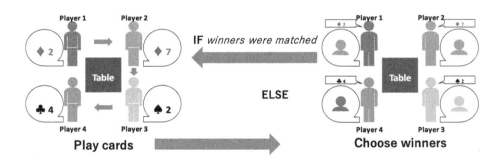

Fig. 1. Flowchart of Game in Barnga (Color figure online)

2.2   How to Play Barnga

When Barnga starts, a dealer distributes seven cards to each player, then, Game starts. After procedure 5 in Game, the winner pile off the cards on the table and next Game starts from the winner. If the players have no hands, *i.e.*, the players play seven Games, the dealer deals seven cards to each player again.

3   Emotional Panel

Players can claim their thoughts and differences of rules by emoting or eyesight in normal Barnga, but, in virtual communication, the players cannot look at faces of the other players, so they can only express with alternative tools, such as Emoji and Stump. Then, we introduce an emotional panel that allows the players to express their inside. The emotional panel has four variations: happiness, anger, sadness, and surprise. According to Ekman [5], the human can distinguish some emotions: happiness, anger, sadness, surprised, disgust and so on, regardless of cultural background. In order to introduce the emotional panel into Barnga, we should not break the premise of Barnga. In short, the emotional panel should be distinguishable for all players, so we introduce the emotional panel with the above four variations of the emotion. However, the players cannot always express their inside such as anger and sadness with the emotional panel. Therefore, we take questionnaires when the end of experiments and analyze the intention, usages, and timing of the emotional panel. By comparing the analysis with the actual players' actions, we analyze the effects of the emotional panel with validity.

Figure 2 shows the *emotional panels* used in experiment. In Fig. 2, the upper right panel is happy, the upper left is anger, the lower left is sadness, and the lower right is surprise.

Fig. 2. Emotional panels

In Barnga, players can use the emotional panels after selecting the winner as an additional procedure. Due to an additional procedure in which the players express their facial expressions, the flowchart of how to play *Game* in Barnga is extended as Fig. 3. The players express their emotions after selecting the winner. After that, if the selections of the winner are matched, Game ends and next Game starts according to the procedures which are described in Sect. 2.1.

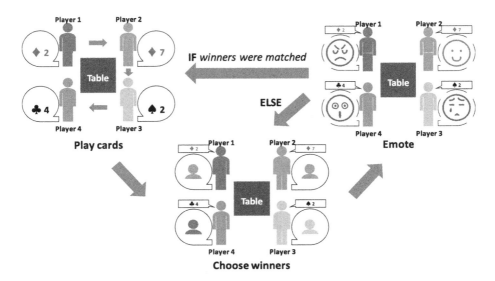

Fig. 3. Flowchart of Game in Barnga with the emotional panel

4   Barnga as Virtual Communication

In order to play Barnga in a non-face-to-face condition, we implement the online-Barnga. In this simulation, players are able to play Barnga through displays without facing to the other players.

Figure 4 shows the screen of simulation after the players finish to play their cards. In this screen, images in the four corners represent the players, the upper left is Player 1, the upper right is Player 2, the lower right is Player 3, and the lower left is Player 4. In addition, the red box represents the hand cards of the player. The player can play a card by clicking an image of a card displayed here. The yellow box denotes the emotional panel which the players can select.

Figure 5 shows the screen of simulation after selecting the winner and the emotional panel. The images of the hand point a player who is selected as the winner by each player. In Fig. 5, Player 1, 2, and 4 selected Player 3, and Player 3 selected Player 2 as the winner, so the winner of the Game is not determined. In addition, Player 1 selects the happiness panels, Player 3 selects the anger panel, and Player 4 selects the surprise panel. If the winner of the Game is determined, images of the field cards, the hands, and the emotional panels are hidden, then, the players play a card from the winner. If not, images of only the hands and the emotional panels are hidden, then, the players select the winner again.

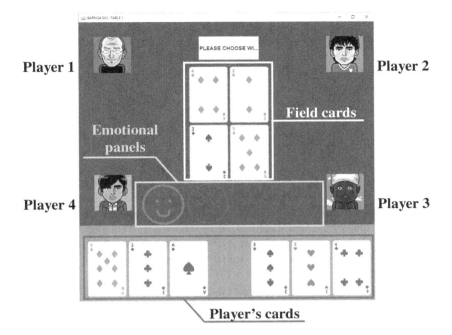

Fig. 4. Screen of online-Barnga (after playing cards)

Fig. 5. Screen of online-Barnga (after selecting the winner and the emotional panel)

5   Experiment 1

We conduct an experiment that employs the online Barnga. This experiment purposes to investigate important elements for consensus-building in virtual communications by analyzing emotional expressions of players just before consensus-building. A point of analysis is the number of using emotional panels before determining the winner of the game.

5.1   Experimental Settings

The number of players is four and the players are taught rules which are shown in Table 1 respectively. They play 28 Games of Barnga. Figure 6 shows scenery of this experiment. The players sit back to back, so they cannot look at the face each other. Because of the rule of Barnga, the players are not allowed to communicate with language, that is, they should imagine the thoughts of the other players from selections and the emotional panels on a display. Under the above condition, we reproduce a virtual situation where information about another person is not informed directly.

Table 1. The rules of the players

	The strongest suit
Player 1	SPADE
Player 2	DIAMOND
Player 3	SPADE
Player 4	HEART

Fig. 6. Overview of the experiment

5.2 Experimental Results

Figure 7 shows the number of emotional panels used just before the winner of the Game in Barnga is determined. In Fig. 7, the vertical axis denotes the number of the emotional panels, the most left bar denotes the happiness panel, the middle left bar denotes anger, the middle right denotes sadness and the most right bar denotes surprise. From the result, the number of the anger panel is the largest and the happiness panel is the smallest. Thus, it is assumed that the anger panel is more effective than other panels, especially the happiness panel, to build consensuses in virtual communication.

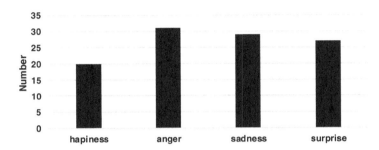

Fig. 7. The number of the emotional panels used just before the winner is determined

6   Experiment 2

This experiment purposes to confirm the effects of the anger panel by comparing this experiment in which players cannot use the anger panel with Experiment 1. Concretely, we analyze the number of turns that is spent until completing 28 Games.

6.1 Experimental Settings

The number of players is four and the players are taught rules which are shown in Table 1 respectively. They play 28 Games of the online Barnga, but the players are not allowed to use the anger panel in this experiment.

6.2 Experimental Result

Figure 8 shows the number of turns which is spent until completing 28 Games, and the vertical axis denotes the number of turns, the left bar denotes the experiments in which players can use the angry panel, that is Experiment 1, and the right bar denotes this experiment in which the players cannot use the anger panel. In Fig. 8, the smaller the number of turns is, the smoother consensuses are built when conflicts happen. From this result, the number of turns in the experiment with the anger panel is smaller than this experiment without the anger panel, thus, the effects of the anger panel for building consensus are confirmed.

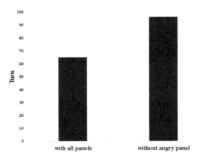

Fig. 8. The number of turn by the end of 28 Games in the non-face-to-face experiments (left: with all variations, right: without the anger panel)

7   Discussion

7.1   Details of the Effect of the Anger Panel

We analyze the effects of the anger panel for consensus-building which is confirmed in Experiment 2. The points of analysis are (1) timings of using the emotional panel and (2) intentions of the players' usage of the anger panel. In point (1), we analyze relationships between the number of the emotional panel used just before consensus-building and turns until consensuses are built.

Figure 9 shows a relationship between the number of used emotional panels just before consensus buildings and a turn when a consensus is built. In Fig. 9, the vertical axis denotes the number of used emotional panels, the yellow line denotes the happiness panel, the red line denotes the anger panel, the blue line denotes the sadness panel and the green line denotes the surprise panel, and the horizontal axis denotes the number of turns when consensuses are built. From this result, the anger panel is used just before consensus building which is reached at fast turn. This result illustrates that the angry panel is effective to build consensuses in short turns and supports the result of Experiment 2.

To confirm the factors of early consensus-building from the anger panel, we took a questionnaire about the usage of the anger panel. Table 2 shows the answer

Fig. 9. Relationships between the number of the emotional panels and the turn

to the questionnaire from each player. It should be noted here is the usage of Player 3. Player 3 used the anger panel toward players who do not grasp the rules shared among the players. In fact, 75% of the anger panel used by Player 3 was used when only one player selected a different winner from the other players, and the winner is determined in the next turn, that is, a consensus was built. Also, Player 1 and Player 4 used the anger panel toward consensus-building, so consensus-building in Experiment 1 is achieved smoother than the Experiment 2.

Table 2. Answers about the usage of the anger panel

	The usage of the anger panel
Player 1	Gathering the selection of the players when winner selections of the other players are different from me
Player 2	Did not use the anger panel, because I did not understand the feeling of anger
Player 3	Announcing the shared rule among the players to a player who does not understand the rule
Player 4	Gathering the selection of the players

7.2   Impressions of Anger Expressions in Virtual Communications

From the answer of the questionnaire from the players, Player 3 used the anger panel to announce shared rules for a player who did not understand the rules. In addition, it is expected that the anger panel is effective to build a consensus in short turns. However, is it true that consensuses are built by the anger panel? in generally, anger expressions are not needed for early consensus building because the expressions can disrupt and stop communications, so it is possible that the consensuses was built as a result of forcing the consensuses by the anger panel. Then, we took a questionnaire about favorability of players. In the questionnaire, a player scores the favorability of the other players in 5 levels from 1 to 5. Also, we discuss if the consensuses are built with agreeing the winner selections or not. If the anger panel is recognized as selfish behaviors or forcing to agree, players who use the anger panel are scored a low favorability. If not, the players are scored a high favorability.

Figure 10 shows the number of the anger panel used by the players. In this figure, the vertical axis denotes the number of the anger panel, the most left bar denotes a result of Player 1, the middle left denotes Player 2, the middle right denotes Player 3 and the most right denotes Player 4 respectively. From the results, Player 3 used the largest number of the anger panel and Player 2 used the fewest number of the anger panel.

Fig. 10. The number of used anger panel

Figure 11 shows the mean of favorability of the players. In this figure, the vertical axis denotes the mean of favorability and the horizontal axis denotes the players. From the results, Player 3 pointed the largest and Player 2 pointed the smallest favorability, and the order of the favorability is matched with the order of the number of the anger panel. Then, in the experiment, it is assumed that the anger panel is not recognized as negative expressions and did not force to change the winner selections of the other players.

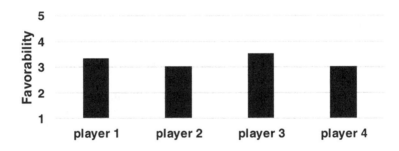

Fig. 11. Favorability of players

8   Conclusion

This paper has aimed to investigate effective emotional expressions for consensus-building in virtual communications. We employed cross-cultural game Barnga with the emotional panel as virtual environments. From the experimental results, the anger panel was effective for consensus-building, and the effect was confirmed by an experiment in which the player cannot use the anger panel. From a relationship between the number of the emotional panel used just before consensus-building and the number of turns spent until consensus-building, it was cleared that the anger panel was effective for early consensus-building. In addition, the anger panel which is generally accepted as negative expressions did not affect the favorability of players who used the anger panel in virtual situations.

Therefore, it is assumed that consensuses are built smoothly by anger expressions without forcing to change selections of opponents in virtual communications.

References

1. Swensen Jr., C.H.: Introduction to Interpersonal Relations. Scott Foresman & Company, Glenview (1973)
2. Tamir, M., Bigman, Y.E., Rhodes, E., Salerno, J., Schreier, J.: An expectancy-value model of emotion regulation: implications for motivation, emotional experience, and decision making. Emotion **15**, 90 (2014)
3. Laurenceau, J.-P., Barrett, L.F., Pietromonaco, P.R.: Intimacy as an Interpersonal process: the importance of self-disclosure, partner disclosure, and perceived partner responsiveness in interpersonal exchanges. J. Pers. Soc. Psychol. **74**, 1238–1251 (1998)
4. Thiagarajan, S., Steinwachs, B.: Barnga: A Simulation Game on Cultural Clashes. Intercultural Press, London (1990)
5. Ekman, P., Friesen, W.V.: Constants across cultures in the face and emotion. J. Pers. Soc. Psychol. **17**(2), 124 (1971)

Learning Support for Historical Interpretation Using Semantically Enhanced Historical Cartoons

Daiki Muroya, Kazuhisa Seta$^{(\boxtimes)}$, and Yuki Hayashi

Graduate School of Humanities and Sustainable System Sciences, Osaka Prefecture University,
1-1, Naka-ku, Gakuen-cho, Sakai, Osaka 599-8531, Japan
seta@mi.s.osakafu-u.ac.jp

Abstract. The importance of cultivating learning attitudes that enable learners not only to memorize key facts but also gain insights into the background of these facts is widely recognized. In this study, we aim to develop a novel learning support system that imparts a positive learning attitude to learners by having them perform historical interpretation activities in an exploratory way using historical cartoons as learning materials that are provided to illustrate historical events. In this paper, we propose a historical interpretation activity support system based on cartoon semantics whereby learners can perform self-exploratory learning in a step-by-step manner according to the historical interpretation process model as well as they are provided with support to encourage their historical interpretation activity according to their interests and learning situations. As a result, we confirmed that the system helps promote the learner's interpretation of history apart from rote learning and has a potential to change their learning attitude of history.

Keywords: Historical cartoon semantics · Historical interpretation · Question generation ontology

1 Introduction

It is important for learners to perform interpretation activities from their own original viewpoints. This not only deepens their knowledge, but also helps to cultivating their logical thinking skills by viewing topics from different angles.

In particular, it is recognized that historical consideration skills are important for studying history [1, 2]. Historical consideration is a knowledge-building activity whereby learners develop their own historical interpretations of historical events by thoroughly investigating their surrounding circumstances. For example, consider the interpretation *Japan's victory in the Sino-Japanese War triggered the advance of western powers into Qing dynasty and opened the door of the imperialist era.* Studying such an interpretation requires a learning attitude whereby learners have access to an extensive range of knowledge about historical facts and causal relations. However, ordinary learners find it hard to identify historical viewpoints that can be used to interpret a historical event (e.g., viewpoints about national strategies from which one can interpret historical events), and often fall back on rote memorization of historical facts [3].

© Springer Nature Switzerland AG 2020
S. Yamamoto and H. Mori (Eds.): HCII 2020, LNCS 12185, pp. 206–218, 2020.
https://doi.org/10.1007/978-3-030-50017-7_14

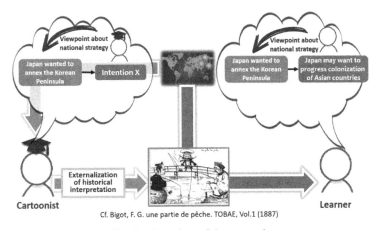

Fig. 1. Overview of the research.

Shindo conducted a questionnaire survey of 159 university students in order to clarify the relationships among their learning strategies and motivation to learn history, and found that students who used deeper strategies such as historical consideration tended to learn in a self-directed and self-exploratory way with higher motivation [4].

It has also been pointed out that self-directed and self-exploratory learning require an enhanced inquiry-based internal self-conversation. Ciardiello showed that a learner's ability to question oneself is the most useful cognitive activity in various learning scenarios because it enhances one's ability to search for an original answer [5].

Yoshikawa proposed a spiral model to explain the generation of inquiries, the transitions of these inquiries in individual learners and learner groups, and the resulting direction of exploratory learning processes in history studies [6]. Based on this model, we built a learning environment where learners are prompted to study historical contexts in greater depth by generating their own inquires [7–9].

In this paper, we focus on 'historical cartoons' as learning materials to prompt self-directed exploratory learning in order to gain a deep understanding of historical events. Our aim is to build a learning environment that uses semantically enhanced historical cartoons to cultivate learning attitudes whereby learners try to understand the background of historical events more deeply and are prompted to develop their own original historical interpretations.

2   Historical Interpretation Activities Triggered by Historical Cartoons

2.1   Historical Cartoons Motivate Learning

It is known that the use of cartoons as learning materials can diminish boredom and enhance the learner's motivation and interest. Takahashi et al. indicated that learners can discover new viewpoints for learning by observing a large amount of information naturally embedded into a cartoon. This is one of the characteristics of cartoons as learning materials [10].

Historical cartoons include strong messages conveyed by the cartoonist, who conveys information about the state and behavior of characters in a historical event by imagining what they might be thinking. The use of historical cartoons as learning materials therefore offers a promising way to encourage learners to move away from rote learning of facts and towards a more investigative and interpretive learning style where they start by interpreting the cartoonist's intentions and interpretations, from where they will be able to investigate the causal relations and background circumstances that led up to this situation.

Figure 1 shows an overview of the research. We use historical cartoons conveying the cartoonist's interpretations from a historical viewpoint as learning materials to enhance the historical interpretation abilities of learners.

2.2 Learning Process Design of Historical Interpretation

To prompt historical interpretation activities using historical cartoons, it is important for us to take into account that ordinary learners do not have the same facilities as history researchers with regard to reading historical documents. Therefore, we need to provide the learners with adequate support for self-directed reading of historical cartoons. In this research, we designed the learning activities shown in Table 1 by referring to three strategies [11] that historians use when reading historical artworks.

2.3 Questions to Prompt Historical Interpretation

Many studies have demonstrated that the usefulness of presenting questions to learners. In the context of supporting history learning, it is also well known that posing questions can help to deepen their historical understanding.

Counsell classifies questions that prompt understanding of history into four types [12]: (i) descriptive questions, (ii) causal questions, (iii) comparison questions and (iv) evaluative questions.

On the other hand, in historical interpretation activities where it is not possible to specify clear and unique answers, learners have to conduct self-directed inference activities. annet van Dire et al. investigated what sort of questions contribute to cultivating the inference activities of learners in the history domain, and indicated that evaluative questions are the most effective [13].

3 Historical Interpretation Activity Support System

3.1 Requirements

It is important that learners do not regard historical interpretations given by teachers as indisputable facts that must be committed to memory without question. Rather, they should seek to deepen their own understanding and construct their own interpretations in a self-exploratory way. However, it is hard for learners to do this without adequate

Table 1. Historical interpretation process via historical cartoons.

Learning process	Learning activities
(i) Read overall components and their relations	Observe and read the states and behaviors of each object
(ii) Analyze facts	(a) Consider what each object represents (b) Consider each object as a representation of a historical background or an expression of some historical viewpoint, e.g., respective national strategies
(iii) Build own interpretation	Consider the effects on subsequent historical movements by interpreting and integrating historical backgrounds and thoughts from various viewpoints based on the results of (ii) (b)

support for self-directed learning. Therefore, the system has to give adaptive support to learners to help them overcome this hurdle. In this research, we try to satisfy the following 2 requirements as well as to adopt historical cartoons as learning materials.

- Learners can perform self-exploratory learning in a step-by-step manner according to the historical interpretation process model shown as Table 1.
- Learners are provided with support to encourage their historical interpretation activity according to their interests and learning situations.

3.2 Learning Support System for Historical Interpretation

We have developed a learning support system for historical interpretation activities that satisfies the above two requirements. This system uses a server-client architecture with a DB server called Virtuoso Open Server, and client systems implemented in the C# programming language. The client systems can capture the learner's eye movements as well as keyboard and mouse operations, and save them as learning log files in CSV format.

Figure 2 shows the interface of our system. The system is designed so that learners can perform historical interpretation activities and then build their own original historical interpretations according to the model shown in Table 1. It comprises four areas: (A) cartoon viewing area, (B) object consideration area, (C) historical background and thought consideration area, and (D) historical interpretation area. In this interface, learners start their historical interpretation activity from area (A) and then gradually build their own historical interpretations in a step-by-step way from (B) to (D). The details of each area are described below.

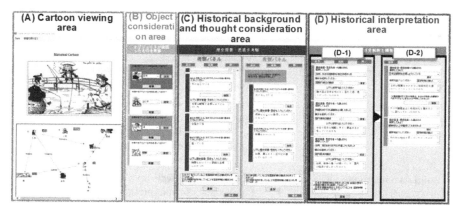

Fig. 2. System interface.

1. **Cartoon viewing area:** This area shows a historical cartoon as learning resource and concept map. The learners examine each object depicted in the cartoon and takes notes on their states and behaviors, e.g., *This man is wearing a kimono, the man on the bridge is watching them trying to fish*, etc.

   When it is detected that the learner's gaze is fixated on a particular object in the cartoon, the system shows a pop-up window that prompts the learner to think more deeply about the object. Then, the representation object the learner tries to think deeply is magnified when the learner gazes at it in more details. The object is also located and visualized in a concept map. Currently, we attach AOIs (areas of interest) to the characters and their states and behaviors in the historical cartoon so as to capture the learners' eye movements on the representation objects.

2. **Object consideration area:** This area is provided for learners to consider each object and the stakeholder it represents (e.g. a nation or organization). The learner associates stakeholders with each object by choosing from a list defined by us (authors of the learning materials).

   The system judges if the results are adequate, and offers suggestions to reconsider based on the historical cartoon semantics of the learning materials specified by us.

3. **Historical background and thought consideration area:** This area is provided for the learners to consider the historical background and the respective stakeholders' thoughts by observing their states or behaviors. It consists of two panels in which they can deepen their thinking about the historical background and thoughts of the stakeholders they wish to consider. By providing plural panels, we aim to encourage learners to make comparisons between different objects.

   The system includes historical cartoon semantics (described in Sect. 3.3) that convey historical background and thoughts (Fig. 3(II)) and historical viewpoints (Fig. 3(III)) with AOIs in the corresponding representation objects. Based on the historical cartoon semantics and question generation framework, this area displays questions that encourage the learner to consider historical backgrounds and thoughts according to the learner's request, e.g., *Let's consider from an international status viewpoint why the Japanese man is depicted with a topknot hairstyle?* This area also features a

Web browser with a search engine that uses Google Custom Search API to support historical queries.

4. **Historical interpretation area:** This is where the learners build their original historical interpretations and historical movements by considering the historical background and thoughts gathered in area (C). Learners indicate their historical thoughts, then either choose a pre-prepared historical viewpoint or create their own interpretation of the historical background. Their historical viewpoint appears based on the specifications in the historical cartoon semantics (Fig. 3(III)). They build their original historical interpretation in Fig. 2(D-I) by deepening their historical thought based on the set of historical viewpoints.

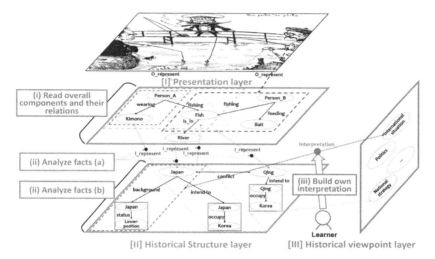

Fig. 3. Historical cartoon semantics model.

When requested, the system asks questions to prompt learners to undertake further historical interpretation with the same mechanism of area (C) (e.g., *Let's consider why Japan wanted to annex the Korean Peninsula by force based on the viewpoint of Japan's domestic economics*). It also provides a search function. When the learner clicks the arrow button, the statement described moves on to area D-2, where the learner can deepen his or her historical contemplation by thinking about its significance and impact on subsequent eras.

3.3 Historical Cartoon Semantics and Adaptive Support

It is important that the content of historical cartoons is represented in a way that can be understood by machine understandable way in order to implement adaptive support mechanisms that can grasp the content of a learning context.

In our research, we propose the three-layered historical semantics model shown in Fig. 3, which corresponds to the historical interpretation process model (shown in

Table 1) as the basis of our historical cartoon learning support system. This model comprises presentation, historical structure and historical viewpoint layers, and can give adaptive support to learners by capturing their historical interpretation model. Table 2 describes detail of each layer.

Table 2. Knowledge layers for the specification of historical cartoon semantics.

Knowledge layer	Knowledge specified
(I) Presentation	Specify respective objects and their behavior and status. They are read in the learning phase (i)
(II) Historical structure	Specify historical background and thoughts of respective objects. They are considered in the learning phase (ii)
(III) Historical Viewpoint	Specify historical viewpoint. They play a fundamental role in historical interpretation in the learning phase (iii)

Furthermore, generally speaking, it is difficult for the system to give appropriate adaptive support by capturing learners' thinking processes according to their interests, since they are tacit and latent. In this research, the system (1) focuses on interactions through gaze recognition and semantically enhanced representation objects to capture their interests and (2) gives adaptive questions based on the historical cartoon semantics based question generation mechanism according to their learning processes.

Regarding (1), by specifying gaze-aware representation object at the presentation layer, the system can capture part of a learner's interests from his or her eye movements on the cartoon, allowing the system to interact with the learner based on the semantics attached to the target representation object.

Regarding (2), by specifying computational semantics according to the historical cartoon semantics model, the system can generate semantics-based questions by using the question generation framework developed in our previous work [14, 15]. More concretely, the system can provide support for historical interpretation activities by giving 'evaluative-type questions' that prompt their inference activities.

On the other hand, one of the things most learners find it hard to understand is the intentions of their instructor when giving evaluative-type questions, because evaluative-type questions tend to appear ambiguous to learners who cannot understand what and how they have to think to answer properly [16].

To overcome this problem, the system provides evaluative questions with 'historical viewpoints' to be considered, e.g., Consider why Japan intended to occupy Qing dynasty as part of its national strategy, based on the historical semantics specified at the historical structure and historical viewpoint layers.

These questions are generated based on the historical cartoon semantics (knowledge base) and evaluative-type question template specified in the question generation ontology. By developing the question generation framework, the system can dynamically generate questions that encourage interpretation activities for various historical cartoons by adding or modifying historical cartoons semantics without having to specify different questions for each individual historical cartoon.

4   System Use and Usefulness Evaluation

4.1   Evaluation Aims and Procedure

We conducted user evaluation trials to confirm whether our proposed system can encourage exploratory history interpretation activities by learners and provide a mechanism that can cultivate a learning attitudes where learners are willing to find out about the backgrounds of and connections between history topics. Table 3 shows a system use flowchart and the task details. Based on the results of a preliminary survey on historical learning awareness [17], we selected 16 undergraduate and graduate students and divided them into two groups of eight people (experimental groups 1 and 2) with no bias in learning awareness. Each group used the history interpretation support system based on the learning design described in Sect. 2.2, and the eight members of experimental group 2 used the system with added adaptive support functions (question display function, historical perspective display function, concept map display function).

Table 3. Knowledge layers for the specification of historical cartoon semantics.

Timing	Details
Learning awareness	• History learning awareness questionnaire [17] • Learning about the Sino-Japanese War • Comprehension quiz (10 questions)
20 min	Historical consideration of the Sino-Japanese War (report writing)
40 min	• Description of historical interpretation using cartoons • Describe system operation and learning activities
15 min	Practice using the system (learning materials: cartoons depicting the first House of Representatives election)
(10 min)	(break)
45 min	Using the system to learn about historical interpretations of the Sino-Japanese War (learning materials: cartoons depicting the situation just before the war started)
20 min	Review of historical study themes (modification of report)
10 min	• Repeat historical learning awareness questionnaire [17] • Answers to functional evaluation questionnaire

Also, since all learners are assumed to have some amount of basic knowledge on the subject they are learning about, the students were asked to conduct preparatory studies on the First Sino-Japanese War (1894–5) and to complete a quiz containing ten questions on the subject (at roughly high school level). As a result, we confirmed that all 16 learners had acquired basic knowledge on this subject (average score: 8.5 points).

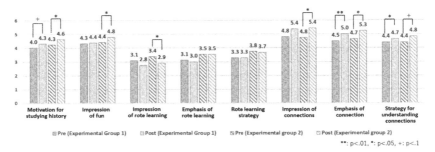

Fig. 4. Results of historical learning awareness questionnaire.

4.2 Analysis Results

Transformation of History Learning Awareness. We investigated the system's effects on history learning awareness by having the students complete a questionnaire on history learning awareness [17] before and after using the system. The results are shown in Fig. 4.

Experimental groups 1 and 2 both showed a tendency of positive transformation in their impressions of history learning (items: (1) Motivation for studying history, (2) Impression of fun). In addition, both groups did not show negative transformations in their impressions of rote learning (items: (3) Impression of rote learning, (4) Emphasis of rote learning, (5) Rote learning strategy), together with increased awareness of strategies for connected understanding (items: (6) Impression of connections, (7) Emphasis of connection, (8) Strategy for understanding connections).

These results suggest that in the context of cultivating a learning attitude where students learn about the background of subjects by supporting historical interpretation activities, it has possible beneficial effects of providing support with this system's history interpretation learning design and support features where historical cartoons are used as learning materials.

In experimental group 1, significant differences were found at the 5% level for two items: (7) Emphasis of connection ($p = 0.008$, $r = 0.81$) and (8) Strategy for understanding connections ($p = 0.033$, $r = 0.71$). In experimental group 2, significant differences were found at the 5% level for five items: (1) Motivation for studying history ($p = 0.017$, $r = 0.76$), (2) Impression of fun ($p = 0.038$, $r = 0.69$), (3) Impression of rote learning ($p = 0.020$, $r = 0.75$), (6) Impression of connections ($p = 0.036$, $r = 0.70$) and (7) Emphasis of connection ($p = 0.014$, $r = 0.78$).

For experimental group 2, which showed significant differences for a greater number of items in the change of awareness of the desire to learn history, it seems that the adaptive support functions incorporated into the system may have contributed to this change. To investigate this possibility, we conducted a detailed analysis of the learner log data, history consideration issue responses and system use questionnaire results of the eight learners in experimental group 2.

Table 4. Some of the description contents reflected in the reports after using the system (experimental group 2).

Learner	Contents of descriptions reflected in reports after using the system
A	After winning this war with large amount of reparation, Japan became more developed, powerful and prosperous, and firmly established its expansion to the south by annexing Taiwan. This may have been the origin of the Greater East Asia War and the Greater East Asia Co-Prosperity Sphere. Perhaps Japan took this as an opportunity to engage in international warfare, resulting in the Russo-Japanese War, the Greater East Asia War and World War II
B	Japan and Qing dynasty were still not fully modernized and were lagging behind other countries, especially Russia. Therefore, Japan was planning to advance into the continent in order to expand its borders and develop economically. It was decided that taking control of Korea was an essential part of this military strategy. In other words, Japan was planning to use Korea as a foothold in order to advance into the Asian continent
C	Since it is connected with the Russo-Japanese War and both World Wars, it seems that this war could be one of the reasons why Japan became the focus of so much attention from the international community

The Usefulness of Concept Maps. In the system used by experimental group 2, a total of twelve representation objects were set with gaze target information by us (the author of the learning materials). Of these, the eight learners in this group looked at 8 objects on average.

The keywords used for web searching included many terms corresponding to the states or actions of representation objects shown in the cartoons, such as "Sino-Japanese War and Fishing" and "Sino-Japanese War and Kimono". Compared with experimental group 1, we found that experimental group 2 tended to use a more diverse range of search keywords.

Although both groups performed history interpretation activities using the same cartoons as their starting points, this difference may have arisen because the function whereby the learners are shown the displayed contents in the form of a concept map by looking at the cartoon directed more attention towards the content of the cartoon, thereby helping to raise awareness of learning taking the cartoon as a starting point.

Usefulness of Presenting a Historical Viewpoint. We examined the average number of types of historical viewpoints set by each group, and found that it was 1.9 types in experimental group 1 and 2.9 types in experimental group 2.

In the system used by experimental group 1, even though no function was added for displaying historical viewpoints, they were able to set historical viewpoints by themselves that could not be set in the preliminary history consideration task. This suggests that the cartoon learning materials contributed to encouraging interpretive activities by proactively setting a historical viewpoint. On the other hand, it is generally difficult for people to create new historical viewpoints by themselves without any support from the system, and in the system used by experimental group 2, the presentation of historical viewpoints that are incorporated into the system beforehand is useful for the students performing their own historical interpretation activities.

Table 5. Correspondence between learner interpretations and answered questions.

Description reflected in report	Contributed question	Learner A's response
After winning this war with large amount of reparation, Japan became more developed, powerful and prosperous, and firmly established its expansion to the south by annexing Taiwan	Let's examine the popularity of topknot hairstyles in Japan from an international status viewpoint	It gives the impression that Japan is not modernized
This may have been the origin of the Greater East Asia War and the Greater East Asia Co-Prosperity Sphere	Try interpreting Japan's international standing from the viewpoint of Japan's opinions of other countries	Since Japan opened its borders, it has aimed to improve its strength through westernization, but this may have resulted in it appearing rather backward to western countries

Historical Interpretations Built Using the System. To investigate the historical interpretation activities performed by experimental group 2 with the support of the system, we analyzed the contents of the reports on historical issues for consideration both before and after using the system.

Table 4 shows some of the historical considerations that learners A, B and C added after using the system. As you can see, the learners constructed their own historical interpretations based on their feelings and on the historical background, and established connections with and effects on subsequent events in history. This suggests that our system—which aims to provide adaptive support based on cartoon semantics—helps promote the learner's interpretation of history apart from rote learning.

Results of Analyzing the Usefulness of Question Presentation. To find out if questions that are dynamically created and displayed by the system based on cartoon semantics and question generation ontology helped to support history interpretation activities, we checked the responses to the questionnaire item "Were the questions helpful for learning?", with possible responses ranging from "1: Not at all" to "5: Yes, very much". The average score of 4.13 suggests that the presentation of questions in history learning activities was positively received by the learners and contributed to the content of the transformation of attitudes to history learning.

To confirm what sort of questions are useful in history interpretation activities, we are currently analyzing which questions contributed to the descriptions reflected in the report after using the system. In this paper, we will examine the statements made by learner A in Table 5 as an example. Table 5 shows the contents of learner A's reflections on the report after using the system, the questions presented by the system that were considered to contribute to the description of the contents, and learner A's answers to these questions. Although this is just one example, it can be seen that the questions presented by the system contribute to history interpretation activities. We plan to analyze other cases in the future work.

5 Conclusion

In this research, with the aim of motivating learners to study the background of topics related to historical events, we developed historical cartoon semantics as a basis for building a novel learning support system that uses historical cartoons as learning materials. and designed the learning activities by referring to three strategies that historians use when reading historical artworks. Then, we developed a system that supports historical interpretation activities whereby learners can perform self-exploratory learning in a step-by-step manner according to the historical interpretation process model as well as they are provided with support to encourage their historical interpretation activity according to their interests and learning situations. As a result, we confirmed that the system helps promote the learner's interpretation of history apart from rote learning and has a potential to change their learning attitude of history.

Further work is needed to develop an authoring tool for expressing knowledge based on this cartoon semantic model.

References

1. Levstik, L.: Negotiating the history landscape. Theory Res. Soc. Educ. **24**(4), 393–397 (1996)
2. Hallden, O., Leinhardt, G., Beck, I.L., Stainton, C.: Teaching and Learning in History. Routledge, London (2016)
3. Spoehr, K.T., Spoehr, L.W.: Learning to think historically. Educ. Psychol. **29**(2), 71–77 (1994)
4. Shindo, T.: Effects of metacognitive strategies on the meaningful learning: precondition to make the learning of history more interesting. Res. J. Educ. Methods **28**, 95–105 (2003). (in Japanese)
5. Ciardiello, A.V.: Did you ask a good question today? Alternative cognitive and metacognitive strategies. J. Adolesc. Adult Lit. **42**(3), 210–219 (1998)
6. Yoshikawa, Y.: The formation and the development of 'questions' about history: on the cases of 'searching history' and 'leaning history'. Bull. Fac. Educ. Yamaguchi Univ. **60**, 337–350 (2010). (in Japanese)
7. Muroya, D., Hayashi, Y., Seta, K.: Semantically enhanced gaze-aware historical cartoons to encourage historical interpretation. In: Proceedings of the 25th International Conference on Computers in Education (ICCE2017), pp. 107–109 (2017)
8. Muroya, D., Hayashi, Y., Seta, K.: Historical cartoons semantics based learning support to enhance historical interpretation. JSAI SIG-ALST-B509-07, 35–42 (2018). (in Japanese)
9. Muroya, D., Hayashi, Y., Seta, K.: Historical cartoon semantics based learning support to enhance historical interpretation. In: 26th International Conference on Computers in Education, pp. 110–112 (2018)
10. Takahashi, S., Takahashi, B. T., Yoshikawa, A., Terano, T.: A systematic approach to manage case method. In: Proceedings of the 23rd International Conference on Computers in Education (ICCE 2015), pp. 154–159 (2015)

11. Kuroda, H.: Sugata To Shigusa No Tyuusei-shi. Heibonsha (1986). (in Japanese)
12. Counsell, C.: Historical knowledge and historical skills. In: Issues in History Teaching, pp. 54–70 (2000)
13. annet van Drie, J., van Boxtel, C., van der Linden, J.: Historical reasoning in a computer-supported collaborative learning environment. In: Collaborative Learning, Reasoning, and Technology, p. 266 (2013)
14. Jouault, C., Seta, K., Hayashi, Y.: Content-dependent question generation using LOD for history learning in open learning space. New Gener. Comput. **34**(4), 367–394 (2016)
15. Jouault, C., Seta, K., Hayashi, Y.: SOLS: an LOD based semantically enhanced open learning space supporting self-directed learning of history. IEICE Trans. Inf. Syst. **E100-D**(10), 2556–2566 (2017)
16. Halldén, O.: On reasoning in history. In: Voss, J.F., Carretero, M. (eds.) Learning and Reasoning in History, pp. 272–278. Woborn Press, Woborn (1998)
17. Kikuma, M.: Analysis of factors influencing high school students': motivation to learn history. Bull. Grad. Sch. Educ. Waseda Univ. **17–1**, 1–11 (2009). (in Japanese)

"Two Way or Go Away": Development of DPP (Digital Presentation Platform) Which Supports to Make a College Teachers Get Two-Way Communication Classroom as a Facilitators

Keizo Nagaoka[1(✉)] and Ryoji Kubota[2]

[1] Waseda University, Tokorozawa, Japan
k.nagaoka@waseda.jp
[2] AVCC, Tokyo, Japan

Abstract. "Two Way or Go Away": If your class isn't a two-way classroom, then you have to go away from your classroom. This gentle call to veteran educators at the university level is the gist of changing the old-style one-way lecturing classroom to a two-way communication venue. The authors developed and started operation of the Digital Presentation Platform (DPP) to serve as the development principle for achieving this call. The DPP has the following three functions: 1) Response Analyzer, 2) Learning Management System (LMS), and 3) Distance Education. In this paper, we report on the Response Analyzer, the core function of the DPP, in terms of its educational function, types and examples of questions, and its effects of some trials. The Response Analyzer is a method for supporting the revitalization of classes required by Japanese higher education in particular: in other words, strengthening the conversion of one-way knowledge-presentation based lectures into two-way discussion-based formats in which students actively participate. The Response Analyzer is very effective in transforming university faculty members, the "teachers" for whom such one-way lectures are the norm, into "facilitators" who can work with the students through two-way communication to lead them towards a network space information world.

Keywords: DPP (Digital Presentation Platform) · Response Analyzer · Two-way communication · Facilitator · University teacher

1 Introduction

1.1 Digital Presentation Platform (DPP)

The authors have developed and started using a system called a Digital Presentation Platform (DPP) in order to contribute to university education in Japan.

The principle behind the design and development of the DPP was to change traditional university teachers, who use old lecture notes to present only their own knowledge, into facilitators who search for the vast amounts of unknown knowledge on the network

© Springer Nature Switzerland AG 2020
S. Yamamoto and H. Mori (Eds.): HCII 2020, LNCS 12185, pp. 219–230, 2020.
https://doi.org/10.1007/978-3-030-50017-7_15

together with their students from the classroom. The goals and methods maybe change as the technological environment changes, but the principle does not. It is stable.

The DPP principle is not just the digitization of educational data, but the digitalization of the educational environment. The DPP has the following three functions.

1) Response Analyzer (also known as the "Audience response system" or "Clicker")
2) LMS (Learning Management System)
3) Distance Education

*1. DPP is a cloud service. If the teaching environment has Wi-Fi, it can be used anytime, anyplace.

*2. DPP is a function of the KK^2 site. Instructors and learners need to register as web members on the KK^2 site to use the DPP. $KK^2 \Rightarrow$ www.kk2.ne.jp.

*3. The DPP aims to ensure learning service quality that meets the basic requirements of ISO29990.

*4. The KK^2 Digital Presentation Platform has been granted a patent as of April 5, 2019, for Media Links Co., Ltd. Patent No. 6507328.

Figure 1 shows the outline of the DPP system.

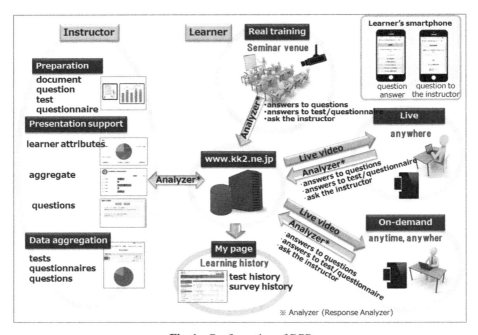

Fig. 1. Configuration of DPP

This paper presents the main function of the Response Analyzer, as it is the function most specialized for two-way interactivity in classrooms, the main purpose of the DPP.

The development and implementation of the first Response Analyzer system, using cellphones supported by AVCC, has already been reported [1].

The DPP that has been developed now is not just about reforming education by getting students to actively participate in classes, but targets what is perhaps the traditional essence of the university lecturer; is something that works on that. Thus, the DPP slogan is "Two Way or Go Away," a stern yet gentle phrase. In other words, it calls on university lecturers to "leave the classroom if your classes cannot be two-way."

The authors have already reported on the former HCIIs, which they developed based on the same goal of support university education as an education and learning system to support two-way style participation in classes and its use in seminars(small and discussion based classes) [2–5].

The development of DPP of this time as an extension of these previous results provides a qualitative assurance.

2   Background to This R&D: The Current Status of Japanese Society and Universities

2.1   The Current Status of Japanese Society

Today, Japanese universities are required to revitalize their on-campus classes even further. There is a policy of reinforcing two-way communication between teachers and students in many classes, and the reason this is happening is because the one-way knowledge presentation education and learning is already shifting to more effective distance education or e-learning formats, which has been already implemented off campus.

The globalization of contemporary society and the influence of ICT that this trend is probably common to any university in the world, but this is a particularly urgent task for Japan.

From the 1970s to the 1990s, Japan succeeded in becoming the most industrialized country in the world, and its economic power was experiencing a golden age as in the book "Japan as Number One" by Ezra F. Vogel [6]. Vogel's book states that the foundation for Japan's rapid economic growth was the interest in learning and the reading habits of the Japanese. As proof of these desires, Vogel noted the fact that the total amount of time spent in reading by Japanese was twice that of Americans, and the huge numbers of newspapers published. This diligence and seriousness, which could be termed the national character of the Japanese, allowed an unrivalled strength among industrial societies.

However, Japan's international competitiveness has tumbled from 1st in 1992 to 30th by May 2019 (according to the IMD World Competitiveness Rankings [7]). Social structures have drastically changed, and Japanese companies, which once were famed throughout the world, are now being swung around by GAFA. The top headline for the Nikkei(Japanese Economics) newspaper on January 1, 2020, was "The Rusting Formula for Growth."

There are a few intriguing and mysterious episodes that explain how Japan came to be this way.

Episode 1: Educational Reforms 75 Years Ago
The General Headquarters (GHQ) of the Allied Occupation of Japan following WW2 carried out the following three educational reforms [8].

(1) The old "injection"-style learning was to be changed into debate-style education which promotes independent activities by students.
(2) Students were to learn not just from textbooks, but going out into the community to see, listen, and learn in hands-on education.
(3) The use of audio-visual materials was to be heavily promoted.

This was 75 years ago. If we replaced "audio-visual materials" in (3) with ICT, then these could be identical with what is being called for today. It is fascinating just how resistant to change Japanese education is.

Episode 2: Undergrounding
"Undergrounding is the replacement of overhead cables providing electrical power or telecommunications" [9]. An egregious example of not changing is the removal of electric poles. In other words, whether or not to bury electrical lines underground. Everyone including Japanese has long understood how their removal has merits both in terms of the visual landscape and in dealing with disasters, but, as shown in Fig. 2, Japanese cities are well behind the curve compared to major cities overseas. This maybe shows a lack of bold resolution based on the gentle national character.

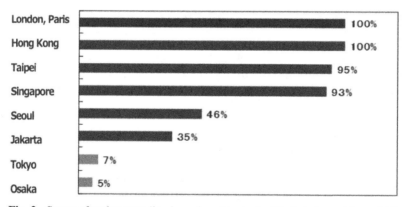

Fig. 2. Status of undergrounding in major cities in the West, Asia, and Japan [10]

In the past, Japan did its best catch up to the industrialized Western world through unifying its citizenry. It succeeded in doing so, joining the ranks of advanced nations. If Japan has a clear goal, like catching up to Western economies, it can unify and use its unequalled diligence as a strength. However, in an era of maturity and uncertainty, Japan appears to finds itself without goals, confused. The issue of burying power lines is perhaps symbolic of its inability to make bold decisions and inflexibility.

Episode 3: A Country of Bold Decisions
There are examples of countries that made successful bold decisions all over the world. One is Finland, which on December 10, 2019, elected the world's youngest female prime minister, 34 years old. Olli-Pekka Heinonen, appointed as Finland's Minister of

Education at just 29 years of age in 1994, took a country where more than 20% of its five million people were out of work and, through bold reforms to education, granting schools a great deal of discretion, turned it into one which was ranked by PISA (Programme for International Student Assessment) as top academic nation in both 2000 and 2003.

We are yet to see this sort of bold decision-making in Japanese education. However, if we aim to restore the unified, knowledge acquisition-based study based on the earlier success story of the "economic miracle," today's Japanese youth, born in a mature society, probably lack both the quality and quantity to compete with the youth of China and India. Japan's university education is faced with the need to make bold reforms. We need the "**advanced education**" to suit the changing times.

2.2 So What is "Advanced Education"?

In the sense of offering a bird's-eye-view of this background, Fig. 3 presents the learning that Japanese students should aim for, along with education and learning-related trends over time. There are various theories discussed elsewhere regarding the learning principles in the figure, but here they have been shown as three stages. As society changes over time, two-way participatory or discussion-based classroom formats become even more necessary.

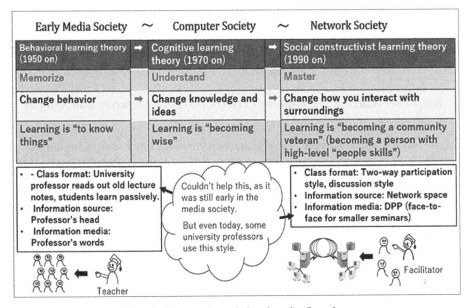

Fig. 3. Temporal trends in education/learning

Today, the knowledge and information that people require exists in the space of the internet. This space contains vastly more knowledge than that previously in the exclusive possession of the university professor. So, it is clear that what humans need to do is to extract that, utilize it, and boldly create new ideas themselves. For students, the role of the university campus is to provide a venue for training towards mastering this essence.

The following section provides an explanation of Fig. 3.

First, as is shown at the left of the topmost line in Fig. 3, shortly after WW2 ended, "**behavioral learning**" theory became popular, and was successful as a knowledge acquisition method suited for an industrializing society. Conditioned responses, as made famous by Pavlov's dog, were applied to human learning, and learning was considered to be changes in actions that could be observed as being able to accomplish something. In plain speech, learning was, as the second line underneath states, "memorizing". In other words, the goal of learning for students was to know things.

However, human learning is not as simple as being able to be explained just by behavioral learning theory. So "**cognitive learning**" theory was then propounded. This is akin to "understanding" on a slightly more advanced level. This is systematizing and mastering knowledge rather than behavior in one's own fashion, and the goal of students shifted to becoming wise.

Whether behavioral learning theory or cognitive learning theory, these are just changes in the knowledge inside one's head. But what the world really needs from learning is social "**constructivism learning**" theory, which considers attaining mastering in more practical terms so as to become a person useful to their community. Rather than memorizing or understanding existing knowledge, students seek out this knowledge themselves, mastering the competency (the forms and characteristics of the behavior of a top performer) in their community, using intellectual behavior located in a more upstream process. The goal of learning here is to "become a veteran".

This would be where the "**advanced education**" that should be aimed at for the time being fits in.

2.3   Response Analyzer is a Toolset to Train University Lecturers into Veteran Facilitators

Over the last few decades, the ICT-based media technology environment for university education has changed in the same way as for general society. Before that, when there was no media technology environment, knowledge only existed in the professors' heads, and students had to carefully note down and remember what the professors were saying in the classroom. This was how classes were conducted back then. Today, however, specialist knowledge exists in a network space that vastly outstrips the professor's head in terms of both quality and quantity, and anyone can easily access it.

University lecturers have taken on the role of facilitators who teach students how to utilize knowledge, and how to spread creative ideas and communicate with others, helping them master it. They may have a lot more experience as a teacher, but these professors are just beginners at being facilitators, so getting support from the Response Analyzer, the core function of the DPP, as a toolset for training them to become veteran facilitators, will allow them to be so for the first time. Preparations for using the Response Analyzer require from university lecturers "**a little effort and much content arrangement**."

3   Response Analyzer, Functions and Effects

3.1   Response Analyzer Smartphone Screens

This paper is mainly concerned with the Response Analyzer, the core function of the DPP. This is because it is a function particularly specialized in making classes two-way interactivity.

Figure 4 shows an example of a student learning process in class using the Response Analyzer.

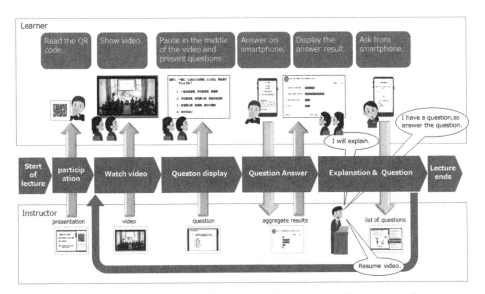

Fig. 4. Example of student learning processes in class using Response Analyzer

There are five Response Analyzer smartphone screens available: the start screen and four types of question screen.

1)   Start
2)   Question
3)   Test
4)   Questionnaire
5)   Asking Instructor

The Figures below, from 5 1) to 5), show illustrations of sample screens for the start screen and the four others listed above. The screen design has a great deal of impact on how easy something is to use in practical terms, so it is important to have an easy-to-use interface. Ease of use is, by extension, an important element in achieving two-way communication that makes use of the DPP Response Analyzer function.

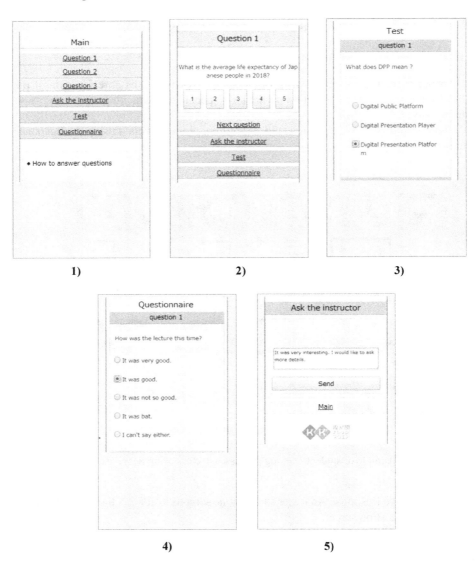

Fig. 5. 1) Start. 2) Question. 3) Test. 4) Questionnaire. 5) Asking Instructor

3.2 Response Analyzer Questions

Based on the authors' experiences, various examples of Response Analyzer questions previously encountered are shown in Table 1.

Table 1. Various examples of Response Analyzer questions

1)	"How do you feel today?": Breaks the ice
2)	"Which is the right answer?": Knowledge-testing (knowledge retaining)
3)	"What do you think?": Views and opinions (encouraging introspection)
4)	"Choose the appropriate one": Questionnaire (understanding situation)
5)	"What do you all think about the 'Social constructivist learning theory' we discussed in today's class?": Questions related to the instructor's lecture (towards deeper understanding)
6)	[Student-posed Question 1] "I'd like everyone's opinions on balancing study and part-time jobs": Learning about the existence of diverse opinions through debate among students regarding class content
7)	[Student-posed Question 2] "Are you seeing anyone?": Using fun questions to enliven the class

This expansion of communication methods brings a new environment to university campuses.

The ice-breaking in 1) above is effective when done at the start of the term or semester, when the instructor and the students meet for the first time. In particular, new students are often nervous about taking their first university classes, and this gives them a sense of security and familiarity. Number 2) is an orthodox method for using the Response Analyzer. It is used to ask about factual knowledge.

As students have been spending the years leading up to their entrance examinations training in giving the only correct answer to test questions, all their mental energy has been directed towards getting the right answer, and they are often deathly afraid of giving the wrong answer. The use of 6) and 7) are especially desirable for emphasizing the action of spreading information rather than correct answers, and creating an opportunity for practicing this.

Table 2. is an example of 3) Views and opinions (encouraging introspection). This question was actually used in the Educational Media Science in the 2017 academic year at Waseda University's School of Human Sciences. The actual responses to this question are shown in Fig. 6.

There are no correct answers to this question. It is about finding out what the students think and feel. Showing the response opinion handouts to the students will lead to even further discussion as they become aware of what the overall answer trends are and what others are thinking and feeling.

Table 2. Example of a question type: views and opinions (encouraging introspection)

Q. Which of the following opinions regarding school fees at Japanese universities do you agree with? (Consider this not just from the perspective of a student, but from the perspective of a leader of society.)

1) I agree that the introduction of mass-production-style education (large classes) would lower fees.

2) Classes need to be smaller to ensure quality is maintained. High fees are an unfortunate but unavoidable consequence.

3) Efforts should be made to reduce the burden of school fees (by giving students tax or economic breaks compared with working people of the same generation).

4) There should be wide-spread introduction of distance learning where people can learn anytime, any place, allowing higher education regardless of age and smashing the current academic career-based society.

5) Other

No.	Response Content	No. of Responses	Response Rate	
1	I agree that the introduction of mass-production-style education (large classes) would lower fees.	7	12.7%	
2	Classes need to be smaller to ensure quality is maintained. High fees are an unfortunate but unavoidable consequence.	13	23.6%	
3	Efforts should be made to reduce the burden of school fees (by giving students tax or economic breaks compared with working people of the same generation).	9	16.3%	
4	There should be wide-spread introduction of distance learning where people can learn anytime, any place, allowing higher education regardless of age and smashing the current academic career-based society.	15	27.2%	
5	Other	3	5.4%	
No response		8	14.5%	
Total		55		

Fig. 6. Responses for question in Table 2

3.3 Effects of Response Analyzer

Effects regarding quality improvement to classes: opinions of students and teachers obtained in trial classes conducted by universities, companies, corporations, etc. are shown below.

1. Bi-directionality: Classes involved the teacher asking questions and thinking about the answers, so I didn't get sleepy.
2. Knowledge retention: Issues raised, answered, and immediate feedback. Easy to remember knowledge.
3. Comparing opinions with others: I liked being able to know what others thought.

4. Thinking about non-regular questions: Debate on questions without a single right answer.
5. Meaning to participatory-style classes: You need to put out your own ideas and actively take part. Unfortunately, some students couldn't get past the idea of scoring points by selecting the most common choices from among what others were saying.
6. Good that attendance is simple: In old-style classrooms, the TA hands out and collects attendance cards, so it takes about five to ten minutes before the actual class can begin.
7. Labor-saving: Attendance data, question response data, and so on, which the instructor would have to do manually before, is now automated.
8. Environmentally-conscious: Not using paper helps save the planet.
9. Saves on storage space: The storage of paper media for class data which university regulations require to be stored. All the data stored on this paper media is now automatically stored electronically, saving space provided by DPP.
10. (Negative!) Unhappiness with individual identification: Initially, there was a function to identify individuals based on their seating positions, but students this semester tend to dislike speaking in front of large numbers and so this function is no longer used as it was not popular.

4   Conclusion

The DPP system was created, developed, and operated based on the experiences and track records of the authors in order to respond to the social expectations placed on Japanese university education today. This paper has presented the construction of principles and development of functions of this research and development, as well as its educational and learning effectiveness of the Response Analyzer.

We believe that the DPP, particularly the Response Analyzer function, is an effective method for strongly supporting revitalizing the classes required in Japanese university education today, or in other words, changing mono-directional knowledge presentation-style university classes into bi-directional discussion-based classes in which students actively participate.

Research and development of the DPP is being actively promoted, and we are currently moving ahead with practical trials in universities and company training sessions to verify its educational effectiveness and deployment of revolutionary methods.

Acknowledgement. The authors would like to thanks everyone at the AVCC and the members of the "Education Digitalization Research group".

References

1. Nagaoka, K.: A response analyzer system utilizing mobile phones. In: Proceedings of The Fourth IASTED International Conference on WEB-BASED EDUCATION WBE 2005, no. 461–38, Grindelwald, Switzerland, 21–23 February 2005, pp. 579–584, February 2005

2. Kometani, Y., Nagaoka, K.: Development of a seminar management system. In: Yamamoto, S. (ed.) HIMI 2015. LNCS, vol. 9173, pp. 350–361. Springer, Cham (2015). https://doi.org/10.1007/978-3-319-20618-9_35

3. Kometani, Y., Nagaoka, K.: Construction of a literature review support system using latent dirichlet allocation. In: Yamamoto, S. (ed.) HIMI 2016. LNCS, vol. 9735, pp. 159–167. Springer, Cham (2016). https://doi.org/10.1007/978-3-319-40397-7_16

4. Kometani, Y., Nagaoka, K.: Development of a seminar management system: evaluation of support functions for improvement of presentation skills. In: Yamamoto, S. (ed.) HIMI 2017. LNCS, vol. 10274, pp. 50–61. Springer, Cham (2017). https://doi.org/10.1007/978-3-319-58524-6_5

5. Kometani, Y., Yatagai, M., Nagaoka, K.: Analysis of student activity in a virtual seminar using a seminar management system. In: Yamamoto, S., Mori, H. (eds.) HIMI 2018. LNCS, vol. 10905, pp. 278–287. Springer, Cham (2018). https://doi.org/10.1007/978-3-319-92046-7_25

6. Vogel, E.F.: Japan as Number One: Lessons for America. Harvard University Press, Cambridge (1979). ISBN 0674472152

7. IMD. https://www.imd.org/news/updates/singapore-topples-united-states-as-worlds-most-competitive-economy/. Accessed Jan 2020

8. Ministry of Education. Culture, Sports, Science and Technology, Editorial Committee for the School System Centennial. https://www.mext.go.jp/b_menu/hakusho/html/others/detail/1317571.htm. Accessed Jan 2020

9. (From wikipedia). https://en.wikipedia.org/wiki/Undergrounding. Accessed Jan 2020

10. Ministry of Land, Infrastructure, Transport and Tourism. http://www.mlit.go.jp/road/road/traffic/chicyuka/chi_13_01.html. Accessed Jan 2020

A Comparison of Cartoon Portrait Generators Based on Generative Adversarial Networks

Yusuke Nakashima$^{(\boxtimes)}$ and Yuichi Bannai

Kanagawa Institute of Technology, Kanagawa, Japan
s1985006@cce.kanagawa-it.ac.jp, bannai@ic.kanagawa-it.ac.jp

Abstract. Cartoon portraits are deformed figures that capture the appearance and characteristics of people, and are often used to express one's image in applications such as social media, games, application profiles, and avatars. Current research regarding the translation of facial images into cartoon portraits focuses on translation methods that use unsupervised learning and methods for translating each part individually. However, studies that reflect the unique personality of professional illustrators have yet to be published. In this study, we examine a suitable network for reflecting the unique personality of a professional illustrator. Specifically, we will consider four networks: pix2pix, Cycle Generative Adversarial Network (CycleGAN), Paired CycleGAN, and Cyclepix. The main difference between these is the loss function. Pix2pix takes the error between the training data and the generated data. However, the main difference in CycleGAN is that it takes the error between the input data and the re-converted data obtained by further translating the generated data. Cyclepix takes both errors. Additionally, pix2pix and Paired CycleGAN require that the input of the discriminator be input data and generated data pairs. The difference between CycleGAN and Cyclepix is that only the input of the discriminator is generated data. Using the cycle consistency loss, considering only the input of the discriminator as generated data, and using the L1 Loss for supervised learning, the experimental results showed that the evaluation of CycleGAN and Cyclepix was high. This is useful for generating high-precision cartoon portraits.

Keywords: Cartoon portraits · Generative Adversarial Network · Deep learning

1 Introduction

Cartoon portraits are used in various contexts such as social media, blog games, application profiles, and avatars. In Japan, it is common to use avatar portraits instead of face photos to express one's identity. Because drawing a portrait requires certain senses and skills, it is difficult for those who do not have such skills to draw a portrait. Therefore, it is becoming increasingly important to create a system that automatically generates portraits.

In previous studies, the website "photoprocessing.com" [1] created images with reduced color and brightness, and added lines to the images to create facial contours. However, "photoprocessing.com" has the following issues: the parameters must be

© Springer Nature Switzerland AG 2020
S. Yamamoto and H. Mori (Eds.): HCII 2020, LNCS 12185, pp. 231–244, 2020.
https://doi.org/10.1007/978-3-030-50017-7_16

adjusted manually, the resulting portrait is a traced image of the photo, and if there are pixels with different RGB values for the face, those pixels are regarded as edges. According to Wu et al. [2], the system acquires features from a facial image, and performs a nonlinear transformation to obtain parameters for drawing a portrait using a neural network. The portrait is generated from the obtained parameters using a portrait drawing tool. As a result, caricatures with similar characteristics may be generated. Currently, several Generative Adversarial Networks (GANs) have been proposed to convert facial images into portraits. CariGANs [3] uses unsupervised learning to convert face photos into portraits, and APDrawingGAN [4] converts each part of the face individually. CariGANs prepares portraits drawn by various illustrators and carries out learning without associating the input images with the portraits serving as teachers. Therefore, the learning that reflects the individuality of each illustrator cannot be performed. APDrawingGAN does not focus on the unique personal touch of illustrators because the teacher data used consists of traced portraits.

In this study, we propose a method for generating a caricature through deep learning with a small amount of training data using a Generative Adversarial Network (GAN). After using a GAN to learn from a pair consisting of a face image and a portrait drawn by a professional illustrator, the test image is input into the GAN to generate a portrait. For the learning process, the training data was prepared so that gender and age could be distributed equally. A comparison is made between the previous methods, pix2pix and CycleGAN; and the proposed methods, Paired-CycleGAN and Cyclepix. Assuming that the training data size was small, we conducted evaluation experiments using the generation results from 90 and 189 input images, and examined the optimal method for generating caricatures from face images.

2   Related Work

2.1   Generative Adversarial Nets

Goodfellow et al. [5] proposed GAN, as a method for efficiently training generative models in deep learning. In GAN, a generator (Generator) and a discriminator (Discriminator) are used and trained. The Generator intends to generate data similar to the training data, and the Discriminator outputs the probability that the generated data is the training data. The Generator performs training, so that the Discriminator identifies the generated data as training data. On the other hand, the Discriminator identifies the training data as training data, and distinguishes the generated data as generator generated data. By training the Generator and Discriminator hostilely in this way, they become methods that compete with each other and improve accuracy. The problem is that learning is not stable.

2.2   Unsupervised Representation Learning with Deep Convolutional Generative Adversarial Network

Radford et al. [6] proposed the Deep Convolutional Generative Adversarial Network (DCGAN) aiming to improve the accuracy of image generation through unsupervised learning. Their points included the elimination of pooling in the convolutional layer, the learning using Batch Normalization for the efficiency of the Generator, the elimination of the fully connected layer, the adaptation of the tanh function in the Generator output layer, and the change to Leaky Rectified Linear Unit (LeakyReLU) for all the activation functions of the Discriminator. As a result, they succeeded in stabilizing the GAN learning process. In this study, we use the method proposed by DCGAN for the network structure of the Generator and the Discriminator.

2.3 Image-to-Image Translation with Conditional Adversarial Networks

Isora et al. [7] proposed pix2pix, a type of image translation algorithm using GAN. By learning and taking into account the relationship between image domains from two pairs of images, they developed a method for generating a transformed image by interpolating from an input image. Pix2pix uses Conditional GAN. It has the same configuration as DCGAN, and uses U-NET as the Generator. The Discriminator uses PatchGAN and focuses on the local rather than the whole, and distinguishes between training data and data generated by the Generator. However, it has been pointed out that a large amount of training data is required and that teacher images must be prepared in pairs.

2.4 Unpaired Image-to-Image Translation Using Cycle-Consistent Adversarial Networks

Zhu et al. [8] proposed CycleGAN, a type of image translation algorithm using GAN and similar to pix2pix discussed in Subsect. 2.3 above. In Cycle GAN, the domain of the image is defined, and the image is collected for each domain and used as training data. The main feature is that there is no need for preparing the training data to be paired. Let the image sets from each domain be X and Y respectively, and prepare a generator that converts them from X to Y and Y to X. In addition, two discriminators corresponding to both cases are prepared. Image generation without pairwise learning is possible using the adversarial loss error (loss) used in GAN and the cycle consistency loss proposed in this paper as the evaluation criterion for learning. However, it is shown that the accuracy is lower than that of pix2pix because of unsupervised learning.

2.5 APDrawingGAN: Generating Artistic Portrait Drawings from Face Photos with Hierarchical GAN

Yi et al. [4] proposed APDrawingGAN, a GAN for drawing portraits. This system is divided into a global net, which converts the entire image, and a local net, which converts the right eye, left eye, nose, mouth, and hair. Finally, these outputs are combined using Fusion net. They proposed the Line-promoting distance transform loss as an error. In addition, they reported the success in generating a highly accurate caricature using a small number of training images by allowing for small deviations often seen in caricatures.

3 Generative Adversarial Networks

3.1 Previous Methods (Pix2pix and CycleGAN)

As mentioned above in the Related Work section, pix2pix [7] is supervised learning, and CycleGAN [8] is unsupervised learning, which is the basis of GANs that perform image-to-image translation. Pix2pix has been reported to successfully convert aerial photographs into maps and generate line drawing bags from color image bags. It is also the basic conversion method of supervised learning. CycleGAN has converted images of horses to zebras and photographs to paintings of various styles, which is the basic conversion method of unsupervised learning. We have decided to use these GANs for portrait generation as examples of previous research. Figure 1 shows the pix2pix network architecture that performs domain conversion through supervised learning. In this network, a pair of images is prepared for the training data, a relationship between the images is learned from the pair of images, and an output image is generated by interpolating an input image based on the relationship. The Generator generates a portrait from a face photo; and the Discriminator receives a portrait and either of the portrait or a training image generated by Generator as a pair, and identifies whether the input portrait is an image generated by the Generator or the training data.

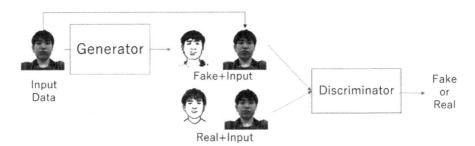

Fig. 1. Pix2pix network architecture.

Figure 2 shows the network architecture of CycleGAN. In CycleGAN, a Discriminator is added to the pix2pix network, and two generators are provided for each Discriminator. The Generator outputs photos from portraits using the inverse conversion of Generator 1. In Fig. 2, there are two types of learning: conversion from a face photo to a portrait, and then reconversion to the face image; and conversion from a portrait to a face photo, and then reconversion to the face image. This network architecture has a reconversion function with the addition of Generator 2, which converts portraits into facial photos. Discriminator 2 discriminates between the face photo generated by Generator 2 and the real face photo, and outputs the discrimination result.

Because the domain conversion of images in CycleGAN is performed without teachers instead of one-to-one mapping (as in pix2pix), overfitting is less likely to occur in CycleGAN than in pix2pix. Although the generation of high-precision images can be expected even with less training data, CycleGAN has a problem in that the generation

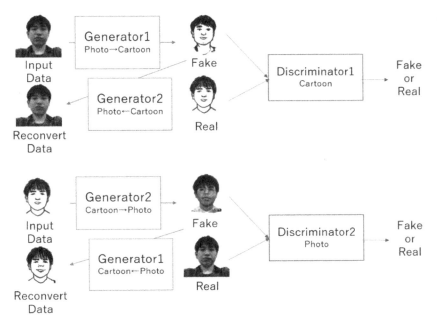

Fig. 2. CycleGAN and Cyclepix network architecture.

of images similar to the training data cannot always be achieved after the learning process. For example, CycleGAN may learn to generate a portrait of another person instead of a portrait of the same person. This may result in the drawing of glasses for a person without glasses or the drawing a beard for a person without a beard. Based on the abovementioned example, CycleGAN is not suitable for generating portraits that reflect the personality of professional illustrators. In addition, pix2pix is not suitable for use in portraits that are deformed and drawn because it is vulnerable to deformation, with resultant overfitting likely to occur.

3.2 Proposed Methods (Paired CycleGAN and Cyclepix)

In this study, we decided to change to supervised learning based on CycleGAN to solve the problem of poor accuracy in pix2pix, and the problem of its inability to learn according to the training data. We propose two methods: Paired CycleGAN and Cyclepix. The first method uses the generated portrait and photo pairs as inputs to the Discriminator, and the latter employs pixel errors between the generated image and the teacher image in addition to adversarial loss. Figure 3 shows the network architecture of Paired Cycle-GAN, which was modified based on CycleGAN. CycleGAN has the problem that it is cannot always learn according to the training data because of unsupervised learning. Therefore, we propose Paired CycleGAN that conducts supervised learning by changing the input of the Discriminator to a pair based on CycleGAN. As shown in Fig. 3, inputs to Discriminator 1 and Discriminator 2 are pairs of face photos and portraits generated by each Generator.

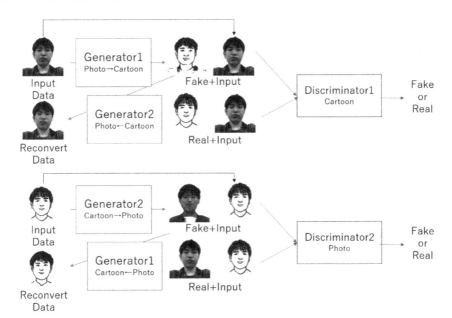

Fig. 3. Paired CycleGAN network architecture

4 GANs Used for the Experiment

4.1 Network Structure

In this study, we employed the same network architecture as CycleGAN [8]. The Generator and Discriminator have a similar structure for all networks in the experiments. Figure 4 shows the structure of the Generator. The Generator consists of an encoder that extracts facial image features, a translator that translates facial feature maps into portrait feature maps, and a decoder that restores facial features into image shapes. In the encoder, the feature map is generated three times using a convolutional layer, and the data size is compressed using stride convolution. The translator uses nine residual blocks called ResNet [9] to perform translation. The residual block has a skip connection, which is a method that outputs the result of performing convolution twice and the input using the skip connection, and is useful for addressing the gradient vanishing problem. The decoder transposes a convolutional layer two times to restore the feature map to the size of the image and then performs a convolutional layer to generate a portrait image. The activation function uses Rectified Linear Unit (ReLU) except for the output layer, and tanh only for the output layer. Batch normalization is performed in the Instance Normalization part.

The Discriminator can take only the generated image as input, or it can take a pair of the generated image and the input face image of the Generator, or the training data and the input face image of the Generator; hence, the number of input channels may change. The structure of the Discriminator adopts a method known as PatchGAN, as described in

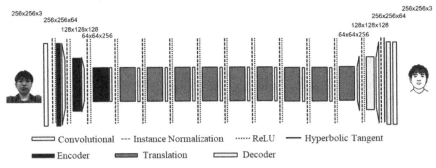

Fig. 4. Generator network structure

Sect. 2.4. One-dimensional convolution is performed while compressing the size using convolution by three times of stride, and a Boolean value of $32 \times 32 \times 1$ as output.

4.2 Loss Function

The learning method and hyperparameters were determined based on CycleGAN [8]. The Generator's loss function is different for each network, whereas the adversarial loss is the same. Equation 1 shows the generator's adversarial loss.

$$L_{Adv} = -\mathbb{E}_x \sim_{px(x)} \left[log D(G(x)) \right] \tag{1}$$

L1 Loss is defined by Eq. 2, where x is the training data, y is the output data, and z is a random noise vector.

$$L_{L1} = \mathbb{E}_{x,y,z} \left[\| y - G(x, z) \|_1 \right] \tag{2}$$

The loss of pix2pix is a weighted sum of L1 Loss, which takes the pixel error between the portrait generated by the Generator and the training data; and adversarial loss, which indicates the error correctly identified as a fake in the Discriminator.

Equation 3 shows the loss function of pix2pix. In the experiment, we set $\lambda_{Adv} = 1.0$ and $\lambda_{L1} = 10.0$.

$$L_G = \lambda_{Adv} * L_{Adv} + \lambda_{L1} * L_{L1} \tag{3}$$

Paired CycleGAN uses the same loss function as CycleGAN. The cycle consistency loss denoted by "Cycle," takes the error between the face image data obtained by further reconversion of the generated data and the face photo of the input data. The loss function of CycleGAN is a weighted sum of the cycle consistency loss and adversarial loss, as shown in Eq. 4. In the experiment, we set $\lambda_{Adv} = 1.0$, and $\lambda_{Cycle} = 10.0$.

$$L_G = \lambda_{Adv} * L_{Adv} + \lambda_{Cycle} * L_{Cycle} \tag{4}$$

The loss of Cyclepix is calculated as a weighted sum of L1 loss, adversarial loss, and cycle consistency loss, as shown in Eq. 5. In the experiment, we used $\lambda_{Adv} = 1.0$, $\lambda_{L1} = 2.5$, and $\lambda_{Cycle} = 10.0$.

$$L_G = \lambda_{Adv} * L_{Adv} + \lambda_{L1} * L_{L1} + \lambda_{Cycle} * L_{Cycle} \tag{5}$$

The Discriminator loss function is the same in all networks. Equation 6 shows the discriminator's adversarial loss.

$$L_{Adv} = \mathbb{E}_{x \sim p_{data(x)}}\big[log D(x)\big] + \mathbb{E}_z \sim_{p(z)} [\log(1 - D(G(z)))] \tag{6}$$

Adam [10] was used as the optimizer with parameters $\beta_1 = 0.5$, and $\beta_2 = 0.999$. The learning rate was set to 0.0002 for both the Generator and Discriminator. For all iterations, both the Generator and Discriminator were updated once, and the learning was terminated when it was considered that the data could be generated with some accuracy for each network.

5 Experiments

To evaluate the differences between the four networks, each network was trained using photos and pairs of portraits as training data. Additionally, we conducted an experiment to obtain a subjective valuation of the portraits using student subjects.

5.1 Datasets

Two datasets were prepared for this study: one consisted of portraits drawn by a student illustrator, and the other consisted of portraits drawn by a professional illustrator. We handed over the same person's face photos to each illustrator. Figure 5 shows some examples of the dataset. The student illustrator draws portraits by faithfully tracing the outline of the face without deforming it from the photo. The professional illustrator, on the other hand, deforms the contours and facial features based on the face image, resulting in a portrait with a shape that is different from the face photo.

In this experiment, a pair of a face photo and a portrait drawn by the professional illustrator was used as training data. In the first step, we collected a total of 100 face photos so that each of the 4 categories (females aged 0–40 and $\geq$41, and males aged 0–40 and $\geq$41) contains 25 photos. Of the 100 face photographs, 90 were used as training data and 10 were used as test data. The test data selection criteria were made equal for each category. As test data, we selected 2 photos each from the photos of women 0–40 years old and men over 40 years old, and 3 photos each from women over 40 years old and men 0–40 years old. Next, we added 99 images with features such as beards, glasses, and gray hair to the training data. The face photo was scanned at 257–300 pixels and trimmed at 256 × 256 pixels. A total of 189 training data were prepared using image processing, such as scaling and horizontal flipping. In this experiment, we show the results under two conditions: 90 and 189 training data.

Input   Illustrator 1   Illustrator 2
                  student   professional

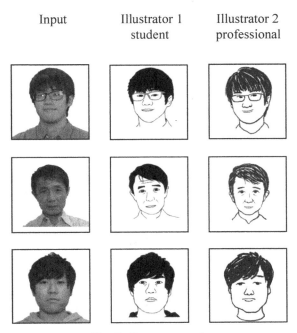

Fig. 5. Dataset example

5.2 Comparison of Generated Results

Figures 6, 7 and 8 show the results generated by each network that learned the test data. Caricatures generated from teacher images of the student illustrator and the professional illustrator are shown in the upper two rows and the lower two rows, respectively. The upper part of the two rows is the result of using 90 training images, and the lower part is that of using 189 training images. The column direction indicates different methods, and the results using the four methods described in Sect. 3 and AutoEncoder [11] as a reference method are listed.

AutoEncoder and pix2pix fail to compose the facial parts of the portraits, whereas Paired CycleGAN creates rather good portraits but often fails.

However, in the portrait generated by the student illustrator in the second column of Fig. 7, the glasses are drawn in the portrait even though they are not worn in the photo. Thus, it was found that there was a case in which the facial features were incorrectly reflected in the portrait.

However, some cases in which the facial features were incorrectly reflected in the portrait were found in the results of CycleGAN. For example, in the second row of Fig. 7, the glasses are drawn in the portrait even though they are not worn in the photo. Cyclepix, on the other hand, did not find any cases that incorrectly reflected facial features. From the results of Cyclepix in Fig. 8, it was found that difficult facial features such as frameless glasses could be best reflected in portraits using various methods. A comparison of each illustrator's portraits demonstrated that the portraits by the student illustrator could be generated in relatively high precision using pix2pix and AutoEncoder, whereas those by the professional illustrator could not compose facial parts using those methods. In other networks, it was also found that portraits from the student illustrator could be generated with higher accuracy than those from the professional illustrator. Regarding the generation of the hair portion, we compared the male portraits shown in Fig. 6 with the female portraits shown in Fig. 7. It can be seen that the hairstyle of the male portrait is close to the teacher image, but that of the female portrait is not well generated. This is because the hairstyle in the portrait of the male is a common hairstyle, while the woman tied her hair back, and there was no photograph of the woman tying her hair back in the teacher data.

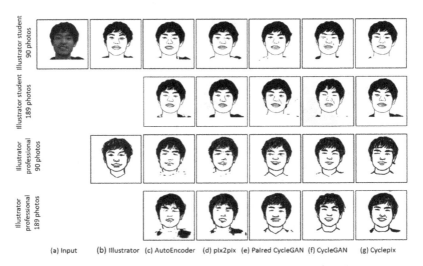

(a) Input   (b) Illustrator   (c) AutoEncoder   (d) pix2pix   (e) Paired CycleGAN   (f) CycleGAN   (g) Cyclepix

Fig. 6. Portrait generation result for male in their 20 s (test data)

Figure 9 shows the portraits generated by the trained networks using the training data. It can be seen that pix2pix and Paired CycleGAN almost reproduced the training data, while CycleGAN did not reproduce the training data accurately. This result indicates that overfitting occurred in CycleGAN as a result of the poor accuracy of the test data. In Cyclepix, the portraits were generated almost as per the training data because of the proper test data, indicating that optimal learning was achieved. From the results of the training data, no differences were found between each illustrator.

Next, Fig. 10 shows some examples in which CycleGAN did not learn according to the training data, whereas Cyclepix did. The image at the top is a face image of a man in his twenties without glasses. As a result of the erroneous learning performed in Cycle GAN, it can be seen that the portrait is generated by erroneously recognizing an area where eyes are shaded as glasses. In the case of the image at the bottom, the shadow of the person's face was incorrectly converted to a mustache. We also observed that Cyclepix was able to learn the clothed areas of face photos according to the training data. The above results showed that Cyclepix can solve the problem of CycleGAN in that it does not always learn according to the training data. From the results of the cases of training and test data, it was considered that pix2pix and Paired CycleGAN were

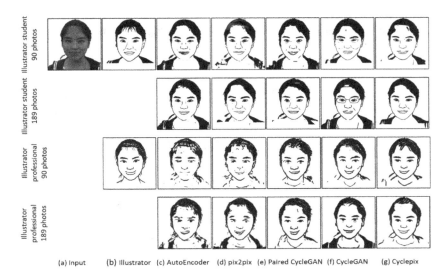

Fig. 7. Portrait generation result for women in their 20 s (test data)

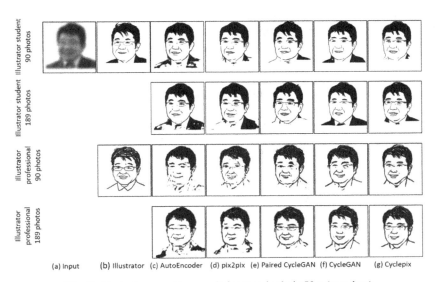

Fig. 8. Portrait generation result for men in their 50 s (test data)

not suitable for generating portraits, because overfitting occurred in these methods for a small amount of test data. On the other hand, in CycleGAN and Cyclepix, accurate portraits were obtained from the test data and they were considered suitable networks for the generation of portraits.

It was found that CycleGAN had a problem, in that training data could not be restored accurately by learning a small amount of training data. On the other hand, Cyclepix was

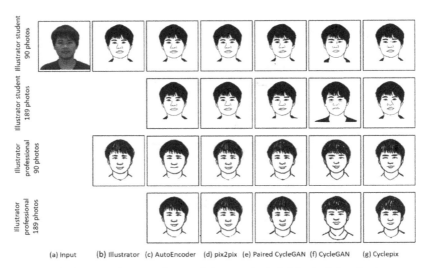

Fig. 9. Portrait generation result for men in their 20 s (training data)

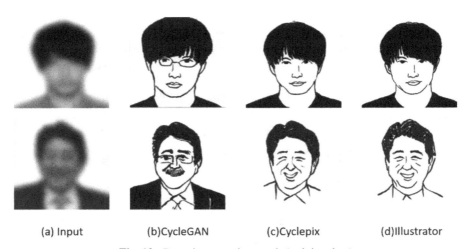

Fig. 10. Portrait generation result (training data)

found to be suitable for portrait generation because training data can be restored by learning using a small amount of training data.

5.3 An Experiment to Evaluate the Similarity of Generated Portraits

Because it is not appropriate to use the error value directly to evaluate a portrait generated by GANs, an evaluation experiment was performed on the subjects using the similarity between the portrait drawn by the illustrator and the portrait generated by each network. In the evaluation experiment, 8 portraits generated with two numbers of training data

(90 and 189) in 4 networks and a portrait drawn by the illustrator were displayed on the screen. 10 subjects aged between 23 and 24 were asked to evaluate for similarity using a 5-point scale (−2: dissimilar, −1: slightly dissimilar, 0: neither, 1: somewhat similar, 2: similar) and to rank 8 portraits of 10 sets. The eight portraits were displayed in random order.

The results of the 5-point scale shown in Table 1 are 1.22 for CycleGAN (189), 1.04 for Cyclepix (90), 0.97 for Cyclepix (189), and 0.4 for CycleGAN (90). It can be said that the subjects judged that the portraits generated by these methods were similar to the original portraits. Paired CycleGAN and pix2pix had negative values, and were evaluated as dissimilar. According to the ranking results, CycleGAN (189) was first, followed by Cyclepix (90) and Cyclepix (189).

Table 1. Evaluation experiment results

GAN	5 point	Rank
Pix2pix [6] 90	−1.65	7.15
Pix2pix [6] 189	−1.42	6.72
CycleGAN [7] 90	0.40	3.59
CycleGAN [7] 189	1.22	2.18
Paired CycleGAN 90	−0.85	5.63
Paired CycleGAN 189	−0.66	5.12
Cyclepix 90	1.04	2.68
Cyclepix 189	0.97	2.91

6 Conclusion and Discussion

We presume that CycleGAN and Cyclepix were highly evaluated because each face part was not blurred and was reproduced clearly, resulting in accurate portraits. For pix2pix and Paired CycleGAN, it is considered that overfitting occurred because the input of the Discriminator was a pair of data, which conditioned adversarial loss. Regarding the cycle consistency loss used for CycleGAN and Cyclepix, we think that cycle consistency loss contributed to an increase the generation accuracy by more than L1 Loss because the accuracy of Paired CycleGAN was better than that of pix2pix. Overfitting occurred in pix2pix because, when deforming like portraits, if the shape of each contour or feature changes, the input and output cannot be consistent and the reproduction accuracy decreases. It was confirmed that CycleGAN did not always provide learning results according to the training data as a result of the unsupervised learning, even in portrait generation. To solve this problem, supervised learning that adds L1 Loss, which is the pixel error between the generated caricature and the teacher's caricature, works well than supervised learning that pairs the input of the Discriminator in Paired CycleGAN. If the input of the Discriminator is a pair, learning will be excessively adapted to the training data because the correspondence of input data is known, while if the input of the Discriminator is only the generated data, the versatility of the learning improves because of the comparisons with plural training data. CycleGAN's evaluation was high in the experiment because facial parts were drawn clearly without causing overfitting for the unsupervised learning, and there were few obvious cases of failure in the experimental data. For this reason, it is considered that in Cyclepix, which uses supervised learning based on pixel errors, the accuracy increases as the data increases and Cyclepix can reflect the characteristics of illustrator drawing.

From the perspective of the difference between illustrators, we found that AutoEncoder and pix2pix can be generated with some accuracy when the input and output shapes match, as in the case of the student illustrator. However, in most cases, the drawn portraits are deformed and the input and output shapes do not match, as in the case of the professional illustrator. As a result, the face parts could not be composed and the generation failed. Therefore, these methods are not suitable for reflecting the individuality of illustrators using a small amount of training data.

Finally, there remains a problem whereby features such as mustache and frameless glasses cannot be completely reflected in portraits because of the small amount of training data, and the problem that the Discriminator is too strong for the Generator. Future challenges include increasing training data and changing the network structure and image size, so that facial features such as mustache and frameless glasses can be extracted. We will also try to reduce the Discriminator's influence by lowering the Discriminator's learning rate or by reducing the Discriminator's learning frequency for the Generator.

References

1. photoprocessing.com. http://www.photo-kako.com/likeness.cgi. Accessed 18 Feb 2019
2. Wu, Y., Enomoto, M., Ohya, J.: Study of subjective discrimination in an automatic system for generating line drawing based portraits from facial images. In: FIT2014, 13th Information Science and Technology Forum, 3rd volume, pp. 247–248 (2015)
3. Li, W., Xiong, W., Liao, H., Huo, J., Gao, Y., Luo, J.: CariGAN: caricature generation through weakly paired adversarial learning. arXiv:1811.00445 (2018)
4. Yi, R., Liu, Y.-J.: APDrawingGAN: generating artistic portrait drawings from face photos with hierarchical GANs. In: CVPR 2019, pp. 0743–10752 (2019)
5. Goodfellow, I.: NIPS 2016 tutorial: generative adversarial networks. arXiv:1701.00160 (2016)
6. Radford, A., Metz, L., Chintala, S.: Unsupervised representation learning with deep convolutional generative adversarial networks. In: ICLR (2016)
7. Isola, P., Zhu, J.-Y., Zhou, T., Efros, A.A.: Image-to-image translation with conditional adversarial networks. In: CVPR (2017)
8. Zhu, J.-Y., Park, T., Isola, P., Efros, A.A.: Unpaired image-to-image translation using cycle-consistent adversarial networks. In: IEEE International Conference on Computer Vision (ICCV) (2017)
9. He, K., Zhang, X., Ren, S., Sun, J.: Deep residual learning for image recognition. In: CVPR (2016)
10. Kingma, D.P., Ba, J.: Adam: a method for stochastic optimization. arXiv:1412.6980 (2014)
11. Hinton, G.E., Salakhutdinov, R.R.: Reducing the dimensionality of data with neural networks. Science **313**(5786), 504–507 (2006)

A Proposal of Estimating Method for Agreement in Face-to-Face Communication

Masashi Okubo[✉] and Yuki Fujimoto

Doshisha University, 1-3 Tatara-Miyakodani, Kyotanabe, Kyoto 6100321, Japan
mokubo@mail.doshisha.ac.jp

Abstract. Generally, in the meeting exchange of opinions, sharing of knowledge, and creation of new ideas are performed through the discussion. However it is difficult to make sure whether the participants agree with the opinion of the speaker. If there is a support system that estimates the agreement of participants with the opinion of the speaker, the meeting may advance more smoothly. In this research, we propose estimation method for agreement by using correlation between participant's motions in face-to-face communication.

Keywords: Non-verbal information · Human communication · Decision making · Nodding · Communication motion

1 Introduction

1.1 Background

Generally, in the meeting exchanging opinions, sharing of knowledge and creation of new ideas are performed through the discussions. In this case, however, there is a problem it is difficult to make sure whether the participants agree with the opinion of the speaker and the meeting may keep continuing without sufficient confirmation of consensus. Meanwhile, non-verbal information such as nodding and facial expression plays an important role in face-to-face communication [1, 2]. Nods are also considered to indicate consent, but also control turn-talking to facilitate the flow of conversation [3]. In this study, we explore a possibility that the meeting can be smoothly supported by estimating the nod.

1.2 Related Works

Nod estimation has been studied by Saiga et al. to classify conversation control of nod in multi-person conversation [4]. In this study swinging motion is acquired by a compact wireless acceleration sensor worn on the forehead and threshold processing is used to estimate of the nods. However, consecutive nods might have been erroneously detected as a noise section, so that the estimation is performed by frequency analysis. Moreover, there are studies of Kimura et al., which evaluates quality of communication between lecturers and students from frequency of head movements [5]. In this research,

© Springer Nature Switzerland AG 2020
S. Yamamoto and H. Mori (Eds.): HCII 2020, LNCS 12185, pp. 245–253, 2020.
https://doi.org/10.1007/978-3-030-50017-7_17

a frequency distribution of acceleration data of each audience is created by measuring three axes X, Y and Z from an acceleration sensor mounted on a smartphone hanging from the neck. The result showed that 3 to 6 Hz corresponds to ordinary nods or hand movements, 6 Hz or more corresponds to quick nod or laughing. From the above, the research indicates that the characteristics of body motion of presenters and audiences may have been estimated from the frequency analysis. However, how the nod and laughing extracted by frequency analysis have an impact on conversation has not been clarified. Meanwhile, Maeda and his colleagues focus on nodding that occurs during face-to-face communication in their research [6]. They aim to analyze the existence of mutual relationships in gesture information such as nodding generated by dialogue. First of all, they recorded the face-to-face conversation between two parties with a prompter, earphone, microphone that has a video camera inside. Then they analyze the gesture expressing during the face-to-face conversation from the recorded data. The result shows that nods, as well as supportive responses tend to occur more frequently in self-speech than in the conversation with the other speakers. The research also indicates that there are many phenomena which nods occur simultaneously in two speakers.

1.3 Purpose of Research

These researches mentioned as above show that characteristic body motions such as nod and laugh can be estimated by frequency analysis. However, the body motions are measured with the acceleration sensor worn on the head or the smartphone hanging from the neck in each research. Assuming an actual face-to-face conversation, we prefer to measure conversation carry out in more natural status. Therefore, we decide to use Kinect enable to acquire the position of the head without contact. In addition, as the nod indicating the consent to the partner's speech is likely to occur simultaneously during the dialogue, we estimate that the correlation value of the head movement on nodding in the face-to-face conversation can be high. That is, there is a possibility that agreement/disagreement can be estimated due to strength of correlation of head movement. If we can support estimation of listener's consent/disagreement on the opinion of the speaker, the meeting will proceed seemingly more smoothly. Therefore, in this research, we propose a consensus formation estimation method with the strength of the correlation of the physical movements of the speaker and the listener as the index of consensus.

2 Acquisition of Head Position by Kinect

In order to estimate the position of the head in a more natural state, we use Kinect which can acquire skeleton information, one of NUI (Natural User Interface) devices. Kinect holding the origin at the main body acquires the position data (X axis, Y axis) of the human head. Figure 1 shows the outline when acquiring position information from Kinect.

The figure on the right is an example of time series data on X axis and Y axis obtained at one nod. This shows, when nodding, a downwardly convex signal is obtained on the time series data of Y axis.

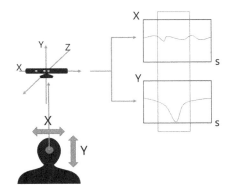

Fig. 1. Position data of head provided from Kinect

However, when acquiring head position data on X axis and Y axis, we have a difficulty to acquire small up-and-down movement of the head due to noises. Solving this problem, we develop an algorithm using quaternion to get rotational motion of the head from 5 points of face, eyes, nose and both corners of mouth. With this algorithm we can get the motion of human's face roll, pitch, and yaw angle.

We focus on the angle (pitch) rotated around X axis of the face particular in this research. Figure 2 shows the outline of the angle rotated around X-axis with the created algorithm when placing Kinect devices across the face. We use θ in this figure for analysis as the movement of the head since it is the angle of the movement of the face.

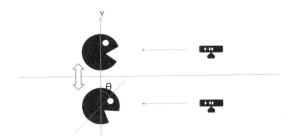

Fig. 2. Angle data of vertical direction of face provided from Kinect

3 Preliminary Experiment

3.1 Purpose of Experiment and Method

We carry out to preliminary experiments to get the frequency band of one nod. Since the study of Kimura and his colleagues indicate the frequency band differs depends on the angel of nod, we seek for the frequency band for two types of motion: deep nod and shallow nod respectively. Each ten experimental talkers perform deep/shallow nod respectively in sets of five and repeat that five times. Next, we seek the power spectrum with 3 s data for both deep/shallow nods from the obtained nodding data and find the maximum frequency value. Figure 3 shows an example of the power spectrum obtained from the data of the first talker's deep nods performed in the first set. Likewise, we seek the maximum frequency of the power spectrum for the other nine talkers.

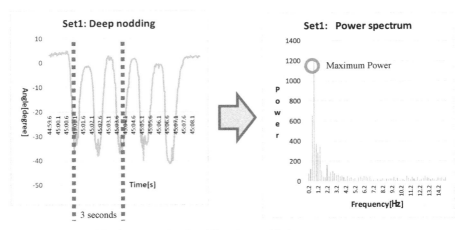

Fig. 3. Example of nodding data and its' power spectrum

3.2   Result of Preliminary Experiment

Figure 4 shows the average of frequency of deep and shallow nods. The t-test was used for the test of the significant difference. There was a significant difference from the average: the average of deep nod is about 0.47 Hz and that of shallow nod is about 1.41 Hz. From this, we learned that the average time taken for one deep nod was 2.13 s, and that for shallow nods was 0.71 s. Here, considering the nod performed in the actual face-to-face conversation, we assume that the frequency of shallow nods is higher than deep nods, and the synchronization of nod meaning consent in the conversation is due to shallow nods. Therefore, we focused only on shallow nods and set to the frequency band of one nodding 1 to 3 Hz.

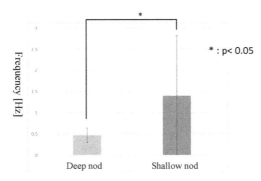

Fig. 4. Average of frequency of deep nod and shallow nod

4 Experiment

4.1 Experimental Purpose and Method

We chose two students from Doshisha University to support the experiment (called as Talker A and B). We aim to examine whether we can estimate listener's agreement on speaker's opinion from the strength of the correlation of their physical movements in their conversation. Firstly, we asked them to answer a questionnaire written with an alternative question in advance. They started the conversation on the question on which they gave different answers. The conversation lasted till either one of them agrees on the other's opinion and reach the agreement. Then they chose the other subject for the next conversation. During the conversation, the behavior of each talker was acquired with Kinect and a video camera. Kinect acquired the angle moved in the vertical direction of their faces, and the video camera recorded the talker's behavior such as expression, body movement and voice during the dialogue (Fig. 5).

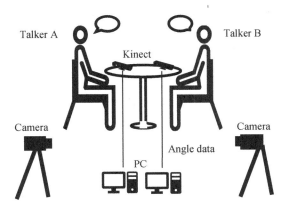

Fig. 5. Experimental setup

We calculated power spectrum with data every 3 s based on the angle data of the vertical direction of each talker's face movement obtained by Kinect. Then we shifted it 1 s and again calculated the power spectrum between 3 s. Figure 6 shows the flow for obtaining the power spectrum of data every 3 s in ten-minute conversation by experimental Talker A. T_1 indicates the power spectrum from the start of the conversation data to 3 s. We obtained the power spectrum up to T_{598} likewise.

Herein we defined the frequency band to be analyzed was from 1 Hz to 3 Hz as previously mentioned in "3.2 Preliminary experiment results". We obtained the correlation value of Talker A and Talker B in the power spectrum every T at 1 to 3 Hz. The figure below shows the time series data of the correlation value for each T of both A and B. In this equation obtaining the correlation value of T_1, A's numerical value of the power spectrum for each frequency of T_1 is described as Ai, and the average is described as A_{ave} (Ditto with Talker B) (Fig. 7).

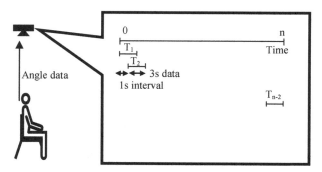

Fig. 6. Flow of obtaining analyzing area

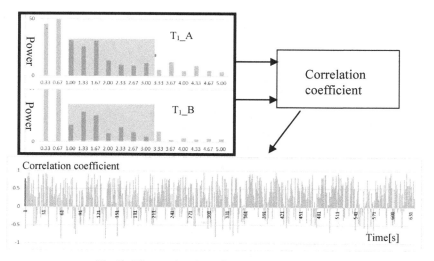

Fig. 7. Time series data of correlating coefficient

4.2 Result

In the time series of the created, we added colors on the sections where had the same tendency of correlation value in more than five intervals, that is, 7 s or more continued in order to show the strength of the correlation. Specifically, the correlation value $[-1.0$ to $-0.31]$ was blue, $[-0.3$ to $0.3]$ was green, and $[0.3$ to $1.0]$ was red. In addition, based on the captured image of the video camera we confirmed the sections where each talker laughed, got excited, agreed with the other person (consensus formation) in the conversation and filed those in the time series graph. Also we put body motions of each talker including nod captured during the conversation in the graph. In this experiment, we recorded the conversation between Talker A and Talker B discussed on three themes. The examples of results of these analyses are shown in Fig. 8 and 9 respectively. In these figures, the pink colored area shows the time when both of talker almost agree something, also the orange colored area shows the time when they made consensus.

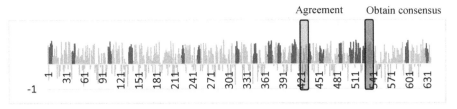

Fig. 8. Analysis result with theme 1 (Color figure online)

Fig. 9. Analysis result with theme 2 (Color figure online)

In place indicated by red where is a continuous section of positive correlation, we have found that laughter, lively conversation and listener's agreement with the speaker were seen in relatively many places. The eye-contact and simultaneous nods were also seen.

In addition, we have found relatively many laughter and simultaneous nods and lively conversation around the part where the listener agreed to the opinion of the speaker. By comparing the two conversations, in continuous section of positive correlation, the second conversation on Theme 2 had more laughter, lively conversation and listener's agreement with the speaker and turn-talking than the first conversation. Also, in the content spoken by each experiment talker in the theme 2, there was no negative statement against the partner's opinion.

After the experiments, the participants answered some questionnaires about the feeling of discussion. Table 1 shows the results. From this table, in theme 1, we can find that Talker A had dissatisfaction, however he felt the sense of unity. And, Talker B felt the satisfaction. In this case, the feel of self-affirmation of both are low. On the other

Table 1. Result of questionnaire

Question	A (theme 1)	B (theme 2)	A (theme 1)	B (theme 2)
Satisfaction	30%	70%	90%	100%
Self-affirmation	40%	40%	100%	0%
Other-affirmation	70%	60%	50%	100%
Consensus	1 of 5	4	4	5
A sense of unity	4 of 5	5	4	4

hand, in theme 2, Talker B agreed with Talker A in short time. In this case, the feel of self-affirmation of B is 0%, however, his feeling of satisfaction, consensus and sense of unity are very high.

5 Discussions

In this research, we aim to propose a method of estimation of consensus formation in face-to-face communication. From the conversation of two university students, we verify whether we can estimate the listener's agreement on the opinion of the speaker based on the strength of the correlation of the body motion during the conversation. The result indicates that consensus formation was often carried out in consecutive sections of positive correlation. We also learn that the number of index showing the listener's agreement where the simultaneous nod and lively conversation was produced needs to be increased depending on the difference of quality of the alternative answers.

First, laughter, lively conversation and the listener's agreement were seen often in the continuous section of positive correlation. In addition, eye-contact and simultaneous nod are found as well in this section. There are many laughs, simultaneous nod and lively conversation around the section where the listener agreed. These result shows that there is a possibility that consensus formation was performed in a continuous section of positive correlation. Also, it is shown that simultaneous nod and lively conversation may be an indicator of consensus formation. On the other hand, in the conversation with two themes, $[-1.0$ to $-0.31]$ which is a continuous section of negative correlation is not found. In addition, by comparing the two conversations, the conversation on theme 2 has more laughter, listener's agreement with speaker, consecutive section of positive correlation and turn-taking than the conversation on theme 1. Also, in the theme 2, there is no negative statement against the other person's opinion. These seem to be due to the difference in the quality of the alternative questions. In theme 1 each talker gave extremely different answers. In theme 2, on contrary, though the answers are divided, they stated that "either answer is acceptable" in the conversation. The analysis results mentioned as above demonstrate that we need to increase the index showing the listener's agreement where the simultaneous nod and lively conversation was produced dependent on the difference in the quality of the two alternative questions. It is necessary to analyze more conversation in the future.

6 Conclusion

In this research, we aim to propose a consensus formation estimation method in face-to-face communication and estimate listener's agreement on the opinion of speaker from the strength of the correlation in the frequency domain of the body motion. The result demonstrated that consensus formation might be performed in a continuous section of positive correlation. It also revealed that we need to increase the index showing the listener's agreement where the simultaneous nod and lively conversation was produced dependent on the difference in the quality of the two alternative questions. In the future, further analysis of various conversations will be necessary to verify for more details.

Acknowledgement. This work was supported by JSPS KAKENHI Grant Number 18K11414.

References

1. Watanabe, T., Okubo, M., Nakashige, M., Danbara, R.: InterActor: speech-driven embodied interactive actor. Int. J. Hum.-Comput. Interact. **17**(1), 43–60 (2004)
2. Watanabe, T., Ogikubo, M., Ishii, Y.: Visualization of respiration in the embodied virtual communication system and its evaluation. Int. J. Hum.-Comput. Interact. **17**(1), 89–102 (2004)
3. Kurokawa, T.: Non-verbal interface, Ohmsha (1994). (in Japanese)
4. Saiga, H., Sumi, Y., Nishida, T.: Function analysis of nodding for conversation adjustment in multi-party conversation. IPSJ SIG Technical report, vol. 2010-UBI-26, no. 1 (2010). (in Japanese)
5. Kimura, M., Kato, Y., Ogisawa, T., Yamamoto, T., Miyake, Y.: Measuring system of communication between a lecturer and students in a class. Human Interface Society Technical report, vol. 18, no. 2 (2016). (in Japanese)
6. Maeda, M., Horiuchi, Y., Ichikawa, A.: Analysis of correlation between interlocutors' gestures in spontaneous speech. IPSJ SIG Tech. Rep. **102**, 39–46 (2013). (in Japanese)

System Design of Community Toward Wellbeing

Katsunori Shimohara[(⊠)]

Doshisha University, Kyoto 610-0321, Japan
kshimoha@mail.doshisha.ac.jp

Abstract. Targeting a community as a system that cannot exist without people's self-motivated involvement, we propose a mechanism through which the selfish behavior of people elicits awareness in their relationship with others, eventually generating an altruistic effect. In this research, we conduct a field experiment in which people utilize the mechanism spontaneously and repeatedly to elucidate and demonstrate that wellbeing in a community is viable. Here, wellbeing indicates that an individual's rights and self-actualization can be secured, and they are physically, mentally, and sociologically in good conditions. Accordingly, we introduce the basic concept of *relationality* and *relationality assets* (RAs). To make people aware of the significance and meaning of relationality in a community, we establish that relationality should be considered as an asset in the social and economic values, expected to provide some utility to a community in the future. This indicates that RAs are valuable for quantizing and visualizing the relationality naturally generated by people through interactions between "Hito," "Mono," and "Koto" while living in a community. In this paper, we discuss the significance and potential of the research concept and research issues to achieve the above goal.

Keywords: Relationality · Relationality assets · Gift and Circulation Model

1 Introduction

Japan is now facing two unprecedented problems, i.e., an abrupt decrease in the population and inevitably super-aging society that human beings have never experienced. People's connection with a community and/or blood relatives has being weakened and lost; social ties after retirement are facing the same consequence. Thus, social hollowing has become increasingly worse in Japan. In other words, local communities as the basis for people's daily life and socioeconomic activities have been devastated. The dissolution of communities, in particular, poses significant problems for the usual wellbeing of a community and emergency responses in the extraordinary situation by disaster. *Irrespective of the introduction of advanced scientific technologies to cope with such hazards, achieving wellbeing without a well-operated and well-managed community that functions as a system would be impractical.*

To the best of our knowledge, rebuilding of a local community has been often attempted from the technological approach to introduce ICT (Information and Communications Technology). However, it was found that such external incentives have limited

S. Yamamoto and H. Mori (Eds.): HCII 2020, LNCS 12185, pp. 254–263, 2020.
https://doi.org/10.1007/978-3-030-50017-7_18

effects and only work well for short-terms. In addition, it is a fact that *we cannot cope with the inherent risks in human relationships, such as mutual misunderstanding, avoidance, conflict, alienation and ignorance in a community with a technological approach.*

Rebuilding a local community founded by mutual trust and connection between the people should be of highest priority at present times. To rebuild and sustain a community facing a super-aging society, internally driven incentives by the people should be indispensable. More concretely, *it is vital to arouse their consciousness and psychology and promote self-motivated behavioral changes that result in mutual understanding and tolerance between them.* That is, the key-scientific question that we pursue in this research is *whether it is viable to accomplish wellbeing in a community by people's self-motivated and repeated utilization of a mechanism through which their selfish behavior elicits awareness in their relationship with others, and eventually generates an altruistic effect.*

2   System Design for Community

Targeting a community as a system that cannot exist without people's self-motivated involvement, we propose a mechanism through which the selfish behavior of people elicits awareness in their relationship with others, eventually creating an altruistic effect. In this research, we conduct a field experiment in which participants utilize the mechanism spontaneously and repeatedly to elucidate and demonstrate that wellbeing in a community is viable. Here, wellbeing means an individual's rights and self-actualization can be secured, and they are physically, mentally, and sociologically in good conditions.

We employ the systems science-based standpoint that a community is a system composed of "Hito," "Mono," and "Koto" as the elements and the relationality between them. Here, "Hito" in Japanese means a person or resident, "Mono" denotes a tangible and physically perceived thing/entity, and "Koto" denotes an intangible and cognitively conceived thing/entity. The concept of *relationality* denotes the *interactions* through which two entities mutually influence each other, *linkage* over time and space, and *context* as a result of accumulated *interactions* and *linkage*. Especially, we utilize the role and functionality of relationality, i.e., the invisible relationships between "Hito," "Mono," and "Koto" in a community. Here, "Hito" implies a resident, "Mono" implies spatial and physical resources such as places and facilities, and "Koto" implies invisible social customs and events, such as town meetings and community gatherings.

The research viewpoints in this study are as follows. 1) The relationships between "Hito," "Mono," and "Koto" created by people in their daily lives should be the assets of the social and economic values that are expected to benefit a community in the future. 2) There is no mechanism that effectively combines and/or correlates individual systems in a community to function as a system through interactions and cooperation. The latter is based on the fact that a community consists of various habitable systems (such as homes, towns, education, medicine, caregiving, and disaster prevention), public infrastructure (garbage collection, water, sewerage, energy utility, telecommunications, traffic), and business sector (selling, manufacturing, logistics, sightseeing, other services).

The originality of this research stems from the belief that *a community cannot sustainably exist or function without people's self-motivated continuous involvement and incentive for community activities.* Second, we challenge *the creation of methodologies for system cooperation in a community by utilizing the proposed mechanism on relationality assets* (RAs). The second aspect of this research is related to System of Systems a significant research issues in the field of system of systems engineering. It is important to realize system cooperation based on the daily lives and socioeconomic activities of people in a community.

3   Research Issues and Methods

To accomplish the abovementioned research objective, we pursue the following three issues.

- Design incentives to prompt people's self-motivated and positive involvement in RAs.
- Demonstrate the effectiveness of the *Gift and Circulation Model (G&CM)* as a mechanism to circulate the RAs through field experiments.
- Build methodologies to create effective system cooperation by utilizing the data acquired through the G&CM.

3.1   Incentive Design to Prompt People's Self-motivated and Positive Involvement in RAs

The following issues should be elucidated through field experiments. 1) How well RAs as quantified and visualized relationality work to elicit awareness in their relationality and prompt their self-motivated involvement in RAs, and 2) whether and/or how long its effect is sustainable.

A mechanism to quantify and visualize an individual's relationality between "Hito," "Mono," and "Koto" has already been implemented [1–3]. Concretely, we have been working on the following issues along with a field experiment;

1) Community modeling [4–6] based on the reality of community activities including participants' incentive structure.
2) Network and behavior analyses of participants' activity data [7–9] to investigate the functionality of relationality between "Hito," "Mono," and "Koto" as assets.
3) Multi-agent system simulations to achieve autonomous regulation considering the liquidity of RAs and people's investment behavior.

Figure 1 shows a platform for field experiments to share the residents' awareness. Additionally, to enable people to mutually share information and problems in a community, we have provided two services, "walking courses recommendation" and "safe and secure map for children," as shown in Fig. 2 [10].

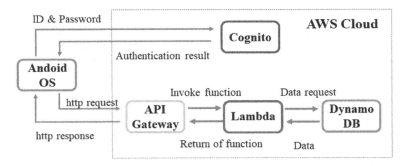

Cognito: Authenication/Authorization **Lambda**: controlling DyanmoDB function
API Gateway: Issuing API   **DynamoDB**: Saving the acquired data

Fig. 1. A platform for field experiments to share local residents' awareness

Walking Course Recommendation Service: Blue pins represent places or points that are posted by residents. They can share photos taken there.

Fig. 2. User interface for walking course recommendation service

Because the RAs include spatial data (such as places and facilities) and time series data, a resident's spatial behavior analysis with KDE (Kernel Density Estimation) and panel data analysis focusing on their time series data should be conducted to reveal the macroscopic reality of their community activities. Figure 3 shows, for example, a result of media spot estimation by applying KDE to sliced location information by DBSCAN (Density-Based Spatial Clustering of Applications with Noise) [8]. The left and right axes represent the latitude and longitude, respectively. The upper axis represents the density. The red part indicates the location of the point's high density. In addition, because RAs between people can be modeled as a network to represent a person's power of influence and personal magnetism, network analysis focusing a specific person or a given role in a community can reveal the significance of the person or the role as microscopic analysis.

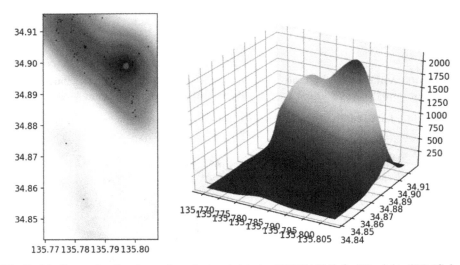

Fig. 3. Media sport estimation using clustered data by DBSCAN (left: 2D, right: 3D) (Color figure online)

Based on the current scheme of the field experiments, we modeled the RAs and G&CM into shape. In addition, we propose a new mechanism to quantify and visualize the data that will be acquired through pedometers and sleep measurement systems [11], targeting seniors who are interested in health and exercise. Moreover, we propose a mechanism for incentive design with nudge and gamification to determine the changes in people's behavioral [12, 13]. When designing the nudge and gamification, we investigate how well they enable for participants to mutually share information while walking toward a goal and to cooperate and collaborate with each other as well as to compete their performance.

We evaluate the effectiveness of this incentive design with objective data acquired by the field experiments and questionnaire filled out by the residents who join in the experiments.

3.2 Demonstration of Effectiveness of G&CM as a Mechanism to Circulate RAs

We investigate the following questions through simulations and field experiments: 1) whether the G&CM works in reality in a community and to what extent, and 2) how to design the new mechanism to ensure efficiency of the G&CM.

We have proposed *the concept of the G&CM to compensate the limitation of Give & Take – the major principle of behavior – that seeks equivalent exchange promptly. In contrast to Give & Take, when we give a gift to someone, we think about how and what he/she feels, and attempt to express diverse values such as love and gratitude, instead of the value of money. The G&CM is a type of mechanism that promotes circulation instead of exchange without asking for prompt returns, by exploiting people's psychology.*

Figure 4 shows a mechanism of the G&CM; its basic features are listed below [14, 15];

- A and B represent individual residents, and every resident has their personal account to store RAs which they acquire through interactions between "Hito," "Mono," and "Koto" while living in a community.
- Each personal account has the leakage mechanism, which is expected to prompt residents to give some gift to others because it should be better to use RAs than lose them.
- The same amount of RA gifted to someone is virtually pooled and accumulated in the public account; the accumulated RA will be redistributed to everyone in a given time period.
- Everyone can check the amount in their personal account along with the information regarding the gifts received ant those given by them.
- Everyone can know how actively the residents in a community interact by the condition of the public account.

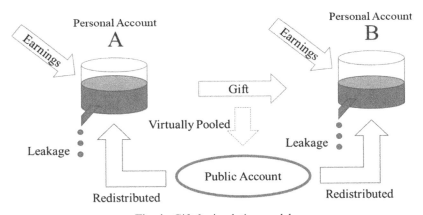

Fig. 4. Gift & circulation model

According to evolutionary psychology, cooperation with a feeling of belonging involves mutual fitness benefits for both actors, whereas altruism refers to the interactions where the actor incurs a fitness cost while benefiting the recipient [16]. Additionally, even when self-interest dominates, reciprocal altruism can evolve between people who are not related to the extent that 1) the benefits provided by one party to another are returned at a later date, and thus, 2) all parties experience a net increase in fitness [17].

It is natural for everyone to want to increase their RAs, which can be considered selfish. Because of leakage, however, an individual would want to give a gift to someone, and then seek someone to whom they can give a gift. It means that they pay attention to others in a community. When they check their personal account, they should be aware of their relationships with others. In addition, an increase in the distribution of the RAs from the public account indicates that an individual is more active and driven to be involved in circulation the RAs in the community. That indicates that the G&CM is expected to work such that people's selfish behavior elicits awareness in their relationship with others and eventually generates an altruistic effect.

First, we will conduct multi agent-based simulations (MASs) on how the rates of gift, leakage and redistribution affect the behavior of agents; how to regulate the rates of leakage and/or redistribution depending on the different rates of gifts of individuals; and how to manage the G&CM as a system through settings such as parameters. Figure 5 shows a preliminary result of MAS which modeled 200 agents referring to a given actual town with 9 km^2 for 90 days [15]. Second, we will implement the G&CM as an application for smartphones, and then conduct field experiments to obtain real-world data in a community. Third, by analyzing the real-world data, we will investigate the changes in motivation of people for acquiring RAs, their attitude and/or interest in relationships with others, and view toward the whole community.

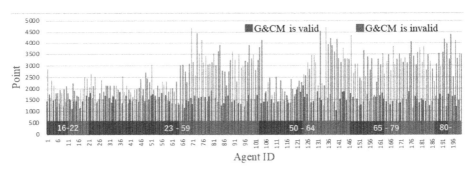

Total points in residents personal accounts in the case of G&CM is valid or invalid. Males and females are in blue and red areas respectively, and numerical numbers show ages. G&CM is effective in reducing the difference in the total points between them.

Fig. 5. Preliminary result of multi-agent based simulations on G&CM

3.3 Building of Methodology to Create Effective System Cooperation by Utilizing Data Acquired Through G&CM

We will attempt here to utilize the real-world data acquired through the field experiment of the G&CM to create real utilities in a community, and build a methodology to create effective system cooperation between individual systems embedded in a community.

For example, we focus on system cooperation between a community and medical and public service systems such as garbage collection, road repair, and street lamp management. Then, we investigate the significance and effectiveness of such system cooperation in a community and extract the problems in both the system and user sides.

Concretely, based on the data analysis on the spatiotemporal behavior of senior citizens, we extract their typical living patterns to build a model of a human-activity-driven System of Systems (SoS) and conduct simulations. Considering the bottom-up-type model for SoS, we have already proposed the interpenetrative model of system boundaries, as shown in Fig. 6 [6], and the boundary-mediated systems cooperation model so far [18–20]. Referring to such models, we build a new model for simulations, and implement the model into field experiments. The real data that will be acquired in the field experiments should be reflected in the simulation model such that the newly proposed model for system cooperation in a community could be refined.

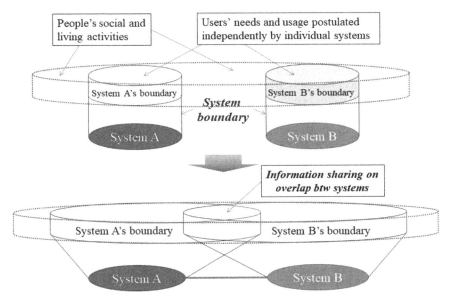

If system boundaries could be interpenetrative, information sharing and transfer between system boundaries can be made.

Fig. 6. Interpenetrative model of system boundaries

As an executional plan, this research will be divided into at least two phases, phase I and phase II. Phase I consists of the designing and modelling stage, wherein field experiments and simulations will be performed and evaluated. Based on the evaluation of phase I, phase II will consist of the re-designing and re-modelling stage, where the re-designed and re-modeled mechanism will be evaluated based on field experiments and simulations.

4   Conclusion

We focused on a community as a system that cannot exist without people's self-motivated involvement and proposed a mechanism through which their selfish behavior elicited awareness in their relationship with others to create an altruistic effect. In this research, conducting a field experiment wherein the proposed mechanism is utilized by the participants spontaneously and repeatedly, we aim to clarify and illustrate that wellbeing in a community is viable.

To accomplish this, the basic concepts of relationality and RAs were introduced. To make people aware of the significance and meaning of relationality in a community, we established that relationality should be considered as an asset in the social and economic values, expected to provide some utility to a community in the future. This implies that RAs are valuable for quantizing and visualizing the relationality that is naturally generated in people through interactions between "Hito," "Mono," and "Koto" in a community.

To achieve the above goal, we discussed the following research issues: 1) incentive design to prompt people's self-motivated and positive involvement in RAs, 2) demonstration of the effectiveness of G&CM as a mechanism to circulate the RAs through field experiments, and 3) building a methodology to create effective cooperation between systems embedded in a community by utilizing the data acquired through the G&CM to provide some utility and/or benefit in the community.

Acknowledgment. The author wishes to thank Ryo Shioya and Mizuki Tanaka (post-graduation students) for their contribution, and Prof. Yurika Shiozu, Kyoto Sangyo University, Prof. Kazuhiko Yonezaki, Taisho University, and Prof. Ivan Tanev, Doshisha University, for their help as research collaborators.

References

1. Shioya, R., Kimura, K., Shiozu, Y., Yonezaki, K., Tanev, I., Shimoahra, K.: Regional revitalization through finding potential hazards by object detection. In: Proceedings of SICE Annual Conference 2019, pp. 498–502 (2019)
2. Shimohara, K.: System for visualizing and managing relationality assets as trust enabling rebuilding of communities. In: Proceedings of the 4th Asia-Pacific World Congress on Computer Science and Engineering, pp. 88–92 (2017)
3. Ogita, K., Kimura, K., Shiozu, Y., Yonezaki, K., Tanev, I., Shimohara, K.: Simulation for visualizing relationality assets in local community. In: Proceedings of SICE Annual Conference 2018, pp. 670–673 (2018)
4. Kimura, K., Shiozu, Y., Tanev, I., Shimohara, K.: Relationality design for local community as system of systems. In: SICE Annual Conference (SICE 2015), pp. 490–493 (2015)
5. Shiozu, Y., Kimura, K., Shimohara, K.: A Measurement of the local community activity by the place. In: SICE Annual Conference (SICE 2015), pp. 494–499 (2015)
6. Shimohara, K.: Interpenetrative model of system boarders based on human activities – weaving trees with rhizome. J. Soc. Instrum. Control Eng. **55**(8), 680–685 (2016)
7. Shiozu, Y., Kimura, K., Shimohara, K.: The temporal analysis of networks for community activity. In: Yamamoto, S. (ed.) HIMI 2016. LNCS, vol. 9735, pp. 63–71. Springer, Cham (2016). https://doi.org/10.1007/978-3-319-40397-7_7
8. Kimura, K., Shiozu, Y., Tanev, I., Shimohara, K.: A leader and media spot estimation method using location information. In: Yamamoto, S. (ed.) HIMI 2016. LNCS, vol. 9735, pp. 550–559. Springer, Cham (2016). https://doi.org/10.1007/978-3-319-40397-7_53

9. Kimura, K., Shiozu, Y., Tanev, I., Shimohara, K.: Visualization of relationship between residents using passing-each-other data toward resident-centered vitalization of local community. In: Proceedings of the Second International Conference on Electronics and software Science (ICESS2016), pp. 122–127 (2016)
10. Shioya, R., Tnaka, M., Yonezaki, K., Shiozu, Y., Tanev, I., Shimohara, K.: Self-motivated information sharing in communities for promoting regional revitalization. IEEE Computer Science and Data Engineering, PID: 97, 4 p. (2019)
11. Takahara, M., Nakamura, K., Huang, F., Tanev, I., Shimohara, K.: Nursing care support system for caregiver and older adults. In: Yamamoto, S., Mori, H. (eds.) HCII 2019. LNCS, vol. 11570, pp. 568–577. Springer, Cham (2019). https://doi.org/10.1007/978-3-030-22649-7_46
12. Shiozu, Y., Kimura, K., Shimohara, K., Yonezaki, K.: Case study about the visualization of GPS data as the nudge and place attachment. In: Proceedings of SICE Annual Conference 2018, pp. 666–669 (2018)
13. Shiozu, Y., Kimura, K., Shioya, R., Shimohara, K., Yonezaki, K.: Relationship between difference of motivation and behavior change caused by visualization. In: Yamamoto, S., Mori, H. (eds.) HCII 2019. LNCS, vol. 11569, pp. 489–499. Springer, Cham (2019). https://doi.org/10.1007/978-3-030-22660-2_36
14. Yonezaki, K., Ogita, K., Kimura, K., Shiozu, Y., Shioya, R., Shimohara, K.: On the relationality assets and gift-and-circulation model in community problem. In: Yamamoto, S., Mori, H. (eds.) HCII 2019. LNCS, vol. 11569, pp. 638–647. Springer, Cham (2019). https://doi.org/10.1007/978-3-030-22660-2_47
15. Tanaka, M., Shioya, R., Yonezaki, K., Shiozu, Y., Tanev, I., Shimohara, K.: Multi-agent simulation of relationality assets to enable community vitalization. IEEE Computer Science and Data Engineering, PID: 80, 6 p. (2019)
16. Trivers, R.L.: The evolution of reciprocal altruism. Q. Rev. Biol. **46**(1), 35–57 (1971)
17. Buss, D.M. (ed.): The Handbook of Evolutionary Psychology, p. 1056. Wiley, Hoboken (2005)
18. Maeshiro, T.: Framework based on relationship to describe non-hierarchical, boundaryless and multi-perspective phenomena. SICE J. Control Meas. Syst. Integr. **11**(5), 381–389 (2018)
19. Shimohara, K.: Boundary and relationality perspective systems approach toward designing system of systems. In: Proceedings of SICE Annual Conference 2019, pp. 491–494 (2019)
20. Shimohara, K.: Boundary and relationality in systems design: toward designing system of systems. IEEE Computer Science and Data Engineering, PID: 83, 6 p. (2019)

Multimodal Interaction-Aware Integrated Platform for CSCL

Aoi Sugimoto, Yuki Hayashi$^{(\boxtimes)}$ (ID), and Kazuhisa Seta

Graduate School of Humanities and Sustainable System Sciences, Osaka Prefecture University,
Osaka 599-8531, Japan
`hayashi@kis.osakafu-u.ac.jp`

Abstract. In collaborative learning in a face-to-face environment, participants exchange verbal and non-verbal cues, including gaze and posture. To realize computer-supported collaborative learning (CSCL) systems that treat a form of multiparty multimodal interaction for different purposes according to the learning objective, executing each activity in the CSCL system life-cycle in a continuous and smooth manner is essential. The research objective is to propose an integrated platform as the basis for multimodal interaction-aware CSCL systems. In this paper, we develop a CSCL analysis support environment to support multimodal interaction analysis activities. The environment allows analysts 1) to utilize basic functions that support multimodal interaction analysis without excessive burden and 2) to analyze collaborative learning session data detected from the learning support system on our proposed platform, including verbal and non-verbal information along with developers' defined learning messages in an integrated way.

Keywords: CSCL · Multiparty multimodal interaction · Verbal and non-verbal information · Analysis support environment · System life-cycle

1 Introduction

Collaborative learning, in which plural participants learn together, is a well-known pedagogical approach to cultivate social interaction skills. Through active interaction processes in collaborative learning, participants reap several benefits from such interactions, ranging from constructing deeper-level learning, shared understanding to developing social and communication skills [1]. However, the quality of learning effects is not always assured due to the negative aspects of small group interactions. To reduce these problems and promote successful collaborative learning interaction, many studies have been conducted to study computer-supported collaborative learning (CSCL) [2].

Moreover, several studies have been conducted to study multiparty multimodal interaction to analyze small-group face-to-face interactions by combining several social signals (i.e., verbal and non-verbal information, such as speech, gaze, and gesture) as multimodal interaction data [3–5]. Using human sensing devices and applying the research findings of the support function of CSCL systems, we can expect the development

© Springer Nature Switzerland AG 2020
S. Yamamoto and H. Mori (Eds.): HCII 2020, LNCS 12185, pp. 264–277, 2020.
https://doi.org/10.1007/978-3-030-50017-7_19

of novel CSCL systems that can assess various interaction situations, e.g. respective participants' commitment to an interaction, and intellectually intervene in real time.

To realize a multimodal interaction-aware CSCL system and gather the findings, supporting the CSCL system life-cycle is essential: 1) developing the CSCL systems by developers, 2) practicing collaborative learning by participants, and 3) analyzing the learning interaction by analysts. Thus, the integrated platform is required whereby stakeholders with varied expertise, along with CSCL system developers and analysts of collaborative learning interactions, can work and accumulate knowledge together.

In this study, we propose a multimodal interaction-aware integrated platform that serves as a basis of the cyclical phases of the CSCL system life-cycle by bridging knowledge accumulated in the fields of multiparty multimodal interaction research and CSCL research. We have so far proposed CSCL development environment where system developers can implement their original learning support tools by using several multimodal interaction data [6]. In addition, in this paper, we focus on the development of a CSCL analysis support environment for analysts on the platform, which successfully accesses not only verbal data but also non-verbal interaction data from CSCL systems implemented on the CSCL development environment.

2 Background and Design Principle of the Integrated Platform for CSCL Systems

2.1 Background 1: Interaction Analysis Based on Multimodal Interaction Data

For analyzing and understanding the conversational structures in multiparty multimodal interaction, Sumi et al. proposed a hierarchical interaction model, as shown in Table 1 [7]. The model represents four types of layers combining elemental verbal and non-verbal communication signals exchanged among the participants to achieve multimodal interpretation processing that elicits contextual information, such as dominant-level transition. In this paper, we adopt the model as a grain size of layered concept for multimodal interpretation.

Many studies, based on low-level layer data, have analyzed the multiparty multimodal interaction for detecting/interpreting the high-level interaction (interaction context layer in Table 1). For examples, for estimating the interaction styles (e.g., discussions, and presentations), McCowan et al. proposed the hidden Markov model-based estimation model that used numerous audio features and visual (head and hand blobs) data as non-verbal features [8]. Hillard et al. proposed a recognition model of a specific type of interaction in meetings (agreement vs. disagreement) based on the number of utterances of each participant and positive/negative words included in their utterances using machine learning [9].

Although the research approach has a similar structure that lifts low-level layer data toward high-level interaction, the type of verbal and/or non-verbal features handled and their processing depend on the analysis target. In addition, analysts need to handle a heavy workload for preparing data before beginning the analysis. For example, for gathering participants' data from numerous video cameras, analysts should construct a multimodal interaction corpus [10] through a huge volume of data shaping work, such as adjustment of synchronously reproduced videos and annotation to target sections by observing each video frame.

Table 1. Hierarchical interpretation model based on interaction corpus (cf. [7]).

Interaction layer	Examples
Interaction context	*Dominant level transition*
Interaction event	*Joint attention, mutual gaze*
Interaction primitive	*Gaze, speech, gesture*
Raw data	*Motion data, wave data*

2.2 Background 2: Diverseness of CSCL Systems

Collaborative learning has various learning types/situations. For example, participants solving the same problems through discussion, creates artifacts cooperatively, and so forth. The forms of collaborative learning are characterized from several viewpoints, such as the number of participants, roles, learning objectives, learning materials, and frequency. To date, many CSCL systems specialized for supporting target learning situations have been proposed.

A CSCL system consists of learning support tool(s) that is/are designed according to the objective of collaborative learning. For example, C-CHINE is a learning support tool whereby participants are promoted to be aware of their own standpoints for the text-based collaborative interaction by providing a restricted set of communicative acts attached to respective each utterance [11]. ReCoNote is a note-sharing tool that requires participants to think explicitly about and comment on the relationships between leaning materials in a diverse perspective [12]. In this manner, system developers should construct specialized learning support tools that scaffold productive target interactions.

In addition, realizing CSCL systems that enable handling multimodal interaction data requires a mechanism to capture participants' verbal and non-verbal information emerging from moment to moment. However, no general platform exists that captures and manages participants' verbal and non-verbal information. Therefore, system developers should build detection functions of the target verbal and non-verbal information from scratch. Furthermore, because the developers' intentions of the developed support function are encoded in a program, conducting data analysis that reflects the developers' intention is difficult.

2.3 Design Principle

Based on the above discussion, realizing a CSCL system that utilizes multimodal interaction data requires developers and analysts to access target verbal and non-verbal information in the development and analysis phases and focus on their own essential work.

Therefore, concentrating on each development/analysis activities without being conscious of non-essential processing, such as detection processing of verbal and non-verbal data by developers and data shaping work of analysts, is essential. ——(i)

In addition, for successfully promoting the CSCL system life-cycle that incorporates the findings of the multiparty multimodal interaction, each stakeholder (developer/analyst) should refer to each other's knowledge without any excessive burden. For practical application, developers should implement CSCL systems that integrate and process learning support tool data, verbal and non-verbal information, while analysts can access the data obtained through the system into their analysis work and they also could apply the data to higher-level of collaborative learning-oriented multimodal interaction analysis, as shown in Table 1. ——(ii)

To satisfy requirements (i) and (ii), we set the following two design principles of the CSCL system development and analysis support environments implemented on our integrated platform.

Design Principle 1 (DP1). The platform allows developers and analysts to focus on their own activities (CSCL system development and data analysis) according to the target collaborative learning.

Design Principle 2 (DP2). The platform provides the mechanism to promote the CSCL system life-cycle in a way that reflects the knowledge of developers and analysts to each other.

3 CSCL System Development Environment Toward Collaborative Learning Analysis

Figure 1 represents the proposed CSCL system development environment to support developers' activities [6]. On this platform, the participants conduct collaborative learning on a remote environment using several sensing devices, such as microphone and eye-tracker, to capture verbal and non-verbal information (Fig. 1(a)). The learning session management function manages fundamental functions such as authentication process and information transmission/reception process exchanged in CSCL systems (Fig. 1(b)). In the development environment, developers can implement their original learning support tools (Fig. 1(c)). In addition, they can embed higher-order interpretation mechanism into their tools by accessing and combining heterogeneous information, that is, verbal, non-verbal, and learning support tool data, as multimodal information, if desired (Fig. 1(d)).

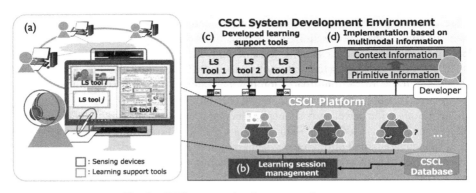

Fig. 1. CSCL system development environment.

3.1 Verbal and Non-verbal Information Based on the Hierarchical Interpretation Model

To lessen the workload in multimodal signal processing based on the hierarchical interaction model, we should present a platform whereby developers can focus on dealing with intended multimodal data without considering the lower-level detection processing (*DP1*).

To concretize this principle, the development environment detects and processes verbal and non-verbal information; *utterance* by a microphone (speech interval, content of utterance), *gaze behavior* by an eye-tracker (eye-coordinates data, gazing interval), *writing action* by a digital pen (timing of writings), and *head movement* by a depth camera (head direction data). It provides these data corresponding to *raw data* and *interaction primitive* layers in Table 1 for the developers as the basis of multimodal signal processing.

3.2 Message Processing

For real-time interaction in collaborative learning, various types of messages among the learning support tools should be controlled, for example, *text-chat message* on a text-chat tool and *writing coordinate message* on a shared-board tool, in addition to allocating the required verbal and non-verbal information to each target learning support tool appropriately.

In the development environment, we use a message processing mechanism that differentiates several types of structured messages; *SystemMessage*, *SessionInfoMessage*, *Multimodal-DataMessage*, and developers' defined *LearningSupportToolMessage* to satisfy the aforementioned requirement. This allows developers to access several target messages readily and concentrate on implementing their original learning support tools without being conscious of the low-order processing.

3.3 Data Management Toward CSCL System Data Analysis

The learning support tools developed in the environment can be built into the CSCL system. Hence, participants can conduct collaborative learning by using necessary learning support tools (e.g., learning support tool i, j, and k in Fig. 1(a)). Based on the recorded data through CSCL systems, analysts analyze collaborative learning interaction. In the analysis, along with the verbal and non-verbal information exchanged among participants, interaction information of learning support tool, such as "inputting characters into text-chat" and "pointing to arbitrary locations," should be considered as collaborative learning interaction analysis. Moreover, analysts should use the higher-level multimodal information originally defined by developers for promoting the CSCL system life-cycle (*DP2*).

To concretize the design principle, the development environment stores each data through message processing, explained in Sect. 3.2 into relational database management system (CSCL database in Fig. 1) and records stream video images of participants for analysis.

4   Requirements of the Analysis Support Environment

In this paper, we set following two requirements to realize an analysis support environment of collaborative learning interaction that follows the design principles in Sect. 2.3.

Requirement 1 (R1). To provide analysts with fundamental analytical functions used in multiparty multimodal interaction analysis (*DP1*: Sect. 4.1).

Requirement 2 (R2). To allow analysts to analyze recorded heterogeneous interaction data as a way to combine them (*DP2*: Sect. 4.2).

4.1   Requirement to Provide Fundamental Function for Multimodal Interaction Analysis

In the multiparty multimodal interaction, several analysis support tools, such as Anvil [13], ELAN [14], and iCorpusStudio [7], have been proposed. These tools serve several fundamental functions such as visualization function of several input multimodal interaction data and annotation support function to construct multimodal interaction corpus. These functions are widely used in interaction analysis that applies data-driven machine learning.

In our analysis support environment, it also provides the fundamental functions to analysts so that various interaction analysis methods can be realized according to the target collaborative learning interaction.

4.2   Requirement to Maintain CSCL System Life-Cycle

CSCL systems include learning tools that support target collaboration based on the learning objectives, and the actions performed on the learning tools are important components of the collaborative learning interaction. Therefore, in addition to verbal and non-verbal information of cooperative learning participants, such learning tool events should be analyzed.

In addition, because the message events that developers independently defined on the learning tools reflect their design intentions, handling these message events in the analysis is important to increase the degree of coupling between the development and analysis for promoting the CSCL system life-cycle.

Furthermore, as the basis toward examining learning tool functions and developing new support functions based on the analytical results, analysis processing based on the hierarchical interpretation model (Table 1) should be declaratively defined as rules (interpretation patterns) that include analysts' intention, and the analysis support environment handles the interpretation patterns by visualizing data corresponding to the patterns.

5   CSCL Analysis Support Environment

Figure 2 represents the module structure of the developed CSCL analysis support environment. The server side contains the CSCL database including the interaction data and video stream server that manages participants' videos of each collaborative learning session. Furthermore, they serve as a server of the CSCL system development environment.

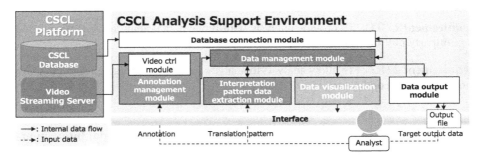

Fig. 2. Module structure of CSCL analysis support environment.

The client side extracts the interaction data based on the analysis target session through database connection module and handles them on the data management module. Analysts can conduct analysis on the user interface of the following four types of modules.

Data Visualization Module. Visualizes each basic analysis target session data in a timeline manner.

Interpretation Pattern Data Extraction Module. Extracts data as *InterpretationData* (Sect. 5.1) that corresponds to the interpretation pattern defined by analysts (Sect. 5.2) and registers them to the data management module.

Annotation Management Module. Manages annotation information as Annotation-Data (Sect. 5.1) and registers them to the data management module. This module equips a simultaneous playback function of participants' videos (video control module), so that analysts can annotate with the clue of the videos.

Data Output Module. Exports the arbitrary timeline data from the analysis.

Section 5.1 explains the features of the data structure managed in the data management module. Section 5.2 describes the analysis support functions that embody two requirements (R1 and R2) of the analysis support environment.

5.1   Data Structure for Interaction Analysis

The data management module handles several types of collaborative learning interaction data. Figure 3 represents the data class category. Each data class is defined as an object-oriented hierarchical structure. The data class inherits the *InteractionData* class that includes ID (*data_id*), layer information of the hierarchical interaction model (*layer*), and data labels (*label*).

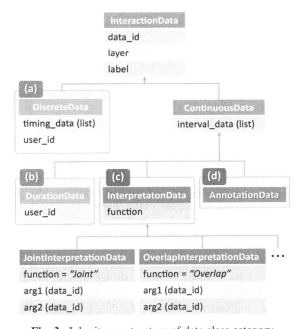

Fig. 3. Inheritance structure of data class category.

InteractionData is classified into two subclasses: (a) *DiscreteData* that is a list form of discrete data and *ContinuousData* that holds a list form of time section information (start and finish timestamp). ContinuousData is further classified into three types: (b) *DurationData*, (c) *InterpretationData*, and (d) *AnnotationData*. They have a basic structure that holds the interaction section occurred in the analysis target session.

DiscreteData (Fig. 3(a)). Consists of the raw data layer data measured in the analysis target session and learning support tool message data defined by CSCL system developers. This data class contains the timestamp information at the time of measurement as a discrete data in a list form, such as a button pressing action of a certain learning tool.

DurationData (Fig. 3(b)). Consists of the interaction primitive layer data, such as speech interval and participants/objects gazing interval provided by the development environment, or developer-defined higher-order data caught by the learning support tools accordingly.

DiscreteData and *DurationData* extracted from the CSCL database corresponding to the analysis target session are used as the initial display data of the visualization module and are specified as a condition in the interpretation pattern data (Sect. 5.2).

InterpretationData (Fig. 3(c)). Represents the data extracted by the extraction function of interpretation pattern data. Because the data used for interpreting and combining depends on the analysis, this data class has a data processing function that explicitly expresses the pattern for interpretation. *OverlapInterpretationData*, *JointInterpretationData*, etc. are defined as subclasses of *InterpretationData*. In these subclasses, each specific processing function is described, and the ID (*data_id*) of the target data is set to the arguments (e.g., *arg1*, *arg2*), which is the input of the function.

AnnotationData (Fig. 3(d)). Represents the data that holds annotation information given to an arbitrary section by an analyst. For example, manually added data of a higher-order interaction level, such as [layer = "Interaction Context", label = "stalemate of discussion"] or [layer = "Interaction Context", label = "topic transition"], are applicable.

5.2 Analysis Support Mechanisms to Follow the Platform Design Principle

Mechanism to Support Multiparty Multimodal Interaction Analysis
To provide analysts with the basic functions of the multimodal interaction analysis (R1), the CSCL analysis support environment has the following functions.

Data Visualization Function. Displays interaction data provided by the data visualization module based on session information (session start/end time, participants, and applying data for analysis) input by analysts. Figure 4 shows the visualization window. Each data of the three participants (A, B, and C) in the same session is displayed as a timeline manner. In the interface, analysts can observe the data in detail by using the zooming in/out button.

Annotation Support Function. Provides analysts with an annotation interface (Fig. 5). In the interface, the video images of the participants are reproduced (Fig. 5(a)), and annotations can be given to specifying sections by dragging operation, as in the conventional annotation support tools (Fig. 5(b)).

Data Export Function. Outputs analysis results through the analysis support environment. In the interface, analysts can select a set of data from the four types of data classes described in Sect. 5.1. The output file takes a CSV format in which rows and columns correspond to the specified frame (milliseconds) and each selected data, respectively. This file can be used as an analysis data set for adapting data-driven machine learning methods.

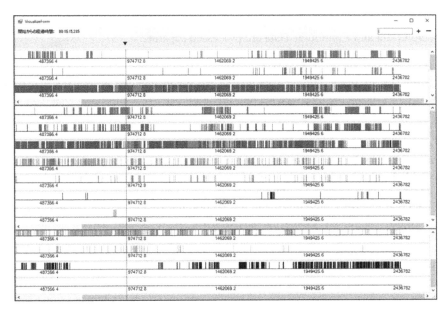

Fig. 4. Visualization window of collaborative learning process interaction data.

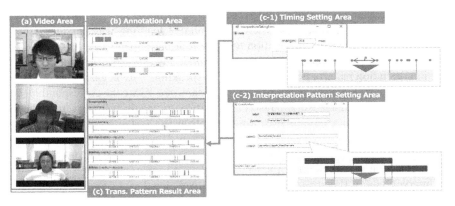

Fig. 5. Interface of annotation and interpretation pattern data extracting function.

Mechanism to Manage Role Definition and Interpretation Pattern Data Extraction

For successful collaborative learning, the "role" played by participants is important [15]. This function realizes the analysis by considering such participants' roles as a specialized function for the collaborative learning interaction analytics. Analysts can assign defined roles such as *Learner*, *Instructor*, *Helper*, and *Observer* as actors of *DiscreteData* and *DurationData*.

In addition, to realize the analysis for promoting the continuity of the CSCL system life-cycle (R2), the analysis support environment comprises a mechanism to manage interpretation pattern data definition/extraction. In this mechanism, the data categorized as DiscreteData and ContinuousData are processed separately.

(i) Interpretation pattern of DiscreteData:
It is a process of interpreting *DiscreteData* for being handled as the interval data. Figure 5(c−1) shows the interface for interpretation pattern definition of *DiscreteData*. On the interface, analysts can select data to be processed (left-side area) and input margin time corresponding to the selection (right-side area).
This example corresponds to the extraction of input timing to the note tool. When the interval of the data is within the set second (200 ms in this case), the combined sections are extracted.

(ii) Interpretation pattern of ContinuousData:
Each data that inherits *ContinuousData* has section information (start and finish timestamp). Figure 5(c−2) represents the interface for interpretation pattern definition of *ContinuousData*. Analysts can define *labels* to be assigned to data sections that match the pattern, *interaction layers* (Table 1) corresponding to interpretation patterns, and processing *functions*. The arguments of the selected function can be set at the bottom of the interface as preconditions. The analysis support environment, currently, provides functions that realize processing of overlapping section (*Overlap*), joint section (*Joint*), and reinterpretation of the section list (*All*).

The data section extracted from the interpretation patterns of *(i)* and *(ii)* is displayed on the visualization area shown in Fig. 5(c). As an example of interpretation pattern extraction, we suppose situations where collaborative learning was conducted using video-chat tools and poster presentation tools by four participants (p_1, p_2, p_3, and p_4). During the startup, *DiscreteData* and *DurationData* in Fig. 3 can be set as the arguments to the interpretation pattern. For example, "$\underline{p_X\ is\ speaking,}$" "$\underline{p_X\ is\ gazing\ at\ p_Y}$," "$\underline{p_X\ is}$ $\underline{gazing\ at\ poster\ area\ Y,}$" and "$\underline{p_X\ is\ pointing\ to\ poster\ area\ Y}$" are the corresponding data recorded in the CSCL database. Analysts can specify participants' roles by setting the role definition function. For example, by setting the role as [$p_1 \rightarrow$ *Learner*, $p_2 \rightarrow$ *Observer*, $p_3 \rightarrow$ *Helper*, $p_4 \rightarrow$ *Learner*], analysts can handle new data such as "$\underline{Helper\ is\ speaking}$" and "$\underline{Learner}$ is gazing at $\underline{Helper}$" that are automatically created by the define roles for the interpretation pattern setting. Based on the data, for example, analysts can extract each interval data of [layer = "Interaction Primitive", label = "$\underline{Helper}$ is observed by others"] by setting the interpretation pattern as [function = Joint ("*Learner*" is gazing at *Helper*", "*Observer*" is gazing at *Helper*")]. In addition, for extracting the interval of [layer = "Interaction Event", label = "$\underline{Helper}$ is explaining the contents of $\underline{poster\ area}$ $\underline{X}$"], the interpretation pattern [function = Overlap ("*Helper*" is speaking", "*Helper*" is gazing at poster area X")] corresponds to the interval data.

The data intervals extracted by set interpretation pattern are managed by the data management module as *InterpretationData* in Fig. 3(c). In addition, they can be set as additional arguments of interpretation patterns. For example, for extracting the interval of [layer = "Interaction Event", label = "$\underline{Learner}$ is observing $poster\ area\ X$ where $\underline{Helper}$ is explaining"], the interpretation pattern [function = Overlap ("*Helper*" is explaining the contents of *poster area X*", "Learner is gazing at *poster area X*")] corresponds to the interval, so that analysts can accumulate higher-order interpretation data based on their previous set patterns.

In this manner, analysts can explicitly define the higher-level interpretation rule in a declarative manner and collect interpretation data based on the interpretation pattern extraction function provided by this analysis support environment. In addition, by enabling data analysis with considering participants' roles, analysis reflecting the collaborative learning theory can be supported and the interpretation patterns can be reused to apply to other sessions in which role configuration of the participants is same as the analysis target session.

6 Discussion

Studies on multiparty multimodal interactions provide knowledge on analysis of communication in face-to-face situations. Collaborative learning can be regarded as a form specialized to the "learning context" of such interactions. In this paper, we discussed the realization of an analysis support environment that uses the method of multiparty multimodal interaction research in the analysis of collaborative learning. In the communication of participants in a distributed environment, we realized a mechanism that analyzes verbal and non-verbal information.

In this section, we discuss the significance of the integrated platform developed from the viewpoint of multiparty multimodal interaction analysis not limited to the learning context and from the one specialized for the CSCL context.

First, as a significance of interaction analysis environment in a situation under a distributed environment not limited to the learning context, we realized the platform at the intersection of top-down and bottom-up analysis approaches. This is realized by annotation support and data analysis functions (*R1* as an embodiment of *DP1*) and an interpretation pattern data extraction function (*R2* as an embodiment of *DP2*). Because the annotation result given by analysts and bottom-up analysis result based on the interpretation pattern along the hierarchical interaction model can be outputted, machine learning can be used as a top-down analysis to these output data.

Second is the significance as a basis to share and accumulate analytical know-how. We realized this through a declarative description of the interpretation pattern (*R2* as an embodiment of *DP2*). The platform provides common operators such as Overlap and Joint for interpretation lifting. Analysts can use them to define interpretation patterns along the hierarchical interaction model. With this mechanism, analysts do not need to embed the process corresponding to the interpretation pattern as a procedural program, and they can declare their interpretation intentions based on the common operators. Thus, comparison of each interpretation pattern and sharing them are relatively easy, and evidence of analysis results, how high-order interpretation is given, can be referred by other analysts/developers.

The third significance is to realize the CSCL analysis environment according to the developers' intentions of the learning support tools. We realized this by defining/processing the learning support tool messages (Sect. 3.2) and interpretation pattern data extraction function. The messages that developers focused on and incorporated them into learning tools were successfully exchanged among various learning support tools, and these messages (e.g., "mutual gaze" captured by the video-chat tools and "joint attention" captured by the poster tools) were set as preconditions of interpretation patterns. Because the analysis results focusing on those messages can be feedback to developers along with the interpretation patterns, communication between developers and analysts is less likely to create conceptual gaps.

The fourth is the significance when setting the second significance as specialized for CSCL analysis as a basis for promoting the comparison of analytical intent by considering the characteristics of collaborative learning and sharing the analytical know-how. Because the environment allows analysts to specify participants' roles that are important features of collaborative learning and set them as preconditions of interpretation patterns, analysts can share and reuse the patterns, beyond a specific analysis target session, for the collaborative learning group consisting of the same participants' roles.

Nowadays, chatting through the Internet, videophone, and other situations where we communicate with other people remotely is a common norm. In the multiparty multimodal interaction analysis in such a distributed environment, the analysis concepts in the face-to-face interaction may not always apply in a directly manner. For example, it is likely that aspects such as joint attention and mutual gaze are different from the face-to-face environment. From this point of view, our proposed environment provides basic analysis functions used for various face-to-face interaction analyses and enables analysis that targets remote synchronous-typed general interaction. In this regard, we believe the environment also has a potential for clarifying the analytical concept unique to distributed human communication.

7   Conclusion

In this paper, while building the foundation to form the bridge between multiparty multimodal interaction research and CSCL research, we proposed an integrated platform to support CSCL system life-cycle activities. As design principles, the platform should allow developers and analysts to focus on their own essential activities according to target collaborative learning, and provide the mechanism to promote the CSCL system life-cycle in a way that reflects the knowledge of developers and analysts. Based on the CSCL system development environment proposed in our previous research, we developed an analysis support environment equipped with these principles. The proposed environment provides analysts with basic functions related to analysis tools of multimodal interaction, and provides role definition and interpretation pattern data extraction functions for collaborative learning interaction analysis.

We recognize that the usefulness of this environment for supporting the CSCL life-cycle is an important future task that needs careful consideration through evidence-based long-term operation. In addition, we intend to refine and enrich the processing functions for interpretation patterns to be provided to analysts by expanding the verbal and non-verbal information provided to CSCL system developers.

Acknowledgements. This work is partially supported by JSPS KAKENHI Grant Numbers 19K12275, 17K18017 and 17H00774.

References

1. Kreijns, K., Kirschner, P.A., Jochems, W.: Identifying the pitfalls for social interaction in computer-supported collaborative learning environments: a review of the research. Comput. Hum. Behav. **19**(3), 335–353 (2003)
2. Jermann, P., Soller, A., Muehlenbrock, M.: From mirroring to guiding: a review of the state of art technology for supporting collaborative learning. In: Proceedings of European Conference on Computer-Supported Collaborative Learning Eu-roCSCL-2001, pp. 324–331 (2001)
3. Gatica-Perez, D.: Automatic nonverbal analysis of social interaction in small groups: a review. Image Vis. Comput. **27**, 1775–1787 (2009)
4. Burgoon, J.K., Magnenat-Thalmann, N., Pantic, M., Vinciarelli, A. (eds.): Social Signal Processing. Cambridge University Press, Cambridge (2017)
5. Thiran, J.P., Marques, F., Bourlard, H. (eds.): Multimodal Signal Processing: Theory and Applications for Human-Computer Interaction. Academic Press, Cambridge (2009)
6. Sugimoto, A., Hayashi, Y., Seta, K.: Multimodal interaction aware platform for collaborative learning. In: Proceedings of 25th International Conference on Computers in Education, pp. 316–325 (2017)
7. Sumi, Y., Yano, M., Nishida, T.: Analysis environment of conversational structure with non-verbal multimodal data. In: Proceedings of International Conference on Multimodal Interfaces and the Workshop on Machine Learning for Multimodal Interaction (2010). Article no. 44
8. McCowan, L., Gatica-Perez, D., Bengio, S., Lathoud, G., Barnard, M., Zhang, D.: Automatic analysis of multimodal group actions in meetings. Proc. IEEE Trans. Pattern Anal. Mach. Intell. **27**(3), 305–317 (2005)
9. Hillard, D., Ostendorf, M., Shriberg, E.: Detection of agreement vs. disagreement in meetings: training with unlabeled data. In: Proceedings of the HLT-NAACL Conference, pp. 34–36 (2003)
10. Sanchez-Cortes, D., Aran, O., Gatica-Perez, D.: An audio visual corpus for emergent leader analysis. In: Proceedings of Multimodal Corpora for Machine Learning, pp. 14–18 (2011)
11. Backer, M.J., Lund, K.: Flexibly structuring the interaction in a CSCL environment. In: Proceedings of the EuroAIED Conference, pp. 401–407 (1996)
12. Miyake, N., Masukawa, H.: Relation-making to sense-making: supporting college students' constructive understanding with an enriched collaborative note-sharing system. In: Proceedings of 4th international Conference of the Learning Science, pp. 41–47 (2000)
13. Kipp, M.: Anvil - a generic annotation tool for multimodal dialogue. In: Proceedings of 7th European Conference on Speech Communication and Technology (2001)
14. Wittenburg, P., Brugman, H., Russel, A., Klassmann, A., Sloetjes, H.: ELAN: a professional framework for multimodality research. In: Proceedings of 5th International Conference on Language Resources and Evaluation, pp. 1556–1559 (2006)
15. Inaba, A., Mizoguchi, R.: Learners' roles and predictable educational benefits in collaborative learning. In: Proceedings of International Conference on Intelligent Tutoring Systems, pp. 285–294 (2004)

The Influence of Human-Computer Sagittal Interaction in Peripersonal Space on Affective Valence Appraisals

Xinyan Wang[1,2](✉) and Yen Hsu[1](✉)

[1] Tatung University, Taipei City 104, Taiwan, People's Republic of China
d10717012@ms.ttu.edu.tw, yhsu@gm.ttu.edu.tw
[2] Jincheng College of Nanjing University of Aeronautics and Astronautics, Nanjing, China

Abstract. This dissertation argues, from an embodied perspective, that people's emotional connection with space is based on their physical structure and their experience of interacting with the environment. Accordingly, the space surrounding the dominant hand and non-dominant hand is associated with different valence appraisals of emotional content (i.e., right hand toward the right space-positive; left hand toward the left space-positive). Rizzolatti regards that the space surrounding us is divided into two parts with the arm length, the space within is called peripersonal space and distant peripersonal space on the contrary. Interestingly, the experiments based on Embodied Cognitive have not been examined with regard to the peripersonal and distant-peripersonal space. Therefore, the study has considered this question and aims to explore the influence of the user's sagittal interaction in peripersonal space (distal-to-proximal or proximal-to-distal touchscreen' locations) on affective valence appraisals.

A total of 80 right-handed participants took part in the experiment. 40 emotional pictures (20 positive pictures and 20 negative pictures) were evaluated after swiping on a touchscreen, either toward or away from the body. Experimental studies aim to explore the association between affective valence with hand dominance (i.e. dominant hand-positive; non-dominant hand-negative) and sagittal movements (far-to-near interaction-positive/near-to-far interaction-negative). Furthermore, to investigate how sagittal actions of the hands may influence affective experiences, for example, in valence appraisals of affective objects that have been manipulated. The results indicated that when interacting with positive pictures, a valence matching between the hand used for the interactions, the picture's valence category, and the movement direction reinforced the valence appraisals of the pictures (i.e. positive pictures were more positively evaluated). Conversely, there is no significant difference when interacting with negative pictures, which means Polarity Correspondence Principle does not apply to negative pictures in peripersonal space. In conclusion, the findings of this study further enrich the Embodied Cognitive theory and Polarity Correspondence Principle in Human-Computer Interaction which can be used to improve user emotional experience.

Keywords: Peripersonal space · Sagittal space · Embodied cognition · Body specificity hypothesis · Polarity correspondence principle · Affective valance

© Springer Nature Switzerland AG 2020
S. Yamamoto and H. Mori (Eds.): HCII 2020, LNCS 12185, pp. 278–288, 2020.
https://doi.org/10.1007/978-3-030-50017-7_20

1 Introduction

Embodied cognition theory posits that a person's environment and physical behavior, both have a certain degree of influence on their cognition and emotions [1–3]. This dissertation argues, from an embodied perspective, that people's emotional connection with space is based on their physical structure and their experience of interacting with the environment [4]. Casasant (2009) concluded from the outcomes of several experiments that an individual's left–right spatial cognition is based on their own body space; this cognition develops as a result of their interactions with the environment with their left and right hands. Therefore, right-handed and left-handed people have different emotional connections with their surrounding space. For example, a right-handed person tends to associate the right side with the positive and the left side with the negative. The opposite holds true for left-handed people [5–7].

During hand-held human–computer interactions, the human body serves as a behavioral carrier, forming the core element that influences the user's emotional experience. According to Embodied Cognition Theory, users interact with the terminal through their body posture and hand movements, triggering the cognition of the body and physical behavior. Studies show that in a touch-screen environment different types of human–computer interactions trigger different emotions in users [8]. Studies that investigate the influence of touch-screen interfaces on users' emotional cognition usually employ large screens in their experiments. Still, it is unclear if the same results can be applied to smaller touch-screen devices.

Rizzolatti, Matelli and Pavesi (1983) assert that the body's three-dimensional space can be divided into two parts with reference to the arms: the space within the reach of the arms is considered peripersonal and the space beyond the reach of the arms is considered distant peripersonal [9]. Li, Watter and Sun (2011) discovered that there is a difference in cognitive processing between peripersonal and distant peripersonal space [10]. The size of a touch-screen might determine the available space for the interactive gestures of users, thus influencing their emotional cognition. This leads to a crucial question: If the experimental device is changed to a small-sized touch-screen, will the interactive gestures still have an influence on users' emotions? Our study employs small tablet computers to display pictures with emotional valences that serve as emotional stimuli. We aim to explore the connection between users' cognition of the pictures' valence and the direction of movement (far-to-near and near-to-far) within peripersonal space. We also investigate the influence of radial human–computer interactions on users' cognition of emotional valences.

2 Literature Review

2.1 Embodied Cognitive and Body Specificity Hypothesis

Embodied cognition theory posits that an individual's cognitive processing is closely related to their environment and that the body and the environment are major elements in the cognition system [11]. Through several experiments, Casasanto (2009) found that discrete individuals develop different interaction experiences when interacting with their environments, thus forming discrepancies in their cognition of the outer world [12].

Humans use their own body as a reference for their emotional cognition of space, which is developed through the interaction of their hands and the surroundings. In their daily lives, right-handed subjects interact with their surroundings mainly with their right hands. Thus, their right hands tend to command better muscle strength, agility, and balance, ensuring a more active experience with the space on the right side. The opposite holds true for left-handed subjects. This is how we know that right-handed and left-handed people have different emotional cognition with regard to spatial locations [4, 13]. For instance, Wilson and Nisbett (1978) discovered that subjects tended to give higher values to socks placed on the right side of a rack than those placed on the left side [14]. Natale, Gur and Gur (1983) discovered in their experiment that subjects tended to label the neutral faces presented on the left side of the screen as "negative" and the neutral faces presented on the right side of the screen as "positive" [15]. Casasanto (2009) developed the body-specificity hypothesis (BSH): since right-handed people command greater motor fluency on their right side, this space is often associated with positive valence [12]. However, they do not command a comparable degree of motor fluency on their left side, so this space is often associated with negative valence. However, based on BSH, studies such as the one performed by de la Vega, Filippis, Lachmair, Dudschig and Kaup (2012) investigate whether the dominant hand's movements are connected to the processing of positive or negative stimuli [16]. The researchers asked all the subjects to choose the part of speech for each word appearing on a screen. The right-handed subjects tended to respond faster when clicking on the active words with their right hands and when clicking on the negative words with their left hands. Left-handed subjects, in contrast, responded faster when clicking on the positive words with their left hands and when clicking on the negative words with their right hands. In other words, consistent polarity helped speed up the subjects' emotional cognition process. This result supports the BSH.

In general, subjects tend to associate the more physically fluent, dominant hand with active emotions and the less physically fluent, non-dominant hand with passive emotions. In line with this thinking, when right-handed subjects use their dominant hand (right hand–positive) and non-dominant hand (left hand–negative) to interact with the valence-laden stimuli on a touch-screen, their emotional experience may differ depending on the hand that they use.

2.2 Polarity Correspondence Principle

Since humans react to positive stimuli faster than to negative stimuli [17], in the stimulus valence dimension, stimuli with positive valence is considered as [+] polarity, while stimuli with negative valence is considered as [−] polarity. In studies about emotion valences in sagittal space, arm movements towards the body are associated with [+] polarity, while arm movements away from the body are associated with [−] polarity [18, 19]. Lakens (2012) developed the Polarity Coding Correspondence Hypothesis with reference to emotions and spatial cognition [20]. In the Polarity Coding Correspondence Hypothesis [21], it is argued that a stimulated emotional meaning (valence) and its cognition type (space) overlap, thus speeding up the emotion cognition process and giving subjects a more positive emotional experience. For example, in Cacioppo's study (1983) [22], it was found that the contraction of arm muscles (extension-away/flexion-toward) influences subjects' cognition of the emotional valence of stimuli. Compared to subjects with their arms moving forward (extension - [−] polarity), subjects with their arms moving backward (flexion - [+] polarity) have a more active valence evaluation of Chinese characters. Cacioppo's study (1983) [22] also shows that arm movement influences subjects' emotional cognition.

When conducting emotional valence research on the sagittal space, positive or negative emotional stimuli (e.g., words or pictures) were displayed on a touch-screen. The subjects completed their interactions with the emotional stimuli by moving their arms forward or backward (i.e., extension or flexion) and evaluating the emotional valences of the stimuli after the interaction [23, 24]. The results showed that swiping the positive pictures toward body (flexion) or swiping the pictures away (extension), both create positive changes in the valence processing of pictures among subjects (with an increase in valence evaluation for positive pictures and a decrease in valence evaluation for negative pictures) [25]. In other words, individuals with different body features interact with their physical environments in different ways and experience varied movement cognition. This will eventually lead to the creation of different psychological representation events that influence the emotional experiences and spatial representations of individuals [12]. In a touch-screen environment, varied operation gestures for human–computer interaction will have diverse influences on users' emotions [8].

2.3 Peripersonal Space

Rizzolatti, Matelli and Pavesi (1983) divide three-dimensional space into two parts: the space that can be reached by the arms is known as peripersonal space and the space that is beyond the reach of the arms is known as distant peripersonal space [9]. Rizzolatti and his colleagues (1990, 1998) argue that since peripersonal space can be physically engaged with, individuals tend to fully process the operational messages of stimuli; in contrast, distant peripersonal space cannot be physically engaged with, so individuals only need to scan and recognize the stimuli instead of processing them [26, 27]. Costantini, Ambrosini, Tieri, Sinigaglia and Committeri (2010) discovered that in peripersonal space, operational representations related to stimuli are processed, while those in distant peripersonal space are not [28]. This result supports Previc's position (1990, 1998) [29, 30].

In the past, experiments and studies have mostly used large multimedia screens [23–25, 31]. Very few studies explore the influence of human–computer interaction on users' emotions in a small-screened environment. Since the touch-screen is smaller, users' hands interactions always remain within the peripersonal space, while most of the movements are limited to the hands rather than the arms. Under these circumstances, the use of hands, the direction of swiping, and the pictures' valence might all exert different influences on users' emotional cognition.

Therefore, this study employs small tablet computers to display pictures with emotional valences that serve as emotional stimuli. We aim to explore the connection between users' cognition of emotional valences and the direction of movement (far-to-near and near-to-far) of both hands (right and left) within peripersonal space. We also investigate the influence of radial human–computer interaction on users' cognition of emotional valences. Through these experiments, we hope to analyze the influence of radial human–computer interactions in peripersonal space on users' cognition of emotional valences when operations carry a stimulus valence.

3   Method

This study was carried out by experimental method, in which the emotional pictures were used as stimulate materials [31]. The participants evaluated the pictures using numbers between 1 (very negative) and 9 (very positive) after swiping them on the iPad, either towards or away from their body.

3.1   Participants

A total of 80 right-handed participants (M_{age} = 20.37, SD = 0.850, 47.5% female) took part in the study in exchange for parts of course credits. The participants were randomly divided into four groups whose visual acuity or corrected visual acuity were normal. Meanwhile, there was no obvious physical disease affecting their hand movements.

3.2   Apparatus and Stimuli

Twenty positive pictures (e.g., plants, landscapes or lovely animals) and twenty negative pictures (e.g., trash, mass or disaster) from the International Affective Picture System (IAPS; Lang, Bradley and Cuthbert 2005) were used as stimuli. An ANOVA on the pictures' valence means confirmed differences between the valence categories ($M_{positive}$ = 5.88, $SD_{positive}$ = 0.16, $M_{negative}$ = 3.40, $SD_{negative}$ = 0.74), $F (1,38)$ = 210.732, $p < 0.001$). A tablet (iPad pro 10.5 (17.4 cm × 25.1 cm)) was used to display the stimuli pictures with a resolution of 4.0 cm × 5.0 cm. The brightness, contrast and other functions of the tablets used by the four groups were set uniformly.

3.3   Procedure

Participants all sat in a natural posture with the tablet putting widthwise on the table in front of them, at a distance of 25 cm to the display screen. The experiment was carried out in two sessions, two days apart. The first session is the pretest which was performed to control for the differences within and between the experimental groups. In this section, participants evaluated the valence of the pictures two days before the formal experiment. The stimuli pictures were randomly displayed middle-centered on the iPad with a 9-point Likert scale (1-very negative, 9-very positive) below to evaluate their valence. The experiment task was introduced to the participants as a procedure, and participants were asked to evaluate the pictures just by watching as soon as possible. The results showed that the evaluated valence of all participants on different pictures were highly consistent in the same dimension, and the internal consistency coefficient was within the accepted range of psychometrics, so the evaluation results were credible. The second session is the formal experiment. In this session, 80 participants were randomly assigned to one of four experimental groups. Two groups of participants touched and swiped the pictures on the screen towards or away from their body only with their dominant right hand, while the other two groups of participants with their non-dominant left hand (see Fig. 1). Those pictures were presented randomly regarding their valence category which were displayed either at the near or far side of the touchscreen from the participants' end. A 9-point Likert scale from 1 (very negative) to 9 (very positive) was used to evaluate digital pictures. Pictures displayed randomly in the middle of the screen after participants logged into the test program, and the participants were asked to touch and move the pictures away or towards their body with their dominant or non-dominant hand to a white square indicated the movement endpoint. After each movement the picture just disappeared, then it appeared again in the middle of the screen together with a 9-point Likert scale below it. Participants had to evaluate the picture using 1 (very negative) to 9 (very positive) and they can rest at any time without time limits.

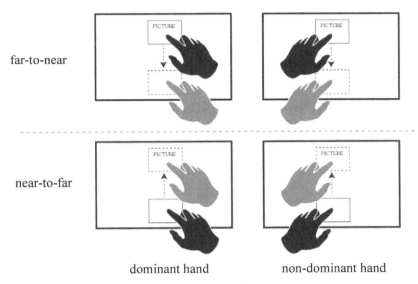

Fig. 1. Participants were randomly assigned into four groups. Two groups of participants touched and moved the pictures using their dominant right hand while the other two groups using their non-dominant left hand. Participants subsequently moved the pictures on the iPad either away or towards their body. Dashed areas represent the final hand's position and the dotted squares represent the final pictures' position.

4   Data Analyses and Results

Experimental studies aim to explore the association between affective valence with hand dominance (i.e. dominant hand-positive; non-dominant hand-negative) and sagittal movement. Furthermore, to investigate how sagittal actions of the hands may influence affective experiences, for example, in valence appraisals of affective objects that have been manipulated. Valence evaluations were analyzed with a 2 (hand: dominant right hand vs. non-dominant left hand) × 2 (movement: forward vs. backward) × 2 (valence category: positive vs. negative), fixed-effects structure.

4.1 Affective Valence Evaluation with Sagittal Movements

A three-way ANOVA was used to analyze the effects of hand, sagittal movements and the pictures' affective valence on emotional cognition. Valence category and sagittal movement were manipulated between subjects, whereas valence category was manipulated within subjects. A summary of the results can be seen in Table 1.

Table 1. Effects of hand, movement and affective valence on affective valence appraisals

Source	SS	df	MS	F	p	η_p^2
within						
Valence	1.08	1	1.08	6.41	.02**	.14
Hand*valence	.37	1	.37	2.20	.15	.06
Error (valence)	6.41	38	.17			
Movement	161.38	1	161.38	157.98	.00***	.81
Hand*movement	.09	1	.09	.08	.77	.00
Error (movement)	38.93	38	1.02			
Valence*movement	1.32	1	1.32	8.73	.01**	.19
Hand*valence*movement	.07	1	.07	.45	.51	.01
Error (valence*movement)	5.73	38	.15			
between						
Hand	2.15	1	2.15	1.39	.25	.04
Error (hand)	58.74	38	1.55			

Note: $^*p < 0.1$, $^{**}p < 0.05$, $^{***}p < 0.01$;

The results of the study showed a significant main effect of the pictures' valence categories, $F(1,38) = 6.41$, $p = 0.016$, $\eta_p^2 = 0.144$, indicating that positive pictures led to more positive evaluations than negative pictures. Sagittal movements also showed a significant main effect indicating that moving towards body led to more positive evaluations than moving away movements.

The two way interaction between valence categories and sagittal movement were significant, $F(1,38) = 8.73$, $p = 0.005$, $\eta_p^2 = .187$. Due to the significant interaction between the two, the simple main effect test was further carried out (seeing Fig. 2). The results indicated that valence categories had a significant simple main effect no matter moving the picture away ($F(1,76) = 420.90$, $p < 0.001$) or towards ($F(1,76) = 602.25$, $p < 0.001$) body. There was also a significant simple main effect on the interaction with positive pictures and sagittal movements, which indicating moving positive pictures towards body led to more positive evaluations than moving away ($F(1,76) = 4.05$, $p = 0.005$, $\eta_p^2 = .051$). But unexpectedly we didn't find any significant effect on the interaction with negative pictures.

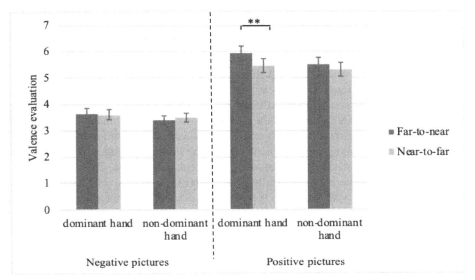

Fig. 2. Valence evaluations of pictures after sagittal movements with the dominant right hand and the non-dominant left hand. Vertical bars indicate 95% confidence intervals. ** represent significant effects at the level of p<0.01.

The analysis of three-way interaction showed no significant difference between hand, sagittal movement and valence category (F (1,38) = 0.45, p = 0.51) (seeing Table 2) indicating that the three of them had no mutual effect on the experimental results. However, in order to gain further insight into the kind of sagittal movement that effects affective valence appraisals most, the results with regard to the influence of the hand used to interact with the pictures will be described below.

Table 2. Simple main effect analyses

Source	SS	df	MS	F	p	η_p^2
Valence categories						
far-to-near (backward)	96.36	1	96.36	602.25	.00***	0.89
near-to-far (forward)	67.34	1	67.34	420.90	.00***	0.85
Error	12.16	76	0.16			
Sagittal movement						
Positive	2.38	1	2.38	4.05	.01**	0.05
Negative	0.00	1	0.00	0.01	.93	0.00
Error	44.65	76	0.59			

Note: **p < 0.05, ***p < 0.01;

4.2 Affective Valence Evaluation with Hand

Swiping positive pictures with the dominant right hand resulted in more positive ratings after far-to-near movements than after near-to-far movements, t (38) = 2.56, p = 0.01. In contrast, interaction with negative pictures by the dominant right hand did not result in any significantly different evaluations between the same sagittal movements, t (38) = 0.11, p = 0.91. The result indicated that when interacting positive pictures with the dominant hand, the codes matching of the pictures' valence, the dominant right hand, as well as the moving towards movements reinforced the valence evaluation of the positive pictures. Likewise, swiping positive pictures with the dominant right hand resulted in more positive evaluations than with non-dominant left hand, t (37) = 2.60, p = 0.01.

However, sagittal interaction with either positive (t (38) = 1.27, p = 0.21) or negative pictures (t (36.132) = −0.22, p = 0.83) by the non-dominant left hand led to any significant difference in valence evaluations. This suggested that, in this case, the valence codes of the pictures' combination of the hand and sagittal movements from the participants' non-dominant left side, made no difference in the valence evaluation. Moreover, it appeared that when moving negative pictures with the dominant right hand (t (37) = 0.69, p = 0.50) or non-dominant left hand (t (36.714) = 0.49, p = 0.63) resulted in no significant difference in valence evaluations, no matter away or towards the participant's body.

5 Conclusion

This study was conducted through experiments and was based on embodied cognition theory. Small-sized tablet computers were chosen as experimental devices. Pictures with emotional valences were used as emotional stimuli to explore the connection between subjects' cognition of emotional valences and interactions with different hands (left and right) in different directions (far-to-near and near-to-far).

1. In a radial movement human–computer interaction, set in a peripersonal space, moving the pictures with active emotions closer by operating the touch-screen has an active influence on the subjects' cognition. This is consistent with the polarity coding correspondence theory. However, when it comes to pictures with passive emotions, the movement type does not have any significant influence on subjects. Furthermore, data analysis shows that when moving pictures with active emotional valences, moving them in a radial direction near-to-far makes subjects who are using their dominant hands (right hands) more active in their cognition of emotional valences than subjects using their non-dominant hands (left hands). This is consistent with the theory of embodied cognition. However, when it comes to pictures with passive emotions, the operation types do not have any significant influence on subjects. This may be because passive emotions are not caused by significant dimensions. According to de la Vega, Dudschig, Lachmair and Kaup (2014), the connection between stimuli and similar encoding may be triggered by significant stimuli [32]. Since passive emotions are not included in significant dimensions, the polarity encoding consistency used in this experiment does not have a significant influence on subjects.

2. Torres (2018) pointed out that when subjects operate the touch-screen, the hands used for the interaction (dominant/non-dominant hand), the valence types (active/passive), and the valence matching between the starting points (left/right) of the touch-screen operation—all increase the subjects' valence evaluations [31]. However, results indicate that when the stimuli are pictures with active emotions, the hands used for the interaction (dominant hand [+]/non-dominant hand [−]), the pictures' valence types (positive [+]/negative [−]), and movement direction (towards [+]/away [−]) do not increase the subjects' valence evaluations of the emotions shown in the pictures. This study result does not completely accord with the polarity coding correspondence theory probably since the experimental space is limited to peripersonal space.

This study result has added to the studies on the application of embodied cognition in human–computer interaction. The result is helpful in understanding how digital information with valences in peripersonal space influences users' emotional cognition. This may help improve users' emotional experience in touch-screen environments and be used as a reference for improving interface experiences. Moreover, by approaching the matter through users' physical location and effects, we may be able to design human–computer interaction products that are easier to use, more desirable, and more satisfying to the users' physical and mental needs.

References

1. Barsalou, L.W.: Grounded cognition. Annu. Rev. Psychol. **59**, 617–645 (2008)
2. Hommel, B., Müsseler, J., Aschersleben, G., Prinz, W.: The theory of event coding (TEC): a framework for perception and action planning. Behav. Brain Sci. **24**, 849–878 (2001)
3. Niedenthal, P.M.: Embodying emotion. Science **316**, 1002–1005 (2007)
4. Pecher, D., Boot, I., Van Dantzig, S.: Abstract concepts: sensory-motor grounding, metaphors, and beyond. Psychol. Learn. Motiv. **54**, 217–248 (2011)
5. Casasanto, D., Henetz, T.: Handedness shapes children's abstract concepts. Cogn. Sci. **36**, 359–372 (2012)
6. De la Fuente, J., Casasanto, D., Román, A., Santiago, J.: Can culture influence body-specific associations between space and valence? Cogn. Sci. **39**, 821–832 (2015)
7. Milhau, A., Brouillet, T., Brouillet, D.: Valence–space compatibility effects depend on situated motor fluency in both right-and left-handers. Q. J. Exp. Psychol. **68**, 887–899 (2015)
8. Gao, Y., Bianchi-Berthouze, N., Meng, H.: What does touch tell us about emotions in touchscreen-based gameplay? ACM Trans. Comput.-Hum. Interact. (TOCHI) **19**, 31 (2012)
9. Rizzolatti, G., Matelli, M., Pavesi, G.: Deficits in attention and movement following the removal of postarcuate (area 6) and prearcuate (area 8) cortex in macaque monkeys. Brain **106**, 655–673 (1983)
10. Li, T., Watter, S., Sun, H.J.: Differential visual processing for equivalent retinal information from near versus far space. Neuropsychologia **49**, 3863–3869 (2011)
11. Wilson, M.: Six views of embodied cognition. Psychon. Bull. Rev. **9**, 625–636 (2002)
12. Casasanto, D.: Embodiment of abstract concepts: good and bad in right-and left-handers. J. Exp. Psychol. Gen. **138**, 351 (2009)
13. Keysar, B., Shen, Y., Glucksberg, S., Horton, W.S.: Conventional language: how metaphorical is it? J. Mem. Lang. **43**, 576–593 (2000)
14. de Camp Wilson, T., Nisbett, R.E.: The accuracy of verbal reports about the effects of stimuli on evaluations and behavior. Soc. Psychol. **41**, 118–131 (1978)

15. Natale, M., Gur, R.E., Gur, R.C.: Hemispheric asymmetries in processing emotional expressions. Neuropsychologia **21**, 555–565 (1983)
16. de la Vega, I., De Filippis, M., Lachmair, M., Dudschig, C., Kaup, B.: Emotional valence and physical space: limits of interaction. J. Exp. Psychol. Hum. Percept. Perform. **38**, 375 (2012)
17. Meier, B.P., Robinson, M.D.: Why the sunny side is up: associations between affect and vertical position. Psychol. Sci. **15**, 243–247 (2004)
18. Centerbar, D.B., Clore, G.L.: Do approach-avoidance actions create attitudes? Psychol. Sci. **17**, 22–29 (2006)
19. Chen, M., Bargh, J.A.: Consequences of automatic evaluation: immediate behavioral predispositions to approach or avoid the stimulus. Pers. Soc. Psychol. Bull. **25**, 215–224 (1999)
20. Lakens, D., Semin, G.R., Foroni, F.: But for the bad, there would not be good: grounding valence in brightness through shared relational structures. J. Exp. Psychol. Gen. **141**, 584 (2012)
21. Proctor, R.W., Cho, Y.S.: Polarity correspondence: a general principle for performance of speeded binary classification tasks. Psychol. Bull. **132**, 416 (2006)
22. Cacioppo, J.T., Petty, R.E., Morris, K.J.: Effects of need for cognition on message evaluation, recall, and persuasion. J. Pers. Soc. Psychol. **45**, 805 (1983)
23. Markman, A.B., Brendl, C.M.: Constraining theories of embodied cognition. Psychol. Sci. **16**, 6–10 (2005)
24. Pecher, D., van Dantzig, S., Zwaan, R.A., Zeelenberg, R.: Short article: language comprehenders retain implied shape and orientation of objects. Q. J. Exp. Psychol. **62**, 1108–1114 (2009)
25. Cervera-Torres, S., Ruiz Fernández, S., Lachmair, M., Riekert, M., Gerjets, P.: Altering emotions near the hand: approach–avoidance swipe interactions modulate the perceived valence of emotional pictures. Emotion (2019)
26. Rizzolatti, G., Berti, A.: Neglect as a neural representation deficit. Revue Neurol. **146**, 626–634 (1990)
27. Rizzolatti, G., Arbib, M.A.: Language within our grasp. Trends Neurosci. **21**, 188–194 (1998)
28. Costantini, M., Ambrosini, E., Tieri, G., Sinigaglia, C., Committeri, G.: Where does an object trigger an action? An investigation about affordances in space. Exp. Brain Res. **207**, 95–103 (2010)
29. Previc, F.H.: Functional specialization in the lower and upper visual fields in humans: its ecological origins and neurophysiological implications. Behav. Brain Sci. **13**, 519–542 (1990)
30. Previc, F.H.: The neuropsychology of 3-D space. Psychol. Bull. **124**, 123 (1998)
31. Cervera-Torres, S., Fernandez, S.R., Lachmair, M., Gerjets, P.: Valence-space associations in touchscreen interactions: valence match between emotional pictures and their vertical touch location leads to pictures' positive evaluation. PloS One **13** (2018)
32. de la Vega, I., Dudschig, C., Lachmair, M., Kaup, B.: Being someone's right hand doesn't always feel right: bodily experiences affect metaphoric language processing. Lang. Cogn. Neurosci. **29**, 1227–1232 (2014)
33. Torres, S.C., Fernández, S.R., Lachmair, M., Gerjets, P.: Coding valence in touchscreen interactions: hand dominance and lateral movement influence valence appraisals of emotional pictures. Psychol. Res. **84**, 1–9 (2018)

A Validation of Textual Expression About Disaster Information to Induce Evacuation

Tomonori Yasui[1](✉), Takayoshi Kitamura[1], Tomoko Izumi[1], and Yoshio Nakatani[2]

[1] Ritsumeikan University, 1-1-1 Noji-Higashi, Kusatsu, Shiga 525-8577, Japan
is0285fk@ed.ritsumei.ac.jp, {ktmr,izumi-t}@fc.ritsumei.ac.jp
[2] Ritsumeikan Trust, 1 Nishinokyo-Suzaku-cho, Nakagyo-ku, Kyoto 604-8520, Japan
nakatani@is.ritsumei.ac.jp

Abstract. An immediate evacuation is essential for safety when a big earthquake and/or a tsunami occurs. For example, the Great East Japan Earthquake in 2011 killed over 10 thousand people, and over 90% of them drowned due to the tsunami. Additionally, people who failed to escape from the tsunami after the earthquake occurred, suffered heavy losses due to the tsunami. If they had evacuated immediately after the earthquake hit, it would have been possible to reduce the losses. In this study, we compare textual expression about disaster information available on smartphones to evaluate the effectiveness of whether this information can induce immediate evacuation. The results of our comparison show that information pertaining to damage caused by disasters and fear-arousing communication is the most effective to induce evacuation. Following the results, we conducted two experiments to evaluate the impact of the most effective sentence in the comparison. This paper shows the results of a comparison study and these experiments.

Keywords: Evacuation behavior · Text-based information expression · Fear-arousing communication

1 Introduction

An immediate evacuation is essential for safety when a big earthquake and/or a tsunami occurs. One example of a large-scale disaster is the Great East Japan Earthquake, which killed over 10 thousand people and over 90% of the victims drowned due to the tsunami [1]. Additionally, the people who failed to escape from the tsunami after the earthquake occurred, suffered heavy losses due to the tsunami. If they had evacuated immediately after the earthquake hit, it would have been possible that the losses could have been reduced. However, people have a tendency to underestimate the threat of a disaster, which is called normalcy bias. This causes people to ignore an immediate evacuation because of the bias.

On the other hand, in Japan, an evacuation advisory is issued when a large-scale disaster occurs. However, the advisory requires no compulsory actions and therefor, during a disaster, people individually decide whether they evacuate or not. However, there are some actions which work to induce immediate evacuation in Japan. One of

S. Yamamoto and H. Mori (Eds.): HCII 2020, LNCS 12185, pp. 289–301, 2020.
https://doi.org/10.1007/978-3-030-50017-7_21

them is education for disaster management to enhance awareness of disaster risk. While there is a positive effect of education on inducing evacuation, it decreases overtime. It is difficult to keep the effect of the education. Another action which can induce evacuation is distributing a hazard map, which provides risk information such as showing certain areas where disasters are more prone. However, a hazard map has a problem. When people inspect the map's damage estimations, they are unlikely to suspect that the damage toll could be much worse than predicted on the map, and therefore could be underprepared [2]. Therefore, these actions have some problems which can negatively affect immediate evacuation in a disaster.

There are many studies about disaster evacuation assists. For example, Fujihara and Miwa [3] proposed a real-time disaster evacuation guidance in which evacuees gather information by themselves and share it using ad-hoc communications between their mobile phones. It can gather and utilize real-time information regarding the disaster areas even if communication channels won't work. Like in Fujihara and Miwa's study, most of the studies that support disaster evacuation focusses on ways of communication. These studies do not explore what kinds of information or expression is effective in inducing evacuation. On the other hand, there are some actions which consider the expression of disaster information. The Japan Meteorological Agency improved bulletin content and expression according to criteria for tsunami warning issuance, and classes of estimated maximum tsunami heights [4]. However, this action utilizes information which is already generally used.

To induce immediate evacuation in a disaster situation, in this study, we focus on the expression of disaster information provided to people in a disaster area on a mobile device. In this study, we consider not only expression of information generally used, but also information which is not used currently. Firstly, we propose some text-based information expressions on a mobile device based on actual cases or psychology, and conduct the comparative survey about the effects of them. Next, we verify the effect of the most effective expression in the comparative survey by conducting two experiments.

2   The Comparative Survey

We compared the effects of some text-based information expression about disaster on inducing evacuation. Some of these expressions include unusual information in addition to information that is in general use. To give people notice to the information, use of some media such as photos, movies, animation, and sounds are considered to be effective. However, in this study, we focus only on the impact of textual expression, and so we do not use these forms of media in our study.

2.1   Information Expressions

This survey takes a look at a situation involving a big earthquake and a tsunami. The details of this situation are shown in Table 1. In the situation, we assume that victims confirm the damage information with an application on a smartphone. The application provides information only in text because we should remove influence of any other content.

Table 1. An assumed disaster situation.

Home location	Kobe city, Hyogo, Japan
Intensity	Lower 6 (in Japanese class)
Estimated maximum height of the tsunami	Three meters
Estimated arrival time of the tsunami	About 88 min after the earthquake
House structure	A two-story wooden home

We set six candidate sentences which seem to induce evacuation (see Table 2). The first sentence describes the scale of the tsunami's height, which is a piece of information generally used in Japan. The second sentence compares the height of the tsunami to an object people often see in order to provide scale. The third sentence counts down the time remaining until the tsunami hits land. It is estimated that evacuees will get impatient from seeing the countdown. Using the effect of fear-arousing communication [5], we set the fourth sentence which represents an estimated damage for evacuees based on the scale of the tsunami. Concretely, this sentence shows the damage that would be inflicted on a wooden house. The fifth sentence shows the expected number of evacuees in the shelters. This expression is applied because people have a tendency to follow the majority, which is called the majority synching bias [6]. We calculate the estimated number of evacuees based on the model proposed in [7]. The sixth sentence suggests a communication failure. We consider that people evacuate in order to get information regarding the situation. So, the last sentence reduces the psychological cost to move to a shelter, and thus increases the likelihood of evacuation.

Table 2. Sentences about assumed damage shown on a smartphone

No.	Sentence
1st sentence	The tsunami will be three meters high
2nd sentence	The tsunami will be the same height as a one story building
3rd sentence	The tsunami will hit in 85 min and 52 s
4th sentence	The tsunami will have the scale to completely destroy a house
5th sentence	The expected number of evacuees in the shelters in Kobe city is 372,191
6th sentence	A communication failure is expected because of termination of 33 base stations

2.2 Results of the Survey

The comparative survey was performed by Macromill Inc., which is a large internet research company in Japan from 17 to 18 July 2019 on the Web. About 600 or more respondents were selected from the registrants living in Japan by a random sampling method so that the selected numbers of the registrants in each generation were almost equal. The registrants living in Hyogo, which is the prefecture including Kobe city, were removed from the respondents because they were familiar with the target area. In addition, we removed people who lived in Yamagata and Niigata from the survey because big earthquakes occurred there one month prior to the date of this investigation.

This investigation was consisted of the following steps: 1) The respondent answers questions about his/her attributes, and then 2) he/she confirms the fictional disaster situation as mentioned above and the map of the target area. After that, 3) he/she sees the screenshot of the application on which one of the sentences is shown. The application is shown in Fig. 1. Finally, 4) he/she answers a question pertaining to the timing of evacuation, selecting from these choices, "after seeing the application", "after seeing an issue of evacuation advisory", "after being alerted by people around you", "after receiving damage to your home or around your home", "after your home is flooded" and "don't evacuate". In this survey, we judge that the sentence is effective for a participant to induce evacuation if he/she chose "after seeing the application" from them. This is because we want to verify whether the sentence on the application induce evacuation, but not warning or surroundings. All of the respondents repeated the steps until they answered for all the sentences.

We obtained the answers from 621 respondents, and 581 of them were valid responses. In terms of effectiveness of the sentences, the fourth sentence, "The tsunami will have the scale to completely destroy a house." is most effective in induce evacuation (See Fig. 2). When applying Cochran's Q test to the results of ratios of effectiveness

Fig. 1. The application which is used in the comparative survey.

between the six sentences, the p value is less than 0.0001. Moreover, from the results of multiple comparisons based on the McNemar test, it is shown that the fourth sentence is the most effective, and the second most effective sentences are, the first, the second, and the third sentences. The fifth and the sixth sentence were the least effective. Therefore, we conclude the fourth sentence based on the fear-arousing communication is the most effective way to induce an immediate evacuation in this study. However, in people over

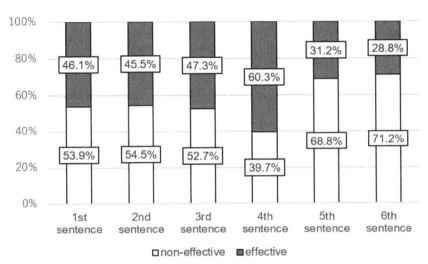

Fig. 2. The results about the effectiveness of the sentences.

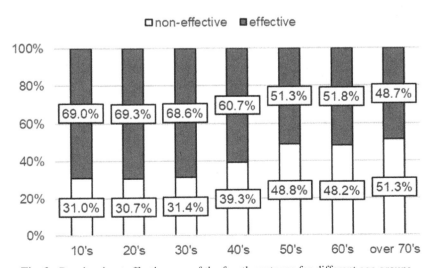

Fig. 3. Results about effectiveness of the fourth sentence for different age groups.

the age of 70, the effectiveness of this sentence is less than half (see Fig. 3). That is, the effect of this sentence is different depending on age.

3 Overview of Demonstration Experiments

According to the results of the comparative survey, we conclude the fourth sentence is the most effective in inducing an immediate evacuation. However, the survey just compared the six sentences, and does not make the impact of the fourth sentence itself clear. Therefore, we conduct demonstration experiments to verify the effectiveness of the fourth sentence based on the fear-arousing communication. In this section, we describe the two demonstration experiments. The first experiment is called "experiment A" and the second one is called "experiment B."

We developed two smartphone applications for the demonstration experiments. One of them shows the fourth sentence (see Fig. 4), and the other does not (see Fig. 5). The first application shows the fourth sentence on a dialog as shown in the left side in Fig. 4 when the application is launched. After closing the dialog, a user can check disaster information (the right in Fig. 4) and evacuation locations (the center in Fig. 4) by choosing them from the menu bar. The fourth sentence is also shown on the top of the screen about the disaster information. The second application is almost the same function as the first application. The only difference between the applications with and without the fourth sentence is the presentation of the fourth sentence (see Fig. 5).

A participant uses one of these applications at random. We compared the results of two groups of participants who use the application showing the fourth sentence and who use the other one.

Fig. 4. The application which shows the fourth sentence.

Fig. 5. The application which does not show the fourth sentence.

4 Experiment A

4.1 Procedure of Experiment A

The procedure of experiment A is based on the study by Tanaka et al. [8]. This experiment objectively aims to verify the impact of the fourth sentence which, was the most effective in the comparative survey. We conducted the Web survey for this verification.

A participant was asked to imagine a disaster situation which shows in Table 1 and watched a movie about how the application is used. In this movie, all of the screens (i.e., Figure 4 and 5) in the application are provided. After watching the movie, the participant answered a question, "What percentage of people do you think will immediately evacuate after viewing this application?" The participant answered the percentage by selecting a value in a slide bar. Then, he/she was required to input a reason for the answer.

4.2 Results of Experiment A

40 Japanese people who are 19 to 24 years old participated in experiment A. Half of them watched the movie about the application which shows the fourth sentence and the others of them watched a movie about the application which does not show the sentence. The average of the answers for the question is 66.7% when the fourth sentence was shown, and the average is 54.45% in the other case. Applying Student's t-test to the results of these percentages, the p value is less than 0.05.

There is a significant difference between the groups which were showed the fourth sentence and which were not. In addition, 8 of 20 participants who checked the fourth sentence answered with positive opinions about the information in the sentence. For these reasons, it is suggested that showing information based on the fear-arousing communication in a disaster situation is an effective way to make people evacuate immediately.

Two out of 20 participants who did not check the fourth sentence stated, "I did not feel a sense of urgent from seeing this application." or "I did not feel a sense of danger from seeing this application." Their percentage of people who evacuate is lower than other participants; 30% and 20%. Form this fact, it is possible that general disaster information does not instill enough sense of danger to evacuees. Therefore, the information such as the fourth sentence is one way to provide a sense of danger in a disaster situation.

5   Experiment B

5.1   Procedure of Experiment B

While the participants in the comparative survey and experiment A only watched the movies about the application, in experiment B, participants used one of the applications in Fig. 4 and Fig. 5 by themselves. We explained the flow of the experiment. First, a participant was explained the situation which is shown in Table 1 by the individual conducting the experiment. Then, the participant used one of the applications which either showed the fourth sentence or not. After that, the participant chose his/her behavior result from "evacuate," "not evacuate," and "see how the situation goes for a while." The participant who answered "see how the situation goes for a while" checked the situation for a few minutes after the first decision, and answered his/her evacuation behavior again. At this second opportunity, they should answer "evacuate" or "not evacuate." After deciding his/her evacuation behavior, we asked for his/her reasoning for the decision, and what information he/she wants to get in a disaster.

However, in the experimental situation, it was possible that participants thought they should answer "evacuate" because they knew it was a good decision in a disaster situation. Therefore, we introduced the cost of evacuation. The rule in Table 3 was applied in this experiment. In this rule, a participant actually takes one of the actions in Table 3 after choosing their evacuation behavior. The actions are defined for each situation where the participant decides to evacuate or not, and receive damage in the disaster or not. Note that participants have to decide their evacuation behavior without knowing whether the disaster imposes human damage. That is, whether human damage occurred or not is told to the participants after they decide their evacuation behavior. The experimenter explained this rule, and whether human damage occurs or not is decided by a hazard map from the local government and the damage of the past disasters similar to the situation in Table 1.

The actions shown in Table 3 are the ones evacuees take in a disaster situation. We set the actions as costs for the corresponding evacuation behaviors. If a participant chooses "evacuate" and gets human damage in the assumed disaster situation, the participant should receive an action I in Table 3. This action imitates a physical cost of walking to an evacuation spot. If a participant chooses "evacuate" and does not get human damage, the action II in Table 3 is imposed on the participant. This action imitates a physical cost of walking to an evacuation spot and back home. For actions I and II, the reason why we set the distance at 850 m is because that is the distance to the nearest shelter from the home in this disaster situation (the center in Fig. 4 and 5). If a participant chooses "not evacuate" and receives human damage in the assumed disaster situation, the participant receives the action III in Table 3. This action imitates the case that the participant does not

Table 3. The rule of experiment B.

| | | Evacuation behavior a participant decides | |
		Evacuate	Not evacuate
Human damage by the disaster	Yes	Walk about 850 m to a building. (I)	Stay in a room for 30 min. (III)
	No	Walk about 850 m to a building and back. (II)	Nothing. (IV)

evacuate, and as the result, he/she gets human damage. Accordingly, a participant stays in a room for 30 min in this action as a penalty. If a participant chooses "not evacuate" and does not get human damage, the action IV in Table 3 is applied to the participant. This action imitates the case the participant does not get losses when a disaster occurs. So, a participant has to take no action. That is, the participant can finish the experiment early.

5.2 Results of Experiment B

As mentioned above, a participant had to decide between "evacuate" or "not evacuate" following if he/she chose "see how the situation goes for a while" as the first decision in this experiment. However, in the case of choosing this decision, the time until the tsunami will arrive become short consequently at the time when the participant gives the second, and the final decision. Therefore, it is possible that the situation forces the participant to answer "evacuate." For this reason, we consider the evacuation behaviors that participants answered at first.

20 Japanese people who are 19 to 24 years old joined experiment B. Half of them used the application which shows the fourth sentence and the others used the application which does not show the sentence. The results of experiment B are shown in Table 4. In the group that was checking the fourth sentence, 4 participants answered "evacuate," 6 participants answered "see how the situation goes for a while" and there was no participant that answered "not evacuate." In the group that didn't see the sentence, 1 participant answered "evacuate", 8 participants answered "see how the situation goes for a while" and 1 participant answered "not evacuate". In the interviews where we asked information that the participants think are necessary for evacuation, most participants answered "Whether people around my home evacuate or not."

Table 4. The result of experiment B.

	Evacuate	See for a while	Not evacuate
Check the fourth sentence	4	6	0
Not check the fourth sentence	1	8	1

5.3   Discussion of Experiment B

Comparing the groups using the application with and without the fourth sentence, there are more participants that answered "evacuate" in the group that checked the fourth sentence. This result suggests that in a similar situation to one assumed in this experiment, the number of evacuees who will evacuate immediately increases by applying information based on fear-arousing communication to the disaster information system. In addition, 2 participants who checked the fourth sentence answered that they felt a sense of danger from the sentence and chose "evacuate". From these opinions, it is possible to say that disaster information using the fear-arousing communication is a factor in the decision of evacuation in a disaster.

In the group which did not check the fourth sentence, 2 of 8 participants who decided "see how the situation goes for a while" answered "Major Tsunami Warnings are not announced." as their reason of the decision. On the other hand, in the group that saw the fourth sentence, 2 of the 4 participants who decided "evacuate" answered "Tsunami Warnings are announced" as their reason. In Japan, when an earthquake occurs that could generate a disastrous tsunami in coastal regions of Japan, Japan Meteorological Agency issue Major Tsunami Warnings, Tsunami Warnings and/or Tsunami Advisories for individual regions based on estimated tsunami heights around three minutes after the earthquake [9]. The participants in this experiment were given announcements about Tsunami Warnings as the assumed disaster situation. From the fact that the participants had different opinions for the same warning, we can see that presenting the information using fear-arousing communication changes the impression of Tsunami Warmings. These results suggest that information using fear-arousing communication is effective in inducing an immediate evacuation.

4 participants answered that they wanted information about another disaster such as a landslide, fire and so on when deciding their evacuation plan in a disaster situation. This is considered information of the fear-arousing communication because these show an estimated damage for the participants. That is, these opinions mean there are other forms of information inducing fear-arousing communication.

6   Comprehensive Discussion

This section shows a comprehensive discussion about the comparative survey and two demonstration experiments.

6.1   Information with Fear-Arousing Communication

In the survey and experiments, it is suggested that the information that uses fear-arousing communications, including estimated damage for evacuees, is effective in inducing an immediate evacuation. In cases where multiple types of damage are estimated for evacuees, we need to discuss which one of them is presented to the evacuees. This study used the damaging of houses as the information. However, this information is less effective for the participants over a certain age. When discussing other expression, there are two points we should consider: The first is that we should look at the experiences and surroundings of an evacuee to maximize the possibility of inducing evacuation. For example, one of the participants of experiment B listed an occurrence of a landslide as necessary information for making an evacuation decision, because a landslide is expected to occur near his home in the event of an earthquake. By optimizing how we present information to an individual victim, it is thought that the effect of inducing evacuation will be improved.

The second point to consider is to moderate the strength of fear within the message to avoid victim's panic. In the comparative survey, there were some opinions such as, "This information may cause panic." pertaining to the fourth sentence. Some studies like Keating [10] dismiss the occurrence of panic in disaster situations. On the other hand, studies about panic in a disaster have also been conducted. For example, Furuta and Yasui [11] developed a simulation system to consider the evacuation behavior in underground malls during the disaster. According to simulation, the underground malls have complicated configurations and connections, which then may cause people to fall into a panic during disasters. Therefore, we need to discuss the level of fear appeal by providing estimated damage depending on a situation.

6.2 Improvement of Information Using the Majority Synching Bias

The effectiveness of the fifth sentence in Table 2, "The expected number of evacuees in the shelters in Kobe city is 372,191." is less likely to induce evacuation than the other sentences in the comparative survey. This sentence was used in order to consider the majority synching bias of humans. However, in experiment B, some participants answered that they want to know whether people around their home evacuate or not, in order to choose whether they should evacuate, which is relevant to the majority synching bias. That is, since the scale of the targeted area in the fifth sentence is too large, (i.e., Kobe City) most of the participants in the comparative survey were unaware of their neighbor's actions and if "people in the neighborhood are evacuating.". As the results show, the effectiveness of the fifth sentence are low. We need to reconsider expression with the majority synching bias so that evacuees are aware of their neighbor's action by reading the expression.

6.3 Inducing Evacuation with a Smartphone

This study used a smartphone as a device to present disaster information. There are some opinions such as "I do not trust information obtained from a smartphone." We had more negative opinions, than the positive ones about using a smartphone. It is considered that each participant who conveyed a negative opinion took into account the problem of misinformation in social networking services. That is, there are some people that do not trust information obtained from the internet. For these people, using a smartphone for transmitting disaster information may decrease the effect of inducing evacuation.

One of the ways to improve trust for a smartphone application is to personalize providing information to a user. As mentioned in Sect. 6.1, it is possible to optimize the presentation of information by considering the individual circumstances or surroundings of a user. This mechanism will improve the effect of inducing evacuation in addition to a trustful information.

7 Conclusions

This study compared the effects of text-based expressions to inducing evacuation. The results of the comparative survey showed that the sentence using fear-arousing communication, which was presented as expected damage to the house, was the most effective among the six sentences. For this result, we conducted the two demonstration experiments to verify the effect of the sentence with the fear-arousing communication to induce evacuation. In the first experiment, we asked the participants what percentage of people in a target area evacuate. We demonstrated a significant difference between the groups given and not given the sentence in the effect to induce evacuation. The second experiment surveyed the evacuation behavior in the case of participants directly use the application on a fictional disaster situation. As the result of this experiment, there were more participants that answered "evacuate" in the group given the sentence than the group that was not given the sentence. From these demonstration experiments, we confirmed that the textual expression based on the fear-arousing communication have a certain effect in inducing an immediate evacuation.

Future works pertaining to this study are to reconsider the sentences which had lower effects, such as the sentence involving the majority synching bias, in the comparative survey with consideration of the opinions obtained in the demonstration experiments. In addition, we will try to adopt a unique experience and expression of expected damage according to the configuration for individual application users.

Acknowledgement. This work is supported in part by KAKENHI no. 16K21484.

References

1. National Police Agency: White paper on police excerpt 2011. (in Japanese)
2. Katada, T., Kodama, M., Saeki, H.: Study on residents' recognition of a flood hazard map and promotion measures of its recognition. J. Proc. Hydraul. Eng. **48**, 233–438 (2004). (in Japanese)
3. Fujihara, M., Miwa, H.: Real-time disaster evacuation guidance using opportunistic communications. In: 2012 IEEE/IPSJ 12th International Symposium on Applications and the Internet, pp. 326–331. IEEE (2012)
4. Japan Meteorological Agency Homepage. http://www.jma.go.jp/jma/en/Publications/publications.html. Accessed 16 Jan 2020
5. Janis, I.L., Feshbach, S.: Effects of fear-arousing communications. J. Abnorm. Soc. Psychol. **48**(1), 78–92 (1953)
6. Takayama, Y., Hirosaki, M.: Quick evacuation method for evacuation navigation system in poor communication environment at the time of disaster. In: 2014 International Conference on Intelligent Networking and Collaborative Systems, pp. 415–429. IEEE (2014)
7. Kumagai, T., Tomita, T.: Mathematical model of time delay to start tsunami evacuation. J. Jpn. Soc. Civ. Eng. Ser. D3 **71**(5), I_171–I_180 (2015). (in Japanese)
8. Tanaka, K., Kato, T.: Perceived danger can be influenced by how the emergency information is expressed. Jpn. J. Cogn. Psychol. **9**(1), 1–7 (2011)
9. Japan Meteorological Agency Homepage. https://www.jma.go.jp/en/tsunami/. Accessed 10 Jan 2020

10. Kearing, J.P.: The myth of panic. Fire J. **76**(3), 57–61 (1982)
11. Furuta, H., Yasui, M.: Evacuation simulation in underground mall by artificial life technology. Applied Research in Uncertainty Modeling and Analysis, pp. 249–265. Springer, Boston (2005). https://doi.org/10.1007/0-387-23550-7_11

Supporting Work, Collaboration and Creativity

Assessing Current HMI Designs and Exploring AI Potential for Future Air-Defence System Development

Zara Gibson[1]([✉]) [ⓘ], Joseph Butterfield[1], Robin Stuart Ferguson[1], Karen Rafferty[1], Wai Yu[2], and Alf Casement[2]

[1] Queen's University Belfast, University Road, Belfast, Northern Ireland
z.gibson@qub.ac.uk
[2] Thales UK, Alanbrooke Road, Belfast, Northern Ireland

Abstract. Designing human-machine interfaces (HMIs) for defence systems (such as vehicle-based weapon terminals) faces numerous challenges such as limited workspace, operation in extreme environments and essential protective gear for operators and equipment. This paper presents a study designed to investigate the HMI and teaming for ground-based air defence systems and reports the findings. The objective of the first stage of the study is to assess the usability, satisfaction, ease of use and design of the current systems to identify avenues for improvement in future system development. The main findings confirm some of the issues identified in the early human factors analysis, such as the lack of space, task complexity and the level of expertise required for efficient system operation. The reported findings do not just help identify the areas for improvement in the HMI, but also identify tasks that could be assisted by Artificial Intelligence (AI) integrated within current system functions, to improve human performance whilst also reducing cognitive load, errors and the risk of poor decision-making.

Keywords: Ergonomics · Human-machine interface · Military · Artificial intelligence

1 Introduction

Recent technological advances in military system development, especially in sensing and networking, have resulted in increased informational processing demands on operators. These operators are often already experiencing high physical and cognitive load, due to the criticality of accurate decision-making. Resultantly, soldiers at all levels are now faced with larger amounts of information in conjunction with their traditional military role requirements. Junior and non-commissioned officers are assigned greater amounts of information, previously only accessible to higher-level commanders [1].

This additional sensory data aims to improve situational awareness, preparedness and assist in making rapid, coordinated and critical battlefield decisions. The armed forces no longer fight as individuals but as a collective system. As a result, the communications and command systems are vital [2], as effective communications allow armies to complete the

© Springer Nature Switzerland AG 2020
S. Yamamoto and H. Mori (Eds.): HCII 2020, LNCS 12185, pp. 305–323, 2020.
https://doi.org/10.1007/978-3-030-50017-7_22

'observe-orient-decide-act' cycle significantly faster. Thereby, complex vehicle systems are required to manage this information.

Unfortunately, tied closely to this increased flow of information, is the rising concern over how the crew will process and use this information effectively in battle scenarios. The risk of information overload is very real for the modern soldier. Due to the lack of time to make decisions and the increased lethality of modern weaponry, the cognitive demands and stress in modern military operations have increased [3, 4]. Elevated stress and higher cognitive demands are linked to an increased likelihood of errors [5], with approximately 80% of military accidents caused by human error [6]. As a result, the human element of these vehicle electronics needs to be considered moving forwards [2] as technological readiness is not enough to wage war and the cognitive readiness of military personnel is key [7].

Effective human-machine interface (HMI) design can be one approach; efficient HMIs use less attentional resources, enabling more efficient information processing [8]. Using salient stimuli can promote faster and more effortless information processing ([9] provides a review). Salient visual designs can direct visual-spatial attention toward critical visual notifications, reducing visual search time and sparing attentional resources [8]. This shows exactly how important the design of the interface is in enabling better human performance. Ineffective HMIs can cause information overload, leading to erroneous decisions. Understanding the impact of existing (and next-generation) HMI designs in conveying multi-source information, is essential to balance information content, and quantity, with user cognitive limitations to improve performance.

Additionally, there is potential to utilise the technological advances in artificial intelligence (AI; such as automation and intelligent agents) to provide the military with a tactical and cognitive advantage. In a military scenario, AI could increase autonomy, sophistication and dispersion of weapons systems and personnel [10]. A challenge, however, is a lack of theoretical understanding of how humans interact with machines in work contexts e.g. in terms of risk management and resiliency [11–13]. In the military, decisions have to be made within tight time schedules, often with incomplete information. Furthermore, mission complexity is outpacing the ability to manage disruptions, which calls for systemic approaches that span technology, human, and mission space [14]. New situational complexity is likely to overload team cognitive resources [15]. As the requirements of systems and their operators are expanded, the tasks approach the operator's response capacity limit; once the limit is reached and exceeded, the system is susceptible to failure [16]. As a result, improved HMIs coupled with AI (to augment human decision-making in complex, high load scenarios) can reduce operational risks associated with poor decision-making.

1.1 Current Study

This paper aims to apply a questionnaire battery method used in previous work [17] to assess user opinions on the design of two variants of a Thales vehicle-based weapon system; a Light Armored Vehicle (LAV) and Heavy Armored Vehicle (HAV). The vehicles are operated by three crew members; a Commander, Operator and Driver. The Commander Console for the LAV (Weapon Terminal- WT) is an updated version of the HAV

Tactical Command Console (TCC). The Operator Control Console (OCC) is the same in both and comprises a display unit and weapon system control panel.

This study was designed to investigate the HMI and teaming for these ground-based air-defence vehicles. The objective was to assess the usability, satisfaction, ease of use, workload and design (from both a physical and cognitive perspective) of the current systems to identify avenues for improvement in future system development. To achieve this, several standardized questionnaires were compiled into a question battery for current users to complete. Firstly, the questionnaires were screened to extract relevant questions to avoid question repetition and to compress the battery to a more manageable size for participants. Additional questions of interest were included to supplement the questionnaires and answer specific design questions such as examining the respective support the interfaces provided in support of mission-critical tasks. The subscales and individual items were extracted to provide insights on key constructs of the system design such as usability, usefulness, satisfaction etc. as well as the workload associated with specific mission tasks. Additionally, the scope for incorporating intelligent elements in the information displays and controls is inferred from the outputs. Table 1 below details the vehicle weapon systems aspects that the questionnaires examined.

Table 1. Components measured by the questionnaires used in this study*

	Physical ergonomics				Cognitive ergonomics			
	DMQ	NMQ	BPDQ	Add. Q's	USE	QUIS	NASA-TLX	Add. Q's
Risk of injury	✓							
Frequency of bad posture	✓							
Recent injuries		✓						
End of shift discomfort			✓					
Visibility				✓				
Space	✓			✓				
Usefulness					✓			
Ease of use					✓	✓	✓	
Ease of learning					✓	✓		
Satisfaction					✓			
Screen						✓		
Information presentation						✓		

(*continued*)

Table 1. (*continued*)

	Physical ergonomics				Cognitive ergonomics			
	DMQ	NMQ	BPDQ	Add. Q's	USE	QUIS	NASA-TLX	Add. Q's
System capabilities					✓			
Level of control					✓			
System logic					✓			
Task demands						✓		
Performance						✓		
Frustration						✓		
Effectiveness								✓

*DMQ- Dutch Musculoskeletal Questionnaire; NMQ- Nordic Musculoskeletal Questionnaire, BDPQ- Body Part Discomfort Questionnaire, USE- Usefulness, Satisfaction and Ease of Use, QUIS- Questionnaire for User Interface Satisfaction, NASA-TLX- Task Load Index

2 Method

2.1 Participants

Thirty-seven participants completed the thirty-minute questionnaire. Twenty-seven (4 female) completed the HAV and ten completed the LAV (all male). HAV users were UK participants recruited from the Ministry of Defence and LAV users were overseas Asian participants recruited via system trainers from the overseas bases. Some users had experience of the both the WT/TCC and OCC so completed all parts, resultantly, sixteen HAV users completed the Commander section and eighteen completed the Operator section of the questionnaire. Both sections were completed by all the LAV users. The experience of the LAV users is unknown but is likely less than 5 years. HAV users demonstrated a diverse range of experience (Fig. 1i). LAV users were all in the 18–24 age bracket whereas HAV users showed more variation (see Fig. 1ii).

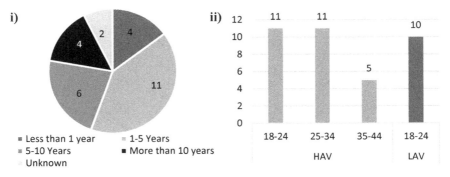

Fig. 1. i) Level of experience indicated by HAV questionnaire respondents. **ii)** Number of participants in each respective age bracket according to type of vehicle used

2.2 Questionnaire Design

Participants assessed the system by responding to a battery of well-established evaluation questionnaires. One part examined the physical aspects of vehicle use, another examined the OCC and the third the WT/TCC.

Physical Ergonomics was assessed using the **Dutch Musculoskeletal Questionnaire** (DMQ; [18]), the **Nordic Musculoskeletal Questionnaire** (NMQ) and the **Body Part Discomfort Questionnaire** (BPDQ [19]). There is supporting research that work intensity correlates with musculoskeletal complaint (MSC) development [20, 21] which results in lost-work-time [22]. Resultantly, MSCs can adversely affect the operational capabilities of defence forces. The DMQ analyses musculoskeletal workload using 5-point frequency rating scales (1-often, 5 never). It exploits the relationship between work tasks and MSCs [23] to identify MSC development risk. The original 63-item questionnaire was reduced to 34-items to remove irrelevant items. For instance, workplace vibration and weather questions were removed as these were outside of the scope of the user's tasks such as 'making short maximal force-exertions'.

An adapted version of the NMQ was used which consisted of users reporting any MSCs (Yes/No) across nine anatomical areas over the past 12 months, indicating the injury impact and whether they required a GP consult. The BPDQ was used to evaluate user discomfort at different body parts on a scale of 0–4 (0 - extremely comfortable, 4 - extremely uncomfortable). Additional questions addressed the visibility and space inside the vehicle as these are potential mitigating factors on user performance.

Cognitive Ergonomics was assessed using the **Usability, Satisfaction and Ease of Use** (USE) questionnaire [24], the **Questionnaire of User Interface Satisfaction** (QUIS) [25] and the **NASA-TLX** [26]. The USE measures the subjective usability of a product or service. The 27-items examined four dimensions of usability; usefulness, ease of use, ease of learning and satisfaction using a 5-point agreement rating scale (1-strongly disagree, 5-strongly agree). The QUIS assessed the HMI usability in specific contexts across four categories (screen, terminology/system information, learning and system capabilities) on 10-point rating scales. The scale anchors vary depending on the statement but generally, the higher score is a more positive response. The NASA TLX is the most cited self-report based workload measure [27]. User's rate their responses to six subscales (mental, temporal and physical demand, effort, frustration and performance) based on their experience of the task (the scale was adjusted to a 10-point scale for consistency). Additional questions on HMI efficiency in task support were included.

3 Results

3.1 Physical Ergonomics

Participants completed the NMQ to indicate any MSCs over the past 12 months. NMQ feedback showed that no LAV users had any MSCs in the timeframe. In contrast, HAV users showed a higher incidence of MSCs with 18 of the 27 (66.7%) reporting a complaint. The most common source of pain was in the lower back followed by knees and neck (Fig. 2i). In line with this, participants also reported the level of comfort they experienced in each area of the body when operating the LAVs and HAVs using the BPDQ

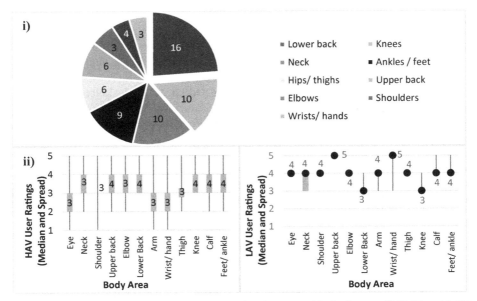

Fig. 2. i) Pie chart showing HAV user MSCs related to a specific body part. ii) HAV and LAV user responses to the BPDQ. A higher score indicates more discomfort.

(Fig. 2ii). From Fig. 2ii, HAV users reported moderate discomfort in their upper and lower back, knees, calves and feet/ankles. The remaining areas were generally acceptable in terms of comfort. In contrast, LAV users reported higher levels of discomfort in the wrists/hands and upper back, corresponding to our knowledge of a smaller workspace associated with the LAV.

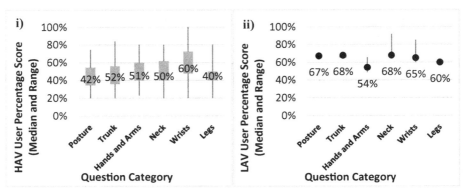

Fig. 3. Box and whisker plots displaying the median and range of i) HAV and ii) LAV user percentage scores for the DMQ body areas. The higher the score the better the physical work environment.

DMQ questionnaire results are displayed in Fig. 3. DMQ responses ranged from 42 to 124 (24.7% to 72.9%) for the HAV and 106 to 115 (62.4% and 67.6%) for the LAV. Average scores of 49.1% and 62.7% in the HAV and LAV reflect moderate MSC risk.

Regarding space, the legroom, headroom and overall space inside the HAV were rated as poor (all items: Mode $\leq$ 1). 'Ability to reach controls' was acceptable (Mode = 4). LAV users were more positive scoring all aspects in the 'Good'/'Very good' range (Mode = $\geq$ 6). Visually, the ability to survey the environment outside the HAV was rated as moderately poor (Mode = 2) whilst the 'ability to see other team members' was rated acceptable (Mode = 4). LAV users again scored more highly, rating the ability to see outside as Good (Mode = 6) and the ability to see inside as Very Good (Mode = 7).

3.2 Cognitive Ergonomics

Commander Console
Twenty-six users completed the Commander questionnaire (sixteen HAV; ten LAV). Both HAV and LAV users scored the systems very positively on the USE with all subscales receiving above 70% except for satisfaction which scored above 65% (Fig. 4).

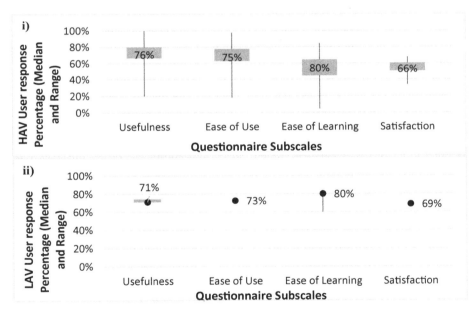

Fig. 4. i) HAV and **ii)** LAV user percentage scores and response range across the USE Questionnaire subscales. A higher the score reflects a more positive review of the interface.

A full range of responses was recorded across HAV USE individual items, hence the modal response was used to indicate a response consensus. In terms of usefulness, HAV users agreed that the interface was successful in improving their own, their teams and mission activity control (all items: Mode = 4). Conjointly they reported that the interface fulfils its purpose and meets their needs (both items: Mode = 4). Less positively viewed was how streamlined tasks were (Mode = 3). LAV users were also generally very positive about their interfaces, agreeing that the console was successful in improving their own and fulfilled its purpose (all items: Mode = 4). LAV users reported lower ratings for how well the console meets their needs, making the missions easier, controlling vehicle operations and streamlining the process (all items: Mode = 3).

HAV users agreed the interface was easy to use by indicating a low operational effort, lack of expertise required and simplicity (all items: Mode = 4). LAV users reported the system as slightly more complex to use, scoring lower on items such as the effort to use, recovery from errors and the number of steps to complete objectives (all items: Mode = 3). They were more positive about the lack of expertise required and the success of each use (all items: Mode = 4). HAV and LAV users gave modal responses of 3 across most aspects of satisfaction such as frustration to use, satisfaction, pleasantness of use, recommending the system and how the system works, making it the lowest scoring of the four USE subscales.

The QUIS assessed interface usability and design during set-up, surveillance/engagement and overall system operation. Figure 5 shows the percentage scores on each subscale of the QUIS. Differences between HAV and LAV users were mainly on the learning aspect of the interface. HAV users reported learning to set-up as more difficult whereas LAV users reported learning the engagement process as more difficult. Secondly, the screen showed some discrepancies between groups with LAV users reporting layout and information sequence being harder to follow in surveillance and overall.

HAV QUIS set-up responses show that most aspects fall within the 'acceptable' response range, i.e. modal values between 4 and 6. The interface appears to excel in is that ability to explore features (Mode = 9, Range = 3–9). The range of responses from HAV users was much larger than LAV users' with most responses ranging from 3 to 9. LAV users responded positively on a range of items including organisation of information, progress updates, system speed and ability to correct mistakes (all items Mode = 6, Range = 6–9). Only the system awkwardness received a score of '4' (Range = 2–4).

Regarding surveillance/engagement, HAV scores indicate that again the interface serves its purpose to an acceptable level. However, in this instance more scales showed more agreeable responses to items such as the task sequences being easy to follow, the task being straightforward and the task being easy to perform (all items: Mode = 7, Range = 1–9). The least positive response was for the understanding of error messages (Mode = 4, Range = 2–9). Again, there was a broad range of responses. LAV users again responded mostly along the 'acceptable' segment of the scale (Mode = 4–6), with only the system 'awkwardness' being less positively reviewed (Mode = 4, Range = 2–4).

Lastly, overall Commander Console feedback followed the previous QUIS trends, showing both LAV and HAV users were generally neutral about the interface. The only aspects that HAV users rated more positively was the ability to read characters on the screen (Mode = 7, Range = 3–9) and that the position of messages was consistent (Mode = 8, Range = 3–9). Again, LAV users were very consistent in scoring the system

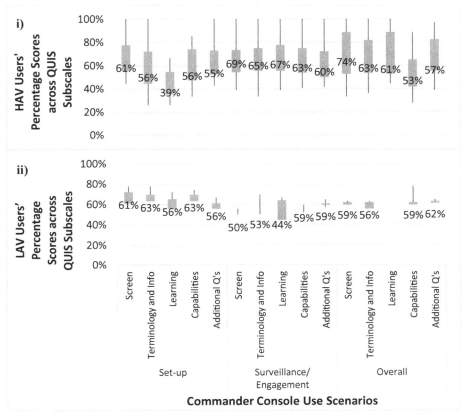

Fig. 5. Box and whisker plot showing the median and range of **i)** HAV and **ii)** LAV user responses to the Tactical Commander Console (TCC) and Weapon Terminal (WT) respectively

between 4 and 6 on the scale. Only one item received a score of '4', being the item 'procedures can be completed by all levels of users (Mode = 4, Range = 4–6).

Operator Console
Eighteen HAV and ten LAV users completed the Operator questionnaire comprising the USE and QUIS questionnaires. Overall, HAV and LAV responses were less positive across all USE subscales for the Operator's console compared to the Commander's console. Figure 6 shows the respective subscale scores.

HAV users responded positively on usefulness items including 'provides good control over mission objectives', meets user needs and fulfils its purpose and is simple and easy to use (all items: Mode = 4). All other elements of the USE showed a modal score of 3, meaning there is room for improvement on aspects such as the steps required to complete procedures and how effective the system is in supporting the crew and user objectives. LAV users responded 'Disagree' with the statements 'I can recover from

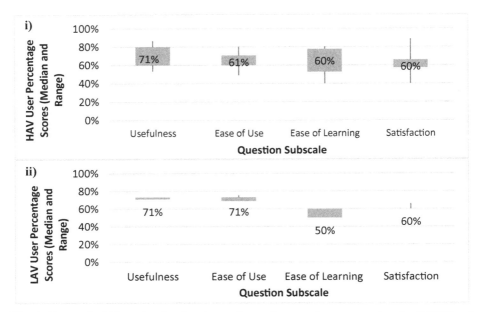

Fig. 6. Box and whisker plot showing the median and range of responses given by **i)** HAV and **ii)** LAV users in the USE questionnaire regarding the Operator's Control Console (OCC)

mistakes quickly and easily' and 'I easily remember how to use it' and 'It is pleasant to use' (all items: Mode = 2) indicating there are some operational issues for LAV users.

The QUIS for OCC set-up showed that for LAV users the organization of information was slightly difficult to follow and the system was slightly awkward to use (all items: Mode = 4, Range = 3–5) but that the interface in its current state is effective in support-ing set-up. All other items scored 5 or 6 indicating the set-up process was effectively supported by the interface. HAV users had a wide range of responses. The users scored the system less favorably on several questions including whether error messages were helpful, the relevance of information on the interface and how streamlined the process is (all items: Mode = 4, Range 0–7). More favorable aspects included the organization of information, following the task sequence and the straightforwardness of engagement (all items Mode = 6, Range = 0–7).

Regarding engagement, LAV users report the system to be somewhat awkward to use (Mode = 4, Range = 3–5). On the other hand, LAV users rate more highly that the information is relevant, there is good control over the task and it is effective in performing the mission (all items: Mode = 6, Range = 5–6). HAV users reported that error messages were somewhat unhelpful, mistakes are quite difficult to correct and that some experience is required to operate the system (all items: Mode = 4, Range = 0–7). They responded positively towards the systems' ability to support engagement, the speed at which it is completed and the organization of information (all items: Mode = 6, Range = 0–9). Users responded similarly to the control panel with LAV users reporting slight problems with the speed of task completion, complexity and awkwardness of use (all items: Mode = 4, Range = 1–6). The panel is, however, good in that controls are appropriate, the number of controls is sufficient and it streamlines the process (all items: Mode = 6, Range 5–8). HAV users responded positively about the organization of information, panel speed and the control it provides (all items: Mode = 7, Range = 1–9) but report it to be somewhat awkward to use (Mode = 3, Range = 0–7). The overall system was again quite neutrally reviewed with scores ranging from 4 to 6 (on mode) for HAV and LAV users (Fig. 7).

Workload

Lastly, participants rated the workload associated with each procedure on their respective interfaces (Fig. 8). The results show that the Commander's WT in the LAV received consistently higher workload scores on all subscales expect performance compared to the TCC in the HAV. This would indicate that the LAV users experience more difficulty in operating the console.

Regarding the OCC, the results were more comparable across demand and performance subscales. Generally, similar levels of mental workload were observed between the groups but LAV users expressed more effort and frustration with procedures using the OCC.

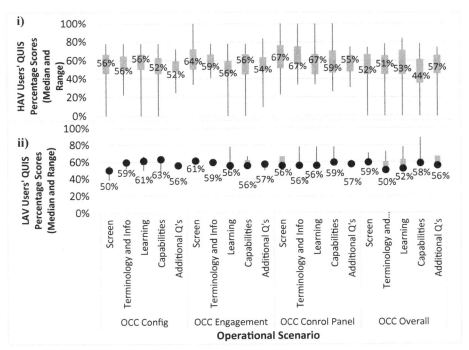

Fig. 7. Box and whisker plot showing the median and range of i) HAV and ii) LAV user responses to the Operator Control Console (OCC).

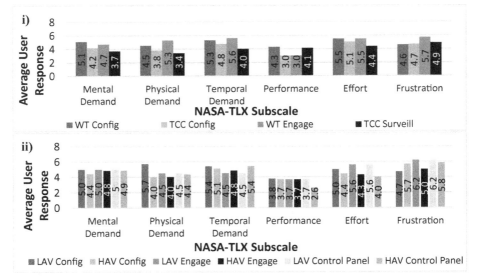

Fig. 8. i) Chart showing the average NASA-TLX scores for each operation on the Commander's respective interface. ii) NASA-TLX scores for operations on the Operator's console

4   Discussion

Overall, the results of the subjective feedback for the LAV and HAV vehicles are generally positive. Physical ergonomics evaluation showed some issues with space and some risk of developing MSCs with prolonged vehicle use. Regarding the weapon system itself, users tended to respond in the mid-range of most items, indicating the system is fit for its purpose but there is room for improvement. The sections below are supplemented with feedback obtained from an HAV user focus group.

4.1   Physical Ergonomics

Regarding physical ergonomics, HAV users reported the physical space available to them as an issue. This corresponds to the current understanding of the system limitations; the interior of the vehicle is cramped and considering the amount of equipment and protective gear users will be wearing the issue is further exacerbated. This is a common feature across military vehicles as evidenced in a report that showed a primary complaint from the Marine vehicle operators was a lack of space to stow personal items during missions, such as rucksacks, rations and spare ammunition [28]. A further study [29], noted that operations in military vehicles are characterised by confined-space workstations which require sustained, relatively static postures, leading to a gradual increase in discomfort levels and fatigue, and a decrease in task performance (speed, accuracy and task completion). Combining the lack of space with the resultant levels of fatigue that HAV and LAV users both report, makes optimal performance difficult to achieve. Considering the impact that discomfort can have, as well as the importance of operator performance in a military context, future workspace designs should consider carefully the organisation and placement of equipment to maximise operator space. This agrees with HAV user consensus in the focus group where users highlighted the future system would likely be more spacious and more in line with the LAV design.

4.2 USE and QUIS Questionnaire Findings

The key difference between the LAV and HAV used in this study was the Commander's operating console. In the LAV, the console receives orders from higher command and the Commander decides whether the vehicle can/cannot follow the order (e.g. based on vehicle status, orientation etc.). In the HAV, the Commander takes on a larger role. Targets are not identified by higher command but are detected, identified and handled by the crew in the vehicle. The TCC (HAV) contains detailed maps of the environment, surveillance options, imaging, IFF (interrogation friend or foe), target tracking and cueing. The WT (LAV) is more simplistic in its function and layout, displaying only a rudimentary target tracking output and engagement status.

What was surprising in our results was the similarity of feedback for the different consoles. User feedback on the USE questionnaire showed very similar ratings across the usefulness, ease of use, ease of learning and user satisfaction across both interfaces (Fig. 4). Here, a user's experience may have a role. A study [30] showed that users with more experience of a product tended to provide higher, more favourable usability scores over those with limited or no experience. The more experienced HAV operators may have reported the interface more favourably than the inexperienced LAV users; potentially explaining why the USE feedback for the HAV was more positive than expected.

In the LAV, USE questionnaire users scored '3' many times, indicating neither agree nor disagree indicating room for improvement in future interfaces. For both HAV and LAV users, streamlining procedures was highlighted concurrently with interface-related frustration. Research has shown that negative emotional states such as frustration may lead to aggressive behaviors and negatively impact the comfort of drivers [31]. Frustration can be a result of the interface diverging from the user's needs, leading to increased dissatisfaction [32]. This can often compliment and relate to how streamlined the process is, i.e. making the system efficient, maximizing its speed and simplicity.

Feedback on the design and layout of the OCC was less positive for HAV users than the TCC. Users generally responded around '3' on the scale indicating neither agree nor disagree with the statements. LAV users reported similarly, only identifying their ability to recover from mistakes, their ability to remember how to use it and the pleasantness of the system, as areas that should be improved. These aspects could also be related to overseas users speaking a different native tongue. The LAV operators speak different languages and have different cultural backgrounds but must learn to use the English-based interface. Users relying on their knowledge a second language will complicate their model of the system and will make remembering system use and correcting mistakes more difficult than those utilizing their primary language. A recent paper highlighted that military personnel are now required to develop 1. Breadth (an expanded set of competencies); 2. Depth (higher levels of skill, e.g., critical thinking, anticipation) and 3. Velocity (gain competencies more efficiently and maintain their relevance in an ever-changing environment) [33]. The language barrier LAV users experience may mean that their method of learning may not easily facilitate three aforementioned requirements of military learning. Furthermore, the focus on cognitive readiness in military units and personnel means that mission-essential tasks need to be tied to the underlying cognitive capabilities to perform missions successfully [34]. This means there is an increased need to develop more context-free, transferable instructional abilities [34].

For the QUIS the LAV and HAV Commander consoles received similar feedback with users generally reporting the interface enabled them to complete the tasks relatively well. Regarding the TCC set-up, users indicated some difficulty with inputting information, correcting mistakes and again with how streamlined the procedure is (scores in the lower 50% of the scale). The engagement process QUIS only highlighted the error messages as a potential cause for concern in this respect, with most of the other items on the scale receiving positive feedback, particularly the task sequences being easy to follow and the ease of performing the task. The WT users reported some issue with the set-up being awkward to perform, which was consistent with what the users reported for the engagement procedure. As the LAV users are non-English speaking perhaps this could be down to a lack of understanding of the system information, leading to confusion regarding what the system requires of them.

On speaking with a training representative at Thales UK, it was clear that language is a significant barrier to training LAV users. LAV users adopt a mimicking approach to learning without any deep understanding or comprehension of the task/procedure. Similar to skill-based approaches, the users are attempting to rapidly acquire the ability to perform the task but when faced with abnormal scenarios this knowledge may fail and impact their ability to adapt. Whilst practicing to perform the specific task they develop routine expertise, but this does not necessarily translate to adaptive expertise i.e. the ability to adapt to non-routine scenarios [35, 36]. The WT NASA-TLX scores could corroborate this suggestion as scores for both configuration and engagement indicate all aspects of demand, as well as effort, was higher for WT users. This suggests that WT users struggle more with its operation than their TCC counterparts.

Regarding Operator QUIS feedback, again the two vehicles' OCC received similar feedback with users generally reporting the interface enabled them to complete the tasks well. LAV users reported some problems with the organization of information and the awkwardness of the system during set-up. HAV users found error messages somewhat unhelpful, they expressed some concern over information relevance and the streamlining of information. These issues reflect some of what was found in the Commanders QUIS. Again, for engagement LAV users reported some level of awkwardness and the HAV users reported some problems with how streamlined the procedure was, the error messages and the ease of correcting mistakes. Interestingly, HAV users report more expertise is required for the OCC than the TCC.

Lastly, when operating the control panel again the concept of awkwardness was apparent in both LAV and HAV users. In this case, the physical awkwardness of operating the panel could be, in part, due to the lack of space inside the respective LAV and HAV vehicles. The OCC control panel has two handles that extend into the legroom of the user and these are responsible for the firing sequence of the weapon system. These were reported as an issue from the qualitative feedback section of the questionnaire, where users suggested removing at least one of the handles. NASA-TLX scores for workload in the OCC reflect the same as above, LAV users scored higher for overall workload than their HAV counterparts. HAV users scored each procedure very similarly on average. Both LAV and HAV user's score frustration the highest dimension on average. What is promising is that although frustration and demand is high, users of both the LAV and HAV report their performance as very good, indicating that they are capable of coping with the workload to perform mission tasks effectively, this coincides with the HAV focus group reporting that generally the system itself is good but it is the vehicle the system is mounted inside that is causing most of the usage issues.

4.3 Design Implications and AI Potential

Questionnaire feedback suggests some design implications for future weapons systems. Firstly, utilizing space available more effectively as users in this study highlighted issues with space when operating inside the AVs. Inefficient use of space could be placing users at a higher risk of MSCs, reducing their effectiveness in the battlefield and during missions. Users noted that the handles of the OCC were obtrusive and effected comfort and posture inside the vehicle. Unfortunately, comments from the focus group indicated that, due to design and weapon system safety considerations, there is little room for adjustment in these aspects. As such, basing the weapons platform on a different vehicle is a more practical solution. Additionally, improving interface accessibility (particularly for LAV users) such as improving the organization of information, deciphering task progress and system complexity could improve usability. Facilitating better training procedures and nurturing adaptive expertise could be an effective approach to these issues. Using better symbology and adapting to local terminology could improve the interface for overseas users. Lastly, improving how streamlined the procedures are for HAV users in the form of removing irrelevant information surrounding task performance, reducing the complexity of the information displayed and improving the organization of the information would be beneficial. This could contribute to workload reduction as well, reducing distraction by making key information easier to locate.

With these in mind, advances in recognition, classification and decision-making algorithms (collectively now referred to as AI) could be embedded in the display and control software of a future weapon system with the aim of reducing user workload and aiding user decision-making. Whilst the level of Operator and Commander workload is comparable between the two vehicles, it is the Commander's role that is essential in determining vehicle actions. Aside from removing the Operator and automating the firing sequence (which has significant ethical and moral considerations; see [37]), improving the layout and design of the interface is the most viable way of improving the operator's workload. This was also agreed with the HAV user focus group.

It seems more likely that AI in the LAV WT or the HAV TCC would be more advantageous to improve Commanders' ability to decide on the correct course of action. In the LAV, AI could assume a large proportion of the Commander's activities including deciding if the vehicle can engage a target by assessing weapon system status (such as missiles available, whether it is in range and in the right orientation). The Commander would be tasked with monitoring the AI to ensure correct decisions are made based on the AI output. In the HAV, AI could acquire and present some of the decision-vital information for the Commander to aid them in their decision-making tasks. An AI system could be adopted that would aid in identifying a target; such as whether a target is located where it should be and the type of target. Ultimately the Commander will still be in control of the final decision which is a property the HAV focus group insisted was vital in future AI integration. Avoiding the system making decisions or causing a confirmation bias was reported as essential in ensuring responsible and carefully considered decisions are made. This form of AI could save Commanders vital seconds in their decision-making, increase efficiency efficient and reduce the number of errors.

4.4 Limitations

One of the main limitations of this study is the subjectivity of the questions and response scales. This is a common problem across questionnaires [38–40]. Terminology can be interpreted differently by individuals. In addition, this study had the added complexity of English being a secondary language, increasing the chances of miscommunication. Moreover, our users in this study had only experienced the use of one of the systems; results may have been more useful had users experienced both the systems, enabling a better comparison between the two vehicles. This may also have helped with the issue of subjectivity as user responses would have been more readily compared between questionnaires. Furthermore, the consistency of LAV user responses could place some doubt over the generalization of the results. Culturally, overseas users are less known for complaining. For instance, Chinese and American politeness behaviors are vastly different, meaning their approaches to complaining may be vastly different [41]. The same rule could apply to the users in this study where, culturally, the LAV users may be less inclined to review their vehicles in any negative way; meaning their results are more positive than their true perspectives. Lastly, user experience levels were unbalanced between the two samples, with LAV users being younger and less experienced. HAV Commanders with more experience tended to score the vehicles more positively in terms of physical ergonomics, whereas users in the middle age group (25–34) scored the interface more favorably across the QUIS. The same is true of the HAV Operators, the 25–34 age group scored the interface more favorably than the younger and older age groups. Workload scoring between the levels of experience was, however, consistent between age groups.

4.5 Conclusion

This study aimed to utilise a questionnaire battery to assess user opinions on the HMI design of two currently used armoured vehicles. Despite the limitations, the results provided valuable insight into the efficiency of the system and prompted avenues for future weapons system improvement. Overall, the study successfully highlighted the concerns users had when using the weapon system and identified how future vehicle development could integrate AI technology. The key conclusions from the study are:

- Users' posture and physical work environment showed a moderate MSC risk. Future system development needs to maximize available space and consider user-system interactions more carefully to promote long-term health and user performance.

- Responses showed users were generally satisfied with the current system with only some refinement suggestions. These include streamlining the procedures and information provided to improve overall system usability and increase user satisfaction which could also aid with the issues reported by LAV users.
- LAV reported higher workload, more difficulty in learning and remembering the system functions and more frustration with system operation. This can be partly attributed to a language barrier in system training and design. Future systems (when designed for a global market) should thereby carefully consider this earlier in the design process, facilitating flexibility as much as possible e.g. by representing functions and information in language-neutral ways such as through symbols.
- Integrating an AI component into the weapon system that would support the Commander's decision-making process appears to be the most beneficial use of the technology. This would save vital seconds in decision-making time, increase efficiency and reduce the number of errors. This approach would also be more accepted by users as it aids the decision-making process whilst also avoiding confirmation bias and coercing/leading users into making a specific decision.

References

1. Krulak, C.C.: The strategic corporal: leadership in the three block war. Marine Corps Gazette **83**(1), 18–22 (1999)
2. Yean, T.C., Hong, M.S., Yew, V.: Fighting Vehicle Technology DSTA Horizons, 62–77 (2013)
3. Friedl, K.E., Grate, S.J., Proctor, S.P., Ness, J.W., Lukey, B.J., Kane, R.L.: Army research needs for automated neuropsychological tests: monitoring soldier health and performance status. Arch. Clin. Neuropsychol. **22**(Suppl 1), S7–S14 (2007)
4. Martinez-Lopez, L.: Cognitive performance in operational environments. Aviat. Space Environ. Med. **76**(7), C2–C3 (2005)
5. Thompson, M.M., McCreary, D.R.: Enhancing mental readiness in military personnel. In; Human Dimensions in Military Operations – Military Leaders' Strategies for Addressing Stress and Psychological Support. Meeting proceedings RTO-MPHFM-134. Neuilly-sur-Seine, pp. 4-1–4-12 (2006)
6. Thomas, M.L., Russo, M.B.: Neurocognitive monitors: toward the prevention of cognitive performance decrements and catastrophic failures in the operational environment. Aviat. Space Environ. Med. **78**(5), B144–B152 (2007)
7. Grier, R.A.: Military cognitive readiness at the operational and strategic levels: a theoretical model for measurement development. J. Cogn. Eng. Dec. Mak. **6**(4), 358–392 (2012)
8. Giraudet, L., Imbert, J.-P., Bérenger, M., Tremblay, S., Causse, M.: The neuroergonomic evaluation of human machine interface design in air traffic control using behavioral and EEG/ERP measures. Behav. Brain Res. **294**, 246–253 (2015)
9. Santangelo, V.: Forced to remember: when memory is biased by salient information. Behav. Brain Res. **283**, 1–10 (2015)
10. Martin, E.W.: Artificial intelligence and robotics for military systems. In: Proceedings. of The Army Conference on Application of Artificial Intelligence to Battlefield Information Management, Washington DC (1984)
11. Gay, C., Horowitz, B., Elshaw, J., Bobko, P., Kim, I.: Operator suspicion and human-machine team performance under mission scenarios of unmanned ground vehicle operation. IEEE Access. **7**, 36371–36379 (2019)

12. Zieba, S., Polet, P., Vanderhaegen, F.: Using adjustable autonomy and human–machine cooperation to make a human–machine system resilient–application to a ground robotic system. Inf. Sci. **181**(3), 379–397 (2011)
13. Bush, L.A., Wang, A.J., Williams, B.C.: Risk-based sensing in support of adjustable autonomy. In: IEEE Aerospace Conference, pp. 1–18 (2012)
14. INCOSE : A world in motion: systems engineering vision 2025. In: International Council on Systems Engineering. INCOSE, San Diego (2014)
15. Carver, L., Turoff, M.: The human and computer as a team in emergency management information systems. CACM **50**(3), 33–38 (2007)
16. Parasuraman, R., Hancock, P.A.: Mitigating the adverse effects of workload, stress, and fatigue with adaptive automation, pp. 45–57 (2008)
17. Gibson, Z., Butterfield, J., Marzano, A.: User-centered design criteria in next generation vehicle consoles. Procedia CIRP **55**, 260–265 (2016)
18. Hildebrandt, V.H., Bongers, P.M., van Dijk, F.J., Kemper, H.C., Dul, J.: Dutch musculoskeletal questionnaire: description and basic qualities. Ergonomics **44**(12), 1038–1055 (2001)
19. Corlett, E.N., Bishop, R.P.: A technique for assessing postural discomfort. Ergonomics **19**(2), 175–182 (1976)
20. Engelbrecht, G.J., de Beer, L.T., Schaufeli, W.B.: The relationships between work intensity, workaholism, burnout, and self-reported musculoskeletal complaints. In: Human Factors and Ergonomics in Manufacturing & Service Industries (2019)
21. Halvarsson, A., Hagman, I., Tegern, M., Broman, L., Larsson, H.: Self-reported musculoskeletal complaints and injuries and exposure of physical workload in Swedish soldiers serving in Afghanistan. PLoS ONE **13**(4), e0195548 (2018)
22. Riches, A., Spratford, W., Witchalls, J., Newman, P.: A systematic review and meta-analysis about the prevalence of neck pain in fast jet pilots. Aerospace Med. Hum. Perform. **90**(10), 882–890 (2019)
23. Dul, J., Delleman, N.J., Hildebrandt, V.H.: Posture and movement analysis in ergonomics: principles and research. In: Proceedings of the Symposium 'Biolocomotion: A Century of Research Using Moving Pictures', vol. 1, Promograph (1992)
24. Lund, A.M.: Measuring usability with the USE questionnaire. Usab. Interf. STC Usabil. SIG Newsl. **8**(2), 3–6 (2001)
25. Chin, J.P., Diehl, V.A., Norman, K.L.: Development of an instrument measuring user satisfaction of the human-computer interface. In: Proceedings of the SIGCHI Conference on Human Factors in Computing Systems, pp. 213–218 (1988)
26. Hart, S.G., Staveland, L.E.: Development of NASA-TLX (Task Load Index): results of empirical and theoretical research. Adv. Psychol. **52**, 139–183 (1988)
27. Grier, R.A.: How high is high? A meta-analysis of NASA-TLX global workload scores. In: Proceedings of the Human Factors and Ergonomics Society Annual Meeting, vol. 59, no. 1, pp. 1727–1731 (2015)
28. Paul, B.: Case study of GPS retransmission in military ground vehicles. In: Proceedings of the 2011 NDIA Ground Vehicle Systems Engineering and Technology Symposium (2011)
29. Delleman, N.J., Colaciuri, V., Wiederkehr, E., Valk, P.J.L.: Sustained operations in confined-space military vehicles. Int. J. Occup. Saf. Ergon. **14**(3), 313–325 (2008)
30. McLellan, S., Muddimer, A., Peres, S.C.: The effect of experience on system usability scale ratings. J. Usabil. Stud. **7**(2), 56–67 (2012)
31. Löcken, A., Ihme, K., Unni, A.: Towards designing affect-aware systems for mitigating the effects of in-vehicle frustration. In: Proceedings of the 9th International Conference on Automotive User Interfaces and Interactive Vehicular Applications Adjunct, pp. 88–93 (2017)
32. Degani, A., Goldman, C.V., Deutsch, O., Tsimhoni, O.: On human-machine relations. Cogn. Technol. Work **19**(2–3), 211–231 (2017)

33. Schatz, S., Fautua, D., Stodd, J., Reitz, E.: The changing face of military learning. In: Proceedings of the I/ITSEC (2015)
34. Fletcher, J., Wind, A.P.: The evolving definition of cognitive readiness for military operations. In: O'Neil, H., Perez, R., Baker, E. (eds.) Teaching and Measuring Cognitive Readiness, pp. 25–52. Springer, Boston (2014). https://doi.org/10.1007/978-1-4614-7579-8_2
35. Bainbridge, L.: Difficulties and errors in complex dynamic tasks. Ergonomics, in press. Retrieved August 2018, vol. 24, p. 2002 (1998)
36. Embrey, D.: Understanding human behaviour and error. Hum. Reliab. Assoc. **1**, 1–10 (2005)
37. Etzioni, A., Etzioni, O.: Pros and cons of autonomous weapons systems. Military Review (2017)
38. Jahedi, S., Méndez, F.: On the advantages and disadvantages of subjective measures. J. Econ. Behav. Organ. **98**, 97–114 (2014)
39. Bertrand, M., Mullainathan, S.: Do people mean what they say? Implications for subjective survey data. Am. Econ. Rev. **91**(2), 67–72 (2001)
40. Redelmeier, D.A., Katz, J., Kahneman, D.: Memories of colonoscopy: a randomized trial. Pain **104**(1–2), 187–194 (2003)
41. Hong, C., Shih, S.: 'You Shouldn't Have Done That!'-a cross-cultural study of perceptions of appropriate complaints. English Teach. Learn. **33**(1) (2009)

How to Design a Research Data Management Platform? Technical, Organizational and Individual Perspectives and Their Relations

Lennart Hofeditz[1], Björn Ross[1(✉)] [iD], Konstantin Wilms[1], Marius Rother[1], Stephanie Rehwald[1] [iD], Bela Brenger[2] [iD], Ania López[1] [iD], Raimund Vogl[3] [iD], and Dominik Rudolph[3] [iD]

[1] University of Duisburg-Essen, 47057 Duisburg, Germany
`bjoern.ross@uni-due.de, ross.bjoern@gmail.com`
[2] RWTH, Aachen, 52062 Aachen, Germany
[3] University of Münster, 48149 Münster, Germany
`d.rudolph@uni-muenster.de`

Abstract. Academic research generates increasing amounts of data that needs to be shared between collaborators, made publicly accessible and/or archived for the long term, all while respecting applicable regulations on topics such as data protection. Good research data management (RDM) is challenging, and despite the growing number of available technical solutions, researchers have been reluctant to use them. We interviewed 64 academic researchers to elicit requirements and explore attitudes towards RDM. Although many funding bodies insist that each project follow published RDM guidelines, only about half the participants considered RDM relevant for their own work, and only one in three reported that they already practiced RDM or were planning to do so. The qualitative analysis of the transcripts revealed three broad categories of requirements for RDM platforms, namely technical, organizational and individual ones. We discuss how these requirements are related to, and sometimes contradict each other.

Keywords: Research data management · Open science · Qualitative research · RDM platform · Design requirements

1 Introduction

Against the background of ongoing digitization in research, an increasing amount of data is being generated by researchers at higher education institutions. As this amount of data seems to grow continuously, researchers will need to change the way they manage their data in order to keep track of it and be able to collaborate effectively. In addition, public funders of research projects such as the European Commission, the German Research Foundation (DFG), and the German Federal Ministry of Education and Research (BMBF) require researchers to maintain their data and make it publicly available. Consequently, academics of all disciplines will need to rethink their data management strategies in order to be able to manage the growing and increasingly complex

© Springer Nature Switzerland AG 2020
S. Yamamoto and H. Mori (Eds.): HCII 2020, LNCS 12185, pp. 324–337, 2020.
https://doi.org/10.1007/978-3-030-50017-7_23

amount of data in the future. To accompany this process, the DFG has published guidelines for research data management (RDM) aimed at researchers and institutions. RDM can be defined as the organization of data, from its collection to its publication and the archiving of results [1]. RDM also includes the management of data through infrastructure, long-term storage, data security, open access, as well as communication between researchers from different disciplines [2].

Vines et al. [3] reported that the availability of data from published studies decreases with the age of publication. Specifically, the probability of data being available decreases by 17% annually after its publication [3]. Open access to research results offers the opportunity to confirm or disprove those results [4]; it consequently offers a control function that ultimately benefits quality. Furthermore, a good and transparent RDM protects against accusations of scientific misconduct [5].

RDM also provides advantages for individual researchers. Researchers who grant access to their research data are cited more often than those who do not [6]. RDM has the potential to positively support individual researchers as well as research groups [7].

Although corresponding specifications exist, there is often a lack of appropriate technical and organizational capabilities to implement a research data management infrastructure in an institution [8]. Knowledge of how to design RDM platforms and services remains very low. But how can an RDM artefact be designed so that it makes a relevant contribution to research? Are there possibly already functionalities in established systems that are used and would, therefore, be suitable to be transferred into a research data management platform? As there are no comprehensive answers to these issues, we derived the following research question:

RQ: *How do RDM platforms need to be designed to support academic research?*

We conducted and evaluated group interviews with researchers in workshops in order to identify requirements for a user-centered RDM platform. We conducted 16 workshops with a total of 64 participants. We evaluated the interviews with a qualitative content analysis following Mayring [9]. From the results we derived technical, organizational and individual requirements for an RDM platform and identified relationships between them.

2 Literature Review and Theoretical Background

RDM is becoming an increasingly important topic, especially in the university context. More and more institutions are beginning to develop their own technical solutions to store research data for the future [10]. One trigger for this could be the research funding of third-party funding bodies, which demand RDM accordingly [11].

Perrier et al. [12] also showed that the number of publications on RDM has increased significantly since 2010, which confirms the growing interest in the topic. Different disciplines have different requirements for research data and its management. For this reason, there is currently no uniform definition of RDM. RDM comprises the organization of data from the collection to publication and archiving of the results [1]. It also includes the management of data through an infrastructure, a long-term storage facility, data security, open access, as well as communication between researchers from different disciplines and research fields [2]. In most cases, however, the aim is to ensure that digital research data is made available to other researchers [13]. However, RDM is not only important for sharing data, but for the entire research cycle. Starting with data collection, through analysis, to the evaluation and interpretation of the data, correct RDM can achieve significant improvements [1]. At the same time, the ongoing digitization creates ever larger amounts of data [14]. Accordingly, researchers today are confronted with an abundance of data and data types [15]. Consequently, researchers need to rethink and change their data management strategies in order to be able to manage the ever-growing and increasingly complex data volumes of the future.

Although data sharing brings many opportunities and benefits and can accelerate the research process, it is still not a common practice [16] and data is more likely to be withheld than published in scientific journals [17]. Citing other researchers is very common and is a reward for the cited researcher [18]. However, sharing data is not based on this formalism and does not offer researchers any perceptible recognition. Thus, data sharing is not yet established as a method of communication within the research community [18, 19]. Nevertheless, researchers are more inclined to share data if they expect it to be beneficial for their own careers and if the risks and effort involved appear low [20].

At the same time, researchers raise questions about privacy and the security of their own data and records [14]. There are also concerns about copyright protection in public cloud storage [21]. Researchers are skeptical as to whether collected data is not passed on to third parties under copyright protection [8].

Furthermore, they are afraid of misinterpretation of their data once they are used and interpreted in other contexts [18], and they fear losing control over their data once it is released [22]. These barriers may therefore have social rather than technical reasons [8, 23].

However, although many open access initiatives exist, there are only moderate results of applications and services [24]. In this context, there are several studies that have examined and compared existing systems and solutions [10, 12, 25, 26]. Süptitz et al. [25] showed that a general distinction can be made between functional (technical) and non-functional (framework conditions such as data security, data protection and usability) requirements [10]. Guidelines have been developed and issued at the international level on how research data should be handled [27]. In addition, researchers are required to explain at the time of application for funding how data will be handled after the conclusion of the project and what measures will be taken with regard to the sustainability of the data [11]. Wilms et al [23] compared the guidelines of ten national and international science and funding institutions. In summary, technical and non-technical factors influencing the use of RDM could be identified. According to the study, technical factors are related to the infrastructure, i.e. the platform itself, and the guidelines of the platform. Further technical factors were data security, data sharing and data maintenance. Non-technical factors were ethical factors, such as the handling of data obtained from human research, the management of, for example, false findings and factors affecting the researcher herself. The main issues here were the protection of intellectual property and incentives to use platforms for RDM.

In summary, it can be said that RDM is not only a national but also an international issue that many institutions, especially universities, are dealing with. In addition, a great deal of money is being invested by both universities and funding bodies to implement and provide technical solutions, such as virtual research environments and repositories, so that researchers can store their research data in a sustainable manner. In this context, those universities and funding institutions have developed and published guidelines for the handling of research data. There are to date no internationally accepted guidelines for handling research data. Guidelines vary by country and sometimes even within countries, which does not simplify the exchange of research data. Correspondingly, the implemented technical solutions are not or only insufficiently used, because the researchers have reservations about the new technologies and the requirements for these systems vary by discipline. Therefore, the requirements of both the disciplines and the individual researchers must be identified. Reservations and concerns must be identified and counteracted. It remains unclear how technical, social and individual requirements are interrelated, and it is essential to find out which functions researchers need in order to feel supported in their RDM.

3   Research Design

Since research in this field is still in an early stage, we chose a qualitative approach. We conducted 16 semi-structured group interviews with researchers as part of workshops on RDM. An open discussion prevented the participants from being influenced too much by given answers. A guide consisting of open-ended questions ensured that the participants' views were given the spotlight and that their statements were as unbiased as possible by the preconceptions of the workshop organizers. The workshops gave the participants a lot of freedom for discussion. The purpose of the workshops was not only to answer the research question, but also to discuss general attitudes towards RDM. The main questions in the guide resulted from the design science approach according to Hevner et al. [28] and from the current state of scientific research on functions and technical properties of research environments for RDM.

In the first part of the interviews, the interviewer gave a short presentation in which RDM was first introduced and a shared understanding of RDM was ensured with the help of a definition of the DFG. In the second part of the interviews, the aim was to find out the current status quo within the research disciplines. We asked to what extent RDM was already important in the participants' daily work, whether and to what extent they had already come into contact with RDM, and which aspects of RDM were already used within their respective disciplines.

The third part of the interview was about finding out the criteria or functionalities that a platform would have to fulfill to be attractive to the researchers and how a technical solution should be designed to support RDM in the future. If the discussion did not make progress, there were topics that were optionally addressed. Possible topics could be data security, the release of research data, long-term storage and the documentation of the research.

We conducted the group interviews in the period from 28/09/17 to 29/11/17 within the context of a project at the University of Duisburg-Essen and RWTH Aachen.

The interviews were conducted face-to-face by three different workshop organizers and the audio recorded electronically. Subsequently, all interviews were transcribed. The completely transcribed interviews were then evaluated using the deductive qualitative content analysis approach described by Mayring [29].

A total of 16 group interviews with 64 participants were conducted. The group interviews were divided into two discussion groups within the life and social sciences discipline, three group discussions within the humanities, three group discussions within the natural sciences, 5 workshops within the engineering sciences and 1 workshop included members of the Commission for Information, Communication and Media Technology at the University of Duisburg-Essen which is responsible for data protection and security. The number of participants per workshop varied between one and nine participants, and the total duration of the audio recordings varied between 12 and 73 min. The number of participants per university and discipline is shown in Table 1.

Table 1. Participants per discipline and institution

Institution	ICM	HUM	ENG	NAT	LIF	Total
RWTH Aachen	0	7	8	10	0	25
University of Duisburg-Essen	7	11	10	8	3	39
Total	7	18	18	18	3	64

ICM = Information, Communication and Media; HUM = Humanities; ENG = Engineering Sciences; NAT = Natural Sciences; LIF = Life Sciences

4   Findings

In general, we were able to determine that RDM is already relevant across disciplines and that its relevance for personal research work has increased. RDM was considered relevant for their work by about 50% of the workshop participants, while for the other half, RDM was less relevant or no precise information was given in the interviews. RDM was considered particularly relevant in engineering and life sciences and was either already applied or its introduction planned.

A majority of the researchers stated that they would store their data on local computers at their workplace or they conducted analog laboratory books to record research hypotheses and experiments. In addition, there are already common standards and set documentation in the life and social science discipline. Commercial services such as Dropbox and Google Drive with version control features were also used to store documents and their history. In the humanities, data reuse also plays an important role, since corpora (collections of texts), some of which are 40 years old, are still in use.

Basically, we could classify the requirements of the researchers into three main categories: Technical, organizational and individual requirements.

4.1 Technical Requirements

The most frequently mentioned aspects were data security and data protection. The interviewees were concerned with protection against misuse, sufficient anonymization or encryption of the data. Data should therefore be adequately protected against unauthorized access.

Another important requirement was data sharing. That means permanent access to data by others who need it in order to ensure smooth cooperation. In addition, sharing data can contribute to research transparency and this could lead to better research quality. Access and release control are also part of data sharing. It should be made clear for whom the data is released, who can access the data and in what role. Finally, technical collaboration and open access requirements were mentioned to improve the use of RDM. More detailed requirements were therefore the ability to work together with shared data, so that one can work on and with the data at the same time.

Another aspect stated by the interviewees was information retention. This includes long-term availability and the sustainability and reusability of data. Long-term availability includes the requirement for (automatic) backups and corresponding specifications from third-party funders, so that the data can still be accessed much later (for example, ten years after the project has ended). The researchers also mentioned the need for a kind of "software asset management" in order to be able to use corresponding, sometimes very special, file formats even at later times. Finally, location-dependent access to research data should ideally be possible so that the necessary data can always be accessed when required. A central point of the reusability of the data is the possibility that other researchers have access to one's research data in order to reuse it. Researchers should be able, or even obliged, to attach the raw data to their publications. This would also have a positive effect on the reproducibility of the results, the researchers' credibility and reputation. In this way, the data would also be tested in new contexts and could thus provide insights that were previously unthinkable.

If the data will be made openly available for other researchers, the systems that make the data available should accept many file formats or, alternatively, standardize the data formats so the researchers can handle them.

According to the interviewees, the possible application of metadata and documentation were other requirements for successfully performing RDM. Standards must be established and, at best, metadata has to be stored automatically as far as possible in order to find the data, if necessary, also with the help of "human data managers" to ensure a certain data quality.

Usability is another aspect that was often mentioned. Simple and intuitive user interfaces should be provided for a technical solution to be accepted.

Hardware and memory, a high bandwidth, faster data transfer, data security, and availability, as well as scalability, were stated as further technical requirements.

4.2 Organizational Requirements

As non-technical or organizational aspects we considered requirements that cannot be implemented through technical functionalities. For an overarching RDM, there must be rules, policies and standards to regulate which data should be tracked and which data types are important.

The interviewees also mentioned finance, personnel structure and administration as organizational requirements. Knowledge about the solution has to be gained, appropriate marketing measures have to be carried out and clarified in order to achieve a high level of technology acceptance.

Those solutions should also be financed and organized accordingly. The system or service could therefore be offered as cheaply as possible by universities (or similar institutions). The existence of good working technical support is also important, according to our findings. This requires long-term preparation and organization by the institutions.

Legal security is also another organizational aspect, especially for data to which a large number of possible users have access. Clear responsibilities, an opportunity for legal advice and legal certainty over the entire research cycle are required.

An additional important aspect is ethics, which is fundamental for RDM since depending on the discipline, sensitive personal data about human participants is collected.

4.3 Individual Requirements

We classified all aspects that could not be classified either in the technical requirements or the organizational requirements as individual aspects. However, this does not mean that there is no overlap with the categories of technical and organizational aspects. Rather, the aim was to show and point out connections and overlaps between subject areas.

The individual aspects were mainly concerned with the individuals in the context of technology and organization. Mostly these aspects were characterized by skepticism or fear, since new developments always bring along uncertainty. We also assigned the researchers' personal attitude towards the RDM to this category.

The participants stated that, according to the specifications of the third-party funding bodies, the research data should be published as early as possible and made available to others. However, the researchers were afraid of "knowledge theft" if the data was released too early (before publication). They would like to prevent another researcher from taking credit for their research achievements.

Due to the pressures of research and publication, it is considered a clear advantage to have sole access to one's own data. This aspect influences the subsequent use of the data accordingly.

The transfer of data was another point of uncertainty mentioned in the interviews. On the one hand, researchers want to release their data according to good scientific practice. On the other hand, researchers wonder which and to what extent data may be passed on and whether a loss of control over the data would be possible. The aspects of data protection and legal certainty played a prominent role.

In the opinions of the researchers, an awareness must be developed that research is done for "eternity", i.e. for more than ten years, and that the data must be documented in such a way that they can still be used for many years to come.

However, it would also require self-discipline, as even today the researchers do not always understand the documentation of their own research from three years earlier.

In order to contribute to traceability, it is important that metadata is also used, and that detailed and comprehensible documentation will be produced.

In spite of self-discipline, the effort to use the technical solution must be kept as low as possible. The researchers described that they would probably use the solution little or not at all if the effort to store the data there or to work with them would be too high. This is mainly due to the fact that the workload of researchers is already high anyway and they want to avoid additional effort. The requirement over the entire cycle, from data sharing to reusability, from (long-term) availability to the documentation of the research, would therefore be to keep the additional effort for the individual researcher as low as possible.

4.4 Relationships of the Requirements

As already mentioned in the description of the individual aspects, there are often inter-relationships within the categories. The interrelationships identified between the aspects showed that in developing an RDM platform, not only individual aspects must be considered, but the "big picture" must not be overlooked. Thus, technical aspects such as metadata and documentation, as well as sharing data in connection with individual and human aspects should be considered together. This concerns the reservations or even fears that researchers might have about certain technical functionalities. But also, the organizational aspects must not be considered separately. Especially regarding personal data, the ethical framework conditions must be discussed and taken into account. The same applies to questions of legal certainty and organization in general.

Of course, these results are only the first indications. Further research should continue to explore overarching connections between the aspects. Our results justify further research in this field to gain further insights into the perception and requirements of the researchers.

5 Discussion

With regard to the research question, it can be seen that researchers make far-reaching demands on an RDM platform. Technical functions still have to be developed to support research data management, but some of them are already available. Researchers also have detailed ideas about what organizational and individual requirements they have so that they feel supported. One important technical aspect that could be derived from the interviews was the aspect of being able to share research data online. For the researchers, this includes collaboration, access and release control and management. An important organizational aspect that we identified was the need for the exact implementation of existing rules and standards. Overarching rules provide researchers with an orientation guide on how RDM should proceed in detail and which workflows need to be run through. The rules and standards do not only refer to discipline-specific metadata, but also to the data formats and the overall workflows regarding research data. Furthermore, we identified some basic functionalities. These include functions for sharing data, for long-term availability for subsequent use and for the protection and secure use of data. In addition, metadata and file format functionalities should be integrated as these functions play a key role. The APIs of existing software were mentioned as particularly important.

Highly specialized functions from the various research disciplines could be implemented by these programming interfaces. As an example, digital laboratory books, such as those from natural sciences, highly complex calculations from the engineering sciences or text corpora considered in social science, could also be integrated. Lastly already established functions from other contexts should be adapted as far as possible.

A key contribution of this study is to show the relationships between the requirements (see Fig. 1). Not always are these easy, or even possible, to meet at the same time. For example, data sharing is an obvious requirement of a good RDM platform, yet researchers also report a need to ensure that their data is not misused. Any form of data sharing feature that allows users to download research data onto their own machine is likely to entail a small possibility that the data might fall into the wrong hands, for example through theft or careless disposal of hardware. The same holds for the requirements of archiving the data for the term and keeping costs low. A solution that meets both requirements is far from obvious: What happens to the data when the commercial cloud service goes out of business, or politicians are no longer willing to extend a publicly funded project?

For managers of research institutions, we derived organizational recommendations. In cooperation with various research disciplines, rules and standards for metadata must be established in addition to the existing guidelines for handling research data. In addition, the issue of legal certainty must be comprehensively regulated. Finally, managers must deal with the topics of human resources, financing and organization. It must be clarified to what extent new human resources must be made available, how these staff members and the provision of the technical solution can be financed and how the organization can plan for the long term, when the political context might change. In Fig. 1 we summarized all identified technical, organizational and individual requirements and their relationships.

Only about half of the participants stated that they considered RDM relevant. Only one in three reported that RDM was already practiced or that it was planned to introduce such a system. One reason for this lack of awareness could be the timeliness of the topic of RDM. It is possible that the topic has not yet "arrived" in many disciplines, as the topic has only gained momentum in recent years, which can be seen in the increasing number of publications on the topic [12]. It could also be possible that international comparisons will slowly increase attention to this topic. The technical aspects that could be derived from the interviews can already be found in similar categories in the literature that describes the requirements of the researchers [25, 30].

Especially technical functions for data sharing, collaboration or access and release control are essential for RDM to be applicable at all. It is certainly important to recognize that, especially with such centralized functions, the effort required to achieve the goal of sharing data with others must be low, since the willingness to share data decreases as the effort increases [31].

The focus on data protection and security is also currently relevant due to the EU's General Data Protection Regulation (EU-GDPR). The principle therefore applies that the more personal the data, the more relevant data protection is. Finally, however, it must be recognized that some research data cannot be released for subsequent use because anonymization of the data would be too costly [32]. At the same time, researchers are rather skeptical about the functionalities of data provision and reusability by others, as they fear data misuse or even loss of control over their self-generated data [30].

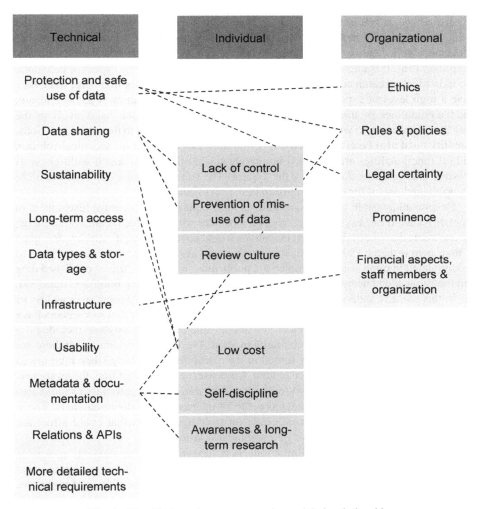

Fig. 1. Identified requirement categories and their relationships

Nevertheless, these functionalities must be in place, as they will become central to research work and are demanded by the various institutions (such as DFG or EU). However, technical functions for mere data storage will not be sufficient to make research data usable in the long term [33]. It must be clarified how the actual information content of the data can be preserved because the added value of information preservation only becomes apparent when the data can be accessed and also analyzed [34].

Research data can also benefit from metadata, as metadata can be used to contextualize and view the data [35]. Thus, the use of metadata also influences the search function and, secondarily, the effectiveness and speed of research. Metadata simplifies data sharing [36]. If there are no standards, this could prevent researchers from ultimately making their data available within the framework of open access [37]. Standards may therefore have to be defined first. These specifications are needed simply because the unification or standardization of workflows, data formats and metadata will ensure that data can be kept clear in the long term and the associated sharing of data will be greatly simplified [36]. It is unclear who is to issue these rules. As with the aspect of metadata, the individual research communities would probably be the best option here, since they have a high level of expertise in the respective fields and thus know what is relevant, and the guidelines are then not simply prescribed by outsiders, but created involving the very communities who will later have to follow them. In addition to the actual functions, usability must also be given priority. It is therefore essential that the technical solution and all functionalities are designed intuitively so that there is as much willingness as possible among researchers to use the system. The functions and tools must therefore be usable and useful for the target group in the first instance [38].

Despite all possible obstacles, initiatives must be taken to encourage researchers to practice RDM. If one asks the researchers themselves what possible incentives might be, the answer is that one of the biggest incentives would be the increased visibility & impact of their own research [30]. For this reason, there are also three major areas that need to be stimulated in open access solutions: the publication of data, the use of published data and the value added using published data and the value added using published data [39].

In this context, individual aspects must also be considered. Aspects such as loss of control or fear of knowledge theft, as well as the perceived effort that researchers have to "take on" in order to provide research data, must be taken seriously and included if a virtual research environment is to be implemented. There is also evidence that there are individual aspects that are deeply rooted in the researcher, especially when it comes to fears of loss of control and knowledge theft. Likewise, the aspect that first, the awareness has to be developed that one's own research will be long-term research that should also be available to others, is a point that has yet to be internalized by the researchers. Those points, in turn, seem to have an influence on technical aspects that could affect the possible acceptance and actual use of a technical solution.

The present study also has its limitations. In groups with seven participants or more, it became difficult to assign all of the statements in the interviews to the correct participants during transcription. The group discussion can also mean that the discussed topics are determined by particularly eloquent or convincing participants who strongly voice their opinion.

In summary, it can be stated that a platform for RDM should be more than just the sum of technical functions. Not only the technical requirements have to be considered, but also the organizational requirements as well as the concerns and fears of individual researchers.

6   Conclusion

The goal of this study was to evaluate how RDM platforms need to be designed to support academic researchers. Three categories of requirements were identified.

In general, basic functionalities should be given so that the system can fulfil its purpose at all. These include functions for data sharing, long-term availability for re-use, and the protection and secure use of data. In addition, functionalities for metadata and file formats should be integrated, as these functions play a key role. In general, however, sufficient infrastructure and usability must be provided for when using the system. In addition, already established functions from other contexts should be adapted if possible, as these functions are then already field-tested and have proven themselves.

In cooperation with various research disciplines, rules and standards for metadata must be established in addition to the existing guidelines for handling research data. Furthermore, the issue of legal certainty must be comprehensively regulated.

Since this study first provides initial indications of connections between various categories and aspects, future studies should deal with the connections between technical and non-technical aspects as well as human concerns and fears in order to be able to make statements in the future as to whether and how these connections could have an influence on user behavior.

References

1. Whyte, A., Tedds, J.: Making the Case for Research Data Management. DCC Briefing Papers. Digital Curation Centre, Edinburgh (2011)
2. Schopfel, J., Chaudiron, S., Jacquemin, B., Prost, H., Severo, M., Thiault, F.: Open access to research data in electronic theses and dissertations: an overview. Libr. Hi Tech. **32**, 612–627 (2014). https://doi.org/10.1108/LHT-06-2014-0058
3. Vines, T.H., et al.: The availability of research data declines rapidly with article age. Curr. Biol. **24**, 94–97 (2014). https://doi.org/10.1016/j.cub.2013.11.014
4. Agarwal, R., Dhar, V.: Big data, data science, and analytics: the opportunity and challenge for IS research. Inf. Syst. Res. **25**, 443–448 (2014). https://doi.org/10.1287/isre.2014.0546
5. Joshi, M., Krag, S.S.: Issues in data management. Sci. Eng. Ethics **16**, 743–748 (2010)
6. Piwowar, H.A., Day, R.S., Fridsma, D.B.: Sharing detailed research data is associated with increased citation rate. PLoS ONE **2** (2007). https://doi.org/10.1371/journal.pone.0000308
7. Link, G., Lumbard, K., Germonprez, M., Conboy, K., Feller, J.: Contemporary issues of open data in information systems research: considerations and recommendations. Commun. Assoc. Inf. Syst. **41**, 587–610 (2018). https://doi.org/10.17705/1cais.04125
8. Yamamoto, S. (ed.): HIMI 2016. LNCS, vol. 9735. Springer, Cham (2016). https://doi.org/10.1007/978-3-319-40397-7
9. Mayring, P.: Qualitative Content Analysis (2014). https://doi.org/10.1016/S1479-3709(07)11003-7
10. Amorim, R.C., Castro, J.A., Rocha da Silva, J., Ribeiro, C.: A comparison of research data management platforms: architecture, flexible metadata and interoperability. Univers. Access Inf. Soc. **16**, 851–862 (2017). https://doi.org/10.1007/s10209-016-0475-y
11. Natural Science Foundation: Data Management & Sharing FAQs (2017)
12. Perrier, L., et al.: Research data management in academic institutions: a scoping review. PLoS ONE **12**, 1–14 (2017). https://doi.org/10.1371/journal.pone.0178261
13. Reuter, C., Ludwig, T., Kotthaus, C., Kaufhold, M.-A., von Radziewski, E., Pipek, V.: Big data in a crisis? Creating social media datasets for crisis management research. i-com 15 (2016). https://doi.org/10.1515/icom-2016-0036
14. Pinfield, S., Cox, A.M., Smith, J.: Research data management and libraries: relationships, activities, drivers and influences, pp. 1–28 (2014). https://doi.org/10.1371/journal.pone.0114734
15. Hicks, B.: UK universities put their faith in the Google cloud
16. Piwowar, H.A., Chapman, W.W.: A review of journal policies for sharing research data (2008)

17. Campbell, E.G., Clarridge, B.R., Birenbaum, L., Hilgartner, S., Blumenthal, D.: Data with-holding in academic genetics: evidence from a national survey. J. Am. Med. Assoc. **287**, 473–480 (2002). https://doi.org/10.1001/jama.287.4.473

18. Borgmann, C.L.: Scholarship in the Digital Age. MIT Press, Cambridge (2007)

19. Tenopir, C., et al.: Data sharing by scientists: practices and perceptions. PLoS ONE **6**, 1–21 (2011). https://doi.org/10.1371/journal.pone.0021101

20. Kim, Y., Zhang, P.: Understanding data sharing behaviors of STEM researchers: the roles of attitudes, norms, and data repositories. Libr. Inf. Sci. Res. **37**(3), 189–200 (2015). https://doi.org/10.1016/j.lisr.2015.04.006

21. Hilber, B., Reintzsch, D.: Cloud Computing und Open Source-Wie groß ist die Gefahr des Copyleft bei SaaS? In: Computer Und Recht: Forum für die Praxis des Rechts der Datenverargei-tung, Information und Automation. pp. 697–702. Otto Schmidt (2014)

22. Feijen, M.: What researchers want - A literature study of researchers' requirements with respect to storage and access to research data (2011)

23. Wilms, K., Brenger, B., Lopez, A., Rehwald, S.: Open data in higher education – what prevents researchers from sharing research data? In: 39th International Conference on Information System, pp. 1–9 (2018)

24. Karkin, N., Janssen, M., Brooks, K.: Open government and data-driven policy making in the digital age. In: Americas Conference on Information System (AMCIS) (2018)

25. Süptitz, T., Weis, S.J., Eymann, T.: Was müssen Virtual Research Environments leisten? -Ein Literaturreview zu den funktionalen und nichtfunktionalen Anforderungen. In: Wirtschaftsinformatik (2013)

26. Bankier, J.G., Gleason, K.: Institutional repository software comparison. UNESCO Communication and Information, Paris (2014)

27. Deutsche Forschungsgemeinschaft: Memorandum Safeguarding Good Scientific Practice. (2013)

28. Hevner, A., Alexander, B.: Roles of digital innovation in design science research. Bus. Inf. Syst. Eng. **61**, 3–8 (2019). https://doi.org/10.1007/s12599-018-0571-z

29. Mayring, P.: Qualitative inhaltsanalyse. In: Boehm, A., Mengel, A., Muhr, T. (eds.) Texte verstehen: Konzepte, Methoden, Werkzeuge, pp. 159–174. UVK Univ.-Verl. Konstanz, Konstanz (1994)

30. Bauer, B., et al.: Forschende und ihre Daten. Ergebnisse einer österreichweiten Befragung – Report 2015. Zenodo (2015). https://doi.org/10.5281/zenodo.31935

31. Kim, Y., Stanton, J.M.: Institutional and individual factors affecting scientists' data-sharing behaviors: A multilevel analysis. J. Am. Soc. Inf. Sci. **67**(4), 776–799 (2016). https://doi.org/10.1002/asi.23424

32. Klemm, M., Liebold, R.: Qualitative Interviews in der Organisationsforschung. In: Liebig, S., Matiaske, W., Rosenbohm, S. (eds.) Handbuch Empirische Organisationsforschung, pp. 299–324. Springer, Wiesbaden (2017). https://doi.org/10.1007/978-3-658-08580-3_13-1

33. Jensen, U.: Leitlinien zum Management von Forschungsdaten: Sozialwissenschaftliche Umfragedaten. Cologne, Germany (2012)

34. Berendt, B., Vanschoren, J., Gao, B.: Datenanalyse und -visualisierung. In: Büttner, S., Hobohm, H., Müller, L. (eds.) Handbuch Forschungsdatenmanagement, pp. 139–148. Bock + Herchen, Bad Honnef (2011)

35. Link, G., et al.: Contemporary issues of open data in information systems research: considerations and recommendations. Commun. Assoc. Inf. Syst. **41**, 587–610 (2017). https://doi.org/10.1016/j.anireprosci.2016.02.027

36. Ribes, D., Polk, J.B.: Flexibility relative to what? Change to research infrastructure. J. Assoc. Inf. Syst. **15**, 287–305 (2014). https://doi.org/10.17705/1jais.00360

37. Vassilakopoulou, P., Skorve, E., Aanestad, M.: A commons perspective on genetic data governance. In: European Conference on Information Systems (ECIS) (2016)

38. Biljon, J. V., Pottas, A., Lehong, S., Platz, M.: Content category selection towards a maturity matrix for ICT4D knowledge sharing platforms. In: International Conference on Information Resources Management (Conf-IRM) (2016)
39. Nugroho, R.P., Zuiderwijk, A., Janssen, M., de Jong, M.: A comparison of national open data policies: lessons learned. Transform. Gov. People, Process Policy **9**, 286–308 (2015). https://doi.org/10.1108/TG-03-2014-0008

Interaction by Taking a Picture for Smartphone Generation

Keita Kaida$^{(\boxtimes)}$, Hirohiko Mori, and Makoto Oka

Tokyo City University, Tokyo, Japan
`{g1981810,hmori,moka}@tcu.ac.jp`

Abstract. In recent years, smartphones have come to pervade people's lives, and people carry their smartphones for whatever they do. With the spread of smartphones, new people called smartphone generation have emerged, and information sharing on SNS using smartphones has become popular among smartphone generations. They began to take pictures in every situation with smartphones, triggered by information sharing on SNS. Considering the characteristics of the smartphone generation like this can lead to computer designs that are easier for them to use. In addition, the number of users having multiple computers has increased, and the opportunity to transfer information between computers has increased. A technology that can quickly and intuitively transfer information between computers is required. In this study, we focus on taking pictures, which is a daily activity, and aim to show the effectiveness of interaction by taking a picture. In this paper, we focused on information transfer between computers as the first step, and we developed a system that is familiar to smartphone generation and that can be operated intuitively. The system allows users to transfer files and web pages displayed on the PC screen to the smartphone by taking a picture of the PC screen with the smartphone. An evaluation experiment of the system showed that the system was effective in three ways. As a result, we showed the effectiveness of the interaction by taking a picture for information transfer.

Keywords: Interaction design · Multi-device interaction · Graphical User Interface (GUI)

1 Introduction

In recent years, many people have smartphones [1], and they share various information using SNS [2]. Most of the people under 25 years old started their experiences of using information appliance with smartphones, and they are called smartphone generation. The smartphone generation uses computers in different ways from other generations. In addition, smartphone generation frequently shares information on SNS and shares various information with text and pictures. They began to take pictures in every situation with smartphones, triggered by information sharing on SNS. Figure 1 shows the results of a questionnaire survey on how to use smartphones for 70 university students. Figure 1 (left) shows the results of cases of using a PC and a smartphone at the same time. 21 respondents answered that they used the PC and smartphone at the same time when

© Springer Nature Switzerland AG 2020
S. Yamamoto and H. Mori (Eds.): HCII 2020, LNCS 12185, pp. 338–349, 2020.
https://doi.org/10.1007/978-3-030-50017-7_24

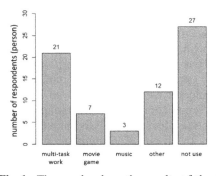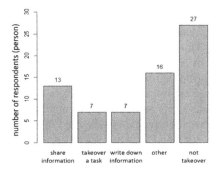

Fig. 1. The graphs show the results of the survey we conducted. The graph (left) shows the situations of using the PC and the smartphone at the same time, and the graph (right) shows the purposes of the users taking the screen of the PC.

working on two screens. For example, in writing a report, they write their report with PC while they examine the necessary information on web pages not with browsers on PC but with a smartphone. Figure 1 (right) shows the results of cases of taking a picture of a PC screen with a smartphone. 43 respondents answered that they took pictures of their PC screens with smartphones for sharing information and taking over work. Taking over work means, for example, to work at a library using a PC and then continue on a train using a smartphone. In taking over work, it is necessary to transfer information from a PC to a smartphone, which is very troublesome. Therefore, instead of information transfer, the smartphone generation takes a picture of the computer screen at work and sees the picture on the train. By realizing information transfer by taking a picture of the PC screen with a smartphone, it is possible to contribute to the design of computers that match the characteristics of the smartphone generation.

In this study, we focused on taking pictures, which young people frequently do in using a smartphone and a PC at the same time, or in taking over work from a PC to a smartphone. The purpose of this study is to show the effectiveness of the interaction with a computer by taking a picture as an input for smartphone generation. In this paper, as a first step, we focus on information transfer between computers.

2   Related Work

2.1   Information Transfer Between Computers

Now, many people have multiple information devices, the way of the quick and intuitive transfer of information between information devices are indispensable. Many studies have been done to realize information transfer between computers quickly and intuitively. For example, Mita et al. [3] developed a system that links two computers by stacking a smartphone on a tablet PC. During the link, the smartphone touch panel can be used as part of the tablet PC touch panel. Then, the file can be moved seamlessly using the direct operation. Sato et al. [4] developed a mechanism that allows Android users to resume their performing work from one device to another. In this mechanism users can restore their work by transferring the state of the current application on another terminal by acquiring the state of the application running on one terminal and sending it to another terminal. This makes it possible to smoothly resume the work after the completion of the information transfer between the computers. These information transfer technologies are more intuitive compared to information transfer methods such as using USB and e-mail.

In order to perform information transfer more intuitively, there has been proposed an information transfer technique that applies an operation performed in human daily life. Rekimoto [5] developed an operation technique called "Pick and Drop", which allows users to transfer information between different computers, like picking up the information with chopstick and dropping it on another device. In that technique, a user first taps and lifts an object on a display with a touch pen. The information can be transferred between the two computers by placing the pen tip anywhere on another display. Pick and Drop is a technology mimics the "lifting and placing" action that is frequently performed in daily life to the transfer of information between two computers in the familiar way to users. Yatani et al. [6] developed Toss-It that enables users to transfer information between different computers by holding the mobile device and throwing it to the device to which information is to be sent. A user can send information to a target device by turning his/her body toward a device to which information is to be sent and slowly lifting his/her arm holding a mobile device from bottom to top. Ikematsu et al. [7] developed Memory Stones that intuitively realizes the information transfer operation between two computers. The user transfers information by touching an object on the display with multiple fingers as if picking up a stone and placing it anywhere on another display without changing the hand shape. Memory Stones realizes intuitive operation as if user can transfer information by hand.

These systems use actions that is frequently used in daily life to transfer information, so they realize intuitive operations. However, when information is transferred, they hold information virtually using a pen, object, or finger. As a result, it is not possible to visually obtain the feeling of actually transferring files. If the feeling of information transfer can be obtained visually, it is considered that a more intuitive operation can be realized. As mentioned in Chapter 1, smartphone users often take pictures when using smartphones in combination with PCs. Therefore, a system using taking a picture as a user interface for operating a smartphone is conceivable, but there is almost no such research.

2.2 Interactions with Taking Pictures

As mentioned in Chapter 1, smartphone users often take pictures to bridge smartphones and PCs. So, there is a need for a system that interacts with computers by taking pictures, but there are almost no such studies. Though there are some commercial applications, such as Office Lens [8] and Google Translate [9], the effectiveness of the application with taking pictures is not shown. Lee [10] developed R-Fii to operate intelligent home appliances by taking a picture, and succeeded to reduce users' load and allowed them to operate them intuitively. In R-Fii, users can operate devices and browse information about devices by taking pictures of the devices they want to interact with in the intelligent space.

Like this, there are commercial applications that use taking pictures, but few studies have been done in detail the effectiveness of interactions by taking pictures. In this paper, we develop an easy-to-use system for smartphone generation and investigate the effectiveness of interaction by taking pictures.

3 Proposed System

The smartphone generation takes a PC screenshot with a smartphone camera, and it is necessary to design the system that considers such situation. Here, a scenario-based approach was taken to develop a system to enhance the user experience based on user behavior. First, the process of grasping the problem from the user's behavior, creating task scenario, and finally forming an interaction scenario is performed.

3.1 Task Scenario

As mentioned in Chapter 1, most people in smartphone generation take pictures of their computer screens using smartphones. The main reason for this is that you want to easily and quickly share your computer screen with your friends or take over the work you were doing on your computer with a smartphone while in a train, but the information transfer between computers is troublesome. Although it is easy to take a picture of a PC screen with a smartphone, the resulting picture has only an image. For example, if you take a picture of a computer screen displaying a file, the picture you take loses the functions of the document creation software, such as file editing and scrolling. Also, when taking a

Fig. 2. Proposed system that realizes information transfer between two computers. It is a state of information transfer of web page (top) and file information (bottom).

picture of a computer screen displaying a web page, the picture taken loses the browser functions such as scrolling and page switching. For the reason, it is desirable to be able to acquire files and web pages instead of images in taking pictures. Therefore, a task scenario was set in which the user took a picture of the PC screen with the smartphone camera, transferred the web page or file displayed on the PC to the smartphone, and continued working on the smartphone.

3.2 Interaction Scenario

First, we will introduce an interaction scenario about the information transfer of web pages. Here, information transfer of a web page means that the same page as the web page displayed on the PC screen is displayed on the smartphone, such as copy and paste instead of cut and paste. In this scenario, we assume that the user is currently surfing the web at home, and he/she displays the interesting web page on the PC screen. Then, the QR code is displayed on the lower right of the screen of the PC (Fig. 2 (top-left)). When the user displays another web page of interest on the computer screen, the QR code changes accordingly. It was time to leave home, and the user wanted to see the continuation of the web page on his smartphone while he was out. When the user takes a picture of the PC screen using the smartphone camera to include the QR code (Fig. 2 (top-center)), the URL of the web page being displayed is transferred to the smartphone and the web page is opened (Fig. 2 (top-right)). In this way, the user was able to quickly and easily transfer work from a PC to a smartphone.

Next, we also introduce an interaction scenario about the information transfer of the file. Here, the information transfer of the file means copying the file displayed on the PC screen to the smartphone and displaying it on the smartphone in the same way as transferring the information of the web page. The scenario assumes that the user is currently working on file editing at home, and he/she displays the file he/she is working on the PC screen. Since the file is opened, the QR code is displayed at the bottom right of the PC screen (Fig. 3 (bottom-left)). When the user displays the other file he/she wants to work in the active window, the QR code changes accordingly. It was time to leave home, and the user wanted to continue the work he/she had done on the PC with his/her smartphone while he/she was out. By taking a picture of the PC screen so that the QR code is included with the smartphone camera (Fig. 3 (bottom-center)), the file path is transferred to the smartphone and the file is opened (Fig. 3 (bottom-right)). At the same time, the file is saved in the Download folder on the smartphone. In this way, the user was able to quickly and easily transfer work from a PC to a smartphone.

4 Implementation

The system was implemented based on the interaction scenario. The system consists of Windows application and Android smartphone application. The terminal uses a Windows 10 PC and Android Nexus 5X. In addition, it is necessary to set the HTTP server on the PC in advance. An HTTP server was built using Internet Information Service, a web server software originally provided on Windows PCs. In addition, access permission is set so that Android Nexus 5X can access the HTTP server.

4.1 The System on PC

This system was implemented as an application on a Windows 10 PC using Visual Studio Community 2017. This system acquires the file or the web page of the active window from the open file and the web page opened by Microsoft Edge, and it displays the URL and file path as a QR code at the lower right of the screen. If the active window is a file, the system creates a QR code which contains the obtained IP address and file path. If the active window is a web page, the system obtains the URL of the web page and displays it as a QR code. The QR code changes when the active window changes.

4.2 The System on Smartphone

This system was implemented as an Android smartphone application using Android Studio 3.1.4. When the QR code is displayed on the lower right corner of the PC screen by the PC system, user uses the smartphone to take a picture including the QR code. This is a system in which the file or web page of the active window displayed on the PC screen transfers to the smartphone and opens. When the user opens the application, a preview of the camera is displayed on the screen. The user can take a picture by touching the screen. When taking a picture, the system looks for the QR code from the image and reads it. By obtaining the file path or URL, and passing it to the browser, the file and web page are transferred to the smartphone and displayed on the smartphone screen. At the same time, the file whose information has been transferred is saved in the Download folder of the smartphone.

5 Evaluation Experiment

We evaluate the usability of the proposed system. By comparing the proposed system with some traditional information transfer methods, we verify whether taking a picture is an effective information transfer method.

5.1 Prerequisite

As mentioned in Chapter 1, many university students take pictures of the PC screens with smartphones, and they share the PC screens with friends, take over the work of the PCs with the smartphones to watch on the train, write down their computer screens. The proposed system is based on such behaviors of the students. Therefore, it is necessary to conduct experiments on the assumption that the proposed system is used by university students. When we asked 70 university students if they had ever transferred files from a computer to a smartphone, 48 respondents described they had transferred files, and 23 respondents E-mail and 19 respondents answered that they moved files mainly through SNS. Therefore, in this experiment, mail and SNS are used as existing information transfer methods in order to reproduce the situation of using the proposed system by university students as a file transfer method.

In addition, there are various methods for transferring file information, so the results of the questionnaire are used. However, since the method for opening a web page displayed on a PC with a smartphone is limited. In this experiment, we subjectively judge that search, URL input, and SNS are the main methods, and we use them as existing information transfer methods.

5.2 Participants

The experiment was performed on 40 university students who had smartphones and PCs (age: 18–24 years old, 27 men, 13 women). They consist of 6 first graders, 9 second graders, 14 third graders, and 11 fourth graders. The reason for limiting participants to university students is to curry out the experiment by reproducing the situation where the smartphone generation uses the proposed system.

5.3 Tasks

The procedure of the experiment is to first explain the whole experiment, then perform task 1, and finally perform task 2. In the explanation of the whole experiment, we explained the flow of the whole experiment to the participants. we also explained how to operate an Android smartphone for iPhone users. They asked to perform the tasks in thinking aloud, and that we took a video of what they were doing from behind.

Next, before performing Task 1, we explained Task 1 to the participants. Task 1 states, "You are using your computer at school to create documents. You want to copy the documents from your computer to your smartphone to continue working on the train. Copy the three files created on your computer to your smartphone." After the explanation of Task 1, we described the procedure for each of the three methods (SNS, e-mail, and the proposed system) for performing the task. In the case of SNS, we described "Log in to SNS from the PC, and send the file you want to transfer information to the group named 'Experimental use'. Open the file from SNS on the smartphone." In the case of using e-mail, we described "Open the university's web mail system (user name and password are already entered) from Favorites or Search. Send an email with the file attached to the smartphone. Open the email from the Gmail app on the smartphone and open the file attached to the email." In the case of proposed system, we described "When a file is opened on the PC, a QR code is displayed at the lower right of the screen. Using the smartphone, take a picture including the QR code with the proposed system. By doing so, you can get and open the file with the smartphone." After the explanation of Task 1, we actually asked the participants to perform the task. After the completion of task 1, we asked the participants to answer the questionnaire.

Next, before performing Task 2, we explained task 2 to the participants. Task 2 states, "You are surfing the Internet at home and have found an interesting web page. You want to view the web page with your smartphone while you go out. Open the page from your smartphone browser." After the explanation of Task 2, assuming that the participant was surfing the Internet, we asked the participant to search for and open an interesting web page on the PC. Then, we described the procedure for each of the four methods (search, URL input, SNS, and the proposed system) for performing the task. In the case of search, we described "Open a browser with the smartphone. Search by entering a search word in the search box and open the web page with the smartphone." In the case of URL input, we described "Open a browser with the smartphone. Input the URL in the address bar to open the web page with the smartphone." In the case of SNS, we described "Log in to

SNS from the PC, and send the URL of the web page you want to transfer information to a group named 'Experimental use'. Open the web page from SNS on the smartphone." In the case of proposed system, we described "When a web page is opened on the PC, a QR code is displayed at the lower right of the screen. Using the smartphone, take a picture including the QR code with the proposed system. By doing so, you can get and open the web page with the smartphone." After the explanation of Task 2, we actually asked the participants to perform the task. After the completion of Task 2, we asked participants to answer the questionnaire.

5.4 Measurement

There are effects, efficiency, and satisfaction as indices for measuring ease of use. The effects are measured by the user's task completion rate (the ratio of the number of people who completed the work), the efficiency is measured by the average task time (the average of the work completion time), the average number of errors (the average of the number of incorrect operations), and the satisfaction is measured by how much you liked the system. To evaluate our systems qualitatively, the questionnaire using a five-point Likert scale was conducted to measure how intuitively you could operate the system, how much you liked the system, and how easy the system is. After evaluating the system, the participants asked to describe their impressions of the system freely. For each of the six items, including three quantitative items and three qualitative items, we statistically examine whether the proposed system is superior to existing information transfer methods. For that we use multiple comparisons.

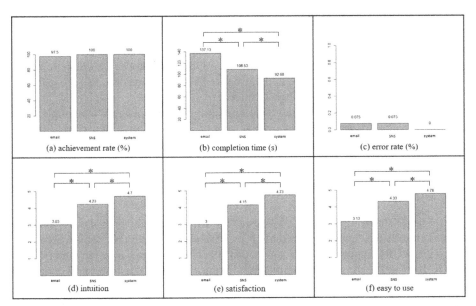

Fig. 3. Results of multiple comparisons between the proposed system and existing information transfer methods in file information transfer.

6 Result

6.1 Task1

Figure 3 shows the results of Task 1. We tested the difference using Steel-Dwass multiple comparisons. In the figure, * represents p < .05. Regarding the task achievement rate (Fig. 3 (a)), all information transfer methods are close to 100%, so there was no significant difference between the proposed system and existing information transfer methods. For a simple task such as the one performed in this experiment, the proposed system can be used accurately enough. Regarding task time (Fig. 3 (b)), there are significant difference among all conditions (p = 2.83e−11 between the proposed system and e-mail, p = 0.018 between the proposed system and SNS, and p = 1.32e−4 between SNS and e-mail). It means that the task can be accomplished in shorter time with the proposed system compared with e-mail and SNS. Regarding the number of errors (Fig. 3 (c)), all information transfer methods are close to 0%, so there was no significant difference among all conditions. Therefore, it was shown that the proposed system was effective for the task time among the quantitative items. Regarding how intuitively you could operate the system (Fig. 3 (d)), there are significant difference among all conditions (p = 4.13e−8 between the proposed system and e-mail, p = 1.05e−3 between the proposed system and SNS, and p = 7.56e−5 between SNS and e-mail). This means that the participants were able to intuitively operate the proposed system compared to e-mail and SNS for transferring file information. Regarding how much you liked the system (Fig. 3 (e)), there are significant difference among all conditions (p = 6.23e−12 between the proposed system and e-mail, p = 3.33e−04 between the proposed system and SNS, and p = 3.06e−07 between SNS and e-mail). This means that participants liked the proposed system compared to e-mail and SNS for transferring file information. Regarding how easy the system was (Fig. 3 (f)), there are significant difference among all conditions (p = 2.69e−11 between the proposed system and e-mail, p = 2.05e−03 between the proposed system and SNS, and p = 3.46e−07 between SNS and e-mail). This means that participants feel that the proposed system is easier to use compared to e-mail and SNS for transferring file information.

From the above, the effectiveness and efficiency are sufficient for the simple tasks performed in this experiment. Also, the results of the qualitative items indicate that the satisfaction is sufficient. Therefore, the proposed system has sufficient values for effectiveness, efficiency, and satisfaction.

6.2 Task2

Figure 4 shows the results of Task 2. We tested the difference using Steel-Dwass multiple comparisons. In the figure, * represents p < .05. Regarding the task achievement rate (Fig. 4 (a)), URL input is a little lower, but other information transfer methods are close to 100%, so there was no significant difference between the proposed system and existing information transfer methods. For a simple task such as the one performed in this experiment, the proposed system can be used accurately enough. Regarding the task time (Fig. 4 (b)), there are significant difference among several conditions (p = 1.11e−13 between the proposed system and URL input, p = 1.02e−5 between the

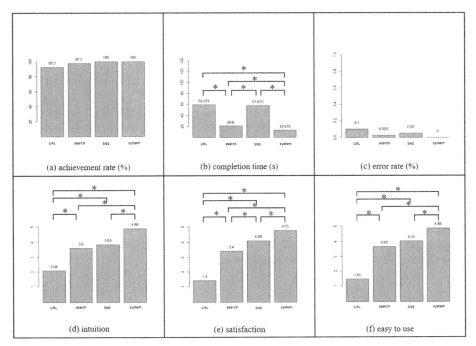

Fig. 4. Results of multiple comparisons between the proposed system and existing information transfer methods in web page information transfer.

proposed system and search, p = 1.01e−13 between the proposed system and SNS, p = 2.06e−12 between SNS and search, and p = 5.09e−11 between search and URL input). This means that the task can be accomplished in shorter time with the proposed system compared with URL input, search, and SNS. Regarding the number of errors (Fig. 4 (c)), all information transfer methods are close to 0%, so there was no significant difference among all conditions. Regarding how intuitively you could operate the system (Fig. 4 (d)), there are significant difference among several conditions (p = 1.16e−13 between the proposed system and URL input, p = 1.42e−7 between the proposed system and search, p = 2.45e−8 between the proposed system and SNS, p = 7.91e−6 between SNS and URL input, and p = 1.42e−4 between search and URL input). This means that participants were able to intuitively operate the proposed system more compared to URL input, search, and SNS for transferring web page information. Regarding how much you liked the system (Fig. 4 (e)), there are significant difference among all conditions (p = 5.42e−14 between the proposed system and URL input, p = 6.03e−9 between the proposed system and search, p = 2.04e−4 between the proposed system and SNS, p = 5.69e−3 between SNS and search, p = 9.67e−14 between SNS and URL input, and p = 3.87e−12 between search and URL input). This means that the participants liked the proposed system better than URL input, search, and SNS. This means that participants liked the proposed system compared to URL input, search, and SNS for transferring web page information. Regarding how easy the system was (Fig. 4 (f)), there are significant difference among several conditions ($p = 4.74e-14$ between the proposed system and URL input, $p = 1.16e-8$ between the proposed system and search, $p = 3.01e-6$ between the proposed system and SNS, $p = 2.71e-13$ between SNS and URL input, and $p = 1.82e-11$ between search and URL input). This means that participants feel that the proposed system is easier to use compared to URL input, search, and SNS for transferring web page information.

From the above, the effectiveness and efficiency are sufficient for the simple tasks performed in this experiment. Also, the results of the qualitative items indicate that the satisfaction is sufficient. Therefore, the proposed system has sufficient values for effectiveness, efficiency, and satisfaction.

7   Discussion

We discuss the results of the free description and multiple comparison of each participant's information transfer method. We discuss three ways about the effectiveness of the interaction using taking pictures in information transfer.

7.1   Takeover of Work

Regarding file information transfer, if you want to transfer information about a file you are working on using the existing information transfer method, e-mail or SNS, close the file you are working on, open e-mail or SNS on your computer, send the file to your smartphone, use it to open mail and SNS, and open files with your smartphone. Thus, you need to take five steps. On the other hand, in the proposed system, information transfer can be realized by two steps of opening the proposed system and taking a picture. In addition, in the proposed system, it is possible to take a picture and transfer information while a file is opening, so taking a picture for information transfer is effective for taking over work.

7.2   Visual Clarity

Three participants described "I felt very intuitive because I could just take a picture of what I was looking at." Also, the proposed system is superior in value to the existing information transfer method in terms of how intuitively you could operate the system, so the proposed system is visually intuitive, which leads to the result of being intuitive. Therefore, as we intended, we found that information transfer using taking a picture was effective in terms of visual clarity.

7.3   The System that Matches the Characteristics of the Smartphone Generation

One participant described "It is convenient to take a QR code because it was difficult to read the text in the picture when taking a picture of the document." Another participant described "I felt that the system is good because the system can easily transfer information to a smartphone when I want to do other work with a PC." From these descriptions, it found that they are participants who have taken a PC screen, or they are participants who use a smartphone and a PC to perform tasks that can be performed only on the PC using the multi-window of the PC. Participants described that the proposed system is convenient, so when the smartphone generation uses a computer, it is effective to transfer information with taking pictures.

8 Conclusion

As a first step to show the effectiveness of interaction with taking a picture, we focused on information transfer between multiple computers. We proposed an information transfer method using taking pictures as a technology to realize an easy-to use system for smartphone generation, and we investigated the effectiveness of interaction by taking pictures. The proposed system displays the URL of the web page being viewed on the PC and the file path being worked on as a QR code at the bottom right of the screen, and transfers information by taking a picture including the QR code on the smartphone. Evaluation experiments by participants showed that the proposed system is superior to the existing information transfer method. In addition, it found that the proposed system was effective for smartphone generation. As a result, the effectiveness of the interaction with taking a picture was shown for information transfer.

References

1. Radicati, S.: Mobile Statistics Report, 2014–2018 (2014). https://www.radicati.com/wp/wp-content/uploads/2014/01/Mobile-Statistics-Report-2014-2018-Executive-Summary.pdf
2. Vaidya, A., Pathak, V., Vaidya, A.: Mobile phone usage among youth. Int. J. Appl. Res. Stud. V(3), 1–16 (2016)
3. Mita, Y., Shizuki, B., Tanaka, J.: Terminal coordination method by overlapping terminals with touch panels. The Special Interest Group Technical reports of IPSJ, pp. 1–7 (2013)
4. Sato, K., Mouri K., Saito, S.: Design and implementation of an application state migration mechanism between Android devices. In: The 7th International Workshop on Advances in Networking and Computing, pp. 696–700 (2016)
5. Rekimoto, J.: Pick-and-Drop: a direct manipulation technique for multiple computer environments. In: Proceedings of the 10th Annual ACM Symposium on User Interface Software and Technology, pp. 31–39 (1997)
6. Yatani, K., Tamura, K., Hiroki, K., Sugimoto, M., Hashizume, H.: Toss-it: intuitive information transfer techniques for mobile devices. In: CHI 2005 Extended Abstracts on Human Factors in Computing Systems, pp. 1881–1884 (2005)
7. Ikematsu, K., Siio, I.: memory stones: an intuitive information transfer technique between multi-touch computers. In: Proceedings of the 16th International Workshop on Mobile Computing Systems and Applications, pp. 3–8 (2015)
8. Microsoft Store. https://www.microsoft.com/ja-jp/p/office-lens/9wzdncrfj3t8?activetab=pivot:overviewtab. Accessed 17 Mar 2014
9. Google Play Store. https://play.google.com/store/apps/details?id=com.google.android.apps.translate&hl=ja. Accessed 20 Dec 2019
10. Ono, K., Lee, J.: A smart phone based interaction in intelligent space using object recognition and facing direction of human. In: Proceedings of the 2013 IEEE/SICE International Symposium on System Integration, pp. 216–221 (2013)

Proposal and Evaluation of Contribution Value Model for Creation Support System

Yoshiharu Kato[1,2]([✉]), Tomonori Hashiyama[1], and Shun'ichi Tano[1]

[1] The University of Electro-Communications, Tokyo, Japan
{hashiyama,tano}@is.uec.ac.jp
[2] Creative Japan Limited, Tokyo, Japan
yoshiharu.kato@creative-japan.co.jp

Abstract. Participants in projects creating new products and services start discussions by formulating a concept or by posing questions. They should exhibit creativity and propose diverse ideas as much as possible. Supporting the connectivity of information and motivation improvement is important to support the creation. Moreover, participants who feel they are meaningfully contributing to the project are usually more motivated. Therefore, in this paper, we propose an evaluation model that visualizes the degree of contribution of each participant as a contribution value when the project reaches points that require creativity to move forward. Through this model, one's own ideas and opinions can be visualized as a chronological contribution value throughout the course of discussions. By visualizing the progress of the discussions as a contribution value through determining the system functions, we found that the motivation support function of the participants worked correctly to contribute to the project and to other discussions. In the future, we plan to have the participants actually use this system to demonstrate its effectiveness.

Keywords: Creation support · Collaboration · Contribution value · Motivation improvement · Evaluation

1 Introduction

1.1 A Subsection Sample

Participants in projects to create new products and services start their investigation from concept making and problem definitions. A new development method known as design thinking [1] is increasingly being used in this context. In contrast to existing projects with established processes, an important point for new service creation projects is the generation of diverse ideas by the participants. Supporting the connectivity of each improvement in information and motivation is important to support the creation process [2, 3].

In projects to create these new products and services, the participants often use brainstorming to generate a diverse array of ideas. However, the reality is that creative activities lack support and that such projects are not necessarily destined to succeed

© Springer Nature Switzerland AG 2020
S. Yamamoto and H. Mori (Eds.): HCII 2020, LNCS 12185, pp. 350–364, 2020.
https://doi.org/10.1007/978-3-030-50017-7_25

because of undue organizational barriers and lack of communication. In particular, the evaluation of discussions tends to be higher among those who make a large number of comments or who present a conclusion. For this reason, those contributing to the problem-solving process, contributing to the support of others, or promoting the discussion will not necessarily be evaluated. Therefore, a new evaluation index is required for objectively evaluating discussions.

This paper presents how we can visualize the whole discussion process, and it proposes the visualization of the degree of contribution to issue resolutions during discussions and to provide evaluation feedback to the participants. In this way, participants can be made aware of evaluations from other people and the value of contributing to promoting discussion. We consider behavior based on their own roles and actions for problem resolutions.

2 Current State and Problems of Contribution Level Evaluations During Discussions

2.1 Related Studies

A couple of structuralization methods make it easier to understand the visualization of discussions after the passage of time. The issue-based information system (IBIS) was developed by Werner Kunz and Horst W. J. Rittel [4] to visualize discussions during a complex development process. Following this, gIBIS [5] was developed to visualize the flow of these discussions. This system uses nodes and links on a graph for the visualization, enabling smooth comprehension of the structure of a discussion and making it easier to join in the middle.

Some prior research has been conducted on evaluating the content of one's comments and on a practical case regarding the contribution to discussions. Quirky [6] has a platform that enables users to propose new products in an open environment, and a community has been formed for co-creating these products with the users, leading to the eventual launch of products. Its most unique feature is a system called Influence, which measures the contribution levels of an individual on the product that is being developed. Compensation that corresponds to one's influence is paid from the funds derived from the sales profit of the product. The contribution levels of the person who proposed the idea, those who voted on it, the designer, and the one who proposed the product name are all taken into account.

Work has been conducted aiming at activating discussions and improving their quality through utilizing a function incentivizing discussions among participants in large-scale discussions such as an online town meeting [7]. Here, a discussion is represented as a tree structure. The system awards activity points according to the content of one's comments during the discussion, and these points provide an incentive to be active. It also awards feedback points, which provide an incentive to encourage constructive comments. Post, reply, and agreement functions are included in the activity points. The feedback points consist of reply points gained by replying to a comment and agree points based on how agreement with one's comment proportionally spreads. Giving incentives to the discussion participants will ideally enable more fruitful discussion.

One method for collaborative learning utilizes the system of discussion activation using online chats and its effects [8]. It monitors the discussion progress and quantifies and displays the role of a learner as an "influence level of positive comments." The idea is to draw useful comments from participants to trigger an active discussion. The intentions of comments are classified and defined before the discussion, and a rule for calculating the influence level of positive comments is established. This enables the character of a participant and his/her role in the discussion to be extracted.

2.2 Awareness of Contribution Level in Discussions

The aforementioned discussion methods can be roughly divided into the evaluation of the content itself and the evaluation of propagation to previously registered content. The evaluation of the content itself involves the already added scores and the registration number. The evaluation of the effect on the registered content involves agreements and disagreements, transmission of such evaluations, and quotation of the content. Both of these serve as methods in which people directly evaluate the registered content themselves.

However, the typical discussion situation is not limited to a direct evaluation of the content by people. For example, there are evaluations of the actions of a person, of the feelings shown through actions such as praising or thanking another participant, and of the role of the facilitator in triggering the progress of the discussion. An example of evaluating the actions toward others is one case in which offering help to another person in trouble led to that person achieving a result. In such a case, the supportive action toward another should be considered. Moreover, content that supports a good idea when it is proposed should also be considered. There have been cases where a person who received praise or gratitude started to participate actively in the discussion afterward. This is because the human desire for recognition was satisfied. Finally, expansion and conclusion of the discussion and activation of a stagnant discussion are also key items to be evaluated because they encourage the discussion to progress.

These items are parts that cannot be assessed through a method in which people directly evaluate the content by themselves. As such, an expanded evaluation, in addition to the evaluation of the content itself, is necessary. The evaluation of the expanded part is also a part that has been left to others to evaluate intuitively. The registered content of each participant can be determined when a discussion concludes within a short period of time or when only a small number of participants are present; however, assessing the overall view of the discussion becomes more difficult when the discussion is prolonged or when it includes many participants. This is because one only remembers the content from the preceding moment and tends to forget more as time passes. Moreover, the relationship between content must be understood, or we must identify how content may change the behavior of people. Because the evaluation of these expanded parts exceeds the scope of human recognition, they cannot be evaluated without using information and communication technology to gain an overall view of the discussion.

We are currently facing three issues here. First, an evaluation of the effects of actions such as supporting others has not been conducted. Second, an evaluation of the changes in behavior triggered by actions such as showing gratitude to others or praising them has not been conducted. Third, an evaluation of discussion progress has not been conducted.

3 Concrete Method

3.1 Visualization of Discussions

The following four functions were implemented to solve the three issues shown in Sect. 2.2.

- Visualization of discussions using a tree diagram
- Evaluations by others
- Recursive evaluations adding to the total score
- Feedback from the system to participants

We will explain each function as follows.

Visualization of Discussions Using a Tree Diagram. A tree diagram is used to visualize a discussion, as shown in Fig. 1. Ideas, opinions, information, etc., which have been expressed as "content" in discussions, are referred to as "nodes." Nodes are pieces of information that participants record. In this paper, the nodes to be registered are classified according to the content, and the point for the classification type is determined in advance. Table 1 shows these node classifications and points. Nodes are classified into three elements: "intellect," "emotion," and "behavior," in addition to "problem" and "solution." Links are used to associate nodes with each other.

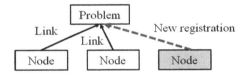

Fig. 1. Connection of nodes and links.

Evaluations by Others. Evaluations by others are when evaluations are given to an already registered host node. The expression of agreement or disagreement with an idea or an opinion, giving points to a good idea through direct evaluation, or demonstrating how a host node was influential are examples expressed through the link information that connects a node with others. As shown in Table 2, a propagation coefficient is added to links as the influence level to the host node. This propagation coefficient is changed according to whether or not it is merely a connection to the host, one's own idea and opinion registering the influence of the host node, or a direct evaluation toward the host node. For example, in the case of the influence classification shown in Table 2, one's own opinion and idea were considered to have been created under the influence of the host node, so 50% of one's point is given to the host. In this system, the node classification point and the evaluation from others is set as the "overall score of the node."

Recursive Evaluations Adding to the Total Score. These explain the mechanism to give evaluation from others to the already registered upper node. An overview of the evaluation method is shown in Fig. 2.

Table 1. Classification of nodes and links.

Node

Large classification	Content		Point
Problem	Setting problem (Identify between AND problem and OR problem)		4
Solution	The solution to the problem		4

Large classification	Medium classification	Small classification	Point
Intellect	Knowledge	Information, analysis, question, opinion	2
	Idea	Inspiration, realization, proposal, ingenuity	4
	Judgment	Evaluation, agreement, disagreement,	1
	Needs	Clients' needs, external environment	1
Emotion	Wish	Longing, ideal form, vision	2
	Will	Encouragment, gratitude	1
Action	Network	Introduction, visit	1
	Plan	Planning, prototype, milestone	1

Link

Large classification	Small classification	Propagation coefficient
Evaluation	Connection to the node tlint gave an evaluation to the host node	0.8
Influence	Iutlueuce. integration, separation	0.5
Result	Result of tlie support, outcome	0.5
Replacement	Replacement, generalization, specifications	0 8
Connection	Connection, explanation	0.2

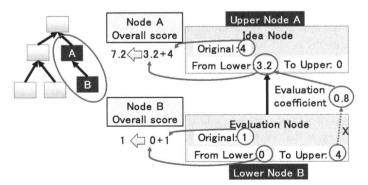

Fig. 2. Evaluation method using nodes and links.

Next, we explain how the system gives an evaluation from others to the already registered host node. The actual calculation is done through the following algorithm (1).

The overall score of a node is only one level if it is on the evaluation of the host node. However, if the nodes are connected through several levels, they are calculated recursively. In the case shown in Fig. 2, the overall score of node S(j) of node N(j) is calculated as

$$S(j) = Nb(j) + \sum_k S(k) * \alpha(k) * \beta(k,j) \qquad (1)$$

- Nb(j): Node classification point of node N(j)
- $\alpha(k)$: Evaluation coefficient of host node N(j)
- The evaluation coefficient is added through the node classification of N(k).
- $\beta(k,j)$: Propagation coefficient from node N(k) to node N(j)

Feedback from the System to Participants. This function displays and notifies the participants' contributions to the project. This is an important function that can improve their motivation.

The system can provide two types of feedback. The first is displaying the results of the analysis of the accumulated data by the system at the request of participants. Specifically, the system has the following three types.

- Changes in the total score of the node over time
- Participant's project contribution
- Monitoring the node registration interval

The details are explained in Sect. 4.2. Second, the system automatically notifies participants. Specifically, subjects are notified when a high evaluation score is given, for praise, for being grateful, for showing good support, or for contributing to revitalizing the discussion.

3.2   Evaluation of Contribution Value

Overall System Configuration. The overall configuration of the system is shown in Fig. 3. The participants discuss using this system to resolve the project issues. A method of displaying using a Web browser is used to display the situation regarding the discussion in real-time to the participants with a tree diagram. The participants use a PC, Tablet, or Smartphone to register nodes, regarding such items as ideas, opinions, or information, and the discussion status is determined from the tree diagram. Remote discussions are also possible. The registered nodes are stored in the database. Similarly, the system analyzes the discussions using the accumulated information, and it notifies the participants by sending them messages displaying the constantly updated information using a graph and table when the participants receive thanks, compliments, or a high evaluation from others.

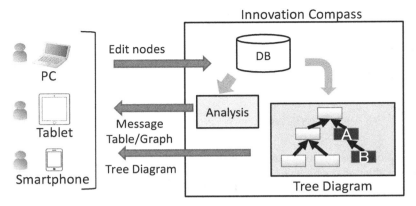

Fig. 3. Overall system configuration.

Function Block. Figure 4 shows a function block in the system. The node information input by the participants is stored within the DB. The node information is managed by project and node, and the node input and tree diagram display between participants is performed using a tree diagram interface. In addition, the information analyzed in the evaluation calculation and node section is displayed in graphs and tables so that participants can easily understand it. The system also sends messages based on the analyzed information in accordance with set thresholds.

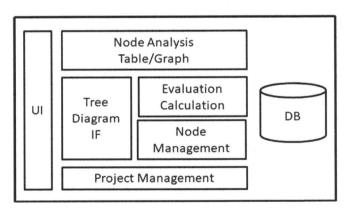

Fig. 4. Functional block diagram.

3.3   User Interface

The user interface on this screen is comprised of three user interfaces. These are the system home screen, node registration/editing/deleting, and the analysis item selection screen. Node registration/editing/deleting are performed from the node selection screen and node edit screen.

System Home Screen. The system home screen is shown in Fig. 5. When registering new nodes or editing or deleting nodes, pressing the respective buttons will display the tree diagram in Fig. 6. Additionally, the bottom of the system home screen has a window that provides notifications of system messages and the total number of nodes registered by the members up to that point.

Fig. 5. System home screen.

Node Registration, Editing, and Deleting. Pressing the new registration button (Fig. 5) adds a new node to the list. A tree diagram of the nodes registered up to that point is displayed. To edit or delete nodes that are already registered, a participant should press the edit and delete button in Fig. 5. Pressing these buttons displays the tree diagram in a separate window, as shown in Fig. 6.

When registering new nodes, if the participant points the mouse at the node to which he or she wishes to connect, an overview is displayed over it.

If the connection point is correct, the node at the top should be clicked. Doing so will display a window to input node details, as shown in Fig. 7.

If a participant wishes to edit or delete nodes that have been registered up to that point, he or she should select the desired node for editing with the same procedure used in Fig. 6 and amend the same one using the node edit screen shown in Fig. 7.

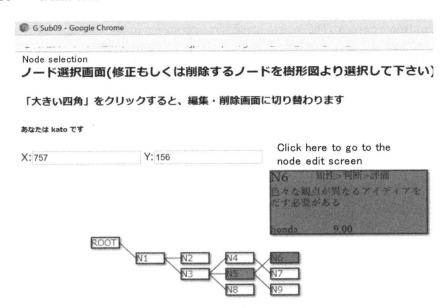

Fig. 6. Tree diagram and node selection screen.

Editing Individual Nodes. He or she can then enter the details for each node as shown in Fig. 7. The text of the outline of the node to be registered is entered in the text. Next, the participant can select the node classification from the pulldown menu. In the same way, the category for the link can be selected with the link classification. When selecting a node that can be evaluated as an upper node, the participant can select the number of evaluation points from the evaluation coefficient pulldown menu.

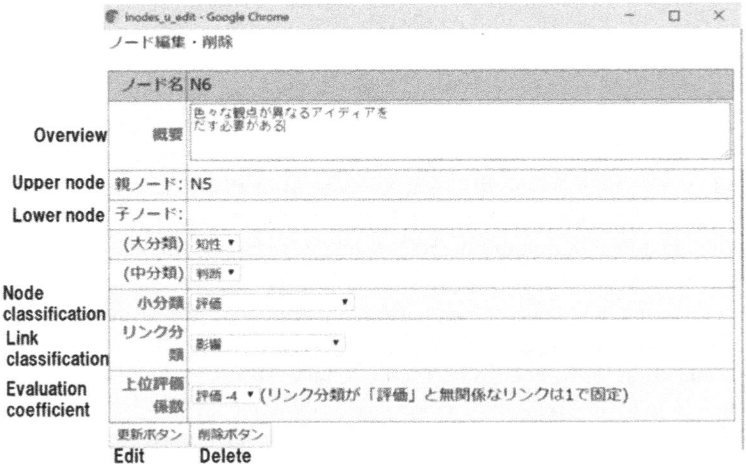

Fig. 7. Node edit/delete screen.

Analysis Item Selection Screen. Participants can press the prepared buttons on the analysis item selection screen shown in Fig. 8 to display a table or graph of monitoring the changes in the total node score over time, the participants' project contributions, and the node registration interval. These enable determining the state of the discussion and the degree of everyone's contributions.

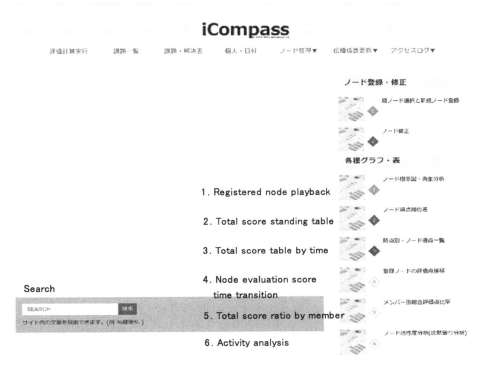

Fig. 8. Analysis item selection screen.

4 System Operation Check

4.1 Check Method

The data used in the evaluation are shown in Table 2. The registered nodes, considering the flow of the discussion, were created as shown in Table 3. Additionally, the discussion was constructed by giving the participants their own respective roles. The node registration time is the virtual time, but the nodes were registered with a time interval that considered the stagnation or activity of the discussion. However, the registration time is not displayed in Table 3.

This evaluation was conducted by entering pre-created data into the system; however, even if real discussion data had been entered, it would have operated according to this algorithm. Thus, this was sufficient for determining system behavior.

The actual node registration status of the five members is shown in Table 3.

Table 2. Evaluation data outline.

Item	Content	Details
Node and Link	Produced 100 nodes	Node/Link clasiffication is based on Table 3
Member	5 participants	Each tasks action suitable to his/her character
Time-stamped record	Set in consideration of discussion flow	Not a real node registration time

Table 3. Registration situation of the node.

Category		Member					
		A	B	C	D	E	Total
Problem		1	9	0	0	0	3
Intellect	Knowledge	6	8	5	5	1	25
	Idea	4	4	3	2	0	13
	Judgment	9	8	13	8	16	54
Emotion	Praising/Gratitude	1	0	1	0	0	2
Action	Support	0	0	1	0	0	1
Solution		1	1	0	0	0	2
Total		22	23	23	15	17	100

4.2 Operation Check Results

The system behavior was determined using the following four evaluation items.

Visualization of the Discussion Using a Tree Diagram. The five people could create a discussion using a dendrogram, as shown in Fig. 9. Additionally, as discussions were carried out for each topic, we could demonstrate that node registrations took place in relation to issues other than the ones focused on during the discussion.

Changes in the Total Number of Points for the Node with the Passage of Time.
We could determine the change in the total number of points for the two nodes with the passing of time. For example, to determine node No. 36 and node No. 80, pressing the time transition in the node evaluation score button on the analysis item selection screen, shown in Fig. 8, enabled us to check the changes in the total number of points for the two nodes with the passage of time on a graph.

Figure 10 displays a graph of the time transition in the total number of points for the two nodes. Both node No. 36 and node No. 80 are idea nodes. We can see that, from a certain point, the number of points obtained by node No. 80 was higher than that for

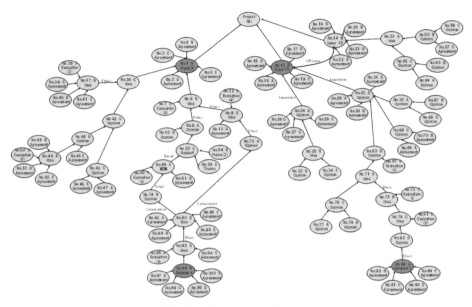

Fig. 9. 100-node tree diagram.

node No. 36. Even with the same idea nodes, node No. 36 did not reach the conclusion. We can see that node No. 80 was the idea that reached the conclusion. In other words, we can see that the total number of points from when No. 80 was registered, with the passing of time from that point, suddenly increased with the evaluations of other people and the development of the discussion. For Node No. 80, we can see that—with the flow of this idea—the discussion developed, and evaluations were added recursively until reaching the final conclusion. Also, the total number of evaluation points for the node increased.

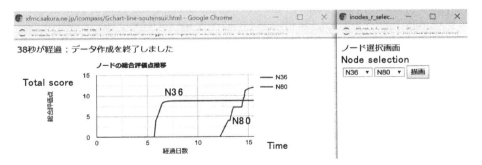

Fig. 10. Time transition in node evaluation score.

Participant Level of Contribution in the Project. The level of contributions by the participants in the project can be determined for each member by pressing the total score ratio using the member button on the selection screen for the evaluation items in Fig. 8. Figure 11 displays the project contribution level for each member. The blue bar shows the ratio of total points for all registered nodes for each member. The red bar is the share of total points for the nodes related to the solution for each member. From this, we can see that the total number of points for the nodes related to the solution was high for both A and B, and both led the discussion. Members C and D had almost the same number of total points, but in terms of total points related to the solution, D had a higher score. Also, member E did not participate in the solution. Thus, we could determine the level of project contribution by the participants.

Fig. 11. Total score ratio by member.

Interval Monitoring of Node Registration. The node registration interval can be monitored in terms of the status of the discussion. Because the system is monitoring the node registration interval, the discussion activity for each topic can be determined. In terms of the topic activity, the level of discussion activity can be seen by pressing the activity analysis button on the evaluation item selection screen, shown in Fig. 8.

For example, as shown in the graph in Fig. 12, node No. 36 is an idea node. However, we can see that—before registering this node—the node registration related to the discussion had stagnated. First, at the point that node No. 36 was registered, its status was evaluated as a node with the potential to enliven the discussion. We can see that, after the registration of Node No. 36, many nodes were registered; moreover, multiple nodes were registered in relation to a topic with a shorter interval than the average interval for the project nodes as a whole. In this way, we can see that the idea of Node No. 36 was the trigger that enlivened the discussion.

Checking these system behaviors enabled us to visualize the evaluations of other people and the project contribution level of the participants and to determine the behavior was as the algorithm predicted.

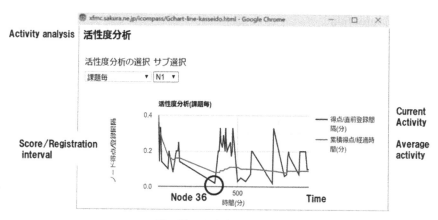

Fig. 12. Activity analysis.

5 Test Plan

5.1 Details

The effectiveness of the system was evaluated in actual use by subjects. Though coming up with a good means of evaluating the system was difficult, we were able to obtain the necessary results.

Purpose. The experiment was conducted to show that our system can support human motivation. The content to validate was as follows.

- From the tree diagram input, in addition to where the discussion is currently focused, are opinions registered in the area, for example, where discussions were registered one day before?
- Do the evaluations and support from others impact the discussion?
- Do the evaluations and support from others impact the progress of the project?

Test Procedure. Each group alternately conducted discussions using this system and discussions using existing SNSs twice. The discussions were performed, in relation to pre-determined project topics, remotely using a PC, tablet, or smartphone. Test compensation and participation compensation was provided to the group that had better discussion content.

Composition of the Test Subjects. Two groups consisting of four or five people were created in accordance with the project issue.

Test Period. The period for one issue was about five days, and each group implemented two issues.

Method of Evaluation

The following evaluations were carried out.

- Quantitative evaluation: Basic data were collected on the number of ideas and the number of compliments.
- Qualitative evaluation: A survey questionnaire was conducted with the test subjects.
- Feature value evaluation: We analyzed the discussions that were conducted using the playback function of the system and the registered node playback in Fig. 8. For example, we checked if change in behavior occurred after subjects were praised.

6 Conclusion

The operation check demonstrated that the following four functions were operating correctly. The first was the visualization of the discussion using a tree diagram, the second was the change in the total score of the node over time, the third was the degree of contribution of the participants to the project, and the fourth was the monitoring of the node registration interval.

Our evaluation method is a key addition to the field of human motivation. To promote the creation of new value, we need to gather the wisdom of many people and translate their insights into action. In order for an individual to think for himself or herself and adapt his or her actions, a clear understanding of one's role and situation is first necessary. We believe that this contribution value is effective for changing one's actions or for personal reform.

In the near future, we will initiate a practical implementation of this system in a real environment and determine whether or not the same results can be obtained. We will also encourage individual inspiration and the bridging of information to implement our system for integrated creation support.

References

1. The Hasso Plattner: Institute of Design at Stanford: An Introduction to Design Thinking Process Guide (2012)
2. Kato, Y., Hashiyama, T., Tano, S.: Innovation compass: integrated system to support creativity in both individuals and groups. In: Yamamoto, S. (ed.) HIMI 2015. LNCS, vol. 9173, pp. 476–487. Springer, Cham (2015). https://doi.org/10.1007/978-3-319-20618-9_48
3. Kato, Y., Hashiyama, T., Tano, S.: Proposal and evaluation of contribution value model for creation support system. In: The 13th International Conference on Knowledge, Information and Creativity Support Systems, pp. 129–134 (2018)
4. Kunz, W., et al.: Issues as Elements of Information Systems, Working Paper No. 131, University of California, Berkeley (1970)
5. Conklin, J., Begeman, M.L.: gIBIS: a hypertext tool for exploratory policy discussion. In: Tool for Exploratory Policy Discussion, CSCW 1988 Proceedings, pp. 140–152. ACM (1988)
6. Quirky. https://www.quirky.com
7. Imi, Y., Ito, T., Ito, T., Hideshima, E.: A large-scale consensus support system called COLLAGREE based on online facilitation functions—a real-world application for Nagoya next generation total city planning. Inf. Process. Soc. Jpn. **56**(10), 1996–2010 (2015)
8. Kotani, T., Seki, K., Matsui, T., Okamoto, T.: Development of discussion supporting system based on the 'value of favorable words' influence. Jpn. Soc. Artif. Intell. **19**(2), 95–104 (2004)

Analysis of Human Factor in Air Traffic Control Unsafe Events Based on Improved DECIDE Model

Jun-jie Liu, Rui-rui Zhang$^{(\boxtimes)}$, Yin-lan Du, and Qian-yu Bao

Civil Aviation University of China, Tianjin 300300, China
13132039969@126.com, zrr18339956340@163.com, 1428476957@qq.com,
baoblair@163.com

Abstract. In order to deeply analyze the human factors of air traffic control unsafe events, air traffic control unsafe event information collected by the Civil Aviation Administration of China in 2018 is used as the sample. Based on the DECIDE model, an improved D^2E model is proposed to analyze the crew errors during the execution of the controller's instructions in the sample events, which can be used as a reference for effective control of safety risks.

Keywords: Analysis of aviation safety information · Human factors · Air traffic control unsafe events · DECIDE model · D^2E model · Flight safety

1 Introduction

Analyzing the causes of ATC unsafe events and taking targeted preventive control measures are important support for improving air traffic safety based on data driving.

ATC unsafe events mainly involved controllers and cockpit crew, which are mainly manifested as crew deviations during the execution of controller's instructions. The controller is both the issuer of the control instruction and the supervisor of the execution of controller's instructions. The cockpit crew is the main body of the execution of the controller's instructions. If there are omissions or deficiencies in the decision-making and execution process, it will cause deviation from the ATC instructions and cause traffic conflicts. The crew's execution of the ATC instructions is not only a process of information exchange, but also a process of collecting information and decision-making. Analyzing cockpit crew errors and error causes are essential in preventing and minimizing safety risks.

Current researches on crew factor mainly include the following two aspects:

(1) Classification and analysis of human errors. Dr. Reason [1] proposed the REASON model, which divided people's unsafe behaviors into unintentional behaviors and intentional behavior, including negligence and forgetting, errors and violations. Yang Shu et al. [2] used the SHEL model to analyze the types of CFIT event risks from the four interfaces of Liveware, Hardware, Environment and Software.

© Springer Nature Switzerland AG 2020
S. Yamamoto and H. Mori (Eds.): HCII 2020, LNCS 12185, pp. 365–374, 2020.
https://doi.org/10.1007/978-3-030-50017-7_26

Shappell, and Wiegmann, [3] proposed the HFACS model based on the REASON model, which classified human errors into skill errors, decision errors, perceived errors, and violations. Ling Xiao-xi [4] analyzed flight accidents and summarized that human errors in the cockpit included operational or decision errors, negligence or misjudgments, inadequate flight skills, improper handling of emergency situations, violations of rules and regulations, crew failure, and improper crew resource management. Sarter, and Alexander, [5] found that a person in error had a 24% self-detection probability and that the errors he made were mainly noticed by other crew members or controllers. Feng et al. [6] studied the human factors affecting flight safety through the analysis of civil aviation incidents (events), and the research showed that the causes of incidents were skill errors, decision errors, and perception errors.

(2) Analysis the crew decision-making behavior and research on the factors affecting the decision-making. Hrebec, et al. [7] studied the relationship between information load and pilot human error, which revealed that the pilot's operational performance is affected by the amount of information and the density of information. Morrow, et al. [8] found that the limited working memory ability was the reason that pilots misunderstood or failed to fully implement the controller's instructions. Rui-shan et al. [9] proposed that the process of crew judgment and decision-making in the cockpit is an important factor to ensure the safe operation of the aircraft. Yi-min [10] proposed a new model of cockpit crew driving behavior, which decomposed the entire crew consideration into "perception-decision-behavior" and analyzed the pilot's driving behavior error mechanism. Hong-bing et al. [11] conducted a qualitative analysis of human error from the psychological and behavioral environment of pilots based on the information processing process and the principle of accident chain. Meng-jie et al. [12] established a P-D-A-F flight cognitive reliability model based on human cognitive reliability, and analyzed the flight error occurrence mechanism from the four aspects of "sense-decision-action-influencing factors".

The research found the source of crew error in the process of the execution of control instructions by analyzing the ATC unsafe events, which helped to take preventive control measures, reduce the occurrence of unsafe incidents, and enhance the safety level of air flight.

2 Sample Selection and Analysis

2.1 Sample Selection

This paper took 1275 ATC unsafe events which were collected by the Civil Aviation Administration of China in 2018 as sample. Unsafe events were divided into five types that require special precautions, including deviation from arrival and departure procedure events, deviation from altitude events, ground taxiing error events, air to ground communication interruption events, course deviation events.

Every event information in the sample contains the following: the place where the event occurred, the time when the event occurred, the description of the event, the type of event, and the cause of the event, etc.

Event description is a brief of the event process and event consequences.

2.2 Sample Overview

The sample involved five types of events: deviation from arrival and departure procedure events, deviation from altitude events, ground taxiing error events, air to ground communication interruption events, course deviation events. The number of events were: 151, 352, 444, 229 and 99. The proportions were: 11.84%, 27.61%, 34.82%, 17.96% and 7.76%.

The sample includes 1275 events. The statistical bar graph of event cause was shown in Fig. 1. 1129 cockpit crew cause events accounted for 88.55%.

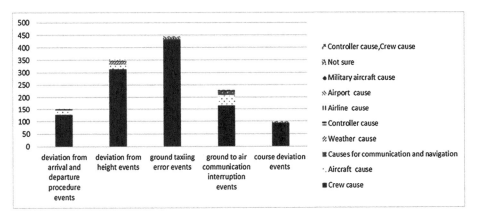

Fig. 1. Event type-event cause stacked bar chart

2.3 Analysis of Basic Characteristics of Sample Information

Analyzing the sample "Event description" item. The description of the unsafe event process includes the following: time, place, flight altitude, involved airline, flight number, aircraft type, aircraft registration number, brief description of the event, controller monitoring and detection situation, and subsequent results, such as the following example:

On April 16, 2018 (time), xx Airlines (airline) AA4842 (flight number) (aircraft type B738, registration number BXXXX) performed the XX to XX flight mission. There were military activities in the XX region. At 12:35 (Beijing time), the flight followed the route to point XX (the location of the incident) and remained at an altitude of 7,800 m. At 12:36, the controller found that the flight did not fly according to the planned route and began to deviate from the route. The controller immediately directed flight AA4842 to XX to join the planned route. The maximum distance of the aircraft from the route was 10 km. No other effects were caused during the period.

However, information in the event description sometimes was not complete enough to determine the cause of the crew error, as shown in the following example.

On March 23, 2018 (time), flight AA3125 performed XX to XX missions. The controller instructed the flight to fly 3 nautical miles from the right flight route while the crew readback correctly. At 13:01, the controller found that the flight was off the right course more than 3 nautical miles, and immediately directed the flight to return to the planned route. No other effects were caused during the period.

The description of the incident affects the process of identifying the cause of the crew error during the analysis of the cause of the crew. Therefore, in order to analyze the 1129 cockpit crew cause events, we need to improve the selected analysis model in order to analyze unsafe events more effectively based on the event description facts.

Event description affected whether the source of the crew error can be found in the process of analyzing cockpit crew causes. Therefore, based on the event description facts, the selected analysis model needed to be improved in order to analyze the 1129 cockpit crew cause events more effectively.

3 D^2E Model Construction

3.1   DECIDE Model Definition

DECIDE Model is a continuous loop process that provides the pilot with a logical way of making decisions.

D - "Detect" means that the decision maker detects the fact that change has occurred.

E - "Estimate" means that the decision maker estimates the need to counter or react to the change.

C - "Choose" means that the decision maker chooses a desirable outcome (in terms of success) for the flight.

I - "Identify" means that the decision maker identifies actions which could successfully control the change.

D - "Do" means that the decision maker takes the necessary action.

E - "Evaluate" means that the decision maker evaluates the effect(s) of his/her action countering the change [13].

3.2   Application of DECIDE Model

The DECIDE model analyzed the crew error in the execution of ATC instructions from six aspects. "Detect" referred to that the cockpit crew can perceive air traffic conflicts in flight and unsafe conditions. "Estimate" referred to that the cockpit crew analyzed and judged the air traffic conflicts and unsafe conditions. "Choose" referred to that the cockpit crew combined their own knowledge, experiences and actual situation, and chose a reasonable and effective way to avoid the accident based on the analysis and judgment of the discovered air traffic conflicts and unsafe conditions. "Identify" referred to that the cockpit crew selected one or more measures collected to be put into practice. "Do" referred to that the cockpit crew put the measures into action. "Evaluate" referred to that the cockpit crew monitored the measures that they have already implemented [14].

3.3   Construction of D^2E Model

According to the description of the sample events, it was difficult to determine the crew errors or mistakes that may occur in every step in the execution of the ATC instructions.

Therefore, the paper proposed an improved DECIDE model. It was a D^2E model which analyzed crew errors from three aspects: Detect, Do, and Evaluate. "Detect" referred to the pilot's perception errors. It means the pilot failed to detect the wrong control instruction, damaged equipment, et al. "Do" referred to the pilot's operation errors. It means the pilot deviated from the control instruction due to lack of skills, operation errors, et al. "Evaluate" referred to the pilot's supervision errors. It means the pilot failed to monitor the expected results after the execution of the instructions.

Based on the description of 1129 unsafe events, the crew errors of the five types of events were analyzed and summarized from the three aspects of Detect, Do, and Evaluate, as shown in Table 1.

Table 1. Event type-D^2E model error analysis table.

Event type	Detect	Do	Evaluate	Fail to judge
Deviation from arrival and departure procedure events	Failure to detect arrival and departure procedure were wrong	1. Not flying according to the arrival and departure ATC instructions; 2. Flying wrong arrival and departure procedures	Not monitoring the expected results after the execution of the instructions	Because the information in the event description was unclear, unspecific, and incomplete, it is impossible to determine the cause of the crew errors from Detect, Do, and Evaluate
Deviation from altitude events	1. Not detecting the altimeter was malfunctioning; 2. Not detecting reference plane was wrong	1. Unauthorized actions without regulatory instructions; 2. Adjusting the altimeter incorrectly; 3. Adjusting the reference plane incorrectly	Not realizing that the command altitude had been breached during the ascent or descent operation, or during the cruise phase	
Ground taxiing error events	1. The understanding of the taxi route instruction was wrong; 2. Not detect that maintenance launched the aircraft without permission; 3. Not detecting that maintenance was executing the opposite launch instruction; 4, Not detecting the wrong ATC instructions	1. Incorrect execution of control instructions; 2. Acting without authorization	Not realizing that the aircraft was slipping past the holding point or line, turning left or right was wrong, etc.	

(*continued*)

Table 1. (*continued*)

Event type	Detect	Do	Evaluate	Fail to judge
Ground to air communication interruption events	1. Not detecting that the communication frequency was wrong; 2. Not detecting that the communication equipment was broken-down	1. No switching frequency when handing off controllers; 2. Using the wrong frequency; 3. Setting the wrong frequency	Not realizing that the communication was interrupted and lost contact with the controllers	
Course deviation events	Not detecting that the planned route in the flight information and the route approved by the controller were inconsistent	1. Unauthorized change of route without the controller's permission; 2. Incorrect execution of ATC instructions; 3. Inputting wrong navigation information		

4   D²E Model Analysis Events

4.1   Analysis Process

Based on the descriptive information in the sample events, such as the source of the crew information, the information content of the control instructions, the person who found deviations from the expected results, and the consequences that deviated from the expectations, et al., 1129 cockpit crew cause events were analyzed using the D²E model. The crew was the receiver, sender and executor of ATC instructions. The realization of control instructions was actually a process of information transmission and processing, mainly including:

① The controller issued an instruction, confirmed that the crew has received and correctly understood the instruction through the crew's readback, and at the same time monitored the status of the flight to evaluate the effect of the crew's execution of ATC instructions.

② After receiving the ATC instructions, the crew controlled the aircraft to execute the instructions, and also monitored whether the expected results were achieved after the operations were performed;

Analyzing the process of the crew obtaining instructions, executing instructions, and supervising the execution effect of the instructions, and finding the errors in the pilot's awareness, implementation, and supervision during the events. The analysis process was shown in Fig. 2.

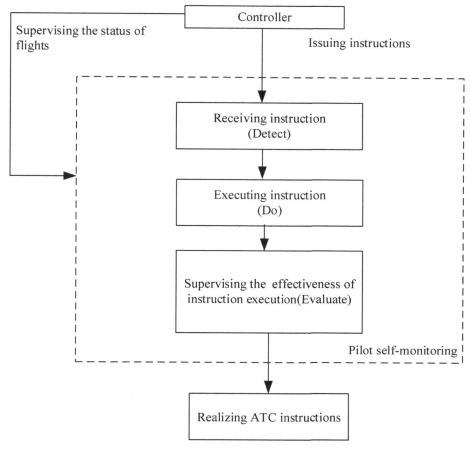

Fig. 2. D2E model analysis flowchart

4.2 Analysis Results

The D^{2}E model was used to analyze the cockpit crew cause events from three aspects: Detect, Do, and Evaluate. The analysis results were shown in Table 2. Regardless of the events that failed to determine the source of the crew error, the pilot's errors were mainly from the Do errors. This indicated that pilots were easy to make mistake in specific operations during the execution of ATC instructions which led to unsafe events.

It can be seen from Table 2 that the Do errors were the most in every event type. It showed that the lack of operating skills of the crew was the most important cause of ATC unsafe events.

Detect errors accounted for the largest proportion of deviations from course deviation events. The approved routes in the navigational information can ensure that the aircraft was flying on the correct route. Inadequate and inaccurate preparation of the crew before the flight will cause the aircraft to fly on the wrong route and deviated from the planned route.

Table 2. D^{2}E model analysis results.

Event type	Detect		Do		Evaluate		Fail to judge	
Deviation from arrival and departure procedure events	7	5.47%	108	84.37	9	7.03%	4	3.13%
Deviation from altitude events	16	5.11%	104	33.23%	5	1.60%	188	60.06%
Ground taxiing error events	4	0.93%	415	96.28%	4	0.93%	8	1.86%
Air to ground communication interruption events	22	13.41%	41	25.00%	2	1.22%	99	60.37%
Course deviation events	34	36.56%	50	53.76	4	4.30	5	5.38
Total	83	7.35%	718	63.60%	24	2.13%	304	26.93%

Do errors accounted for the largest proportion of ground taxiing error events. The crew's unfamiliarity with the taxiing route of the airport, the excessive speed of maneuvering the aircraft, and the unclear information of the signs et al. would lead the aircraft to taxi on the ground incorrectly.

Evaluate errors accounted for the largest proportion of deviation from arrival and departure procedure events. Takeoff and landing phases were the most prone to unsafe events. The cockpit crew did not supervise the attitude of the aircraft after the execution of ATC instructions, which would cause flight conflicts and emergency go-arounds.

Clear ground signs, correct communication frequencies, accurate flight plans, et al. were the prerequisites for implementing the ATC instructions. If the crew could not correctly identify these prerequisites, it would result in the inability to execute the ATC instructions correctly. The crew operating ability and compliance with the standard operating specifications were the guarantee conditions for realizing the ATC instructions. If the crew could not operate accurately and strictly adhere to the operating specifications, it would result in the inability to implement the ATC instructions accurately. That crew can supervise the operation results after the implementation of ATC instruction was a supplementary condition for the realizing ATC instruction. Insufficient supervision would result in previous operations failing to achieve the intended goals. Therefore, finding out the source of errors and proposing preventive control measures could achieve the purpose of preventing ATC unsafe events. The analysis results were shown in Table 3.

Table 3. D^2E error source analysis-preventive control measures.

D^2E model	The source of errors	Preventive control measures
Detect	1. The obtained instruction information was wrong; 2. Misunderstanding the instruction information; 3. The equipment that completed the instruction message was broken-down; 4. The environment in which the instructions were implemented was not feasible	1. The cockpit crew must be fully prepared in advance. a. When receiving flight information, navigation information, and communication information, the information required for inspection and proofreading was complete, up-to-date, and valid b. Investigate information about takeoffs, landings, and alternate airports, routes, or flight areas c. Understand the weather situation and proof the navigation information of the routes and areas d. Cooperate well between the crew e. Receive a medical check-up by the aviation doctor before flight attendance to avoid crew failure 2. The crew should do the pre-flight inspection of the aircraft. a. Strictly stick to the checklist and carefully check the effectiveness of the equipment on board. b. Plan the input procedure strictly in accordance with the route flight, check and verify that the route coordinates were correct
Do	1. Unskilled movements; 2. The operation speed was slow; 3. Action error; 4. Actions were not standardized; 5. The instruction was executed incorrectly	Airlines should do a good job in training the crew 1. Strict assessment during the training process; 2. During the training process, the pilot's operational skills should be improved in accordance with the actual situation, such as training for new aircraft models, actual flight training for new captains, and learning of navigational data 3. The pilot should operate the aircraft in accordance with standard operating procedures
Evaluate	Means that the crew have not supervised the execution results after the execution of the ATC instruction	1. In the process of piloting the aircraft, the crew should do a good job of controlling and monitoring the aircraft 2. Monitoring the instrument, attitude, flight altitude, and heading of the aircraft during the flight, especially during the automatic driving

5 Conclusion

In the case of insufficient event description information, the D^2E model simplified the analysis of unsafe events and only analyzed the three key steps to implement the control instructions, including the three processes of receiving the control instructions, executing the control instructions, and monitoring the results of the execution of the instructions. In order to find the source of the Detect, Do, and Evaluate errors of the crew.

The cockpit crew cause was the main cause of the ATC unsafe events. The D^2E model analyzed the causes of the crew, and found that the crew Do error were the most important error that leaded to the occurrence of unsafe events. It showed that the crew operation skills were the key factors affecting flight safety.

The realization of ATC instructions was a process of receiving, executing and supervising information, as well as a process for the crew to collect information and make decisions. The D^2E model could be used to analyze the crew's decision-making process, find out the influencing factors of decision-making errors, find the source of errors that needs to be accurately prevented, and further develop control measures to fundamentally prevent unsafe events and improve flight safety.

References

1. James, R.: Human Error, 1st edn. Cambridge University Press, Cambridge (1990)
2. Yang, S., Luo, X., Li, J.: Risk factors analysis and the system structural model investigation of the CFIT of the aircraft. J. Saf. Environ. **18**(3), 866–871 (2018)
3. Shappell, S.A., Wiegmann, D.A.: Applying reason: the human factors analysis and classification system (HFACS). Hum. Fact. Aerosp. Saf. **1**(1), 59–86 (2001)
4. Ling, X.: Research on human factors affecting aviation safety. Southwest Jiaotong University, Chengdu (2007)
5. Sarter, N.B., Alexander, H.M.: Error types and related error detection mechanisms in the aviation domain: an analysis of aviation safety reporting system incident reports. Int. J. Sviat. Psychol. **10**(2), 189–206 (2000)
6. Zhang, F., Yu, G., Li, Y., et al.: Individual and organizational factors affecting Chinese Civil Aviation Safety: event analysis based on HFACS framework. China Saf. Sci. J. **17**(10), 67–75 (2007)
7. Hrebec, D.G., Fiedler, F.E., Infield, S.E.: The effects of datalink on flight deck intra-crew communication patterns. In: International Symposium on Aviation Psychology, 8th, Columbus, OH (1995)
8. Morrow, D.G., et al.: Environmental support promotes expertise-based mitigation of age differences on pilot communication tasks. Psychol. Aging **18**(2), 268 (2003)
9. Sun, R., Wang, X.: Application of failure probability of CREAM for judgement and decision-making in the cockpit. J. Saf. Sci. Technol. **6**(6), 40–45 (2010)
10. Gong, Y.: Study on Reliability of Pilot Operation in Cockpit Based on Correlation. Civil Aviation University of China, Tianjin (2014)
11. Du, H., Liu, M., Jin, H.: Study on a structured pilot error model based on information processing and accident chain principle. China Saf. Sci. J. **21**(6), 25–31 (2001)
12. Li, M., Sun, R.: Establishment of impact factor system for flight error based on cognitive reliability. J. Safe. Sci. Technol. **9**(12), 148–154 (2013)
13. FAA-H-8083-25B. Pilot's Handbook of Aeronautical Knowledge. FAA. U.S. Department of Transportation (2016)
14. Qin, G.: Analysis of flight error behind the human factor based on DECIDE model. Guide Sci-tech Mag. (12), 83 (2012)

Expanding and Embedding a High-Level Gesture Vocabulary for Digital and Augmented Musical Instruments

Eduardo A. L. Meneses[1,2(✉)], Takuto Fukuda[2,3], and Marcelo M. Wanderley[1,2]

[1] Input Devices and Music Interaction Laboratory (IDMIL),
Montreal, QC H3A 1E3, Canada
eduardo.meneses@mail.mcgill.ca, marcelo.wanderley@mcgill.ca
[2] Centre for Interdisciplinary Research in Music, Media and Technology (CIRMMT),
Montreal, QC H3A 1E3, Canada
takuto.fukuda@mail.mcgill.ca
[3] Digital Composition Studios (DCS), Montreal, QC H3A 1E3, Canada
http://www.idmil.org, http://www.music.mcgill.ca/dcs/,
http://www.cirmmt.org

Abstract. This paper reports ongoing initiatives to explore how digital and augmented musical instruments gestural vocabulary is developed over time, and how embedding the high-level gesture descriptors in those instruments can fomenting their use and contribute to their maturity toward established music instruments. The instruments included in this research are the T-Stick (Digital Musical Instrument), and the GuitarAMI (Augmented Music Instrument). Finally, we discuss present and future strategies for instrument longevity for the presented instruments.

Keywords: Digital Musical Instruments · Gestural control · Embedded synthesis

1 Introduction

Augmented and Digital Musical Instruments (AMIs and DMIs) use several sensors in their construction, such as inertial measurement units (IMUs), resistive or capacitive sensors, electromagnetic transducers, Force Sensitive Resistors (FSRs), etc. DMIs and AMIs are often used exclusively by their designers and builders, a problem known as *the problem of the second performer* [5]. One of the possible reasons for the problem of the second performer is that proficiency in computer programming languages and electronics is required for composers and performers to work with DMIs and AMIs using the raw sensor data, usually the only available information provided by the instrument/controller.

To use this raw sensor data (such as angle or acceleration) in performances or compositions, the user needs to transcode low-level sensor data into

© Springer Nature Switzerland AG 2020
S. Yamamoto and H. Mori (Eds.): HCII 2020, LNCS 12185, pp. 375–384, 2020.
https://doi.org/10.1007/978-3-030-50017-7_27

meaningful high-level gesture descriptors (such as "jab" , "squeeze" , or instrument orientation) to be used in compositions, mastered by performers and performed on stage.

This transcoding process is often inconsistent between compositions and performers, making the gestures unique to a particular piece/performance, impeding different performers to develop expertise in a particular digital instrument, and different composers to dialog with material already composed.

2   Instruments in Maturity Stage

To investigate the impact of music programming languages and low-level sensor data on the usage of DMIs and AMIs, we decided to analyze the use of some instruments in the maturity stage. We understand that a particular instrument enters the maturity stage when he is still performed/developed after several years while still not possess enough repertoire or formed a user base of composers and performers.

The instruments chosen are the T-Stick and the GuitarAMI. The T-Stick is a Digital Musical Instrument originally conceived by Joseph Malloch and D. Andrew Stewart, and it is being developed at the Input Devices and Music Interaction Laboratory (IDMIL) and the Centre for Interdisciplinary Research in Music Media and Technology (CIRMMT) since 2006. The instrument has a tube (cylindrical) shape, and it is equipped with capacitive sensors, an inertial measurement unit, a piezoelectric transducer, a force sensitive resistor, and, in some prototypes, an infrared, an air pressure and a light sensor. The T-Stick has been widely used in compositions and performances in Canada, USA, Brazil, Italy, Norway, and Portugal [9]. Several T-Sticks of different sizes can be seen in Fig. 1.

Fig. 1. Instruments of the T-Stick family. Sopraninos on top, Alto in the middle, and Soprano at the botton of the picture.

The GuitarAMI uses sensors that generate data from gestures to control algorithms that overcome some of classical guitar intrinsic sonic limitations such as short sustain and the lack of sound intensity control after the attack [8]. The instrument has been used in improvisations and performances in Brazil and Canada since 2015. The GuitarAMI can be seen in Fig. 2.

Fig. 2. GuitarAMI Module and Processing Unit, connected to a standard classical guitar.

3   Establishing an Instrument's Gestural Vocabulary

Even though there is no high-level gestural vocabulary explicitly shared between different performers and composers of a particular DMI or AMI, users tend to organize their work by first processing sensor data (cooking data), and later mapping this processed data into sound synthesis parameters. This strategy could be observed during the *Workshop on the T-Stick*[1], organized by CIRMMT and IDMIL. This workshop is part of a larger T-Stick project, discussed in Sect. 4.

This data process can vary from simply rescaling the data to perform sensor fusion or extract high-level gestural descriptors. One of the main issues regarding the *cooking data process* is that DMI/AMI users (and often instrument designers) don't necessarily understand sensor technical specifications and don't take into account factors such as drift, precision, resolution, etc. [6].

Even though instrument designers usually build their instruments with some interactions (gestures) in mind, instrument exploration and the creation of a gestural vocabulary happen mostly during composition and performance.

The process of embedding high-level gesture descriptors in DMIs/AMIs, discussed in Sect. 4, can also be useful to minimize the data process problem since

---

[1] More information about the Workshop on the T-Stick can be found at https://www.cirmmt.org/activities/workshops/research/stick_workshop/workshop_tstick.

during the embedding process, the instrument designer can not only reprogram gesture descriptors used by composers and performers to be more computationally efficient, but also take into account all technical aspects previously neglected by composers and performers. Those steps are critical when working with embedded microcontrollers, usually less powerful than computers.

Sections 3.1 and 3.2 will briefly discuss two possible procedures to explore DMIs/AMIs and develop their gestural vocabularies.

3.1   From Gesture: Instrument Affordances

The T-Stick is an interesting example of an instrument with an already established gestural vocabulary created by performers and composers. T-Stick composer D. Andrew Stewart notably explored the instrument affordances, envisioning meaningful gestures according to the instrument shape and data acquired by the sensors [12]. Gestured used in Stewart works are also classified according to the movement nature as *malleable* or *intractable*. Repeatable gestures (malleable) are easily repeatable and reproduce gestures used to trigger sounds, while fluid subtle movements (intractable) are used for sound modification. The gestural vocabulary created with this approach is developed similarly to a traditional musical instrument, i.e. interaction with the physical object is the main exploration method to access the DMI affordances.

In other words, the question to be answered to create the T-Stick's gesture vocabulary was: what gestures naturally emerge from interaction with the instrument? Those gestures tend to be easily assimilated to the specific instrument vocabulary and can be used in different contexts (music compositions, learning how to play the instrument, etc.) not necessarily being associated with a particular sonic outcome.

3.2   From Sound: Meaningful Gestures

The GuitarAMI is an example of AMI that is yet to establish a standard gestural vocabulary commonly used in different contexts. GuitarAMI performances were created exploring the desired sonic outcome, based on digital sound modifications designed to modify the classical guitar's sustain and audio feedback. Gestures used to control the sound modification parameters were chosen accordingly to the expected sonic outcome [7]. Due to the nature of augmented instruments and the GuitarAMI design choices, the AMI's gesture vocabulary tends to be mostly used for sound modification.

In this particular scenario, the question to be answered to create the GuitarAMI's gesture vocabulary is: what gestures can be associated with the intended sonic outcome? Those gestures tend to be correlated with the resulting sounds, similar to the relationship between the tremolo technique for classical guitars and the inseparable sonic outcome expected by the physical act. Time-Control, reverb, and freeze gestures are part of the gesture vocabulary used on the GuitarAMI.

4   Embedding High-Level Gesture Descriptors in DMIs/AMIs

A research project organized by CIRMMT, IDMIL, and Digital Composition Studios (DCS) aims to explore the possibility to embed algorithms in digital instruments to process raw sensor data and provide high-level gestural descriptors as the DMI/AMI output.

The first goal of this project is to provide possibilities to explore and expand the instrument's gestural vocabulary. The established gestural vocabulary will be available to users as a set of data provided by the AMI/DMI, allowing those instruments to output both raw data and high-level gestures. It is expected to allow composers/performers to use high-level descriptors directly in their compositions, as well as expand the instrument's gestural vocabulary using raw sensor data to create new high-level descriptors.

This is an ongoing project consisting of the development of a new T-Stick generation, two workshops, a call for composers, and two concerts.

A new T-Stick generation was developed at IDMIL during Summer and Fall 2019. The main goals for the new instrument iteration were increasing reliability for data transmission (this T-Stick generation operates wirelessly) and update the firmware to allow the instrument designers to embed high-level gestural description algorithms maintaining the remaining characteristics untouched.

The first workshop, entitled *Workshop on the T-Stick*, explored the development of compositional and performance practices for the T-Stick Sopranino. During the workshop the participants discussed the instrument design and compositional possibilities, followed by a hands-on workshop for the practical use of the T-Stick, including how to set up, perform and notate. The workshop included the participation of Joseph Malloch[2]—the T-Stick designer (Dalhousie University)—and D. Andrew Stewart[3]—composer/T-Stick instrumentalist (University of Lethbridge).

Simultaneously to the Workshop on the T-Stick, CIRMMT released a public call for five composers of any nationality and age interested in composing for the T-Stick. The call asked specifically for new live electroacoustic solos for the T-Stick, but later also accepted ensemble proposals for any formation as long as included the T-Stick. The selected composers were introduced to the current modes of performance on the T-Stick during the first workshop, exploring musical and physical playing gestures and the development of new playing techniques and sounds for the instrument. D. Andrew Stewart and Joseph Malloch also participate as tutors for the composers during the composition phase.

Composers are currently working on the T-Stick works that will be performed in February 2020 in two concerts: live@CIRMMT[4] and improv@CIRMMT[5].

---

[2] More information on Joseph Malloch can be found at https://josephmalloch.wordpress.com/.

[3] More information on D. Andrew Stewart can be found at http://dandrewstewart.ca/.

[4] https://www.cirmmt.org/activities/live-cirmmt/cirmmt_composers_february.

[5] https://www.cirmmt.org/activities/special/improv_feb2020_tstick.

Information gathered from users during the first workshop from T-Stick, and also from the selected composer's compositional process between the workshop and the performances are being used to extract the instrument's high-level gestural descriptors. Those descriptors are being reprogrammed to run inside the ESP32, used in the T-Stick to receive sensor data and send OSC messages over the network. The process and a partial outcome of this process can be seen in Fig. 3.

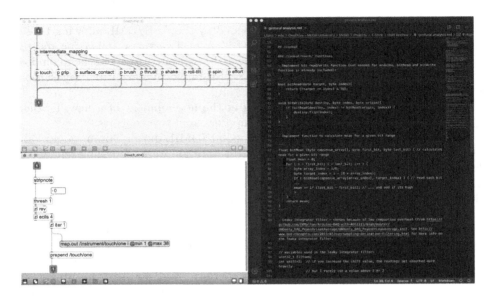

Fig. 3. Example of Max/MSP patch in analysis to extract high-level gesture descriptor algorithms. Those algorithms are described in markdown files using pseudocode or C++ Arduino compatible language.

5   Impact of High-Level Gesture Descriptors on Compositions and Performers

The high-level gesture descriptors are created using raw sensor data mapped or fused using algorithms, then classified into categories of gesture presented to the user. This gesture classification approach opens up a possibility to integrate a gesture type and electronic sounds into a hybrid expression. In recent years, there has been increasing interest in studies on hybrid expressions as in the Gestural-Sonorous Objects [3] and Kinesonic approach [4]. These researches synthesize two different preceding research fields, that are, sound typology and gesture typology. While sound typology has been explored in electroacoustic music studies such as typo-morphology by Pierre Schaeffer [10] and Spectromorphology by Denis Smalley [11], gesture typology was developed in DMI researches such as Claude

Cadoz [1] and Marcelo Wanderley [2]. In the context of compositions for T-Stick, hybrid expression has been explored by D. Andrew Stewart as in *fan, lasso and airplane* [12], combining a specific sound synthesis techniques with high-level gesture types.

From a composer's perspective, high-level gesture types can be used as compositional materials which can form a hierarchical gesture complex that mirrors the hierarchy of grouped discrete sounds (e.g., notes grouped as a motive, motives grouped as a melody) seen often in Western music composition. The concept of high-level gestures demonstrates the match of the auditory grouping with the body movement, unifying the aural and visual elements not only in a micro temporal level, but also at a macro temporal level of music.

While the hybrid approaches expanded the expressivity in T-Stick performances, it also raises the height of the "ceiling" [13] to master the instrument. Composers and performers have to shift the approach from: 1) harvest gestural data from the T-Stick by learning body movements that excite particular gestures and use raw data; to 2) learn appropriate body motions to reproduce pre-defined gestures, now acquired by a complex relation between several raw sensor data. This raise the challenge to master the instrument that comprises "low entry and high ceiling" for performers.

6   Strategies for the Longevity of T-Stick

The longevity of new musical instruments matters to achieve a greater diversity of instruments. There have been several musical instruments developed and extinct throughout the history of Western Music, such as the *arpeggione* and the *Wagner tuba*, while some instruments survived, such as the clarinet, the saxophone, and the *Ondes Martenot*. What swayed the extinction and survival? We hypothesize the following four factors as influential factors for longevity of musical instruments:

- Repertoires;
- Uniqueness of instrument;
- Playing techniques;
- Notation for instrument;
- Learning opportunities.

The existence of repertoires creates a social and economic demand for the instrument and its players. The larger repertoires for the instrument there are, the more frequently some of those pieces in the repertoires for the instrument may be performed, so, the more opportunities for the performer to perform with the instrument. As a result, the repertoires bring out the economic sustainability of the instrument and the performers. For example, *Ondes Martenot* and its performer is frequently required for performances of *Turangalila Symphonie* (O. Messian, 1948). In order words, existing repertoires for a specific instrument answer the question: what do players master the instrument for?

The uniqueness of an instrument is another influential factor that sways the survival of a new instrument. If an instrument can be replaced with other more popular and accessible one, why should the piece be performed by that particular new instrument? While *Turangalila Symphonie* requires the large continuous glissandi that are specific for the unique instrumental feature of *Ondes Martenot*, *Arpeggione Sonata* (F. Schubert, 1824) is nowadays often performed by a cello or a viola in place of the *arpeggione*, the instrument the piece was originally composed for.

The development of playing techniques (e.g., *pizzicato*, *battuto*, and double stops in the violin performance practice) results in the wider range of musical expression that encourages to generate new repertoires for the instrument. These new repertoires, in turn, increase the demand for the advanced expertise of performers. As a result, the development of playing techniques creates a creative spiral in which new repertoires and advanced expertise call for each other. This spiral contributes to the sustainable demand for the instrument.

The notation system for an instrument enables to make the repertoires for the instrument more portable, repeatable and archivable. Portability enables the repertoires to prevail over the wider society. Repeatability contributes to make the repertoires sustainable over time. Archivability enables to store and to pile up new repertoires on top of the inherited works. The development of the notation system brings out these three possibilities, which can minimize the spatiotemporal limits inherent in the ephemerality of musical performance. This minimization benefits for geographically wider and chronologically longer demand for the instrument.

The opportunity for leaning an instrument is important for the longevity of the instrument. Numerous new musical instruments are developed at institutions and laboratories. While these places are open to researchers and students, people outside the institutes are only seldom able to get access. This problem of academic isolation may narrow accessibility to the instrument, preventing a development of new repertoires and a transmission of new playing techniques to posterior players.

To address the four factors (i.e., repertoires, uniqueness of instrument, playing techniques and learning opportunities), we organized the *workshop on T-Stick* and the *T-Stick music creation project* mentioned in Sect. 4.

6.1   Workshop on T-Stick

The workshop offered a learning opportunity for beginners. The workshop brought the T-Stick instrument outside the lab to make the instrument more accessible from non-academics with the aim of removing the technological difficulty for setup, introducing existing playing techniques and notation strategies.

The workshop took place at CIRMMT on November 16, 2019. This workshop invited two tutors, Joseph Malloch-the developer of T-Stick-and D. Andrew Stewart-the composer/performer who have extensively generated repertoires for T-Sticks. There were more than 30 participants mainly from academic institutes in Montreal area such as McGill university and University of Montreal. Only two non-affiliated participants were reported.

6.2   Music Creation Project

The T-Stick music creation project aims at creating new repertoires and fostering new skilled T-Stick performers, as well as developing new playing techniques for T-Stick throughout the compositional process. As discussed in Sect. 4, through an open call for composers, five composers are invited for creating new work for T-Sticks.

This project foresees to develop not only new repertoires, but also new playing techniques throughout the compositional process, and new skilled performers for having these new compositions performed by the composers themselves. Thus, this open call contributes to the dissemination of the instrument as well as the development of the performance practice for the instrument, which are both essential for the longevity of the instrument.

7   Conclusion and Future Work

We hypothesize that providing an expanded and tested gestural vocabulary will foment the use of the AMIs and DMIs in music compositions and allow performers to develop expertise in playing digital instruments. Moreover, the use of different instruments may lead to particular gestural taxonomies that are yet to be explored by composers and performers. New gestures emerging from that use can feedback this instrument vocabulary, and be embedded within the instrument.

Finally, we expect project outcomes in the form of both compositions and performances, as well as gather information about the creation and dissemination of gestural vocabulary for DMIs and AMIs.

As a particular digital instrument moves towards maturity, the gestural vocabulary slowly evolves through the work of composers, performers, and instrument designers. Creating tools that allow direct access to these high-level gestures will foster the adoption of the instrument and enable better communication between the areas of composition, performance, and music technology.

References

1. Cadoz, C.: Instrumental gesture and musical composition. In: ICMC 1988 - International Computer Music Conference, pp. 1–12. Cologne, Germany, February 1988. https://hal.archives-ouvertes.fr/hal-00491738, http://computermusic.org/
2. Cadoz, C., Wanderley, M.M.: Gesture-music. In: Wanderley, M.M., Battier, M. (eds.) Trends in Gestural Control of Music, pp. 71–94. Editions IRCAM - Centre Pompidou, Paris (2000)
3. Godøy, R.I.: Gestural-sonorous objects: embodied extensions of schaeffer's conceptual apparatus. Organ. Sound **11**(2), 149–157 (2006). https://doi.org/10.1017/S1355771806001439

4. Hsu, A., Kemper, S.: Kinesonic approaches to mapping movement and music with the remote electroacoustic kinesthetic sensing (RAKS) system. In: Proceedings of the 2nd International Workshop on Movement and Computing, pp. 45–47. MOCO 2015, Association for Computing Machinery, New York (2015). https://doi.org/10.1145/2790994.2791020, https://doi.org/10.1145/2790994.2791020
5. McPherson, A.P., Kim, Y.E.: The problem of the second performer: building a community around an augmented piano. Comput. Music J. **36**(4), 10–27 (2012)
6. Medeiros, C.B.: Advanced instrumentation and sensor fusion methods in input devices for musical expression. Ph.D. thesis, McGill University, Montreal, Canada (2015)
7. Meneses, E.A.L.: GuitarAMI: desenvolvimento, implementação e performance de um instrumento musical aumentado que explora possibilidades de modificação de características intrínsecas do violão. Master's thesis, Universidade Estadual de Campinas (UNICAMP), Campinas, Brazil (2016)
8. Meneses, E.A.L., Freire, S., Wanderley, M.M.: GuitarAMI and GuiaRT: two independent yet complementary augmented nylon guitar projects. In: Proceedings International Conference on New Interfaces for Musical Expression (NIME), pp. 222–227. Blacksburg, USA (2018)
9. Nieva, A., Wang, J., Malloch, J.W., Wanderley, M.M.: The T-Stick: maintaining a 12 year-old digital musical instrument. In: Proceedings International Conference on New Interfaces for Musical Expression (NIME), pp. 198–199. Blacksburg, USA (2018)
10. Schaeffer, P.: Traité des objets musicaux essai interdisciplines. Pierre Vives, University Of California Press, nouvelle édition edn. (1977). http://www.sudoc.fr/008265623
11. Smalley, D.: Spectromorphology: explaining sound-shapes. Organ. Sound **2**(2), 107–126 (1997). https://doi.org/10.1017/S1355771897009059
12. Stewart, D.A.: Catching air and the superman. Ph.D. thesis, McGill University (2010)
13. Wessel, D., Wright, M.: Problems and prospects for intimate musical control of computers. Comput. Music J. **26**(3), 11–22 (2002)

Visual Compiler: Towards Translating Digital UI Design Draft to Front-End Code Automatically

Jiemao Pan[1]([✉]), Xiang Chen[1], Ting Chen[1], Bin Tang[1], Junbiao Yang[1],
Yuhong Chen[1], Yixiong Lin[1], Chao Xiao[1], and Jian Meng[2]

[1] Deep Blue, Tencent, Shenzhen, China
{stevenpan,ralychen,chrisschen,bowentang,chironyang,yonechen,
yixionglin,alltasxiao}@tencent.com
[2] IM Web, Tencent, Shenzhen, China
erasermeng@tencent.com

Abstract. One assignment of a front-end engineer is to transform the User Interface (UI) design drafts to arrangements with program compatibilities. To furnish the customer requirement, engineers usually need to consider various factors for different terminal devices such as a wide range of screen sizes. Such process usually contains a lot of tedious work and much of them is repetitive which can be done by machine. In this paper, we propose Visual Compiler, a tool trying to bridge the gap between UI design draft and front-end code. We combine expert heuristics and techniques in computer vision to improve the readability and usability of generated code, making the generation process more intelligently. In practice, users just need to input the design drafts obtained from UI designers, then our method can produce clean and well-organized front-end code. Compared with existing approaches, Visual Compiler is able to reduce the size of output files by approximately 80% while maintaining the same appearance as in the original draft. We hope our tool can help UI designers and front-end developers collaborate more efficiently.

Keywords: User interface design · Front-end code · Computer vision · Artificial intelligence

1 Introduction

User Interface (UI) is one of the most important components in modern mobile applications. Good UIs can attract customers at first sight and may contribute a lot to application's final success. The development of specific UIs needs the cooperation between UI designers and front-end developers. To produce UI design drafts, UI designers need to create wireframes with pencils or computers. The wireframe mainly depicts the basic structure of a specific UI. After more details are added, a wireframe becomes a higher fidelity draft [9]. Excellent drafts require designers to have the knowledge of human interaction and a good sense of art.

These drafts are then passed to front-end developers and prepared to be converted to computer languages. Engineers have to firstly understand the spatial layout of a draft

© Springer Nature Switzerland AG 2020
S. Yamamoto and H. Mori (Eds.): HCII 2020, LNCS 12185, pp. 385–394, 2020.
https://doi.org/10.1007/978-3-030-50017-7_28

and the functionality of each element within it. After that, they are required to implement all details using a specific UI skeleton. In practice, such draft-to-code process can be tedious and cumbersome because there are a great number of factors to be considered. For instance, front-end developers need to carefully choose the type of every element to make them visually acceptable in a wide range of screen sizes. On the other hand, drafts from designers usually have poor hierarchy which makes them hard to understand. Thus, industrial engineers may have to optimize the detailed structures of these drafts to produce well-organized and compact frontend code. Moreover, good engineers also make preparation for the secondary development and function expanding, which put higher requests forward the produced code.

There are a lot of work focusing on releasing front-end developers from lengthy converting process. Most projects try to directly generate front-end code from sketch or screenshot. These work usually have two characters: (a) the underlying structure of an input image is simple and (b) we do not ask the generated code to behave like real programmers' work. In Fig. 1, we mainly show the results of UI2Layout, Sketch2Code and our Visual Compiler. UI2Layout [3] is the most recent work which turns UI design image to GUI skeleton code. From Fig. 1a, we can see that UI2Layout is able to produce simple layout code, however, it lacks the ability to focus on image details such as icons and figures. When we come to Sketch2Code (Fig. 1b), it is obvious that Sketch2Code cannot well handle the complex case whose output HTML is quite crude. Compared with UI2Layout and Sketch2Code, Visual Compiler seems to be more "intelligent". Our generated code can exactly reflect the hidden structure and logic of the original design draft. Also, the produced code is well-organized and reusable which provides an opportunity for secondary development.

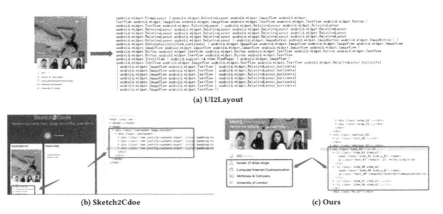

(a) UI2Layout

(b) Sketch2Cdoe

(c) Ours

Fig. 1. In this figure, we display the results of UI2Layout, Sketch2Code and our Visual Compiler. UI2Layout is mainly designed for generating spatial layout Android code while Sketch2Code aims to transform design sketch to HTML which is the same as ours. However, the front-end code from our Visual Compiler seems to be more well-organized, logical and reusable.

Our contributions can be summarized as follows:

1. We present Visual Compiler to bridge gap between UI designers and front-end engineers. Our approach is able to translation UI design draft to front-end code automatically.

2. Visual Compiler is built with various capabilities, such as unifying figure pieces and produce intuitive components combinations.
3. Compared with previous image (sketch & screenshot) to code techniques, Visual Compiler makes the produced code more understandable and suitable for secondary development. Experiments have verified this aspect.

In the rest this paper, we will first review the related work and then introduce different modules in details.

2   Related Work

In this section, we mainly review existing tools trying to bridge the gap between UI designers and front-end developers. Most of them focus on generating code from input images (sketches or screenshots) using vision techniques.

REMAUI [7] proposed the first technique to automatically reverse mobile application UIs. It uses classical computer vision and optical character recognition (OCR) techniques to identify UI elements, such as images and texts in drawings and screenshots. REMAUI is able to recognize item collections and produce readable layout Android code. However, REMAUI is not flexible and cannot well generalize to diverse interfaces because it heavily relies on the combination of classical vision techniques which usually have poor recognition rates. In comparison, Visual Compiler incorporate recent deep AI models into expertise to deal with image uniting and develop tree-based strategies to generate reasonable layouts.

The prevalence of deep learning [4, 5, 10] in computer vision and machine translation [1, 11] brings energy to this topic. Almost all tools treat the AI module as the main body part. Robinson [9] proposed to develop interface code from website wireframes using deep learning which outperforms classical vision approaches by a large margin. pix2code [2] showed that deep learning methods can be leveraged to train a model end-to-end to automatically generate code from a single screenshot for different platforms. pix2code is based on Convolutional and Recurrent Neural Networks and follows an end-to-end manner to produce HTML/CSS code. Recently, UI2Layout [3] presented a neural machine translator that combines recent advances in computer vision and machine translation for translating a UI design image into a GUI skeleton. The translator learns to extract visual features in UI images, encode these features' spatial layouts, and generate GUI skeletons in a unified neural network framework, without requiring manual rule development. The major problem of most deep learning based tools can be summarized as two points:

a) Poor readability and reusability of the generated code. The fact is that neural translators often produce strange code snippets because it does not understand the hidden structures.
b) Hard to debug and explain. This is because recent deep learning is a black-box tool and lacks the ability to explain itself.

The two points above make pure AI based methods hard to exist in industrial applications. However, our Visual Compiler carefully integrates deep learning into the image uniting module and aids AI with expert heuristics. Moreover, we add tree-based approaches to increase interpretability of the translation process.

3 Visual Compiler

We provide an overview of Visual Compiler in Fig. 2. Unlike previous approaches which produce front-end code directly from screenshots or sketches, our method is based on metadata extracted from UI drafts. We employ a parser module to interpret metadata and turn it to JSON tree. After that, we develop an image uniting module to assemble figure entities. Meanwhile, we utilize a cascaded template matching algorithm and a type of render technology to generate DSL. Finally, figures and code are combined to produce the wellorganized front-end code. In this section, we will talk about each module displayed in Fig. 2.

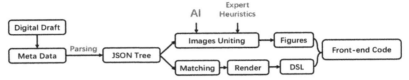

Fig. 2. An overview of Visual Compiler. "DSL" represents Domain Specific Language. We firstly extract metadata from UI drafts and then parse the data with JSON tree. We deal with figure entities using a uniting module and develop a cascaded matching method to produce DSL. Finally, we fuse processed figures and rendered DSL to produce final front-end code.

3.1 From Digital Draft to Json Tree

Metadata Extraction. Digital Drafts are usually accompanied by metadata. For example, it is easy to extract metadata from Sketch files by changing its suffix to .zip and unpackage the zip file. For Adobe Photoshop and XD files, we developed software plugins to extract their metadata. We provide an example in Fig. 3 to show what metadata usually looks like.

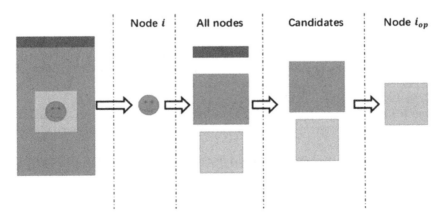

Fig. 3. The structure reconstruction process.

Node Tree Construction. After we obtain the metadata, we will use different parsers to interpret the data based on layer types. We transform different layers into four types of nodes: Group, Shape, Text and Image. Group node usually contains hierarchical organizations. The whole tree is named as node tree.

JSON Tree Construction. Although the node tree already has better organization compared with metadata, there is still room to optimize. In this part, we employ three strategies to generate the final JSON tree which can be described as follows:

Node Cleaning. We will traverse every node to see if it is visible. If not, we will remove it from the node tree. There are three cases where the node can be invisible:

a) the node is covered by other nodes
b) the node is fully transparent
c) the color of node is the same as that of its group

Structure Reconstruction. The goal of this strategy is to discover the reasonable hierarchical relationship among different nodes and reconstruct the node tree. The main idea can be summarized as: we apply Depth-First-Search (DFS) to the node tree. For each node i, we try to find its optimal parent node i_{op}. We denote the current parent node of i as ip. If iop is different from i_p, node i would be moved to i_{op}. We define iop as the parent node which has the best visual effect. To seek out i_{op}, we need to first find out all candidates nodes $i_{\{op1,op2,....,opn\}}$ which visually contain node i. The optimal parent node i_{op} is the candidate with minimal area. An example of discovering i_{op} is shown in Fig. 3.

Tree Compression. When UI designers make drafts, it is common that they may add some invisible layers which then become blank nodes in the node tree. To solve this problem, we recursively remove the blank nodes and thus compress the node tree. We offer an illustration in.

After applying these strategies, we will get a more compact version which is shown as JSON tree in Fig. 4.

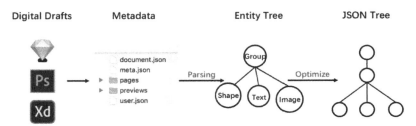

Fig. 4. From Digital Draft to Json Tree. We mainly studied how to deal with drafts from Sketch, Adobe Photoshop and Adobe XD.

3.2 Image Uniting

The drafts produced by UI designers usually contain scattered figures. If we do not process these small entities, they would slow down the response of cloud servers. In this section, we propose an Image Uniting module to deal with scattered figures. As shown in Fig. 5, the original draft has dozens of figure entities. However, our algorithm is able to merge small figures and produce two independent large figure entities. In practice, the proposed method can produce better figure organizations and reduce redundancy of generated code.

Fig. 5. An overview of the Image Uniting module.

In the Images Uniting module, our goal is to produce large figure entities from small ones. To do it, we have to first obtain all figure pieces that need to be united. Each figure piece can be paired with the other figures and we are supposed to have many figure pairs. Each pair will be passed to a scoring system to obtain its combination score. We use power and exponential functions to process the score so that figure entities have high scores and disparate figures achieve low numbers. It is worth noting the scoring system jointly utilizes artificial intelligence (AI) and expert heuristics to determine the combination score. Each evaluation method has independent weight which will be multiplied by its score. The weighted sum of AI and expert heuristics is taken as the final score to tell whether two figure entities should be united or not. We will discuss how AI and expert heuristics work in the rest of this section.

Artificial Intelligence (AI). In this part, we make use of recent deep learning techniques to determine whether small figure pieces can be united as a whole or not. To be specific, we train a deep model to recognize various types of icons. The model thus learns what an integrated figure looks like so that when we apply it to scattered figure entities, it can produce a probability score to tell if entities should be merged.

Dataset. We collected approximately 2,000 UI interfaces and built a dataset containing 14 classes. The class names are as follows: icon, icon description, image, image description, button, tab, banner, dialog, tips, list, scroll, feeds, text and signal Bar. For each class, there are about 2,000 to 4,000 label boxes. All labels are manually labeled and each box is checked by three persons on average.

Icon Detection. We use ResNet-101 [4] as the backbone model which has 101 layers with residual connections. For the detection method, we build Faster R-CNN [8] on top of ResNet. Faster R-CNN is one of the most popular methods in computer vision. To further improve the detection accuracy, we also add Feature Pyramid Network [6] to Faster R-CNN because most icons are small and feature pyramid helps enhance the ability to capture small objects.

Expert Heuristics. To measure the similarity of figure pairs, we manually propose seven rules to produce similarity scores. We report these rules in Table 1. We mainly evaluate the pair similarity from three aspects: area&shape, hierarchical relationship and color. For area&Shape, we compute the interaction of union (IoU) of a figure pair. We also compare their areas and positions. As for hierarchical relationship, we focus on if two figure entities belongs to the same parent node. If not, we also measure their hierarchy distance because small distance usually means two entities are homogenous. Also, color similarity is necessary to report similarity scores. In this aspect, we calculate the similarity of color histograms and numbers of color types. It is worth noting that each rule has its own weight which will be added to produce the score of expert heuristics.

Table 1. Heuristic rules. These rules are used to measure the similarity of two adjacent figure entities.

Area & Shape	Hierarchical relation	Color
1. Interaction of union	1. Whether have the same parent node	1. Color Similarity
2. Area similarity	2. Hierarchy distance	2. Color complexity similarity

In our scoring systems, the weight of AI is 0.7 while expert heuristics takes the rest 30%. Our experience is that AI prefers to look at figure entities from the big picture and heuristic rules pay more attention to the details. In practice, they complement each other and jointly predict the combination score.

3.3 Cascaded Model Matching

Translating design draft to interface code has been a hot issue in front-end field. However, most tools on the market can only generate crude code which means that their productions are usually difficult to understand and hard to do further development. For example, these methods usually do not consider code redundancy. Also, they cannot generate code with logic. A typical case can be described as that they cannot recognize the loop structures appeared in different design drafts.

There are currently two solutions to tackle the translation problem: (a) recognize code for specific components and (b) generate code for every node separately. It is obvious that the first strategy is not flexible enough because it cannot generalize to new components. As for the second method, it would increase the redundancy of code snippets and may make them look stupid. In this paper, we propose to incorporate the structure into the code generation process. To be specific, we come up with a cascaded template matching strategy to eliminate disadvantages of existing solutions.

We interpret each component as a visual model. In modern interfaces, there are various types of components with different complexity. Thus, we further divide the visual model into element model and component model. For convenience, we reorganize the node types in JSON tree and propose four types of node: text, icon, image and shape. Each variation of element model is a simple combination of different node types which usually takes only one line in the draft. We give some examples of element models in Table 2. The component model aims to reflect the relative spatial correlation of different element models. In practice, a component model can be regarded as a composite of various element models which usually takes more than one line.

Table 2. We show some members of element models. Note that "icon-text" means icon is at the left of text. "shape(text)" means shape contains the text. "$\frac{shape}{text}$" tells text is at the top of shape. shape

One element	Two elements	Three elements
text	icon-text	shape(text)-text
icon	text-icon	text-shape(text)
image	shape (text)	image(text)-text
shape	$\frac{shape}{text}$	text-image(text)
		icon(text)-text
		text-icon(text)
		text-shape-text

The core idea of cascaded matching strategy can be described as iteratively scoring all node combinations based on element and component models. To reduce the computing effort, we develop two strategies (which makes it a cascading process):

a) Divide the UI interface space into regions and perform the matching operation within each region.
b) During the matching process, we follow a "coarse to fine" manner. We first match the element models, after which we would match the component ones.

The reason why we take the first strategy is that nodes far away often cannot be organized as a visual model. Also, the second strategy helps us to exclude some useless matchings and focus on the reasonable ones.

After we finish matching the component models, it is necessary to pick out the most suitable combination. To achieve this goal, we manually design sixteen empirical rules to score possible element and component models. Some of them are based on alignment and specific interval. For example, to be the best element or component model, the nodes of a candidate model should be aligned and not far from each other.

3.4 Render

After getting different element and component models using the matching module, we can easily generate a reasonable layout for each model. However, how to intelligent combine different layout code thus becomes a problem. In this part, we introduce our technique to generate code snippets for different models with appropriate spatial layout.

Similar to the construction process of JSON tree, we make use of a node tree to generate reasonable layout code. Note that before we render visual models, we need to rasterize the JSON tree to produce node patches.

In Fig. 6, we give an example to show how render works. The real process is simple and intuitive. Our render tries to extract all nodes and build a layout tree based on their relative and inner (for element and component models) spatial positions. The generated tree brings code logic and helps make them well-organized.

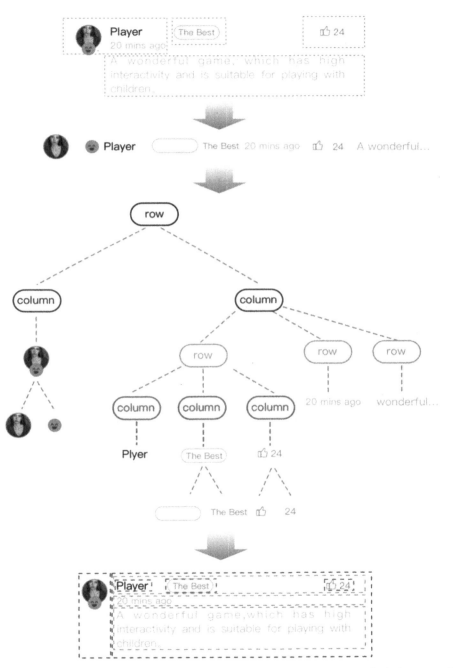

Fig. 6. An example of the rendering process. Gray dash boxes represent matched element and component models.

References

1. Bahdanau, D., Cho, K., Bengio, Y.: Neural machine translation by jointly learning to align and translate. arXiv preprint arXiv:1409.0473 (2014)
2. Beltramelli, T.: pix2code: generating code from a graphical user interface screenshot. In: Proceedings of the ACM SIGCHI Symposium on Engineering Interactive Computing Systems, p. 3. ACM (2018)
3. Chen, C., Su, T., Meng, G., Xing, Z., Liu, Y.: From UI design image to GUI skeleton: a neural machine translator to bootstrap mobile GUI implementation. In: Proceedings of the 40th International Conference on Software Engineering, pp. 665–676. ACM (2018)
4. He, K., Zhang,, X., Ren, S., Sun, J.: Deep residual learning for image recognition. In: Proceedings of the IEEE Conference on Computer Vision and Pattern Recognition, pp. 770–778 (2016)
5. Krizhevsky, A., Sutskever, I., Hinton, G.E.: Imagenet classification with deep convolutional neural networks. In: Advances in Neural Information Processing Systems, pp. 1097–1105 (2012)
6. Lin, T.-Y., Dollár, P., Girshick, R., He, K., Hariharan, B., Belongie, S.: Feature pyramid networks for object detection. In: Proceedings of the IEEE Conference on Computer Vision and Pattern Recognition, pp. 2117–2125 (2017)
7. Nguyen, T.A., Csallner, C.: Reverse engineering mobile application user interfaces with REMAUI. In: 2015 30th IEEE/ACM International Conference on Automated Software Engineering (ASE), pp. 248–259. IEEE (2015)
8. Ren, S., He., K., Girshick, R., Sun, J.: Faster R-CNN: towards real-time object detection with region proposal networks. In: Advances in Neural Information Processing Systems, pp. 91–99 (2015)
9. Robinson, A.: Sketch2Code: generating a website from a paper mockup. arXiv preprint arXiv: 1905.13750 (2019)
10. Simonyan, K., Zisserman, A.: Very deep convolutional networks for large-scale image recognition. arXiv preprint arXiv:1409.1556 (2014)
11. Sutskever, I., Vinyals, O., Le, Q.V.: Sequence to sequence learning with neural networks. In: Advances in Neural Information Processing Systems, pp. 3104–3112 (2014)

Research on Design of Tai-Chong and Yong-Quan Acupoints Physiotherapy Apparatus Based on Traditional Chinese Medicine Theory

Huabin Wang$^{(\boxtimes)}$, Baoping Xu, and Yu-Chi Lee

South China University of Technology, Guangzhou, China
{Hbwang,liyuqi}@scut.edu.cn, 575646780@qq.com

Abstract. This research is to inherit and carry forward China's extensive and profound traditional Chinese medicine (TCM) theory, combining TCM massage with novel technology and design methods to develop a newly foot acupoint physiotherapy instrument to enhance the user experience. The first step is to summarize the principles and functions of Tai-chong acupoint and Yong-quan massage through in-depth literature research. The second step is to use the existing foot scanning image and TCM theory to locate the Tai-chong and Yong-quan acupoints. The third step is to establish a design and application model of the massage therapy instrument by applying the theory of microelectronics technology, Kano model, anthropometric data, and design methodology. Finally, the foot microelectronics Tai-chong and Yong-quan acupoints physiotherapy device was used for verification and evaluation. Conceptual fuzzy was used in the design evaluation. Reasonable calculations were made through the weight matrix, fuzzy relationship matrix and decision matrix to form a more scientific evaluation result. The results showed that the design and application model of the Tai-chong and Yong-quan acupoints massage physiotherapy apparatus is effective way for physiotherapy. The study provided a certain reference value for the application of TCM massage theory in product design.

Keywords: Industrial design · Traditional chinese medicine theory · KANO model · User experience · Massage · Tai-chong acupoint · Yong-quan acupoint

1 Introduction

For a long time, the combination between the medical mechanism of traditional Chinese medicine (TCM) massage and modern science and technology has been widely studied. For instance, Gao et al. [1] used sensor information fusion technology, human-computer interaction technology, and three-dimensional simulation to implement TCM massage with robots as a carrier. They developed a robotic system, which consists of a multifunctional massage mechanical arm integrating multiple massage techniques, a vision system for judging the acupoint position, and a control and monitoring system for real-time monitoring. It realized the intelligentization of multiple massage techniques as well

© Springer Nature Switzerland AG 2020
S. Yamamoto and H. Mori (Eds.): HCII 2020, LNCS 12185, pp. 395–406, 2020.
https://doi.org/10.1007/978-3-030-50017-7_29

as the timely monitoring and feedback of user data. Firouzeh and Bozena [2] from Simon Fraser University of Canada designed a smart massage patch model based on the hot stone massage mechanism to transfer heat to the body. Especially for tight muscles or injured bodies, it could relieve body pain or relax the body. Based on reflexology and electro-acupuncture of foot massage, Felix and Gerald [3] of Applied Science University in Austria developed an electronic foot-reflex therapy stimulation device and stimulated the acupoints of the foot via microcurrent. In this way, it achieved massage effect, thereby enhancing the physical health of the user. Lu [4] of Dalian University of Technology designed and implemented a multifunctional electric pulse physiotherapy instrument, and proposed the method of using a switching power supply step-down circuit to improve power efficiency and ensure output power. He also designed a user-defined mode to meet the special needs of different users by adjusting the efficiency of the switching power supply and forming a therapeutic waveform. The waveform showed a significant TCM massage effect. As above mentioned, in most of the existing studies, TCM massage was mainly achieved with heat conduction technology, automated machinery, electric pulse technology, etc. However, little attention has been paid to the application of TCM massage into product design. Herein, microelectronic technology was used to realize the function of TCM massage. In combination with TCM massage theory, foot scanning data, and design methodology, we built a design model and then applied it to the design project to improve the user's health and use experience.

2   TCM Foot Massage Theory

Foot massage as an external treatment of TCM belongs to the category of traditional TCM massage and modern Chinese medicine. The feet to a human being is just like the roots to a tree; roots dry up before a tree gets withered, and the feet exhaust before a human being gets old. Foot massage means to compress, rub, shove and knead in the acupoint reflection area of the foot to achieve yin-yang balance, dredge the meridian, promote blood circulation to remove blood stasis, and regulate viscera. It is aimed to promote the transition from the sub-healthy state to healthy state. The theory of foot massage is still under discussion. The mainstream theories are summarized below: ① Theory of meridians: Chinese medicine believes that the foot connects viscera through the meridian; while the meridian passing through viscera and connecting limbs serves as the channel for blood circulation. Foot massage can act on the meridians and acupoints to dredge the meridians, balance the internal organs, improve the healthy level, and enhance immunity. ② Theory of nerve reflex: Each organ of the human body has a corresponding reflexion area on the foot, and it realizes regulation mainly by neuromodulation. When the massage is performed in a reflexion area of the foot, the effect is conveyed to the organ via nerve reflexion, thereby achieving the regulation of the corresponding body part. ③ Qi and blood circle theory: The foot is farthest from the heart and subject to the slowest blood flow. Metabolites and unused minerals in the blood are easily deposited on the foot. When the human body or organs are in a bad state, the circulation of Qi and blood on the foot at one tip is poor, making it easier to deposit waste. Foot massage can help expel these deposits, thus promoting qi-blood circulation and bringing the deposits back to the organs for elimination. ④ Holographic biomedicine: This theory holds that each body is composed of a number of holographic embryos. The feet are a holographic embryo, where each area has similar biological characteristics to those of corresponding organs. Massaging the reflexion areas on the feet corresponding to the organs can regulate and improve the functions of organs, thus contributing to the mitigated diseases and enhanced health [5].

3 Positioning and Function of Tai-Chong and Yong-Quan Acupoints

3.1 Tai-Chong Acupoint

Taichong acupoint was first proposed in "Lingshu Jing Bensu". It is the original point of the foot Jueyin and liver meridian, and the place where the original Qi of the liver passes and stays. The body surface of Taichong acupoint is located in the depression before the 1st and 2nd metatarsal joints on the dorsal side of the foot, as shown in Fig. 1. Acupuncture and massage on Taichong acupoint can achieve the functions of clearing channels, promoting circulation of qi and blood, nourishing blood, softening the liver, and nourishing liver and kidney. It has a good therapeutic effect on the diseases of limb meridians, qi and blood fluid, the heart system, the kidney system, gynecology and face [6]. For the mitigation of diseases, Tai-chong acupoint is usually found according to the meridians. Acupoint matching treatment not only expands its use range, but also displays the synergistic effect [7].

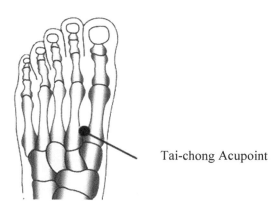

Fig. 1. Location map of Tai-chong acupoint

3.2 Yong-Quan Acupoint

Yongquan acupoint was derived from "Lingshu Bensu": "Yong-quan acupoint is the origin of kidney and located at the heart of feet, just like the supporting wood under a well." Yong-quan acupoint, also known as "Juexin", "Dichong" or "Diqu", is one of the commonly used acupoints in foot-Shaoyin kidney meridian. It is located at the bottom of the foot, specifically, the depression in the front of the foot when the foot is stomped, the point of intersection between the first 1/3 and the second 2/3 of the connection line between the head end of the 2nd and 3rd plantar toe seam and the heel of the foot, as shown in Fig. 2 [8]. Yong-quan acupoint is the first acupoint of the kidney meridian. As we know, the kidney not only is the innate foundation and the root of life, but is closely related to the internal organs. Therefore, it can be used to adjust qi in the kidney meridian and enhance the health throughout the whole body [9]. In medicine, it can not only mitigate acute conditions but also benefit the treatment of chronic diseases. Massaging Yong-quan acupoint is found to strengthen the kidney, unblock the yin meridian and the kidney meridian and also regulate Qi and blood of the kidney, thereby improving various functions of the kidney. Existing research has shown that TCM Yong-quan acupoint massage has a very obvious effect in improvement of appetite and sleep, as well as the prevention and treatment of sub-health [10].

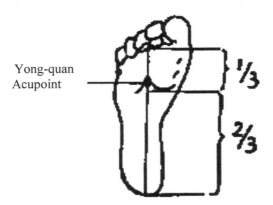

Fig. 2. Location map of Yong-quan acupoint

4   The Application Model of the Massage Therapy Instrument on Tai-Chong and Yong-Quan Acupoints

The purpose of the design is not to develop products, but to meet people's needs [11]. Thus, the application model was built based on the three levels of user needs, which were obtained from the analysis by the Kano model. Then, the TCM acupoint theory, foot scanning image, novel technology, design methodologies and other tools were combined to solve existing demand problems. Finally, the corresponding functions were determined to meet three levels of needs. The application model of the massage physiotherapy instrument on Tai-chong and Yong-quan acupoints is depicted in the figure below (Fig. 3).

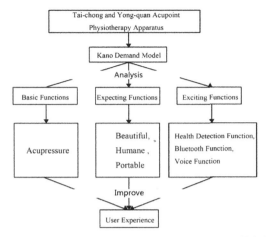

Fig. 3. The application model of the massage therapy instrument on Tai-chong and Yong-quan acupoints

4.1 User Analysis

Foot massage is found to be significantly effective in improving human health [12]. Therefore, sub-healthy people are the main target users of the foot massage physiotherapy instrument. Since both Tai-chong and Yong-quan acupoints are located on the feet, this study specifically focused on the young, middle-aged and elderly people in the sub-health state and having no change in foot size.

4.2 Kano Model-Based Demand Analysis of Massage Therapy Instrument on Tai-Chong and Yong-Quan Acupoints

The Kano model was officially proposed by Noriaki Kano, a professor of Tokyo Institute of Technology, at the 12th Japan Quality Management Conference in 1982. This model is a useful tool for categorizing and prioritizing user needs, which analyzes the impact of user needs on user satisfaction and reflects the non-linear relationship between the extent to which user needs are met and user satisfaction [13]. The Kano model divides user needs into three levels: basic needs, expectation needs, and excitement needs. Basic needs refer to the needs that the product function must meet. If this level of needs is satisfied, user satisfaction is guaranteed; otherwise, the user satisfaction will decrease. Expectation needs means that the user expects the product to have certain function; the extent to which the user's demand is meet has a linear relationship with the level of user satisfaction. The more satisfied this level of needs is, the higher the user satisfaction is, and vice versa. Excitement needs refer to an attribute or function that is unexpected by users. When this level of needs is met, it will surprise users; if not, user satisfaction will not decrease at any time.

According to literature review, expert interviews and questionnaire surveys, the demand analysis of the massage therapy instrument on Tai-chong and Yong-quan acupoints is shown in Table 1.

Table 1. Demand analysis of Massage Therapy Instrument on Tai-chong and Yong-quan Acupoints

Demand category	Specific requirement
Basic needs	Improve physical health
Expected needs	Beautiful, humanization, portable
Excited needs	Health Detection, intelligent control

4.3   Function Definition

According to the above three levels of needs, three levels of functions can be defined correspondingly: basic functions, expectation functions, and excitement functions.

1.   Basic Functions

(1) Massage positioning

The massage therapy instrument on Tai-chong and Yong-quan acupoints is a product related to the human foot. Therefore, it is necessary to conduct research on the feet of mature youth, middle-aged and older users in a sub-health state. Middle-aged men and women in China belong to mature user groups, so the foot scanning data of this group are applied to this product design research. Figure 4 and Table 2 show the foot size and characteristics of Chinese middle-aged men and women, which are as the reference data. Then, the TCM theory was used to locate Tai-chong and Yong-quan acupoints, and find out the approximate size range of acupoints. According to the above theory and foot scanning data, the location of Tai-chong acupoint can be acquired from 95% of male data and 5% of female data, so as to meet the needs of most people. According to the above data and principle, the location of Yong-quan acupoint is 51.33 mm–56.66 mm from the line connecting the 2nd and 3rd toe seam heads with the heel. Thus, the Yong-quan acupoint massage head should cover a 2.7 mm radius circle centered on the 54.0 mm from the line connecting the 2nd and 3rd toe seam heads with the heel. Similarly, the location of Yong-quan acupoint is 50.00 mm–60.00 mm from the 1st and 2nd metatarsal joints along the depression at an inclination of 10°–15°. Therefore, the Yong-quan acupoint massage head should cover the three-dimensional space area of a sphere with a radius of 2.7 mm from the 55.0 mm from the 1st and 2nd metatarsal joints along the depression with a slope of 12.5°.

(2) Massage Techniques

TMC massage techniques refer to specific standardized technical movements of hands or other parts of the limbs, which rub on specific acupoints to produce a benign stimulus and hence prevent or mitigate diseases. There are many types of massage techniques, which can be divided by kinematic characteristics to rolling, vibrating, rubbing, friction, hitting, pinching, and pressing. Various stimulation modes can be set on kneading, tapping, acupuncture, and massage [14]. At present, the technical methods applying these stimuli include the physical stimulation of the mechanical arm and the electronic stimulation

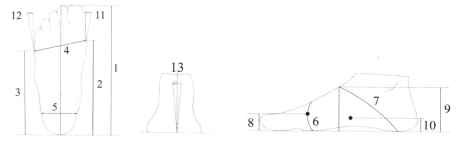

Fig. 4. 13 Foot features and schematics

Table 2. 13 Foot characteristic parameters

		Middle-aged Man				Middle-aged Women			
		5% lie	95% lie	Average ± Standard Deviation (A)	Standardized Parameters (B)	5% lie	95% lie	Average ± Standard Deviation (A)	Standardized Parameters (B)
1	Foot Length	236.9	273.0	255.3 ± 11.2	100%	218.0	248.1	232.9 ± 9.3	100%
2	Medial Instep Length	171.7	200.1	185.9 ± 8.8	72.8%	156.9	182.3	169.6 ± 7.9	72.8%
3	Lateral Instep	153.4	181.2	166.7 ± 8.5	65.3%	138.9	164.1	151.4 ± 7.4	65%
4	Foot Width	95.3	112.1	103.9 ± 5.1	40.7%	87.2	103.6	94.7 ± 4.7	40.6%
5	Heel Width	61.6	73.4	67.9 ± 3.7	26.6%	55.8	68.0	61.9 ± 3.7	26.6%
6	Foot CircumFerence	230.9	268.0	250.5 ± 14.5	98.2%	210.9	244.1	226.7 ± 10.3	97.3%
7	Instep CircumFerence	229.2	267.8	249.3 ± 14.6	97.7%	206.5	240.3	221.9 ± 10.1	95.3%
8	1st Metatarsal Bone Height	36.0	47.1	41.0 ± 4.3	16.1%	33.0	42.1	36.6 ± 3.0	15.7%
9	Dorsal Height	53.9	69.4	61.8 ± 5.3	24.2%	48.9	61.0	54.2 ± 3.7	23.2%
10	Scaphoid	31.7	52.2	41.8 ± 6.5	16.3%	26.6	48.0	36.1 ± 6.0	15.5%
11	Big Toe Angle	−6.7	10.7	1.9 ± 5.6	–	−4.2	15.0	4.7 ± 5.6	–
12	5th Toe Angle	−2.0	12.1	5.7 ± 4.4	–	−4.1	11.1	3.9 ± 4.8	–
13	Heel Angle	−3.4	6.2	1.6 ± 2.9	–	−3.2	6.5	1.7 ± 2.9	–

A: Foot size sex difference effect, B: Gender differences in standardized parameters, *: $p < 0.05$, *: $p < 0.01$, ***: $p < 0.001$

of the microelectronic electrical pulse. The mechanical arm simulates the human hand to perform a specific standard massage technique. The electric pulse of microelectronic technology simulates the stimulation of massage through different current waveforms.

2. Expectation Functions

(1) Portable and Beautiful

The product designed must be portable. A small-size product is easy to carry. Since the designed instrument is aimed at the two acupoints of Tai-chong and Yong-quan, the required functional parts should meet the miniaturization to make it convenient for users to take. Good products need not only internal and practical functions, but also external aesthetics. Product appearance reflects practical functions and emotional functions. The instrument designed in this study is a medical care product, and users have soft, safety, peace and other emotional needs. Therefore, the shape of the instrument should be round and soft in a curved way.

(2) Humanization

The humanization of the Tai-chong and Yong-quan acupoint acupressure massage therapy instrument is mainly reflected in the use of the product, materials, operation interface and other aspects. In terms of use, since the Tai-chong and Yong-quan acupoint are located on the upper and lower sides of the foot, respectively, it is possible to consider the use of the foot toe clamp. The clamping use should meet the comfort of the user. The shape of the clamping part and the contact part of the foot should be closely fitted, and the material should be soft. In terms of materials, different materials can give users different visual and tactile sensations. Foot acupressure massage therapy device is a medical care product that needs to be used in contact with the human foot. Therefore, the material in contact with the human body should be selected to be soft and not harmful to the skin. Soft products are easy to make people feel comfortable, and soft materials can also cushion the pressure of interaction forces when users use the products. Materials that are harmless to the skin would guarantee the health and safety of users. The operation interface should be consistent with the user's basic usage habits, and keep it simple. For example, set the commonly used function key requirements in an obvious location to facilitate the user's use.

3. Excitement Functions

Excitement functions involve health detection, Bluetooth technology, and voice functions. Sub-healthy people are at the tipping point of health and disease, physically and mentally unhealthy. For example, to increase the humanization of the product by, it is advisable to provide the functions of health detection and voice reminders, or to connect the instrument to the user's mobile phone terminal via Bluetooth technology. This connection will allow to record and analyze the health status and give corresponding suggestions. It eventually helps the user to maintain a positive mental state from the aspects of vision and hearing.

5 Product Design of the Foot Microelectronics Physiotherapy Instrument on Tai-Chong and Yong-Quan Acupoints

5.1 Foot Microelectronics Physiotherapy Instrument on Tai-Chong and Yong-Quan Acupoints

The acupoint massagers in the market can be mainly divided into non-energy-consuming and energy-consuming types, which rely on physical power and electric power respectively. In the energy consumption category, most of the foot massagers are household multi-acupoints massagers, which can perform deep-level massage, but are not portable. Non-energy-consuming foot massage devices require users to have a certain knowledge of TCM acupoints; in addition, the use mode is not modern enough. As a result, foot massage devices cannot achieve good results in most cases. It is urgent to develop a small massage product that can accurately act on fixed acupoints and realize the professionalization and convenient use of acupoint massage.

In the specific design, the foot microelectronics physiotherapy instrument on Tai-chong and Yong-quan acupoints consists of 1) the pulse generator end body, 2) the massager connector with a toe grip in the middle, 3) the Tai-chong acupoint massage head, and 4) the Yongquan acupoint massage head, as shown in Fig. 5. According to the above analysis, the fixed position of the massage head is determined to realize the massage positioning, and different radio waves of the microelectronic technology are used to implement the massage technique. In terms of aesthetics, the instrument mainly has a simple and round shape with the off-white as the main color, making users feel comfortable visually. In terms of portability and humanization, the overall instrument is small and the massager connector with a toe grip in the middle is easy to take. In addition, the left and right sides of the middle toe grip are inwardly curved and concave, in order to maintain the comfort of the clamping between the first toe and the second toe. Also, the instrument is a plastic shell outside and a circuit inside which connects the massage heads of Tai-chong and Yong-quan acupoints. A model of the designed instrument is given in Fig. 6.

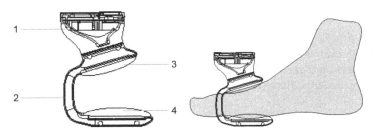

Fig. 5. Product schematic

Fig. 6. Product physical map

5.2 Evaluation of the Designed Instrument

1. **Fuzzy Evaluation Model**

   (1) Determine the evaluation indicator set and the weight matrix. Evaluation indicator set U={$u_1, u_2,..., u_n$}. Each indicator data is kept as parallel as possible, so that there is no crossover factor. A weighting coefficient is assigned to each indicator to obtain a weight matrix A = [$a_1, a_2,..., a_n$], which satisfies $\sum_{i=1}^{n} a_i = 1$. The level of the user's recognition and satisfaction with the indicators are expressed by fuzzy concepts such as excellent, good, general, and poor. The evaluation indicators are evaluated to obtain the evaluation set V = {$v_1, v_2,..., v_m$}. In the following evaluation schemes, the satisfaction level of V = (100, 75, 50, 0) is extracted.

   (2) Determine the fuzzy relation matrix. The evaluation index u_i($i = 1, 2,..., n$) is evaluated accordingly, and the evaluation value r_{ij} ($j = 1, 2,..., m$) in the j-th semantic of the i-th index is obtained to satisfy $\sum_{j=1}^{m} r_{ij} = 1$. Similarly, the fuzzy concepts such as excellent, good, average, and poor are used as the set of evaluation vocabulary j to evaluate each evaluation index u_i. Then, the proportion of the number of people in the comment set in each indicator is got to generate the fuzzy relationship matrix:

$$R = \begin{bmatrix} r_{11} & r_{12} & \cdots & r_{1m} \\ r_{21} & r_{22} & \cdots & r_{2m} \\ \cdots & \cdots & \cdots & \cdots \\ r_{n1} & r_{n2} & \cdots & r_{nm} \end{bmatrix}$$

Calculate the decision matrix. Based on the fuzzy relation matrix and the weight matrix, the decision matrix is calculated as:

$$B = AR = \begin{bmatrix} a_1 & a_2 & \cdots & a_n \end{bmatrix} \begin{bmatrix} r_{11} & r_{12} & \cdots & r_{1m} \\ r_{21} & r_{22} & \cdots & r_{2m} \\ \cdots & \cdots & \cdots & \cdots \\ r_{n1} & r_{n2} & \cdots & r_{nm} \end{bmatrix} = \begin{bmatrix} b_1 & b_2 & \cdots & b_n \end{bmatrix}$$

where $bj = \sum_{i=1}^{n} a_i a_{ij}$. Each evaluation result denotes the membership degree of each comment set.

2. Design Evaluation

A total of 50 senior product designers were invited to evaluate the product and score the specific functions according to the three functional categories above. From literature review and the above discussion, it can be concluded that the influence weight of the three functional categories on user experience is: A = [0.3, 0.5, 0.2] for basic, expectation and excitement functions respectively. In terms of the excitement function, the influence weight of health detection, Bluetooth function and Voice function is 0.6, 0.2 and 0.2, respectively. The user experience score of each category function is equal to the value of B • VT, as shown in Table 3.

Table 3. Evaluation score of the designed instrument

	Functional analysis	Evaluation score
Basic functions	Acupressure	94.00
Expecting functions	Beautiful, humanization, portable	85.10
Exciting functions	Health detection function, bluetooth function, voice function	0.00
User experience	Basic functions, expecting functions, exciting functions	70.70

From the above table, the score of basic function of the instrument developed in this study is 94.00, indicating an excellent satisfaction of basic needs. The score of expectation function is 85.10, suggesting a good satisfaction of expectation needs. The score of excitement function is 0.00, presenting a poor satisfaction of excitement needs. User experience is scored to be 70.70 points, in an average level. In terms of the excitement function, health detection, voice function and Bluetooth technology have not been applied in practice. Thus, the performance of the excitement function requires a further study.

6 Conclusion

Based on the Kano demand model, the three functions of the foot microelectronics therapy instrument on Tai-chong and Yong-quan acupoints were defined. The design model was established in a combination with the modeling design theory, man-machine engineering, color design theory, acupoint theory of TCM and foot scanning data. Finally, through the evaluation of the designed instrument, it is concluded that this acupoint physiotherapy device can improve the user experience from three functional levels and effectively perform deep-level massage on the acupoints, thereby enhancing the health of users. The evaluation results prove the validity of this model. Still, this study is subject to some limitation. The future study should examine the accuracy of the acupoint location. This paper not only expands the application of the Kano demand model, but also provides new insights into the innovative design of acupoint physiotherapy products.

References

1. Gao, H., Lu, S., Tao, W., Liu, C., Kang, B., Ji, Y., et al.: Research and development of traditional chinese medicine massage robots. Robots 05, 43–52 (2011). (in Chinese)
2. Himmelstoss, F.A., Haas, G.A., Strummer, M.F., Votzi, H.L.: Electro foot-reflexology stimulator. In: 2007 International Symposium on Signals, Circuits and Systems. IEEE 2007, vol. 8, pp. 962–967 (2007)
3. Kume, M., Morita, Y., Yamauchi, Y., Aoki, H.: Development of a mechanotherapy unit for examining the possibility of an intelligent massage robot. In: IEEE/RSJ International Conference on Intelligent Robots & Systems, IEEE (1996)
4. Lu, C.: Design and Implementation of Multifunctional Electric Pulse Physiotherapy Apparatus. (Doctoral dissertation, Dalian University of Technology) (2011). (in Chinese)
5. Lu, Y., Wang, D., Lu, G.: Analysis of the principles and functions of traditional chinese medicine foot massage (in Chinese). Chinese and Foreign Medicine 27(20), 94 (2008)
6. Song, H., Wang, W.: Exploring the acupoints and clinical application of acupuncture points in Dacheng of Acupuncture and Moxibustion (in Chinese). Sichuan Traditional Chin. Med. 08, 8–10 (2015)
7. Gao, L., Ren, Y., Guo, T., Li, D., Tang, Y., Liang, F.: Literature research on the rules of Taichong and its common compatibility. Shizhen Traditional Chin. Med. Traditional Chin. Med. 06, 257–258 (2013). (in Chinese)
8. Huang, L.: World Health Organization Standard Acupuncture Meridian Location (Western Pacific), pp. 131–132. People's Medical Publishing House, Beijing (2010). (in Chinese)
9. Wang, C., Zhang, Q.: Exploration on the indication function and mechanism of Yongquan Point). Western Chin. Med. 7, 81–82 (2007). (in Chinese)
10. Sun, Y.: Research on the effect of "Yongquan massage method" on the prevention and treatment of sub-health under the theory of traditional Chinese medicine. China Health Ind. 35, 176 (2012). (in Chinese)
11. Li, Y.: Introduction to Art Design, pp. 87–93. Hubei Fine Arts Publishing House, Hubei (2009). (in Chinese)
12. Wei, Y., Dian, Y.: Mechanism of foot massage on human sub-health status. Henan Traditional Chin. Med. 23(4), 7 (2003). (in Chinese)
13. Tang, Z., Long, Y.: Research on personalized demand acquisition method based on kano model (in Chinese). Soft Sci. 02, 131–135 (2012). (in Chinese)
14. Wang, G.: Massage Techniques, pp. 58–67. China Traditional Chinese Medicine Press, Beijing (2003)

Developing an AR Remote Collaboration System with Semantic Virtual Labels and a 3D Pointer

Tzu-Yang Wang[1]([✉]) [iD], Yuji Sato[1], Mai Otsuki[2] [iD], Hideaki Kuzuoka[1,3] [iD], and Yusuke Suzuki[4]

[1] University of Tsukuba, Tsukuba, Japan
st900278@gmail.com
[2] National Institute of Advanced Industrial Science and Technology, Tokyo, Japan
[3] The University of Tokyo, Tokyo, Japan
[4] Oki Electric Industry Co., Ltd., Tokyo, Japan

Abstract. Referential communication is common in physical remote collaboration. To successfully transfer instructions, remote instructors have to refer objects in the local worker's environment. However, it is known that nonverbal behaviors are hard to be transferred correctly through modern remote collaboration systems. We focused on enhancing verbal communication and developed an AR-based remote collaboration system. Past research has shown that annotation and labels can support communication in collaboration. Thus, we proposed combining the two functions to achieve a smooth remote collaboration. Concerning the labeling function, we improved Chang et al's work [1] and introduced semantic virtual labels that were attached to the objects in local workers' environment. Besides, concerning the annotation function, we introduced a 3D pointer and the instructor can easily draw workers' attention by moving the 3D pointer. In addition, the 3D pointer can highlight the virtual labels to improve the mutual understanding between the instructors and the workers. Later, a simple experiment was conducted to evaluate the usability of the proposed system.

Keywords: Augmented reality · Remote collaboration · Virtual label · 3D pointer

1 Introduction

Nowadays, physical remote collaboration is widely used in many places (including education, manufacturing, etc), and two participants who live far away from each other use remote collaborative tools to work together. Among all types of remote collaboration, we focused on the physical remote collaboration. In a physical remote collaboration, participants not only interact with each other but also interact with the objects in the environment. In order to refer to objects during collaboration, participants use many expressions and non-verbal (e.g. gestures, gaze) behaviors to reduce the misunderstandings.

© Springer Nature Switzerland AG 2020
S. Yamamoto and H. Mori (Eds.): HCII 2020, LNCS 12185, pp. 407–417, 2020.
https://doi.org/10.1007/978-3-030-50017-7_30

However, it is known that nonverbal behaviors are hard to be correctly transferred through modern teleconferencing tools. Thus, referential communication could not be successfully conducted [4]; consequently, remote collaboration usually does not have the same quality as face-to-face collaboration. In this research, we focused on verbal communication and increased the efficiency of referential communication to improve the quality of remote collaboration.

There were several existing systems that aimed at improving verbal communication during the collaboration. Gauglitz [2] developed an AR system that allowed instructors to draw circles and arrows on tablets which showed the worker's working environment. It helped participants to understand what their interlocutor was talking about. Chang et al. developed a tablets-based remote instruction system that allows instructors to give objects unique alphabetical names (e.g. A, B, C), and the given names were shown as virtual labels on both instructor and worker's tablets [1]. By giving objects names, both participants built up a mutual understanding of how to refer to the objects during the remote instruction.

However, we considered that providing new names to each object improves communication only when the working area is narrow. In a wide working area, there are many chances that participants are not able to see the labels and it is hard for participants to remember and use the labels. We considered that providing virtual labels with semantic meanings can improve the quality of collaboration. Thus, in this paper, we first conducted a pilot experiment to understand if labels with semantic meanings support collaboration or not. Later, based on the result, we developed an AR-based remote collaboration system which supports semantic label and 3D pointer. In addition, a simple experiment for evaluation was conducted to evaluate the usability of the proposed system.

2   Pilot Experiment

2.1   Experimental Design

Hypothesis. In the pilot experiment, we investigated how participants used two types of AR labels: AR labels with unique names (Simple Label) and AR labels with detailed features describing the corresponding object (Detailed Label). We assumed that both types of AR labels supported participants building up mutual knowledge and resulted in a better quality of collaboration than remote collaboration without AR labels.

Method. This experiment is a within-participant design, and the independent variable is the label type: detailed label, simple label, and no label. In the detailed label condition, for each Lego block, we attached a virtual semi-transparent label with two or three features that can be used to describe the corresponding Lego block. The features included the color, size and shape (Fig. 1). In the simple label condition, for each Lego, a virtual semi-transparent label with a unique alphabet was attached to provide the Lego a new name (Fig. 2). The font size and label size were the same in both conditions to reduce the bias. In the no label condition, no label was shown.

Regarding the task, we chose an assembly task which is common in manufacturing as our task. We used Lego blocks which are widely used in other remote collaboration tasks. Although the assembly task of Lego blocks is not a task in the real world, it has many components which are similar to real-world task (e.g. seeking, pointing, grasping, releasing). For each task, participants had to pick up 11 Lego blocks from 16 Lego blocks and they had to assembly two shapes. One shape contained 5 Lego blocks; another shape contained 6 Lego blocks.

Fig. 1. As for the detailed label condition, a virtual semi-transparent label with two or three features were attached to each Lego block.

Fig. 2. As for the simple label condition, a virtual semi-transparent label with a unique alphabet which represented the Lego's name was attached to each Lego block.

Participants. Two participants from University of Tsukuba were recruited to attend this experiment. Both of them were male and the ages were both 23.

Procedure. At the beginning of this experiment, the experimenter explained how to use the system. The participant played the role of the worker was asked to wear the HMD of HTC VIVE; the participant played the role of the instructor was asked to sit in front of a table with monitor (Fig. 3). Two participants were separated by a curtain. They could not see each other, but the voice can be transmitted clearly. A manual was given to the instructor. Later, the instructor was informed that he can see the worker's working environment on the screen and he had to give instructions to the worker. On the other hand, the worker was informed he could see the real environment through the HMD and was asked to follow the instruction and assemble the corresponding Lego blocks.

The experiment consisted of four trials. A practice trial was followed by three main trials. In each trial, two participants were asked to conduct the Lego block assembly task. After each task, two participants were requested to fill in the questionnaire. At the end of the experiment, a short unstructured interview was conducted.

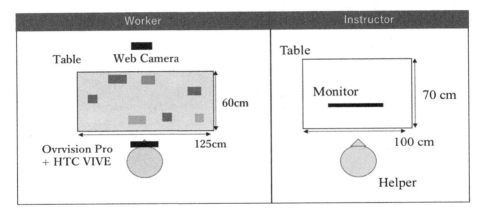

Fig. 3. Two participants were separated in two areas. The worker wore a HMD of HTC VIVE and stood in front of the Lego blocks; the instructor sat in front of a table with a monitor.

Measure. To assess the effect of labels, we considered two aspects: workload and quality of collaboration. Regarding workload, we chose NASA-TLX which is a standard method to assess workload. The NASA-TLX was developed by Hart and Staveland [3] to assess a person's subjective workload. It consists of six sub-scales: mental demand, physical demand, temporal demand, performance, effort, and frustration. The NASA-TLX contains two stages: rating scales and pairwise comparison. In the rating scale stage, participants answered each sub-scales with a rating scale with 20 five-point steps, from 0 to 100 (Table 1 Q1–Q6). In the pairwise comparison stage, the participants compared each pair of sub-scales and judge which sub-scale was more important to the task.

Regarding the quality of collaboration, we adapted the questionnaire used in Chang's research. The questions were shown in Table 1, from Q7 to Q13. In addition, we also interested in if the labels have a negative effect on visibility, so we added a question "can clearly see the screen during the experiment" (Q14). The questionnaire was a 7-point rating scale.

Table 1. 14 questions include NASA-TLX, the quality of collaboration

---

Q1: How much mental and perceptual activity was required (e.g. thinking, deciding, calculating, remembering, looking, searching, etc)? Was the task easy or demanding, simple or complex, exacting or forgiving?

Q2: How much physical activity was required (e.g. pushing, pulling, turning, controlling, activating, etc)? Was the task easy or demanding, slow or brisk, slack or strenuous, restful or laborious?

Q3: How successful do you think you were in accomplishing the goals of the task set by the experimenter (or yourself)? How satisfied were you with your performance in accomplishing these goals?

Q4: How much time pressure did you feel due to the rate of pace at which the tasks or task elements occurred? Was the pace slow and leisurely or rapid and frantic?

Q5: How hard did you have to work (mentally and physically) to accomplish your level of performance?

Q6: How insecure, discouraged, irritated, stressed and annoyed versus secure, gratified, content, relaxed and complacent did you feel during the task?

Q7: I would like to use this system for remote collaboration in the future

Q8: I am willing to recommend friends to use this system for remote collaboration in the future

Q9: I felt happy during the task

Q10 (detailed label and simple label): I felt that the label is useful for communication.

Q10 (no label): It is hard to communicate with another person without labels.

Q11: I successfully finished the task with another person.

Q12: I communicated with another person efficiently

Q13: I am satisfied with another person's collaboration.

Q14: I can clearly see the screen during the experiment.

2.2   Result and Discussion

To calculate the score of NASA-TLX, we summed up each sub-scale's score with their weight. The result was shown in Fig. 4. Regarding the worker side, we found that the simple label condition had the lowest workload. However, the detailed label condition had the highest workload. According to the interview, we found that it was mainly because the detailed label contained too much information and then it lowered down the visibility. Regarding the instructor side, we found that the workloads of both conditions with labels provided were lower than no label condition, and it is an evidence that providing either type of label can reduce the instructors' workload. The reason might be because the instructor did not have to think about how to explain the objects.

Fig. 4. Result of NASA-TLX

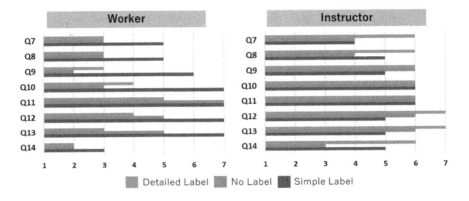

Fig. 5. Result of questionnaire about quality of collaboration

On the other hand, the result of the quality of collaboration was shown in Fig. 5. Since this study is an exploratory study, no statistical analysis was performed. However, we found that the worker and instructor had a different opinion on the quality of collaboration. The worker rated the simple label condition a higher score, but the instructor rated the detailed label condition a higher score. According to the interview, the two participants also mentioned that the task was simple and the labels were often useless.

Overall, we found that both simple labels and detailed labels are possible to support remote collaborations. However, the visibility issue might cause a negative effect on collaboration.

3   Proposed System

In this section, we introduced our proposed system. It is a dependent-view AR remote collaboration system while both the instructor and the worker share the same viewpoint. The architecture was shown in Fig. 6. In this system, we designed two different functions to improve the remote collaboration: virtual label and 3D pointer. The details are explained below.

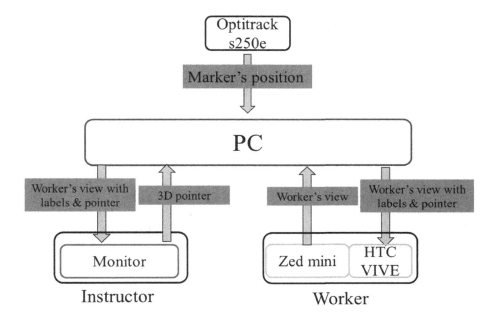

Fig. 6. The architecture of the proposed system

3.1 Environment Capturing

In our proposed system, we used a video see-through AR instead of optical see-through AR to provide a wide view angle. We used the ZED Mini, an RGB-based stereo-camera to capture the real-world environment and transfer to Unity 3D. The resolution was 2560×720 and the frame rate of the system $60\,\mathrm{Hz}$.

3.2 Virtual Label

Regarding the implementation of the function of virtual labels, we attached Aruco markers, a type of AR marker, to each object. Three video cameras were set up to capture the Aruco markers and the captured videos were streamed to the Unity 3D.

Then, in order to get blocks' positions, we used OpenCV for Unity to estimate the position. Later, semi-transparent virtual labels were attached to the blocks' positions to the support instructors and workers building up mutual understandings.

3.3   3D Pointer

In addition to providing virtual labels to achieve a better mutual understanding, we considered including a 3D pointer which is a metaphor of human's finger (Fig. 7). A ball shape pointer was created with Unity 3D and augmented to the real-world environment. The instructor can move the cursor with a mouse and the worker can easily understand what the instructor is referring to.

Besides, the instructor can use the pointer to change the color of the virtual labels. This function can further support the instructor to draw the worker's attention.

Fig. 7. A ball shaped 3D pointer that can support the instructor to communicate with the worker

4   Evaluation Experiment

4.1   Experimental Design

Hypothesis. To evaluate the proposed system, we conducted a simple experiment. As we mentioned in Sect. 1, our system is designed for a wide area; thus, in this experiment, we asked participants to conduct assembly tasks in a wide environment. In addition, based on the result of the previous experiment, we found that visibility is an important issue. Thus, we would also like to know how the participants behave after we remove the virtual labels. We assumed that the quality of remote collaboration with the virtual labels with semantic meanings (Detailed Label) was better than the baseline (with the virtual labels with non-semantic contents) (Simple Label). Also, we assessed how remote collaboration changed after the virtual labels were removed.

Method and Participant. It was a between-participant design experiment to reduce the learning effect. We compared two types of virtual labels: the simple label and the detailed label. Other settings were similar to Sect. 2.1. The only difference is that we prepared more types of Lego blocks to increase the task's complexity. Four male participants from the University of Tsukuba were recruited to participate in the experiment.

Procedure. After two participants entered the room, the participant played the role of the instructor sat in front of the table with a monitor and the participant played the role of the worker stood between three tables (Fig. 8). After explaining the system, participants were asked to conduct a practice task. In the practice task, several spray cans with different colors, sizes, and shapes of caps were put on the three tables. The participants followed the given manual and switched the positions of the spray cans. Later, the participants were asked to conduct two main tasks. In each main task, the participants assembled and dismantled the Lego blocks based on the manual. In the first main task, participants saw different virtual labels according to their groups; in the second main task, participants conducted the task without virtual labels. Both participants were asked to answer the questionnaire after each main task. At the end of the experiment, a brief unstructured interview was conducted.

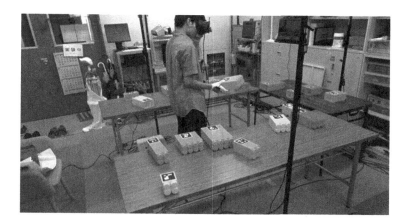

Fig. 8. The worker followed the instruction and assembled the Lego blocks.

4.2 Result and Discussion

The result of the workload was shown in Fig. 9; the result of the quality of collaboration was shown in Fig. 10. According to Q14, we found that the visibility issue was addressed. Regarding the workload, the NASA-TLX scores of both the instructor and worker were higher in the simple label condition than the detailed label condition, and it meant that both the instructor and worker experienced low workload in the detailed label condition. Regarding the quality of collaboration, we found that the effect of the virtual label differed between the instructor and the worker. The instructor rated that the simple label higher than the detailed label when the virtual labels existed, but the instructor rated oppositely after the virtual labels were removed. However, the worker did not have a big difference. Based on the interview and observation, we found another interesting finding that while the instructor in the detailed label condition was trying to describe a feature of a Lego block, he tended to create his own description based on other labels attached to other Lego blocks. However, this phenomenon did not appear in the simple label condition.

However, this was a very simple evaluation to initially test the proposed system. As future work, we should recruit enough participants to investigate the effect of virtual labels with semantic meanings. In addition, we should conduct conversational analysis to analyze how the virtual labels changed users' behaviors.

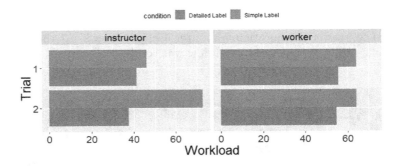

Fig. 9. Result of NASA-TLX

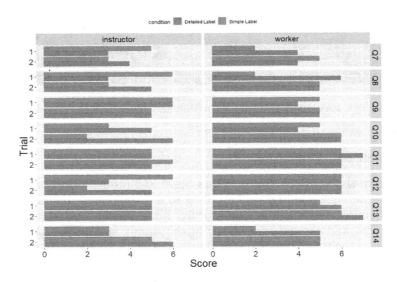

Fig. 10. Result of questionnaire about the quality of collaboration

5   Conclusion

In this paper, we demonstrated a novel AR remote collaboration system. The function of the virtual labels and 3D pointer allowed users to have smooth communication, and further improve the quality of remote collaboration.

Acknowledgement. This work was supported by JSPS KAKENHI Grant Number 17H01771.

References

1. Chang, Y.C., Wang, H.C., Chu, H.k., Lin, S.Y., Wang, S.P.: Alpharead: support unambiguous referencing in remote collaboration with readable object annotation. In: Proceedings of the 2017 ACM Conference on Computer Supported Cooperative Work and Social Computing, CSCW 2017, pp. 2246–2259. Association for Computing Machinery, New York (2017). https://doi.org/10.1145/2998181.2998258,
2. Gauglitz, S., Nuernberger, B., Turk, M., Höllerer, T.: World-stabilized annotations and virtual scene navigation for remote collaboration. In: Proceedings of the 27th Annual ACM Symposium on User Interface Software and Technology, pp. 449–459 (2014)
3. Hart, S.G., Staveland, L.E.: Development of NASA-TLX (task load index): results of empirical and theoretical research. Hum. Ment. Workload **1**(3), 139–183 (1988)
4. Jones, B., Witcraft, A., Bateman, S., Neustaedter, C., Tang, A.: Mechanics of camera work in mobile video collaboration. In: Proceedings of the 33rd Annual ACM Conference on Human Factors in Computing Systems, CHI 2015, pp. 957–966. Association for Computing Machinery, New York (2015). https://doi.org/10.1145/2702123.2702345

Will the Process of Creation Impact the Viewer's Appraisal of the Creativeness of Artificial Intelligence Artworks?

Rui Xu[1,2] and Yen Hsu[1(✉)]

[1] The Graduate Institute of Design Science, Tatung University, Taipei 104, Taiwan
635524937@qq.com
[2] School of Art and Design,
Fuzhou University of International Studies and Trade, Fuzhou 350202, China

Abstract. At present, artificial intelligence products and programs are widely utilized in every aspect of people's daily life, including artistic creation. The viewer usually sees the outcome rather than the process in the case of artworks. However, the production process of an artistic work often influences the viewer's appraisal of the creativity of the work. Nowadays, however, most studies concentrate on artificial intelligence artwork performance while ignoring the process of creation. This study conducted experiments with the ARS scale on the theoretical basis of schema theory to analyze whether there is any difference in the viewer's appraisal of artistic works after realizing the process of artistic creation. The goal is to examine whether the process of creation can influence the viewer's appraisal of creativity on the outcome generated by artificial intelligence. The results show that the appraisal of artificial intelligence artistry is influenced by the creative process to a certain extent, and the appraisal of the works with more diversified colors are affected more than those with monochrome color.

Keywords: Artificial intelligence · Process of creation · Artworks

1 Introduction

With the development of technology, artificial intelligence has involved various tasks usually performed by humans, such as the game of Go, language, theory, and many other fields, including artistic creation. The artistic creation of artificial intelligence has produced tremendous success. However, studies have shown that viewers have certain aesthetic biases against artificial intelligence work of art (Kirk et al. 2009). People prefer works created by human artists. The origins of this prejudice are currently unclear. Some researchers believe that many factors can influence the classification and appraisal of the works of art. This prejudice in aesthetic experience is likely to be conveyed by physical aspects other than the work of art. For example, the impact of observers on the assumptions of overall creative processes (Dutton 2003, 2009). When assessing an artwork, the viewer will project the feelings of creativity about the work to the artist according to different aspects of the work. The viewer may try to figure out the process of

© Springer Nature Switzerland AG 2020
S. Yamamoto and H. Mori (Eds.): HCII 2020, LNCS 12185, pp. 418–429, 2020.
https://doi.org/10.1007/978-3-030-50017-7_31

creating the artwork (intellectual, practical, or otherwise). They may use this information to make judgments on the creativity of the artists themselves, and ultimately apply that judgment to the appraisal of the artwork. The more creative the process of producing a work, the better is the appraisal of the outcome. In other words, the creation process of the artist is more likely to elicit the resonant response of the observer than the work, reinforce the emotions of the viewer to the work, and increase appreciation for the ingenuity of the works. Computer-based artworks are created in various ways, and little is known about the artistic processes involved (Colton 2008). At present, most of the research in this field focuses on how to assess the achievement of artistic creation by artificial intelligence, trying to analyze and discuss the audience's reaction to the artistic work created by human or artificial intelligence. This study argues that the results of artificial intelligence creation cannot be the sole criterion for measuring the creativity or other aesthetic value of their artistic works independently. Combining the art creation process of artificial intelligence will make the results more convincing. The goal of this study is therefore to achieve the following objectives:

- Conduct the creativity assessment of artificial intelligence by combining schema theory and ARS scale.
- Based on the literature review, this study attempts to discuss whether there is a priori bias in the viewer towards the creation of artificial intelligence artworks.
- This study takes the category of painting as an example to examine whether there is more prejudice in color painting than in monochrome (black and white) sketch.

2 Literature Review

2.1 Schema Theory

According to the meaningful research framework provided by schema theory, we can think that according to the identity of artists and their creation process, viewers try to express their views on artistic works based on some fixed schema. The so-called schema refers to "an active processing data structure that organizes memory and guides perception, performance, and thought." (Norman and Rumelhart 1981). For example, a schema for artistic creation would include knowledge about artistic concepts, giving us a more or less artistic view on art, whether we have seen and appreciated art, and the circumstances in which we have seen art, etc. It can be said that schema and prejudice (or stereotypes) have similar functionalities in the cognitive process. Schema is a heuristic feature that allows us to make decisions when we receive new information, drawing on previous experience. Schema theory is widely used in media influence studies. Researchers are interested in how prejudice affects individuals' media portraying certain races and influence perceptions of media users. Since art is a medium for conveying information, schema theory is applicable to the research focusing on artworks. Previous studies have shown that vision is particularly effective in triggering patterns. Therefore, this theory is applicable to understanding how stereotypes about artificial intelligence change the perception of artificial intelligence works of art. McCarthy pointed out that some people would wonder if artificial intelligence has truly "humanized" manifestations, even if their performance is objectively indistinguishable. Even though there is no distinction between artificial intelligence produced artwork and those created by humans, people may still claim that artificial intelligence cannot produce art because they believe that art should be human-created works (McCarthy 2007). Moreover, several studies have revealed the prejudices of the viewer against computer artworks. The image marked as Photoshop has relatively low aesthetic value when the source of works with the same visual effect is labeled as "Art Gallery" and "Photoshop" respectively. Hawley-Dolan and Winner (2011) labeled artworks as being created by professional artists or children. Viewers' preferences and value judgments on artworks would not be affected too much. However, there is a prejudice against computer-based artworks. In the face of the artistry of artificial intelligence, creativity is often attributed to programmers. This can be viewed as a twofold standard or prejudice. Because when faced with human works of art, the creativity of the work is not usually attributed to the instructor who teaches students how to create works of art (Colton 2008). Therefore, this study intends to examine the different reactions of artworks labeled as artificial intelligence when there is a process of human-like creation and when there is no process of human-like creation, in order to judge whether there is a bias in appreciating artificial intelligence artistic composition.

2.2 Impact of the Course of Events on Artworks

The artistry of artificial intelligence has made remarkable progress, some of which have even passed the so-called Turing Art Test. That is, whether people can differentiate between which one of the two paintings was created by artificial intelligence and which one was created by a human artist. Relevant studies have shown that in general, 75% of human subjects cannot clearly identify whether a work of art was created by a human artist or artificial intelligence. In the context of abstractionism, over 85% of subjects classified artworks created by artificial intelligence as those created by human beings, and described them as "inspiring" and "visually structured" (Mazzone and Elgammal 2019). Yet Simon Colton pointed out that the public often overpraises artificial intelligent artworks passing the Turing Art Test. Actually, this is not a proper question. Simon Colton also argues that when consumers and viewers of paintings evaluate them, they do not strictly distinguish between the course of events and the outcome. At least when it comes to the artistic assessment of graphic visual arts, it should not stop at the evaluation of the results of artificial intelligence artwork, otherwise, it is biased. The process of creating artwork should be the decisive factor in evaluating it (Colton 2008). The key explanation is that it is difficult for people to regard computer programs as independent entities from programmers (Sundar and Nass 2000). As mentioned above, the independent classification and aesthetic value of artificial intelligence generated art maybe restricted by a variety of factors. The viewer, for example, maybe influenced by the superficial nature of the artwork or by higher-level cognitive biases about the personal and social values inherent in artistry generated by artificial intelligence. Because the general impression is that a machine or program cannot be creative, it will influence the assessment of its artwork (Colton 2008). Similarly, Kruger et al. (2004) and Jucker (2013) proved that works of art that seemed to require more time and effort to produce were rated higher in terms of quality, value, creativity, and liking. Kruger et al. (2004) illustrated effort heuristics through works of art, i.e., if a painting seems to take longer to paint, it is considered more aesthetic, innovative, and desirable than a painting that seems to be drawn quickly with less effort. Considering that robots and other artificial intelligence systems are often designed to reduce human effort and burden, and that art is a series of creations that require a long time and full devotion, the combination of the two that mistakenly lead viewers to conclude that artificial intelligence produces art that takes less work or avoids the required effort.

This potentially biased assumption may largely affect the viewer's judgment on the achievement of artificial intelligence art. Just like the drip paintings of Jackson Pollock were once considered as worthless and unplanned graffiti. It was not until his arduous creation process was exposed that art critics and the public gradually embraced his works (Kruger et al. 2004). Secondly, Newman and Bloom (2011) found that the economic value of an artwork depends to some extent on the degree to which it is viewed as a unique creative act and the degree of contact between the original author and the artwork. The longer the contact, the greater the aesthetic benefit and the economic advantage. This view is also supported by Hawley-Dolan and Winner (2011). They stressed that objective process evaluation (i.e. value measurement) is more important than subjective evaluation (i.e., artistic preference) in the assessment artworks (Hawley-Dolan and Young 2013). After reviewing the literature, we can conclude that although there is a default phenomenon of simplified appreciation and evaluation of artistic works by appreciators in the society, there are also other more complicated models of appreciation and evaluation of artistic works. In particular, when it comes to artistry generated by artificial intelligence, the model of true appreciation is as follows: the spectator strives to discover the process behind the production of a particular artwork. They then evaluate the work based on 1) the commitment behind the process, 2) the creativity of the process, and 3) the skills required to perform the process. On this basis, this study assumes that the process would impact the assessment of artificial intelligence artwork by viewers. Compared with those who only see the results of creation, viewers who watch the creation process of artificial intelligence will consider the works of artificial intelligence more creative.

2.3 Why Use ARS

The role of the non-human in the artistic process is increasingly recognized in the field of art as they become increasingly important in creative practice. More and more researchers are now trying to measure the subjective assessment of art by individuals (Lindell and Mueller 2011). Among them, one of the most popular methods for assessing creativity relies on judgments. Art professionals or other experts are usually invited to judge the creativity of artworks (Runco Runco, M.A., Mccarthy, K.A., Svenson, E.: Judgments of the Creativity of Artwork from Students and Professional Artists 2015). ARS (2012) aesthetic perception questionnaire, widely used in art learning or practice context, will be used in this study to describe and evaluate their feelings towards each artwork in order to assess the creativity of artificial intelligence artworks. There is no doubt that one of the motivations for experiencing art as a viewer is to enjoy the intrinsic qualities of the artwork. This appreciation is often referred to as the judgment of pleasure, preference, or aesthetic feeling. Several studies use this and Turing test as the basis for designing the binary artistic Turing test questionnaire. Yet the latest findings from aesthetic studies suggest that aesthetic judgments are far more complex. In particular, the perception of various emotional and cognitive aspects plays a central role in the assessment of visual arts. Other studies used a simple creativity scale (Joo-Whahong 2018) for evaluation and ignored the emotional and cognitive level of the viewer. The ARS model is based on previous models, instead of continuing to rely on the assessment of the viewer's cognition and emotion. In particular, human related characteristics, such as art experience, declarative knowledge, as well as personal interests and preferences, are classified as the basis for classification and applied to the scale. The ARS scale is essentially divided into seven categories. These items can be roughly classified into several categories. Artistic works are assessed from the perspectives of cognitive stimulation, negative emotion, professional knowledge, self-awareness, artistry, positive attraction, and creativity. Up to now, there are numerous scales regarding aesthetic emotions and experiences. ARS is chosen to assess the creativity of artificial intelligence artworks in this experiment for the following four reasons. First, it is clear that the dimensions of aesthetic perception and creativity evaluation of artworks are not universal. Usually, the scale is used only to evaluate a particular aesthetic field, such as music, dance, and literature, etc. ARS is a scale for the aesthetic experience of paintings. Second, during the development stage, the ARS scale tries to avoid setting the scale as something related to explicit content to ensure that the scale can be applied to the assessment of a variety of paintings (Joo-Whahong 2018). Third, much of the research on the creativity and aesthetic perception of artwork has simply assessed a single aesthetic response to an object, asking whether the painting is attractive, pleasant, or enjoyable. Although these measurement criteria may be a standard of aesthetic perception that is relatively consistent with a wide range of cognition, aesthetic experience, and creative evaluation are multi-level, and the viewer's emotions after admiring a work of art are rich and subtle. The scale must, therefore, be very precise. If artwork is assessed by ARS, researchers will not only learn about the viewer's personal preference, but also discover the viewer's subjective evaluation of other aspects of the art. This includes the creative dimension, which can be analyzed and discussed as a key object. Lastly, under creative stimulation, we contrasted ARS with other scales. Both the reliability and validity have exceeded the expectation, which can allow researchers to clearly distinguish the variations of artworks in different aspects, which is beneficial to the study in various fields of art. In conclusion, ARS has been evaluated as a valuable and versatile tool for future research in the field of empirical aesthetics and can be used in this study.

3   Research Methodology

3.1   Research Approach

According to the goal of the study and the above-mentioned literature review, this paper puts forward two hypotheses about the experimental results. 1) Viewers have a certain prejudice against artificial intelligence created artistic works, believing that their creativity is low. However, this prejudice will be improved by observing the creation process. 2) As far as the main forms are concerned, artworks created by artificial intelligence can be divided into two types: color and monochrome sketch. Many studies have shown that colored is more creative, attractive, and interesting than monochrome (Clarke 2000). Furthermore, the researchers found that colored is multifaceted (Tucker 2004), and can stimulate emotional responses under certain circumstances. This experiment assumes that the degree to which the creative assessment of colored artificial intelligence affected by the process is more significant than that of the monochrome works. Based on these two hypotheses, there are two premises in this experiment. The first is the type of images created by an artificial intelligence robot, AI-DA. The artwork is selected from a computer art database on the Internet. The collection of images consists of two types of images, one being monochromatic sketch and the other being aquarelle. Second, whether there is an activation video. The process group was asked to watch a three-minute video on how artificial intelligence conducts artistic creation, namely its creation process, before observing the works of artificial intelligence, while the outcome group did not. 244 subjects with high similarity in age, major of study, and education level were selected to participate in the study. Subjects were randomly divided into four groups with the same number of participants according to the differences in the two variables of image type and video activation. They are monochrome sketch process group, monochrome sketch result group, colored process group, colored result group. It is helpful to distinguish the subjects to support the validity of the experimental data (Table 1).

Table 1. Grouping situation

Control variables	Monochrome sketch	Color
Without watch the video (result)	Monochrome sketch result group	Color result group
Watch the video (process)	Monochrome sketch process group	Color process group

3.2 Participants

All the 244 participants in the sample study had received higher education at least with a bachelor's degree. All of them had art and design-related professional background or had received art related training, including 104 males and 136 females.

3.3 Procedures

Participants need to fill out an online form and basic personal information (including age, level of education, and whether accepted the professional training in art, etc., in front of the color set of test to confirm there is no color blindness, visual or measured normal vision correction) before experiment to ensure the validity of the random sampling and the reliability of test results, then the viewer will be focused on a projector capacious space (room), in the process of experiment, in order to eliminate indoor environment, light and other interference factors on the measured and the effect of measured according to the category of the classification, Video and image observations were made in the same classroom at the same time. The display time of each image lasted about 27–30 s. All the images and videos observed in the experiment were connected to the computer (Apple model: Mac Book Pro (Retina, 15-in., Mid 2014, resolution 2880 × 1880) and projected onto a large screen for display (the projector was EPSON, eb-c2040xn, size 1024 × 768). The lighting and screen resolution have been adjusted to ensure that all the boot stimuli are in optimum condition.

The process group (single color sketch, color, 2) will be asked to sit in front of the big screen for video and image, and the result group (single color sketch, color, 1) need only observe the image by ARS scale of artificial intelligence after creating works of art on each score, scale using Likert five-levels scale (1 = low, strongly disagree, 5 = high, strongly agree).

4   Result Analysis

A total of 244 questionnaires were collected for this study. Among them, 4 questionnaires were invalid and eliminated because the age is not accord with the requirement of this lab control variables, thus finally 240 valid questionnaires were kept for analysis. Respectively, monochrome drawing process group (n = 60), monochrome drawings result group (n = 60), color process group (n = 60), color group result group (n = 60). All of the 240 participants in the sample study all had received higher education with a bachelor's degree or above, and were all with professional background in art and design or had received art-related training. Among them, 106 were male and 138 were female, aged between 18 and 27.

Due to ARS scale's questions were various, as many as 75, involving seven level aesthetic perception of color, including cognitive stimulation, negative emotions, professional knowledge, self-knowledge, artistic quality, positive emotions and creativity, because this research mainly discusses the AI art creativity performance, so the results analysis focuses on discussed in (part 7) creativity.

In order to measure whether viewers were biased against the creativity of artificial intelligence in creating works, first of all, the four groups tested were classified according to the image type and observation mode: the monochrome sketch process group (n = 60), the monochrome sketch result group (n = 60), and the color process group (n = 60), the color result group (n = 60). One-way ANOVA was used to compare scores of different groups in some items to analyze whether image types and observation methods have an impact on creative evaluation. 18. The composition of this picture is very good (using the new space combination), 19. This picture is very creative, 34. This painting is full of originality, 45. This painting makes me feel a change from the previous one (hereinafter referred to as 18, 19, 34, 45). Besides, SNK - q (Student - Newman - Keuls) test for post hoc multiple comparisons.

The results showed that: Firstly, it is true that viewers' aesthetic feelings and judgment of creativity for artificial intelligence creations will be affected by its procedural work. Secondly, the creativity of his works and other aesthetic feelings vary according to different themes and types of works. In conclusion, the results were consistent with the experimental hypothesis (Table 6).

Table 2. Analysis of scores of different groups (Mean ± SD)

Group	Q18	Q19	Q20	Q21
Monochrome sketch result group	3.03 ± 1.149	3.38 ± 1.329	3.25 ± 1.244	3.13 ± 1.065
Color result group	3.23 ± 1.254	3.92 ± 1.154	3.75 ± 1.188	3.02 ± 1.295
Monochromatic sketch process group	3.57 ± 1.184	3.68 ± 1.228	3.55 ± 1.185	3.15 ± 1.313
Color process group	4.75 ± 0.773	4.73 ± 0.756	4.67 ± 0.857	4.53 ± 0.929
F	28.956	15.531	17.558	22.991
P	<0.001	<0.001	<0.001	<0.001

Table 3. The result of Post Hoc tests for Q18

Group	N	Subset for alpha = 0.05		
		1	2	3
Monochrome sketch result group	60	3.03		
Monochromatic sketch process group	60	3.23	3.23	
Color result group	60		3.57	
Color process group	60			4.75
Sig.		0.323	0.100	1.000

Table 4. The result of Post Hoc tests for Q19

Group	N	Subset for alpha = 0.05		
		1	2	3
Monochrome sketch result group	60	3.38		
Monochromatic sketch process group	60	3.68	3.68	
Color result group	60		3.92	
Color process group	60			4.73
Sig.		0.150	0.262	1.000

Table 5. The result of Post Hoc tests for Q34

Group	N	Subset for alpha = 0.05		
		1	2	3
Monochrome sketch result group	60	3.25		
Monochromatic sketch process group	60	3.55	3.55	
Color result group	60		3.75	
Color process group	60			4.67
Sig.		0.147	0.333	1.000

Table 6. The result of Post Hoc tests for Q45

Group	N	Subset for alpha = 0.05	
		1	2
Monochrome sketch result group	60	3.02	
Monochromatic sketch process group	60	3.13	
Color result group	60	3.15	
Color process group	60		4.53
Sig.		0.805	1.000

Table 7. Analysis of scores of different groups (Mean ± SD)

Group	Q18	Q19	Q34	Q45
Monochrome sketch result group	3.03 ± 1.149a	3.38 ± 1.329a	3.25 ± 1.244a	3.13 ± 1.065a
Color result group	3.23 ± 1.254ab	3.92 ± 1.154ab	3.75 ± 1.188ab	3.02 ± 1.295a
Monochromatic sketch process group	3.57 ± 1.184b	3.68 ± 1.228b	3.55 ± 1.185b	3.15 ± 1.313a
Color process group	4.75 ± 0.773c	4.73 ± 0.756c	4.67 ± 0.857ac	4.53 ± 0.929c
F	28.956	15.531	17.558	22.991
P	<0.001	<0.001	<0.001	<0.001

Note: The different letters "abcd" indicate that there are statistically significant differences in post hoc comparisons among the four methods in each column; For example: "ab" indicates that there is no statistical significance in comparison with "a" or "b".

The results (Table 2 and Table 3) showed that there were statistically significant differences in the scores of the four groups in Q18 (F = 28.956, P < 0.001), and the score of color process group (4.75 ± 0.773) was significantly higher than those of the other groups (P < 0.05), and the score of color result group was higher than Monochrome sketch result group (P < 0.05), but there is no significant difference between monochrome sketch groups (P > 0.05), as did monochromatic sketch process group and color result group (P > 0.05).

The findings (Table 2, Table 4 and Table 5) of Q19 and Q34 was similar to Q18. There were statistically significant differences between color groups and monochrome sketch groups, as did result groups and process groups (P < 0.05). The results of the scores of Q45 showed as bellows. There was significant difference among color process group (4.53 ± 0.929) and the other groups (P < 0.05). But there were no significant differences among monochrome sketch result group, monochromatic sketch process group and color result group (P > 0.05).

In conclusion, the results (Table 7) showed that there were statistically significant differences in the scores of the four groups in Q18 (F = 28.956, P < 0.001), and the score of color process group (4.75 ± 0.773) was significantly higher than those of the other groups (P < 0.05), and the score of color result group was higher than Monochrome sketch result group (P < 0.05), but there is no significant difference between monochrome sketch groups (P > 0.05), as did monochromatic sketch process group and color result group (P > 0.05) (Fig. 1).

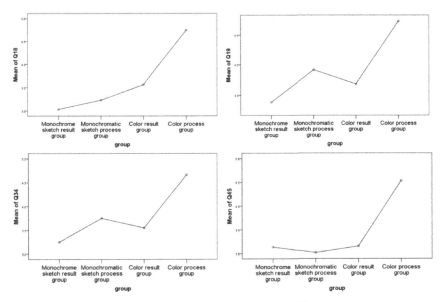

Fig. 1. The scores of Q18/Q19/Q34/Q45 in different groups

5 Discussion

This study seeks to explore how spectators assess the creativity of artworks known to be generated by computers or artificial intelligence agents before and after witnessing the process of artistry creation, and whether significant differences exist in this assessment. The results show that the spectators are influenced to some extent by the surface characteristics of artificial intelligence generated artworks and the negative value of artificial intelligence works of art. Such influence is even more obvious in the creation of more diversified colors. Based on these findings, recommendations can be made to improve the anthropomorphism of robotics and computational art, increase social participation, and potentially reduce spectators' hostility to future representations of artificial intelligence works of art.

References

Hertzmann, A.: Can computers create art? In: Arts, vol. 7, no. 2, p. 18 (2018)

Lindell, A., Mueller, J.: Can science account for taste? Psychological insights into art appreciation. J. Cogn. Psychol. **23**(4), 453–475 (2011)

Baggi, D. (ed.): Readings in Computer Generated Music. IEEE Computer Society Press, Los Alamitos (1992)

Bringsjord, S., Bello, P., Ferrucci, D.: Creativity, the turing test, and the (better) lovelace test. In: Moor, J.H. (ed.) The Turing Test. Studies in Cognitive Systems, vol. 30, pp. 215–239. Springer, Dordrecht (2003). https://doi.org/10.1007/978-94-010-0105-2_12

Binsted, K., Ritchie, G.: Computational rules for generating punning riddles. Int. J. Humour Res. **10**(1), 25–76 (2007)

Bartneck, C., Croft, E., Kulic, D., Zoghbi, S.: Measurement instruments for the anthropomorphism, animacy, likeability, perceived intelligence, and perceived safety of robots. Int. J. Soc. Robot. **1**, 71–81 (2009). https://doi.org/10.1007/s12369-008-0001-3

Cohen, H.: Parallel to perception: some notes on the problem of machine-generated art. In: Computer Studies, vol. 4 (1973)

Collomosse, J., Hall, P.: Cubist style rendering of photographs. IEEE Trans. Visual. Comput. Graph. (TVCG) **9**(4), 443–453 (2003)

Nass, C., Moon, Y.: Machines and mindlessness: social responses to computers. J. Soc. Issues **56**(1), 81–103 (2000)

Colton, S.: Automatic invention of fitness functions with application to scene generation. In: Giacobini, M., et al. (eds.) EvoWorkshops 2008. LNCS, vol. 4974, pp. 381–391. Springer, Heidelberg (2008). https://doi.org/10.1007/978-3-540-78761-7_41

Desmet, P.M.A.: Faces of product pleasure: 25 positive emotions in human-product interactions. Int. J. Des. **6**(2), 1–29 (2012)

Dutton, D.: Authenticity in art. In: Levinson, J. (ed.) The Oxford Handbook of Aesthetics, pp. 258–274. Oxford University Press, New York (2003)

Dutton, D.: The Art Instinct: Beauty, Pleasure, and Human Evolution. Oxford University Press, Oxford (2009)

Norman, D.A., Rumelhart, D.E.: The LNR approach to human information processing. Cognition **10**(1), 235–240 (1981)

Gervas, P.: WASP: Evaluation of different strategies for the automatic generation of spanish verse. In: Proceedings of the AISB-00 Symposium on Creative and Cultural Aspects of AI. (2000)

Han, H., Back, K.-J., Barrett, B.: A consumption emotion measurement development: a full-service restaurant setting. Serv. Ind. J. **30**(2), 299–320 (2010)

Hawley-Dolan, A., Winner, E.: Seeing the mind behind the art: people can distinguish abstract expressionist paintings from highly similar paintings by children, chimps, monkeys and elephants. Psychol. Sci. **22**, 435–441 (2011)

Hawley-Dolan, A., Young, L.: Whose mind matters more: the moral agent or the artist? The role of intent in ethics and aesthetics. PLoS ONE **8**(9), e70759 (2013)

Clarke III, I., Honeycutt Jr., E.D.: International business-to-business print advertising. Ind. Mark. Manage. **29**, 255–261 (2000). Elsevier Science Inc.

McCarthy, J.: From here to human-level AI. Artif. Intell. **171**(18), 1174–1182 (2007)

Hong, J.-W., Curran, N.M.: Artificial intelligence, artists, and art: attitudes toward artwork produced by humans vs. artificial intelligence. ACM Trans. Multimedia Comput. Commun. Appl. 15(2s) (2019). Article 58. Publication date: July (2019)

Kruger, J., Wirtz, D., Van Boven, L., Altermatt, T.W.: The effort heuristic. J. Exp. Soc. Psychol. **40**(1), 91–98 (2004)

Kirk, U., Skov, M., Ulme, O., Christensen, M.S., Zeki, S.: Modulation of aesthetic value by semantic context: an fMRI study. NeuroImage **44**(3), 1125–1132 (2009)

Laros, F.J.M., Steenkamp, J.-B.E.M.: Emotions in consumer behavior: a hierarchical approach. J. Bus. Res. **58**(10), 1437–1445 (2005)

Runco, M.A., Mccarthy, K.A., Svenson, E.: Judgments of the Creativity of Artwork from Students and Professional Artists (2015)

Hager, M.: Assessing aesthetic appreciation of visual artworks—the construction of the Art Reception Survey (ARS). Psychol. Aesthet. Creat. Arts Am. Psychol. Assoc. **6**(4), 320–333 (2012)

McFarland, M.: What AlphaGo's sly move says about machine creativity; Google's machine is leaving the smartest humans in the dust. The Washington Post (2016). https://www.washingto npost.com/news/innovations/wp/2016/03/15/what-alphagos-sly-move-says-about-machine-creativity/?utm_term=.e213e59a2038

Coeckelbergh, M.: Can machines create art? Philos. Technol. **30**(3), 285–303 (2017)

Solly, M.: Christie's will be the first auction house to sell art made by artificial intelligence. In Smithsonian Magazine (2018). https://www.smithsonianmag.com/smart-news/christies-will-be-first-auc tion-house-sell-art-made-artificial-intelligence-180970086/

Mazzone, M., Elgammal, A.: Art, creativity, and the potential of artificial intelligence. Arts **8**, 26 (2019). https://doi.org/10.3390/arts8010026

Newman, G.E., Bloom, P.: Art and authenticity: the importance of originality in judgments of value. J. Exp. Psychol. Gen. **141**(3), 558–569 (2011)

Adams, R.L.: 10 Powerful examples of artificial intelligence in use today. Forbes. (2017). https://www.forbes.com/sites/robertadams/2017/01/10/10-powerful-examples-of-artifi cial-intelligence-in-use-today/#658cdafc420d

Colton, S.: Creativity Versus the Perception of Creativity in Computational Systems (2008)

Sundar, S.S., Nass, C.: Source orientation in human-computer interaction: Programmer, networker, or independent social actor. Commun. Res. **27**(6), 683–703 (2000)

Theune, M., Slabbers, N., Hielkema, F.: The automatic generation of narratives. In: Proceedings of the 17th Conference on Computational Linguistics in the Netherlands (CLIN-17) (2007)

Tucker, M.: No title. In: Baas, J., Jacob, M. (eds.) Buddha Mind in Contemporary Art, pp. 75–86. University of California Press, Berkeley (2004)

Veale, T.: Tracking the lexical zeitgeist with WordNet and Wikipedia. In: Proceedings of the 17th European Conference on Artificial Intelligence (2006)

Information in Intelligent Systems and Environments

Experimental Study on Improvement of Sign Language Motion Classification Performance Using Pre-trained Network Models

Kaito Kawaguchi[1], Zhizhong Wang[1], Tomoki Kuniwa[1], Paporn Daraseneeyakul[2], Phaphimon Veerakiatikit[2], Eiji Ohta[3], Hiromitsu Nishimura[1], and Hiroshi Tanaka[1](✉)

[1] Department of Information and Computer Sciences, Kanagawa Institute of Technology, Atsugi, Kanagawa, Japan
{s1621099,s1621031,s1721140}@cce.kanagawa-it.ac.jp,
{nisimura,h_tanaka}@ic.kanagawa-it.ac.jp
[2] Department of Mechanical Engineering, Chulalongkorn University, Bangkok, Thailand
paporn.d@gmail.com, phaphimon.v@gmail.com
[3] Freelance, Iruma, Saitama, Japan
eiji.ohta@gmail.com

Abstract. Sign language is a major means of communication for people with hearing disabilities. However, there are very few hearing people who have learned sign language, and this is a great barrier to communication between hearing-impaired and hearing people. While automatic speech interpretation has already been put to practical use in some fields, there remains a lot of difficulties in putting sign language interpretation into practical use. Considering the variety of sign languages, the complexity of their motions and many subtle differences, it seems that there is bound to be a limit to any method of artificially extracting feature elements from motions and inputting them to a classifier to decide sign language motions. The authors are now investigating a method for automatically extracting feature elements using a pre-trained network model that has been trained by deep learning, and for classifying each motion. The problem of using deep learning is that it requires a large amount of training data to create a trained model. The acquisition of sign language motion data in order to satisfy this requirement seems to be difficult in practice. This paper presents a method of artificially creating data by data augmentation under conditions where the number of data items that can be collected is limited, and improving classification accuracy. It is shown that the proposed method has obtained a result of about 10% improvement in classification accuracy. In addition, the application of ensemble learning, which is another techniques for improving accuracy, is also described. The author shows that classification performance after integrating the results using a plurality of trained models built on the feature elements obtained from each pre-trained network model, resulted in a significant improvement in accuracy of more than about 10%.

Keywords: Sign language motion · Classification · Pre-trained network model · Data augmentation · Ensemble learning

© Springer Nature Switzerland AG 2020
S. Yamamoto and H. Mori (Eds.): HCII 2020, LNCS 12185, pp. 433–446, 2020.
https://doi.org/10.1007/978-3-030-50017-7_32

1 Introduction

Sign language is widely used for communication between hearing-impaired people [1]. However, learning sign language is extremely difficult, and the barriers to communication with hearing people are very large. Currently, handwriting and character input devices are usually used, but communication takes more time than it does with sign language, and it cannot be denied that there remains a high barrier to communication. As in the case of speech translation, which has already been partially commercialized [2], if sign language translation becomes possible, it is thought that the communication barrier between a hearing-impaired person and a hearing person can be largely eliminated.

To make sign language translation a reality, the classification of sign language motions is an extremely important factor. In the conventional classification of the sign language motions, the hand movement and shape of the finger are detected, and feature elements indicating the specific features of the sign language motions are extracted from the detected data. Sign language motions have then been classified by inputting them to a classifier such as SVM [3, 4]. Sign language motions are complex and comprise many movements, and the method of extracting feature elements with empirical skills and using classifiers seems to have limitations in responding to the increases in the number of target motions as well as in ensuring classification accuracy.

It has been found that remarkable performance improvement can be achieved in the classification of still images by using deep learning, and deep learning has also been effectively applied to the classification of time series data from acceleration sensors, and various other classification problems [5, 6]. One of the issues in applying these kinds of deep learning schemes is that a huge amount of training data is required to ensure good performance. For this reason, a method of processing existing data and adding it as training data has been applied to still image training [7]. This method is called data augmentation. In addition, a general method, known as ensemble learning, in which weak classifiers are combined to improve classification performance, has also been widely applied [8].

The authors are studying a method for classifying sign language motions using pre-trained network models such as AlexNet, in which automatically-extracted features are used to classify the many sign language motions. This paper presents methods for enhancing sign language motion classification using a pre-trained network model. The authors propose two methods and show the performance enhancement produced by (1) data augmentation and (2) ensemble learning using a plurality of trained models.

2 Final Goal and Current Research Target

Figure 1 shows the final application image of this research technology as assumed by the authors. For voice translations, dedicated terminals have already been commercialized, and machine translators in different languages have been made available. The ultimate goal is to expand this into sign language interpretation. It is assumed that sign language motions will be measured with a built-in camera in a device such as a smartphone, which will then transmit the video information to a sign language recognition server, receive the recognition result, and output word-by-word voice synthesis or text/characters on a display.

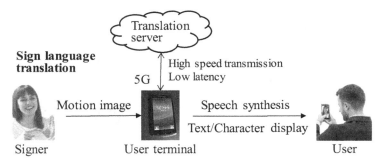

Fig. 1. Final usage image

By using an optical camera, not only the motion of the hands and fingers in sign language but also the facial expressions and movements of the lips can be detected. This provides a merit as compared to the other detectors. In addition, with the advancement of mobile communication technology, that is, high speed and low latency in 5th generation systems, it seems likely that it is going to be possible to realize a sign language interpretation service whose use is unrestricted by time, place and occasion.

To make sign language recognition a reality, a lot of technical developments are required. Fundamentally, it is considered necessary to combine motion classification focusing on sign language motion with linguistic prediction. Figure 2 shows the configuration of sign language recognition technology and indicates the focus of our current study. Our research area relates to the classification of sign language motions described in the yellow area. This paper shows the results of examining a method to improve the classification performance under the condition of a limited volume of motion data with which to create a trained model.

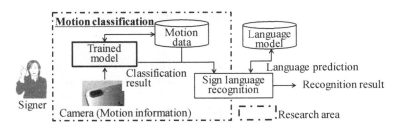

Fig. 2. Current research area

3 Motion Data Acquisition

The authors used colored gloves [9] to detect the motions of sign language with an optical camera built into a smartphone. The distinction between the front and back of the hand and the identification of each finger were facilitated by the color information. The motion of the entire hand was detected by the movement of the colored area of the wristband. Figure 3 shows the colored gloves and wristbands currently used.

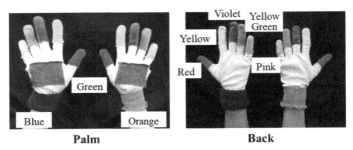

Palm   **Back**

Fig. 3. Appearance of colored gloves and wristbands

The sign language motions of a signer wearing colored gloves were acquired at a 30 fps (frames per second) time interval. The resolution was 600×800 pixels. The distance between the camera and the signer was 1 m, assuming a realistic conversational situation. Video data was obtained under the supervision of the actual sign language user, who confirmed that each sign language motion was correct. The acquired data was pre-processed as sign language motion data by conducting background subtraction and extracting the colored regions of the colored gloves and wristbands. This data was used to create trained models and evaluations described hereafter. The authors used color-extracted video because the classification method using data after color extraction provided better classification performance than the method used in our previous studies, which relied on unprocessed images [10].

4   Classification Method

This chapter describes a feature extraction and trained model creation method using a pre-trained network model for sign language motion classification.

4.1   Feature Extraction

The authors obtained the motion trajectory, position, speed, and other features of sign language motion from the position and size of the colored regions extracted from images of the colored gloves and wristband. Classifiers such as SVM etc., were applied to classify the motion. However, the number of sign language actions is enormous, and the actions themselves are often similar. These factors make it difficult to enhance classification performance, so the authors started to investigate a method using a pre-trained network model such as AlexNet to extract the feature elements from motion data.

Figure 4 shows the sequence for creating a trained model. The feature element is extracted for each frame of the sign language motion data using a pre-trained network model that has a proven track record, such as AlexNet, and the trained model is created using an LSTM (Long Short Time Memory) model. In the classification, the feature element of the sign language data to be classified is input to the trained LSTM model, and the maximum value from the probability of each sign language motion (each word) is selected as the classification result. The structure and parameters described in the figure are selected based on the results of previous studies [11]. The layers for feature extraction in each network model are, in order, AlexNet, VGG16, VGG19, GoogleNet, ResNet50 and ResNet101, pool5, pool5-7×7_s1, pool5, pool5, avg_pool and pool5.

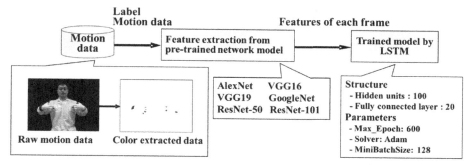

Fig. 4. Sequence for creating trained model

4.2 Target Words

The words that were classified in this investigation are shown in Table 1. Twenty words were selected from words included in the "Health/Illness" category of the video database "SmartDeaf" [12], which is a library of learning video material for sign language motion, meeting the required condition of movement involving both hands. Table 2 shows the sign language motion data used to make the trained model, and for evaluation. Twenty samples per word from three signers A, B, and C for a total of 60 samples per word for training, and 10 samples for each word of three signers D, E and F for a total of 30 samples per word for evaluation, were used in this experiment. The total number of original data items was 1800, that is, 60 * 20 + 30 * 20.

Table 1. Targeted sign language words

Bone	Bone fracture	Complexion	Developmental disability
Diet	Doctor	Get drunk	Glasses
Irritation	Kidney	Limit	Myopia
Nude	Obesity	Obstetrics and gynecology	Strong
Sweat	Sweaty	Tears	Wheelchair

4.3 Creation of Trained Model

Figure 5 shows an example of a training curve, that is, a history of loss convergence (epoch set to 600) of the LSTM model using the extracted features. These features were

Table 2. Data for making trained model and evaluation

	Signer	Sample/signer	Total/word
Data for training	A, B, C	20	60
Data for evaluation	D, E, F	10	30

obtained when training data (1200 samples (60 samples per word × 20 words)) was input to the VGG16 network. The horizontal axis shows epoch and the vertical axis shows loss. Loss is calculated from the cross entropy error. Since the number of training data items is 1200 and the mini-batch size is 128, one epoch comprises 9 iterations. The convergence situation differs for each training process. In this study, the training process was terminated when the average of the loss values in the last six iterations satisfied the condition of 1E−3 or less. In cases where features from other pre-trained network models were used, the trained model was created without changing the structure of the LSTM model.

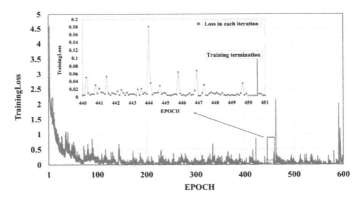

Fig. 5. History of loss convergence

The operating environment was OS: Windows 10, 64-bit; CPU: i7-8700 k, 3.70 Hz; GPU: NVIDIA GeForce GTX 1080Ti; memory: 48 GB; and the training time required to produce this graph was about 270 min. For the classification, the feature element of the sign language data to be classified was input to the trained LSTM model, and the maximum value from the probability for each sign language motion (each word) was selected as the classification result.

5   Data Augmentation and Results

In static image classification, data augmentation has been proposed as a method for improving classification performance and has a number of benefits. Deep learning requires a large amount of training data but there is a method of artificially creating and adding image data by enlarging, reducing, or rotating the original images.

When sign language motion data is acquired, a relative displacement between the camera and the signer occurs in addition to a slight difference in the physique of each signer and their sign language motion. Due to these effects, the obtained motion data features slight variations. In order to accurately classify such subtly differentiated data, it is desirable to perform training using a sufficient number of data items to allow for these fluctuation ranges. However, it is quite difficult to gather training data items that fully cover these differences.

Therefore, in this investigation, a limited volume of motion data was modified and augmented to cope with various fluctuations in sign language motions. Then, an attempt was made to realize more accurate classification than with a trained model created using only conventionally acquired training data.

5.1 Data Creation

Data augmentation was performed using the original motion data (A, B, C in Table 2) in consideration of the following fluctuation factors.

(1) Expansion/reduction in size taking into account differences in the physique of signers and the range of sign language motion
(2) Rotation considering the posture of the signer and the tilt of the camera
(3) Horizontal/vertical translation to reflect the difference in the positional relationship between the signer and the camera.

Table 3 shows the data augmentation methods and their quantities. Assuming an actual use situation with a distance of 1 m between the camera and the signer when acquiring the training data, the amount of variation considered to actually occur was given. Augmentation was performed for all training data.

Table 3. Data augmentation method and quantities

Method	Quantity
Expansion	1%, 3%, 5%
Reduction	1%, 3%, 5%
Rotation	1°, 2°, 3°
Horizontal translation	20 mm, 40 mm, 60 mm
Vertical translation	40 mm, 80 mm, 120 mm

5.2 Results

Training was performed with a total of 2400 data items, 1200 original data items and 1200 data items augmented by each method. The network used for feature extraction was a VGG16 pre-trained network model. The learning time was twice that used without augmentation.

The trained model differs depending on the influence of the initial value used when creating it. Therefore, in order to confirm the change of the classification rate, three models were created using the same feature data extracted from VGG16, and the classification rate was examined. The result is shown in Fig. 6. The result at the left end of the figure is the classification rate before augmentation. From this result, it can be confirmed that the classification rate is improved by any of the augmentation methods.

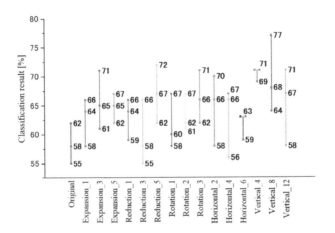

Fig. 6. Classification enhancement by data augmentation

The average value of the classification rates of the three trained models was as follows: expansion: 64.3% (1%: 62.6%, 3%: 65.6%, 5%: 64.6%); reduction: 63.2% (1%: 62.9%, 3%: 59.6%, 5%: 67.0%); rotation: 63.7% (1%: 61.7%, 3%: 63.1%, 5%: 66.3%); horizontal translation: 63.1% (1%: 64.7%, 3%: 63.0%, 5%: 61.5%); and vertical translation: 65.1% (1%: 69.8%, 3%: 65.4%, 5%: 61.2%) (in parentheses, rate in each case). On average, it was found that the classification rate was improved in all 15 cases of expansion, reduction, rotation, horizontal translation, and vertical translation. It has been confirmed that the accuracy of classification can be improved by about 6% using data augmentation that simulates realistic fluctuations in actual motion data.

5.3 Discussion

Looking at the results of the signers individually, the classification rate of the smaller signers was greatly improved after the data augmentation. Figure 7 shows the confusion matrix as a result of classifying the sign language motion of the signer D, that is, it shows the results before and after the augmentation, respectively. This is a result of performing data augmentation by means of a translation in the vertical axis. Accuracy increased from 45% to 57% after augmentation. The effects on the words "get drunk" and "tears" were particularly significant.

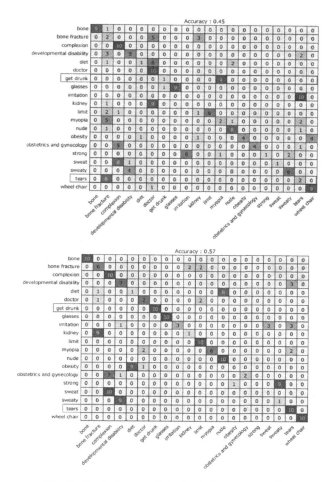

Fig. 7. Confusion matrix before/after augmentation

The motion of the signed word "get drunk" is shown in Fig. 8. The left column shows frames from a moving image used for training, and the right column shows frames from the data used for evaluation. With a smaller signer, the sign language motion is located at a lower position in the frames. It is considered that by augmenting the data by moving the training data in the vertical axis, the sign language motion of a smaller person can be equivalently added to the training data. In this sense, the proposed data augmentation method can absorb fluctuations in sign language motion caused by differences in the physique of signers, subtle differences in motions, and differences in the positional relationship between the camera and the signers, and can contribute to improved classification accuracy.

Data for training   Data for evaluation

Fig. 8. Difference of motion for signing of "get drunk"

6   Ensemble Learning and Results

As a method for improving classification accuracy, ensemble learning is widely known. It obtains a classification result by combining a plurality of trained models, and various algorithms have already been proposed [13]. Here, the simplest Bagging method is applied to improve the performance in this investigation.

6.1   Ensemble Method

The method applied on this occasion is shown in Fig. 9. The probability value of each motion (word) with respect to the input data from each classifier was added as indicated.

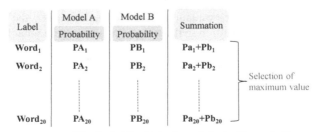

PX_n : Probability P of n-th word obtained by model X

Fig. 9. Ensemble method

Since the LSTM model has the same structure for each feature element from the pre-trained networks, the probability values for each motion of the Softmax layer were added, and the motion that obtained the maximum value was selected as the classification result.

6.2   Results

The improvement in the classification result was investigated by two methods. In the first case, classification results from six trained models created using feature elements from VGG16 were used. In the second case, all six different trained network models (AlexNet, VGG16, VGG19, GoogleNet, ResNet50, ResNet101) were used. Tables 4 and 5 show the results. It was confirmed that the performance was greatly improved irrespective of the pre-trained network model used. In the case of VGG16, the average classification accuracy rate was 61.3% to 74.3%, and the results of the trained model created from six different network models showed that the rate was significantly improved from 54.4% to 74.7%, an improvement of over 20%. In this experiment, the improvement of the performance was larger when using a trained model created by using the feature elements of different pre-network models.

Table 4. Result of integrating six trained models (using VGG16)

VGG16	VGG16	VGG16	VGG16	VGG16	VGG16	Average	Ensemble
58.0%	55.2%	61.5%	68.8%	55.7%	68.8%	61.3%	74.3%

Table 5. Result of integrating six trained models (using 6 kinds of network)

AlexNet	VGG16	VGG16	GoogleNet	ResNet50	ResNet101	Average	Ensemble
61.8%	68.8%	56.3%	40.8%	41.3%	57.2%	54.4%	74.7%

6.3   Discussion

Figure 10 shows the confusion matrix. These are the results of the fourth and sixth values in Table 4 when the classification accuracy is 68.8%. Although the overall accuracy is the same, in particular, the results differ greatly between the motions of "diet" and "obstetrics and gynecology". The reason that the performance was improved by integrating the results from the trained models seems to be that the individual classification results are different. This is considered to be the same reason that the improvement in the classification rate of the results from the six models from the different pre-trained networks is larger than that from VGG16 alone. On the other hand, the results in Fig. 10 may indicate that the trained model is not optimized. It seems there is a need to continue studying the structure of the trained model.

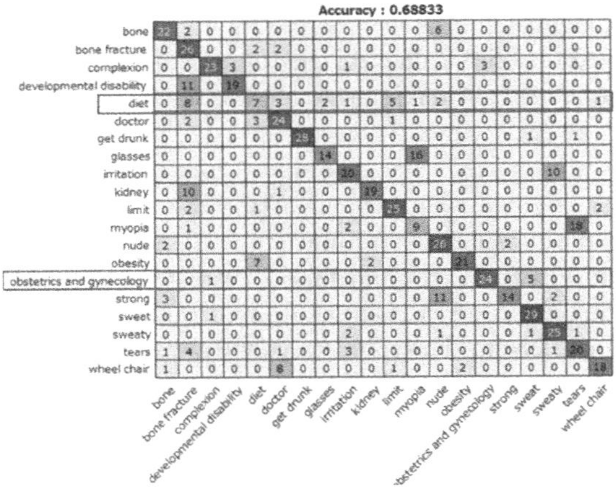

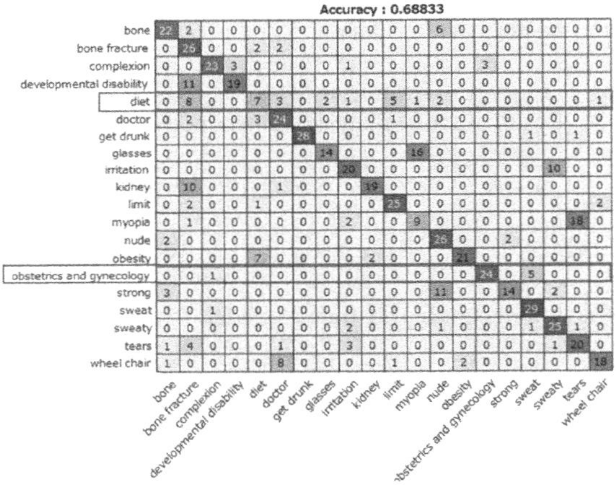

Fig. 10. Confusion matrix of each model created using VGG16

7   Conclusion

This paper has described the results of an investigation into the improvement of a sign language motion classification method using features extracted from pre-trained network models. Since there are many types of sign language motions and subtle differences in each movement, it is impossible to collect sign language motion data corresponding to all of these fluctuations. Therefore, new data is artificially created from existing sign language motion data by data augmentation, and added as supplementary data for creating a trained model. Here, variations arising from differences in the physique of each signer, their range of motion, and the positional relationship between the camera and the signer are added to the original sign language motion data. As a result, the performance improvement was different depending on the additional data, but an average improvement of about 6% was confirmed.

In addition, many pre-trained network models with a proven track record are available. By using these, it is possible to obtain different feature elements with each extraction method. This makes it possible to create a trained model having different properties for classifying sign language motions. The authors tried to improve the performance using the ensemble learning method applied as a method for enhancing classification performance. As a result, it was confirmed that the average classification rate of 61.3% and 54.4% improved to 74.3% and 74.7%, respectively, by integrating the results of various trained models.

Future issues include the need to automatically and accurately detect the color regions of colored gloves and wristbands, which are currently performed manually in advance; to optimize LSTM model structure; and to evaluate the accuracy improvement when combining the proposed data augmentation and ensemble learning. It is also necessary to compose a demonstration system using the current technology in order to realize a concrete usage concept.

Acknowledgement. The authors would like to thank KCC Corporation for their cooperation in acquiring sign language motion data.

References

1. Pfau, R., Steinbach, M., Woll, B.: Sign Language: An International Handbook, p. 1138. Walter de Gruyter, Berlin (2012)
2. Sourcenext Corporation, Pockettalk. https://pocketalk.jp/. (in Japanese)
3. Kumar, P., Gauba, H., Roy, P., Dogra, D.: Coupled HMM-based multi-sensor data fusion for sign language recognition. Pattern Recogn. Lett. **86**, 1–8 (2017)
4. Singha, J., Das, K.: Hand gesture recognition based on Karhunen-Loeve transform. In: Mobile & Embedded Technology International Conference 2013, pp. 365–371 (2013)
5. Yang, J., Nguyen, M., San, P., Li, X., Krishnaswamy, S.: Deep convolutional neural networks on multichannel time series for human activity recognition. In: Proceedings of the Twenty-Fourth International Joint Conference on Artificial Intelligence (IJCAI 2015), pp. 3995–4001 (2015)
6. Zheng, Y., Liu, Q., Chen, E., Ge, Y., Zhao, J.: Time series classification using multi-channels deep convolutional neural networks. In: International Conference on Web-Age Information Management (WAIM), pp. 298–310 (2014)
7. Xie, S., Yang, T., Wang, X., Lin, Y.: Hyper-class augmented and regularized deep learning for fine-grained image classification. In: The IEEE Conference on Computer Vision and Pattern Recognition (CVPR), pp. 2645–2654 (2015)
8. Dietterich, T.G.: Ensemble methods in machine learning. In: Kittler, J., Roli, F. (eds.) MCS 2000. LNCS, vol. 1857, pp. 1–15. Springer, Heidelberg (2000). https://doi.org/10.1007/3-540-45014-9_1
9. Ozawa, T., Shibata, H., Nishimura, H., Tanaka, H.: Investigation of feature elements and performance improvement for sign language recognition by hidden Markov model. In: Antona, M., Stephanidis, C. (eds.) UAHCI 2017. LNCS, vol. 10278, pp. 76–88. Springer, Cham (2017). https://doi.org/10.1007/978-3-319-58703-5_6
10. Losuwanakul, N., Sakamoto, K., Ozawa, T., Nishimura, H., Tanaka, H.: Trial report on applying deep learning to sign language recognition. In: The 9th Asian Symposium on Printing Technology (ASPT2018), Poster-Session, pp. 39–40 (2018)

11. Kawaguchi, K., Wang, W., Ohta, E., Nishimura, H., Tanaka, H.: Basic investigation of sign language motion classification by feature extraction using pre-trained network models. In: IEEE Pacific Rim Conference on Communications, Computers and Signal Processing (PacRim2019), 4 p. (2019)
12. KCC Corporation, Smart Deaf. http://www.smartdeaf.com/. (in Japanese)
13. Erp, M., Vuurpijl, L., Schomaker, L.: An overview and comparison of voting methods for pattern recognition. In: Eighth International Workshop on Frontiers in Handwriting Recognition, pp. 1–6 (2002)

An Intermediate Mapping Layer
for Interactive Sequencing

Mathias Kirkegaard$^{(\boxtimes)}$, Mathias Bredholt, and Marcelo M. Wanderley

Input Devices and Musical Interaction Laboratory - IDMIL,
Centre for Interdisciplinary Research in Music Media and Technology - CIRMMT,
McGill University, Montreal, Canada
{mathias.kirkegaard,mathias.bredholt}@mail.mcgill.ca,
marcelo.wanderley@mcgill.ca

Abstract. The definition of mapping strategies between input devices and sound generating algorithms is an essential process in computer music. Traditionally, mapping has been considered in the context of digital musical instruments where the control of low level sound features (note articulation, timbre) is the goal. This paper describes the motivation, implementation and example application of an intermediate mapping layer for interactive sequencing. Building upon the mapping literature, we expand it by exploring the control of predefined musical sequences, focusing on the ability to make spontaneous musical decisions, creative exploration by browsing, and easy mapping between devices. It involves a parameterization of rhythm, melody, and harmony along with collaborative mappings in both libmapper and Ableton Link.

Keywords: Mapping · Sequencing · Collaborative performance

1 Introduction

The importance of mapping within design of DMI's has been elaborately discussed in [6] and [3], and it has been used in several contexts, synthesis engines [5], physical models [15], audio effects [14], and envelopes [7]. In these contexts, mappings are usually focused on the direct control of timbral parameters, to define the feel and responsiveness of a musical instrument. The work described in this paper focuses on expanding the concept of mapping into sequencing. The *sequencer*, a recording and playback system, which can send and receive the control and performance data needed to regenerate a series of musical events [11], lets music makers organize and control more layers and dimensions of musical structure than possible with traditional acoustic instruments, giving access to extended timescales of rhythm, polyrhythmic grids or extreme uptempo performance [11]. The concept of sequencing can be seen as a mapping problem by considering a sequencer as an intermediate mapping layer that translates a control input to multiple musical events. This is the idea behind the *algorithmic sequencing layer* (ASL), an intermediate mapping layer that maps 18 control

© Springer Nature Switzerland AG 2020
S. Yamamoto and H. Mori (Eds.): HCII 2020, LNCS 12185, pp. 447–456, 2020.
https://doi.org/10.1007/978-3-030-50017-7_33

parameters to real-time generated MIDI events, by means of a parameterization of rhythm, melody and harmony. The parameters can be mapped to a gestural controller with complex mappings such as one-to-many or many-to-one. In a performance situation, the generated MIDI events would trigger a synthesis engine, which generates the audio.

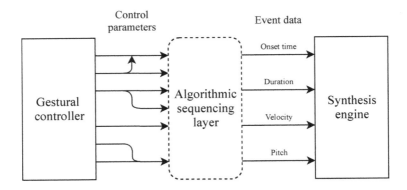

Fig. 1. An example of a complete sequencer application

The following keywords are used as guidelines for the mapping strategy

- **Spontaneity.** The ability to make spontaneous musical decisions by controlling multiple musical events simultaneously.
- **Serendipity.** Creative exploration by browsing.
- **Collaborative.** Easy mapping between devices to increase musical coherence between multiple performers.

1.1   Spontaneity

In a live performance situation, the performer should be able to change the generated sequence spontaneously. It should be possible to quickly make drastic changes to tempo, event onset density, and melodic/harmonic content.

1.2   Serendipity

In [2] S. Fels proposes the use of metaphors to increase the transparency of a mapping. Fels argues that the perceived expressivity of an instrument depends on the transparency of the mapping, as the communication between the player and the audience involves an understanding of the link between the player's actions and the sounds produced [2]. The metaphor of browsing is used in the design of the ASL, in order to allow for "scrolling" through different rhythms and chords. This is related to the concept of serendipity, as the user can discover new musical ideas without having imagined them beforehand.

1.3   Collaboration

When gestures are mapped to timbral parameters as in [3,5–7,14,15], the auditory feedback is often instantaneous. On the contrary, when changing parameters for a musical sequence, the auditory feedback is distributed over time. This can result in lack of coherence between performers in a collaborative improvisational musical setting. The proposed strategy enables a mapping between multiple sequencers and gestural controllers, in order to accommodate this issue.

2   Algorithmic Sequencing Layer (ASL)

The ASL was developed as part of the hardware sequencer $T-1$, which features 18 control parameters for algorithmic sequencing. This section describes the implementation of the most important parameters of the ASL, specifically the parameterizations of rhythm, melody, and harmony.

2.1   Rhythm

In this work the concept of musical rhythm is considered as a sequence of events, defined by their amplitude, duration, and onset time. A parameterization of rhythms can be regarded as a divergent mapping to multiple rhythmic events, that results in a sequence with musically relevant properties. This allows for an interaction, which uses the metaphor of browsing. By changing the parameters of the rhythm, a user can browse through different musically relevant rhythms. In [13] G. Toussaint studies a large range of traditional rhythms, and especially those of Sub-Saharan African music. They share an important property, that their onset patterns are distributed as evenly as possible. Toussaint also demonstrates, how the *euclidean algorithm* can be used to generate rhythmic sequences that share this property. This is the basis for the parameterization of onset time in the ASL.

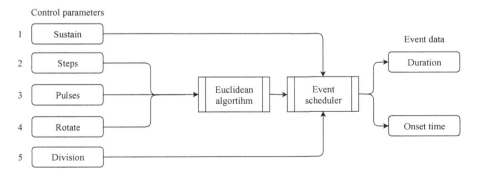

Fig. 2. Internal mappings to onset time and duration of musical events

Euclidean Rhythms. are represented by 2 parameters, *steps* and *pulses*. For a euclidean rhythm $E(n, k)$, there is n steps, $k < n$ pulses, and $k - n$ rests. The euclidean algorithm, a procedure that computes the greatest common divisor, is used to place the rests among the pulses as evenly as possible. The position of a pulse determines the onset time of a rhythmic event, and the duration of each event corresponds to the number of rests succeeding it.

Fig. 3. Illustration of 3 euclidean rhythms with different number of pulses. From left to right: $E(8,3), E(8,4), E(8,5)$

The ASL control inputs that maps to duration and onset time include:

1 Sustain. Percentage of the full duration of a rhythmic event
2 Steps. Length of the euclidean rhythm
3 Pulses. Number of onsets in the euclidean rhythm
4 Rotate. Starting position of the euclidean rhythm, which corresponds to a rotation of the graphical representation in Fig. 3
5 Division Temporal resolution of the euclidean rhythm.

Accentuation. An important feature of rhythmic patterns is accentuation, i.e. amplitude modulation over time, as it allows for emphasizing certain events by means of a louder sound. P. Pfordresher concludes that accents function as temporal landmarks that listeners can use when tracking the time structure of musical patterns [10]. In the ASL, a parametrization of accentuation is obtained by considering the amplitude envelope of a rhythmic phrase as discrete steps in an accent phrase. An overview of the accentuation mapping is seen in Fig. 4. A collection of perceptually relevant accent phrases can be used as input to the ASL.

The ASL control inputs that maps to amplitude include:

1 Force. Addition and subtraction to the accent phrase, effectively controlling the average amplitude of a rhythmic sequence.
2 Dynamics. Multiplication of the accent phrase, effectively controlling the amount of accentuation.

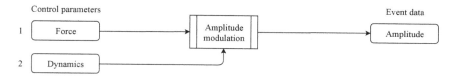

Fig. 4. Internal mapping to amplitude of rhythmic events

2.2 Melody

By considering a musical phrase of a melody as a discrete sequence of degrees in a musical scale, the first phrase of the melody *Brother John* can be represented as

$$[0, 1, 2, 0, 0, 1, 2, 0]$$

which in the C-major scale translates into the sequence of pitches

$$[C, D, E, C, C, D, E, C]$$

In this paper, this is defined as the *scale degree representation* of a musical phrase, and it allows for doing arithmetic operations on melodies. Addition and subtraction corresponds to the concept of diatonic transposition i.e. transposing a melody sequence within the given musical scale. Multiplication and division corresponds to changing the melodic range of the melody i.e. the distance between the lowest and highest note. As the scale degree representation is independent of the chosen musical scale, a phrase can easily be translated between major and minor. As with accent phrases, a collection of melody phrases can be used as input to the ASL. The control inputs that map to pitch include:

1 *Scale.* Musical scale (major, minor, pentatonic etc.)
2 *Ambitus.* Multiplication of the melody phrase, effectively controlling the melodic range of the phrase
3 *Degree.* Addition and subtraction to the melody phrase, effectively doing diatonic transposition.

2.3 Harmony

Harmony can be parameterized using voice leading principles i.e. the theory of progressions of individual melody lines and how they interact with each other to create harmony. An important principle within voice leading is that a good chord progression has common tones between each successive chord. In scale degree representation this means that each successive chord should have at least 1 integer in common. This chord sequence follows that principle

$$\begin{bmatrix} 0 \\ 2 \\ 4 \end{bmatrix} \rightarrow \begin{bmatrix} 0 \\ 2 \\ 5 \end{bmatrix} \rightarrow \begin{bmatrix} 0 \\ 3 \\ 5 \end{bmatrix}$$

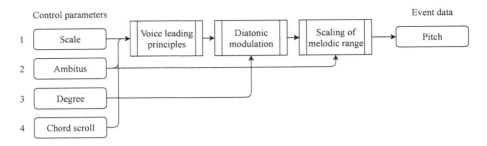

Fig. 5. Internal mapping to pitch height

In C-major the chords above represent the progression

$$C \to Am \to F$$

The ASL includes a simple algorithm that adds or subtracts to a single tone, T, in the chord at a time. After each addition/subtraction, T points to the next tone in the chord, such that a new chord is created at each step. The new chord always has 2 common tones with the previous chord. As with the euclidean algorithm, this algorithm allows an interaction which uses browsing as metaphor. By stepping through the algorithm a user can scroll through musically relevant harmonic progressions. This is implemented with the control input *Chord scroll*:

4 *Chord scroll*. A single step of the voice leading algorithm

3 Hardware Platform

$T-1$ is a hardware platform, developed by the two first authors, that utilizes the ASL to implement a MIDI sequencer with 16 polyphonic tracks [12]. Parameterizations of rhythm, melody, and harmony, enables the design of a sequencer interface where all control inputs are space multiplexed, and thus immediately accessible. This limits the need for a display, and instead animations of multicolored LED's are used as visual feedback.

3.1 Interface

The interface consists of 18 rotary encoders and 23 rubber keypad buttons with LED's. A drawing of the interface is seen in Fig. 6. The 18 encoders are mapped in a one-to-one manner to the ASL, effectively controlling the rhythm, melody and harmony generation of a selected track. The 16 buttons to the bottom left represent the 16 tracks, which can be edited by pressing the corresponding button. The 7 buttons to the bottom right represent the *performance tools*, which activate a one-to-many mapping between the interface and the ASL.

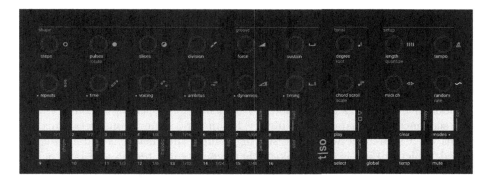

Fig. 6. Front panel of the T − 1

3.2 Performance Tools

Controlling 16 tracks simultaneously can be both time consuming and confusing in a musical performance. In order to allow for spontaneous musical decisions, a set of tools for multi-track editing are developed with the aim of minimizing *speed of performance* for tasks that are deemed typical in a musical performance.

> **Global.** Apply relative changes to all enabled tracks simultaneously i.e. adds or subtracts the same value to all parameters
> **Temp.** Apply temporary changes to different tracks one at time, and revert all changes simultaneously
> **Mute.** Mute/unmute multiple tracks simultaneously.

4 Collaborative Sequencing

The parametrization implemented in the ASL, enables the possibility of a shared reference of musical parameters. Each parameter can be represented as a signal, which can be shared with peers in an collaborative musical setting. This allows for the creation of one-to-one and many-to-many mappings between multiple instances of the ASL. A one-to-one mapping is relevant for parameters such as tempo, musical scale/key and meter, where uniformity is desired. A many-to-many mapping is relevant for rhythmic and melodic parameters where coherence but not necessarily uniformity is desired. Some examples include:

Constant Note Density. A mapping of *pulses* across performers. When a performer increases their *pulses* parameter, the number of pulses decrease on the their peers thereby keeping the combined note density constant.

Pizzicato. A mapping between the sustain of one performer to velocity of all performers, where the sustain is inversely proportional to the velocity, effectively implementing a pizzicato mode when sustain is low.

Shared Global Mode. A mapping between all the parameters of multiple ASL's, effectively implementing the global mode explained in Sect. 3.2 across multiple performers.

4.1   Technology

Collaborative mappings are obtained by utilizing *libmapper* [8] to connect multiple sequencers. libmapper is a library for making connections between data signals on a shared network. For sharing tempo and meter, *Ableton Link* [4] is used. Ableton Link is a technology that synchronizes tempo and beat across applications running on multiple devices connected on a shared network. The 2nd author has ported the Ableton Link and libmapper technologies to the *ESP32* microcontroller platform to allow for synchronization and mapping between multiple instances of the $T-1$ and other music applications [1].

Collaborative Performance with 2 T-Sticks During the porting of libmapper a demonstration of mappings on a shared network in a collaborative performance and was created. The demonstration used two T-Sticks [9], a gestural controller made from a pipe equipped with a range of sensors. Two performers had one T-Stick each and controlled different aspects of a single sequence of sounds. By using libmapper, it was possible to experiment with and dynamically change mappings between the gestures of multiple performers and a single stream of musical events.

5   Discussion and Future Work

In Sect. 2, it is mentioned that the ASL uses accent and melody phrases as input for the parameterization of accentuation and melody. On the $T-1$, phrases are generated using a pseudo random algorithm. More work should be put into making the generation and collection of phrases motivated by music- and perceptual theory. Alternatively, it would be interesting to develop a system that allows for recording these phrases on a gestural controller, to add more expressive possibilities to the system.

The euclidean algorithm is used for parameterizing rhythms, and while it offers a large range of rhythmic patterns, it also simplifies the musical output to sequences with an even distribution of onsets. This limits the possibilities of making fills and uneven rhythms. Additional features, not described in this paper, were added to the $T-1$ [12] to accommodate this issue.

The work described in this paper simplifies musical sequences to discrete musical events. This simplification resulted from the development process of the $T-1$, which outputs MIDI messages, that are defined by only pitch, velocity, sustain, and onset time. Thus, perceptually important information regarding the temporal evolution of a musical event is disregarded. Future work could combine the findings in [7] on parameterizations of temporal envelopes, with the ASL, in order to increase the dimensionality of the sequenced musical events.

Another simplification is the assumption of independence between the dimensions of musical events. For instance, some acoustic instruments has inherent internal mappings between sustain and pitch, or amplitude and sustain, which are not accounted for here. Though, as the proposed mapping system enables internal mappings (through libmapper), an interesting next step would be to experiment with inter-dependency of these dimensions, by means of complex many-to-many mappings.

6   Conclusion

In this paper the motivation of an intermediate mapping layer for interactive sequencing is presented. The proposed mapping layer, the algorithmic sequencing layer (ASL), provides a mapping between linear control variables and discrete musical events. A detailed description of how the ASL parameterizes rhythm, melody, and harmony is provided, and the hardware sequencer $T-1$ is presented as an example application that utilizes the ASL. Additionally, a mapping strategy for collaborative performance with multiple sequencers is proposed. Finally, the simplifications of the suggested framework is discussed, emphasizing that the musical output of this work has a limited range.

Acknowledgements. The ideas presented in this paper are the result of the more than 3 years of development of the $T-1$ sequencer by Torso Electronics, a company founded by Mathias Bredholt, Mathias Kirkegaard, Lars Buchholtz, and Jonas Kenton. The first two authors send a big thanks to our colleagues, Jonas and Lars, for helping us with the development.

References

1. Bredholt, M.: libmapper for arduino. https://github.com/mathiasbredholt/libmapper_arduino. Accessed 24 Jan 2020
2. Fels, S., Gadd, A., Mulder, A.: Mapping transparency through metaphor: towards more expressive musical instruments. Organ. Sound **7**, 109–126 (2003). https://doi.org/10.1017/S1355771802002042
3. Garnett, G.E., Goudeseune, C.: Performance factors in control of high-dimensional space. In: International Computer Music Conference (ICMC) (1999)
4. Goltz, F.: Ableton link - a technology to synchronize music software. In: LAC, pp. 39–42 (2018). https://doi.org/10.14279/depositonce-7046
5. Hunt, A., Wanderley, M.: Mapping performer parameters to synthesis engines. Organ. Sound **7**, 97–108 (2002). https://doi.org/10.1017/S1355771802002030
6. Hunt, A., Wanderley, M.M., Paradis, M.: The importance of parameter mapping in electronic instrument design. In: New Interfaces For Musical Expression (NIME) (2002). https://doi.org/10.1076/jnmr.32.4.429.18853
7. Levitin, D.J., McAdams, S., Adams, R.L.: Control parameters for musical instruments: a foundation for new mappings of gesture to sound. Organ. Sound **7**(2), 171–189 (2002). https://doi.org/10.1017/S135577180200208X
8. Malloch, J., Sinclair, S., Wanderley, M.: Libmapper (a library for connecting things). In: CHI (2013). https://doi.org/10.1145/2468356.2479617

9. Malloch, J., Wanderley, M.: The t-stick: from musical interface to musical instrument. In: New Interfaces for Musical Expression (NIME) (January 2007). https://doi.org/10.1145/1279740.1279751

10. Pfordresher, P.: The role of melodic and rhythmic accents in musical structure. Music Percept.: Interdiscip. J. **20**, 431–464 (2003). https://doi.org/10.1525/mp.2003.20.4.431

11. Roads, C.: Composing Electronic Music, a New Aesthetic. Oxford University Press, Oxford (2015)

12. Torso Electronics Homepage. https://www.torsoelectronics.com. Accessed 02 Jan 2020

13. Toussaint, G.: The euclidean algorithm generates traditional musical rhythms. In: BRIDGES: Mathematical Connections in Art, Music and Science, pp. 47–56 (2005)

14. Verfaille, V., Wanderley, M.M., Depalle, P.: Mapping strategies for gestural and adaptive control of digital audio effects. J. New Music Res. **35**(1), 71–93 (2006). https://doi.org/10.1080/09298210600696881

15. Wang, S., Wanderley, M.M., Scavone, G.: The study of mapping strategies between the excitators of the single-reed woodwind and the bowed string. In: Conference on Sound and Music Technology (CSMT), pp. 107–120 (2019). https://doi.org/10.1007/978-981-15-2756-2_9

Drowsy Bather Detection Using a Triaxial Accelerometer

Hisashi Kojima, Chika Oshima$^{(\boxtimes)}$, and Koichi Nakayama

Saga University, Saga, Japan
knakayama@is.saga-u.ac.jp

Abstract. Japanese people like soaking in bathtubs; however, the number of deaths by drowning among those over the age of 65 is increasing year by year. We focused on the problem that there are no popular solutions for those accidents caused by nodding off while bathing. Today, lightweight wireless earbuds often feature accelerometers. Further, more and more people enjoy music with such earbuds while bathing. Therefore, if a person's drowsiness in the bathtub can be detected using these accelerometers, wireless earbuds worn while bathing may prevent serious accidents before they happen. This paper proposed a drowsy bather detection system using an accelerometer. When a person nods off, their head tilts gradually, and the direction of gravity applied to the head changes. The system detects drowsiness by detecting these changes with the accelerometer. In the experiment, the usefulness of the algorithm in the system was evaluated by comparing the drowsiness level estimated by the system with by data from a sleep tracking device. The detection rate tended to increase as the stage of non-REM sleep increased. These results suggest that the system may be useful for preventing accidents due to nodding off while bathing.

Keywords: Bathtub · Gravitational acceleration · Nod off · Stages of sleep

1 Introduction

The number of deaths by drowning in Japan among those over the age of 65 is increasing year by year [1, 2]. In many cases of drowning during bathing, the cause is thought to be heat shock [3]. "Heat shock" is a phenomenon in which a myocardial infarction or stroke is caused by the increased burden on the heart due to a rapid change in temperature. In an 11-year retrospective study conducted in Maryland, 71.7% of 92 bathtub deaths were attributable to drowning [4]. Further, it is possible to nod off while bathing. This is dangerous, too. It is known that bathing before sleeping facilitates earlier sleep onset in a cold environment [5]. Heat shock can, to some extent, be prevented by checking the room temperature difference between the bathroom and the dressing room [6], or by refraining from taking a bath after drinking. However, it is difficult to take precautionary measures against nodding off while bathing, because it can happen even if a person has not been drinking, and regardless of age. Tokyo Gas Co., Ltd. and Purpose Co., Ltd. have developed a water heater remote control [7]. It detects when there is no movement

© Springer Nature Switzerland AG 2020
S. Yamamoto and H. Mori (Eds.): HCII 2020, LNCS 12185, pp. 457–468, 2020.
https://doi.org/10.1007/978-3-030-50017-7_34

from a bather for a certain time, noting it as an abnormality conveyed via a door sensor, a water level sensor, and a person-detecting sensor. If a bather does not move, the system assumes they are likely sleeping deeply or losing consciousness. With this in mind, it is necessary to detect drowsiness before a bather becomes unable to move. One drawback to this method is that it requires sensors to be installed in the home.

Many studies have been done to detect drowsiness using eye-shape [8], eye-blink [9], and eye-tracking [10] technologies. However, these have intended to detect drowsiness while driving, not in a bathtub. Placing a camera in a bathroom is not practical, because of privacy concerns and the need for a bather to sit in a fixed position. A detection system for drowsy driving with an accelerometer affixed to the surface plane of a steering wheel has been proposed [11]. Vural, et al. [12] measured the head movements of drivers using accelerometers. Their results showed that head motion increases as drivers become drowsy, but just before falling asleep, the head becomes still.

Today, some lightweight wireless earbuds feature accelerometers [13]. Many people enjoy music with such earbuds during bathing because, oftentimes, these earbuds are water-resistant. Therefore, if a person's drowsiness in the bathtub can be detected using the onboard accelerometers, wireless earbuds worn for listening to music may prevent serious accidents before they happen.

In this paper, we focus on the head movements seen before falling asleep and develop a system that detects bathers' drowsiness using an accelerometer.

2   System

2.1   System Structure

This system consists of two parts: a data acquisition part and a data analysis part. In the data acquisition part, an accelerometer transmits acceleration data with elapsed time to a computer via Bluetooth technology. The computer receives the data and writes them to a text file. In the data analysis part, the computer reads the text file, analyzes them, and detects drowsiness.

2.2   Acquisition of Head Movement Data

In this paper, we develop an algorithm for detecting drowsiness during bathing using an accelerometer. The accelerometer used is the TSND121, made by ATR-Promotions [14]. Table 1 shows the main specifications of the accelerometer.

Table 1. The main specifications of the accelerometer.

Size	37 mm (W) × 46 mm (H) × 12 mm (D)
Weight	About 22 g
Communication	Bluetooth Ver2.0 + EDR Class2
Sample rate	4 Hz – 1000 Hz
Acceleration range	±16G

In this experiment, the accelerometer transmits data every 5 ms. In other words, the data output frequency is 200 Hz. The accelerometer is fixed on one ear with a headband in the experiment. In the future, we will use an accelerometer that is built into earbuds.

When a person nods off, their head tilts gradually. Figures 1, 2 and 3 show the change of the direction of gravity applied to the head as it tilts gradually.

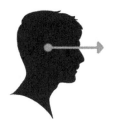

Fig. 1. The normal direction of gravity.

Fig. 2. The direction of gravity when a person nods off.

Fig. 3. Rotated Fig. 2.

We define the vector g, which is the gravitational acceleration applied to the accelerometer in the normal state. We have:

$$a = p + r, \tag{1}$$

where a is the acceleration applied to the accelerometer, p is the vector projection of a on g, and r is the vector rejection of a from g (see Fig. 4).

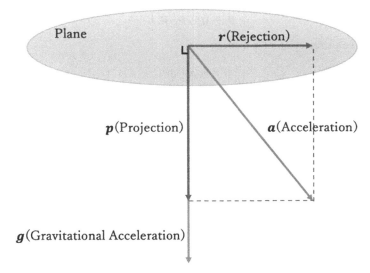

Fig. 4. Relationship between acceleration, gravitational acceleration, projection, and rejection.

When the direction of gravity applied to the accelerometer changes, p and r change. Therefore, p and r are useful for detecting movements that change the direction of gravity, even if the movement is not large, such as bending the neck. p is not affected by horizontal movement, and r is not affected by vertical movement. In this paper, large movements such as standing up and sitting down are not considered. Moreover, we do not care about effect of small movements on p and r because the effect of small movements on them is much less than that of change in direction of gravity applied to the accelerometer on them.

We detect two motions with p and r. One motion is that the head tilts from the upright position (tilt motion). The other is that the head returns to the upright position (return motion). The first author measured his head movements and used the data to develop the algorithm for detecting these two motions.

2.3 Detection Algorithm

The accelerometer transmits three-dimensional acceleration data:

$$a = (a_x, a_y, a_z).$$ (2)

After the data acquisition and before their analysis, we find the acceleration when the head does not move in the upright position and define it as the gravitational acceleration:

$$g = (g_x, g_y, g_z).$$ (3)

p is the vector projection of a on g:

$$p = \frac{a \cdot g}{|g|^2} g,$$ (4)

$$p = (p_x, p_y, p_z).$$ (5)

r is the vector rejection of a from g:

$$r = a - p,$$ (6)

$$r = (r_x, r_y, r_z).$$ (7)

$|p|$ is given by:

$$|p| = \sqrt{p_x^2 + p_y^2 + p_z^2}.$$ (8)

$|r|$ is given by:

$$|r| = \sqrt{r_x^2 + r_y^2 + r_z^2}.$$ (9)

To reduce the amount of calculation and the influence of random errors, the averages of every 20 acquired accelerations are used for analysis. We collected 200 acceleration data acquired from the accelerometer for one second at 200 Hz and 10 averages of acceleration are obtained from 200 acceleration data for one second. Figures 5 and 6 show the difference between $|p|$ without the average processing and with the average processing.

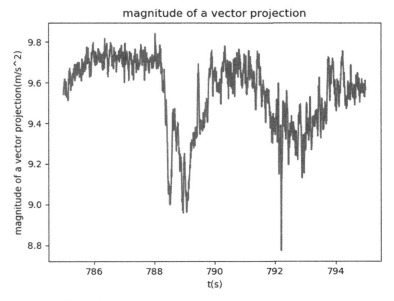

Fig. 5. $|p|$ vs. time graph without the average processing.

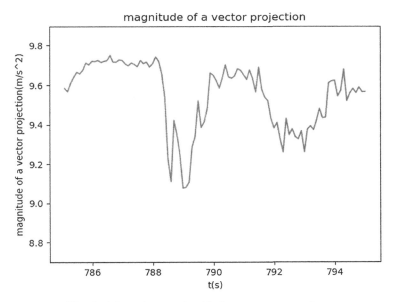

Fig. 6. $|p|$ vs. time graph with the average processing.

When the head does not move, $|p|$ and $|r|$ are constant. However, $|p|$ and $|r|$ change when the head moves. The change is detected using the linear least squares method. We use it to determine the straight line of best fit for changes in $|p|$ or $|r|$ for two seconds.

The slope of a least squares regression line is given by:

$$A'_{|p|} = \frac{\sum_{i=1}^{n}\{(t_i - \bar{t})(|p|_i - \overline{|p|})\}}{\sum_{i=1}^{n}(t_i - \bar{t})^2}, \tag{10}$$

$$A'_{|r|} = \frac{\sum_{i=1}^{n}\{(t_i - \bar{t})(|r|_i - \overline{|r|})\}}{\sum_{i=1}^{n}(t_i - \bar{t})^2}, \tag{11}$$

where $A'_{|p|}$ is the slope from a $|p|$ vs. time graph, $A'_{|r|}$ is the slope from a $|r|$ vs. time graph, and t is time. A motion is regarded as a tilt motion if $A'_{|p|} < -0.1$ and $A'_{|r|} > 0.1$. A motion is regarded as a return motion if $A'_{|p|} > 0.1$ and $A'_{|r|} < -0.1$.

Figure 7 shows the drowsiness detection algorithm. Our system detects the drowsiness if the last minute has more than 9 and less than 21 instances of a tilt/return motion starting moment. The reason for setting the threshold to less than 21 times is that, if the head moves more than 20 times per minute, the person is not likely sleepy, but more likely moving with the beat of the music they are hearing. The system is set not to detect drowsiness for the first five minutes of use, because we assume that it takes the bather some time to relax. In addition, the interval of the same motion is one second or more. In other words, it is determined that the motion is continuous if $A'_{|p|}$ and $A'_{|r|}$ exceed the threshold again within one second.

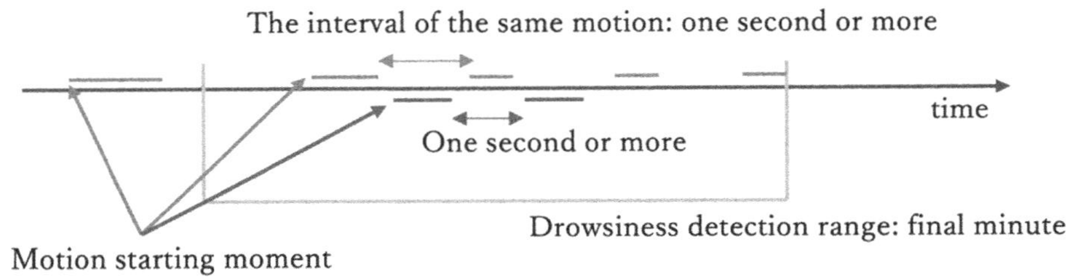

Fig. 7. Drowsiness detection algorithm.

3 Experiment

3.1 Aim

The experiment aims to show that the algorithm developed in Sect. 2 can detect drowsiness.

3.2 Method

The participants were seven university students who had never learned Russian. Six of them were men. They participated in the experiment one at a time. Six of them participated in the experiment twice, while one participated only once, due to scheduling issues.

The experiment was conducted in a soundproof room installed in the laboratory; the lights in the room were turned off, and only the lights in the laboratory were left on, to prompt drowsiness in the participants.

Participants fixed the accelerometer [14] on one ear using a headband and put GO2SLEEP [15] on the finger of the left hand. GO2SLEEP is a wearable sleep measurement device made by Sleepon. It estimates the depth of sleep by measuring the user's heart rate, pulse rate, and blood oxygen levels through finger sensors.

Participants were instructed to sit on a sofa and watch a Russian language video about an hour long [16] and to count the number of Russian words in the video using a Yumqua wireless mouse [17].

Before the experiment, they received the explanation that, while they would be recorded during the experiment, their personally identifiable information would not be disclosed in the research presentation. We collected signed informed consent documents from all participants.

3.3 Analysis

Our system determines tilt and return motions from the data measured by the accelerometer fixed on one ear. The system detects the drowsiness if the last minute has shown more than 9 and less than 21 instances of tilt or return motion starting moments. The participants' actual drowsiness is estimated using a GO2SLEEP monitor. The GO2SLEEP outputs six stages: Awake, REM (Rapid Eye Movement), Light Sleep N1, Light Sleep N2, Deep Sleep N3, and Deep Sleep N4. REM is the stage of sleep during which the eyes jerk rapidly in various directions; it usually occurs about 70–90 min after falling asleep [18]. Light Sleep N1, Light Sleep N2, Deep Sleep N3, and Deep Sleep N4 are the stages of non-REM sleep.

In this experiment, we examine whether the system's drowsiness detection matches the GO2SLEEP's non-REM sleep estimation.

3.4 Results

(1) Missing data

Participant A's first and second acceleration data and Participant B's first acceleration data were lost due to an incorrect setting. In addition, Participant C's first video data were lost because the video camera ran out of power. These missing data were not used for analysis. Moreover, the second experiments of Participants B and D were inadvertently conducted using a different Russian language video [19]. Although the experiment time was shortened by this unexpected event, we determined this had no effect on the experiment, so these two data sets were used in the analysis. In all, we used data from a total of nine participants (nine experiments) for the analysis.

(2) Head movements when drowsy

When the participants were drowsy, several motions were observed: nodding, yawning, and sleeping with the head tilted. Figure 8 shows the change of $|\boldsymbol{p}|$ at the time of nodding. The graph has a valley because the tilt motion decreases $|\boldsymbol{p}|$ and the return motion increases $|p|$. Figure 9 shows the change of $|p|$ when the participant made a return motion and then a tilt motion. $|p|$ increased when the head returned to the upright position.

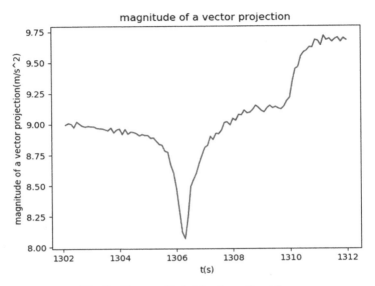

Fig. 8. Change of $|p|$ at the time of nodding.

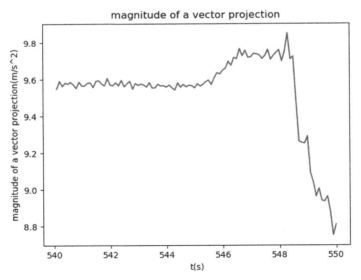

Fig. 9. Change of $|p|$ when a return motion is followed by a tilt motion.

(3) Drowsiness detection
Figure 10 shows the stages of sleep for each participant per minute measured by the GO2SLEEP using colors and numbers/letters. There are six stages: Awake (0), Light Sleep N1 (1), Light Sleep N2 (2), Deep Sleep N3 (3), Deep Sleep N4 (4), and REM Sleep (R). Deep sleep N4 was not measured in all experiments. In Fig. 10, the horizontal axis represents the time from 0–64 min, while the vertical axis represents the participants and the number of the experiments. Moreover, the numbers/letters of the sleep stages at the time when the system detected drowsiness are circled. For example, (D, 1) at 13 and 14 min indicates that light sleep N2 and drowsiness were detected in the first experiment with Participant D.

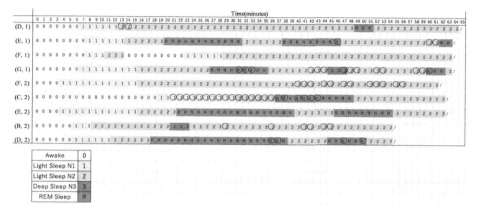

Fig. 10. Stages of sleep and drowsiness detection results.

In Fig. 10, the sections that consecutively indicate the same stage of sleep are regarded as a line. For example, 0–6 min in Participant D's first experiment are a line, because the sections of the stage of sleep are consecutively Awake (0). Throughout all experiments, Awake has 10 lines, and all the lines appeared from the beginning to the middle of the experiments. There were no Awake lines at the end of the experiments. Light Sleep N1 had 10 lines, and all the lines appeared from the beginning through the middle of the experiments. Light Sleep N2 has 22 lines and is longest of all stages in the experiments. Deep Sleep N3 has 2 lines. REM sleep has 11 lines and appeared in the middle and end of six experiments.

We examined whether the system detected drowsiness at each stage of non-REM sleep. Drowsiness was detected in 1 out of 10 lines (10%) in N1, 7 out of 22 lines (31.8%) in N2, and 1 out of 2 lines (50%) in N3. Drowsiness was not detected in Awake.

3.5 Discussion

The system did not detect drowsiness in the awake stage, and sometimes detected drowsiness during light sleep. The detection rate tended to increase as the stage of sleep increased, so it is suggested that the system may be useful in preventing accidents due to falling asleep while bathing. The reason why drowsiness was not detected by N3 in Participant B's second experiment was that the head was tilted and did not move.

It was also observed in other participants that their heads tilted and did not move. When the head tilts and does not move, the only force acting on the accelerometer is gravity, and $|p|$ is less than 9.8 m/s^2, which is the gravitational acceleration (see Fig. 9). $A'_{|p|}$ at that time is near 0, because $|p|$ is constant until the head starts to move. Therefore, it is likely detectable that the head tilts and does not move. In addition, a person can drown without their head tilting. For this reason, it is necessary to examine whether the motion is detectable with an accelerometer.

Moreover, large movements were not considered in this paper. By setting a threshold for magnitude of acceleration, it is likely that large movements can be distinguished from small movements.

REM sleep was measured 11 times throughout all the experiments, which lasted about an hour. However, REM stage usually occurs about 70–90 min after falling asleep. The cause for this discrepancy may be the sleep measurement device (GO2SLEEP). We will conduct further experiments regarding this in consultation with a sleep expert.

4   Conclusion

In this paper, we proposed a system to detect a drowsy bather using an accelerometer. The detection rate tends to increase as the stage of non-REM sleep increases, so it has been suggested that the system may be useful for preventing accidents due to falling asleep while bathing.

5   Future Work

In future work, we will develop the system outlined below (see Fig. 11). Accelerometers built into earphones will measure the acceleration of the user's head movements and send the data to an application. The application will receive the data and analyze them. The application will warn the user if they are likely to doze off. The warning is highly likely to wake them up if they doze off. However, if they do not respond to the warning, the application will send a notice to registered devices. It is possible to detect an abnormal state, such as the user losing consciousness, early because the application not only warns the user but also sends a notice to family members or others if the user does not respond to the warning.

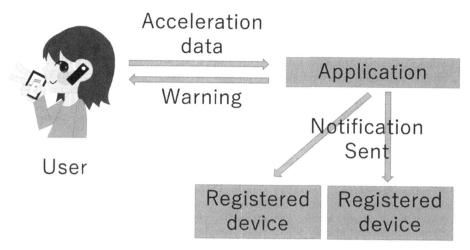

Fig. 11. Future structure of the system.

Acknowledgement. This work was supported by JSPS KAKENHI Grant 17H01950.

References

1. The Consumer Affairs Agency (in Japan): Let's prevent elderly people from accidents. https://www.caa.go.jp/policies/policy/consumer_safety/caution/caution_009/pdf/consumer_safety_cms204_191218_01.pdf. Accessed 30 Jan 2020
2. The Consumer Affairs Agency (in Japan): Beware of bathing accidents, which occur frequently in winter. https://www.caa.go.jp/policies/policy/consumer_safety/caution/caution_009/pdf/caution_009_181121_0001.pdf. Accessed 30 Jan 2020
3. Japan Medical Association: What is heat shock? http://www.kagoshima.med.or.jp/people/topic/2010/308.htm. Accessed 30 Jan 2020
4. Okuda, T., Wang, Z., Lapan, S., Fowler, D.R.: Bathtub drowning: an 11-year retrospective study in the state of Maryland. Forensic Sci. Int. **253**, 64–70 (2015)
5. Sung, E.J., Tochihara, Y.: Effects of bathing and hot footbath on sleep in winter. J. Physiol. Anthropol. Appl. Hum. Sci. **19**(1), 21–27 (2000)
6. INTEC Company Limited (in Japan): Heat shock sensor. https://grus.tokyo/product/detail.php?pid=4. Accessed 30 Jan 2020
7. Tokyo Gas (in Japan): Joint development of water heater remote control with safe bathing support functionality. https://www.tokyo-gas.co.jp/Press/20190711-01.html. Accessed 30 Jan 2020
8. Galindo, R., Aguilar, W.G., Reyes Ch., R.P.: Landmark based eye ratio estimation for driver fatigue detection. In: Yu, H., Liu, J., Liu, L., Ju, Z., Liu, Y., Zhou, D. (eds.) ICIRA 2019, Part V. LNCS (LNAI), vol. 11744, pp. 565–576. Springer, Cham (2019). https://doi.org/10.1007/978-3-030-27541-9_46
9. Soleimanloo, S.S., et al.: Eye-blink parameters detect on-road track-driving impairment following severe sleep deprivation. J. Clin. Sleep Med. **15**(9), 1271–1284 (2019)
10. Nguyen, T.P., Chew, M. T., Demidenko, S.: Eye tracking system to detect driver drowsiness. In: 6th International Conference on Automation, Robotics and Applications, pp. 472–477. IEEE (2015)

11. Lawoyin, S., Fei, D.Y., Bai, O.: Accelerometer-based steering-wheel movement monitoring for drowsy-driving detection. Proc. Inst. Mech. Eng. Part D J. Automob. Eng. **229**(2), 163–173 (2015)
12. Vural, E., Cetin, M., Ercil, A., Littlewort, G., Bartlett, M., Movellan, J.: Drowsy driver detection through facial movement analysis. In: Lew, M., Sebe, N., Huang, T.S., Bakker, E.M. (eds.) HCI 2007. LNCS, vol. 4796, pp. 6–18. Springer, Heidelberg (2007). https://doi.org/10.1007/978-3-540-75773-3_2
13. Apple: AirPods (2nd generation) Technical Specifications. https://www.apple.com/airpods-2nd-generation/specs/. Accessed 30 Jan 2020
14. ATR-Promotions (in Japan): TSND121 specifications. https://www.atr-p.com/products/TSND121.html. Accessed 30 Jan 2020
15. SLEEPON: GO2SLEEP HST. https://www.sleepon.us/go2sleep/. Accessed 30 Jan 2020
16. World Language School: Russian 19. https://youtu.be/6zH3Qw6mIeo. Accessed 30 Jan 2020
17. Yumqua: Yumqua Y-10 W 2.4 GHZ Portable Finger Handheld Wireless USB Trackball Mouse For PC Laptop Mac Lovers. https://www.yumqua.com/collections/trackball-mouse-flexible-keyboard/products/y-10w-2-4-ghz-portable-finger-wireless-ambidextrous-trackball-mouse-for-left-right-handed-users-1. Accessed 30 Jan 2020
18. American Sleep Association: What is Sleep and Why is It Important? https://www.sleepassociation.org/about-sleep/what-is-sleep/. Accessed 30 Jan 2020
19. World Language School: Russian 21. https://youtu.be/ata5hIkB2Wo. Accessed 30 Jan 2020

Development of a Prototyping Support Tool for a Data Utilization Skill-Development Program

Development and Evaluation of a Camera Sensor Pod with an AI-Based People-Counting Function

Yusuke Kometani[1]([⊠]), Koichiro Yonemaru[2], Naoto Hikawa[3], Kyosuke Takahashi[1], Naka Gotoda[1], Takayuki Kunieda[1], and Rihito Yaegashi[1]

[1] Kagawa University, 2217-20 Hayashi-Cho, Takamatsu-shi, Kagawa, Japan
kometani@eng.kagawa-u.ac.jp
[2] NEC Corp, 5-7-1 Shiba, Minato-Ku, Tokyo, Japan
[3] Kagawa Information Service Co., Ltd., 2-1 Sunport, Takamatsu-shi, Kagawa, Japan

Abstract. Citizen-centered design is essential for global data utilization in smart cities. We developed a data utilization skill-development program that features a prototyping support tool for data utilization services. We implemented the program in a seminar course for citizens. In this paper, we describe the development of a datafication tool with a people-counting function for camera images. We show usefulness and limitations of the tool for use in a data utilization skill-development program based on results of a case study.

Keywords: Smart city · Data utilization · Data utilization skill · Data utilization services · FIWARE

1 Introduction

We previously developed a data utilization skill-development program [1] with the aim of encouraging citizen-centered data-driven innovation [2] for data utilization in smart cities [3]. The program started in 2018 as a seminar course for citizens of Takamatsu City, Kagawa Prefecture in Japan. We developed a prototyping support tool as a set of programming libraries and applications to support datafication and data utilization, and applied it to the program. The tool complements users' knowledge and skills and encourages idea creation.

This 2018 implementation revealed some issues, such as nonuse of registered open data and users not knowing what could be done with the data. The flow of data disclosure in Internet of things (IoT) applications can be divided into three stages: data generation, storage, and utilization. Effective use of open data requires data generation based on utilization in applications. Unless a mechanism for accumulating effective data to some extent is established, data utilization will not spread and there is no room for consideration of ideas.

© Springer Nature Switzerland AG 2020
S. Yamamoto and H. Mori (Eds.): HCII 2020, LNCS 12185, pp. 469–478, 2020.
https://doi.org/10.1007/978-3-030-50017-7_35

In response to the above issues and with the aim of improving the program, we developed a tool for data utilization services based on an AI camera sensor pod and an IoT platform. The AI camera sensor pod extracts information from video captured by a camera and converts that information into data. In this research, we developed a sensor pod with a function that counts arbitrary objects, allowing users to specify the type of object counted, thereby enabling datafication in various situations. We applied this tool to a case study to demonstrate its usefulness and limitations.

2 Data Utilization in a Skill-Development Program and a Prototyping Support Tool

The targeted program is a continuing education course jointly run by Kagawa Prefecture and Kagawa University at e-Topia Kagawa, an interactive ICT education facility near the Japan Railway Takamatsu Station in Kagawa Prefecture. Table 1 shows the course schedule. There are eight lessons of 3 h each. The first four lessons teach web app design, with participants learning how to register and visualize data. The last four sessions are about the IoT, and teaches participants about collecting and accumulating historical data using sensors. Each unit concludes with an idea contest, in which participants evaluate each other's ideas.

Table 1. Data utilization skill-development program schedule.

Course	#	Date	Topic
Web app design	Web1	2019/7/13	Use and visualization of open data
	Web2	2019/7/20	Use and visualization of moving object data
	Web3	2019/8/3	Design and development of data utilization web applications
	Web4	2019/8/10	Presentation of ideas and peer assessment
IoT app design	IoT1	2019/9/14	Collection of sensor data using IoT
	IoT2	2019/9/21	Use of sensor data in data utilization applications
	IoT3	2019/9/28	Design and development of data utilization IoT application
	IoT4	2019/10/5	Presentation of ideas and peer assessment

The program allows non-programmers to participate, so opinions are gathered from a variety of local citizens. Support for developing a data utilization service is therefore needed. To achieve this, we have developed and refined a prototyping support tool. Figure 1 shows the relation between this research and the data utilization skill-development program. By providing a prototyping support tool, we support idea creation by citizens in the data utilization skill-development program. As a result, we can improve our prototyping support tool based on participant opinions obtained through the program.

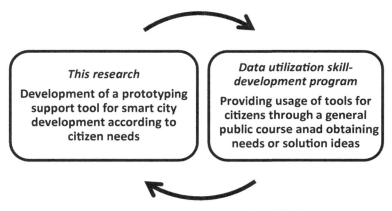

Fig. 1. Relation between this research and data utilization skill-development programs.

Figure 2 shows development of a bus location system as an example of utilizing the prototyping support tool developed in the previous research. The tool consists of libraries and apps [1]. Various data can be registered to the IoT platform via a static data registration tool, and registered data can be visualized using the data visualization tool.

The IoT platform uses FIWARE [4], a standardized platform in Europe and was first introduced in Japan in Takamatsu City. Data registered in FIWARE can be shared between applications, and dynamic data collected by sensors such as GPS loggers and temperature sensors can be added. By installing GPS loggers on buses, bus location

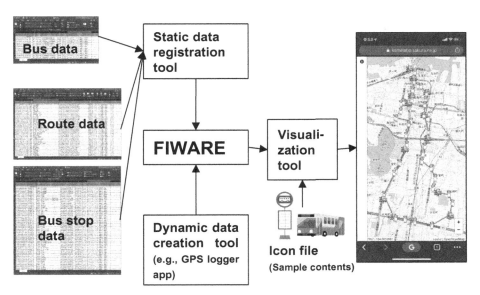

Fig. 2. Scheme for smart city application development based on our prototyping support tool.

information can be visualized to show where buses are located. Program participants can create similar systems by combining libraries and apps.

3 Tool Design

3.1 Data Utilization Flow and Target Data

The flow of open data disclosure using the IoT can be divided into three stages: data generation, storage, and utilization. In the data generation stage, the number of arbitrary objects is counted by detecting objects in captured images by machine learning and extracting information using devices and camera sensors supporting AI calculations. Only the number of objects extracted from the image is sent to the IoT data platform. In the data storage stage, generated data are automatically registered and aggregated on the IoT data platform. The aggregated data are then released according to rules and formats defined by the local government. In the data utilization stage, the tool user creates ideas for utilizing the data, such as visualization.

In this study, the generated data were the number of arbitrary objects. For example, if the target objects are people, the degree of congestion at a service window can be known by counting people in line. If the arbitrary objects are cars, then parking availability can be known by counting cars in a parking lot. Using cameras to capture data can raise concerns about privacy, but such issues can be avoided by extracting the number of detected objects through processing and sending only that information to the IoT data platform. We therefore consider it useful to count arbitrary objects whose number continually changes and to convert those numbers into open data in real time.

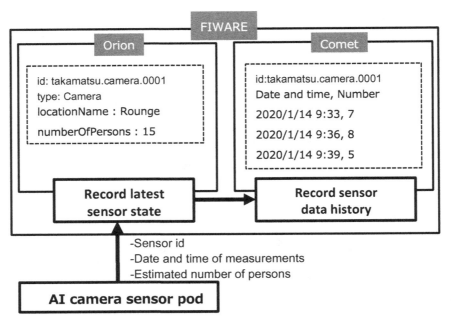

Fig. 3. System configuration and data example.

3.2 Requirements for a Datafication Tool

Figure 3 shows a system configuration diagram and an example of registered data, along with a mechanism for counting people and storing the counts on a data platform. Requirements for realizing this mechanism are as follows:

- Requirement 1: Object detection can be performed
- Requirement 2: Data from detection results can be processed
- Requirement 3: Limited prerequisite knowledge for users
- Requirement 4: Easy to carry and install when verifying prototypes

4   Tool Implementation

Table 2 shows hardware and software configurations for the AI camera sensor pod, and Fig. 4 shows its appearance. From Requirements 1 and 4, the sensor pod needs to be a small AI device that can perform high-speed calculations for machine learning. From Requirements 2 and 3, different object types should be detectable with a single algorithm and data processing should be possible via a programming language.

Table 2. AI camera sensor pod configuration.

Task	Hardware
Computer for AI calculations	Jetson Nano
Image acquisition	Web camera, tripod
Network connection	Wi-Fi router
I/O devices	Mouse, keyboard, display
Task	Software
Photographing	OpenCV
Object detection	YOLO v3 [5]

We developed the sensor pod based on these requirements. YOLO [5], which can simultaneously detect and classify objects, is used as the object detection algorithm. Various object types can thus be simultaneously detected from camera images, allowing efficient collection of information at the shooting location. Aggregation of detection results and transmission of data to the IoT data platform were implemented using the Python programming language.

Fig. 4. The developed AI camera sensor pod.

5   Implementation and Evaluation of the Tool

5.1   Case Study for Evaluation

We conducted a case study to clarify accuracy of the data collected by this tool and the value of utilizing the data. The theme of this case study was reducing waiting times at the Takamatsu City Hall reception desk.

The flow at the citizen's section reception desk is as follows:

1. A visitor fills out an application form (often for issuance of an official document).
2. The visitor takes a numbered ticket from a ticket dispenser and waits until their number is called.
3. Visitor numbers are displayed on a monitor and a panel at the reception counter.
4. The visitor will receive a second numbered ticket after acceptance of their form.
5. The visitor waits until called again when their application is complete.

As described above, visits to the reception desk incur waiting times, and reducing these wait times was positioned as an issue to be addressed for resident services at the city hall. By tracking the number of waiting people by time, it becomes possible to determine the days and times when there are relatively few visitors, allowing citizens to plan to minimize their wait times.

5.2   Results

The above-described datafication practice has been in place since 6 January 2020. The sensor pod performs datafication every 3 min, due to performance limitations of the controlling computer. Table 3 shows a descriptive analysis of the estimated number of waiting people each day. We additionally investigated the number of applications each day for comparison with the estimated counts. Average values are calculated between

8:30 and 17:00, the time during which the service window is open. The analysis shows crowding on the first business day of the year and the first business day of the week.

The graph in Fig. 5 compares days when estimated waiting times were long and short. This shows that on 6 January 2020, when there were many visitors, there were

Table 3. Descriptive analysis of estimated number of waiting people by day.

Date	Day	Average number of waiting people	S.D.	Max	Number of applications	Number of documents issued	Notes
2020/1/6	Mon.	10.8	4.5	20	811	1067	First open day of the year
2020/1/7	Tues.	7.9	3.7	17	719	940	
2020/1/8	Wed.	6.6	2.8	14	630	794	
2020/1/9	Thurs.	7.6	3.1	15	654	866	
2020/1/10	Fri.	6.8	2.9	13	632	832	
2020/1/13	Mon.	–	–	–	–	–	National holiday
2020/1/14	Tues.	9.5	3.2	16	740	958	First open day of the week
2020/1/15	Wed.	8.4	3.4	16	671	903	
2020/1/16	Thur.	7.5	3.5	16	684	873	
2020/1/17	Fri.	7.3	3.1	15	639	866	

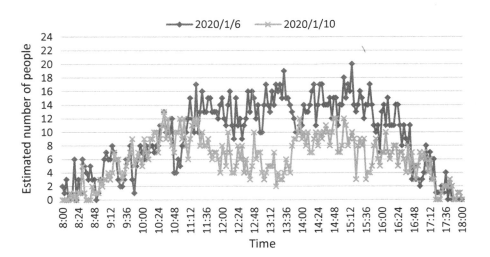

Fig. 5. Time course of estimated number of waiting people.

many people waiting even after noon. Moreover, on days when there were few visitors, waiting times shorter in the afternoon.

Figure 5 shows slight variations in estimated values. Figure 6 shows an example of object detection, in which objects other than the targets, such as passersby, are also counted. In other cases, however, the number of waiting people was underestimated, due to counting multiple overlapping people as one person, introducing error into the data.

Fig. 6. Example of object detection.

Figure 7 shows a scatter plot comparing average estimates for the number of people (from Table 3) and the actual number of applications. Similarly, Fig. 8 shows a scatter plot comparing the number of waiting people and the number of issued documents. These observations suggest that the estimated number of waiting people is strongly correlated with the actual processing work done at the city hall. Correlation between the number of waiting people and the number of issued documents is slightly stronger than the correlation between the number of waiting people and the number of applications.

5.3   Availability of the Tool

Figure 5 shows fluctuations in estimated values. Figure 6 further shows that error arises in the number of measurements due to erroneous detection. Even so, Figs. 7 and 8 show strong correlations with number of applications and documents issued each day and the number of waiting people. Therefore, this tool is not suited to applications requiring precision, but it can be used where approximate degrees of congestion are sufficient, such as reducing waiting times at a reception desk.

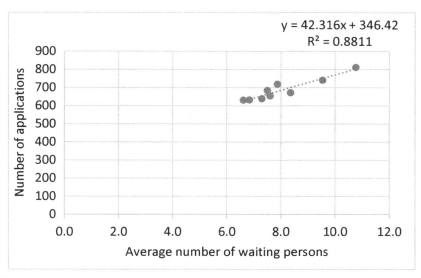

Fig. 7. Correlation between the average number of waiting people and the number of applications each day.

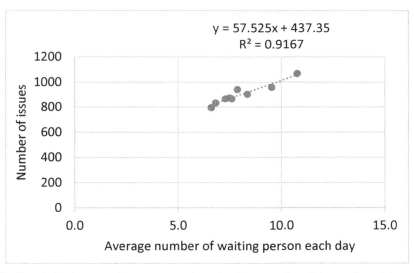

Fig. 8. Correlation between the average number of waiting people and the number of documents issued each day

6 Conclusion

The purpose of this research was to develop a prototyping support tool for a data utilization skill-development program. We designed a datafication tool that uses AI to count objects in images. A case study in Takamatsu City suggested that this tool could collect useful data.

In future work, we will consider the usefulness of detecting objects other than humans. Since we used YOLO v3, a deep-learning-based algorithm for generic object detection, we can count any object registered in the learning model. For example, counting cars is expected to be useful in transportation applications. Further, modifying the machine learning model according to local issues will be useful as an educational program teaching AI methodologies. We will also attempt to adapt machine learning model creation procedures to teaching materials for use in educational programs.

References

1. Kometani, Y., et al.: Development of a data utilization skill development program-development of prototyping support environment for data utilization services, and its practical use. J. Japn. Soc. Inf. Syst. Educ. **37**(2). In Press (in Japanese)
2. OECD: Data-driven innovation for growth and well-being. https://www.oecd.org/sti/ieconomy/data-driven-innovation.htm. Accessed 20 Dec 2019
3. Bibri, S.E.: The anatomy of the data-driven smart sustainable city: instrumentation, datafication, computerization and related applications. J. Big Data **6**, 59 (2019). https://doi.org/10.1186/s40537-019-0221-4
4. FIWARE Foundation: FIWARE. https://www.fiware.org/
5. Redmon, J., Farhadi, A.: YOLOv3: An Incremental Improvement, arXiv: 1804.02767, p. 6 (2018)

Data Paradigm Shift in Cross-Media IoT System

Shih-Ta Liu[1], Su-Chu Hsu[1(✉)], and Yu-Hsiung Huang[2]

[1] Research Center for Technology and Art, National Tsing Hua University,
Hsinchu 30013, Taiwan
{shihta,suchu}@mx.nthu.edu.tw
[2] Department of New Media Art, Taipei National University of the Arts, Taipei 11201, Taiwan
eric@techart.tnua.edu.tw

Abstract. In 1962, Kuhn proposed the "Paradigm Shift". This term used to describe the changes in basic scientific concepts and experimental practices in science. Such changes also affect the development of scientific research. The new technologies and information are constantly changing and dissemination in the era. In this paper, we propose the "Cross-Media IoT System", which takes IoT technology and cloud server as the core. In this system, we used mobile phones, servers, social media, installation arts, as the media and objects of IoT to transmission data by different kinds of sensors. When data is transformed in different media, it will be deconstructed and recombined, also role of data(input/output) will be changing, and data may change from text to images, from images to sounds, and even from digital to analog forms and data will be to control installation art, we call this phenomenon "Data Liquidity". This is due to the advancement of digital technology, which allows data to be the change in liquidity state. We call this is "Data Paradigm Shift".

In Cross-Media IoT System is based on the IoT environment, and we develop the Cross-Media Control System and embed them in each interactive installation. For different artworks, we design different Mobile APPs. When users take the Mobile APP to participate in different interactive installation art in the space, the data through Mobile APP, use the Cross-Media Control System to transfer into artworks and control that to interact. The interaction of results will be generated data in liquidized through IoT to transfer, once again controlling another installation art. Data sculpture is transferred between different media and liquefied to form the "Data Paradigm Shift". This system has been applied in "Tsing Hua Effects 2019: Cross-Media Technology and Art Festival" of National Tsing Hua University in Taiwan. We have created "Morse Code" and" Cross-Media Representor" that are artworks in the art festival, we cited as an example to illustrate the operation of our system and the concept of "Data Paradigm Shift".

In the past, most of the artworks are participated and appreciated individually. In our system, the data can cross different media among different interactive artworks by formation-liquidity, In the future, our system is not only be applied to outdoor interactive artworks but also the education fields such as "mobile learning".

Keywords: Data Paradigm Shift · Cross-Media · Internet of Things · Formation-liquidity · Interactive installation art

© Springer Nature Switzerland AG 2020
S. Yamamoto and H. Mori (Eds.): HCII 2020, LNCS 12185, pp. 479–490, 2020.
https://doi.org/10.1007/978-3-030-50017-7_36

1 Introduction

Due to the rapid development of the science and technology industry, the way of data exchange between people, people, and technology, people and field have no boundaries. In 2014, the World Semiconductor Council is showing the next big thing is the internet of things [1]. In recent years, the Internet of Things has been widely used in the smart life, and gradually applied to artistic creation. Through the Internet of Things and sensors, data can act a control and presentation role in interactive art. In 2018, we curated the "2018 Tsing Hua Effects – IoT Technology and Art Festival" [2], integrating the data of Tsing Hua University into artworks. We store big data in the cloud. Through sensing and access to the Internet of Things, we also integrate and control outdoor public artworks for an interactive interface. The data in the artwork can be appreciated, discussed and accessed, and even become a part of the artwork. However, most the interactive art works are appreciated and participated individually, and the data between works is rarely connected. Therefore, we curated "2019 Tsing Hua Effects – Cross-Media IoT Technology and Art Festival" [3], and developed "Cross-Media IoT System", let data cross between different media, such as mobile phones, computers, social media, etc. and input into artworks, or even cross from one of artwork into another. When data is transformed in different media, it will be deconstructed and re-combined, also role of data (input/output) will be change, and data may change from text to images, from images to sounds, and even from digital to analog forms and data will be to control installation art, we call this phenomenon "Data Liquidity". This phenomenon is like water, it will change the shape of the convergence with different containers. In our research, data will change its format and role of input and output with different applications. This is due to the advancement of digital technology, which allows data to be change in liquidity state. We call this is "Data Paradigm Shift".

2 Related Work

This chapter will explain the related works of paradigm shift in the field of humanities and arts. With the advent of the digital and technological age, the digital paradigm shift was proposed which influenced the creative methods of technology and art. We will discuss related creations and works of IoT applications in scientific and technological works.

2.1 Paradigm Shift Related Studies in Humanities

This chapter will explain the related research of Paradigm Shift in the field of humanities and arts. With the advent of the digital and technological era, the digital paradigm shift was proposed, which influenced the creative methods of science and technology. We will discuss the related creation and research of IoT applications in scientific and technological works.

Kuhn proposed the Paradigm Shift in 1962. This term was used to describe the changes in the basic concepts and experimental practices of science in the scientific category which also affected the development of scientific research [4]. Kolay proposed a digital paradigm shift in 2016 when classic paintings in Indian culture were transformed into digital forms. The human characters in traditional Indian classic paintings are translated into digital forms that are more easily understood by the general public through the conversion of digital media. This makes it easier to protect and disseminate the cultural heritage value of traditional Indian art [5]. Bowen and Giannini and others mentioned in 2018 that there is a paradigm shift in the Digital Ecosystem. Through the Internet, people's identities and spaces easily meet in virtual events, which is also a case of digital paradigm shift. [6]. The above-mentioned paradigm shift is mostly a common paradigm shift application. In our thesis, we emphasize that data is transferred between installation art works in the context of the Internet of Things. The format and characteristics of the data will be changed. We call it "Data Paradigm Shift". This will be explained further in later chapters.

2.2 Research on IoT Technology and Art Works

The development of wireless transmission technology in the past few years has been quite rapid. From the transmission methods of 802.11, Bluetooth, and 4G networks to the large-scale technological advances of LoRa, WiFi6, and 5G net-works proposed today, the idea of "interconnecting everything" has gradually evolved. come true. The performance of our internet technology and smart phones is getting stronger and stronger. People can appreciate the form of artistic creation through different interactive interfaces. The Internet of Things technology extended from wireless sensing network technology also brings more possibilities for viewers to appreciate artistic creation.

Bill Fontana of the United Kingdom proposed the "Harmonic Bridge" work using wireless sensing network technology in 2006 [7]. They use the vibration or wind strength collected by the sensors and calculate it through wireless sensing technology, so that participants will produce pleasant harmony music when walking across the bridge. In the first Taipei Digital Arts Festival and ACM Multimedia seminar in 2006, Su-Chu Hsu, Jing-Yao Lin, Caven Chen and others proposed the "One Million Heartbeat" interactive art work [8]. This work collects participants' identity data, including gender and blood type, through a wireless sensing network. After the system has collected one million heartbeat data, the identity data of the participants will determine the gender and blood type of the twins in the work.

Aaron Koblin, Nik Hafermaas, and Dan Goods of the United States established the "eCLOUD" project at San Jose International Airport [9]. Since its establishment in 2007, it has used electrical variable glass technology and the Internet of Things (IoT) system to collect climates around the world and create a dynamic and optoelectronically changing public sculpture. The work can dynamically let people passing by understand the weather changes in the cities they are visiting, like clouds in the sky.

The "ALAVs 2.0 (Autonomous Light Air Vessels)" project created by Jed Berk in the United States in 2012 [10] is to use indoor small flying boats combined with wireless sensing network technology to feed the spacecraft through the participants like or dislike, so the spacecraft Has an anthropomorphic form and personality.

An interactive artwork of "Mushroom Story" produced by Su-Chu Hsu, Shih-Ta Liu, Po-Yao Wu in 2018 [11]. This work uses a mobile phone to scan the QR-Code to open the WebAPP. After entering any text and uploading it to the cloud server, the system performs text-to-speech and then automatically downloads it to the outdoor mushroom modeling art installation. When participants approach the mushroom modeling installation, voice data will be automatically activated after being detected by the sensor. At the same time, the latest three artificial speeches are played randomly. This makes speech data a part of interactive art-work.

3   Cross-Media IoT System

We designed a Cross-Media IoT System mainly to allow data to be streamed between different artworks, and the format of the data can be transformed due to the appearance of different artworks, and the data is liquidity. Figure 1 Cross-Media Control System is one of the subsystems and the core part. It's embedded in every interactive installation. For different forms of artwork, we use an embedded sensor IC to detect interactive in the installation art. It can also use the mobile phone's interactive method to use G-Sensor to dynamically detect and make decisions, and then send data to the server. The data will be returned to the mobile phone in time through processing on the server-side, showing different interactive feedback.

On the mobile phone, we designed related APPs and WebAPPs for each artwork, and both types of APPs can interact with the artwork. Users who download apps, in general, can turn on Bluetooth connection support via native apps. Conversely, WebAPP can only be connected through account binding. Through the mobile APP/WebAPP program development, the built-in G-Sensor and wireless transmission of the mobile phone will be used to allow users to take the mobile APP/WebAPP to participate in different Interactive Installation Arts in the space. The data is inputted into the artworks through the Cross-Media Control System through the mobile phone's APP/WebAPP as the medium, and the artworks are controlled to interact.

3.1   The Structure of Cross-Media IoT System

The Cross-Media IoT System includes IoT Server and multiple interactive installation art, as shown in Fig. 1. Each interactive installation art is embedded in the Cell Phone APP/WebAPP included in the Cross-Media Control System. The IoT Server is responsible for receiving the sensing signal of the Cross-Media Control System, and the mobile phone is used as a carrier for data sending and receiving in the system. Use the G-Sensor of the user's mobile phone to perform "scoop" and "pour-in" motion detection, and input data into the installation art or output from the installation art. The format of the data will be transformed into different artworks, and the roles of input and output will be changed.

Cross-Media Control System is the core unit of the entire Cross-Media IoT System. It includes two parts, one is the Cell Phone APP/WebAPP and Non-Contact Capacitive Data Control Interface. When the user interacts with the artwork using the Cell Phone APP/WebAPP, the input data is transmitted to the server through the interactive control interface, and the server converts the information into data, which is then returned to the user's cell phone for presentation. Then the user must detect the flipping movement of the hand through the G-Sensor of the cell phone, make the Non-Contact Capacitive

Data Control Interface sense, and trigger the operation of the interactive device at the same time so that the artwork produces different interactive results. As a result of the interaction, data is generated, and the format of the data may be converted from the text, digital codes, audio and video, and even digital and analog conversion. The converted data controls different installation arts to do different creative interactive presentations, and even the data streams are in different installation arts, affecting each other.

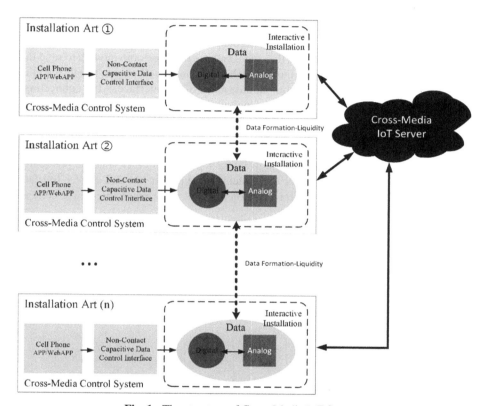

Fig. 1. The structure of Cross-Media IoT System

3.2 Cross-Media Control System

Cross-Media Control System is embedded in each interactive installation art. The purpose is to allow users to use two interactive operation methods designed by "Data Retrieval" to input data and "Data Pouring In" to output data, as shown in Figs. 7 and 9. The main technologies include: "Non-Contact Capacitive Data Control Interface" and "Tangible Interface in Mobile Phones". The Non-Contact Capacitive Data Control Interface uses a capacitance sensor as the main interface to detect the piezoelectric change of the sensed capacitance. The output signal is sent to the microcontroller to receive data and then transmitted to the IoT Server through the wireless transmission module. The data is transmitted to the cell phones with Tangible Interface through the processing of the IoT Server. In the following, these two control interfaces will be described in detail.

Non-Contact Capacitive Data Control Interface. Non-Contact Capacitive Data Control Interface is mainly used to achieve two interactive operation methods: "scoop" and "pour-in". This interface contains high-sensitivity capacitive sensing ICs. In this part, we use Azoteq's IQS128 sensing IC. IQS128 is highly penetrating and can be easily embedded in materials containing wooden exhibits or acrylic exhibits, and it can pass through a material of about 6 mm or a glass material of 10 mm and can sense a sensing area of about 15 cm. In the part of the signal changes when processing capacitance induction, we use Arduino to process the signal and use the Bluetooth module to send the Beacon signal. When a user opens the APP while holding a cell phone, it will scan the Bluetooth device and find the Bluetooth module name of the interface. After connecting, you can connect and bind the cell phone. On the contrary, WebAPP users need to login into account to perform the cell phone binding status, and the user can choose one of the methods to interact. After binding, the system will start to detect whether there is any "scoop" or "pour-in" action using the cell phone. When the capacitive sensing module detects that the user uses the cell phone to interact with each other, and the proximity area is less than 5 cm, it can trigger the system to connect to the IoT Server for data transmission through the wireless transmission module, and change interactive content on the APP/WebAPP.

Tangible Interface in Mobile Phones. This chapter will introduce the research results of G-Sensor control technology that we have developed in the past with smart phones as tangible interface [12]. It uses the X, Y, and Z axis (Fig. 2. left) data results sensed by the acceleration sensor in the tangible interface to analyze the characteristics of the following three actions, including: bottom to top, Scoop from left to right, Scoop from right to left (Fig. 2. Right) [13].

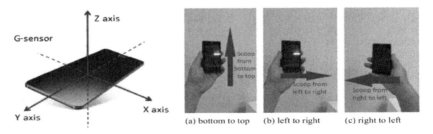

Fig. 2. Tangible interface with G-Sensor

Figures 3, 4 and 5 below are the results of experiments we have done in the past. Figure 3 below is an analysis chart from bottom to top. It can be seen from the figure that during the "scoop" action, the Y-axis data will increase and the Z-axis data will decrease.

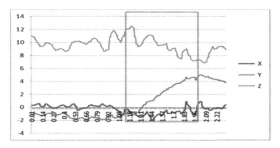

Fig. 3. G-Sensor with left to right

The part of scoop from left to right is shown in Fig. 4 below. In the blue frame, because the mobile phone is moving to the right, the acceleration on the X axis is negative until it stops. Due to the effect of gravity, the acceleration of the Z axis is positive and continues to increase.

Fig. 4. G-Sensor with bottom to top

Figure 5 below is the data analysis of scooping from right to left. In the orange box, the mobile phone is moving to the left, so the acceleration of the X axis is positive. Because the mobile phone is horizontal after completing the scooping action, the final X axis data trend Nearly zero; in addition, the Z-axis data rose significantly because the mobile phone was going to lift up and was affected by gravity.

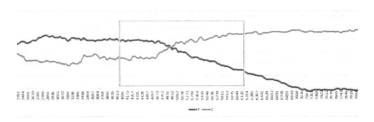

Fig. 5. G-Sensor with right to left

Based on the above-mentioned research on the G-Sensor component control technology, the Tangible Interface can detect two gestures, "scooping" and "pour-in" of the phone through the acceleration sensor, and transmit the analysis results via wireless transmission To Cross-Media Control System. If the coordinates of the mobile phone match the position sensed by the non-contact capacitance data control Interface, the work data can be transmitted while the mobile phone is tilted for "scooping" or "pour-in".

After analyzing these motion detection data, we combined the two data interaction methods of "data retrieval" and "data pouring in" to allow users to input and output data when interacting with the device. When the user interacts through the mobile phone's APP/WebAPP interface, the mobile phone and the non-contact capacitance data control interface perform calculations. The mobile phone's APP/WebAPP will also determine whether the current state is "data retrieval" or "data pouring in". The interactive behavior of the interactive device makes the result appear different content.

4   Implementations

This section mainly exemplifies and explains the implementation of Cross-Media IoT System. All the works of "Tsing Hua Effects 2019 – Cross-Media Technology and Art Festival" run under our Cross-Media IoT System and practice the concept of Data Paradigm Shift. To develop this system, we must obtain government subsidies, and we especially appreciate the Ministry of Education Republic of China (Taiwan) [14]. In festival, there are about 10 interactive artworks scattered on the campus. We use "Morse Code" and "Cross-Media Representor" to explain Data Liquidity (data liquefaction), how data can be transferred be-tween different works, and explain the concept of Data Paradigm Shift.

4.1   The Steps of Cross-Media in Installation Art Implementation

The "Morse Code" artwork author is Ya-Lun Tao, and this artwork is one of the works exhibited by the "Tsing Hua Effects 2019 -Cross-Media Technology and Art Festival" at National Tsinghua University in Taiwan [15]. The author is Ya-Lun Tao. The creative concept of the work comes from the message that different objects want to express. Through this device, I want to speak to the God in the sky, to the loved ones in the sky, to the creatures in outer space, to the past, to the future and the desire to speak to yourself is realized through this interactive device.

It mainly contains the following steps:

Fig. 6. Scan QR-Code and enter text of blessing words

Step1: Data input from cell phone
People took their cell phones and walked to the "Morse Code", scanned the QR Code of the artwork, obtained the corresponding APP or WebAPP and bound them, and entered the text of blessing words on the cell phone, and then enter the text to convert Morse code from IoT server, as shown in Fig. 6.

Step2: "Data Pouring In" installation art
People took the cell phone to the front of the "Morse Code" installation, there is a Non-Contact Capacitive Data Control Interface embedded in the installation, people through the cell phone's G-Sensor detection and transition, let text of blessing converted into Morse code data, that can be "Data Pouring In" to installation art, as shown in Fig. 7.

Fig. 7. Using cell phone for "Data Pouring In" to installation art

Step3: Data cross into "Liquidity Transfer"
"Morse Code" after receiving the Morse code data, the installation activates the shutter control to let the light beam reach the sky with the Morse code. At this time, the format of the data has changed from digital to the analog state of the motor control shutter structure, as shown in Fig. 8.

Fig. 8. Receiving the Morse code data and turning the shutter mechanism

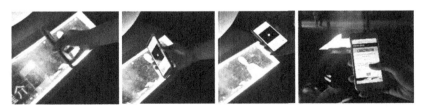

Fig. 9. Using cell phone for "Data Retrieval" from installation art

Step4: "Data Retrieval" from installation art

Anyone can "retrieval" the words that have recently been converted into the Morse code from the "Morse Code" installation, and then walk to another installation art "Cross-Media Representor" in Pigeon Plaza, as shown in Fig. 9. That is, the input of the blessed discourse text data of "Morse Code" is outputted to another work "Cross-Media Representor" by being retrieved.

Step5: 'Data Pouring In" another installation art

People walked to Pigeon Plaza and similarly transmitted through the cell phone G-Sensor detection and Non-Contact Capacitance Data Control Interface, so that the retrieved data was poured into the installation art of "Cross-Media Representor", as shown in Fig. 10.

Fig. 10. Participants pouring in the retrieved data into the installation art

Step6: Data cross into installation art and data "Liquidity Retransferred"

"Cross-Media Representor" After receiving the data, the device deconstructs the Morse code data into the original blessing words and transforms it into a Laser Projector to the projection on the wall that is animated and displayed on Pigeon Square, as shown in Fig. 11.

Fig. 11. Morse code data is restored and transformed into an animated projection on the wall

4.2 Data Paradigm Shift in Liquidity of Format

In the above example, through the "Cross-Media IoT System" that we have developed, the blessing text originally entered in the work of "The Morse Code" was transferred to the Morse code, poured into the device and turned into an analog beam. Then the Morse code was retrieved, poured into another work, and then restored to the original blessing text and presented in animation. The entire data, from text, Morse password, analog beam, to the original text to animation, this is what we call "Data Liquidity". The format of the data is changed during transmission, and the characteristics (input/output) of the data are also changed. In the field of digital art, we developed the Cross-Media IoT System, which breaks through the past when digital artwork data is restricted to be presented in the same work. Our system allows data to perform a "Data Paradigm Shift".

In all the works of "Tsing Hua Effects 2019 – Cross-Media Technology and Art Fe Festival", participants can interact with each other by means of "fishing" and "pouring in" the data, which adds interest to the entire festival of science and technology, and creatively allows data to travel across different media and devices Art work.

5 Conclusions

The currently proposed Cross-Media IoT System has achieved 10 outdoor installation art works in the "Tsing Hua Effects 2019 – Cross-Media Technology and Art Festival". The user uses the mobile phone to input and output data, so that the data can be transferred to different devices for format conversion and role conversion. In the past, many large-scale outdoor art festivals' interactive installation works are presented in a way preset by the art creators themselves. There are relatively few works for the audience to participate interactively. If there is an interactive form, it can only be achieved through a single. The mode of interaction also lacks the interconnected relationship between several different works. The Cross-Media IoT System we have proposed uses mobile phones to do "scoop" (input) and "pour-in" (output), so that the interactive experience of the works adds a lot of fun. The participant-centered approach makes the dialogue between the participants and the work deeper. At the same time, the liquidity of the data can also make the interactive control of the work more diverse and interesting.

In the future, our Cross-Media IoT System is expected to be applied to more large-scale outdoor public art or technology art performances. The Cross-Media control System can be embedded in works or performers, and allows data to be streamed between different works and performers. Data is appreciated in different media. In addition, our system can also be applied to mobile learning in the field of education, allowing data to be learned in different media. The boundary between teachers and students can be crossed through our system to open various learning opportunities.

Our system breaks through the way users experience humanities and arts. Advances in technology also allow different data to span across different devices. This has become the key to breaking the old norms and cognitions and giving different possibilities for the interactive public art installations of science and art in the past. When data is transformed in different media, deconstructed and reorganized, the data format can be changed to control the production work, and the role of data (input/output) can be streamed between different works. In this the-sis, we want to use our system development and application to interpret the concept of Data Paradigm Shift.

References

1. SciTech Report: Celebrities Talking about New Trends in Internet of Things. SciTech Report **390**, 25 (2014)
2. Tsing Hua Effects – IoT Technology and Art Festival, Hsichu City, Taiwan (2018)

3. Tsing Hua Effects – Cross-Media Technology and Art Festival, Hsichu City, Taiwan (2019)
4. Kuhn, T.S.: The Structure of Scientifi Revolutions, vol. 2, p. 90. The University of Chicago Press, Chicago (1962)
5. Kolay, Saptarshi: Cultural heritage preservation of traditional Indian art through virtual new-media. Procedia-Soc. Behav. Sci. **225**, 309–320 (2016)
6. Bowen, J.P., et al.: States of being: art and identity in digital space and time. In: Electronic Visualisation and the Arts, pp. 1–7 (2018)
7. Fontana, B.: Harmonic Bridge (2006)
8. Hsu, S.C., Lin, J., Chen, C.: Application of wireless sensing network in digital creative learning. In: The Fifth Digital Archives Symposium (2006)
9. Goods, D., Hafermaas, N., Koblin, A.; The eCloud (2010)
10. Berk, J., Mitter, N.: Autonomous light air vessels (ALAVs). In: Proceedings of the 14th ACM International Conference on Multimedia (2006)
11. Hsu, S.-C., Liu, S.-T., Wu, P.-Y.; Mushroom dialogues. In: 2018 Tsing Hua Effects – IoT Tecnology and Art Festival, Hsichu City, Taiwan (2018)
12. Shih, K.-P., et al.: On a tangible interface in interactive media display using mobile phones. In: 2016 International Conference on Networking and Network Applications. IEEE (2016)
13. Hsu, S.C., et al.: TmP-the study and application of tangible mobile-phone interface of emerging presentation in culture creative industry. In: Achievement Report of the Special Research Project of the Ministry of Science and Technology, NSC 104-2627-E-119-001- (2014)
14. The Application of Technology and Art in the Intelligent and Creation Space. University Industry Innovation R&D Program of the Science and Technology Innovations in Cultural Industries Research Service Company (RSC), Ministry of Education Republic of China (Taiwan) (2019)
15. Tao, Y.-L.: Morse code. In: 2019 Tsing Hua Effects - Cross-Media Technology and Art Festival, Hsichu City (2019)

Optimizing Combinations of Teaching Image Data for Detecting Objects in Images

Keisuke Nakamura, Ryodai Hamasaki, Chika Oshima$^{(\boxtimes)}$, and Koichi Nakayama

Saga University, Saga 840-8502, Japan
karin27@sa3.so-net.ne.jp, knakayama@is.saga-u.ac.jp

Abstract. Recently, large amounts of images serving as teaching image data can be prepared when a system detects objects in images using deep learning. However, the accuracy of detecting these objects is often low, because the system has not previously learned the background images of the objects. This paper proposed a method that optimizes a combination of images as teaching image data using dynamic programming (DP). First, the system created mask data, which serves as a reference for comparing with the teaching image data. The system calculated an image feature distance and a similarity of colors between the mask data and each image. Then, the system calculated the sum of the optimum feature's distance at each specified similarity rate using DP. Then, the system determined whether each image was selected using a suitable combination of the teaching image data in the process of DP via back-calculating. It was expected that the proposed method would be effective for detecting objects in an image with a more complicated background.

Keywords: Dynamic programming · Histogram comparison · Mask R-CNN

1 Introduction

People with visual disabilities often memorize where the things they need for daily use are in their home. They can then gather these things when they are needed, without depending on others. However, it is difficult for them to find things if someone moves them without telling them. Recently, a tag [1] that can be attached to an object to detect its location when lost has been developed. However, it is not realistic for all objects in one's home to be tagged in this way. Therefore, if a moving object can be detected using a fixed point camera in the room, a person with a visual disability will be able to find the object easily, even if it has been moved.

Many studies have developed systems to detect the classification and position of specified objects in an image. This is called "object detection." It is important to detect the feature points of these objects, so that the system can determine their location. In many earlier studies, systems have been able to detect the corners of objects (feature points) according to changes in color and/or luminance [2]. Later, a system was proposed using a method to describe a local feature value that is calculated based on the pixel and difference values of each feature point [3]. The Scale-Invariant Feature Transform (SIFT)

© Springer Nature Switzerland AG 2020
S. Yamamoto and H. Mori (Eds.): HCII 2020, LNCS 12185, pp. 491–505, 2020.
https://doi.org/10.1007/978-3-030-50017-7_37

method [4] describes a feature value that is invariant to image scale and rotation. This method can calculate the feature value of each pixel and compare two images to detect the objects in them. These methods were once the mainstream means of detecting objects, when there was not yet enough power within computers and when the quantity of image data for calculation was lacking.

However, during the ImageNet Large Scale Visual Recognition Challenge 2012 (ILSVRC2012) [5], an image recognition system that could learn a subset of the large, hand-labeled ImageNet dataset and then estimate the objects in the images using deep learning [6] techniques won the competition. Following this, the convolutional neural network (CNN), a new method for detecting objects using deep learning became the mainstream approach to image recognition. Recently, higher-resolution cameras have become available, and a large amount of image data is available. By contrast, because a calculation amount should be suppressed, a method that automatically selects beneficial images from a large amount of image data has been anticipated. Inappropriate teaching images disturb the improvement of accuracy in object detection. Further, images obtained from a fixed camera in a room typically include an unknown background. Because the system cannot learn the previous background, the accuracy of detecting objects is diminished.

With the above in mind, this paper proposes a method for optimizing the combination of teaching images data using a dynamic programming (DP) approach [7]. Mask data, which is a set of reference data created by repeating all teaching image data at the same transparency, is used as a criterion for optimizing the teaching image data. Then, two evaluation indices, a feature distance and a similarity on the basis of the mask data, are calculated for each teaching image. It is expected that this proposed method contributes to higher accuracy when detecting objects, because the learning model will learn the teaching image data without depending on their backgrounds.

2   Optimizing the Combination of Teaching Image Data

2.1   Creating Mask Data

Mask data are reference data created by repeating all teaching image data at the same transparency (alpha channel). Formula (1) calculates the degree of transparency.

$$\begin{cases} rate_i = \frac{1}{i}, \\ mask_i = 1 - rate_i, \end{cases} \tag{1}$$

where $rate_i$ means the degree of transparency. i is defined as follows:

$$\{i \in N | 1 \le i \le M\}. \tag{2}$$

Figure 1 shows the procedure when M teaching image data are repeated at the same degree of transparency, $\frac{1}{M}$. The last image in this figure shows the mask data. The system calculates the distance between the image feature of the mask data and each piece of teaching image data.

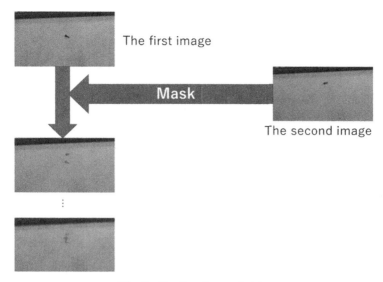

Fig. 1. Creating the mask data

2.2 Evaluation Indices for Dynamic Programing Method

Learning accuracy often depends on the background of an image. As much as possible, the system should optimize the combinations of teaching image data that do not depend on the background. For example, there are 435 ways if we chose two possible combinations from 30 teaching image data. The number of ways to chose all possible combinations is 107,374,182. A calculation of all searches (107,374,182) to find suitable combinations cannot finish within finite time. Therefore, the system optimizes the combinations of the teaching image data using a DP approach [7] that solves the least-cost path problem. The DP can calculate the most suitable combination in a defined solution space.

The system uses two evaluation indices for DP. One is an image feature distance between the mask data and each piece of teaching image data. The other is the similarity of colors between the mask data and each piece of teaching image data.

The image feature is extracted using ACCELERATED-KAZE features (A-KAZE) [8], which is based on KAZE features [9]. An A-KAZE algorithm can extract the image features faster than KAZE can because it uses an original feature descriptor, "Modified-Local Difference Binary (M-LDB)," and an original method that speeds up a pyramid structural calculation [8]. A matching of the image feature vectors between the mask data and each piece of teaching image data is performed using the k-nearest neighbor algorithm [10], which selects the nearest k units label among a search space and assigns a class label by a majority vote. Then, the feature distance is calculated using brute force.

The similarity is calculated by comparing a histogram of the background colors of the mask data with that of the teaching image data. Formula (3) shows that the similarity of colors between the mask data and each piece of teaching image data is calculated using a histogram intersection algorithm [11].

$$H_l = \sum_{k=0}^{255} \frac{\min(H_{Mk}, H_{ik})}{D}, \tag{3}$$

where H_l means the similarity of two images, the mask data and each piece of teaching image data, D refers to a pixel, and H_M and H_i are histograms that show the colors of the object's region of the mask data and the teaching image data, respectively. H_l takes from the lower limit, 0, to the upper limit, 1. The similarity is higher as H_l gets closer to 1.

2.3 Obtain the Sum of Optimum Feature Distance with DP

The system optimizes the combination of the teaching image data on the basis of the image feature distance and the similarity with DP. The system's user (the model's creator) specifies an upper limit value for an accumulative similarity. Then, the system calculates the sum of the optimum feature distance at each specified similarity. Formula (4) calculates the sum of the optimum feature distance:

$$dp[i+1][j] = \begin{cases} dp[i][j] & (j < similarity[i]), \\ max(dp[i+1][j - similarity[i]] + feature[i], dp[i][j]) & (j \geq similarity[i]), \end{cases} \tag{4}$$

where *feature* means the image feature distance between the mask data and each piece of teaching image data, and *similarity* refers to the similarity between the mask data and each teaching image data. i and j are defined as follows:

$$\{i \in N \mid 1 \leq i \leq images\}, \tag{5}$$

$$\{j \in N \mid 1 \leq j \leq max\_simirality\}. \tag{6}$$

Table 1 shows examples of the *similarity* and *features* of seven fictional images. Table 2 shows the data structure of a process for calculating the sum of the optimum feature distance. We can see that the system obtains 1312, which is the sum of the optimum feature distance in the row for Sample7.jpg and the *similarity* column 50.

Table 1. The similarities and features of seven fictional images.

Image	Similarity	Feature
Sample1.jpg	92	689
Sample2.jpg	83	647
Sample3.jpg	14	650
Sample4.jpg	22	662
Sample5.jpg	72	620
Sample6.jpg	36	639
Sample7.jpg	43	688

Table 2. Process for calculating the sum of optimum feature distance.

Image/Similarity	1	..	14	..	22	..	36	...	50
Sample1.jpg	0	0	0	0	0	0	0	0	0
Sample2.jpg	0	0	0	0	0	0	0	0	0
Sample3.jpg	0	0	650	650	650	650	650	650	650
Sample4.jpg	0	0	650	650	662	662	1312	1312	1312
Sample5.jpg	0	0	650	650	662	662	1312	1312	1312
Sample6.jpg	0	0	650	650	662	662	1312	1312	1312
Sample7.jpg	0	0	650	650	662	662	1312	1312	1312

Table 3 shows the sum of the optimum feature distance at each combination of the images (Samples1–7.jpg). The accumulative similarity was 0.5 when Sample3.jpg and Sample4.jpg were selected. When Sample3.jpg, Sample4.jpg, and Sample7.jpg were selected, the accumulative similarity was 1.0; it was 2.0 when Sample2.jpg, Sample3.jpg, Sample4.jpg, Sample6.jpg, and Sample7.jpg were selected. The accumulative similarity when all images except Sample5.jpg were selected was 3.0. When all images on Table 1 were selected, the accumulative similarity was 3.62.

Table 3. Sum of optimum feature distance at each combination of the images.

Accumulative similarity	Sum of optimum feature distance
0.5	1312
1.0	2000
2.0	3286
3.0	3975
3.62	4595

2.4 Determine Whether the Image Is the Selected Image

As shown in Sect. 2.3, the system could calculate the sum of the optimum feature distance at each specified similarity. However, the system had not yet acquired the suitable combination of the teaching image data. At this point, the system back-calculated to determine the optimum combinations of the teaching image data according to the optimum feature distance, as calculated in Sect. 2.3. Each piece of teaching image data was determined as *True* or *False* as follows:

$$\begin{cases} images[image] = False(condition == 1) \\ images[image] = False(condition == 2) \\ images[image] = True(condition == 3) \\ similarity_{current} = similarity_{current} - similarity[image](condition == 3) \end{cases}, \quad (7)$$

where *True* means that the teaching image data are among the selected data, and *False* means that the teaching image data are not selected in the process of optimizing the combination of the images. The system considered the upper limit value of the specified accumulative similarity as the current accumulative similarity. If the image was selected in the process of optimizing the combination of the images, the system subtracted the *similarity* of the selected teaching image data (*similarity[image]*) from the current accumulative similarity (*similarity_{current}*).

Referring to *True* or *False* in Formula (7), the system can determine whether each piece of teaching image data was selected or not based on the last line of the DP process of calculating the sum of the optimum feature distance of the suitable combinations (see Table 2), as follows:

$$
condition = \begin{cases}
1\,(similarity_{current} < similarity[image]), \\
2\,(similarity_{current} \geq similarity[image] \\
\quad \wedge \max\left(\begin{array}{l} table[image][similarity_{current} - similarity[image]] + \\ feature[image], table[image][similarity_{current}] \end{array} \right) == \\
\quad table[image][similarity_{current}]), \\
3\,(similarity_{current} \geq similarity[image] \wedge \\
\quad \max\left(\begin{array}{l} table[image][similarity_{current} - similarity[image]] + \\ feature[image], table[image][similarity_{current}] \end{array} \right) == \\
\quad table[image][similarity_{current} - similarity[image]] + feature[image]),
\end{cases}
$$

$$(8)$$

where, in the case of *condition* 1, the similarity of the teaching image data (*similarity[image]*) is higher than the current accumulative similarity (*similarity_{current}*). Hence, the teaching image data were considered not to be selected.

In the case of *condition* 2, the similarity of the teaching image data (*similarity[image]*) is less than the current accumulative similarity (*similarity_{current}*). Moreover, the sum of the feature distance at the current accumulative similarity (*table[image][similarity_{current}]*) is higher than the sum of the feature distance, which is added the feature distance of the teaching image data (*table[image][similarity_{current} - similarity[image]] + feature[image]*). This means that the teaching image data (*images[image]*) might have been selected according to the current accumulative similarity at the point. However, in the end, the teaching image data were not selected, because other, more suitable teaching image data, were selected.

In the case of *condition* 3, the similarity of the teaching image data (*similarity[image]*) is less than the current accumulative similarity (*similarity_{current}*). Moreover, the sum of the feature distance, which is added the feature distance of the teaching image data (*table[image][similarity_{current} - similarity[image]] + feature[image]*), is higher than the sum of feature distance at the current accumulative similarity (*table[image][similarity_{current}]*). The teaching image data were considered selected by the system.

2.5 Creating Teaching Image Data Sets and Learning

The COCO Annotator [12] creates a COCO data set [13] based on the selected teaching image data. The data set acquires an annotation in a *json* file from the COCO Annotator. The learning model of the system then learns the data set, which includes the images and the *json* files using Mask R-CNN [14]. Figure 2 shows that four screws are annotated.

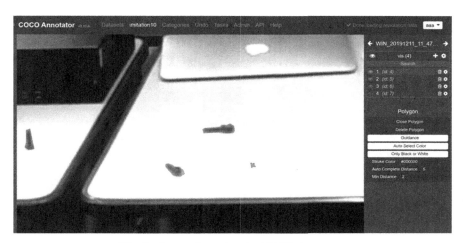

Fig. 2. Annotation using the COCO Annotator

3 System Setup

Figure 3 shows the entire structure of the system that detects the objects in the teaching image data and determines whether the objects have moved, when compared with a past image.

In the first stage, as explained in Sect. 2, the teaching image data are photographed by a fixed point camera and include the objects. The system optimizes the combinations of the teaching image data for learning that do not depend on the background with DP. Then, the COCO dataset [13] is created based on the selected images. The learning model of the system learns the objects in the selected teaching image data using the Mask R-CNN [14] learning program. After learning this, the system is able to detect objects in the images.

In the second stage, the system determines whether each object in the time-series image data is the same as the object that was detected in the past. At first, the objects in the time-series image data are detected by the learning model of the system with Mask R-CNN [14]. A motion-detection program receives the information about the detected objects. An object information storage system stores the information about the objects that have been detected in the past. The motion-detection program refers the information of detected objects to each piece of object information in the object information storage system. If the similarity is smaller than a given threshold, the system determines the detected object is new. The second stage is explained in the next section.

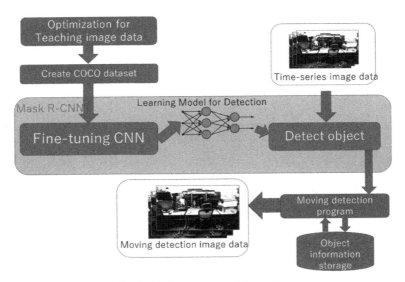

Fig. 3. Entire structure of the system.

4 Determining Whether an Object is the Same as the Object in the Motion-Detection Storage System

4.1 The Full Motion-Detection Process

Figure 4 shows the full process of the motion-detection program. First, the program receives the time-series images. Then, the objects in the images are detected using Mask R-CNN [14]. The program acquires the information about the detected objects, their classification, region, and coordinate values. Then, the motion-detection program adds a label to the detected objects and sends the information as a query to the object information storage system. The system refers the color of the segmented region of each detected object to that of each object in the storage system. If the similarity is smaller than a pre-set threshold, the system determines the detected object is new. The new object's information is then added to the storage system.

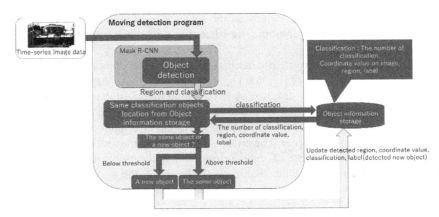

Fig. 4. Motion detection program

4.2 Determining Whether the Object is the Same as an Object Already in the System, to Detect Motion

In the object information storage system, the region and position data acquired from all previously detected objects are preserved in a map format. The system delivers the classification of the detected object to the storage system. The system can acquire the object's classification number, its region, position data, and label. If the classification number is "0," the detected object is considered a new object, and the information about the detected object is stored in the system.

If the classification number is not "0," the colors of the regions detected currently and detected in the past are converted into the histogram. The similarity of colors between the regions detected currently and in the past are normalized from 0–1 using a histogram intersection algorithm (Formula (3)). This normalized similarity is the criteria for determining whether the current detected object is the same as an object already in the system.

Figure 5 shows the process wherein a currently detected object is tied to a previous object in the storage system. Object 1 is most closely associated with the object of "label C" in storage, because they have the highest similarity value. The system determines that the

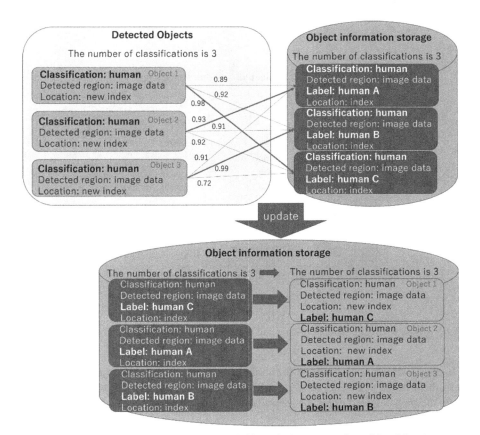

Fig. 5. A case where the number of the detected objects is the same as that of the object in storage.

current detected object is the same as the object with label C. Then, the information about the object with label C in storage is updated to match the information about Object 1.

Figure 6 shows a case where the number of current detected object is greater than the number of the objects in storage. The object whose similarity rating is the lowest among the current detected objects is considered a new object.

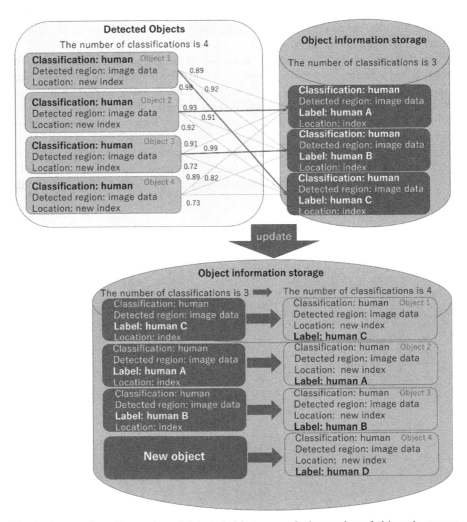

Fig. 6. A case where the number of detected objects exceeds the number of objects in storage.

Figure 7 shows a case where the number of current detected objects is less than that of the number of objects in storage. The object whose similarity value is the lowest among the past detected objects is considered to have disappeared.

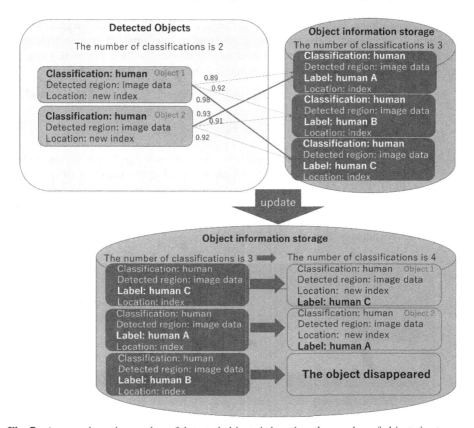

Fig. 7. A case where the number of detected objects is less than the number of objects in storage.

4.3 Updating Coordinate Values

When the current detected object is the same as the object in the object information storage, the position data (coordinate value) of the object in the storage is updated.

The newest coordinate value of the object in the storage is shown as:

$$prev_i\left\{i \in x, y, prev_x, prev_y \in N\right\}. \tag{9}$$

The newest coordinate value of the detected object from the time-series image data is shown as:

$$current_i\left\{i \in x, y, current_x, current_y \in N\right\}. \tag{10}$$

The comparison between *prev* and *current* using Formula (11),

$$\text{different (prev, current)} = \begin{cases} false(prev = current), \\ true(prev \neq current), \end{cases} \tag{11}$$

The system gives the coordinate values of the objects in the storage and the time-series image data to augments. If the object is considered to have moved, *true* is returned. Then, the coordinate value of the object in storage is updated to the coordinate value of the detected object from the time-series image data as follows:

$$\text{prev} = \text{current} \ (\text{prev} \neq \text{current}). \tag{12}$$

4.4 Indicating Moving Objects

Figure 8 shows an example of objects enclosed by red bounding boxes. In the upper image of Fig. 8, four different-length screws are detected in the image at time t_1 and enclosed by red bounding boxes. Next, the system acquires the information about the detected objects in the image at time t_2. Three of the four screws at time t_2 are considered to have moved. Therefore, the three screws are enclosed by the red bounding boxes, as shown the lower image of Fig. 8.

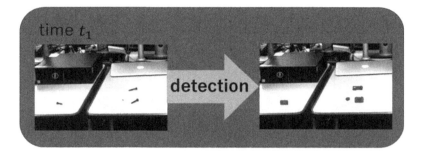

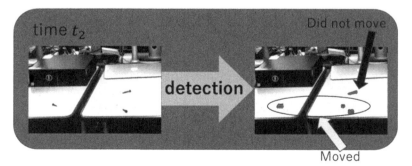

Fig. 8. Moved objects are enclosed by red bounding boxes. (Color figure online)

5 Experiment

5.1 Aim and Method

This section compares the accuracy of detecting the movement of objects from among some accumulative similarities. Thirty pieces of teaching image data are input to the system. The system optimizes the teaching image data at *similarity* 10–30, which is the upper limit of accumulative similarity. The learning model learns using the selected teaching image data. Then, the system detects which objects have moved or been moved.

The estimated region of the moving object that the learning model detects is compared with a correct region of the objects, which an experimenter determines in pixels. The accuracy of detecting the moving objects is calculated in terms of precision, recall, F-measure, and intersection over union (IoU) as follows:

$$\text{Precision} = \frac{TruePositive}{TruePositive + FalsePositive}, \tag{13}$$

$$\text{Recall} = \frac{TruePositive}{TruePositive + FalseNegative}, \tag{14}$$

$$\text{F} = \frac{2 \cdot \text{Recall} \cdot \text{Precision}}{\text{Recall} + \text{Precision}}, \tag{15}$$

$$\text{IoU} = \frac{TP}{TP + TN + FN}, \tag{16}$$

where a *True Positive* means that the number of pixels where the estimated regions and the correct regions of the moving object intersect; a *False Positive* means the number of error pixels in which the system estimated the regions of the moving object; a *False Negative* means the number of error pixels in which the system estimated that the region is not the moving object, even though these pixels are the region of the moving object in actuality; and a *True Negative* means that the number of pixels where the estimated regions and the correct regions that are not the moving object intersect.

The conditions of the experiment are *All, similarity* 10, 20, and 30. *All* is the learning model that learned using the 30 pieces of teaching image data. *Similarity* 10, 20, and 30 are the learning models that are learned with 16, 22, and 27 optimized teaching image data, respectively.

5.2   Results

Table 4 shows the results of recall, precision, F-measure, and IoU. The results show that there is little difference among these conditions.

Table 4. Comparing the accuracy of detecting moving objects among the upper limit accumulative similarities.

	Recall	Precision	F-measure	IoU
All	0.62332	0.62844	0.62578	0.456557
Similarity 10	0.62330	0.62850	0.62580	0.456574
Similarity 20	0.62338	0.62845	0.62582	0.456590
Similarity 30	0.62315	0.62858	0.62577	0.456541

6 Discussion

The system of the proposed method uses colors (histogram) to determine the similarity between a detected object and objects in storage to detect the movement of an object. The system often outputs an incorrect detection of a moving object, when it detects several objects that have similar colors. Therefore, it may be necessary for the system to determine similarity according to another determination method apart from color.

The results of this experiment indicate that there is little difference among the conditions. The teaching image data for the experiment included only one object and a simple background. If the system learns teaching image data that includes many objects, namely those with a complicated background, as a real room would have, there will be more differences in the accuracy among the accumulative similarities.

7 Conclusion

This paper proposed a method in which a combination of teaching image data is optimized using dynamic programming, so that the learning model does not learn teaching image data dependent on those backgrounds. The system used image feature distances and color similarities as evaluation indices for DP. This method was expected to show accuracy in detecting moving objects more accurately than other approaches can, despite there not being a lot of teaching image data. The results of the experiment showed that there was little difference among the conditions, and there were some accumulative similarities in the accuracy of detecting moving objects.

In the future, we will propose another method for determining the similarity between two regions to supplement the method based on colors.

Acknowledgement. This work was supported by JSPS KAKENHI Grant Number 17H01950.

References

1. Tile. https://thetileapp.jp/
2. Harris, C.G., Stephens, M.: A combined corner and edge detector. Proc. Alvey Vis. Conf. **15**(50), 147–151 (1988)
3. Lindeberg, T.: Scale-space theory: a basic tool for analyzing structures at different scales. J. Appl. Stat. **21**(1–2), 225–270 (1994)
4. Lowe, D.G.: Object recognition from local scale-invariant features. In: Proceedings of the Seventh IEEE International Conference on Computer Vision, vol. 2, pp. 1150–1157. IEEE Press, New York (1999)
5. Large Scale Visual Recognition Challenge 2012 (ILSVRC2012). http://www.image-net.org/challenges/LSVRC/2012/
6. Krizhevsky, A., Sutskever, I., Hinton, G.E.: Imagenet classification with deep convolutional neural networks. In: Advances in Neural Information Processing Systems, pp. 1097–1105. NIPS, San Diego (2012)
7. Bellman, R.: Dynamic programming. Science **153**(3731), 34–37 (1966)
8. Alcantarilla, P.F.: KAZE. http://www.robesafe.com/personal/pablo.alcantarilla/kaze.html

9. Alcantarilla, P.F., Bartoli, A., Davison, A.J.: KAZE Features. In: Fitzgibbon, A., Lazebnik, S., Perona, P., Sato, Y., Schmid, C. (eds.) ECCV 2012. LNCS, vol. 7577, pp. 214–227. Springer, Heidelberg (2012). https://doi.org/10.1007/978-3-642-33783-3_16
10. Dudani, S.A.: The distance-weighted k-nearest-neighbor rule. IEEE Trans. Syst. Man Cybern. **4**, 325–327 (1976)
11. Wu, J., Rehg, J.M.: Beyond the Euclidean distance: creating effective visual codebooks using the histogram intersection kernel. In: 12th International Conference on Computer Vision, pp. 630–637. Computer Vision Foundation (2009)
12. COCO Annotator. https://github.com/jsbroks/coco-annotator/wiki
13. Lin, T.-Y., et al.: Microsoft COCO: common objects in context. In: Fleet, D., Pajdla, T., Schiele, B., Tuytelaars, T. (eds.) ECCV 2014. LNCS, vol. 8693, pp. 740–755. Springer, Cham (2014). https://doi.org/10.1007/978-3-319-10602-1_48
14. He, K., Gkioxari, G., Dollar, P., Girshick, R.: Mask R-CNN, [1703.06870] (2017)

Optimal Route Search Based on Multi-objective Genetic Algorithm for Maritime Navigation Vessels

Ryosuke Saga$^{(\boxtimes)}$, Zhipeng Liang, Naoyuki Hara, and Yasunori Nihei

Osaka Prefecture University, 1-1 Gakuen-cho, Naka-ku, Sakai, Osaka 599-8531, Japan
saga@cs.osakafu-u.ac.jp, mcb04032@edu.osakafu-u.ac.jp,
n-hara@eis.osakafu-u.ac.jp, nihei@marine.osakafu-u.ac.jp

Abstract. Ocean research requires regular collection of ocean data, wherein an autonomous robotic ship is usually used. However, in contrast to collecting land-based data, collecting sea level data face the following problems. First, robot ships are affected by sea surface winds, waves, and tides, with constantly changing strength and direction. Second, hull collisions must be prevented when multiple ships are working simultaneously. Third, given the limitation of the electric power of the autonomous sailing ship, the electric power consumption of the robot ship must be considered when collecting over a wide sea. Fourth, fixed obstacles, such as an island on the sea surface, must be avoided. Given such issues, no effective navigation route search system is currently available. In this work, a navigation route system for complex situations on the sea surface was designed on the basis of the actual situation. Clustering method was used to classify collection points according to distance based on the number of robot ships, and a multi-objective genetic algorithm was used to determine the optimal path for each classification.

Keywords: Ocean research · Multi-objective genetic algorithm · Optimal route search

1 Introduction

Related fields combining aquaculture and IT have become widespread recently, and many examples have emerged with the development of IT technology. However, the basis of the research is the collection of aquaculture data. Autonomous robotic vessel is a highly efficient method to collect data frequently, especially in the field of marine aquaculture.

Autonomous vessels attract attention rapidly due to their potential to solve problems in the marine field. Such solutions include realizing high safety and efficiency of ships and improving marine data collection and working environment. An automatic navigation ship is to be in use with some coastal vessels in the early 2020s, and the realization of the automatic navigation ship that was completely made no person in the future after having utilized IoT is expected abroad at the earliest [1].

© Springer Nature Switzerland AG 2020
S. Yamamoto and H. Mori (Eds.): HCII 2020, LNCS 12185, pp. 506–518, 2020.
https://doi.org/10.1007/978-3-030-50017-7_38

However, the current research is mainly aimed at large ships facing the following problems: hull communication, obstacle detection and collision avoidance, location estimation, surrounding environment identification, and automatic desorption technology. For special aquaculture such as oyster aquaculture, high frequency data collection in a fixed sea area using a small electric self-operated ship is also a meaningful study. In addition, the robot ship can improve the accuracy of seawater flow simulation and further improve the efficiency of aquaculture and fishery. One representative is the four-hull robot ship [2] designed by Nihei and colleagues. Figure 1 shows the basic structure and physical appearance of the four-body robot ship. It can be automatically navigated by setting a well-established route and has a fixed-point hold function, so that the acquisition point of the sea surface can be used for data collection. It has been developed to collect marine data from farms at high frequencies and to establish big data systems for farms to improve farming efficiency.

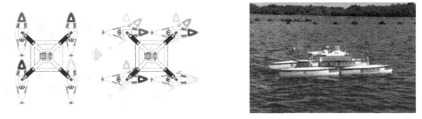

Fig. 1. Quad–maran automated vessel [2].

This study takes oyster farming at Nanao Bay as an example; this area covers about 183 km^2, housing many oyster farms [3]. Periodically collecting data on each cultivation point is necessary to study the growth status of oysters. However, in contrast to large autonomous vessels, small autonomous vessels, such as four-hull robot vessels, are limited. Therefore, their portable power is limited, and energy consumption during navigation is affected by wind waves. Therefore, efficient data collection for many aquaculture points is the key to enhancing the practicality of four-body robot ships. In other words, one of the key topics for the practicality of small autonomous vessels is to design the most suitable navigation routes based on the sea surface wind and waves and their own power conditions.

An autonomous ship must face the following problems when navigating at sea level:

1. Autonomous vessels are affected by sea surface winds, waves, and tides, with constantly changing strength and direction.
2. The collision of the hull must be prevented when multiple ships work simultaneously.
3. Given the limited power of autonomous ships, their power consumption must be considered when collecting over a wide sea.
4. Fixed obstacles, such as an island on the sea surface, must be avoided.

However, no effective navigation route search system that satisfies the above requirements is available.

Therefore, this study designs an efficient navigation route generation system for small automatic navigation vessels, such as a four-hull robot ship, according to the complicated situation on the sea surface. Specifically, in this system, the optimal navigation route, navigation distance, and power consumption in the current situation are considered outputs when the navigation start time, sampling point position, obstacle position, obstacle size, and navigation speed are given as inputs.

On the basis of the problems in this study, the goal of this work is transformed into a multi-objective optimization of multiple traveling salesman problem (mTSP) [4], which is a time-dependent combinatorial optimization problem. In addition, the actual route deviates to a certain extent from the planned route because of the influence of wind waves when the autonomous ship is sailing on the sea. The distance between sampling points is used as an indicator to prevent collision between hills. Clustering the sampling points according to the number of operating vessels and generating an optimal track for each generated cluster are recommended. This method reduces the direct intersection of navigation routes as well as the possibility of collisions between hulls. Considering that the sailing boat is operating, the route faces different requirements under various conditions. For example, traversing the sampling points in the shortest time is necessary when the weather is bad. The most efficient path is needed when power is low and distances are long. In this study, we propose an improved multipurpose genetic approach. This method automatically avoids obstacles, calculates the best solution set, and selects the best navigation route according to the situation. We developed this method using Java language to visualize the optimized route of autonomous boat.

2 Time-Dependent Traveling Salesman Problem (TDTSP) in the Ocean

2.1 General TDTSP Problems and Solutions

The time-dependent traveling salesman problem (TDTSP) is a traveling salesman problem, in which the cost of traveling to the next city varies depending on the location where the city appears in the solution [5]. The problem is to find the one with the lowest total moving cost among the fixed Hamiltonian cycles. Figure 2 shows a conceptual diagram of the TDTSP solution search. When the most suitable course of TDTSP is greatly related with placed time to show it in the figure and solves TDTSP by time because the cost between two points is different, it is necessary to predict the cost between two points in each time. Furthermore, I demand an optimization course in the whole time.

A typical example of the TDTSP problem is the mail delivery problem. Given that the actual traffic may be congested, the running speed of the vehicle is not constant but changes according to the degree of traffic congestion. The general method of solving TDTSP is to perform a research every time the moving cost changes. In this study, we explain this scenario using a typical traffic problem. In the actual TDTSP problem, the time consumption between two cities is generally calculated by predicting traffic volume.

For different real problems, the functional relationship between speed and time varies. It must be set according to the actual situation. For example, in the study of

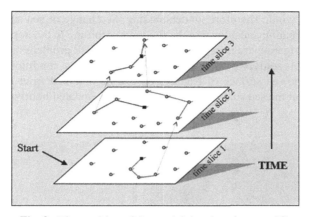

Fig. 2. The partition of the model time in subspaces [6].

"Solving Time-Dependent Traveling Salesman Problems using Ant Colony Optimization Based on Predicted Traffic and Its Application to Wide Area Road Network" [6], the following definition is used. The travel cost between cities is defined as travel time. If the travel time between cities i and j is t_{ij}, then the change in traffic volume can be represented by the change in t_{ij}. The variation of travel time at this time is defined by the following equation:

$$t_{ij}\big(n_{up}(T)\big) = t_{ij}\big(n_{up}(T) - 1\big) \times \Big(1 + C_f' \times rand\Big), \tag{1}$$

$$C_f' = \begin{cases} C_f & if\ rand \geq 0 \\ \frac{C_f}{1+C_f} & otherwise \end{cases}, \tag{2}$$

$$n_{up}(T) = \frac{T}{\Delta T}, \tag{3}$$

$$t_{ij}(0) = d_{ij}, \tag{4}$$

where T is the current time, $t_{ij}\big(n_{up}(T)\big)$ is the travel time between cities i and j when the departure time from city i is T, C_f is the travel time variation coefficient, and Δt is the update interval. The calculation formula is defined as follows:

$$T_s = \sum_{i=1}^{n} t_{N_{i-1}N_i}\big(n_{up}(T_{i-1})\big) \tag{5}$$

2.2 The Electricity Consumption of the Automatic Observation Ship

The TDTSP problem for the marine environment is more complicated than the general TDTSP described above. The autonomous navigation vessel in this study is a small autonomous robot vessel developed by the team of Nihei and colleagues. The hull is small, and the effect of wind waves during navigation is large. Therefore, $t_{ij}\big(n_{up}(T)\big)$

changes with the wind. Therefore, understanding the change of sea surface wind and waves during navigation and adjusting the function according to the impact of wind and waves on ship navigation are necessary to study the TDTSP problem facing the marine environment. In this study, we discuss based on the sea surface condition of Nanao Bay. Information on the sea surface of Nanao Bay can be obtained from Sea Weather.jp. (Fig. 3). Given that the sea surface wind information is updated hourly, Δt is one hour in this study.

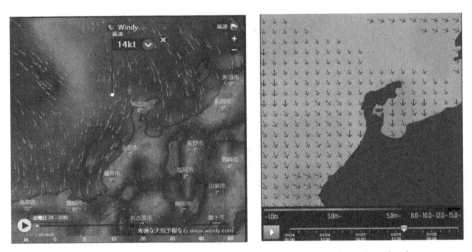

Fig. 3. Prediction of wind and tidal current in Nanao Bay from Weather.jp.

The power consumption according to the wind conditions is analyzed as shown in Fig. 4. When the observing ship sails from i to j at speed V, the wind received by the ship (Based on wind strength and direction at the time of departure), the acute angle α in the horizontal direction, and the intensity can be obtained from the sea weather forecast information in that time zone. β indicates the angle between the navigation direction and the horizontal direction, and is the angle γ $(=\alpha-\beta)$ between the wind and the navigation route. At this time, the wind force w received by the observation ship is decomposed into w_c and w_s in the figure. Since w_c is perpendicular to the navigation direction, it exerts a force to deviate from the navigation channel, so that maintaining the navigation route requires electric power to offset the effect of w_c. On the other hand, the effect of w_s is useful when the wind direction is the same as the navigation direction. Power is required.

From these, in order to convert the influence of the wind into the power consumption of the observation vessel, this study assumes that the power consumption per unit time is proportional to the wind intensity. That is, $E = \rho w$. Here, ρ is a coefficient depending on the observation ship. Assuming that E is decomposed into $w_c = \rho w \, sin(\gamma)$ and $w_s = \rho w \, cos(\gamma)$ as E_c and E_s, respectively, the power consumption between the i and j points is calculated by the following equation.

$$E_{ij} = t_{ij}\big(n_{up}(T)\big) \times (E_{v0} + E_s + |E_c|) \tag{6}$$

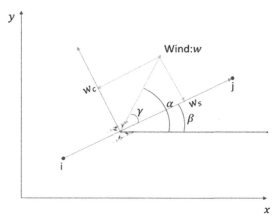

Fig. 4. Analysis of observation ship affected by wind

Here, E_{v0} is power consumption per unit time when there is no influence of wind waves when the automatic robot ship is at the speed V, and E_{v0} depends on the navigating ship used.

2.3 Dual-Purpose Optimization Distance and Power Consumption

When an autonomous ship sails on the sea surface, the effects of wind waves are significant in addition to the navigation time. Substantial electric power is required to cancel the effects of sea surface winds during navigation particularly when the volume of the self-operating ship is small. As a result, each boat can only visit a limited distance. Therefore, we consider the travel distance for this actual problem and the power consumption of each route, that is, two objective functions of travel distance and power consumption. By contrast, we referred to research on multi-objective optimization.

Optimization is to optimize evaluation index under given constraint conditions. Optimization is a concept deeply involved in many fields, such as engineering, industry, and economy. Optimization generally refers to a single-objective optimization that performs optimization for one evaluation (objective). However, the evaluation criteria are not necessarily unique in many problems. For example, when evaluating a product, multiple evaluation criteria, such as product function, price, appearance, weight, and size, are involved. The evaluation criteria that often have a trade-off relationship are mutually contradictory, and no product in which all the evaluation criteria are optimal exists. A problem in which such a plurality of evaluation criteria exists and the evaluation criteria have a trade-off relationship with each other, which is called a multi-objective optimization problem. A multi-objective optimization problem generally consists of k competing objective functions that deal with n design variables [7].

$$f_i(x_1, x_2, \ldots x_n)(i = 1, 2, \ldots k). \tag{7}$$

With m inequality constraints,

$$g_j(x_1, x_2, \ldots x_m) \leq 0(j = 1, 2, \ldots k). \tag{8}$$

In a multi-objective optimization problem, all objective functions $f_i(x)$ generally cannot be minimized simultaneously. This observation is due to the existence of a trade-off relationship between the objective functions. Therefore, in the multi-objective optimization problem, no optimal solution that takes the best value for all objectives is generally available. Therefore, a Pareto optimal solution is used as a new solution concept instead of the optimal solution in the multi-objective optimization problem. This concept of Pareto optimal solution was first defined by economist Pareto [8].

There are several researches and solutions for multi-objective optimization problems. In this study, we solve them using a multi-objective genetic algorithm [9]. Genetic algorithms have multiple approximate solutions within a population of search spaces. Therefore, by presenting the solution by the multipurpose GA to the user, it is possible for the user to select a route that suits them preference from among them, and it is possible to generate a route that considers the user's preference. Further, even if the solution search is terminated in a fixed time, a solution candidate can be obtained, so that the search can be performed in a practical time.

3 Proposed Algorithm

3.1 Basic Policy

When generating automatic navigation routes on the sea, various practical conditions must be considered. For example, a line with the lowest power consumption under a specific time limit and a case with the shortest navigation time under a specific power limit are needed. Therefore, we should choose the optimal path under different conditions, that is, the Pareto optimal solution space. This study proposes a method for generating a Pareto optimal solution space using a multi-objective genetic algorithm. The algorithm has multiple approximate solutions in the entire search space. Therefore, the user can be presented with multiple routes and can select a route that suits his or her preferences. A route that considers the user's preferences can be generated. In addition, even if the solution search is terminated within a fixed time, a solution candidate can be obtained. Therefore, the search can be performed in real time.

In this study, two objective functions are used and defined by the following formula:

$$Fitness1 = \sum\nolimits_{i=1}^{n} t_{N_{i-1}N_i}\left(n_{up}(T_{i-1})\right) \times v_{N_{i-1}N_i}. \tag{9}$$

$$Fitness2 = \sum\nolimits_{i=1}^{n} E_{N_{i-1}N_i}. \tag{10}$$

Equation 9 calculates the navigation distance, and Eq. 10 calculates the amount of power consumed for navigation. In this paper, we use the NSGA-II [10] algorithm to generate the Pareto optimal solution space. The NSGA-II algorithm is characterized by good search performance and wide range of Pareto optimal solution set generated by congestion degree calculation. Therefore, the generated route selectivity is good, and a more realistic problem can be solved. In this paper, we make improvements based on NSGA-II and add an obstacle avoidance function.

Various methods are available for fixed obstacle avoidance, such as the A* algorithm [11]. The principle in implementing A* algorithm is to detour around obstacles. However, the effect of the A* algorithm is not good because a gap exists between the navigation and planned routes in actual navigation, and bypassing obstacles may not be possible. In this study, we propose adding an obstacle collision judgment step to the genetic algorithm. In this way, the path generated can avoid obstacles directly. When the current route passes through the obstacle area by adding the determination condition to the performed step, the distance of this route is set to the maximum value.

In actual data collection, multiple observation robot containers are usually used simultaneously to improve the collection efficiency. In this case, the route generated by the solution usually has many intersections, but the navigation route may deviate from the planned route because of wind and waves when observing the robot ship sailing at sea. The possibility of collision between hulls is high. This study proposes to use the improved k-means [12, 13] method to first cluster the collection points according to the number of observation ships and then calculate the best path for each category separately to avoid this problem. As such, collisions between hulls can be effectively prevented.

3.2 Algorithm Overview

As input to the algorithm, (1) Observation point location and starting point: Cities, (2) Obstacle location: D, (3) Sea surface wind information: Wind, (4) Number of autonomous vessels: ShipNum, (5) The speed of the autonomous ship: v and the start time: StartTime. The output is a set G of Pareto optimal solutions. Figure 5 shows the entire algorithm.

In this algorithm, first, clustering is performed according to the number of observation vessels, and then an improved multi-objective GA is executed in each cluster based on the clustering results. After that, an optimal route for each cluster is generated, and the result is returned.

In this study, we increased the method of avoiding obstacles in the Multi-objective GA algorithm. The specific procedure is shown in Fig. 6.

The details of each operation are described below.

1. Initialization: Initialize by setting each parameter of NSGA-II. Chromosomes are generated based on the number of observation points, and the population is initialized. Regarding chromosome generation in this paper, a fixed number of observation points can be obtained by clustering, and fixed-length chromosomes are generated according to the number of observation points.
2. Obstacle avoidance: By adding an obstacle collision determination step in the NSGA-II algorithm, a route around the obstacle is directly generated. If the current route passes through the obstacle area, the distance and power consumption of the route are set to the maximum values, and this route is eliminated when a next generation population is generated.
3. Fitness calculation: Calculate the objective function of each chromosome in the population. The chromosome of each individual is decoded into a problem space to obtain an individual evaluation value. Generally, a fitness value of an individual is determined based on the evaluation value. The fitness value is a value indicating the degree to which the individual is adapted to the environment, and quantitatively indicates the likelihood of survival for the next generation.

Algorithm 1 Overall algorithm

Input : Cities
     D_i
    Wind
    ShipNumber
    StartTime
    v
OUTPUT : G[ShipNumber]
1:   **if** (ShipNum == 1)
2:       Do GA Algorithm:
3   G[0] = **function GA**(Cities, D_i, Wind, StartTime , v);
4   **return** G[0];
5: **else**
6:       Do Cluster by K-means: Cities[ShipNumber]:=K-means(ShipNumber);
7:       **for** each i ∈ [1, ShipNumber];
8:           Do GA Algorithm;
9   G[i] = **function GA**(Cities, D_i, Wind, StartTime , v);
10   **end for**;
11:      **return** G[i];

Fig. 5. The whole algorithm.

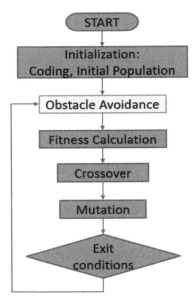

Fig. 6. Specific procedure.

4. Crossover: Crossover exchanges chromosomal information between individuals. If individuals having a part of the individual representing the optimal solution cross each other, there is a high possibility that an individual closer to the optimal solution can be obtained. In this paper, we use PMX crossover [14]. This method ensures that the stations in the newly produced route do not overlap.

5. Mutation: Mutation is a technique that maintains population diversity. It is effective in escaping from the local optimal solution. However, when the mutation rate is increased, the state becomes closer to a random search, so a smaller value is usually used. This paper uses 0.2.
6. End condition judgment: Judge based on the set number of generations, add 1 each time a new generation number counter is generated, terminate the program when the set value is reached, and return the latest solution set.

4   Simulation

4.1   Goal and Simulation Environment

The purpose of this experiment is to achieve the following:

1. Verify the effectiveness of this technique, including whether the best route can be generated based on sea conditions, whether the generated route can avoid obstacles, and whether the generated routes can avoid intersections in the presence of multiple ships.
2. Under different data volumes, the implementation effect of this technique and the parameters and execution time are required to generate the best route.

In this simulation, the data of the observation point uses the data of traveling salesman problem library [15]. The wind wave data is generated randomly by referring to the forecast data of Nanao Bay. Moreover, the simulation environment used a computer with a CPU Intel Core i7 2.6 GHz, memory 16 384 MB, and OS Windows10. The parameters of the multipurpose GA are set as follows (Table 1):

Table 1. GA parameters.

Population	3000
Crossover rate	1.0
Mutation rate	0.2
Generations	50000

4.2   Effectiveness of Proposed Method

The test was performed using the at 48 dataset, which is a collection of TSP questions, as the city coordinate points to test the execution result of the system. Figure 7 shows the program execution results. The black area on the screen indicates the obstacle area. Consequently, this study showed that effective evacuation is possible for obstacles fixed on the sea surface and obstacles moving within a certain range.

The result of the Pareto optimal solution is shown in Fig. 8. The red line indicates the optimal distance solution for this problem set, and the algorithm can obtain a value close to the optimal solution from the distribution of the solution space.

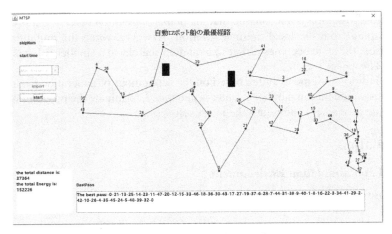

Fig. 7. Program running results.

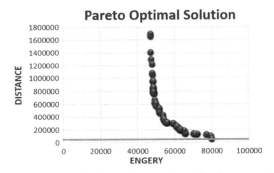

Fig. 8. Pareto optimal solution results (Color figure online)

4.3 Verify the Effect of This Method on Different Datasets

We conducted experiments with four datasets selected to verify the effect of this method on different datasets. These datasets are the at 48, kroA 100, kroA 200, and at 532 data sets. Table 2 shows the experimental results. According to the result analysis, calculations can be performed efficiently for data with fewer than 100 observation points with the current parameter settings. As the data increases, the effect of the current parameters decreases. The accuracy can be improved by increasing the number of generations, but the program execution time increases.

4.4 Analysis of Results

Based on the analysis of the results of this experiment, this method can achieve the effect close to the ideal value if only the distance is used for evaluation. Considering the optimization of distance and power, this method can choose the appropriate land based on time.

Table 2. Simulation result of multi-objective GA algorithm.

Cities	Shortest distance	Simulated distance	Generation	Calculation time (seconds)
48	10628	10628	3000	65
100	21282	21282	9000	177
200	26524	27653	20000	598
532	27686	29624	60000	1156

For different data volumes, experiments show that this method can obtain ideal results, but calculation time increases with data volume. Therefore, appropriate parameters can be designed according to data requirements.

5   Conclusions

This study focuses on the problems faced by small electric boats when sailing on the sea surface and proposes clustering and multipurpose optimization techniques. Experiments show that this method is effective for the proposal of the small robotic ship's navigation route. This study only considers the effects of wind and waves on ships presently. Influential factors will be added in subsequent studies, and the effect of this method will be verified through actual sea surface navigation experiments.

References

1. Yoshida, K., Shimizu, N., Hirayama, K., Arima, M., Ikeda, Y.: A basic study on development of automatic ships. Japan Soc. Naval Architects Ocean Eng. **22**, 335–340 (2016)
2. Srinivasamurthy, S., Sakamoto, H., Nishikawa, T., Nihei, Y.: Numerical hull resistance and hydrodynamic characteristics of an independently rotating multi-hull vessel. In: 38th International Conference on Ocean, Offshore and Arctic Engineering (OMAE2019), 9–14 June 2019, Glasgow, Scotland (2019)
3. http://www.ikgyoren.jf-net.ne.jp/seiwan_html/seiwan/index.html
4. Matsuura, T., Numata, K.: Solving min-max multiple traveling salesman problems by chaotic neural network. In: NOLTA2014, Luzern, Switzerland, 14–18 September 2014 (2014)
5. Malandraki, C., Daskin, M.S.: Time dependent vehicle routing problems: formulations, properties and heuristic algorithms. Transp. Sci. **26**(3), 185–200 (1992)
6. Kanoh, H., Ochiai, J.: Solving time-dependent traveling salesman problems using ant colony optimization based on predicted traffic. In: Omatu, S., De Paz Santana, J.F., González, S.R., Molina, Jose M., Bernardos, Ana M., Rodríguez, Juan M.Corchado (eds.) Distributed Computing and Artificial Intelligence. AISC, vol. 151, pp. 25–32. Springer, Heidelberg (2012). https://doi.org/10.1007/978-3-642-28765-7_4
7. Shamshirband, S., Shojafar, M., Hosseinabadi, A.R., Abraham, A.: A solution for multi-objective commodity vehicle routing problem by NSGA-II. In: 14th IEEE International Conference on Hybrid Intelligent Systems (HIS), pp. 12–17 (2014)
8. Atsushi, H., Takashi, O., Seiichi, K., Hironori, H.: Analysis and improvements of the pareto optimal solution visualization method using the self-organizing maps. SICE J. Control Meas. Syst. Integr. **8**(1), 34–43 (2015)

9. Liang, J.J., Yue, C.T., Qu, B.Y.: Multimodal multi-objective optimization: a preliminary study. In: 2016 IEEE Congress on Evolutionary Computation (CEC), pp. 2454–2461 (2016)
10. Deb, K., Pratap, A., Agarwal, S., Meyarivan, T.: A fast and elitist multiobjective genetic algorithm: NSGA-II. IEEE Trans. Evol. Comput. **6**, 182–197 (2002)
11. Chen, Y.S., Juang, J.: Intelligent obstacle avoidance control strategy for wheeled mobile robot. In: 2009 ICCAS-SICE, Fukuoka, pp. 3199–3204 (2009)
12. Bouguessa, M., Wang, S., Jiang, Q.: A K-means-based algorithm for projective clustering. In: 18th International Conference on Pattern Recognition (ICPR 2006), Hong Kong, China (2006)
13. Majd, L.: Solving multiple TSP problem by k-means and crossover based modified ACO algorithm. J. Eng. Tech. Res. **5**, 430–434 (2016)
14. Singh, V., Choudhary, S.: Genetic algorithm for traveling salesman problem: using modified partially-mapped crossover operator. In: 2009 International Multimedia, Signal Processing and Communication Technologies, pp. 20–23 (2009)
15. Reinelt, G.: TSPLIB—a traveling salesman problem library. ORSA J. Comput. **3**, 376–384 (1991)

The Integration of Web-Based and Mobile-Based Participatory Sensing Interfaces Apply to the Identification and Assessment of Contextual Features in the City

Yang Ting Shen[1], Pei Wen Lu[2(✉)], and Feng Cheng Lin[3]

[1] Department of Architecture, National Cheng Kung University, Tainan, Taiwan
10808028@gs.ncku.edu.tw
[2] Department of Geography, National Changhua University of Education, Changhua, Taiwan
peiwenlu@cc.ncue.edu.tw
[3] Department of Information Engineering and Computer Science, Feng Chia University, Taichung, Taiwan
fclin@fcu.edu.tw

Abstract. In this paper, we propose the integration of mobile-based and web-based Interfaces called City Probe system for the spatial identification and assessment driven by citizens' participation. The City Probe system provides the potential method to engage the power of citizens' participation in the city governance. It allows citizens' on-site and off-site identification and assessment of contextual features. The City Probe system sets up the measuring rule from -10 (most negative) to $+10$ (most positive) to standardize citizens' participation. Individual citizens can quantify their contextual feature identification into assessable standard. Three kinds of maps including DOT, BLOCK, and HEAT modes can be made and visualize the quantitative results.

The experiment based on the City Probe Mobile APP is conducted according to the features pre-made by subjects. It demonstrates how the City Probe system could be adopted to almost any contextual feature. The results also use visualized maps to present the potential positive (blue) and negative (negative) areas of target features derived from subjects' participation.

Keywords: Participatory sensing · Geo-visualization · City governance · Contextual feature · UGC

1 Introduction

Today, 55% of the world's population lives in urban areas, a proportion that is expected to increase to 68% by 2050 [30]. With the trend to more urbanization, effective engagement citizens to the city governance holds the promise of improving the quality of life of urban residents, improving the governance of cities and making cities prosperous, inclusive, sustainable and resilient [21]. When we talk about citizens' participation in the city governance, by contributing the development of Internet technologies, people

© Springer Nature Switzerland AG 2020
S. Yamamoto and H. Mori (Eds.): HCII 2020, LNCS 12185, pp. 519–528, 2020.
https://doi.org/10.1007/978-3-030-50017-7_39

have the chance to become "netizens" of web social community. More and more citizens choose dual identity to participate in the city governance. However, it can't be easily divided into offline and online statuses. The board line between the two statuses has become fuzzy and mixed due to the popularization of ICT devices. For example, when a citizen participates in an on-site activity, he may also hold an online streaming through his ICT device. In the same time, a mass of off-site citizens may also join this event synchronously. Sometimes they even can feed their comments back to on site. The internet and ICT devices indeed blur the time-space status of citizens' participation. Therefore, the most important issue of citizens' participation is not about the methods of participation but is about the participation of content generation. The idea called UGC (user-generated content) [7, 11, 17] facilitates and accelerates citizens' participation in the city governance. From another point of view, UGC derived from citizens can provide the third-party evidences for the scientific city governance.

In this paper, we are going to discuss about the participatory sensing application and its geo-visualization method. The integration of mobile-based and web-based Interfaces called the City Probe system for the spatial identification and assessment driven by citizens' participation will be presented to demonstrate the bottom-up city governance. In the end, the experiment operated by City Probe is conducted to realize the citizens' participation of contextual feature identification and assessment.

2 Literature Review

2.1 Participatory Sensing

By contributing the popularization of Internet-enabled and GPS-enable devices, many people have become "netizens" of the Web social community [27]. The use of terminal devices to upload UGC (user-generated contents) gives citizens the ability to act as sensors [25]. Comparing with robotic sensors, citizens have the cognitive ability to perceive the complex events or phenomena. For example, the safety of a place. It is difficult to determine how safe of a place just according to robotic sensors. Thus, the detectable environmental data such as wind, light, heat, air or water are not the target reason to engage citizens. Citizens' participation in the city governance should address on the qualitative feature exploration of living context. In addition, another advantage of citizen's engagement is mobility. Not like fixed sensors, citizens can migrate in the city to access almost any target place. The mobility of citizens provides the opportunity to build the dynamic sensor network [13, 22].

The advance in location-aware technologies coupled with ubiquitous citizens have paved the way for an exciting paradigm shift for accomplishing urban-scale sensing, known in literature as participatory sensing [3]. Participatory sensing forms interactive, participatory sensor networks that enable public and professional users to gather, analyze and share local knowledge [3, 15]. BikeNet [8] is a mobile sensing system for mapping the cyclist experience. It uses several sensors embedded into a cyclist's bicycle to gather quantitative data such as current location, speed, CO_2, burnt calories, and galvanic skin response etc. The peripheral sensors interact with the mobile phone over a wireless connection to upload data. The individual data can be merged with other cyclists' data to build the complete map for the cycling community. NoiseTube project [19] monitors noise pollution involving citizens (people) and built (environment) upon the notions of participatory sensing and citizen science. It enables citizens to measure peripheral noise exposure by using GPS-equipped mobile phones. The geo-localized UGC automatically upload and form the collective noise mapping of cities.

The use of robotic sensors for environment detection like we mention above provides the accurate source feedback. However, citizens play less role and just act as vehicles. The power of citizens should not only about mobility but also cognition. Streetscore [20] engages the citizens' perception power to assess spatial issues. Streetscore developed by MIT Media Lab is a scene understanding algorithm that predicts the perceived safety of a streetscape, using training data from an online survey with contributions from more than 7000 participants. One of most interesting part is the online participatory sensing interface [22]. The interface randomly shows two different geo-tagged images and asks participants to choose which one is safer. Finally, the algorithm analyzes crowdsourcing data and presents the safety map. The participants' cognition ability is really engaged in the identification of safety context that sensors or computers are difficult to tell.

The application of participatory sensing can generate vast data from participants. How to visualize the location-based data to deliver the meaningful information will be discussed in the next section.

2.2 Geo-Visualization

Realizing the potential of participatory sensing result as a data source requires developing appropriate methodologies [9]. We need a proper way for meaningful explanations from newly massive scales and complexities of digital data that are emerging through UGC. Techniques from information visualization, geo-visualization, and spatialization offer ways of reducing the complexity of information and clarifying relationships in big data [10, 28, 29]. For instance, Kramis has developed an XML-based infrastructure to enhance c interactive Geo-visualization of large data sets [16]. Bailey and Grossardt use information visualization to create collaborative geospatial/geovisual decision support systems (C-GDSS) for the supporting of public decision making [1]. Both cases give the idea that information visualization is not only provide the function of efficient data interpretation, but also induce the potential of decision making supporting for authority units or anonymous citizens.

The key of valuable Geo-visualization is to visualize the big data and map them according to coordination. It provides the spatial clues which allow users to discern massive data and build their relationship. Currid and Williams use a unique data set, Getty Images and geo-coded over 6000 events and 300,000 photographic images taken in Los Angeles and New York City, and conduct GIS -based spatial statistics to analyze macro-geographical patterns [6]. The project effectively identifies the hot spots to understand cultural industries and city geographic patterns. In addition to large-scale quantitative approaches, scholars in the social sciences argue that qualitative geo-visualization methods are equally important in our efforts to draw meaning from UGC [2, 14]. The terms computer-aided qualitative GIS and geo-narrative analysis adapt existing geospatial technologies for interpretive analysis of geographic information expressed as qualitative information [5, 18]. Cidell shows how content clouds with geo-location can be used to summarize and compare information from different places on a single issue [4].

In sum, with internet-enable technologies, the basic components of a widespread participatory sensing network already exist. The participatory sensing based on citizens brings a lot of opportunities to the city governance. In the same time, citizen-based participation also means the vast production of UGC. It needs well visualization methods to analyze the patterns and deliver meaningful information. Geo-visualization integrates the location and information to arouse context awareness. We believe the integration of participation sensing and geo-visualization will enable citizens to co-govern the city in a new way.

3   City Probe

Bring citizens to the city governance can reverse the traditional top-down leading management to the bottom-up collaborative governance. It provides potential opportunities from citizens' participation to achieve 1. the reflection of citizens' needs, 2. the deep and broad exploration of places, 3. the spatial interpretation based on human cognition. Under those premises, one of the most important issues is how to engage citizens' cognition ability for place features recognition. As we know, the human brain can perceive the complex context and interpret it into abstract but comprehensive concept. For instance, the safety of a place. Some urbanology scholars call it "sense of place" [13, 24]. Here we try to augment the place sensing ability of human and apply it to the identification and assessment of contextual features in the city.

We propose the participatory sensing system called City Probe to quantify citizens' perception of cities [25, 26]. In following sections, we will introduce the methodology and interface design of City Probe to explain how we engage citizens in the city governance. In addition, the visualization map will show how the collective data from citizens can be visualized to assist the citizens' decision making.

3.1   Identification and Assessment of Contextual Features

Comparing with robotic sensors, taking citizens as sensors presents more qualitative dimension of city features identification. The cognition ability of citizens allows them to perceive the complex and contextual phenomenon. The City Probe system we developed try to engage this kind of cognition ability for the identification and assessment of contextual features in the city. The critical challenges include 1. how to identify the contextual features, 2. how to record them, 3. how to assess them.

The City Probe system designs serial operating steps to identify and assess the contextual features. In the beginning, the manager of city probe system presets several features to make the feature pool. The manager can create any kind of features; but remember, try to make the features qualitative but NOT calculating or static. For example, "I feel comfortable" is better than "the temperature is....". From this example we can understand that former one is the comprehensive contextual phenomenon rather than the later one only. In addition, no any robotic sensor can detect the former feature but human brain.

Then citizens can choose one of the features provided from the pool to start their participatory sensing. When citizens pick up one target feature, it means the place fills or lacks this kind of feature worth to identify. Therefore, the City Probe system need to crate the measuring rule to quantify the citizens' identification. The measuring rule sets up the scale from -10 (most negative) to $+10$ (most positive). According the shared scale, citizens can quantify their identification into assessable standard. In the same time, it also makes contextual features countable in order of further urban metrology application.

3.2 Interface Design

We present twin participatory sensing interfaces to quantify citizens' perception of cities. Two interfaces called City Probe Mobile and City Probe Web (Fig. 1) are based on place ratings from citizens. Those two interfaces share the similar participatory sensing idea but aim to two different citizen groups: on-site citizens and off-site citizens. The on-site citizen group means the citizens who really visit places and participate in the place rating via City Probe Mobile APP. In the other site, the off-site citizen group means the citizens who "surf" the street view and participate in the place rating via City Probe Web. In the beginning, we only provided the City Probe Mobile APP to citizens. After several small tests, we found the City Probe Mobile APP users could dig into the city places provide high quality local place rating due to the on-site observation and mobility. However, after a period, the rating amount and rage went down due to the constrain of citizens' familiar area. Therefore, we develop the City Probe Web which could present the photorealistic street view to engage the off-site community into the place rating. Two City Probe modes show complementarity for the identification and assessment of contextual features in the city.

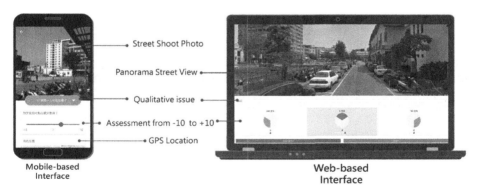

Fig. 1. City Probe interface design: mobile-based interface (left) and web-based interface (right)

When citizens use City Probe interfaces, the system not only quantifies their assessment, but also records their coordinates. The mobile-based interface reports the location via GPS. The web-based interface also extracts the location from Google map. Based on the location, we can map the quantified assessment information and visualize it.

3.3 Visualization Methods

We design three kinds of map mode to visualize the citizens' participatory sensing outcomes of contextual features (Fig. 2). 1. DOT mode: the map shows the individual assessment locations and visualizes the score with gradient red (negative) to blue (positive) dots. It provides the method to view the density and location of assessment data. 2. BLOCK mode: the map calculates the average score in 50 m by 50 m square and visualizes the score with gradient red (negative) to blue (positive) blocks. It provides the method to view the regional assessment data. 3. HEAT mode: the map places variables in the rows and columns and coloring the cells within the table. It provides a warm-to-cool color spectrum to show the heat of assessment data.

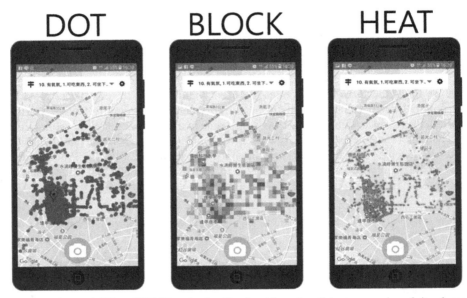

Fig. 2. DOT, BLOCK, and HEAT mode visualize the citizens' participatory sensing of city places. (Color figure online)

4 Experiment Design and Analysis

The City Probe tool allows us to investigate the city features by citizens' participatory. In this paper, we conducted the interesting experiment to demonstrate how the City Probe worked in almost any contextual feature. We invited 60 student subjects and deployed the City Probe Mobile-based Interface APP in their smartphones. In the beginning, we asked subjects to discuss the issue of "dating place features". After serial discussions, subjects submitted 10 potential features including having a great view, having a secret path, having an atmosphere, etc. We adopted the features and created the feature pool in our City Probe Qualitative Issue field. Then we asked subjects to start their field trip and use the City Probe APP by walking in 180 min.

The outcomes from 60 subjects in 180 min were amazing. First, the spread of features identification was quite fast and vast. In Fig. 3, we could see the progress and distribution of subjects' action. They reported around 3000 data covering an area of 4 km^2.

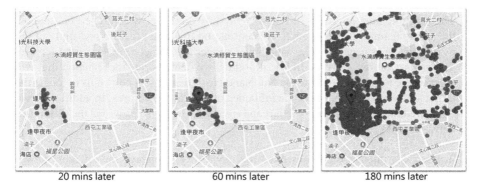

| 20 mins later | 60 mins later | 180 mins later |

Fig. 3. The progress and spread of subjects' place features identification.

Second, the outcomes provided the new method to observe the distribution of different features in the city. The reported features coupled with coordinates could be visualized in the Google map. Each feature was regarded as a layer. Therefore, we could check out the single or multiple features by turning layers on/off individually. For example, in Fig. 4, we chose the BLOCK mode to visualize the reported data. The left figure showed the result which turned on all the layers, the middle one just turned on No. 5 (having a great view) and No. 7 (having a secret path) layers, and the right one only turned in No. 7 layer.

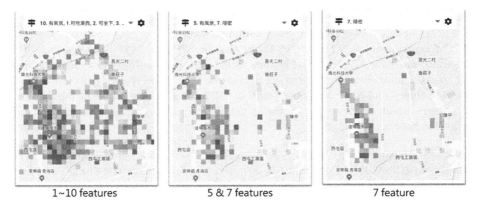

| 1~10 features | 5 & 7 features | 7 feature |

Fig. 4. The feature layers can be turned on/off individually.

The visualized map provided 3 potential analysis methods via layers' mapping.

1. Overall features analysis: In Fig. 4 left, we turned all layers on to map 10 features in the same diagram. The diagram showed the overall assessment results and visualized them by blue (positive score) and red (negative score) blocks. We could locate the target areas according to the shade of blocks. It helped us to find out the most positive or negative areas which were under the influence of all reported features.
2. The single feature analysis: In Fig. 4 right, only one layer was turened on to show the single feature. It helped us to concentrate on the target feature and find out the most positive or negative areas which were under the influence of the target feature.
3. The cross-features analysis: In Fig. 4 middle, we demonstrate the function that two layers were turned on to show the No. 5 and No. 7 features. It helped us to locate the target areas which were under the influence of two target features. In addition, if we compared the middle figure with left and right figures, it also provided the difference between cross features.

In this experiment we demonstrated the novel way to engage the citizens' power driven by the City Probe system. The experiment tool was based on the City Probe Mobile APP. However, we also noticed the shortage of subjects' mobility during the time constrain. Therefore, after the experiment, we lock the vacant areas visualized map and use the City Probe Web to fill them up. In other words, the City Probe web played the complementary tool to complete the identification and assessment of contextual features.

5   Conclusion

The City Probe system provides the potential method to engage the power of citizens' participation in the city governance. Two interfaces called City Probe Mobile and City Probe Web are developed to allow citizens' on-site and off-site identification and assessment of contextual features. Both of them share the same measuring rule from −10 (most negative) to +10 (most positive). Individual citizens can quantify their identification into assessable standard. Therefore, 3 kinds of maps including DOT, BLOCK, and HEAT modes can be made and visualize the quantitative results.

The experiment based on the City Probe Mobile APP presented the valuable results to demonstrate how the City Probe system could be adopted to almost any identification and assessment of contextual feature. However, the City Probe Web only worked as the complementary tool after our experiment. In the future, we may conduct the parallel experiment which adopts two City Probe interfaces in the same time to compare the difference between them.

Acknowledgements. The financial support from Ministry of Science and Technology (MOST) project "ProBIM" (MOST 105-2627-M-035-008 -), the technical support from Cheng Yang Shih, the partition class and participants support from Yi Shiang Shiu, are greatly acknowledged.

References

1. Bailey, K., Grossardt, T.: Toward structured public involvement: justice, geography and collaborative geospatial/geovisual decision support systems. Ann. Assoc. Am. Geogr. **100**(1), 57–86 (2010)
2. Bodenhamer, D.J., Corrigan, J., Harris, T.M. (eds.): The Spatial Humanities: GIS and the Future of Humanities Scholarship. Indiana University Press, Bloomington (2010)
3. Burke, J.A., et al.: Participatory sensing (2006)
4. Cidell, J.: Content clouds as exploratory qualitative data analysis. Area **42**(4), 514–523 (2010)
5. Cope, M., Elwood, S. (eds.): Qualitative GIS: A Mixed Methods Approach. Sage, London (2009)
6. Currid, E., Williams, S.: The geography of buzz: art, culture and the social milieu in Los Angeles and New York. J. Econ. Geogr. **10**(3), 423–451 (2010)
7. Daugherty, T., Eastin, M.S., Bright, L.: Exploring consumer motivations for creating user-generated content. J. Interact. Advert. **8**(2), 16–25 (2008)
8. Eisenman, S.B., Miluzzo, E., Lane, N.D., Peterson, R.A., Ahn, G.S., Campbell, A.T.: BikeNet: a mobile sensing system for cyclist experience mapping. ACM Trans. Sens. Netw. (TOSN) **6**(1), 1–39 (2010)
9. Elwood, S.: Geographic information science: visualization, visual methods, and the geoweb. Prog. Hum. Geogr. **35**(3), 401–408 (2011)
10. Fabrikant, S.I., Buttenfield, B.P.: Formalizing semantic spaces for information access. Ann. Assoc. Am. Geogr. **91**(2), 263–280 (2001)
11. Girardin, F., Calabrese, F., Dal Fiore, F., Ratti, C., Blat, J.: Digital footprinting: uncovering tourists with user-generated content. IEEE Pervasive Comput. **7**(4), 36–43 (2008)
12. Goodchild, M.F., Li, L.: Assuring the quality of volunteered geographic information. Spatial Stat. **1**, 110–120 (2012)
13. Hay, R.: Sense of place in developmental context. J. Environ. Psychol. **18**(1), 5–29 (1998)
14. Jung, J.K., Elwood, S.: Extending the qualitative capabilities of GIS: computer-aided qualitative GIS. Trans. GIS **14**(1), 63–87 (2010)
15. Kanhere, S.S.: Participatory sensing: crowdsourcing data from mobile smartphones in urban spaces. In: Hota, C., Srimani, Pradip K. (eds.) ICDCIT 2013. LNCS, vol. 7753, pp. 19–26. Springer, Heidelberg (2013). https://doi.org/10.1007/978-3-642-36071-8_2
16. Kramis, M., Gabathuler, C., Fabrikant, S.I., Waldvogel, M.: An XML-based infrastructure to enhance collaborative geographic visual analytics. Cartogr. Geogr. Inf. Sci. **36**(3), 281–293 (2009)
17. Krumm, J., Davies, N., Narayanaswami, C.: User-generated content. IEEE Pervasive Comput. **7**(4), 10–11 (2008)
18. Kwan, M.P., Ding, G.: Geo-narrative: Extending geographic information systems for narrative analysis in qualitative and mixed-method research. Prof. Geogr. **60**(4), 443–465 (2008)
19. Maisonneuve, N., Stevens, M., Niessen, M.E., Hanappe, P., Steels, L.: Citizen noise pollution monitoring. In: Proceedings of the 10th Annual International Conference on Digital Government Research: Social Networks: Making Connections between Citizens, Data and Government, pp. 96–103). Digital Government Society of North America, May 2009
20. Naik, N., Philipoom, J., Raskar, R., Hidalgo, C.: Streetscore-predicting the perceived safety of one million streetscapes. In: Proceedings of the IEEE Conference on Computer Vision and Pattern Recognition Workshops, pp. 779–785 (2014)
21. Percivall, G., Rönsdorf, C., Liang, S., McKenzie, D., McKee, L.: OGC smart cities spatial information framework. OGC Internal Reference, pp. 14–115 (2015)
22. Salesses, P., Schechtner, K., Hidalgo, C.A.: The collaborative image of the city: mapping the inequality of urban perception. PloS one **8**(7) (2013). https://www.ncbi.nlm.nih.gov/pmc/articles/PMC3722224/

23. Schade, S., et al.: Citizen-based sensing of crisis events: sensor web enablement for volunteered geographic information. Appl. Geomat. **5**(1), 3–18 (2013)
24. Shamai, S.: Sense of place: an empirical measurement. Geoforum **22**(3), 347–358 (1991)
25. Shen, Y.T., Shiu, Y.S., Lu, P.: City Probe: the crowdsourcing platform driven by citizen-based sensing for spatial identification and assessment. In: Luo, Y. (ed.) CDVE 2016. LNCS, vol. 9929, pp. 69–76. Springer, Cham (2016). https://doi.org/10.1007/978-3-319-46771-9_9
26. Shen, Y.T., Shiu, Y.S., Liu, W.K., Lu, P.W.: The participatory sensing platform driven by UGC for the evaluation of living quality in the city. In: Yamamoto, S. (ed.) HIMI 2017. LNCS, vol. 10274, pp. 516–527. Springer, Cham (2017). https://doi.org/10.1007/978-3-319-58524-6_41
27. Sheth, A.: Citizen sensing, social signals, and enriching human experience. IEEE Internet Comput. **13**(4), 87–92 (2009)
28. Skupin, A., Fabrikant, S.I.: Spatialization methods: a cartographic research agenda for non-geographic information visualization. Cartogr. Geogr. Inf. Sci. **30**(2), 99–119 (2003)
29. Spence, R.: Information Visualization, vol. 1. Addison-Wesley, New York (2001)
30. UN World Urbanization Prospects (2018). https://esa.un.org/unpd/wup/Download/

Home Care System for Supporting Caregivers and Elderly Care Receivers

Madoka Takahara[✉], Kakiha Gosho, Fanwei Huang, Ivan Tanev, and Katsunori Shimohara

Doshisha University, Kyoto 610-0394, Japan
takahara2012@sil.doshisha.ac.jp

Abstract. In recent years, the aging population of Japan is rapidly increasing at an alarming rate and Japan is called a super-aging society. Therefore, people desire high-quality nursing care for elderly adults. This study focuses on problems of both care giver's and receiver's mind and body especially on sleep. For this reason, we propose a new system for improving their sleep qualities by decreasing the burden of caregivers. Specifically, we have developed a system that adjusts home appliances for a room environment such as illumination and air conditioning to enable the elderly to have much better sleep situation. Moreover, the system gives suggestions to them every day using the voices of their intimate people such as their granddaughters/sons and their supporters. This study has the following three research issues: A. Sleep quality evaluation mechanism of the first 90 min from the beginning of users' sleep state, B. Conversation mechanism to enable care receivers to undertake behavior modifications leading to improving their minds and bodies, C. Information-sharing mechanism to foster mutual understanding and acceptance between the care receivers, caregivers, and relatives such as their supporters. In this paper, we mention our research concept, scheme, and approach, as well as a discussion of their significance based on the results of field experiments.

Especially, in this paper, we describe a sleep quality evaluation mechanism of the first 90 min from the beginning of users' sleep state.

Keywords: Home care · Sleep quality · Care receiver · Care giver · The first 90 min from the beginning of sleep

1 Introduction

Given the rapid progression into a super-aging society in Japan, one of the typical problems in a 24-h society is nursing care for care receiver during the night. Specifically, caregivers suffer from the burden of providing long-term care because care receiver need periodic care for the night. They have to monitor and check care receiver' sleeping situation periodically, give suggestions or advice when care receiver have difficulty sleeping, and control the room environment, such as illumination and air conditioning. Consequently, caregivers themselves experience sleep problems, which may negatively affect their attitude to care receiver. Such a situation seems to drive a vicious circle, and it is obviously worse for both caregivers and care recipient.

S. Yamamoto and H. Mori (Eds.): HCII 2020, LNCS 12185, pp. 529–538, 2020.
https://doi.org/10.1007/978-3-030-50017-7_40

A lot of caregivers are middle aged, and they often have to quit their job to care for care receiver, as providing care and working are hardly compatible. According to an employment status survey in 2017, about 100,000 workers annually leave their jobs, most of whom are aged 55–59 years. Half of them want to keep working even while being caregivers. However, in the present situation, it is difficult for them to provide care for care receiver and invest in their regular work [1].

The population of care receiver is estimated to keep increasing more and more in the future. Achieving effective and high-quality care support for care receiver while reducing the burden for caregivers are pressing concerns in Japan. Special care is due not only for care receiver but also for caregivers; the care stress and irregular daily rhythm experienced by caregivers drain them physically and mentally. Sleep problems among care receiver and caregivers are clearly serious. Caregivers cannot sleep well, because they have to care for care receiver all day. Sleep deprivation increases risk of depression, dementia, lifestyle-related diseases, and obesity. In other words, the lack of sleep can cause diseases in many people. Thus, caregivers are at risk of contracting diseases and be new care receivers themselves. Accordingly, the care problem in Japan can be expected to become serious in the future. However, studies on sleep care support system has not emphasized the needs of both care receiver and caregivers in home care.

In this research, our final goal is to develop a caregiver support system for nursing care of care receiver. This system supports sleep not only care receiver but also caregivers. As a first step for constructing the caregiver support system, in this paper, we describe a new sleep quality evaluation mechanism of the first 90 min from the beginning of users' sleep state.

2   Reducing Caregivers' Burden of the Long-Term Care and Caregiver Support System

To reduce caregivers' burden of the long-term care, we propose a caregiver system that automatically executes a caregiver's functionality. It aims not to replace caregivers but to support them by reducing the number of their periodic tasks. Caregivers have conversation skills, know-how, experience, and knowledge of nursing care, which has been cultivated over many years. The system should, therefore, achieve functionality by substituting caregivers' performance through data acquisition and learning mechanisms. Moreover, to foster reliable relationships, mutual understanding, and acceptance among care receiver, their family members, and caregivers, it is indispensable for the system to provide them with an information-sharing mechanism on the care recipient's sleep data. Thus, the goal of this research is to improve and resolve the serious sleep problems of both caregivers and care receiver.

Figure 1 shows the system configuration of the proposed system. It is composed of a smart watch to measure a person's biometric data related to their sleep state, smart desk to that provides suggestions and/or advice, a home appliances controller to control home appliances linked with a smart desk, and a PC to control these devices and execute the system's functionality.

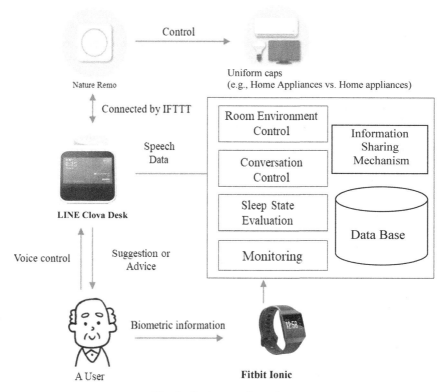

Fig. 1. System configuration.

3 Related Works

Japan is ranked tenth in the world in the number of people suffering from mental diseases. It is also ranked first in number of beds in mental hospitals. The percentage of people who have sleep disorders in worldwide ranges from 9% to 15%; that in Japan is 20%. At present, the economic loss attributed to sleep loan is JPY 35 trillion/year in Japan. Further, sleep loan causes depression, obesity, dementia, and other disorders. On average, it takes three weeks (12 h/day) for people to return the sleep loan [1].

Sleep disorders increase the risk of lifestyle-related diseases and depression. This problem has been observed in Japan owing to changes in lifestyle. Meanwhile, the quality and duration of sleep vary greatly with age and are determined by numerous other factors. Previous studies have shown that sleep disorders commonly occur in care receiver.

Professor Takadama and his team focused on this problem and proposed a concierge-based care support system to provide a comfortable and healthy life for care receiver. The system estimated a user's daily sleep stage and stores such personal data as big data, thereby enabling care workers and doctors to design personal care plans for specific users more effectively [5–7].

Professor Takahara et al. proposed an indirect biofeedback mechanism that helps patients keep track of their sleep quality and condition by monitoring a device that displays a virtual plant. They also proposed a mechanism through which the patient, family members, and medical staff can share indirect biofeedback information. An experiment was conducted in a senior care home using five elderly people and two healthy people as subjects, with family members and medical staff participating in the experiment. The experiment attempted to clarify the usefulness of indirect biofeedback in the improvement of a patient's sleep. They also aimed to confirm that patients, their family members, and medical staff could deepen their mutual understanding and mutual acceptance by sharing indirect biofeedback information. Consequently, they may be able to judge whether indirect biofeedback through the virtual plant is useful for improving patients' sleep condition [8].

Professor Nishino and his team emphasized how humans spend a significant part of our lives sleeping, which is essential for our physical and psychological well-being. However, sleep can be easily impaired by psychological and physical disorders [2, 3]. Shimamoto and his team suggested that a decline in the quality and total duration of sleep decreases physical activity levels and increases daytime sleepiness as well as the risk of lifestyle-related diseases and depression [4].

Moreover, Professor Nishino said that the characteristics of sleep are notably expressed in an introductory sleep phase for 90 min. We focus on and adopt the introductory sleep phase as an indication of sleep quality evaluation. In this research, we adapt this 90 min mechanism to our proposed system and mechanism.

4   Proposed Method

To develop the proposed system, we addressed the following research issues:

- Subject A: Sleep quality evaluation mechanism of the first 90 min from the beginning of users' sleep state
- Subject B: Conversation control to enable a care recipient to undertake behavior modifications leading to sleep improvement
- Subject C: Information-sharing mechanism to foster mutual understanding and acceptance between the care recipient, caregivers, and related people.

In this paper, specially, we describe "Sleep quality evaluation mechanism of the first 90 min from the beginning of users' sleep state" of Subject C.

4.1   Tools in This Research

In this research, we use the following tools for nursing care of care receiver.

- Nature Remo
  Nature Remo is a smart remote controller that can control every home electronic appliance though Wi-Fi. This can be accessed by Smart desk or a mobile phone.

- LINE Clova Desk
  LINE Clova Desk is a smart desk speaker. It controls every home electronic appliance by voice. In the experiment, when the participant asks Smart desk about his/her sleep information, Smart desk provides feedback of the previous day's sleep information, suggests their ideal wake-up time/bedtime, and turns on/off the lights automatically.
- Fibit Ionic
  Fitbit is a wearable smart watch with sensors. In this research, we collect sleep data of the participants using Fitbit Ionic.
- Fitabace database
  Fitabase has databases of sleep data which are acquired through Fitbit products. In this research, we get sleep data of the participants through this service.

4.2 Subject A: Sleep Quality Evaluation Mechanism of the First 90 Min from the Beginning of Users Sleep

The proposed system can acquire a care receivers' sleep data, including "time", "sleep stage," for 90 min from the beginning of sleep through Fitbit Ionic developed by Fitbit. In this study, we incorporate a new sleep evaluation mechanism to extract the regularity of sleep quality from the beginning 90 min of their sleep.

The characteristics of sleep are notably expressed in an introductory sleep phase for 90 min. We focus on and adopt the introductory sleep phase as an indication of sleep quality evaluation. Figure 2 shows the image of the proposed mechanism.

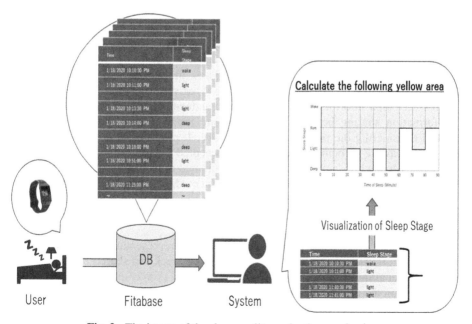

Fig. 2. The image of the sleep quality evaluation mechanism.

We get user's sleep data using Fitbit Ionic though a database of Fitabase. Moreover, we calculate the user's 90 min sleep quality using the sleep data.

4.3 Subject B: Conversation Control Enabling Behavior Modifications Leading to Sleep Improvement

In this research, we aim to solve issues in generating suggestions and/or advice based on the evaluation of a care recipient's sleep state, controlling the conversation with a care recipient in the proposed system, and controlling the room environment, such as illumination and air conditioning. Moreover, utilizing a bedside Smart desk is important given that older adults mainly use voice communication.

Based on veteran caregivers' conversation skills and experiences, several basic pieces of advice on such topics as optimal wake-up time, bedtime, and bath time, as well as typical conversation templates, are preset. The lights in the bedroom are controlled depending on the optimal waking and sleep time.

In this research, we introduce the voices of the participant's relative people as a feedback tool and we verify how the speeches of human real voice affect the participants' mind and body.

4.4 Subject C: Information-Sharing Mechanism

We propose a model of information sharing to foster mutual understanding and acceptance not only between care recipients and caregivers but also between them and related people, such as the recipient's family. They can monitor the change in the care recipient's sleep state and then confirm sleep improvement.

The sleep quality of a care recipient is deeply related to his/her relationship with the caregiver. To improve a care recipient's sleep quality, it is necessary for a care recipient and a caregiver to improve their relationship. Thus, in this research, we facilitate the sharing of information of both care recipient and caregiver using a web application. The system shares their information to foster mutual understanding and acceptance.

Information sharing between the patient and medical staff should be carefully designed considering the points mentioned above. It might be quite significant for a patient to be aware of being understood and accepted by others through information sharing [8]. Meanwhile, a patient's extremely personal information that cannot be usually seen and known by others may need to be protected. In general, the patient does not want others to know his/her extremely personal information. In addition, direct numerical feedback, displayed as drastic numerical changes, might be perceived as unfamiliar data and give users a negative feeling.

As such, we consider the significance of indirect representation, that is, indirect biofeedback. Information represent as indirect biofeedback and shared by others is the patient's personal information, but it is not too specific or too comprehensive, enabling acceptability on the part of the patient that the personal information is seen and known by others.

5   System Structure of Sleep Quality Evaluation Mechanism

The following Fig. 3 is showed in the image of sleep data from fitabase using Fitbit. The following Fig. 4 is showed the image of the sleep stage for 90 min.

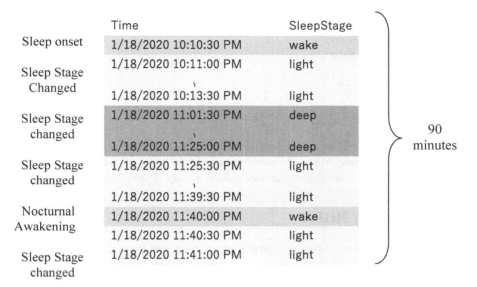

Fig. 3. Image of sleep data from fitabase using Fitbit.

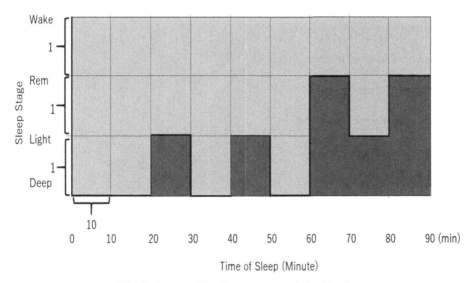

Fig. 4. Image of the sleep stage graph for 90 min.

We construct the sleep stage graph such a Fig. 4 with the first 90 min sleep data from the beginning of user's sleep. We set the following values for calculating the 90 min sleep graph area.

- Length (Sleep Stage)

  - Wake – Rem: 1 Score
  - Rem – Light: 1 Score
  - Light – Deep: 1 Score

- Width (Time of sleep)

  - 10 min: 10 Score

The minimum of the 90 min sleep graph is 0 score and the maximum of the 90 min sleep graph is 270 score. When the sleep score is high, the user's sleep quality means high, when the sleep score is low, the user's sleep quality means low.

6   Experimental Method

In order to study how the different effects to the participants in their sleep qualities, we conduct a experiment with 2 participants (2 females, 50s) in 2 months, each experiment is 1 month after the pre-experiment about one month.

After the experiments, we evaluate the participants' sleep qualities using the questionnaires and sleep areas of the participants.

- Participants

  - 2 people (Gender: females, Age: 50s)

- Experiment Terms

  - Experiment term: 2 months

- Evaluation methods

  - Subjective evaluation
    10 VAS Questionnaires during the experiment.
  - Objective evaluation
    Sleep area from the first 90 min from the beginning of users sleep though Fitbit

We calculate the participants' usual sleep qualities using the participants' 90 min of sleep data. Moreover, we compare the participants' sleep results through our proposed mechanism and the results of the subjective questionnaires. Finally, we verify the effectiveness of our proposed mechanism.

7   Conclusion

We have proposed a caregiver support system for nursing care of care receiver to decrease the burden of caring for caregivers. In this paper, especially we described a sleep quality evaluation mechanism of the first 90 min from the beginning of users' sleep. This mechanism helps to evaluate care receivers' and caregivers' sleep qualities. Furthermore, we can recognize the sleep qualities of care receivers and caregivers in-home nursing care and we can develop the caregiver support system for improving their sleep qualities.

To embed this mechanism to our propose home nursing care system, the care giver support system periodically checks the care receivers' sleeping situation, gives suggestions or advice when they have difficulty sleeping, and controls the room environment, including illumination and air conditioning. Furthermore, the system helps both care receiver and caregivers to be aware of their sleep quality and condition, by monitoring a device that is displayed on a web application. Thus, they can deepen mutual acceptance and understanding.

In future work, we will develop the following proposed mechanism and system: A. Sleep quality evaluation mechanism of the first 90 min from the beginning of users sleep, B. Conversation control to enable a care recipient to undertake behavior modifications leading to sleep improvement, and C. Information-sharing mechanism to foster mutual understanding and acceptance between care receiver, caregivers, and related people.

Further, we will conduct preliminary experiments at a normal home for developing the sleep quality evaluation mechanism firstly. Afterward, we will perform field experiments with care receiver in their own home, with their permission for the mechanism.

Acknowledgement. This study was supported by JSPS KAKENHI Grant Number 18H05725. Moreover, we would like to thank all of the members who supported me during this study. We would especially like to express my sincere gratitude to Orylab Inc., who not only imparted the professional knowledge necessary for this research but also provided full assistance.

References

1. Nishino, S.: The Stanford Method for Ultimate Sound Sleep. Sunmark Publishing, Tokyo (2017)
2. Nishino, S., Taheri, S., Black, J., Nofzinger, E.: The neurology of sleep in relation to mental illness. In: Charney, D.S., Nestler, E.J. (eds.) Neurobiology of Mental Illness, pp. 1160–1179. Oxford University Press, New York (2004)
3. Mignot, E., Taheri, S., Nishino, S.: Sleeping with hypothalamus, emerging therapeutic targets for sleep disorders. Nat. Neurosci. **5**, 1071–1075 (2004)
4. Shimamoto, H., Shibata, M.: The relationship between physical activity and sleep, a literature review. Center Educ. Lib. Arts Sci. **2**, 75–82 (2014)
5. Takadama, K.: Concierge-based care support system for designing your own lifestyle. In: AAAI Spring Symposium, pp. 69–74 (2014)
6. Harada, T., et al.: Real-time sleep stage estimation from biological data with trigonometric function regression model. In: AAAI Spring Symposium Series, pp. 348–353 (2016)

7. Takadama, K., Tajima, Y.: Sleep monitoring agent for care support and its perspective. IEICE ESS Fundam. Rev. **8**(2), 96–101 (2014)
8. Takahara, M., Huang, F., Tanev, I., Shimohara, K.: Sharing indirect biofeedback information for mutual acceptance. In: Yamamoto, S. (ed.) HIMI 2017. LNCS, vol. 10273, pp. 617–630. Springer, Cham (2017). https://doi.org/10.1007/978-3-319-58521-5_49
9. Huang, F., Takahara, M., Tanev, I., Shimohara, K.: Emergence of collective escaping strategies of various sized teams of empathic caribou agents in the wolf-caribou predator-prey problem. IEEJ Trans. Electron. Inf. Syst. **138**(5), 619–626 (2017)

Development of Multi-DoF Robot Arm with Expansion and Contraction Mechanism for Portability

Taiga Yokota$^{(\boxtimes)}$ and Naoyuki Takesue$^{(\boxtimes)}$

Faculty of Systems Design, Tokyo Metropolitan University,
6-6 Asahigaoka, Hino-shi, Tokyo 191-0065, Japan
yokota-taiga@ed.tmu.ac.jp, ntakesue@tmu.ac.jp
https://www.sd.tmu.ac.jp/en/

Abstract. In recent years, it becomes popular to use robots that clean houses. In the future, it is expected that various robots having arm are used at home. But the robot arms used in factories are large and heavy, so it is difficult to use them at home. In this study, an expansion and contraction mechanism, which has a capability of portability and easiness of put-away, have been proposed and the robot arm have been developed using it. The previous robot arm was manually expanded and contracted. In this paper, we improved the robot arm so that can automatically expand and contract and have a wide movable range.

Keywords: Portable robot · Expansion and contraction · Wire drive · Robot arm

1 Introduction

In recent years, it becomes popular to use robots that clean houses. In the future, it is expected that various robots are used at home. The current vacuum cleaning robots only move and clean on the floor. If robot arms are used at home, it is possible to manipulate and carry objects. Furthermore, by using robot arms mounted on mobile robots [1] and unmanned aerial vehicles (UAVs) [2], people with physical disabilities can carry things to their hand without bending over. However, the present robot arms used in factories are generally large and heavy, hence fences are needed for safety. Therefore, home robots need to have a capability such as miniaturization and weight reduction for safety and furthermore portability and easiness of put-away, which are different from functions required so far.

From these backgrounds, several expansion and contraction mechanisms have been proposed. By expanding and contracting, robots can be extended greatly when the robots work in large workspace, and can become smaller when the robots are put away. However, there are some issues in the proposed mechanisms. A prismatic joint mechanisms using a rigid body, such as the Spiral Zipper robot [3], have a high expansion/contraction ratio, but they have no driving joints in

© Springer Nature Switzerland AG 2020
S. Yamamoto and H. Mori (Eds.): HCII 2020, LNCS 12185, pp. 539–550, 2020.
https://doi.org/10.1007/978-3-030-50017-7_41

the body. As a result, they have a few degree. Those that expand and contract by a compressed air [4] are not rigid, hence they can move flexibly even through constrained environment. But the air compressor must always be running and it may be difficult to carry a heavy object.

Based on a Mandala (Flex-Sphere), which is a geometric toy from ancient India shown in Fig. 1(a), a wireframe robot was developed using expansion and contraction mechanism [5] (Fig. 1(b)). The expansion/contraction ratio of the robot was 9 from 60 mm to 540 mm. The robot arm was operated using wire drive as shown in Fig. 2. It could self-stand as shown in Fig. 2(a) and also was deformed due to the flexibility as shown in Fig. 2(c).

However, the robot arm was manually expanded and contracted. To use it for people with physical disabilities, the transformation between the expansion and the contraction should be actuated. Although the robot arm was deformed by

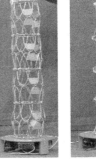

(a) Mandala (Flex-Sphere),   (b) Mandala-inspired wireframe robot arm
a wireframe toy from ancient India   with expansion and contraction mechanism

Fig. 1. Mandala and previous mandala-inspired robot [5]

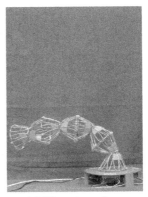

(a) Initial posture   (b) Intermediate posture   (c) Target posture

Fig. 2. Motion of wireframe robot [5]

wire drive taking advantage of flexibility of the robot arm, this method realized only a narrow range of motion.

Therefore, in this study, we aim to improve the operability for actuating the expansion and contraction motion and the movable range. For the purpose, we developed a new expansion and contraction component and change a bending operation method. Finally, it is experimentally verified that the performance is improved.

2   Improvement of Expansion and Contraction Component

2.1   Previous Expansion and Contraction Component

The previous expansion and contraction component consists of a base part (CC: Center-Circle) and a semicircular part (SC: Semi-Circle) shown in Fig. 3, and two base parts and several semicircular parts are connected with revolute pairs with one degree of freedom as shown in Fig. 4. The semicircular parts that adjoin each other are constrained by a point-contact pair of thin rods, and all the semicircular parts move in conjunction with each other. As a result, this mechanism has only one degree of freedom.

2.2   Problem of Expansion and Contraction Component

As described above, the base part and the semicircular part are connected by a revolute pair. The axis of rotation is straight as shown in the red line in Fig. 5(a) although the base part is circular. Therefore, the diameter of the connecting part between the base part and the semicircular part must be large. As a result, it has redundant degrees of freedom, and it works as the flexibility.

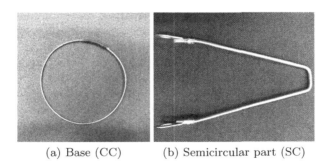

(a) Base (CC)   (b) Semicircular part (SC)

Fig. 3. Elements of previous expansion and contraction component

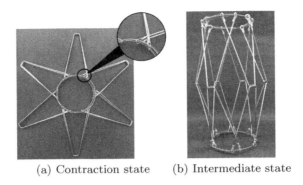

(a) Contraction state   (b) Intermediate state

Fig. 4. Overview of previous expansion and contraction component

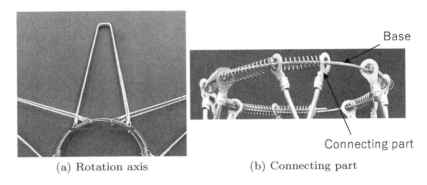

(a) Rotation axis   (b) Connecting part

Fig. 5. Redundancy of rotation axis (Color figure online)

2.3   Improvement of Expansion and Contraction Component

To solve the problem described in the previous section, we developed a new base part whose all rotation axes were straight without the redundancy, as shown in Fig. 6. Paying attention to the point-contact pairs of one semicircular part, we found that there are rods located on the upper side and the lower side as shown in Fig. 7(a). All the adjacent semicircular part must be constrained by the point-contact pair of rods and move in conjunction with each other. Therefore, the vertical distance r between joints (Points P and Q) shown in Fig. 7(a) must be larger than the diameter (3 mm) of the stainless steel rod used for the semicircular part.

In addition, the red part shown in Fig. 8 includes a fixture (length: 25.92 mm) for connecting the base part and the semicircle part. Therefore, the contact point of adjacent semicircular part must not enter the red area and the base part needs to satisfy the following conditions (1) and (2).

$$r = l \sin \alpha \cos \alpha > 3 \,\mathrm{mm} \tag{1}$$

$$s = \frac{t}{\tan(\pi/6)} > 25.92 \,\mathrm{mm} \tag{2}$$

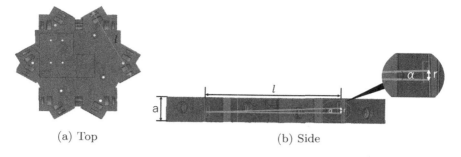

(a) Top   (b) Side

Fig. 6. Improved base part of expansion and contraction component

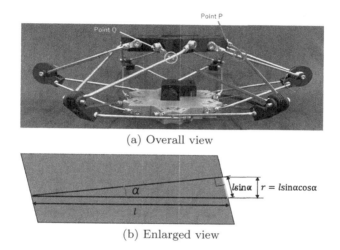

(a) Overall view

(b) Enlarged view

Fig. 7. Contact condition 1 of base part

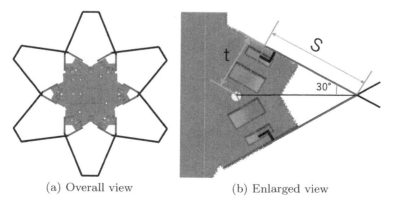

(a) Overall view   (b) Enlarged view

Fig. 8. Contact condition 2 of base part (Color figure online)

Table 1. Size of base part

Parameter	Size
l	80 mm
a	15 mm
t	10 mm
α	2.0°

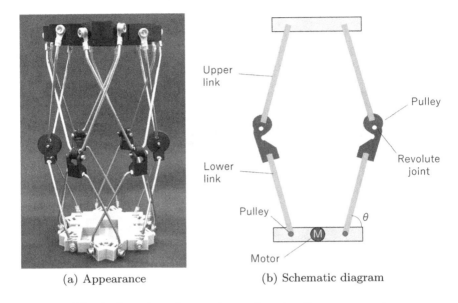

(a) Appearance   (b) Schematic diagram

Fig. 9. Overview of expansion and contraction component

Table 1 shows the parameters of the base part based on the above conditions. Based on the condition 1, as a candidate for the angle α, we tested it in increments of 0.1° from 1.9° to 2.3°. As a result, 2.0° showed good performance in both the redundancy of freedom and the incoherence, hence we decided $\alpha = 2.0°$.

Figure 9 shows the newly developed expansion and contraction component based on the above conditions.

3   Automatic Transformation Between Expansion and Contraction

In this section, we propose a method for the automatic transformation of the expansion and contraction component shown in Fig. 9. In this paper, we define that the frame angle θ in Fig. 9(b) increases as "the component expands." On the other hand, we define that θ decreases as "the component contracts."

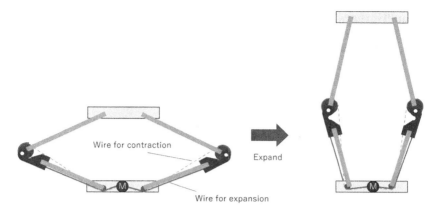

Fig. 10. Expansion method of component (Color figure online)

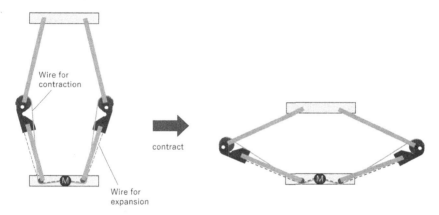

Fig. 11. Contraction method of component (Color figure online)

3.1 Expansion Method

Figure 10 shows how the component expands. The solid red lines represent wires for expansion, and the dotted green lines represent wires for contraction. The one end of the wires for expansion were fixed at the pulleys on the upper links and wound from the outside of the pulleys. Hence, if they are wound up using a motor at the bottom, the links rise toward the center.

3.2 Contraction Method

Figure 11 shows how the component contracts. In contrary to the expansion method, the solid green lines represent the wires for contraction, and the dotted red lines represent the wires for expansion. The one end of the wires for contraction were also fixed at the pulleys, but they were wound from the inside of the pulleys unlike the wires for expansion. Therefore, if the motor at the bottom is rotated in the opposite direction of the expansion and winds up the contraction wires, the links lower while being pulled outward.

4   Joint Drive Method

As shown in Fig. 2, in the previous wireframe robot, the expansion and contraction components are deformed by winding the wire to move the arm. However, the movable range is limited. In this section, therefore, we propose a new driving method.

4.1   Pitch Joint

Kim proposed a wire driven method of tension amplifying mechanism [6] as shown in Fig. 12. Figure 12 shows that the rolling joint rotates counterclockwise when the red wire is wound up and the green wire is released. It is also possible to rotate clockwise by reversing the wire of winding up and releasing. The range of motion is increased by using the rolling joint, and the amount of wire wound up and released is equalized by using circular pulleys, hence its control is easy. Furthermore, the payload is enhanced by wrapping the wire multiple times as shown in Fig. 12.

If the rolling circular joint used in the above method is applied to the robot arm with expansion and contraction components, the height of the contracted robot arm increases. Therefore, we developed a low rolling joint shown in Fig. 13. The basic method is the same with Fig. 12, but two motors are needed for two

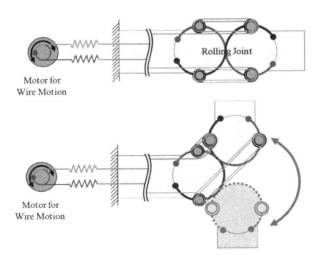

Fig. 12. 1-DOF tension amplifying mechanism proposed by Kim [6] (Color figure online)

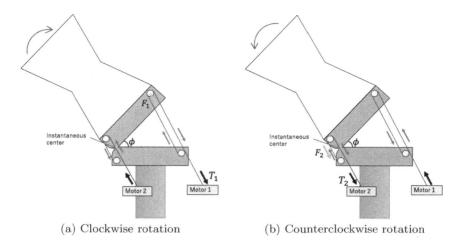

(a) Clockwise rotation   (b) Counterclockwise rotation

Fig. 13. Developed joint driving method

wires each. In the case of the developed joint, the joint rotates clockwise when the wire is wound up by motor 1 and the other wire is released by motor 2 as shown in Fig. 13(a). On the other hand, the joint rotates counterclockwise when motor 1 releases the wire and motor 2 winds up the wire as shown in Fig. 13(b).

4.2 Yaw Joint

Figure 14 shows the developed robot arm that consists of three expansion and contraction components, two pitch joint drive and one yaw joint drive. The motor for the yaw joint is arranged at the center of the yaw joint drive shown in Fig. 14(b).

5 Specifications of Developed Robot Arm

Figures 14, 15, 16 and Table 2 show the overview, size and weight of the developed robot arm.

Regarding one expansion and contraction component, the automatic transformation mechanism has successfully expanded and contracted under the same load as its own weight, but it hasn't been implemented to the robot arm yet.

6 Payload Experiment

6.1 Experimental Method

We examined how much weight can be lifted from the initial bent state as shown in Fig. 17(a). If the bending angles (ϕ_1, ϕ_2) of the pitch joints can be set to $0°$, we make a judgment that the robot arm completed lifting the weight. We increase the weight from $200\,$g to $1000\,$g in $100\,$g increments in the experiment (Fig. 16).

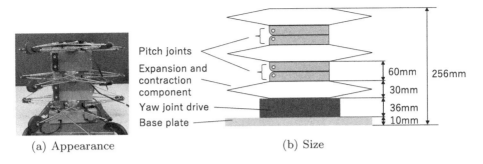

(a) Appearance   (b) Size

Fig. 14. Overview of robot arm (contraction state)

Table 2. Weight of components

Component	Number	Weight[g]
Base plate	1	1,306
Yaw joint drive	1	533
Expansion and contraction component	3	519
Pitch joint	2	237
Total		3,870

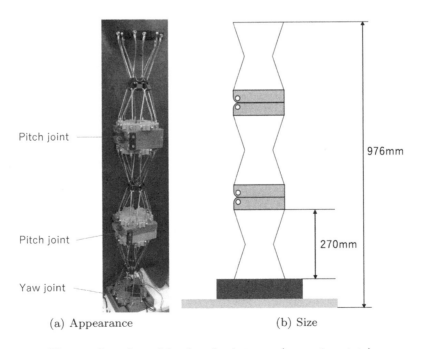

(a) Appearance   (b) Size

Fig. 15. Overview of developed robot arm (expansion state)

(a) Pitch and yaw joints

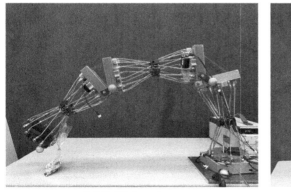

(b) Pitch joint bending

(c) Yaw joint rotation

Fig. 16. Overview of developed robot arm (pitch and yaw joints)

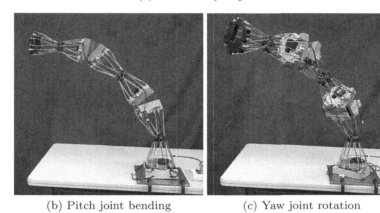

(a) Initial posture

(b) Lift-up posture of 900g

Fig. 17. Payload experiment

6.2 Result

Figure 17(b) shows the robot arm applied a load of 900 g in the payload experiment. The robot arm completed lifting although the first expansion and contraction component was slightly deformed due to the payload.

7 Conclusions

In this study, we solved the redundant degree of freedom of joints in the previous
robot arm and developed the automatic transformation by improving the expansion and contraction mechanism. Furthermore, by changing joint drive method,
we expand the movable range of the robot arm. As a result, operability has been
improved. As future works, the rigidity should be improved.

References

1. Srinivasa, S.S., et al.: Herb: a home exploring robotic butler. Auton. Robots **28**(1),
   5–20 (2010)
2. Keemink, A., Fumagalli, M., Stramigioli, S., Carloni, R.: Mechanical design of a
   manipulation system for unmanned aerial vehicles. In: Proceedings 2012 IEEE International Conference on Robotics and Automation, pp. 3147–3152 (2012)
3. Collins, F., Yim, M.: Design of a spherical robot arm with the spiral zipper prismatic joint. In: Proceedings 2016 IEEE International Conference on Robotics and
   Automation, pp. 2137–2143 (2016)
4. Hawkes, E.W., Blumenschein, L.H., Greer, J.D., Okamura, A.M.: A soft robot that
   navigates its environment through growth. Sci. Robot. **2**(8), eaan3028 (2017)
5. Takei, Y., Takesue, N.: Design of wireframe expansion and contraction mechanism
   and its application to robot. In: Proceedings the 9th International Conference on
   Intelligent Robotics and Applications, pp. 101–110 (2016)
6. Kim Y. J.: Design of low manipulator with high stiffness and strength using tension
   amplifying mechanisms. In: Proceedings 2015 IEEE/RSJ International Conference
   on Intelligent Robots and Systems, pp. 5850–5856 (2015)

Author Index

Printed in the United States
By Bookmasters